HTML 4 Bible,
2nd Edition

HTML 4 Bible, 2nd Edition

Bryan Pfaffenberger and Bill Karow

IDG Books Worldwide, Inc.
An International Data Group Company

Foster City, CA ✦ Chicago, IL ✦ Indianapolis, IN ✦ New York, NY

HTML 4 Bible, 2nd Edition

Published by
IDG Books Worldwide, Inc.
An International Data Group Company
919 E. Hillsdale Blvd., Suite 400
Foster City, CA 94404
www.idgbooks.com (IDG Books Worldwide Web site)

ISBN: 0-7645-3473-4

Printed in the United States of America

10 9 8 7 6 5 4 3 2 1

1B/RX/QY/QQ/FC

Distributed in the United States by IDG Books Worldwide, Inc.

Distributed by CDG Books Canada Inc. for Canada; by Transworld Publishers Limited in the United Kingdom; by IDG Norge Books for Norway; by IDG Sweden Books for Sweden; by IDG Books Australia Publishing Corporation Pty. Ltd. for Australia and New Zealand; by TransQuest Publishers Pte Ltd. for Singapore, Malaysia, Thailand, Indonesia, and Hong Kong; by Gotop Information Inc. for Taiwan; by ICG Muse, Inc. for Japan; by Intersoft for South Africa; by Eyrolles for France; by International Thomson Publishing for Germany, Austria, and Switzerland; by Distribuidora Cuspide for Argentina; by LR International for Brazil; by Galileo Libros for Chile; by Ediciones ZETA S.C.R. Ltda. for Peru; by WS Computer Publishing Corporation, Inc., for the Philippines; by Contemporanea de Ediciones for Venezuela; by Express Computer Distributors for the Caribbean and West Indies; by Micronesia Media Distributor, Inc. for Micronesia; by Chips Computadoras S.A. de C.V. for Mexico; by Editorial Norma de Panama S.A. for Panama; by American Bookshops for Finland.

For general information on IDG Books Worldwide's books in the U.S., please call our Consumer Customer Service department at 800-762-2974. For reseller information, including discounts and premium sales, please call our Reseller Customer Service department at 800-434-3422.

For information on where to purchase IDG Books Worldwide's books outside the U.S., please contact our International Sales department at 317-596-5530 or fax 317-572-4002.

For consumer information on foreign language translations, please contact our Customer Service department at 800-434-3422, fax 317-572-4002, or e-mail rights@idgbooks.com.

For information on licensing foreign or domestic rights, please phone +1-650-653-7098.

For sales inquiries and special prices for bulk quantities, please contact our Order Services department at 800-434-3422 or write to the address above.

For information on using IDG Books Worldwide's books in the classroom or for ordering examination copies, please contact our Educational Sales department at 800-434-2086 or fax 317-572-4005.

For press review copies, author interviews, or other publicity information, please contact our Public Relations department at 650-653-7000 or fax 650-653-7500.

For authorization to photocopy items for corporate, personal, or educational use, please contact Copyright Clearance Center, 222 Rosewood Drive, Danvers, MA 01923, or fax 978-750-4470.

Library of Congress Cataloging-in-Publication Data

Pfaffenberger, Bryan, 1949-
    HTML 4 Bible / Bryan Pfaffenberger and Bill Karow.--2nd ed.
        p.   cm.
    ISBN 0-7645-3473-4 (alk. paper)
    1. HTML (Document markup language) I. Karow, Bill. II. Title.
QA76.76.H94 P494   2000
005.7'2--dc21   00-040993

ABOUT IDG BOOKS WORLDWIDE

Welcome to the world of IDG Books Worldwide.

IDG Books Worldwide, Inc., is a subsidiary of International Data Group, the world's largest publisher of computer-related information and the leading global provider of information services on information technology. IDG was founded more than 30 years ago by Patrick J. McGovern and now employs more than 9,000 people worldwide. IDG publishes more than 290 computer publications in over 75 countries. More than 90 million people read one or more IDG publications each month.

Launched in 1990, IDG Books Worldwide is today the #1 publisher of best-selling computer books in the United States. We are proud to have received eight awards from the Computer Press Association in recognition of editorial excellence and three from Computer Currents' First Annual Readers' Choice Awards. Our best-selling *...For Dummies*® series has more than 50 million copies in print with translations in 31 languages. IDG Books Worldwide, through a joint venture with IDG's Hi-Tech Beijing, became the first U.S. publisher to publish a computer book in the People's Republic of China. In record time, IDG Books Worldwide has become the first choice for millions of readers around the world who want to learn how to better manage their businesses.

Our mission is simple: Every one of our books is designed to bring extra value and skill-building instructions to the reader. Our books are written by experts who understand and care about our readers. The knowledge base of our editorial staff comes from years of experience in publishing, education, and journalism — experience we use to produce books to carry us into the new millennium. In short, we care about books, so we attract the best people. We devote special attention to details such as audience, interior design, use of icons, and illustrations. And because we use an efficient process of authoring, editing, and desktop publishing our books electronically, we can spend more time ensuring superior content and less time on the technicalities of making books.

You can count on our commitment to deliver high-quality books at competitive prices on topics you want to read about. At IDG Books Worldwide, we continue in the IDG tradition of delivering quality for more than 30 years. You'll find no better book on a subject than one from IDG Books Worldwide.

John Kilcullen
Chairman and CEO
IDG Books Worldwide, Inc.

Eighth Annual
Computer Press
Awards ≥1992

Ninth Annual
Computer Press
Awards ≥1993

Tenth Annual
Computer Press
Awards ≥1994

Eleventh Annual
Computer Press
Awards ≥1995

Credits

Acquisitions Editors
David Mayhew
John Gravener

Project Editor
Sharon Eames

Technical Editor
Greg Guntle

Copy Editor
Laura J. Hester

Proof Editor
Patsy Owens

Project Coordinators
Danette Nurse
Louigene A. Santos

Graphics and Production Specialists
Bob Bihlmayer
Darren Cutlip
Jude Levinson
Victor Pérez-Varela
Ramses Ramirez

Quality Control Technician
Dina F Quan

Permissions Editors
Jessica Montgomery
Carmen Krikorian

Associate Media Development Specialist
Jamie Smith

Media Development Assistant
Marisa Pearman

Media Development Managers
Stephen Noetzel
Laura Carpenter

Book Designer
Drew R. Moore

Illustrator
Gabriele McCann

Proofreading and Indexing
York Production Services

Cover Illustration
Larry S. Wilson

About the Authors

Bryan Pfaffenberger is the author of more than 75 books on computers and the Internet, including the best-selling *Discover the Internet,* from IDG Books Worldwide. He teaches advanced professional communication and the sociology of computing in the University of Virginia's Division of Technology, Culture, and Communication. Bryan lives in Charlottesville, Virginia, with his family and an extremely spoiled cat.

In addition to writing several computer books, **Bill Karow** has served as a contributor or technical editor on more than 30 other books. Formerly in charge of systems development for Walt Disney Entertainment, Bill now serves as a computer consultant in the Orlando area when he's not out riding his bicycle. He also has the distinction of having stood atop many of the buildings at Walt Disney World, fanfare trumpet in hand (with their permission, of course).

To Suzanne and Farris

Preface

Remember all that late-1980s talk about the Information Superhighway? You learned you'd get 500 cable channels, not just 50 (or, as comedians put it, 500 terrible channels instead of 50 terrible channels). Like most predictions involving technology, this one was way off the mark. (Add this one to the growing catalog of predictions gone awry, such as the famed remark by a 1950s IBM executive that the world would need, at most, a dozen or so computers.) The Information Superhighway didn't happen at the TV; instead, it happened at the personal computer, connected to the Internet and the World Wide Web.

Far more important, though, the Information Superhighway that has developed isn't like TV at all. TV is a broadcast medium, in which corporate content providers determine what you're going to see. The Web, from the beginning, was designed to transform couch potatoes into content producers. You can do nothing but consume Web content, to be sure, and millions of Web surfers are out there who are happy to flit from site to site without making their own contribution. And WebTV, of course, brings the Web-as-TV to the TV — and in so doing, robs the Web of part of its power.

What makes the Web such a powerful medium is, unlike all other mass media, it's inherently a two-way street, content-wise. Anyone who can consume content on the Web can also produce it, using HTML, the easy-to-learn page definition language that underlies the Web's appearance. It's as if you got a morning paper, but by afternoon, you could publish your own take on the news — and make it available, potentially, to millions of people.

The Web is probably the most important development in support of free speech since the invention of the printing press, in that it enables virtually anyone to originate content cheaply and make this content available to a potentially massive audience.

Unquestionably, the Web is good for the environment: millions of tree-killing publications are moving to the Web. Within corporations, for example, voluminous publications — directories, employee manuals, procedure manuals, agendas, reports, and meeting minutes — appear in Web-based internal networks called intranets; the environmental plusses, coupled with significant cost savings, make this innovation a no-brainer.

For even the smallest business, the Web provides a way to get your message out, stay in touch with customers, and provide needed information, but without running up a huge bill at the printer. And the best part of all is no one can tell how big or small you are. No reason exists for them ever to know only one little scientist is behind the curtain in the Emerald City.

The list of Web impacts could go on for dozens of pages, but the pattern's clear: the Web is fast becoming an indispensable new way to make information available to others. This doesn't mean the Web is going to replace other media anytime soon. If you're running a retail business, you'd be wise to advertise in the local newspaper as well as set up a Web page, but it does mean the Web is no longer something you can prudently ignore. No matter what your message might be, you want to get it out on the Web.

Who Should Read This Book?

What all this means for you is simple: Whatever your walk of life — whether you're a businessperson, a manager, a student at any level, a retired person, a homemaker, or the vice president of the United States (a confessed Web junkie) — you owe it to yourself to learn how to originate Web content. And this means learning HTML. To do this, you need a book — a comprehensive book, and what's more, a book that teaches you how to take full advantage of this exciting new version of HTML, Version 4.01. Whether you're a complete beginner or someone who's already delved into previous versions of HTML, you'll find this book is absolutely the right one for learning and mastering HTML 4.01 — and in so doing, assure your place in the Web's future.

What's So Special About This Book?

The *HTML 4 Bible, 2nd Edition* is your ticket to mastery of the newest version of HTML, Version 4.01. As you learn in the next section, HTML 4 is the most significant revision of the Web's publishing language to appear since the language's invention. You need a book that recognizes these novel features and takes a novel approach.

For the first time, HTML provides Web publishers with the power and flexibility to create page layouts rivaling those found in professionally designed magazines and newsletters. HTML 4 requires a new approach to HTML, however. If you've learned previous versions of HTML, you need to unlearn some old habits — a lot of old habits. If you're learning HTML for the first time, you need to learn it the *right* way, by reading a book that's not just a quickie rehash of a book on some previous version of HTML.

From the first sentence to the last item in the final appendix, this book was written from scratch to emphasize the HTML 4 Way, the radically new approach to Web publishing made possible by this exciting new version of HTML. Not a single word of this book appeared in any previous edition that focused on an earlier, flawed version of HTML. This book teaches a new approach to learning and using HTML 4, one that fully enables you to realize HTML 4's incredible layout potential. Once you learn what HTML is and understand the important implications of HTML Version 4, you'll understand why you need a book that's been written from the ground up to emphasize HTML 4's incredible new capabilities.

How This Book Is Organized

This book has seven parts. All of them adhere strictly to the HTML 4 Way.

Part I focuses on getting you up to speed on Web publishing: what's in it for you, and what's involved.

Part II helps you understand HTML — where it is today, and where it's heading in the future with XML and XHTML. Part II includes a review of the latest HTML-editing software on the market with special attention to whether it supports the HTML 4 Way (and all of it is included on the CD-ROM in the back of the book).

Part III teaches document structure with HTML.

Part IV helps you design the look of your site with graphics and cascading style sheets.

Part V teaches advanced page layout and cascading style sheets — something not covered in any other book of this type about HTML 4.

Part VI explains how to add bells and whistles to your site with multimedia and interactivity.

Part VII explains what has become known as *dynamic* HTML and its animation with JavaScript.

Using This Book's Special Features

Because this book can't make use of hypertext, it implements several special conventions to draw your attention to things you might want to know or need to know outside the text.

To help you become familiar with new terms, we introduce new terms and acronyms (and, boy, are a lot of acronyms associated with HTML!) in special vocabulary boxes. You'll know them when you come across them by looking for this Vocabulary icon.

This book addresses the needs of a number of audiences, each of which desires a different level of technical detail. To accommodate all levels, the main text covers what you need to know to publish your pages successfully. When there is more you might want to know, the topic is covered in-depth because we set it apart from the text with this icon.

Tip

If we suggest a particularly useful way to achieve something, a marvelous shortcut, or a clever alternative, we identify it with this icon to save you both time and frustration . . . at no extra charge!

Caution

Many of you are already familiar with HTML 4.0 and earlier versions. For you, knowing both how HTML 4.01 does it and when doing it the pre-HTML 4.01 Way might get you into trouble with subsequent versions of browsers is important. The W3C calls certain uses of elements and attributes deprecated. Rather than ignoring deprecated elements and attributes, in which case you might go ahead and use them, this book flags them with an icon, along with any other special information you should know.

On the CD-ROM

Content you find included on this book's CD-ROM is flagged with a CD icon for your convenience.

Cross-Reference

Sometimes you are directed to other sections of the chapter or other chapters in the book for more information on a topic. In addition, each chapter ends with a section telling you where you go next in the book — a particularly useful feature if you're not following the book sequentially.

We didn't include anything unimportant. If you read a chapter every night, you can be as knowledgeable as the pros in less than two months! In what other career could you know what the experts know this quickly? What are you waiting for? Begin!

Acknowledgments

Writing this book has been a real adventure. So many people have helped us along the way. With the breadth of material this book covers, we occasionally turned to specialists to make sure everything we said was up-to-the-moment correct. Many thanks to Peter Dalianis for his professional and thoughtful comments on defining the message. Thanks also to Rick Provine for his invaluable assistance with digital audio. Michael Tuite provided thoughtful assistance with digital video and a host of other issues, for which we are grateful. We are indebted to Chuck Moran and Debra Weiss, who generously assisted with professional design advice for the section on site design. Thanks also to Tim O'Brien for his help with Java rapid development environments.

Thank you to Carole McClendon and Chris Van Buren at Waterside Productions for pulling this opportunity together and making it happen.

Thanks to *everyone* at IDG Books Worldwide; a more professional group has never been assembled. Thanks to project editor Sharon Eames, acquisitions editors David Mayhew and John Gravener, technical editor Greg Guntle, copy editor Laura Hester, and proof editor Patsy Owens. Also working behind the scenes were permissions editor Jessica Montgomery, graphics coordinator Danette Nurse, layout supervisor Chris Pimentel, project coordinator Louigene Santos, and a multitude of others at IDG Books, too numerous to mention here.

Extra special thanks also should go to Rick Darnell for his assistance with the last part of this book, and to Michele Davis, for jumping in to ensure this book would make it out to you, the reader. Thanks!

Finally, Bill would like to thank Suzanne and Farris for their patience and support while he disappeared for many hours at a time. This wouldn't have been possible without you both.

Contents at a Glance

Contents

Part V: Lay It Out Like the Pros   359

Chapter 32: Essentials of Web Page Design 361

Chapter 33: Understanding CSS Positioning Options 381

Part VI: Adding Sensory Excitement and Interactivity   431

Chapter 37: Creating Still Graphics for the Web 433

Chapter 38: Creating Animated Graphics for the Web 445

Chapter 45: Accessing External Databases 511

Chapter 46: Building a Community: Incorporating Discussion Groups and Chat 519

Introduction

Short for HyperText Markup Language, *HTML* is one of many markup languages that have appeared in recent years. In brief, a *markup language* provides guidelines for adding markup — in the form of special symbols — to text documents. These symbols describe the parts of the document. For example, you can use a markup language to identify a portion of the text as an *abstract,* a brief summary of the document's contents. HTML is a markup language designed for Internet documents.

Introducing markup languages

Markup is needed because computers are quite stupid when it comes to understanding text. A computer can't really tell whether a certain portion of a text is an abstract, a title, a heading, or a paragraph. Without some kind of additional coding, the computer doesn't know how to display the text so that it looks like an actual document.

Word processing programs provide the necessary coding by means of proprietary formatting codes, but these have a gigantic downside: They work only if you're looking at the document using the same word processing program and type of computer that created it. If you ever tried to exchange a WordPerfect file with a Macintosh MS Word user, you can understand the difficulties involved.

Markup languages solve the file-compatibility problem by using nothing but *ASCII* (plain text) characters and, what's more, by breaking the connection between structural markup and presentation.

In structural markup, you identify the parts of a document — in effect, you say *this is a title* or *this is a heading* — but you say nothing about how this part of the document should be presented using specific formatting (fonts, alignment, and so on). You mark up the document's structure by identifying the document's parts (title, abstract, headings, paragraphs, lists, and so on).

But there's more. *Presentation* — how the document is formatted for display or printing — is left entirely up to a *browser,* a program designed to read the marked-up document for display on a specific type of computer hardware.

The distinction between structure and presentation is important, for in it lies the key to a markup language's capability to work smoothly in a cross-platform environment (a computer network in which people are using many different types of computers).

With a markup language, you can create just one version of a document. People can run browsers designed to function on Macintoshes, UNIX computers, and all the various versions of Windows (3.1, 95, 98, NT, and 2000), and they can display your document with absolutely no trouble. For each of these computers, a browser knows how to display the marked-up document on a given system.

Does a downside exist to markup languages? Yes. If you do pure structural markup, with no presentation at all, you give up control over how your document appears. On one system, it may appear with black Times Roman text — but, on another, some crazy user may have set up his or her browser to display your text in 28-point Demented Bold. And there's nothing you can do to stop this user.

HTML — a hypertext markup language

HTML is a markup language with all the advantages of other markup languages when it comes to separating structure from presentation. But HTML has something more: HTML is a hypertext markup language.

What's hypertext? In brief, *hypertext* is a way of organizing information so readers can choose their own path through the material. Instead of clicking through sequentially organized pages, a hypertext user clicks specially highlighted text, called a *hyperlink* (or just a *link* for short), to go directly to information of interest. There's more to say about hypertext but, for now, the important point is this: HTML is the first markup language to incorporate markup for hyperlinks. When you mark up a document with HTML, you can define some of the text as a link, within which you embed the computer address of another resource on the Internet. This could be a document, a movie, a sound, an animation, or a file to download.

Eroding the structure/presentation distinction

As you just learned, the whole purpose of a markup language lies in separating structure from presentation and, in so doing, enabling content developers to create documents that can be displayed faultlessly on any type of computer. But this distinction hasn't fared well. By the time HTML got to Version 3.2, it had been seriously eroded.

Why did this erosion occur? The reason lies in the Web's rapid commercialization. Actually, HTML was initially designed to enable physics researchers to make their preliminary papers available to other physics researchers, and the humdrum appearance of plain-vanilla HTML wasn't an issue. As the Web migrated to the private sector and became an important way for giant corporations to get their message out, Web developers couldn't ignore presentation anymore. They needed to emulate the page layout designs of professional newsletter and magazine designers. They didn't like the idea of a pure markup language, which would let someone display America, Inc.'s pages using 28-point Demented Bold font.

So what did Web developers do? They learned a whole series of tricks to fake layout. For example, they used tables — initially designed to group data in tabular form — to emulate newspaper columns and magazine layouts. Browser publishers, including both Netscape and Microsoft, tried to expand their market share by creating browsers that support *extensions,* nonstandard additions to HTML that provide presentation capabilities. (The most egregious of these is probably Netscape's notorious blink extension, which enables Web authors to create text that blinks away annoyingly while you're trying to read the page.)

What's the result of HTML's commercialization? In brief, a mess. You can use the tricks and extensions to fake presentation with a Web page, but how it's going to look on a given computer and monitor is anyone's guess. HTML pages are crammed with HTML code that's been elaborated to a ridiculous extent to emulate magazine layouts, but editing and maintaining these pages is a costly nightmare. To correct errors in the text, you have to pick through reams of messy code. And suppose you create a whole series of pages, but later find they look terrible when displayed on a Macintosh. You'd have to go back into each page and change the offending code.

In short, the erosion of the structure versus presentation distinction has seriously damaged HTML's underlying purpose. What's worse, it's slowing down the Web's development. To be sure, creating a simple page is easier. But the cost of creating and maintaining HTML that generates professional-looking results is so prohibitive, many would-be content providers are shying away — a bad scene!

HTML 4 and the HTML 4 Way

Realizing that something drastic had to be done to rescue HTML, the *World Wide Web Consortium* (W3C) — the nonprofit, standards-setting body responsible for HTML — has published a specification for a new version of HTML, Version 4.01. Although HTML 4.01 is downwardly compatible with previous versions of HTML, the new version is designed to restore the lost balance between structure and presentation. What's more, it does so in a way that gives Web-content developers precisely what they want: total control over document layout. The secret? Cascading style sheets (CSS).

Introducing cascading style sheets

The W3C-originated cascading style sheets (CSS) specification is a dream come true for Web-content developers. To understand why it's such a big deal, think about word processing.

The earliest word processors gave you formatting commands, but made you use them over and over. For example, suppose you wanted to format a paragraph with a first-line indent, double line spacing, and Times Roman text. With early programs, you had to apply three different formatting commands to every paragraph you typed. What a hassle! Then along came Microsoft Word. Word enabled you to define a named style. You could create a style called Body Text, and then define this style with all the formats you want. You then apply this style to any paragraph you type. When you apply the style, Bingo! You get all the formats you assigned to the style. Once you've tried this, you can never go back—and that's one reason Microsoft Word has an overwhelming market share in the word-processing world.

Harnessing the power of styles

Cascading style sheets bring the power of styles to HTML and the Web. Using CSS, you define styles, which tell Web browsers how to display the text you marked up with HTML. Suppose, for example, you marked up some of the text as a heading. With CSS, you can define the heading so it appears with the following formats: centered, 12 points above and below, 14-point Helvetica, and bold. The marked-up text is clean, structure-only HTML—no gobbledygook designed to hassle HTML into a presentation language. And what's more, you get all the benefits of styles. Make one change to the underlying style definition and you change every instance of text to which the style is assigned. Even more powerfully, you can use external style sheets, which define the styles appearing in dozens or even thousands of documents. One little change to the underlying style and all the linked documents are changed, too.

CSS is easy to learn, easy to use, and—once you grasp what CSS can do—totally indispensable. And the benefits are amazing. By removing the presentation from HTML, you let HTML do what it does best—namely, define structure. Your HTML will be cleaner, much more readable, and much easier to edit. What's more, CSS does a far better job of presentation than HTML ever could. For example, the latest version of CSS enables *absolute positioning,* in which you can nail down the precise location of text or graphics on the page. You can create newspaper-column effects, and even superimpose text on graphics.

What about the structure versus presentation distinction?

Wait a minute! Doesn't CSS violate the structure versus presentation distinction? In some ways, yes. Admittedly, it's a compromise, but an elegant compromise. The CSS authors recognized Web developers wanted and needed to control their documents' presentation aspects. But they wanted to give authors presentation control without harming the basic benefit of a markup language, namely, the ability to create documents that function well in a cross-platform environment.

CSS does enable you to define presentation—in fact, that's its point. With CSS, you can, indeed, define presentation aspects such as fonts, and a CSS-compatible browser respects your choice. The guy who wants to look at your page with 28-point Demented Bold sees your Times Roman instead. Unlike a word processor's formatting codes, though, CSS doesn't lock users into a rigid straightjacket. If Times Roman isn't available, the browser looks for fonts you listed as likely alternates. And, if these aren't available, the browser defaults to a fallback font. All this is totally automatic, so no one is prevented from reading your page. In short, CSS pulls off something word processing programs can't: CSS creates richly formatted documents that are easily exchanged and used in a cross-platform environment.

What's more, CSS enables you to move the presentation out of HTML. To be sure, you can include CSS style specifications within your HTML, but this book doesn't recommend this practice. It's much better to move the style specifications out of the HTML entirely, either in a grouped style specification within the document's header or (better yet) in a separate file. With the presentation code out of the way, you can write pure, structure-only HTML. And this is precisely the controlling theme of the HTML 4 revision.

Back to pure structure with HTML 4

Although HTML 4 supports the various presentation features and extensions shoehorned into previous versions of HTML, this new version's real significance lies in its reassertion of pure structure. By moving the presentation to CSS, your HTML goes back to what it should be: clean, easy to read, inexpensive to maintain, quick to process and display, and — most of all — ideal for a cross-platform environment.

The HTML 4 Way

This book teaches an entirely new approach to HTML, one you won't find in competing books that explore HTML as extensively as this one. It's called the HTML 4 Way.

The *HTML 4 Way* takes full advantage of the exciting new possibilities of HTML and CSS, and calls for learning both, from the beginning. That's why this book's approach is unique. Almost all HTML books begin with HTML, teach all those horrible presentation tricks that have accumulated over the years, and then throw in a chapter on CSS as an afterthought. Not so with this book. As you'll see, you begin by writing pure structural HTML, with absolutely no presentation included. You then learn how to weave CSS into your documents to obtain total, impressive control over every aspect of your documents' presentation. You produce code that's beautifully simple and clear, easy and inexpensive to maintain, and absolutely stunning onscreen.

HTML 4
Quick Start

HTML 4 Basics

When you learn a language, you need to learn rules, called *syntax*. Unless you follow these rules, your statements don't have any meaning. Consider this statement, for instance: "Extra! Pizza, with a bring pepperoni me; cheese." The word order is out of whack and so is the punctuation. You can say this to a waiter, but good luck getting your pizza! Like any language, HTML has syntax rules. Fortunately, they're simple and easy to learn. Before you start trying to write HTML, you'll be wise to spend a little time learning these rules. It doesn't take long and there's a huge payoff: You'll avoid confusion and find it much easier to track down your errors.

This chapter introduces the basic building blocks of HTML, including elements, attributes, and entities. (Don't worry about defining these terms right now; that's done in this chapter.) You also learn the basics of nesting tags and about the basic, underlying structure of every HTML document. Once you learn these concepts, you're ready to starting writing HTML.

Introducing the Basic Building Blocks: Elements

When you write your HTML, you use *elements* to define the structure of the document, to define the presentation of your document, to define links to other documents, and to specify desired behavior. Examples of elements are: HEAD, BODY, P, BLOCKQUOTE, and UL. When you actually go to insert these elements into your text, you surround them with < (less than) and > (greater than) symbols, which are collectively referred to as *angle brackets*. Once you have done this, you have <HEAD>, <BODY>, <P>, <BLOCKQUOTE>, and <UL>. These are no longer called elements; they are now called *tags*.

Who makes the rules?

Every organization has its own rule-making body. In the case of the Web, the rule-making body is the World Wide Web Consortium (W3C). The W3C is composed of representatives from over 400 member companies who want to have a say in the standards. The W3C tries to balance the interests of the academy, the companies producing the Web browsers (notably Netscape and Microsoft), and the technology. The W3C pulls together committees with representatives from interested members and puts the specifications in writing for HTML, CSS, XML, and other essential technologies. If the W3C weren't maintaining a standard, all browsers might eventually be unable to talk to all Web servers. You can visit their Web site at http://www.w3c.org.

Elements versus tags

The World Wide Web Consortium (W3C) uses the word *elements* in two ways, which is rather confusing. You may have noticed this book does the same thing. In this chapter, we discuss elements in the *tag* sense of the word. The other kind of element is the *element of structure* of a document (for example, title, paragraph, blockquote).

Even elements have parts

Unlike the elements in the Periodic Table, elements in HTML usually have three parts: start tags, content, and end tags. Most elements have start tags and end tags. The *start tag* is the element name surrounded by angle brackets: <HEAD>, <BODY>, <P>, <BLOCKQUOTE>, and <UL>. The *end tag* is the element name, preceded by a / (called a *forward slash*), surrounded by angle brackets: </HEAD>, </BODY>, </P>, </BLOCKQUOTE>, and </UL>.

When the browser sees a start tag, it knows the text to come will all be of the type defined by the start tag. Not until the browser sees an end tag does it stop expecting the text to be of that type. Because elements can often be nested — not all elements can be nested within all other elements, but there are valid element nestings — it doesn't automatically assume a different start tag indicates the previous element type has ended. In fact, the browser assumes nothing. Forget about the benefit of the doubt. The browser takes everything you send it absolutely literally.

Note   To add another layer of confusion, some elements will display correctly without their end tag, as long as the end of an element can be clearly determined from other surrounding elements. For example, the LI (list item) and P (paragraph) tag don't require end tags, since their end can be clearly determined by the beginning of the next element. Still, you won't go wrong by always including end tags.

Definition   **Nesting.** Placing elements within other elements. For example, in a table, the rows are nested within the table element, and the cells are nested within the row elements.

Recap: This stuff is really important!

Every element has a *name*.

The *start tag* is the element name surrounded by angle brackets.

The *end tag* always starts with a slash, has the element name, and is surrounded by angle brackets.

Most elements have content, which occurs between the start and the end tags.

Some elements have no content.

Some elements have no end tags.

Some elements don't take any content, such as BR, which forces a line break. Some elements have optional end tags, such as LI and P, which are list item and paragraph elements. When we explain an element, we tell you whether it has any content and whether it has a required end tag. Elements are case-insensitive: <TITLE>, <Title>, and <title> are all the same to the browser. To make reading your markup easier, though, we recommend you write your element names in all caps. This is the convention this book uses.

Between the start tag and the end tag, you place the *content.* In reality, you usually write the content first and put the start tag before your content, and then put your end tag after your content. A major cause of errors in HTML documents is forgetting the slash in the end tag. Be careful when you type your HTML and be sure you spell your tag names correctly, include both angle brackets, and include your slash. Three examples of syntactically correct HTML follow:

```
<H1>This is the <B>bolded title</B> of the page</H1>
<B>This statement will be in bold.</B>
<I>This statement will be in italics.</I>
```

Understanding Your Options: Attributes

Elements have attributes that give you flexibility in writing your HTML. Each element has its own unique attributes. You see patterns, but you can't just apply any old attribute to any old element.

Couples only

Attributes have values. In fact, they come in pairs. If you are going to include an attribute, you have to include the value for that attribute. The value for the attribute is always enclosed in double quotation marks. Examples of attribute-value pairs are as follows:

```
align="center"
width="33%"
size="12"
name="first_name"
```

Always shop from a list

The values for some attributes come from a list of acceptable values that the W3C creates, when it sets the standards. In the case of *valign* (an attribute frequently used to tell the browser where on the page you want an image or a table to appear, relative to text), your choices are top, middle, bottom, and baseline. In the next chapter, you learn the shorthand for the element rules.

Please take a number

Some attributes take numbers as their values. In some cases, the numbers can be either a set number (usually of pixels, which are just the dots on your screen — comparable to dpi, the measurement for dots on your printer) or a percentage. For example, when you define a table, you may want the first column to be 25 percent of the screen width, the second column to be 50 percent of the screen width, and the third column to be 25 percent of the screen width. Regardless of how the screen is sized, it changes size to fit in proportionately. If you were to assume the screen was 636 pixels and divide it yourself, the last column of the table may not be visible if the visitor to your page didn't have the browser open in full-screen mode. For a form, however, when you indicate the *size* (one of the attributes for text fields) of a field, you are indicating the number of characters. For an image, when you indicate the *width* (one of the attributes for object elements), you are indicating the number of pixels.

The colors of the world

In both the HTML document itself and in the style sheet, some attributes take a color for a value. As you may have noticed, colors don't appear the same from one monitor to the next. You can, however, say a lot with colors. For example, take a page where everything is in seafoam green or watermelon; this page says *beach*.

 Cross-Reference   Not only do colors not look the same from one monitor to the next, Macs and PCs actually use different system palettes. Chapter 37 covers this topic in detail.

Just as with everything else, an HTML way exists to convey information about colors. HTML gives you two choices: the name of the color (from their approved list) and the hex (hexadecimal) representation of the color. Only 16 named colors exist, so if you are picky about the color you use, then you'll want to find the hex representation of that color.

Another thing you should know about colors on the computer is that colors are composed of red, green, and blue, thus the *RGB scale*. In hex, the first two digits are the amount of red, the next two are green, and the next two are blue. So FF0000 would be pure red. Did we mention the highest any digit can go is *F*? We discuss this next. One more thing: 000000 is black; FFFFFF is white. That's not very intuitive, so you just have to remember when you add color to the screen, it gets lighter. Unlike paper, which is white when blank, the screen is black when blank.

When you indicate the value of an attribute is a color and you use hex representation, you need to precede the hex value with a # (pound sign). The 16 named colors are listed in Table 1-1 with their hex names. If you know you want a color between two of the colors in the chart, try selecting the value between the two hex values. First, you must know how to count in hex. Hex counts from 1 to 9, then A, B, C, D, E, and F. If you need to add 1 to F, you go to 10 (that's one-zero, not ten). Try this math problem along with us: 5 plus 6 is B. Plus 5 is 10. Plus 7 is 17. Minus 9 is E. That's not too hard, is it? Fortunately, we don't need to multiply or divide in hex!

Table 1-1 Color Codes in Hex	
Color Name	**Hex Representation**
Black	#000000
Green	#008000
Silver	#C0C0C0
Lime	#00FF00
Gray	#808080
Olive	#808000
White	#FFFFFF
Yellow	#FFFF00
Maroon	#800000
Navy	#000080
Red	#FF0000
Blue	#0000FF
Purple	#800080
Teal	#008080
Fuchsia	#FF00FF
Aqua	#00FFFF

> ### Recap: More important stuff!
>
> Attributes are specific to the elements they modify.
>
> Attributes always have values.
>
> Attribute values must be enclosed in double quotation marks.
>
> Attribute values can be one from a list, a number, a percentage, or a name of your creation.

Creativity counts

For some elements, the attribute value is something you make up yourself. For example, if you want to create a form and you want people to enter their first names, you assign the value of the attribute *name* to be "first_name." Normally, when you are working with fields, some server-side scripting is going on. Your field names should match the names you expect in your script.

Using Special Characters: Entities

Another example of the W3C's penchant for academic vocabulary, *entities* are simply characters you may want to display that don't appear on your keyboard or are characters with special significance to HTML (notably <,>,&, and "). The most common of these are (©) (copyright) and (™) (trademark). Three ways exist to write a code for an entity in your HTML. Whichever way you choose, you will find all entities begin with an ampersand (&) and end with a semicolon (;):

✦ Using character notation. While this is the easiest way to show an entity, there isn't a character notation for every single entity. For the most common ones, there are character representations. For example, © is the entity for the copyright symbol. Character notation to indicate entities is one of the rare parts of HTML that is case-sensitive.

✦ Using decimal notation. The decimal representation of a copyright symbol is ©. Sure, you knew that!

✦ Using hex notation. Programmers dig this method. Instead of © to indicate the copyright symbol, they get to type ©, which is obviously way cooler. For the rest of the population, knowing A9 in hex (hexadecimal notation) equals 169 in the decimal system is useful. All hex numbers are preceded by a lowercase *x*.

Entities exist for many foreign languages, mathematical symbols, and English symbols that either can't be produced on a normal keyboard or are special to HTML.

For example, if you wanted to write "Good idea" in Greek, but the bulk of your document was English, you'd write:

```
&Kappa;&alpha;&lambda;&eta;&eta;&delta;&epsilon;&alpha;
```

which would render as: Καλιηιδεα.

Table 1-2 has the entities you will need most often, if you aren't planning to include foreign languages in your pages to any great extent. A complete list of entities can be found in Appendix D.

	Table 1-2 **Common Entities**	
Character notation	*Hex notation*	*Entity created*
		nonbreaking space
&iexcl;	&#161;	inverted exclamation mark
&cent;	&#162;	cent sign
&pound;	&#163;	pound sign
&curren;	&#164;	currency sign
&yen;	&#165;	yen sign
&brvbar;	&#166;	broken bar
&sect;	&#167;	section sign
&uml;	&#168;	Diaeresis
&copy;	&#169;	copyright sign
&ordf;	&#170;	feminine ordinal indicator
&laquo;	&#171;	left-pointing double-angle quotation mark
&not;	&#172;	not sign
&shy;	&#173;	discretionary hyphen
&reg;	&#174;	registered trademark sign
&macr;	&#175;	Macron
&deg;	&#176;	degree sign
&plusmn;	&#177;	plus or minus sign
&sup2;	&#178;	superscript two

Continued

Table 1-2 *(continued)*		
Character notation	*Hex notation*	*Entity created*
&sup3;	&#179;	superscript three
&acute;	&#180;	acute accent
&micro;	&#181;	micro sign
&para;	&#182;	paragraph sign
&sup1;	&#185;	superscript one
&ordm;	&#186;	masculine ordinal indicator
&raquo;	&#187;	right-pointing double-angle quotation mark
&frac14;	&#188;	fraction one quarter
&frac12;	&#189;	fraction one half
&frac34;	&#190;	fraction three quarters
&iquest;	&#191;	inverted question mark

Adding Comments to Your HTML

You have spent so much time with your HTML, no way could you ever forget what you were thinking when you wrote it, right? Maybe, maybe not. Most people can't remember where they put the bank statement they meant to balance from last month. How can you expect to remember what you were thinking if you have to modify your HTML in six months?

Realistically, you want to use comments in your HTML to tell yourself — and anyone who inherits your files — basic information about what you are doing in there. For example, putting a comment line near the top of your document telling who created the file and on what date is pretty standard. If you expect your HTML to be a teaching tool at all, with people viewing the source to see how you did things, then you want to have especially helpful comments.

Begin your comment with <!–. Any text you put after the two dashes is comment. The browser will not even try to read it. Even if you use special characters, such as ampersands and slashes and quotation marks and angle brackets, your browser ignores everything it comes across until it sees –>. Your comments can span multiple lines. The browser doesn't care. It is only looking for –>.

 Cross-Reference Later, in Chapter 8, we discuss the use of special programs that increase your productivity when you write your HTML.

One of the nice features of most of these programs is colored tags. If your editor changes the color of the tags, then you can see visually whether you have remembered to close your comments — or whether the rest of your document will be processed as a comment (usually not what you want).

Making Your HTML Readable

Most of the markup of your HTML document (that is, the actual HTML elements that mark up your content) is case-insensitive. This means you can pretty much type your HTML as you please. You don't want to work this way, though, because you want your HTML to be readable both to you and to others. Consider the following HTML:

```
<html><head><title>Over the Web, Inc.</title></head><body>
<object type="img/gif" src="logo-f.gif" height="155" width
="90"><h1>List, Email, and Relationship Management 1.15</h1>
<p>Would you like to have a more effective and effortless way
to solicit your potential customer base on the Web?</p> <p><i>
Over the Web Stay in Touch&reg;</i> List, Email, and Relation
ship Management allows you to add a page to your Web site where
your customers can sign in. You can then send mail to them
based on the interests they indicate. The system is entirely
configurable by you. You can change the background color, add
your logo to the top of your page, and customize the interests
your customers indicate.</p>
```

What a mess! Even if you know what all the tags mean, you won't want to dive into that! Now consider:

```
<HTML>
<HEAD>
<TITLE>Over the Web, Inc.</TITLE>
</HEAD>
<BODY>
<OBJECT type="img/gif" src="logo-f.gif" height="155"
width="90">
<H1>List, Email, and Relationship Management 1.15</H1>
<P>Would you like to have a more effective and effortless way
to solicit your potential customer base on the Web?</P>
<P><I>Over the Web Stay in Touch&reg;</I> List, Email, and
Relationship Management allows you to add a page to your Web
site where your customers can sign in. You can then send mail
to them based on the interests they indicate. The system is
entirely configurable by you. You can change the background
color, add your logo to the top of your page, and customize
the interests your customers indicate.</P>
```

This is much friendlier on the eyes. We encourage you to make use of white space in your file (as well as in your pages, which we discuss later). The file won't be any larger (each line of blank space is only sent as one or two bytes of data).

Another convention you may have noticed is the use of all caps for element names and lowercase for attribute-value pairs. You needn't be fanatical about this. If the editor you use does something else, don't worry. Being consistent and leaving lots of white space when you write your markup, though, makes maintenance easier.

Avoiding Common Syntax Errors

Syntax isn't a tax on cigarettes and beer. *Syntax* is the rules of a language. In English, you don't even think about syntax. You know most sentences have a syntax of subject-verb-object. You know not to say (poets excluded): "Wrote the book me."

HTML has syntax, too. When you break the rules, it is politely referred to as a syntax error. When you sit down to start writing HTML, you may find one of the following in your page:

✦ Everything from the first italicized word on is italicized.

✦ You can see one of your tags in your browser.

✦ A form field does not appear, even though you know you created it in HTML.

Figure 1-1 shows some of these syntax errors appearing on a Web page.

Checklist for avoiding common errors when writing HTML

✓   Do you have angle brackets surrounding the start and end tags?

✓   Do you have a slash at the beginning of your end tag?

✓   Do you have quotation marks around the values of your attributes?

✓   Are all the attributes for your tags valid?

Italic begins but never ends

Bold begins but never ends

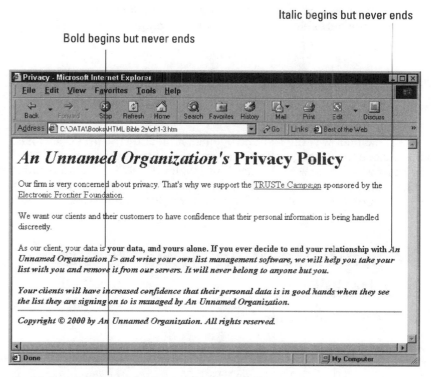

Oops! Forgot the less than sign and the slash (< /)

Figure 1-1: Common syntax errors

Understanding Nesting

As we discussed, sometimes you want to nest elements within other elements. For example, you may want to italicize something that occurs in a paragraph. You've seen the paragraph element, P, in all our examples. The italics element is I. In the previous code example (see "Making Your HTML Readable"), the words *Over the Web Stay in Touch* are italicized within a paragraph.

Many valid types of nesting exist. For example, nearly any element you put within the BODY element is valid, except for the HEAD element. You can't nest some elements, such as a link inside a link.

What is important to remember about nesting is you must close the inner element before you close the outer element. Consider this example of *invalid* HTML:

```
<H1>Over the Web Presents <I>Stay In Touch</H1></I>
```

The *valid* equivalent of this would be:

```
<H1>Over the Web Presents <I>Stay In Touch</I></H1>
```

Because the I element was the last one opened, it must be the first one closed. Be careful to close the inner element before you close the outer element. Most browsers know what to do with the previous invalid HTML, but as more and more elements become available, browsers will enforce rules more strictly. A day may come when the previous invalid HTML does not render properly.

The Basic Structure of an HTML Document: HEAD and BODY

A valid HTML 4 document has three parts:

1. **Version information.** This is also called the document type declaration used by this document. Earlier, we discussed that HTML is a document type declaration (DTD) of SGML. Three HTML DTDs exist; the version information should include which DTD you are using. If you are using an HTML editor, it takes care of this for you. If not, you will be safe using `<!DOCTYPE HTML PUBLIC "-//W3C//DTD HTML 4-01 Frameset//EN""http://www.w3.org/TR/html4/frameset.dtd">`, which is the most permissive of the three.

2. **The HEAD.** The HEAD, in addition to being part of the HTML element, is an element of its own. The HEAD element can contain the title and meta data.

3. **The BODY.** Everything else you want to put into an HTML document belongs in the BODY. The BODY, like the HEAD, is also an element.

What we haven't mentioned yet is that HTML itself is an element. The HTML element has both a start tag and an end tag. The start tag should be placed after the version information and before the start tag of the HEAD element. The end tag goes at the very end of your document, after the end tag of the BODY element.

```
<!DOCTYPE HTML PUBLIC "-//W3C//DTD HTML 4-01 Frameset//EN"
"http://www.w3.org/TR/html4/frameset.dtd">
<HTML>
<HEAD>
<TITLE>My Valid HTML document</TITLE>
</HEAD>
```

```
<BODY>
If this had been an actual HTML document, this is where we
would have put the content.
</BODY>
</HTML>
```

The previous code example shows how a valid HTML document is structured. Notice how the BODY element is closed before the HTML element is closed.

From Here

 For the more practical-minded, proceed to Chapter 2 to begin creating a Web page.

Summary

HTML syntax is straightforward. If you follow a few simple rules, you won't find your HTML document full of syntax errors and, more important, your pages will look right in a browser. The basic building block of HTML is an element. Elements have attributes that enable you to customize them. Attributes require values. Values should be enclosed in double quotation marks.

Most elements have both start tags and end tags. These tags surround the content. Both the start tags and end tags consist of the element name surrounded by angle brackets. The end tag has a slash before the element name, within the angle brackets.

An HTML document should have version information at the top. After that comes the HTML element, which consists of a HEAD and a BODY. To ensure you have nested elements properly, always close the inner element before you close the outer element.

✦   ✦   ✦

The HTML 4 Way

Let's talk for a moment about history. Not ancient history but, say, mid-1997 Web-publishing history. What were people's biggest concerns about publishing a page back then?

+ **Compatibility across browsers.** Would a page that looked awesome in Internet Explorer 4 look right in Netscape Navigator 4? Would JavaScript, which animated a figure perfectly in Navigator 4, work in Internet Explorer 4? And what if a visitor to your site was using Netscape Navigator 2? Did you really have to maintain a nonframes-compatible version of every single page?

+ **Keeping content fresh.** People expect to come to your Web site to get accurate, up-to-date answers to their questions. Can you afford to be constantly updating your content when it is buried in a bunch of HTML? You practically need a Web developer just to correct a misspelling, when the content and the design are so closely interwoven.

+ **Keeping a current look.** The standards for gorgeous Web page design are climbing every week. Keeping your site looking hot is both costly and time-consuming.

HTML 4 can't completely solve all these problems, but it can reduce the magnitude of these problems. This chapter explains how.

The Extension Problem

In America, we value innovation. We celebrate people who make a lot of money by being the first to implement great ideas. This culture of reverence for mavericks creates a lot of problems for Web developers when the mavericks are producing the browsers that have the lion's share of the market.

Both Netscape and Microsoft are to blame (don't try to pin it all on Bill Gates, founder of Microsoft, the world's richest man, and the subject of an entire genre of humor); both these companies have introduced proprietary *extensions* (ways of marking up HTML) that only work on their own browsers.

AOL's purchase of Netscape hasn't changed the browser race drastically, but it has added a layer of mystery to the continuing evolution of Netscape Communicator. Of course, Netscape and Microsoft aren't doing anything car manufacturers don't do every year. When the first minivan manufacturer added cupholders, did anyone complain? This feature may have made you purchase that minivan instead of the competitor's. Today, every minivan has cupholders — so it goes with great innovations!

So what do cupholders and mavericks have to do with your Web site? Everything. The people who make browsers are trying to get more people to purchase and use their own browsers — rather than the competitors — by adding more new features. Of course, you're thinking, isn't this contrary to the idea of the Web, that everything would be standard so everything could be seen on every computer, regardless of platform or software installed? You've obviously been paying attention. It is, indeed, antithetical to the very basis of the Web. In fact, if these motivations had been in place when the Web got off the ground, we'd probably have two or three different Webs and nothing from one could be viewed on either of the others!

Let's look at the specific problems browser manufacturers introduce when they add new features no one else has.

Compatibility across browsers

When Netscape introduced frames with Version 3 of Navigator, designers had a problem: Did they start using a feature that not only couldn't be seen by a visitor who came to their sites from any other browser, but couldn't even be seen by a visitor who came to their sites from all previous versions of Netscape Navigator? The answer is many of them started to use frames, but maintained two separate sites: one for people coming to the site with Netscape Navigator 3 and one for everyone else. They also put little icons (provided by Netscape at no charge) on their pages saying: This site looks best when viewed with Netscape Navigator. What could be more of a pain for designers?

What could be better for Netscape? As it turned out, Microsoft ended up adding support for frames to their own browsers, making frames a standard. Now, both Netscape Communicator 4.7 and Internet Explorer 5.0 support frames. Most sites look identical in either Netscape or IE, as long as you're running the newest version of the browser.

So, didn't it all end happily ever after? Not exactly. This constant battle for market share that rages between Microsoft and Netscape means as a Web designer, you will constantly evaluate your material to see what works with which browser. You will always have to assess the trade-off between the following three positions:

1. **Don't use any tags that aren't widely supported.** The result of this decision is you will only have to support one set of pages (rather than one for the latest set of extensions and one for everyone who has browsers that don't support those). But — and this is the major drawback — your site will never look as cool as the sites of those who do use the latest extensions. You won't be able to implement the latest and greatest design features.

2. **Use the proprietary tags and to heck with people who haven't upgraded.** Arrogant but, for certain sites, this works. If your site is about design, you don't have any choice but to use the latest design tools. (No one attends fashion shows of last year's clothes.) If, however, you are trying to sell something on your site (other than your own design services), then you'd better be a little less cavalier about your visitors' experiences. If your site appeals to education or social causes — where you can do the most good if you reach the maximum number of people — then you should probably not adopt this attitude.

3. **Support two versions of the same site: one that uses the latest extensions and one that doesn't.** Later in this book, you learn how to use JavaScript to find out which browser your visitors are using when they come to your page and then to show them the appropriate page for their browsers. Of course, this approach is the most expensive, because you have to maintain the site in two versions — what a pain!

How did it happen that on this cross-platform Web, where everything was supposed to work on every computer, we ended up in a situation where we are writing browser-specific pages? Isn't someone supposed to keep this from happening?

Indeed, someone is trying.

The World Wide Web Consortium

The World Wide Web Consortium (W3C) is the organization created to set standards for the Web. However, the W3C has no means of enforcement (and no inspection teams to make sure soon-to-be-released browsers comply). The W3C has a small staff of its own, but most of the people on the committees (about which you'll soon hear more) who write the standards come from the academy and industry. Sometimes those who sit on committees represent specific interests.

While the theory goes that the W3C sets a standard and the industry follows, the reality is, the W3C is usually following the actions taken by the largest browser manufacturers: Netscape and Microsoft. Because Microsoft and Netscape continue to add their own proprietary extensions, the W3C is often in the position of simply compiling a list of the features already in use on either browser and deciding which ones will be declared standard. The W3C also does a lot of interesting work in developing standards for ancillary Web technologies.

The Ideal: Separating Structure from Presentation

The most expensive thing about publishing a Web site isn't the cost of your account with an ISP. It isn't the cost of any tool you may purchase to increase your productivity when writing HTML. It isn't the time spent learning HTML. What is it? It's the time spent maintaining your site.

HTML 4 tackles this problem head-on by storing all the information about the way things should look in a separate location (either in a separate place in the same document or, better yet, in a separate file altogether) from the content. You simply indicate what type of element (paragraph, title, list, heading) each block of text is, using HTML, and then, in a style sheet, you describe how you want each element to look.

Cluttered HTML (the pre-HTML-4 universe)

Unless you are content to let your content get stale and your style become dated, you need to put time into updating both your design and your content. In the pre-HTML-4 world, you needed to hire a Web developer to do both of these, which became expensive. Why did you need a Web developer simply to update your content? Consider the following HTML:

```
<li><FONT SIZE="+1" FACE="comic sans ms" FAMILY="sans-serif"
COLOR="#0000FF"><P><A name="do"></a><B>What does <i>Stay In
Touch</i> do?</B></P></FONT>
<FONT SIZE="-1" FACE="comic sans ms" FAMILY="sans-serif"
COLOR="#000000"><P><i>Stay In Touch</i> allows you to harness
the power of the World Wide Web to communicate with people who
visit your web site. Using <i>Stay In Touch</i> list management
service you can set up a sign-in page on your web site today
```

and customize it to match the rest of your web site. Your
visitors can sign into your site when they visit, then you can
send mail to your visitors based on a number of criteria: the
interest they indicate, the publications they read, etc. To see
an example of this, go to the Demo and view the Send Mail
option.</P></FONT>
<li><FONT SIZE="+1" FACE="comic sans ms" FAMILY="sans-serif"
COLOR="#0000FF"><P><A name="security"></a><B>How secure is my
list?</B></P></FCNT>
<FONT SIZE="-1" FACE="comic sans ms" FAMILY="Sans Serif"
COLOR="#000000"><P>Only you have access to your list. Access to
your list is available exclusively from secure pages residing
on our server. You have enough to worry about. The security of
your list needn't be one of those things.</P></FONT>

Figures 2-1 and 2-2 are what it looks like in your browser on a PC and then on a Mac
(notice the font is slightly different).

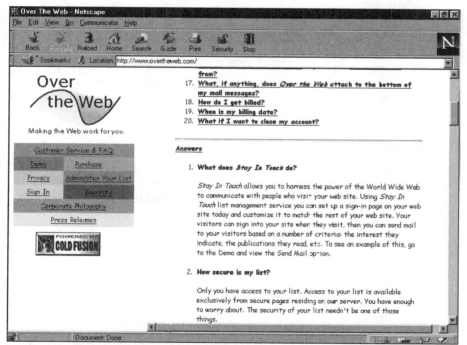

Figure 2-1: The previous text displayed in a browser on a PC

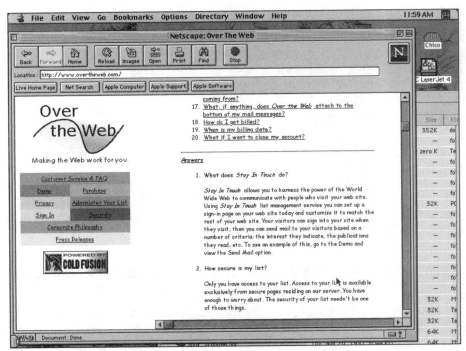

Figure 2-2: The previous text displayed in a browser on a Mac

The maintenance nightmare

From looking at the HTML and then seeing the HTML interpreted by the browser, you can pretty much tell what part of the text is instructions to the browser and what part is the content. But would you feel comfortable making changes to the content — say, adding another bulleted set of questions and answers? Probably not. And you probably wouldn't want someone else who didn't know what all those codes meant doing it either.

HTML 4 almost eliminates this need to have an HTML expert perform site maintenance. This means HTML 4 helps reduce the cost of maintaining your Web site! When was the last time you heard anything about reducing costs being associated with the Web?

Consider the site map in Figure 2-3. Every screen should have the same formatting: same font, same heading sizes, same alignment, same text color, and same background color. Wouldn't it be nice if you could put all this information in one place and have every page look to that page for formatting instructions?

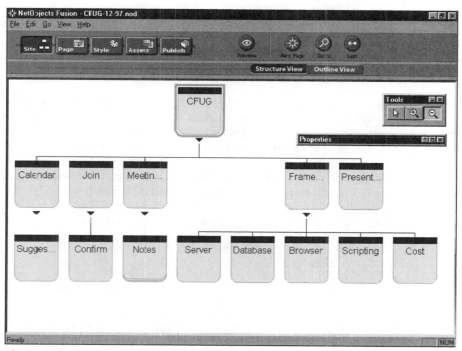

Figure 2-3: Site map

HTML 4 defines structure

A brief outburst of history—Standard Generalized Markup Language (SGML), approved by the ISO in 1988, is the basis for HTML. SGML is a standard for electronic document exchange, and in fact, was used in the publication of this book. In the publication process, the book publisher marks up a text using SGML and then tells the printer to print it by providing a list of how each element of SGML should appear.

Title:	Make this blue. 18pt. Times New Roman. Also center it.
Section headings:	Make them black (the rest of the book should all be black, by the way) and 18pt. The font should be Times Roman. They should be left-justified and triple-spaced.
Paragraphs:	Each paragraph should be indented ¾ inch. Font should be 12pt. And Times Roman.
Examples of code:	These should be in Courier 12pt. They should be indented from each margin by ¾ inch.

The publisher uses SGML to indicate where titles, section headings, paragraphs, and code examples (referred to collectively as *elements*) begin and end. When HTML was first created, this was how it was supposed to work. But designers weren't happy with the lack of control over formatting, so they started to use it in a way that never had been intended.

HTML 4 enables us to return to the ideal of HTML. What does this mean to you and your ability to maintain a site? If the only codes that appear in your HTML are structure codes (with the presentation codes appearing elsewhere), then no reason exists why you can't use less expensive talent to maintain your content.

Consider the following code. It produces the same results as the previous example in the browser. Notice there is no formatting. All the HTML you see is related to the structure. We discuss the formatting code in the next section. For now, just remember we put the information related to presentation into a style sheet.

```
<LI>What does <i>Stay In Touch</i> do?
<P><i>Stay In Touch</i> allows you to harness the power of the
World Wide Web to communicate with people who visit your web
site. Using <i>Stay In Touch</i> list management service you
can set up a sign-in page on your web site today and customize
it to match the rest of your web site. Your visitors can sign
into your site when they visit, then you can send mail to your
visitors based on a number of criteria: the interest they
indicate, the publications they read, etc. To see an example of
this, go to the Demo and view the Send Mail option.</P>
<LI>How secure is my list?
<P>Only you have access to your list. Access to your list is
available exclusively from secure pages residing on our server.
You have enough to worry about. The security of your list
needn't be one of those things.</P>
```

How comfortable would you be updating the previous HTML? How about if you needed to add another set of questions and answers? Already, you can see using HTML 4 makes a world of difference. The information the browser must know to format the previous text is stored separately, in a style sheet.

Introducing Cascading Style Sheets

A *style sheet* contains information about how you want your page to look. The idea and the name come from the publishing industry, where style sheets are still used today. But why *cascading* style sheets (CSS)? Good question. Most of the time, when you create a site, you want a uniform look across the site. You probably don't want each different section of a site to use a different font or a different background color. You probably also don't want one section to have all the text left-justified (like this book) and have another section right-justified, just for the heck of it. If you are creating the site yourself, this kind of uniformity is easier to maintain, but even you may sometimes forget how you did it on another page.

The answer to uniformity is a style sheet. Define your style sheet outside any of your pages (give it a name like `MyStyleSheet.css`) and link all your pages to it. Now, any element you have described in your style sheet will look the way you want it to look (and the same) in every page where that element is used.

But what if you want the color of some text to be different on one page? Say, to indicate this is a new addition to your site or a limited-time offer? Easy. Just define the style for this element right there, in that tag. Isn't this the way pre-HTML-4 worked? Exactly. Except you will use style definitions within elements only as the exception, not as the rule.

The browser knows to look in the external (global) style sheet for style definitions about each element it encounters (see Figure 2-4). It uses those unless it finds locally defined styles, and then those locally defined styles override the globally defined styles. Finally, you can define styles for an entire page. Element-level styles override page-specific styles, which override global styles.

As confusing as this sounds, most often you only have a globally defined style sheet. Still, it's nice to know you can override the global style sheet if you like.

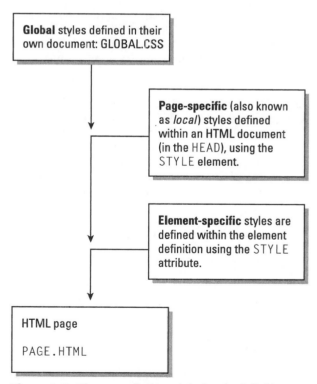

Figure 2-4: The cascading model of style definitions

The HTML 4 Way

So what is the HTML 4 Way? The *HTML 4 Way* is using HTML within your document only to define structure and putting all information your browser needs about presentation into a style sheet.

The rest of this book focuses on the HTML 4 Way. If you are already a veteran Web developer, then you may have to break some bad habits. If you are new to Web development, then you have it easier; you can learn it right — right from the beginning.

The Future: XML

Let's go back to SGML — standard generalized markup language — again. HTML came from SGML, but those folks who live and breathe SGML in publishing and the academy were not satisfied with what HTML could do. They kept complaining to the W3C about the things HTML couldn't do that SGML could.

The W3C tried to appease these SGML-zealots (using the term advisedly) who complained about the shortcomings of HTML — now remember the reason HTML became so popular so quickly was it was simple — by expanding the HTML specification. Each time a new version of HTML came out, the SGML fanatics complained at greater length (if you ever see SGML, you'll see it is not known for its brevity, unlike HTML) about its failure to perform like SGML.

You can see where this is going: XML. Extensible Markup Language (XML) was approved in January 1998 by the members of the W3C, and recommended by the W3C shortly thereafter. To help you understand why the W3C had delayed supporting the demand of the SGML advocates, note that, at the time XML was approved, neither of the major browsers supported it (please recall that every feature of HTML 4 was already supported in one of the two major browsers — and had been for almost a year — by the time it was approved). So why would you want to know or use XML? Two reasons:

✦ **Flexibility.** Unlike HTML, XML gives you the ability to define your own tags.

✦ **Power.** Unlike HTML, XML enables the use of variables you can define externally to your page. This makes XML more like a programming language. Before XML, you had to use server-side scripting, JavaScript, or Java to include variables in your documents. Because XML isn't implemented (at the time of this publication), you still must use one of these.

And why wouldn't you want to use XML?

✦ **Flexibility.** With flexibility comes responsibility. You have to define each of your tag definitions properly in a document type definition (DTD).

✦ **Complexity.** XML is a lot like a programming language. None of the programming languages have taken off the way HTML has. The average Web developer isn't ready for this kind of complexity.

We'll cover XML basics in subsequent chapters, but for the whole story, look for the *XML Bible* by Elliotte Rusty Harold (IDG Books, 1999).

The Ideal Versus the Reality

While HTML 4 addresses all three of the major concerns of Web developers outlined as we began this chapter—compatibility across browsers, keeping content fresh, and keeping a current look—as a designer, you are still somewhat trapped by the dilemma that has frustrated all previous Web designers contending with new versions. Until all browsers support all features of HTML 4 and you can be sure all visitors to your site are using HTML-4-compatible browsers, you are left with the following options:

✦ **Don't use any HTML-4-specific tags or methodology.** Just keep doing things the way you have been. Clutter up your document with formatting and structural HTML and take a new job when the mess becomes too unmanageable.

✦ **Use HTML 4 and to heck with people who haven't upgraded to HTML-4-compatible browsers.** Use HTML for structure only within your documents. If people are viewing your site with a browser that doesn't support HTML 4, then they will see minimalist formatting, but this is basically their problem.

✦ **Support two versions of the same site: one that uses HTML 4 and one that doesn't.** Keep the content up-to-date in your current site. Apply any face-lifts to the HTML 4 version of your site.

Where's All This Going?

Without question, the direction of the Web is toward the HTML 4 Way. Whether it is with HTML 4 this year or XML next year, you can count on the need for the separation of structure from design. As HTML becomes more sophisticated and more and more formatting features are added, the need for separation will become even clearer.

Web designers want to make their pages more visually compelling, taking the best practices from print and the best practices from television. Management wants the ever-spiraling cost of maintaining a Web site to level off or drop—why should they have to pay high-priced Web designers just to update the text on a page? HTML 4 meets both these needs in a concrete way.

Unlike previous versions of HTML, HTML 4 is pretty well implemented in both Navigator and Internet Explorer. With HTML 4, you'll find you can do things you only dreamed of before now. Indenting a paragraph? No problem. Indenting every paragraph? No problem. Change the text color of every heading? No problem.

The die is cast, and even though you may have to change the way you think about creating and maintaining a Web site, it is for the better. Never before have you had the kind of control over formatting you have now. Never before have you had the flexibility to make your text do whatever you want, including moving!

What Should You Do Now?

Get excited! The face of the Web will never look the same. You are going to be part of the story, whether you are an example in the next version of this book of the bad, old way people used to write HTML or an award-winning Web designer, implementing HTML 4 to bring traffic and recognition to your Web site.

Don't necessarily look to the Web for the future of design. Few places exist where you can see the power of HTML 4 in action. Look to print — where few formatting constraints exist (although they, unlike we, are constrained by two dimensions). Look to television where animated text is something we take for granted.

From Here

If you are an old hand at HTML and you have been bearing with us to see what this HTML 4 Way is all about, you can jump right into Part IV to learn about enhancing your presentation with Cascading Style Sheets.

If you are just getting started with HTML, proceed to Chapter 3 to learn the basics of creating your first Web page.

Summary

The HTML 4 Way is, indeed, the future of Web publishing. It reduces the cost of maintaining a Web site, increases the speed of giving your site a periodic face-lift, and completely changes the paradigm of Web development by separating presentation from structure.

XML may or may not take over as the king of the Web for reasons, principally, of complexity. In any case, the design choices available to you as a Web designer continue to increase. Even if the W3C didn't have this as a goal, Netscape and Microsoft continue to try to sell their own browsers, which necessitates the inclusion of new features.

While it is true you can't assume every visitor to your site has the most recent browser supporting HTML 4, you can still provide adequate content to your foot-dragging visitors and stunning design to your visitors who are keeping up.

✦   ✦   ✦

Creating Your First Web Page

Now that you've gotten a little background on HTML 4 and the importance of separating your content from formatting, it's time to get your hands dirty (figuratively speaking, of course). By the end of this chapter, you'll have a working Web page. We won't make it do tricks yet, but it will have all the basics. Later, we can add the bells and whistles.

Fire Up Your Editor

For this first Web page, you use the plain text editor that came built into your computer. If you are on a PC running Windows 95/98/2000 or NT, from the Start Menu, select Program and then select Accessories and then select Notepad. You will see something similar to Figure 3-1. If you are on a Mac, open SimpleText and you will see something similar to Figure 3-2. If you are in a UNIX environment, open your text editor of choice (vi, pico, jove, or emacs).

Even if you have some fancy tool that was bundled with your computer when you purchased it, or you downloaded from the Web, or you purchased yourself, don't use it yet. There's time for productivity-enhancing tools later. Right now, you need to learn some basic HTML and, depending on the HTML-development program you have, it may get in your way.

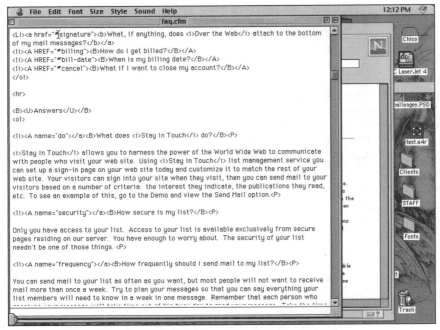

Figure 3-1: Notepad is the text editor that comes with the Windows operating systems.

Figure 3-2: SimpleText comes with the Mac operating system.

Titling Your Page

Have you ever tried to set a bookmark for a page, only to find the bookmark had a meaningless name? This was a particular problem in earlier browsers, which didn't permit you to edit bookmark properties. Why didn't a meaningful name — or, sometimes, any name at all — show up in your bookmark list? The Web developer hadn't put a title into the page.

The TITLE element is among the simplest elements. It takes no attributes. In previous versions of HTML, a title was not required. Under HTML 4, absence of a title is a syntax violation. Both a start tag and an end tag are required.

Using as descriptive a title as possible is always a good idea. In addition to showing up in the bookmark folder, the title also displays across the top of your browser. Some Web developers have been in the habit of titling all their pages with the same title — usually the name of the company. This isn't a useful practice because the title should impart useful information. Unlike book titles, where publishers may be imposing limits, with Web page titles, you can take all the words you need to convey your message — within limits, of course. The two major browsers support title length up to 96 or 100 characters. Because search engines frequently use the title of your page as the heading for the entry to your page, it is triply important for you to use a good, descriptive title.

First things first

As you learned in the last chapter, the TITLE element goes in the HEAD element. But where does the HEAD element go? That's right — in the HTML element. So, before you can really put a title on your page, you want to write the following into your empty document:

- ✦ Version information
- ✦ The HTML element start tag
- ✦ The HEAD element start tag

Consider this your first quiz. We give you the answer to the requirement for version information, so you don't have to flip back a few pages, but you must remember what the HTML and HEAD start tags look like.

```
<!DOCTYPE HTML PUBLIC "-//W3C//DTD HTML 4.0 Strict//EN"
"http://www.w3.org/TR/html40/Strict.dtd">
```

Go ahead and add the HTML element start tag and the HEAD element start tag next. Be sure to put each of these on a separate line. If you want, you can leave blank lines between these tags, as well.

Next, we add the title, which requires the `TITLE` element start tag: `<TITLE>`. The content for the `TITLE` element should be your actual page title, so put that next. At the end of your content, put the `TITLE` element end tag: `</TITLE>`.

Identifying the Author

If you recall, we said one other thing went into the `HEAD` of an HTML document, which is metadata. *Metadata* is information about the information on your page. This would include the name of the author, the software used to write the page, the company name (if there is any), contact information, and so forth.

We won't go into the syntax of the `META` element right now. You want to indicate you are the author, and there is a `META` element perfect for this:

```
<META name="Author" content="put your name here">
```

As you can see, the `META` element has at least two attributes. We have two in the previous example. The `META` element is unique because, instead of having content between a start tag and an end tag, the `META` element has a `CONTENT` attribute. And there is no end tag. You will see a variety of uses for the `META` element.

In general, you won't see anything from `META` elements displayed in your browser. The W3C leaves the implementation of the `META` element to the discretion of the browser. In the future, it is conceivable some of this data could be viewed from within your browser — yet another reason to include it.

Defining key words for better retrieval

While we realize you probably won't try to get this initial Web page listed with a search engine — although you certainly can — you might as well get into using good habits. A good habit to have when creating a Web page is adding a `META` element for keywords.

Add the following tag to your document:

```
<META name="keywords" content="list of keywords">
```

where *list of keywords* is a comma-delimited list such as "list management, email, crossware, relationship management, guestbook, sign-in page." With some search engines, capitalization matters, so it is to your advantage to include *guestbook*, *Guestbook*, and *Guest Book* as three different keywords. Unfortunately, other search engines might interpret this as *spamming* — trying to fool them into listing you higher for a more relevant match.

A note about search engines

Most of the search engines use the metadata you provide about keywords to help index your page. Rules exist about these things, but they change from search engine to search engine. Extensive resources are also on the Web for finding the techniques to get your page listed higher in the search engines. For example, one search engine automatically ignores any word listed more than seven times in the keyword string—even if it is listed in different ways. Knowing the rules when you submit with search engines is important. They are getting harder and harder to fool.

An interesting tool, which can help you identify the ranking of your page on a variety of search engines, is WebPosition Gold. At publication date, this was the only commercial software that could go out to a variety of search engines and find what number your site is, based on the keywords you provide. Many services will do this for you, but WebPosition Gold enables you to do it yourself on a scheduled basis, if you wish, from your own desktop. A trial version of WebPosition Gold is available as a free download at www.webposition.com/download.htm. The following figure shows a screen from WebPosition Gold.

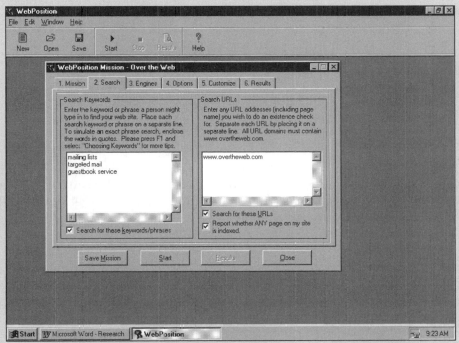

WebPosition Gold finds your site in all the search engines and reports back to you.

A variety of newsletters can tell you about tips and tricks to get your site listed higher. WebPosition Analyzer publishes its own newsletter. Another excellent one is Danny Sullivan's *Search Engine Report,* which you can subscribe to from the Search Engine Watch page (www.searchenginewatch.com).

Beginning the BODY

What do you have to do before you can begin the BODY element? Close the HEAD element. Go ahead and add the end tag for the HEAD element. Then add the start tag for the BODY element.

The BODY element has several attributes that you can use to customize the look of your document. In previous versions of HTML, this is where you set the background image, if there was one. This image would tile across the screen, which could look nice or could look horrid. This is also where you would set the background color, the text color, the link color, the visited link color, and the active link color. With the HTML 4 Way, these presentational qualities are all set in the style sheet. This keeps down the amount of markup in your document and keeps the visual clutter to a minimum when you are editing your document. The W3C refers to those BODY attributes as deprecated. A deprecated element or attribute is one the W3C would rather you not use. In future versions of HTML, that element or attribute might not work in browsers or might do something unexpected. For now, all the major browsers support deprecated elements. This means you won't have any problems with them, but it is a good idea to try to steer clear of them as you develop new pages.

Adding an Apparent Title

Going along with these instructions and typing junk every time we instruct you to type content would be easy. Instead, let's stop for a minute. Think about what you want on your page. We are finally at the point where what you type will appear in your browser window.

What did you entitle your page, using the previous TITLE element? Is this really what you want to call your page? If not, go back and change it. Later on in the book, we focus at length on the content of your page, but that doesn't mean you want to publish junk until then.

To add a title to your page, we use the heading elements. In the HTML 4 Way, all we do is tell the browser this is a heading, along with the importance of this heading (number 1 being the most important and number 6 being the least important). As far as presentation goes, we can either let the browser have its way with our headings or we can use style sheets to define the presentation.

 Note Don't be confused by the terms used here. When we discuss the TITLE element, you see the term as uppercase code font. In this discussion of using heading elements on pages, we use title in lowercase.

The heading elements are H1, H2, H3, H4, H5, and H6 Don't try to make them look the way you want your page to look. We can do this later with style sheets. For now, just assign them to headings in order of importance. If you have been in the habit of adding an align attribute, you want to stop doing that. W3C deprecates the use of align as an attribute of heading elements (that's why style sheets are used).

Figure 3-3 shows how you may use elements H1, H2, and H3 to indicate varying degrees of importance in your page.

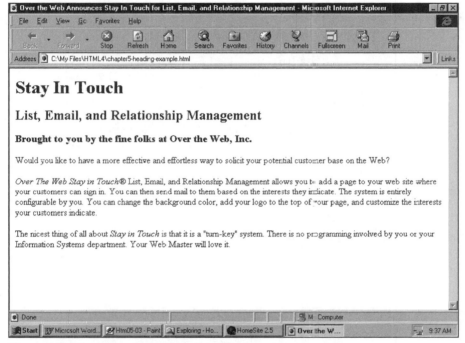

Figure 3-3: Example of using heading elements on your page

This is also a good time to check your own HTML. If the following markup doesn't match your own, you'll want to review your own and see what you missed. Of course, the content won't match.

```
<!DOCTYPE HTML PUBLIC "-//W3C//DTD HTML 4.0 Strict//EN"
"http://www.w3.org/TR/html40/Strict.dtd">
<HTML>
<HEAD>
```

```
<TITLE>Over the Web Announces Stay In Touch for List, Email,
and Relationship Management</TITLE>
<META name="author" content="Alexis D. Gutzman">
<META name="keywords" content="list management, relationship
management, email, mailing lists, turn-key">
</HEAD>
<BODY>
<h1>Stay In Touch</h1>
<h2>List, Email, and Relationship Management</h2>
<h3>Brought to you by the fine folks at Over the Web, Inc.</h3>
<P>Would you like to have a more effective and effortless way
to solicit your potential customer base on the Web?</P>
<P><I>Over The Web Stay in Touch&reg;</I> List, Email, and
Relationship Management allows you to add a page to your web
site where your customers can sign in. You can then send mail
to them based on the interests they indicate. The system is
entirely configurable by you. You can change the background
color, add your logo to the top of your page, and customize the
interests your customers indicate.</P>
<P>The nicest thing of all about <I>Stay in Touch</I> is that
it is a "turn-key" system. There is no programming involved by
you or your Information Systems department. Your Web Master
will love it.</P>
</BODY>
</HTML>
```

Typing and Editing Text

Now you want to enter your text—the main content of your page. You may want to use two types of text: paragraphs and blockquotes.

Paragraphs

Most prose is divided into paragraphs. HTML provides the P element to identify paragraphs. The P element has a start tag and an end tag. You put your content between the two. For our purposes in this section, we won't include any attributes. The one you may have seen or used in the past was the align attribute, but as we noted, that is deprecated by the W3C.

Blockquotes

The other kind of prose you may want to include is a quote from someone else. If this quote extends beyond a line or two, you will want to set it off in its own block. This is the way we often see reviews of software or reviews of pages. Figure 3-4 shows two quoted paragraphs from Marc Andreessen in a Netscape White Paper:

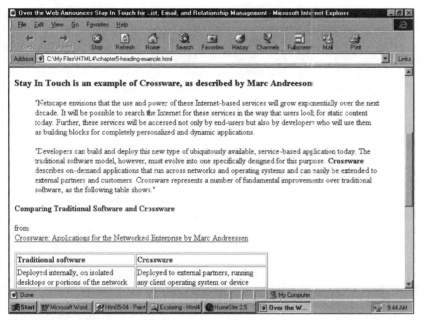

Figure 3-4: A blockquote

Breaking Lines and Starting New Paragraphs

Sometimes you want to add extra blank space. Perhaps you have text that doesn't belong in a paragraph. In the previous example, after the table heading, we have the word *from* on its own line. To achieve this, we inserted the BR element after the table heading. We wouldn't have wanted this word to be a paragraph by itself, in part, because, structurally, it is not. Had we made this word a paragraph, and in a style sheet indicated that paragraphs should have a half-inch indentation on the first line, then this word would have been indented a half inch. Wouldn't that look strange?

The BR element takes no attributes. It only has a start tag. There is no content and no end tag. This is the easiest element to get right.

```
<H4>The Netscape Application Platform</H4>
<p>from <BR>
<A HREF= "http://developer.netscape.com/docs/wpapers/crossware/index.html">The
Netscape Application Platform by Marc Andreessen</a>
```

Preventing line breaks

The opposite of creating a line break is preventing a line break. Sometimes you want a string of words to appear all on the same line. For example: March 1788. For a variety of reasons, you may always want March and 1788 to appear on the same line. You can prevent automatic wrapping of lines resulting in March appearing at the end of one line and 1788 appearing at the beginning of the next line by inserting a nonbreaking space between `March` and `1788`. The nonbreaking space is an entity (remember, in entities — unlike the rest of HTML — capitalization *does* matter), but it is not a printable character. To insert a nonbreaking space, you can use either the character representation of ` ` or the decimal representation of ` `. Thus, March 1788 would look like:

```
March 1788
```

Adding horizontal lines

Your page may benefit from horizontal lines. For example, it is not unusual to see a horizontal line between the page and footer text. *Footer text* is text that appears on every page and is not specifically related to the content of the page. For example, you almost always see footers on magazine pages, which may include the page number.

On a Web page, a footer usually includes copyright information, perhaps the date of publication of the page, and how to contact the Webmaster. Many pages include *hit counts,* which actually in no way represent the actual number of visitors, even if they say they do.

Figure 3-5 is an example of a page the effectively uses horizontal lines.

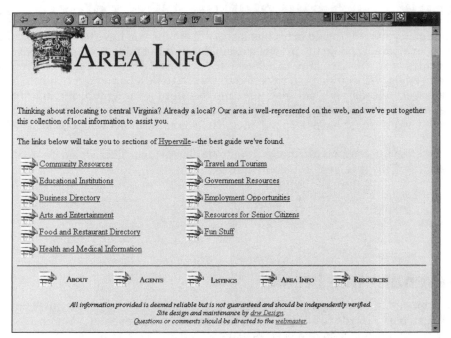

Figure 3-5: The horizontal rule element is right at home at the bottom of this page.

The horizontal rule HR element is almost as foolproof as the BR element. It requires a start tag, forbids an end tag, and has no content. If you have any memories of using attributes with the HR element, forget them. The W3C deprecates any formatting attributes.

Creating a List

You may want to include a list for many reasons:

✦ You think in lists.

✦ You are trying to persuade people and you want to make your evidence clear.

✦ You use lists as shorthand.

✦ You want people to know the sequence of events in instructions.

✦ You know people more often remember material set apart from the main text.

✦ You just want an example of a list.

Whatever your reasons, HTML accommodates your wish for a list. Three types of lists actually exist in HTML:

✦ Bulleted lists (called unordered lists)

✦ Numbered lists (called ordered lists)

✦ Definition lists

We discuss them all in further detail later in the book, but for now we plan to discuss only bulleted lists and numbered lists.

Bulleted lists

We may call them bulleted lists, or simply bullet lists, but HTML calls them *unordered lists*. An unordered list is created with the UL element. For each item in the list, you need the LI element.

The UL element requires a start tag and an end tag. Between those go each item on your list. You can, of course, include other text between the start and end tags, but unless that other text is part of the LI element, it won't appear with a bullet in front of it.

The LI element requires a start tag. The end tag is optional. Following the start tag, you put whatever you want in the list. Each item in your list gets its own LI element. Witness:

```
<UL>
<LI> Have a custom sign-in page on your Website today!
```

```
<LI> Collect information from your customers right on your Web site
<LI> Send email to your customers
<!--LI> Export customer information to spreadsheet, database, or word processing
software for paper mailings-->
<LI> Add your logo, set the background color or graphic to match the rest of
your Web site
</UL>
```

Cross-Reference   You can do other interesting tricks with unordered lists such as nesting them, but we save this for Chapter 16, where we cover lists in depth.

Numbered lists

A numbered list uses the OL element (ordered list). The OL element requires a start tag and an end tag. Each item in the list is part of its own LI element. You use the exact same LI element as in the ordered list. Look at the following code:

```
<H2>Setting up your list is as Easy as 1-2-3</H2>
<OL>
<LI> Get a Stay in Touch Account
<LI> Click through our easy set-up wizard to customize your pages
<LI> Link to your list from your Web site
</OL>
```

Figure 3-6 shows what the browser does with your lists.

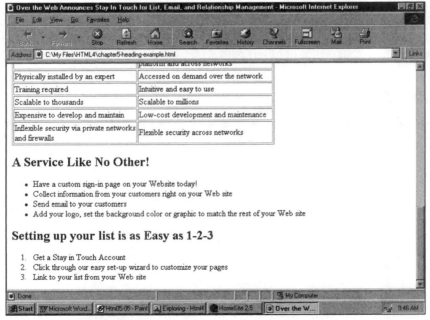

Figure 3-6: Two kinds of lists

Adding a Link

How can you create a hypertext page without a link—*at least one* link? The syntax for linking is quite simple. You use the A (anchor) element to create a link. Just for fun, let's put one link in your document to something else in your document. The other link, we'll put to the IDG Books Web site. For now, we'll use text to link to the IDG Books Web site, but before you know it, we'll use an image from the CD-ROM in the back of the book. You wondered what was on the CD, didn't you?

Simply, here is the syntax for the A element. Both a start tag and an end tag are required. For the *hot text* (that is, the text that can be clicked to jump elsewhere), content is required. For the destination of the link, content is optional, but we recommend you do include content because some browsers won't find a named anchor (the W3C term for destination) that does not have content.

Adding an internal link

The interesting part of the A element is the attributes. To add an internal link, you use the A element to create both the link and the destination. First, we create the destination. To do this, you need to use the name attribute of the A element, thus:

```
<A name="Features">Features of this product include:</A>
```

Where did we get the value of the name attribute? We made it up. What good does it do to have a destination in our page right now? None. But we can use it in conjunction with hot text elsewhere in the page to make it valuable.

Let's dissect the previous A element, just for review:

Start tag:	`<A name="Features">`
Attribute-value pair:	`name= "Features"`
Attribute:	`name`
Value:	`Features`
Content:	`Features of this product include:`
End tag:	`</A>`

Now, let's link to the named anchor we previously created. We use the href attribute to do this. As with all attributes, the href attribute needs a value. What do you suppose the value of the href attribute will be in our example? If you guess features, you are getting good at this. We just need to add one little twist. We need to add a # (pound sign) in front of the value, inside the double quotation marks.

```
Stay in Touch is loaded with <A href="#Features">
features</A> that no other product has.
```

When you look at this code in a browser, you can't see the named anchor, but if you click the highlighted word *features*, you can jump to the features list. The browser knows where the named anchors are, but it doesn't show them to you.

You've done the harder version; now let's do the easy version.

Adding an external link

When you link to someplace outside your page, whether this is within your site or on some distant server, you use the A element with the href attribute, such as in the previous example. Pointing to a page somewhere else requires a little more than is required when pointing to a place within your document. The value of the href attribute will be a bit longer.

For this example, you are going to point to the IDG Books Worldwide page. You decided that somewhere on your page you mention you're using the HTML 4 Way. This should look familiar to you, with one twist. The value of the href attribute is a URL: the home page of IDG Books.

```
<A href="http://www.idgbooks.com">This page was created the HTML 4 Way</A>
```

That's not the most appealing text, but later we'll replace it with an image, anyway. For now, you have a working link to a distant server. Isn't that the point of this whole hypertext thing, anyway?

Caution

STOP: Save your file now! Call it **MyFirst.html** unless you are working in Windows 3.1, in which case, you need to call it **MyFirst.htm**. If you are working in Windows 3.1, you'll want to remember that every time we talk about your files as **something.html**, your files will actually be **something.htm**, okay? This is the last time we'll mention it.

Preview Your Page

Now that you've saved your page, you can open it in a browser and look at it. If anything doesn't look the way you expected, you'll want to review the "Checklist for avoiding common errors when writing HTML" that appears at the end of Chapter 1. Check for end tags (and those pesky slashes). Be sure you have double quotation marks around all your attributes.

You are probably used to opening Web pages in your browser by clicking on the *location* line and typing a URL. The page you have created isn't sitting on a Web browser, so there isn't a URL for it yet. But you can still see your page in your browser. How? On the File Menu of your browser, you'll see either Open Page or Open (depending on the browser maker and version). Select whichever one you have.

Select either Choose File or Browse, depending upon which you have on your screen. Using the standard file management dialog box that opens up, find your HTML file, called MyFirst.html. Select it. Then click Open.

For the remainder of this session, when you make changes to your HTML file, you can just click the Reload or Refresh button at the top of your browser to see your changes.

Finishing Touches

Break out that CD-ROM!

Because you've been good and followed the HTML 4 Way, you're about to be rewarded. We have created four different style sheets to make your page look truly marvelous, darling! This last section tells you where to find the style sheet files, where to copy the style sheet files, and how to link to them.

Loading your style sheets

You could certainly link to style sheets on your CD-ROM without ever copying them, but, because we assume someday you may want to use your CD-ROM drive for something else, we'll tell you how to get them loaded onto your computer.

 Copy the four files located in the **Chap3** folder on your CD to the same directory where you stored your HTML file called MyFirst.html.

The files are called

```
prof.css
wild.css
retro.css
earthy.css
```

If you want to, you can open them in your text editor and look at them. We tell you what this all means later. If you do open them to read, don't modify them yet. There's time for that later.

Linking to style sheets

Linking to a style sheet requires the use of the LINK element. This is a completely different type of link than linking to another page. The LINK element takes a start tag, no end tag, no content, and three attributes (when we use it to link to an external style sheet).

The first attribute is the `href` attribute. You should recognize the `href` attribute from the previous A element; it does exactly the same thing here. In this case, the value of the `href` attribute is the name of your style sheet. Because all four style sheets are in the same directory where your HTML file is located, you needn't add any directory information in the `href` attribute. We discuss later how you do this when your style sheets are stored elsewhere.

The next attribute is the `rel` (relationship) attribute. This attribute specifies the relationship of this link to your page. The two most common relationship values are *stylesheet,* which means this is the default style sheet for this page, and *alternate stylesheet,* which means this is the alternate style sheet for this page. Because this page only has one style sheet (be patient — we get to the fancy stuff later), you use *stylesheet* as the value of the `rel` attribute.

The final attribute should tell you the `LINK` element has more than one use. In this case, we use the `LINK` element to link to a style sheet, so the value of the `type` attribute is *text/css* (meaning the file is only text and the extension of the file is *css,* which happens to be the extension of the files you copied from the CD-ROM).

This gives us the completed tag:

```
<LINK href="prof.css" rel="stylesheet" type="text/css">
```

You want to put this tag into your HEAD element. It can go anywhere in the HEAD, but we suggest you put it after your META elements. Then you want to save your file and pull it up in your browser. Don't feel you must close out your text editor to see your file or close your browser to edit your file. This will only slow you down. The text editor hardly takes up any resources, anyway.

Note

In case you aren't used to having more than one software program open at a time, you'll find it useful to know, first, that you can have more than one program open and, second, how to switch between them. If you are using any flavor of the Windows operating system, you can switch between open software packages by holding down your Alt key and pressing Tab. You will cycle through all the open software packages (including the Program Manager in Windows 3.1). When you see the icon of the package you want to use, let go of the Alt key. The software you left is still there; it is just in the background.

For a Mac, click the icon in the upper right-hand corner of the screen. You will see the icons of all open software. Click the one you want to use.

Change your style

Now, flip back to your text editor and change the value of the `href` attribute. Use one of the other style sheets. Save your file and look at it. Try them all out and see which one you like best.

Remember, you must first save your HTML file in your editor; then Reload or Refresh your page *before* you can see the changes you made.

The sequence is as follows:

1. Edit your file in your text editor; save your changes.

2. Reload or Refresh your page in your browser.

3. View your changes.

HTML Elements in Shorthand

We intended this chapter to get you up to speed on the basics of marking up your text with elements. If all elements in this book and their attributes were explained in such length as those in this chapter, this book would be three times as thick as it is. This book uses shorthand to give you the basics of each element. This shorthand includes whether there is a start tag, whether there is any content, whether there is an end tag, and whether any of those are forbidden or optional. This shorthand also includes a list of attributes along with information about which, if any, are required, optional, deprecated, or obsolete. We will explain new attributes at length. Attributes you have seen before won't be explained.

Here are two examples:

List Item `<LI>`

Start Tag:	required
Content:	optional
End Tag:	optional
Attributes:	none

Blockquote `<BLOCKQUOTE>`

Start Tag:	required
Content:	required
End Tag:	required
Attributes:	`cite`: URL
	`id,class`: document-wide identifiers
	`lang`: language information
	`dir`: text direction
	`title`: element title
	`style`: inline style information

From Here

Proceed to Chapter 4 and learn about publishing your page. After all, everyone won't get to see your masterwork until it resides on a Web server.

Already tired of typing all those tags? Jump to Chapter 8 and find the HTML-development software program that's right for you.

Summary

Once you understand the structure of HTML, actually assembling your page is a snap. You want a title, some metadata about your page — those go into the HEAD of your document. Most pages have some headings in the BODY of the page. Add some text, perhaps a blockquote, some lists, and, of course, some links, and you have a solid foundation. You understand the structure of HTML, so actually assembling your page is a snap.

It really gets exciting when you add the style sheets. In one line of code, you can completely change the look of your page. Later, you learn to write your own style sheets, but you can always find some on the Web and link to those (why not?).

✦   ✦   ✦

Going Public!

Now that you have something to publish, you need to know how to get it to your Web server. Do you have a Web server? Do you have your own domain? What is your platform? In this chapter, we have a worksheet to help you get answers to the right questions.

Once you get your files up to your server, you want to organize them effectively so you always know how to link between files. We discuss the various approaches to organizing your files and weigh in with our opinion on the best way (as if we could resist). Finally, we discuss the methodology of testing your files. When you finish this chapter, you'll be ready to publish your files correctly, manage the directory structure, and test your site thoroughly.

Getting Your Facts Straight

To publish your page in a way that enables visitors to your site to view it properly, you should know a few things. This section helps you ask the right questions of your system administrator, or ISP, if you have one, or to make the right decisions about deploying your own Web server, if you are thinking about that option.

We start with the worksheet. If you already have this information at your fingertips, you can skip the definitions of each item and go directly to the detailed instructions about publishing.

Information on the Web site publishing worksheet

The following worksheet is for you to fill out. Having this information in writing should be helpful, especially if you are doing something other than publishing for a month or so. You may well have forgotten how you did everything. You obviously don't need to write down your password. Many times a systems administrator creates a standard password for you and then you're expected to change it to something no one can guess. This would be the place to write the password the administrator gives you.

Web Site Publishing Worksheet

My Web server is:
____ on my desktop
____ not on my desktop

My Web server administrator is:
____ me
____ someone within my organization
____ someone outside my organization

My Web server platform is:
____ UNIX
____ Windows NT/2000
____ Mac

My desktop platform is:
____ Windows 95
____ Windows NT/2000
____ Mac
____ UNIX

My Web server name is:
DNS: _____
IP address: _____
NT domain: _____
NT name: _____
NT share name: _____

Contact information:
Name: _____
E-mail: _____
Phone: _____

My account information is:
Account ID: _____
Password: _____

Desktop Web Servers

Do you have your own Web server? If you hunt around on your computer, you may find you do have Web server software on your computer. The most common Web server software for your desktop is Personal Web Server by Microsoft, which is free from the Microsoft Web site, but others exist. You are most likely to have acquired one of these packages when downloading some Web-related software from a Web page.

You can install a desktop Web server, if you wish. Should you? Probably not. The disadvantages of using your desktop machine for a server outweigh the advantages. Consider the following pros and cons:

Pros	Cons
No charge for disk space usage. Most ISPs charge you by the megabyte you use, after some small initial amount included with your monthly fee. Many organizations have disk quotas enforced on their servers and getting more space is difficult or impossible. If you have a 2GB hard drive and you want to have 1GB of images on your Web site, you can do it free on your desktop. (We discuss why you don't really want 1GB of images in your Web site later.)	**You can't ever turn off your machine.** You have to think twice when you want to install new software and would need to restart your computer for the software to take effect. This is doubly true if you have any downloads from your site. Having a Web site going up and down all the time doesn't look professional.
You have control over the directory structure. Many of these pros are autonomy issues. This is certainly one. You may be working within an organization or with an ISP that has strict rules about where you can put HTML files, where you can put images, where you must put anything you want to execute (scripts), and where style sheets must be stored. If you can't live with those constraints, then you may need your own Web server.	**You have to solve all your server problems yourself.** Are you ready to start worrying about registry entries in Windows 95 or NT? Do you want to handle security issues from your desktop? The alternative is to turn your whole server administration over to someone else. Don't think of this as some big loss of autonomy. You don't learn how to dry-clean just so you can dry-clean a few suits and sweaters, do you? No. You are willing to depend on the dry cleaner to do it right because doing it yourself for the little you do simply isn't worth the trouble.
	You must have a high-speed direct connection to the Internet with a permanent IP address. A dial-in connection to the Internet is inadequate.

Continued

Pros	*Cons*
You can create as many mappings as you like. Consider the URL `http://www.overtheweb.com/purchase`. You know there is a server called `www.overtheweb.com`, but is there really a directory called *purchase?* It doesn't matter. Your Web server can create virtual directories, called *mappings,* that point visitors to some remote location on the Web server with one easy-to-remember virtual directory name. Some ISPs charge you for creating mappings. They are convenient for you as a developer—creating links between documents—and for visitors, too.	
You can associate as many server-side applications with your Web site as you like. If you want to run any server-side processes, such as forms processing or database interaction, you may want to use something that isn't built into your desktop Web server. Most ISPs charge for the software and again for setup. Some ISPs charge by the month for using specialized server-side applications. Some organizations won't install server-side applications on their Web servers for maintenance reasons. On your own computer, you can install whatever you want.	
Ease of publishing a page. This one applies to everyone. Publishing a page is as simple as saving it to the right directory on your hard drive.	

Enterprise Web Servers

The alternative to a desktop Web server is an enterprise Web server. Many varieties of these exist: O'Reilly Web Site Pro, iPlanet Web Server Enterprise Edition, Netscape Enterprise Server, Microsoft Internet Information Server, Apache, and many others. Generally, they run on UNIX or Windows NT, although they can also run on Macs.

An enterprise Web server can be within your own organization or with your Internet service provider. In either case, there is a systems administrator who should be able to answer all your questions.

An enterprise Web server is usually a robust, turnkey environment for your Web site. It is directly connected to the Internet (as opposed to being connected by a modem). Usually there are backup procedures and an uninterruptible power supply (UPS) to prevent downtime due to power outages.

Publishing on Your Own Server

If you have your own server, you should know just where to save your files. If your server is an enterprise server, you may have to transport them using FTP, but you probably know about all this. When you are publishing to your own server, it's easy to forget good practices of file organization. Heck, no one enforces any rules on you. For this reason, deciding on a directory structure and being disciplined about following your own rules is even more important. If you don't impose discipline on yourself, you can have a big mess on your hands in no time.

Cross-Reference Skip down to the section called "Developing Directories to Store Your Pages and Graphics" to learn more about the philosophy choices you have. Make some rules for yourself and follow them.

When you are the systems administrator

For some lucky few, you will have your own Web server and it will reside on a dedicated server—then you are a systems administrator. You are the person everyone else must come to for answers to these questions. You are the top dog.

As the systems administrator, you can have all the hard drive space you want, all the mappings you want, and, as long as it doesn't conflict with other vital services your server provides, you can install all the additional applications you want.

Publishing on Your Service Provider's Server

Mere mortals must consign themselves to publishing their pages on someone else's server. The major disadvantage is loss of autonomy: You have to play by someone else's rules. However constraining this sounds, its advantages are overwhelming:

✦ **A functioning, reliable server provides a turnkey environment for your site.** You needn't pull anything out of a box, install any software, or find answers to difficult technical questions. You just sit at your desk, develop your site, and then when the time comes, you publish to your site and everything works (from the server side, anyway).

✦ **Someone else already has answers to your questions.** Even though your systems administrator may be hard to find, he or she does have answers to your questions. Heck, at one time, your systems administrator didn't know the answers and had to find them out by doing research. It is so much easier for you to be able to ask your systems administrator instead of digging out the answers yourself!

✦ **More time to create Web sites. What do systems administrators do?** They install software. They answer questions from their users. They create new accounts. They answer questions from their users. They perform backups and restores. They answer questions from their users. They create Web sites. Oh, yeah, and they answer questions from their users. You can spend your time developing great Web sites instead of all these other fun things.

As an industry, ISPs have grown out of nowhere. This isn't the place to discuss everything you need to consider before selecting an ISP, but know both great ones and awful ones exist. Ask for referrals. Let someone else keep an account at the awful one. If your ISP isn't great, switch. Even though they can't guarantee the network will always be up, your ISP should take great pains to keep you informed. This is the minimum you should demand.

Platform Issues

Now that you have found out who your systems administrator is, you can find out on what platform your Web server runs. How you move files between your desktop and your server depends on three things:

1. **Your desktop platform.** Are you sitting at a Mac, a PC, or a UNIX workstation, or at a terminal running X-Window? Even if you are at a PC or a Mac, if you operate within the UNIX environment, for example, from a telnet session, UNIX is your platform.

2. **Your server platform.** Ask that elusive systems administrator.

3. **The HTML editor you use.** We discuss this in depth in Chapter 8. The good HTML editors have built-in publishing capabilities. You can even save your file directly to a UNIX server from a PC or a Mac.

Because we don't yet know which HTML editor you'll like the best or even whether you want to fork out the dough to get one, and because your plain old text editor did such a nice job in the last chapter, we proceed assuming you don't have any fancy tools to get your pages to your server.

Extra: Publishing to a Windows NT/2000 server

Publishing to a Windows NT/2000 server is easier than publishing to a UNIX server. Unlike UNIX, an NT server can be mapped as a hard drive on your PC or on your Mac. This means, instead of using FTP, which we discuss next, you can copy your files as if you were just copying them from one directory (or folder) to another. This won't work if you are running Windows 3.1 on your desktop (but why would anyone still be running Windows 3.1?).

From Windows 98

You can connect your Windows 98 desktop computer to an NT server in two ways: the easy way and the other way. The easy way isn't available to everyone, but everyone can use the other way.

First, the easy way:

1. **Make sure you have Client for Microsoft Networks and NetBEUI running.** You can do this by

    a. From the Start Menu, select Settings and then Control Panel.

    b. Select the Network Control Panel.

    c. On the Configuration tab, make sure you have both Client for Microsoft Networks and NetBEUI listed, as shown in Figure 4-1.

2. **If you don't, you must add them and then restart your computer.** Client for Microsoft Networks is a *Client* and NetBEUI is a *protocol*. Chances are, if these weren't already running, you won't be able to use the easy way.

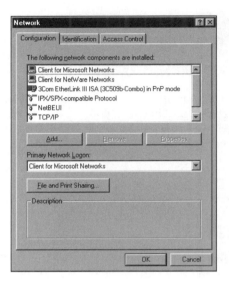

Figure 4-1: Network Control Panel in Windows 98

3. **Open your Network Neighborhood.** If you see your NT server on the list of available machines, you're in luck. Try checking under Entire Network. Otherwise, skip down to the other way. You still need to have accomplished Step 1.

4. **Double-click the NT server that is your Web server.** This opens a window with all the share names on the NT server. These are directories or disks available to be shared, if you have permissions.

5. **Right-click the share name you were instructed to use.** This brings up a list of the things you can do with the share.

6. **Select Map Network Drive.** This brings up a dialog box in which you can select the drive letter you want to associate with the server, as shown in Figure 4-2. You can actually map more than one drive from a single NT server; each would get a drive letter.

Figure 4-2: Mapping a network drive in Windows 98 is easy when your NT server is in your Network Neighborhood.

7. **Select the drive letter you want to associate with the NT server.**

8. **Check the Reconnect at Logon box, if you want to map to this drive each time you log in.** If you don't check this box, you must repeat Steps 2–6 each time you want to copy or save files to your NT server.

Now, you can either save your HTML files directly to your Web server directory or save them to your local hard drive, wherever you want to put them, and then copy them to your Web server directory when you are ready to publish. Graphics files, which can sometimes be tricky, move over correctly if you just copy them this way.

Now, the other way:

1. **Make sure you have Client for Microsoft Networks and NetBEUI running.** See Step 1 under the easy way for instructions.

2. **Edit your HOSTS and LMHOSTS files.** These can be found in your Windows directory. Both these files have no extensions. There may also be HOSTS.SAM and LMHOSTS.SAM files, but those are different files. Don't touch those! If you don't have either file, create them. If you create them using Notepad, it adds .txt to the end of the file name. You must find these files in your Windows directory and rename them without an extension.

   You need both the name, the domain name, and the IP address of your server. Your systems administrator can provide these for you. You can get the IP address from your systems administrator or, if he or she gives you the domain name (such as nautilus.minerva.net), you can go to a DOS prompt on any computer hooked up to the Internet and type **ping your.domain.name** and the system will return the IP address of your.domain.name. The domain name sometimes has four parts, as in nmc.itc.virginia.edu. Here is what your files need to have:

   LMHOSTS file:

   ```
   206.55.47.87 nautilus  #pre #dom:minerva
   ```

   HOSTS file:

   ```
   206.55.47.87 nautilus.minerva.net
   ```

   The second item in the LMHOSTS file is the NT name of the server. You have to get this from your systems administrator. The #pre tells your system to preload this network connection. The #dom: tells the system it should find the minerva domain. Again, you need to get the domain name from your systems administrator. In the HOSTS file, the item after the IP address is the server's domain name.

3. **Restart your computer.**

4. **Sign into the Microsoft Networking dialog box with the ID and password provided by your systems administrator** (even if this isn't what you normally do). You may get weird errors from your regular servers, if you normally sign into a server other than the NT Web server (such as a different NT server or a Netware server), but just click through them.

5. **Right-click Network Neighborhood.** You get a list of the things you can do with networking.

6. **Select Map Network Drive.** This brings up the dialog box, shown in Figure 4-3, where you can indicate what you want to map (your NT server) to which drive letter.

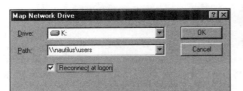

Figure 4-3: Mapping a network drive to a remote host in Windows 98

7. **Enter the NT server name, followed by the share name in the first blank as follows:**

   `\\nautilus\users`

   Again, you don't actually type `nautilus\users`; you type your machine name, followed by the share name given to you by your systems administrator. Be sure to type backslashes (\), not forward slashes (/), or it won't work.

8. **Enter the drive letter to which you want to map in the second blank.** This will default to the next available letter of the alphabet.

9. **Check the Reconnect at Logon box, if you want to map to this drive every time you log in.** If you don't check this box, you must repeat Steps 4–8 every time you want to copy or save files to your NT server.

From Windows NT/2000

You can attach a Windows NT/2000 workstation to a Windows NT/2000 server in three ways. For all these methods using Windows NT, you must have Client for Microsoft Networks and NetBEUI running. If your server is Windows 2000, you can use IP, and NetBEUI is no longer needed. You can see which protocols are running by checking the Network Control Panel, under the Services tab. If these are already running, try the easy way explained in the previous section on Windows 98. If these aren't already running, you need administrator privileges on your NT workstation to install these services. If you can't use the easy way, use this other method:

1. Right-click Network Neighborhood. This brings up a list of system options.

2. Select Map Network Drive. A dialog box like the one in Figure 4-4 pops up.

3. Enter the following in the first blank:

`\\206.55.47.87\users`

The first part is your IP address and the second part is your share name. Make sure you use backslashes (\) or it definitely won't work.

Figure 4-4: Mapping a network drive using an IP address in Windows NT

4. Enter your login ID in the second blank.

5. Indicate the drive letter you want to assign.

6. Check the Reconnect at Logon box.

Now you can save or copy files to the drive letter you indicated. If you click My Computer (or whatever you have renamed your computer), you see a list of all your drives, including the one you just mapped to your NT server.

From a Mac

The only way to map an NT server as a local drive on a Mac is if you are sharing a network and the NT server has Services for Macintoshes turned on. If this is the case and you can find the NT server in the right zone in the Chooser, then you can sign on to the NT server, using the share name the systems administrator gave you. Then you can save or copy files directly to your NT server directory.

If you save or copy HTML or CSS files from your Mac to the NT server and then you try to open them from a PC, they will look strange, but they will still work properly. Figure 4-5 shows a file with a line-length problem.

If you save or copy from a PC and then open on a Mac that has a mapping to the NT server, then your file will look like the one in Figure 4-6.

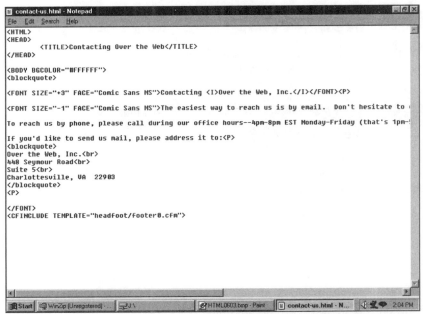

Figure 4-5: This is what your HTML or CSS file looks like if saved or copied from a Mac and then opened on a PC.

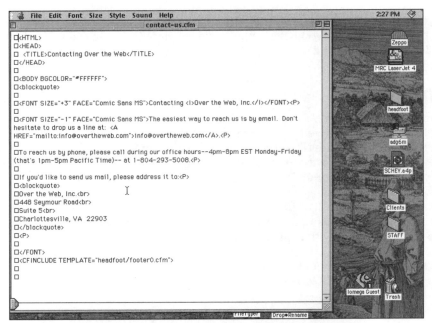

Figure 4-6: This is what your text files look like if opened on a Mac, after having been saved or copied from a PC.

Introducing FTP

The other way to move files from your desktop to your Web server—if you don't have an NT server or you can't connect to it for some reason—is the tried and true method of transferring your files, called File Transfer Protocol (FTP). FTP is a fast, easy way to move your files from any desktop to any server.

In the early days of FTP and still today in non-X-Window environments on UNIX, all file transfers relied on a text-based interface. Commands were short and sweet, but only one file could be moved at a time. This was the entire vocabulary: open, get, put, bini (for binary file transfer), and bye. Figure 4-7 shows an example of FTP commands.

Figure 4-7: Text-based FTP client

You will upload two kinds of files: binary and text. When you think about it, everything on your computer is binary, even your text files. *Binary* just refers to the way the data is stored: as ones and zeros. With a *text file,* every set of 8 ones and zeros translates neatly into a letter, a number, or a special character on your keyboard. With a binary file, all the ones and zeros translate into something bigger, such as an image. If you open a text file with a plain text editor, you see text. If you open a binary file in a plain text editor, you see junk. The plain text editor has tried to turn every set of 8 ones and zeros into a number or letter.

FTP predates the Web

Before there was a World Wide Web, there was an Internet. The World Wide Web relies on the HyperText Transfer Protocol (HTTP). The Internet relied on the File Transfer Protocol (FTP). FTP is a simple concept. One computer establishes a connection with another computer using TCP/IP (more on this follows). Then the first computer tells the second computer whether the data about to be passed will be text or binary data (*binary data* is any file that looks like gobbledygook when opened in a plain text editor; this would include word processing documents, spreadsheets, and image files). Then the first computer either puts one file onto the second computer or gets one file off the second computer. All this assumes the first computer has the necessary permissions to read or write files on the second computer. That's all: so simple, so elegant.

FTP takes advantage, as does HTTP, of TCP/IP. This is a double-decker protocol. The Transmission Control Protocol (TCP) part packages the data a certain way so when the packages get to the other side, the computer over there knows how to unpackage them and reassemble the data into the right file. When the receiving computer gets data, it needs to know whether it is putting together an e-mail message (plain text) or an image. The Internet Protocol (IP) part handles getting those packets to the correct address. TCP is like the mailroom and IP is like the post office.

Introducing FTP clients: CuteFTP, WS_FTP, Fetch

Once every computer had a mouse, drag-and-drop FTP software was not long in coming. Today, several visual FTP clients are available. For the Mac, it is easy: Fetch. Fetch even guesses whether your file is text or binary (what it calls *raw data*). You can drag a file right out of the folder on your desk into the Fetch client and watch the dog run. Figure 4-8 shows Fetch capabilities on the Mac.

For the Windows environments, the most common are WS_FTP, for which a lite version is available, and CuteFTP (shown in Figure 4-9), which is shareware. In both of these packages, you can set up a list of the most common places to which you connect, including your login ID, your password, and the directory on the remote machine. Then you can drag-and-drop files or directories full of files from your desktop machine (by pointing the software to the right directory) to the Web server (or any remote machine that has an IP address). This software makes a reasonably accurate guess as to whether your file is binary or text.

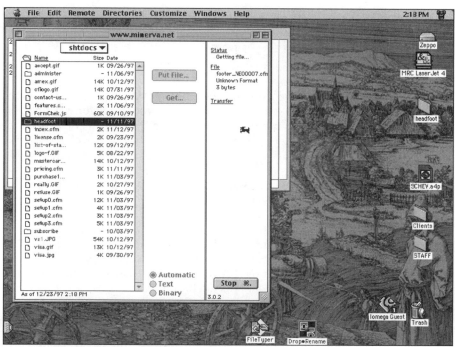

Figure 4-8: Fetch makes FTPing easy on the Mac.

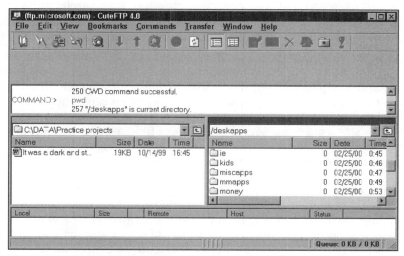

Figure 4-9: CuteFTP makes light work of FTPing files and folders.

Developing Directories to Store Your Pages and Graphics

Before you start uploading those pages, you should decide how you want to structure your directories. You have three choices: put everything into one directory, put your files into a directory structure that mirrors your site (for example, one directory per page), or put your files into directories by type. Making this decision early and enforcing discipline on yourself to keep your structure clean is important. The alternative is to recode all your links when you rearrange your files.

 Some of the tools to make this easier are found in Chapter 8 — but it is still not much fun.

Unless your site is small (one page with a photo of your cat and your grandmother's baklava recipe), you don't want to put all your files into one directory. This leaves two choices: having your directory structure match your pages, which we tell you in the next section heading is generally a bad idea, or structuring your directories by file type, which is, generally, a better way.

The reason we include an explanation of both theories is, for some organizations, having your directory structure come closer to matching your pages than to being by file type does make sense. This is the case in a large organization when dozens of people publish pages to one site. You probably don't want everyone to have permission to overlay everyone else's files. Breaking up the directory structure by functional group enables you to protect each group's files from carelessness by anyone in any of the other groups (say, two people naming their files the same thing).

Directory structure to match your pages

The idea behind this is pretty straightforward. For each page, you create a directory. You call it something related to what's on the page. You can either use a flat directory structure, where every page is on the same level, or a hierarchical directory structure, where a page that serves as a pointer to four other pages is actually closer to the root than those four pages, which are under it. Figure 4-10 shows a directory structure that matches the pages in the site.

Having one directory per page doesn't make sense, but it may make sense to have one directory per functional unit involved in creating your site. You could modify the previous diagram by removing the directories for features (a subset of sales), FAQs (a subset of support), and purchase (a subset of sales), and lumping those three in with the pages they modify. If you have a handful of people working on each unit, you can protect your site better by restricting the permissions of the people in each group only to the folder where all their files go. Figure 4-11 shows an even more convoluted directory tree with one page per directory using hierarchical structure.

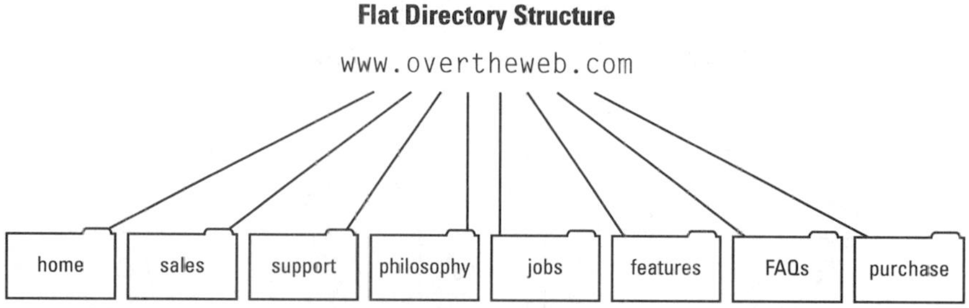

Flat Directory Structure

www.overtheweb.com

Figure 4-10: Flat directory structure with one directory per page

Hierarchical Directory Structure

www.overtheweb.com

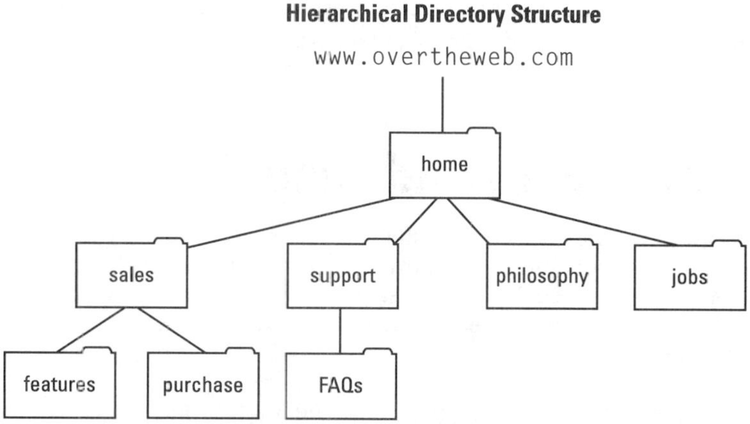

Figure 4-11: Hierarchical directory structure with one directory per page

It's hard to imagine where this model makes sense because it just doesn't scale. If you rearrange your site, you may as well start over.

Directory structure by file type (generally a better idea)

HTML files go into the root directory for your site. Style-sheets files go into a style-sheets directory (as shown in Figure 4-12). All media go into subdirectories of a media directory based on media type (if you think you'll have more than just images — be realistic). If you think you'll have only images, skip the media directory and have a directory in your root directory named images.

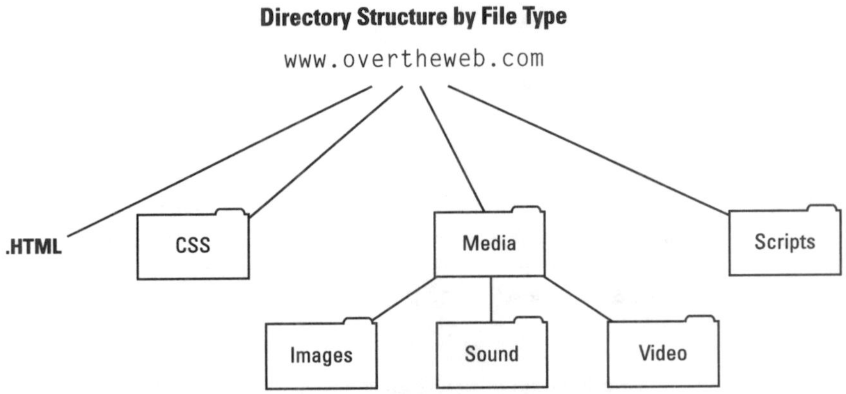

Directory Structure by File Type

www.overtheweb.com

Figure 4-12: Nice and simple. Directory structure by file type. Especially good for small sites.

Uploading Your Pages and Graphics

Earlier in this chapter, we mentioned text files are binary files where every set of 8 ones and zeros neatly convert into one character. This is almost perfectly true. Text files are more than what you see. If text files were only text, each file would be one long line of text. In fact, at the end of each line in a text file is at least one character indicating this is where a line ends.

PCs use two characters: carriage return (CR) and line feed (LF). Macs use only CR and UNIX uses only LF. What a pain! Indeed it is, but when you FTP your files, your FTP client can take care of this for you. If you tell your FTP client (or let it guess) your file is a text file, then it automatically makes the proper adjustments to the end of the lines to correct for the file's new platform. If you tell your FTP client your text file is actually binary, then it leaves the whole file alone. This means when you open your file on the new platform, the line ends won't be right.

What if you upload your binary file as text? Disaster. The FTP client has conveniently gone through your file and changed every string of 8 ones and zeros that translate into an LF or CR and tried to convert them as if they were text. You won't recognize your file and neither will a browser.

If you are working on either a Mac or a PC and your Web server is UNIX, or if you are working on UNIX or a Mac and your Web server is Windows NT, then try this experiment: upload a text file (any old HTML file will do) to your Web server as text and then download it as binary. Your end of file characters will be wrong because you didn't let the FTP client fix it on the way back down.

DNS

What will you call your site? Do you have a domain name (like ibm.com)? You can do this from the official organization that registers domain names, called InterNIC: www.internic.net. You can also get your ISP to do it for you, but they usually charge something extra. One enterprising group on the Web chose to call itself www.internic.com. Guess what it does? It registers your domain name with the official group and charges you twice as much! The group has easy online forms, but usually your ISP will do it for less than twice the registration amount.

Before you can get a domain name, you must have the technical information from your ISP, such as the IP address of your ISP. This is yet another good reason to let your ISP register your domain name for you.

Permissions

In addition to needing an account on your Web server, you also need permissions to perform basic file management tasks. You must be able to create new directories within your root directory, unless your systems administrator is a real dictator and creates them for you according to a prescribed system. You need permissions to write to your directory to upload files.

When visitors come to your site with their browsers, they either read or execute files on your Web server. The permissions for the directories must be set to permit this. Your systems administrator will probably want all your executable files (scripts and programs) in one directory so just that directory can be marked as executable.

Testing Your Work

You have to test your work. Because of the informal system of creating pages and publishing them, which most of us work in, this is easy to forget. Don't wait until you receive mail from someone who visited your site telling you links don't work to learn this. Your visitors shouldn't be your beta testers.

Where should you test? On your server. While this sounds dangerous, you can ask your systems administrator to create an obscure mapping name, so if a browser comes to www.overtheweb.com, it returns a 404 not found error while you are testing your site. You will know the only way to see the site is to go to www.overtheweb.com/blahblah. When you are done testing, you ask your systems administrator to delete the blahblah mapping and reinstate www.overtheweb.com to point to your home page.

What about testing on a desktop server? Good reasons exist not to do it this way. The following chart discusses the pros and cons of testing on a desktop Web server, if this is not where you ultimately plan to publish.

Pros	*Cons*
Permissions are not an issue because you should have God-like permissions on your own workstation. The exception to this is if you are running Windows NT Workstation or Windows 2000 Professional on your computer. If you are running NT and you don't have administrator privileges, then you may not even be able to install a desktop Web server.	**Permissions may be different on your production Web server.** If your permissions aren't the same on your desktop server as they are on your production Web server, then you need to make changes. How will you know they're different? You have to test. This means you will test your page twice.
Testing is instant. Just save your HTML file, as we did in the last chapter, and reload your page.	**Testing is less thorough.** Why? Because you know you have to test again anyway. You'll be better off using the mapping suggestion we made previously and doing your testing once on your production server.
No special file manipulation is required. Just save your pages to your Web server's home directory, which is right on your local hard drive.	**Unless you are doing server-side scripting, you get the same results as if you just opened the file locally.** Let me explain. In Chapter 3, we taught you how to open a local file from your browser. If you install a desktop Web server, you can pull up the file using the IP address of your computer, if you know it, or `http://127.0.0.1/yourpage.html`, if you put your page into your desktop Web server's root directory. Instead of opening the file locally, it opens the file as if it were coming from somewhere on the Internet. Your page looks exactly the same as it did by opening it locally. The only time this kind of round-about page loading is necessary is if you are doing some kind of server processing of your page. In this case, you would also have some other software on your desktop computer (such as Cold Fusion, Tango, FileMaker Pro, and so on).

The most important points to remember when you test are as follows:

✦ Look at your site, clicking through all the links from a variety of browsers (both Netscape and Internet Explorer in their most recently released versions and one or two versions earlier). Looking at your site from a few versions of AOL's browser is also not a bad idea because they have such a large installed base.

✦ Look at your site from both Macs and PCs.

✦ Look at your site after setting your screen resolution to 640×480, 800×600, and 1024×768.

✦ Look at your site with the browser sized to the full screen and with the browser taking up only part of the screen.

✦ Look at your site from within your domain and then from outside your domain. Permissions may be different if you are coming to your site from outside your domain.

✦ Look at your site from the desk of someone who doesn't have privileges on your server.

Note Both Windows NT/2000 and Windows 98 send your login data to an NT/2000 Web server (pretty tricky, huh?), so if you are authorized to see a certain page because of your ID and password, the Web server already knows this and doesn't even bother to ask you to sign in. If you are not authorized, you get a sign-in screen. Of course, as the Webmaster, you never see this screen — thus, you never know everyone else can't get to your site — unless you try this from someone's computer who doesn't have the permissions you have. In fact, if you didn't know this, you'd never be able to duplicate this permissions problem from your own desk and you'd assume everyone coming to your page was doing something wrong, because it worked for you!

Complete a testing worksheet, something like the one shown in Figure 4-13, and you won't go wrong.

From Here

Cross-Reference Find servers fascinating? Wish you could be a systems administrator and have your own enterprise Web server? Then jump to Chapter 11 to learn more about server options.

Proceed to Chapter 5 and get your feet wet with an introduction to HTML.

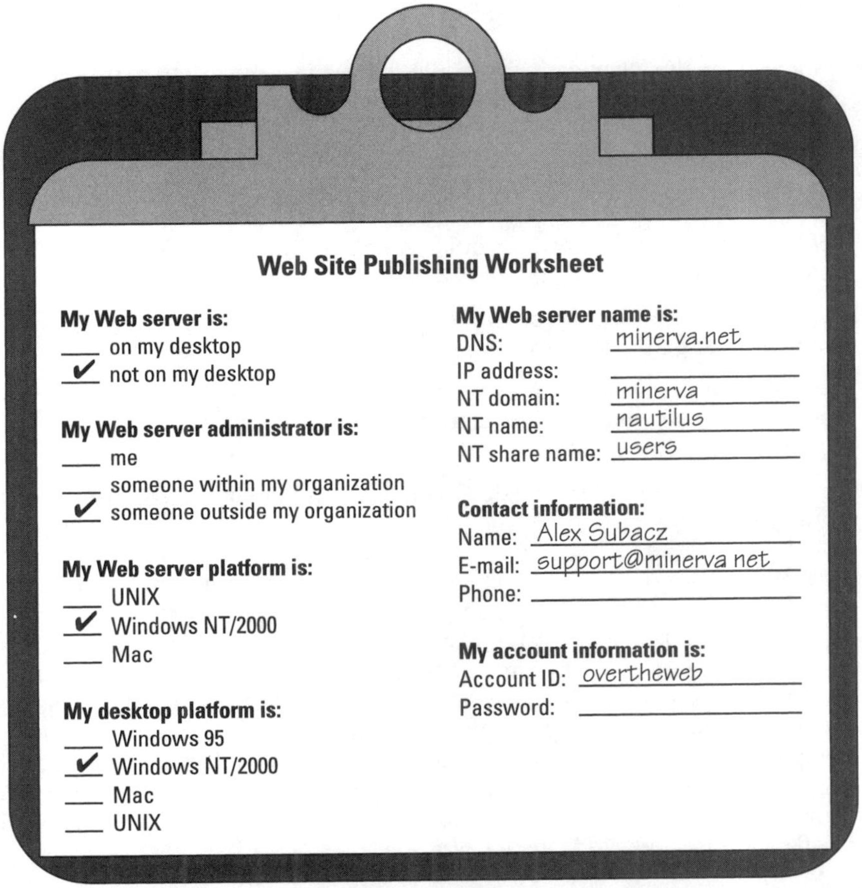

Web Site Publishing Worksheet

My Web server is:
___ on my desktop
✔ not on my desktop

My Web server administrator is:
___ me
___ someone within my organization
✔ someone outside my organization

My Web server platform is:
___ UNIX
✔ Windows NT/2000
___ Mac

My desktop platform is:
___ Windows 95
✔ Windows NT/2000
___ Mac
___ UNIX

My Web server name is:
DNS: _minerva.net_
IP address: _____
NT domain: _minerva_
NT name: _nautilus_
NT share name: _users_

Contact information:
Name: _Alex Subacz_
E-mail: _support@minerva.net_
Phone: _____

My account information is:
Account ID: _overtheweb_
Password: _____

Figure 4-13: This is what your worksheet may look like once you've completed it.

Summary

You now have everything you need to begin publishing your pages. You have a completed worksheet with all the information you need about your server. You understand file types. You have made some decisions about how you want to structure your directories. You know how to get your files to your server using an FTP client. Or, if you have an NT Web server, you know how to map a drive to your NT server.

You're ready to publish your files correctly, manage the directory structure, and test your site thoroughly.

✦ ✦ ✦

Understanding HTML 4

Introducing HTML

So you want to publish a Web site. Why? Unless you have a clear purpose, you won't be able to create a compelling site. Who is your audience? Surely you must have some idea of who cares about what you have to say (other than your mother, and she's just being polite). What do you want to tell people? Your message must be crystal clear. No fancy design will compensate for a murky message. What do you suppose your audience wants to know? Don't assume what you want to tell them and what they want to know are the same. Because you probably can't influence what they want to know, you may have to modify what you want to tell them to answer their needs.

This book teaches HTML 4, but, as mentioned earlier, not everyone who comes to your Web page will be running a browser that supports HTML 4 features. The browsers your visitors use affect how they see your site. In this chapter, you also get a brief overview of the process involved in getting a version of HTML recommended by the World Wide Web Consortium (W3C). You also see examples of the document type definitions that SGML uses to specify HTML. This chapter introduces HTML by taking you through the evolution of HTML from Version 1.0, which was never even published by the W3C, to Version 4.01, the current version.

Standardization is the name of the game on the Web. Because everyone agrees that Web pages should be loaded using the HTTP protocol, every browser can load every standard Web page. When people or companies stop conforming to the standard or, more frequently, develop new standards in areas that aren't yet well developed, standardization becomes a problem. This chapter sorts out the thorny history of standardization. You learn why much of what HTML has to offer (JavaScript, the DOM, Java implementation, and CSS implementation) isn't yet standardized between the major browsers. You also learn a bit about the process that exists within the W3C for creating standards.

What's Your Purpose?

Think of the last time you saw a presidential press conference or speech. Do you suppose the speechwriter planned ahead which of the president's quotes would make it onto the evening news? You bet the writer did! Did you notice after the speech how all the high mucky-mucks in the president's party had exactly the same thing to say? Sure, they used different words, but they all had the same message. Of course, this is no accident.

You have to plan your own Web site with the same single-mindedness. What is the purpose of putting up your Web site? First, will your site be a transit point or a destination?

Transit point

A *transit point,* like a train station, is a place people pass through to get where they really want to go. A search engine is a transit point. A list of places to find 100-percent cotton, organic baby clothes is a transit point. Lots of people put up pages full of pointers to other pages. Whether they realize it or not, these are transit points.

Want to put up a commercial Web site? You can make money from advertising banners, if you can attract a crowd to your transit-point Web site.

How long will you stay at a page that does nothing more than point you to other pages? What if you want people to stay in your site and look around, read all the pages, and perhaps contribute their opinions or purchase something? Then you don't want to put up a transit point site; you want to put up a destination site.

Destination

A destination Web site is the site where you spend time looking for something. You normally won't leave a destination Web site until you have found it or you've given up trying. Then you may take one of the links off one of the pages and see what you can find there.

Five types of destination Web sites exist:

✦ **Educational.** Teach your visitors about something.

✦ **Motivational.** Motivate your visitors to take some action.

✦ **Informational.** Tell your visitors something.

✦ **Persuasive.** Convince your visitors of something.

✦ **Sales.** Sell your visitors a product or service.

Frequently, elements of more than one of these exist in a site.

Educational

Once upon a time, the Web was primarily populated with educational sites. Because the Web's first inhabitants were primarily academics and researchers, this only made sense. Although times have changed, you can still find excellent educational resources on the Web. Figure 5-1 is an excellent example of an education site on the Web.

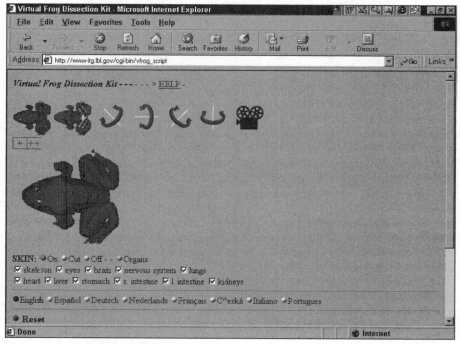

Figure 5-1: A frog dissection Web site

Motivational

Perhaps you are putting up a Web site to get people to take action: give money to their favorite charity, volunteer their time with their local library, call their member of Congress to demand stricter enforcement of immigration laws, or start exercising regularly. You may or may not be able to assume your visitors already believe in the value of your cause. You may have to do some persuading, as well.

Motivational sites are what you probably have in mind if your message is related to improving your community, the society, or the environment. Giving people information (education) is not enough. You probably also want them to take action: join the PTA, drop off food at the soup kitchen, or recycle.

You may not need to get your visitors to call the president, but you may want to assist them in managing their time so they can find time to exercise. Or, you may list local public health clinics in your state where they can get their children vaccinated. If you are going to motivate your visitors to do something, you must give them all the information they currently need to take action.

Informational

In an informational site, you simply want to tell your visitor something. It could be your family history, the cute tricks your cat does, or the services provided by the local United Way. If your page is strictly informational — such as design tips for quilting (see Figure 5-2) — then you are under less pressure to conform to standards. However, you still want to have a clear message, good content, and a clean design, as this page has.

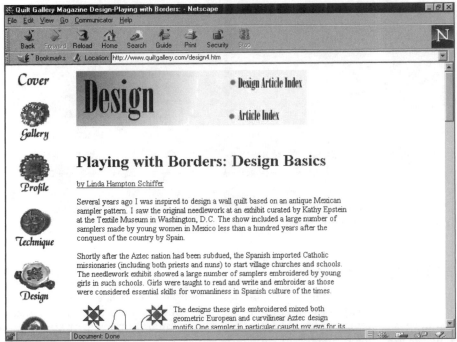

Figure 5-2: Quilting design basics — a lovely example of an informational page

Persuasive

With a persuasive site or page, you have a clear message. You want your visitor to agree with you about something. Your job is to explain your cause and then support it with enough evidence to win your visitor over to your way of thinking.

If you don't have a clear idea of what you want your visitors to take away from your site — what you want them to remember — then they won't either.

Sales

This is perhaps the most straightforward purpose of a Web page: selling. In other words, you want your visitor to buy a product or service. What does it take to convince your visitor to make a purchase? You have to educate, inform, persuade, motivate, and finally, sell! On a sales site, you probably want to have some sort of server processor to handle payments and security to insure that information for payments is safe. Figure 5-3 shows a form used on the Anvil Bikes site to capture a prospective buyer's information.

Figure 5-3: Most sales sites should culminate in a form that requests basic purchasing information.

Understanding Your Tools

Have you clarified your message at all since the beginning of this chapter? What is the purpose of your site or page? What kind of site or page will it be? Will it have elements of more than one type of site? Fortunately, you have a few more topics to cover before you begin writing.

As you probably guessed from the title of this book, the primary tool you use to create your Web site is HTML 4. So what is HTML anyway?

Simply put, HyperText Markup Language is a set of rules for marking up text so a browser knows what to do with that text. Do you want to see some HTML right now? While browsing any page on the Web, select View Source or View Document Source from the View menu at the top of your screen. Just in case you're not currently online, here is some HTML from the IDG Books Worldwide Web site.

```
<!-- Hot and Happening -->          <font size="4"><b><tt>Hot and
Happening</tt></b></font><br>
<!-- Help your Valentine get more out of Windows 2000 with
Brian Livingston's <a href="/cgi/fill_out_template.pl?idgbook:
0-7645-3413-0:book-idg::~uid~"> Windows&reg; 2000 Secrets&reg;.
-->          <p><!-- Windows 2000 Trade Show -->
<a href="http://www.idgbooks.com/bookstore/win2000.html"><font
size="4"><b><tt>Windows 2000 is Here</tt></b></font></a><font
size="4"><b><tt> </tt></b></font><br>
```

As you can see, HTML looks like text with other things inserted between less than (<) and greater than (>) signs. If you try to read the previous HTML, you should be able to extract the following text from it: "Hot and Happening Help your Valentine get more out of Windows 2000 with Brian Livingston's Windows 2000 Trade Show."

Your browser makes sense of the tags within the < and > (often referred to collectively as angle brackets) so the text between the codes looks exactly as the designer wants it to look. What a great idea! You write the content, and then you mark up the text to look the way you want using HTML.

SGML

Standard Generalized Markup Language (SGML) is the basis for HTML. Actually, HTML is a subset of SGML. What you probably didn't realize is that HTML is actually specified in SGML. In other words, SGML is used to define HTML. SGML uses document type definitions (DTDs) to specify itself, the elements of HTML, and XML. (DTDs are covered in detail in Chapter 6.)

SGML became standard in 1988, when it was approved by the International Standards Organization (ISO). Why should you care? You will better understand where HTML is going if you understand where it came from. Briefly then, SGML is a standard for electronic document exchange. It was, in fact, used in the publication of this book!

How does SGML work? When you read a book manuscript, each element on the page (paragraph, section heading, block quote) has its own typographical convention. For example, in this book, anything representing HTML code appears in courier font, such as the previous HTML code. The publisher communicates to the printer that the code sample should be typeset a certain way by marking up the text with special codes and then telling the printer that whenever he sees those codes, he should change the font to the appropriate font for that element (the publisher gets to define this).

If you've ever tried to write your own Web page, you've noticed you can't always get it to look precisely the way you want. Why is that? You are like the publisher: You mark up your text and tell the printer how you want it to look. The browser is like an arrogant printer, who reads what you have to say and, sometimes, does it his own way despite your instructions.

As a Web-page designer, you are at the mercy of the browser. If a publisher doesn't like the way the printer follows directions, he can take his business elsewhere. If you don't like the way a particular browser handles your Web page, you can't do much about it. Fortunately, this is changing with HTML 4.

HTML

When the first graphics-capable browser (Mosaic 1.0) was released in 1993, it handled only a small subset of all the SGML tags. Essentially, as a designer, you could center text, choose from one of four font sizes, separate paragraphs with a blank white line, and do a few other things to make your text look nice.

We've come a long way since then. Today you have extensive control over white space and formatting. However, HTML is still only a small subset of SGML. HTML is definitely growing in the direction of SGML.

The HTML Standardization Process

But how are changes made to the HTML standard? Who controls this gradual movement of HTML towards SGML? The standards-setting body for the World Wide Web is the W3C. Its membership is derived from companies, not individuals. The W3C has a process for recommending versions of HTML and other Web-related technologies. Currently in the hopper are CSS level 3, XML, PICS, and the Web Accessibility Initiative (WAI).

Buzz and scrambling

How does the W3C decide when a new technology must be standardized or a new version of an existing technology must be developed? Newsgroups and mailing lists exist where leading figures in the relevant field talk about the shortcomings of an existing version or the idea of a new technology (that's the buzz). If a ground swell of support seems to exist for a new technology or a new version, the W3C begins the process of specifying it.

Something else, however, carries more weight and more urgency than discussion by agitators and activists. This is ongoing development by software developers (that's the scrambling). Nothing gets the W3C activated quite so quickly. In reality, the W3C is mostly involved in trying to standardize the proprietary extensions developed by software developers, such as Netscape and Microsoft. If the W3C didn't do this, within two versions of their browsers, HTML might not run the same (or at all) on both systems. The W3C reins them in to some degree. Neither one wants to produce a browser that lacks support for recommended HTML elements, so even if Netscape introduced a new element, Microsoft will incorporate that element in the subsequent version of their own browser — after an official recommendation by the W3C (and vice versa).

Committees and working drafts

When a new technology or a new version of an existing technology is required, the W3C convenes a committee of interested parties to write the specification. The committee publishes its work on an ongoing basis as a working draft. The point of publishing these working drafts is this: Software developers who want to implement the new technology or the new features of the new version can get a jump on things and build their new product to incorporate the new features. When the specification is finalized and developers are ready to use it, products are on the market that implement it.

There is also the issue of books. You want books on new technologies to be in the bookstores the day the recommendation is finalized. For this to happen, authors must write the books using the working drafts — a moving target — as the reference materials. Working drafts have changed during the writing of this book. Sometimes this works and sometimes it doesn't. If the specification changes radically from the working draft to the final version, then the book will be inaccurate. Most of the time, working drafts only get thicker as they approach approval time.

Voting process

Democracy: You just can't get away from it. When a working draft reaches a point where the committee is pleased and believes it is complete, the working draft is released to the public as a proposed recommendation. Members of the W3C have up to six weeks to vote on it — votes can take the form of any one of three choices: yes, yes if certain changes are made, or no. At the conclusion of the voting process, the W3C can recommend the specification officially, make the requested changes and recommend the specification with the changes, or discard the proposal.

HTML 1.0

HTML 1.0 was never formally specified by the W3C because the W3C came along too late. HTML 1.0 was the original specification Mosaic 1.0 used, and it supported few elements. What you couldn't do on a page is more interesting than what you could do.

You couldn't set the background color or background image of the page. There were no tables or frames. You couldn't dictate the font. All inline images had to be GIFs; JPEGs were used for out-of-line images. And there were no forms.

Every page looked pretty much the same: gray background and Times Roman font. Links were indicated in blue until you'd visited them, and then they were red. Because scanners and image-manipulation software weren't as available then as they are today, the image limitation wasn't a huge problem. HTML 1.0 was only implemented in Mosaic and Lynx (a text-only browser that runs under UNIX).

HTML 2.0

Huge strides forward were made between HTML 1.0 and HTML 2.0. An HTML 1.1 actually did exist, created by Netscape to support what its first browser could do. Because only Netscape and Mosaic were available at the time (both written under the leadership of Marc Andreesen), browser makers were in the habit of adding their own new features and creating names for HTML elements to use those features.

Between HTML 1.0 and HTML 2.0, the W3C also came into being, under the leadership of Tim Berners-Lee, founder of the Web. HTML 2.0 was a huge improvement over HTML 1.0. Background colors and images could be set. Forms became available with a limited set of fields, but nevertheless, for the first time, visitors to a Web page could submit information. Tables also became possible.

HTML 3.2

Why no 3.0? The W3C couldn't get a specification out in time for agreement by the members. HTML 3.2 was vastly richer than HTML 2.0. It included support for style sheets (CSS level 1). Even though CSS was supported in the 3.2 specification, the browser manufacturers didn't support CSS well enough for a designer to make much use of it. HTML 3.2 expanded the number of attributes that enabled designers to customize the look of a page (exactly the opposite of the HTML 4 Way). HTML 3.2 didn't include support for frames, but the browser makers implemented them anyway.

 Definition

Frames. A page with two frames is actually processed like three separate pages within your browser. The outer page is the *frameset.* The frameset indicates to the browser which pages go where in the browser window. Implementing frames can be tricky, but frames can also be an effective way to implement a Web site. A common use for frames is navigation in the left pane, and content in the right.

HTML 4.0

What does HTML 4.0 add? Not so much new elements — although those do exist — as a rethinking of the direction HTML is taking. Up until now, HTML has encouraged interjecting presentation information into the page. HTML 4.0 now clearly deprecates any uses of HTML that relate to forcing a browser to format an element a certain way.

All formatting has been moved into the style sheets. With formatting information strewn throughout the pages, HTML 3.2 had reached a point where maintenance was expensive and difficult. This movement of presentation out of the document, once and for all, should facilitate the continued rapid growth of the Web.

Tip   Use the Web Page Purifier, available at `www.delorie.com/web/purify.html`, to check your HTML against most of the versions mentioned in this chapter.

Enough about the history of HTML.

HTML editors

Where do you write your HTML? One of the nice properties of HTML is it is just text. The content is text and the tags are text. As a result, you can write your HTML in any text editor. If you are running any flavor of Windows, you can use Notepad, which comes installed with Windows. If you have a Mac on your desk, you can use SimpleText, as shown in Figure 5-4. If you work in UNIX, you can use emacs, vi, jove, pico, or whatever you normally use to edit text.

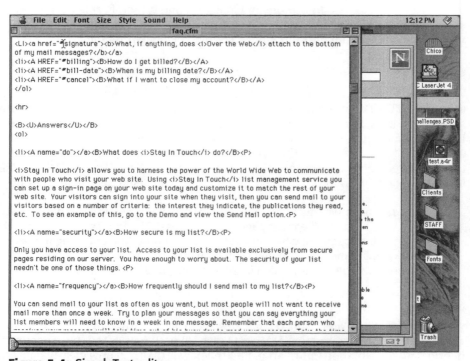

Figure 5-4: SimpleText editor

Cross-Reference For your first page, we use your regular text editor. Chapter 8 is dedicated to HTML-editing programs that increase your productivity over a plain old text editor. But for now, we focus on the fundamentals: HTML elements and content.

Writing HTML

What else do you need to know to write your HTML? Presumably, by now, you know:

✦ What your purpose is (at least generally)

✦ You need to write your content from your focused message

✦ You mark up your content with HTML tags

✦ You can write your page with a text editor that is already installed on your computer

Obviously, you need to know the elements. But before discussing those, here are a few guidelines about how you should and shouldn't use HTML.

HTML shouldn't be used to format your text: It should be used to structure your document.

Desperate men and women

As we discussed in Chapter 2, the lengths to which Web designers have gone to format their pages the way they wanted was quite absurd. HTML had a limited tag set, meaning everything you may have wanted to do to your text wasn't necessarily possible. Yet visitors' expectations for graphically appealing pages were still high. Web designers, before HTML 4 came along, had to get creative. One devious device to force indentation of paragraphs or a set amount of white space between paragraphs was the clear GIF. A *GIF* is an image file (called *somename.GIF*). It is possible (in a software package designed for image creation, such as Photoshop) to create a 1×1-pixel image. A *pixel* is the smallest unit of measurement on the screen. Then with HTML, the image can be stretched to fill the desired space. The evil tag would look something like this:

```
<img src="clear.GIF" width="18" height="1">
```

Then the Web designer would write the text for the paragraph. The result would be 18 pixels of white space (or about ¼ inch on most monitors) before the first word of that paragraph. You can imagine what this did to the readability of the HTML when all that junk went at the beginning of the paragraph!

Format your text

If you are already writing HTML pages, you may need to break your bad habits. You probably already think in terms of getting the browser to make your page look the right way. And you use HTML to make it do this. If you are really underhanded, you may even use goofy conventions such as 1-pixel-wide clear image files (usually GIFs) and stretch them to indent your paragraphs.

With HTML 4 you needn't out-maneuver the browser. Browsers that support the HTML 4 standards display your pages as you define them — no more of that arrogant printer stuff! And fortunately, with HTML 4, you can define the way you want your pages to look outside of the content, so your HTML won't be all cluttered with tags.

Structure your document

So, if you are not supposed to use HTML to format your pages, how should you use HTML? Glad you asked.

HTML defines your document's structure. Then, outside the main body of the document (or even in a separate file, if you prefer), you define the appearance of each element of the structure. Just like the publisher and the printer in the previous example.

With few exceptions, you want all your paragraphs to be formatted the same — uniform margins, indents, fonts, spacing between lines, and color.

So, within the main body of your document, you type your text for each paragraph and mark up your document to indicate where each paragraph begins and ends. Then, in a separate location and only once, you define how you want all your paragraphs to look. Ways exist to override this universal definition, but we discuss them later.

The most important concept to remember — and this is a big change for you if you've already been writing HTML 3.2 or earlier versions — is that the HTML only defines the *structure* of your document. The *formatting* of your document is handled separately.

What is so great about this? First, your text doesn't get all cluttered up with tags. And second, you can define the look for your whole site in one place. You simply have every page in the site (even if some pages in your site are being written by people you have never met) point to the style sheet (the place where you put all those style definitions).

Including Multimedia

Throughout this explanation, we have been talking about text. What if you want to include images? Sound? Video? Animations? 3D models? HTML 4 supports the use of multimedia in your pages. Chapters 40 and 41 go into detail on adding sound and video to your site.

Two ways exist to include multimedia features in your page: inline and out-of-line, and uses exist for both. The only way to insure your visitor sees or hears your multimedia, however, is to put it inline. For example, advertising banners wouldn't get seen much if they weren't inline!

Inline

Visitors to your page can see or hear an inline element without taking any additional action. Inline elements are supported by HTML directly. Examples of inline elements are images, sound, and animated images (called *animated GIFs*, because this is the only type of image that supports animation). Figure 5-5 is an example of an inline image.

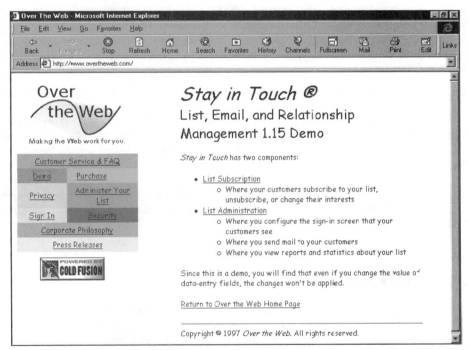

Figure 5-5: The Over the Web logo in the upper left-hand corner is an inline image.

Unless an image is huge (and justifiably so), meaning greater than the size of your screen, you probably want to keep your images inline. Exceptions always exist. Say you want to show a map of Chicago. You may allow your visitors to click a neighborhood and see a more detailed map of only that neighborhood. In this case, you need both inline and out-of-line images. A really large image may, indeed, be justified — as in a map — where detail matters. If you are only showing a photo of Monticello (Thomas Jefferson's home), that level of detail probably isn't necessary. You would be better off, in this case, to show the entire house in one photo and then show separate smaller images of the details you want to discuss.

Out-of-line

When your visitors have to take additional action, such as click an image or agree to initiate a plug-in to see or hear your element, then it is an out-of-line element. Examples of out-of-line elements are images, sound, video, 3D models to be navigated, and animations.

Your visitors may get annoyed if they must take action too often to see or hear your multimedia. A good use of out-of-line sound is a music store that lets you click an icon to hear a music clip from an album. This enables the store to list many album titles on one page — obviously, there wouldn't be any way for you to hear the music clips from every album concurrently. Then the detail page from each album may have inline sound, with a clip from the most popular song on the album.

Objects

Because the number of types of multimedia you can add to your page — many of them proprietary (meaning the technology is owned by only one company) — is growing faster than anyone can count, the WC3 isn't trying to keep up. Instead, it has defined a type of element, called an *object,* which you define when you want to refer to any of these proprietary multimedia types (RealAudio, Worlds, and Shockwave come immediately to mind).

Cross-Reference   Chapter 42 explains how to incorporate proprietary multimedia technologies into your page. It also introduces some of the more common "plug-ins" that Web sites use.

Standardization

This section is being written in reverse order. First, you read about the rational process in place to ensure that every new technology is compatible with every existing technology and that all the major players in these industries sing songs holding hands. Then you read about the actual process an individual company goes through to bring a new technology to market before its competitors get it done. This includes all the compelling reasons why a company can't stop and wait for everyone else to agree (and catch up) with what it is doing. By the end of this section, you understand why standardization rarely precedes technical innovation and why developers will always be in a position of having to make trade-offs between universal access to their page (by every browser that has ever been written) and implementing the latest, coolest technologies. Eventually, after a technology has aged a bit, all the players can come together and agree on a standard.

Understanding the Standardization Process

The process of setting standards for Web-related technologies is run by the World Wide Web Consortium (W3C), based at MIT in the United States and at INRIA in Europe. The W3C is led by Tim Berners-Lee, "creator of the World Wide Web," as the W3C pages tell you repeatedly. The W3C is a consortium. The vocabulary used to define a *consortium,* how it runs, and how it works is a study in nonconfrontation. The person who runs it is a *director.* The people who get paid to do what Berners-Lee says are his *team.* The companies that pay to participate and get a vote in what is decided are *members.* When the W3C is thinking about setting a standard for a technology, it *initiates an activity.* When a W3C committee has decided upon what it thinks is a standard, it issues a *proposed recommendation.* After the membership votes to support the proposed recommendation, it becomes a *recommendation.*

No wonder the W3C doesn't claim to have any enforcement power. With a passive vocabulary like this, it couldn't enforce a bedtime!

Participation in the standardization practice is similar to participation in social activities. If you are going to show up, you'd better behave according to accepted norms.

Activities

If a member of the W3C (members are universities, corporations, and organizations) thinks the W3C should look into setting a standard, then members can initiate an activity. Members may initiate activities both for technologies and for social issues affected by technology. If the W3C agrees some interest exists in this activity, then committees and mailing lists are formed to determine which direction that technology should go.

The Activity Proposal needs to answer some hard questions:

✦ What is the market? Who are the major players? Who stands to benefit from a standard? Are the players and the beneficiaries members of the W3C or will they join? Is the market new, growing, or a niche market? What alternatives to this technology are there? Who owns these technologies?

✦ How many resources of the W3C will this require?

✦ What is the scope of the project?

✦ Is there a deadline? What are the timelines?

✦ Are there any intellectual property conflicts?

✦ Is anyone else setting standards for this technology? Will there be a conflict? Whom will this affect?

✦ Is an activity already in place that covers this technology?

Groups

If the director accepts an activity proposal, then a working group is formed to begin work on the activity. The goal of most *working groups* is to produce a statement or a proposed recommendation. The composition of the working group is important. Any technology company in any way affected by the recommendations regarding an activity will want to be part of this working group. You can bet both Netscape and Microsoft were represented on the HTML 4 working group. Only members can participate in working groups for activities.

Consensus

Not surprisingly, the W3C operates by consensus. A working group must address the concerns of all participants and make an effort to resolve them before reaching a conclusion. A simple majority rule is not enough. The idea is the working group hashes through every possibility until either everyone is in agreement, the people who dissent are convinced the position arrived at is the best possible position given the constraints, or the people in the minority think the problem is no longer worth fighting over.

This philosophy protects small start-ups that come to the table with new technology to protect. It gives every party — whether Sun, Microsoft, or Midge's New Technology Company — equal weight.

Proposed recommendations

Not all activity proposals result in proposed recommendations, but many do. When a working group has resolved the conflict raised by its membership and has drafted what it thinks is a pretty good attempt to set a standard, it publishes what is called a *proposed recommendation*. A proposed recommendation — along with working drafts that are developed along the way — is published to the W3C Web site. Most materials you purchase in bookstores explaining the newest technologies are actually written with the working drafts or the proposed recommendations as the reference materials.

Voting

By following the process of consensus building that takes place during the drafting of the proposed recommendation, the hope is all major conflicts have been resolved by the time the proposed recommendation is issued. During the voting period, all members of the W3C—whether or not they participated on the working group (and most wouldn't have)—vote on the proposed recommendation.

At the end of the voting period, the director, ever the facilitator of good will, has three choices:

1. Issue the proposed recommendation as a recommendation

2. Reject the proposed recommendation

3. Issue the proposed recommendation with comments

When members vote, they can make comments in addition to their vote. If the comments are substantial, especially if the comments that accompany no votes are substantial, then the director will not accept the proposed recommendation as a recommendation. Thus far, the process of consensus has been effective in dealing with the comments of members *before* the activity is no longer a draft; most proposed recommendations do become recommendations.

Recommendations

Even after all these steps are taken to ensure that every member's viewpoint is heard, considered, and incorporated as much as possible, the conclusions regarding standardization that the W3C reaches are still only recommendations. Why? First, the W3C is an international standards body and does not yet have access to United Nations troops to enforce its resolutions. Second, all companies in the community of corporations are trying to develop the best new technologies without antagonizing *you,* the developer. Making up new and different ways to do the same thing, just to be different, doesn't serve the company's own interests. Each company is best served by having the largest pool of developers developing in that technology. This logic enticed Microsoft to offer native support for JavaScript in its Internet Explorer browsers. (Of course, Microsoft's native support isn't the same as Netscape's.) Companies that insist on "my way or the highway" often find themselves on the shoulder—alone.

Players in the Standardization Process

So who gets a vote when the W3C asks? Members of the W3C. Membership in the W3C isn't exclusive, however. Any organization or company can join. Of course, a rather high membership fee exists, which pays the administrative costs of running the W3C.

Who would want to get involved in the W3C? Technology vendors, content providers, corporate users, research laboratories, standards bodies, universities, and governments. If you develop a new technology, you need to be at the table when the standards for related technologies are being set. Otherwise, you run the risk of being written right out of the standard. If your operations are affected by new technologies, then you want to be on the working group, pushing for that standard in which you've already invested. If you develop content that makes use of new technologies, then you want to be well-positioned to know what resources you need to have in place when a new standard is implemented.

The major players, of course, are Microsoft and Netscape. They develop the browsers most widely used to visit Web sites. Microsoft and Netscape both want to see standards set that

✦ are backward-compatible with their own browsers

✦ make use of the newest technologies they are implementing—the way they are implementing them

✦ don't require them to add any features or elements coined by their competitors

But realistically, both browsers want to meet all the needs of the developers. If you, as a developer, find your site looks much better with one browser than with another, you may finally put a "Best Viewed with . . ." logo on your page and call it a day, rather than trying to make a silk purse out of a sow's ear with the other browser.

It might surprise you to learn Microsoft has been far quicker to adopt the technologies developed by others than has Netscape. Despite the bad rap Microsoft receives for its anticompetitive practices (so says Senator Arlen Specter), Microsoft implemented JavaScript as soon as it was clear this was what developers preferred (over its own VBScript). Netscape invented JavaScript, but it still hasn't opened everything in its browsers to scripting with the Document Object Model (DOM), the way Microsoft has.

The Extensions Game

How do you get the standards set in your favor? You create extensions you know aren't standard and implement them on your browser. If they catch up in the developer community, the other browser maker will be forced to become compliant with the de facto standard you have set. At this point, if the W3C accepts it, this is just icing.

Consider the FONT element. The FONT element has never been part of an official W3C specification, but Netscape introduced it, Microsoft adopted it, and until CSS is fully and uniformly implemented in both browsers, the FONT element will continue to give the best results for formatting text available. At some point, standardization is irrelevant. Finally, with the HTML 4 specification, the W3C recognized the FONT element just enough to deprecate it!

From Here

Cross-Reference

Proceed to Chapter 6 to learn about XML and XSL.

Go to Part III and begin learning about HTML structure in depth.

Summary

HTML has come a long way from the days all pages had black, Times Roman text on a gray background. Today you can place text over graphics, layer images, and define paragraphs with indentation. With patience and an understanding of the standards currently in use, you can make your design visible as you intended to a majority of Web users.

Standards are a Web developers dream. Oh, for the day when you can implement a fabulous new technology and *know* it will work on all platforms on all browsers in the same way. But, alas, that day will never come. Browser makers and other purveyors of technology don't make money by finishing neck-and-neck with their competitors. They need to be the first one across the finish line to deliver on a new technology.

Even with the W3C spelling out standards as fast as they can, it will never be able to anticipate technology to such a degree that the standards precede the technology. All you can hope for is that within a reasonable period of time *after* a new technology is introduced, the competitive browser makers will implement it in a reasonably similar fashion. W3C or no W3C, the market is still the primary factor that drives standardization in this industry.

✦ ✦ ✦

What About XML/XSL?

HTML is a markup language—HTML actually stands for HyperText Markup Language. It gives you a way of marking text so that browsers interpret the text correctly, yet you can still look at the HTML code in a text editor and make some sense of the content.

But HTML has its drawbacks. Unless new definitions are added to HTML, such as when a new version like HTML 4.01 was introduced, there are not a lot of options available to a content author.

Help is on the way. This chapter gives you an overview of XML, or Extensible Markup Language. (And yes, you are correct, that acronym doesn't match the words too well.) XML is a language that enables you to design your own markup and share it with others. It also plays an important role in the evolution of HTML. XML is a complex topic and would take an entire book to describe. Conveniently, you can refer to the *XML Bible* by Elliotte Rusty Harold (IDG Books Worldwide, Inc., 1999) for great coverage of XML.

What Is XML?

XML is a subset of SGML, or Standard Generalized Markup Language. HTML itself is defined in SGML. XML is intended to offer most of the flexibility of SGML without the complexity of that language. Think of XML as a set of rules that enable you to establish different sets of markup rules for different classes of documents, and to easily share those sets of rules.

XML is a meta-markup language, or a means of formally defining a markup language. For example, if you're creating a Web site to share written music, you may need to describe composers, instrumentation, and a grade to indicate to conductors who is best suited for that arrangement. Using XML, you can mark these specific descriptors — and any others you may consider relevant — using tags to contain the information. These tagged items can then be manipulated, such as displaying them in a certain font or other formatting method, depending on how the tags are defined in the Document Type Definition, or DTD.

Document type definition

DTDs are the syntax of a specific XML subset. They contain all the definitions created for a specific application, such as the composers and instrumentation in our music Web site example. The real beauty of this extensibility is that you are no longer constrained by what browser vendors opt to support in their latest version — you can define a specific set of definitions to suit your needs, whether it is for one specific application or a project that has broader application.

You have the option of including a DTD directly in the document it describes, or posting the DTD online and referencing that Uniform Resource Identifier (URI) in your document. There are reasons for both approaches. If you anticipate this DTD would be used widely, posting it may be the best approach. You may also create a single task-specific DTD, and it might make better sense to include it directly in the document for which it was created.

XML namespace

A namespace is the collection of available elements and attributes that work in a specific XML application, and is identified by a URI reference. The namespace gives a method of overriding conflicts between documents. For example, if two different XML applications share a document, and these two separate applications have used the same attribute or element name differently, the namespace gives a means of arbitrating these potential collisions by linking the attribute names with their specific namespace.

What Is XSL

In XML, CSS style sheets apply only to elements, not attributes. Attribute content will appear blank when a CSS style sheet is applied. XSL (Extensible Style Language) is the answer. XSL has two sections: transformations and formatting.

Transformations

Transformations in XSL enable you to replace one tag with another. You can use this process to reorder elements or to add data that wasn't included in the XML document, but its simplest purpose is to replace XML tags with HTML tags. You can also assign CSS attributes during this transformation.

Formatting

XSL *formatting* is extremely powerful, but not yet supported by the major browsers. With XML formatting, you can define the appearance of a page that flows text around graphics, separates text into multiple columns, and includes a variety of fonts. Even more important, you can define a page to appear one way on screen, and then print out in a way better suited for the printed page.

From Here

XHTML, covered in the next chapter, is the direction of HTML in the future. It is actually an XML application designed to mimic HTML 4.01. Proceed to Chapter 7 to learn more about it.

Jump to Part IV to compare XSL to HTML's Cascading Style Sheets (CSS).

Summary

XML, like HTML, came from SGML. Unlike HTML, XML offers a convenient way for new attributes and elements to be defined and shared with others, either on a specific project or as a new markup language for a group of projects with common interests. XML in concert with XSL offers exciting new steps in the presentation of your information as you want it to appear.

✦　　✦　　✦

Introducing XHTML: HTML's Future

In Chapter 6, you learned about XML. In this chapter, you'll see how XHTML, or XML with a specific Document Type Definition (DTD), is serving as the jumping point for future revisions of HTML.

What Is XHTML?

XHTML is an XML application. The DTDs, or Document Type Definitions, used with XML are actually close copies of HTML 4.01, close enough that XHTML can be viewed as simply a stricter enforcement of HTML. It doesn't offer any exciting new tags. Instead, it has been created with two specific goals — extensibility and portability.

 Chapter 6 provides a detailed explanation of XML.

Extensibility

Previously, a new version of HTML was introduced every so often, with new elements and attributes that were probably already in use. The major browsers often leapfrogged the HTML specification with new goodies they thought were beneficial, and then Microsoft and Netscape would go to the W3C and campaign for their newly defined tags to be included in the next new HTML specification. This method of defining new tags led to complications we discuss throughout this book. But what it really led to were more headaches for HTML authors who just wanted their pages to look good in any browser.

XML elements must be well formed, which will be discussed shortly. To change or introduce new HTML elements, the language itself must be changed. But in XML, all that is required is for the new elements to be internally consistent and well formed before they can be added to a DTD. This makes adding new elements much simpler.

Portability

We are moving rapidly away from a time when the Web was only accessed via computer. New electronic devices, such as cellular phones and personal digital assistants (PDAs), are Web-enabled. In the past, sheer horsepower from the computer could be used to fill in sloppy or ill-formed HTML code, often invisibly to the user.

New devices don't have this kind of spare processor power. Instead of interpreting the bad code, these new Web devices may simply sit there and wait to be told what to do. By more rigidly enforcing the HTML DTD, this type of code error is better prevented, and is thus less likely to be the source of PDA panic.

Differences Between HTML and XHTML

Current browsers correctly interpret omissions in HTML instructions. In contrast, XHTML code must be well formed by adhering closely to established standards. To give an example, if there is a missing `</table>` end tag, Internet Explorer will fill it in. In XHTML, this would be an example of ill-formed code and it would probably result in a failure to show the table.

There are a number of considerations in writing well-formed XHTML code. Keep in mind that some of these provisions are a stricter enforcement of things that should have been done in HTML 4, but you could get away with errors and the browser would correct many of them. This is no longer true in XHTML.

Required tags

In XHTML, the head and body tags must be included. Since including them is part of well written HTML code anyway, this shouldn't be a problem.

Tags must be properly nested

Tags must be closed in the proper order. In HTML, if you were using the italic tags in a paragraph, it didn't matter which tag you closed first, and which tag was closed second. In XHTML, tags need to be closed in reverse order — the last tag opened is the first closed. The following code is an XHTML example:

```
<!DOCTYPE html PUBLIC
          "-//W3C//DTD XHTML 1.0 Transiticnal//EN"
          "DTD/xhtml1-transitional.dtd"    >
<html    xmlns   = "http://www.w3.org/1999/xhtml">
<head>
          <title>Quick Example</title>
</head>
<body>
<h1>      Quick Example
</h1>
<a        href    = "http://validator.w3.org/check/referer">
<img      src     = "http://validator.w3.org/images/vxhtml10"
          height  = "31"
          width   = "88"
          border  = "0"
          hspace  = "16"
          align   = "left"
          alt     = "Valid XHTML 1.0!"
          /></a>
<p>       Note that the layout (with tabs and alignment) is
          purely for readability - XHTML doesn't require it.
</p>
</body>
</html>
```

This example is code that wouldn't pass XHTML requirements:

```
<!DOCTYPE html PUBLIC
          "-//W3C//DTD XHTML 1.0 Transitional//EN"
          "DTD/xhtml1-transitional.dtd"    >
<html    xmlns   = "http://www.w3.org/1999/xhtml">
<head>
          <title>Quick Example</title>
</head>
<body>
<h1>      Quick Example
</h1>
<a        href    = "http://validator.w3.org/check/referer">
<img      src     = "http://validator.w3.org/images/vxhtml10"
          height  = "31"
          width   = "88"
          border  = "0"
          hspace  = "16"
          align   = "left"
          alt     = "Valid XHTML 1.0!"
          /></a>
<p>       Note that the layout (with tabs and alignment) is
          purely for readability - XHTML doesn't require it.
</body>
</p>
</html>
```

Note   Notice the last closing paragraph tag comes after the closing body tag in this example; this one occurrence of swapped tags makes this invalid XHTML.

Lowercase tag and attribute names

In HTML, tags are often written in uppercase to make the code easier to follow. This is no longer acceptable. While attribute *values* are still case-insensitive, elements and attributes must be written in lowercase.

Empty elements are not allowed

Empty elements are those that have no closing tag, like `<hr>`, `<br>`, or `<img src>`. These elements must be closed using the XML syntax for empty tags, which requires a forward slash (/) immediately before the closing bracket, also known as the greater than sign. For example, `<hr>` becomes `<hr />`. An image reference changes from `<img src="pony.gif">` to `<img src="pony.gif" />`. The following code is an example of closing empty elements.

```
<img    src     = "http://validator.w3.org/images/vxhtml10"
        height  = "31"
        width   = "88"
        border  = "0"
        hspace  = "16"
        align   = "left"
        alt     = "Valid XHTML 1.0!"
        /></a>
```

Note   Notice the closing bracket for `img src` has a forward slash (/).

Nonempty elements have to be closed

Many elements in use don't currently require end tags. For example, in HTML 4 the `<li>` tag is used to list elements, and since the next element is marked by another `<li>` tag; this tag effectively closes the previous list element. But not any more. XHTML requires that nonempty elements be closed. This affects tags such as `<li>`, `<p>`, `<body>`, and many table-related tags.

```
<p>     Note that the layout (with tabs and alignment) is
        purely for readability - XHTML doesn't require it.
</p>
</body>
</html>
```

Note Notice the presence of the closing paragraph tag, `</p>`.

Attribute values must be quoted

All attribute values, whether alphabetic or numeric, must now be enclosed in quotation marks. For example, when setting attributes such as height and width for an image element, the numbers must be surrounded by quotation marks.

```
<img    src     = "http://validator.w3.org/images/vxhtml10"
        height  = "31"
        width   = "88"
        border  = "0"
        hspace  = "16"
        align   = "left"
        alt     = "Valid XHTML 1.0!"
        />
```

Note Notice the double quotation marks before and after the attribute values, for example, `"31"`.

Attribute values must be expanded

Attributes are considered minimized when there is only one possible value. XML doesn't allow this type of minimization, so attributes must be expanded. For example, `<ul compact>` becomes `<ul compact="compact">`.

From Here

Cross-Reference Proceed to Chapter 8 to learn about HTML development software.

Not ready to take the XHTML plunge? Jump to Chapter 24 to find out about testing and validating your HTML.

Summary

HTML 4.01 is the final version of HTML. In order to allay portability concerns and address new extensions to the language for specific needs, an XML-based framework, XHTML, has been developed. While it requires a bit more attention to writing well-formed code, these habits will pay off in easier adoption of new elements and better support across many new platforms. XHTML 1.0 takes over where HTML 4.01 left off.

✦   ✦   ✦

Choosing an HTML Editor

In the early days of the Web, everyone was stuck with just one option: creating HTML with plain old text editors. These are simple word-processing programs designed for writing software. This was, of course, part of the appeal of HTML; it could be created in a text editor, such as vi, WinVile, or Notepad. Compared to word processors, text editors are small, fast programs optimized for writing programming code. Although many people still prefer to write HTML using a text editor, those no-choice days are gone. Today you can choose from many HTML-creation programs.

The program choices are full of cool, new options for developing Web sites. This chapter uses the term *HTML editor* to describe *any* program that includes at least some features that help you write HTML, however simple or complex. The simplest programs are text editors souped up with a few HTML-savvy features. At the other extreme are expensive, big-ticket programs that enable you to create your pages in an entirely visual environment. Pros and cons exist to each approach. For a beginner, the visual environment is often the most painless way to get started.

This chapter discusses the features good Web-page-development software has, and then moves on to review the gamut of programs. Included are both the HTML editors that provide a graphical environment for Web page creation, and those that give you a place to type your HTML and content, providing a variety of cues and programs to assist with the HTML creation.

To WYSIWYG or Not to WYSIWYG?

That's the question, and it's a biggie. On the one hand, you find *graphical environments,* which enable you to create fantastic-looking Web pages without writing any HTML code. These programs enable you to see your Web page just the way it looks in the browser; that's why these programs are called *What You See Is What You Get* (WYSIWYG, pronounced wiz-ee-wig).

On the other hand, *tag-based editors* force you to edit HTML code directly. These programs enable you to enter and modify HTML tags, but you'll need to know HTML.

WYSIWYG editors: Easy to use, but hands-off

WYSIWYG programs give you a visual drag-and-drop environment for Web-page creation. They are well suited for beginners or for people who don't plan to use more advanced features. Using Netscape Composer, the WYSIWYG editor that comes with Netscape Communicator, you can quickly and easily create a nice-looking Web page.

But WYSIWYG editors exact a price for their ease of use:

✦ Often, they don't include advanced features. For example, Netscape Composer doesn't handle frames. That's ironic, because Netscape invented frames in the first place.

✦ They often don't let you edit the HTML directly. If you don't know HTML, that's a plus. However, experienced HTML authors know few WYSIWYG programs generate wholly satisfactory output. Often, they require some HTML tweaking to get everything working, and looking great.

✦ They may introduce proprietary extensions that prevent your pages from working with all browsers. If you can't see the HTML, you don't know what code is written. Microsoft's FrontPage Express, supplied gratis with Microsoft Internet Explorer 5.0, enables you to create scrolling marquees — but what you don't know is Netscape Navigator (and most other browsers except Internet Explorer) doesn't recognize the MARQUEE element, one of Microsoft's unilaterally introduced extensions. However, FrontPage Express does allow you to alter your HTML code manually.

✦ The bottom line: For advanced HTML coding, WYSIWYG editors won't cut it. Sooner or later, you realize you need to dive into the underlying HTML. At this point, you need a program that enables you to edit your HTML code directly.

Getting serious: Tag-based programs

Tag-based editors don't hide the underlying HTML; instead, they stick it in your face. That's uncomfortable for beginners, but it's heaven for experienced HTML authors. Sooner or later, you need to see and directly edit the code — and this is particularly true if you want to write "real" HTML 4, as this book advocates. You could use a simple text editor, such as the Windows Notepad utility, but you might wind up using a tag-based editor for ease of use.

These programs are called *tag-based* because they provide easy-to-use tools for entering tags with a click of the mouse. For example, to code a heading, you select the heading text and click one of the heading buttons. The program automatically enters the HTML tags. This is easier, and less prone to error, than typing tags yourself. There is also an added plus: You can manually tweak the underlying HTML. And, more to this book's point, you can also make sure the code conforms to the HTML 4 Way.

XHTML 1.0 is the W3C's recommendation for the latest version of HTML, following on from earlier work on HTML 4.01, HTML 4.0, HTML 3.2, and HTML 2.0. With a wealth of features, XHTML 1.0 is a reformulation of HTML 4.01 in XML, and combines the strength of HTML 4 with the power of XML. XHTML 1.0 can be put to immediate use with existing browsers by following a few simple guidelines. Even though this new recommendation occurred in January 2000, for our purposes we are creating HTML the 4.01 way.

What's the downside of a tag-based editor? You can't look at your page the way browsers display it. This makes it tough to enter and proofread text because all those HTML tags get in the way. Also, you can't immediately see the results of your coding. To see what your page looks like you have to click an option that sends the page to a browser. If you find a mistake, you have to go back to the editor and make the change. Tag-based editors, in short, aren't very interactive.

What's the difference?

Want to see the difference between a WYSIWYG program and a tag-based editor? Look at Figure 8-1, which shows a WYSIWYG editor, and Figure 8-2, which shows a tag-based editor.

For example, if you're working in a WYSIWIG program, like the one shown in Figure 8-1, and you want to add a horizontal line in the middle of your page, you would place the cursor where you want the line to appear and then click the horizontal line tool. The program automatically enters the horizontal line and you see it right away on your page, just the way it's going to look when displayed by a browser.

In a tag-based editor, you would scroll through your HTML to the point where you want to place a horizontal line and either type <HR> (that's the HTML tag that enters a horizontal line), or click a button indicating a horizontal rule tag should be added at that point in the page. You would then have to take the extra step of viewing your page in a browser (or a browser facsimile that's built into the editor) to see your horizontal line.

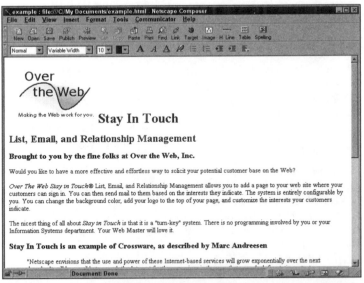

Figure 8-1: A simple Web page in a WYSIWYG program (Netscape Communicator 4.7)

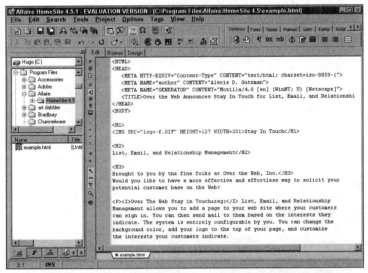

Figure 8-2: The same simple Web page in a tag-based editor (HomeSite 4.5)

Exploring HTML Editor Features

Whether you choose a WYSIWYG or a tag-based editor to create your HTML, you'll be wise to spend some time exploring the various features offered by the current crop of HTML software. Depending on your needs, some of them may offer features and programs that may make you work more efficiently. If you don't choose carefully, you might get stuck with a program that doesn't do something you need — and this means more tedious, manual work for you.

Work-wise, creating and launching your Web site is just the beginning of a creative adventure. All sites should take their guests on an interesting journey, and the first visit should offer a reason to return, and on subsequent visits, the guest needs to experience a site that grows and evolves over time. Web sites are living, dynamic documents. For this reason, you'll want a program that makes updating them easy. WYSIWYG HTML editors make producing your initial site easy, but often come up short when it's time to update. Whichever route you take, WYSIWYG or tag-based, you need to be able to make changes to your pages frequently.

The following sections explore some of the features found in today's HTML editors. To select the right features for your needs, consider what you're planning to do. You won't necessarily need all the features listed. If you want to create a few simple pages, for instance, you won't need site maintenance features. But you won't want to live without those features if you plan to create a huge, complex site with dozens, or even hundreds, of Web pages.

Considerations

Before you can select the right program, you must decide what features you need. This section explains all the features considered valuable in an HTML-development program.

Note

Colored tags is a valuable feature to have in your HTML editor. With colored tags, each type of tag is displayed in a different color. For example, comments might be gray, tags related to tables might be green, script tags might be red, and so forth. This way, if you forget to close your comment, the rest of the code will be colored gray — a useful visual cue.

Some features, however, are absolutely essential. These include the capability to have multiple pages open for editing at the same time, the capability to do multiple-file search-and-replace, tag cues to tell you what attributes are available to the tag you are editing, colored tags, and the capability to add custom tags so you don't need to add or cut and paste sequences of tags you use frequently.

Note   Why will you fail to see your scripting if you open files with server-side scripting from the Web? Server-side scripting has already executed by the time you see the page. If you go to a page with server-side scripting (CGI scripts, server-side JavaScript, server-side Java, server-side includes, or Cold Fusion) and view the source, you won't see any of the code. Unlike client-side JavaScript — what most people think of when they think of JavaScript — and VBScript, these other types of scripts are interpreted on the server. This means you only see the results of what the script told the server to do, not the actual instructions, or script.

HTML 4 support

The HTML 4 Way separates presentation from structure. This is different from previous versions of HTML. Not all HTML-development programs encourage this dichotomy. Most development programs available at publication are not well suited to the HTML dichotomy between structure and content. Even if you are happy with your HTML-development program, you might want to evaluate it in light of how well it supports this dichotomy.

Simple migration between editors

One of the nice things about HTML is, even if you create it in one tag-based editor, you can easily edit in another one. This means you can move between tag-based editors without having to perform file conversions, the way you would have to if you moved between word processing packages.

Many of the programs discussed in this chapter provide the capability to import your entire site. This means you can open the site you created with one program in a different program. If you are managing a growing site, this is a definite feature to remember.

One drawback of importing a site into a WYSIWYG editor is that it often uses its own rules to make your HTML more cumbersome. When you evaluate HTML editors, be sure to open some of your existing pages in them to see what, if anything, each one does to the readability of your HTML. At the least, most of them add a <META> tag to the top of the document, claiming credit for generating it.

On the CD-ROM   Most of the editors discussed in this chapter are on the CD-ROM at the back of this book.

Wizards: A quick start

Some elements of Web pages — those that come in groups — are best created with wizards. Wizards, tools, dialog boxes, or whatever the marketing department wants to call them, are a great way to get something done quickly and accurately. The HTML page structure, tables, forms, style sheets, and channels fall into this category. The best programs give you the option of completing a simple dialog box or a series of simple dialog boxes to define these elements and then create the HTML for you.

Definition

Channels. One of the interesting features most browsers permit is the creation of "subscription to channels." Channels are basically a feature you can define in your page that enables visitors to indicate they want to receive any updates to your page or your site in the background. This means people who *subscribe* to your channel will always have a completely current version of your page loaded locally on their own clients.

Of all these wizards, the style-sheet wizard is the most essential. Figure 8-3 shows the Bradsoft TopStyle Lite 1.51 style-sheet wizard, which was included with Home-Site 4.5. You shouldn't be creating that many style sheets, because the point of the style sheet is to apply the same one to your entire site. Still, you definitely won't want to memorize or look up the syntax every time. Each program handles style sheets differently; some have wizards and some have entire applications dedicated to the creation of CSS.

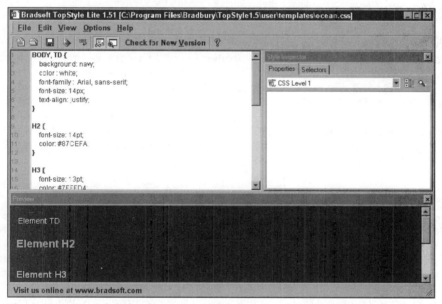

Figure 8-3: Useful dialog box in a style-sheet wizard (Bradsoft TopStyle Lite 1.51)

Version control

Even the most organized Webmaster appreciates support for version control, a feature that automatically assigns version numbers to each modified version of your pages. Before too long, you may find your mirror site (a copy of your site located elsewhere) doesn't perfectly mirror the source site (where the original version is stored). You might have made just one small change to a file on the server or from someone else's workstation. However you arrive at this moment of panic, version control can help you identify the most recent version of your HTML file.

Definition

Mirror site. A *mirror site* is either a place where you test your pages before publishing them to the public site or a copy of your public site. In either case, it's easy to find that your mirror site is not identical to your public site. Keeping the two in sync is facilitated by version-control software.

Unfortunately, few programs support this feature. One of the few that does is NetObjects Team Fusion. NetObjects Fusion 5.0 is discussed later in this chapter. Team Fusion is an add-on to this application, which is actually a collaborative development tool. You can purchase third-party products to fill the version-control need, if you purchase a program that doesn't offer this valuable feature.

Group collaboration programs

Only a lucky few get to make all decisions related to their Web sites. Most Web developers have to work with a team at some point. If you have a number of individuals working on your site, then this feature will ease your task. Group collaboration programs can make the process of team Web-site building easier.

Starbase offers a complete family of user-friendly software products that enable teams of people to collaborate in the production of Web sites, e-commerce applications, and other mission-critical applications. The Starbase technology provides a framework for digital asset management. This framework supports integration of products like StarTeam Enterprise, which provides collaboration and configuration management across the whole project life cycle. The Starbase Server and the StarGate SDK enable you to "plug in" other life cycle development products to the framework and bring the deliverables under StarTeam control. These applications are available from the Starbase Web site (www.starbase.com).

Make yourself right at home: Customization

Any good Web-page-development program enables you to customize it extensively. You should be able to see only the program bars you need. If you don't create forms, you don't need all the tags related to forms represented on your screen. These take up valuable space that could be used for the editor. You should also be able to create a custom color palette and be able to view or hide it, according to your preferences.

You may have strings of HTML you use frequently in combination. Wouldn't it be nice to click one button and have all those tags pasted right into your document? Whether this feature is marketed as *tag snippets* or *custom tags,* this is a nice feature to have.

Finally, the capability to create custom templates that provide the shell of your document without any additional typing — say, to provide metadata — is also a nice feature to have. Fortunately, customization is widely available.

Open sesame

Where are your HTML files located? For most Webmasters, files are located on a remote server and are only available via FTP. For this reason, an integrated FTP client is usually essential to enhancing your productivity. If your server is NT, you can easily access the remote directory by mapping a drive letter to it. You'll be able to access your Web files by the mapped drive's letter, just like your local drives. If you have trouble accessing the files, ask your administrator for help.

Tip

Mapping a local drive to your NT server. To do this, you have to be running Windows 95/98/2000/NT, or Mac OS. You also need access privileges to the server. Talk to your server administrator about getting these privileges and setting up your LMHOSTS and HOSTS files (not required for Mac OS) so you can save your files to your server as easily as you save them to a floppy disk. Licensing issues are also related to using this approach, but once you're set up, it does make things easier.

If you don't use server-side scripting or you don't know what it is, you might also want to take advantage of the "Open from the Web" feature. This enables you to open the page you want to edit without having to use FTP or sign onto your Web server. You get exactly what you would get if you opened the page with your browser and saved the source. Because you need FTP to save your files when you are done editing, this feature isn't as valuable as an integrated FTP client.

Caution

If you are taking advantage of the "Open from the Web" feature, remember: You should make backup copies of all files before working. This way, if a program bombs, you can still retrieve the original file from the Web server.

Speaking of saving files, you might need the capability to save your files as either DOS, Mac, or UNIX files. The difference among these formats is the presence or absence of carriage returns (CR) or line feeds (LF). If you save the files in one format and open them in another, either you will have no end-line markers or you will have extra characters (^M) at the beginning of each line. If you develop your files on a PC and publish them to an NT server, this won't be an issue for you.

You also need the capability to have more than one page open at once. Fortunately, support for multiple open documents is part of several of the programs.

Syntax compliance: How much is too much?

When selecting a Web-page creation program, you will find various levels of *syntax checking* (a feature that scrutinizes your code to make sure it's free from errors and conforms to HTML standards):

✦ **None.** The program makes no attempt to check whether your HTML code conforms to HTML standards.

✦ **Continuous.** Syntax checking can be turned on or off. When it is on, any errors or incomplete tags are marked in color, whether or not you are done with them.

✦ **On-demand built in.** Syntax checking is only a click away. When you are ready to have your syntax checked, you can request it.

✦ **On-demand as a plug-in.** After you install a plug-in (which may or may not cost more money), syntax checking is only a click away.

✦ **Forced continuous.** Syntax checking is always, annoyingly, on.

✦ **Forced on-save.** When you try to save, it forces you to correct any errors it finds.

The only unacceptable levels are "continuous" and "forced" anything. Can you imagine a word processor that wouldn't let you save a file that had a word it didn't recognize? This is the mentality behind forced syntax compliance. Continuous syntax checking is a waste of your processor. What is the point of telling you that you need a `</CENTER>` tag while you are still in the middle of typing the content you want centered? This feature is a lot like Microsoft Word's continuous spelling checker (offered in Versions 6, 7, 97, and 2000), which, gratefully, you can turn off.

You will want to check your syntax to make sure you comply with the latest set of rules, but you will want to do it on your schedule, not your editor's.

Another nice feature beginning to appear in these programs is support for browser-specific tags. Microsoft Internet Explorer and Netscape Navigator are not perfectly in synch when it comes to tag support. If you know your visitors are running a certain browser (for example, in an intranet) and that browser supports extra tags, it is nice to use those tags without being hassled by the syntax checker.

Tag assistance

A good HTML-development program helps you out with your tags — letting you know which attributes are available to the tag you are using — without imposing itself on you. Some editors provide *tag completion,* automatically filling in a `</CENTER>`, when you finish typing `<CENTER>`. Some editors offer visual assistance by color-coding the tags by type. While this may sound annoying, once you know what to look for, you will appreciate it.

Some editors provide dialog boxes, enabling you to fill in values for the attributes you want to include. The only truly time-wasting tag assistance in this set of programs is the "feature" that automatically inserts every attribute for the tag you select with the values of the attributes set to blank.

Viewing your work in progress

While you work in a tag-based editor, you will probably want to see how your page is developing. It is convenient, but not essential, to have an internal browser in your development program. The alternative is to save your file and open it locally from your browser or publish it to your Web site and view it in your regular browser. If there is an internal browser, it should be accurate. An inaccurate internal browser is as bad as none at all. Best of all is the capability to select more than one internal browser of your choice.

Tip   To open a page on your local computer from your browser without publishing it to your remote server, select *Open* or *Open Page* from the File menu, select the file you want to view, and click Open.

Support for advanced tags

Server-side scripting may become a part of your Web site before you know it. If you want your visitors to be able to sign into your database to enter a contest on your site or to complete a survey, you need to use Cold Fusion, Active Server Pages (ASP), CGI, server-side Java, or server-side JavaScript.

If you are going to use JavaScript, applets, style sheets, or ActiveX controls, you want a development program that facilitates the use of these tags. You will get frustrated fast if you have to wrestle with your editor every time you want to use one of these tools. Figure 8-4 shows the HoTMetaL PRO Wizard for adding ActiveX controls.

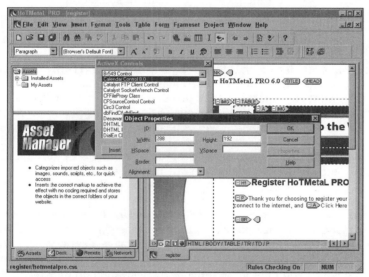

Figure 8-4: Inserting an ActiveX Control (made easy with HoTMetaL PRO 6.0)

Other niceties

Most programs offer the following features:

✦ **Automatic word wrapping.** With this feature—a no-brainer, you would think—you can see your entire paragraph of text or all the attributes of your tag without having to scroll right.

✦ **Global find and replace.** This feature searches all the files in your project or your site and makes changes. If you don't use style sheets, this is the only practical way you can make formatting changes that affect large numbers of pages, that is, unless you want to go into each one and make all the changes manually. This feature isn't as important if you're using style sheets, which enable you to define presentation styles for all the documents you link to it, but it is nice if you find you've been spelling the president's name wrong.

✦ **Link checking.** Confirms all your links work.

✦ **Link manager.** Gives you some sort of graphical representation of the relationship between your pages.

✦ **Link repair.** Automatically attempts to repair links that get broken from moving pages around in your directory tree.

✦ **Spell checking.** Essential and, fortunately, universally available in these programs.

✦ **Site Manager.** Shows you all the pages in your site in some graphically meaningful way.

Comparing HTML editors

By now you should have an idea of what features you need in an HTML editor. In the following table, use the column on the left to mark your needs and then compare your needs with what is available. All the programs listed in Table 8-1 can be downloaded from the Web for 15- to 45-day evaluations. Take advantage of these downloads to find the program that works best for you.

The rest of this chapter discusses each of the programs in Table 8-1 in brief. Each description includes information on evaluation downloads, URLs for each company, and pricing.

While you might be tempted to go down Table 8-1 looking for the program with the most yeses under it, realize not all features are essential or even good. For example, if you are maintaining a site alone, collaborative development tools probably aren't necessary. If you publish your pages to an NT server and you have the NT drive on which you publish files mapped locally, then an integrated FTP client won't matter. If you use any server-side includes or scripting that is interpreted on the server, you can't use the "Open from the Web" feature without losing your scripting. Finally, an example of a downright annoying feature of some programs is *forced syntax compliance*. While you might want to enforce syntax compliance on others, you won't enjoy having it forced on you. The HTML standard is constantly evolving. If you are working with an editor that enforces compliance to a fixed HTML set of tags, then you will need to upgrade the editor to work with the newest HTML standard.

Table 8-1
Comparison of HTML-Development Programs

	TextPad 4.2	Hot Dog Pro 6.0	HomeSite 4.5	HoTMetaL 6.0	CoffeeCup	Dream-weaver	FrontPage 2000	PageMill 3.0	HTML-Kit 1.0	NetObjects Fusion 3 with TeamFusion
WYSIWYG	No	No	No	Yes	Yes	Yes	Yes	Yes	Yes	Yes
View source	Yes	Yes	Yes	Yes	Yes	Yes	Yes	Yes	Yes	No
Supports HTML 4.0 dichotomy	Yes	Yes	Yes	Yes	Yes	Yes	Yes	Yes	Yes	Yes
Imports a Web site	No	Yes	No	No	Yes	Yes	Yes	No	Yes	Yes
Web page importing	Yes	Yes	Yes	Yes	Yes	Yes	Yes	Yes	Yes	Yes
Wizards	No	Yes	Yes	Yes	Yes	Yes	Yes	Yes	Yes	Yes
Tables Wizard	No	Yes	Yes	Yes	Yes	Yes	Yes	Yes	Yes	Yes
Frames Wizard	No	Yes	Yes	Yes	Yes	Yes	Yes	Yes	Yes	Yes
Form Wizard	No	Yes	Yes	Yes	Yes	Yes	Yes	Yes	Yes	Yes
Style-sheets Wizard	No	Yes	Yes	Yes	Yes	Yes	Yes	No	Yes	No
Channel Wizard	No	Yes	No	No	No	No	Yes	No	No	No
Imagemap creation	No	Yes	No	Yes	Yes	Yes	No	Yes	Yes	Yes
Version control	No	No	No	No	No	No	No	No	No	No

Continued

Table 8-1 (continued)

	TextPad 4.2	Hot Dog Pro 6.0	HomeSite 4.5	HoTMetaL 6.0	CoffeeCup	Dream-weaver	FrontPage 2000	PageMill 3.0	HTML-Kit 1.0	NetObjects Fusion 3 with TeamFusion
Collaborative site-creation tools	No	No	No	No	No	Yes	Yes	No	Yes	No
File Manager	Yes	Yes	Yes	No	No	Yes	Yes	Yes	Yes	No
Project Manager	No	Yes	Yes	Yes	No	Yes	Yes	Yes	Yes	No
Custom tags	Yes	Yes	Yes	Yes	No	Yes	No	No	Yes	No
Customizable interface	Yes	Yes	Yes	Yes	Yes	Yes	Yes	No	No	No
Customizable templates	No	Yes	Yes	Yes	Yes	Yes	Yes	No	Yes	Yes
Integrated FTP client	No	Yes	Yes	Yes	Yes	Yes	Yes	Yes	Yes	Yes
Open files from Web	No	Yes	Yes	No	Yes	Yes	Yes	No	Yes	Yes
Multiple pages open at once	Yes	Yes	Yes	Yes	Yes	Yes	Yes	Yes	Yes	No
Save files in multiple formats	No	Yes	Yes	Yes	No	Yes	No	No	Yes	No
Integrated syntax checker	No	Yes	Yes	Yes	No	Yes	No	No	Yes	No

	TextPad 4.2	Hot Dog Pro 6.0	HomeSite 4.5	HotMetaL 6.0	CoffeeCup	Dreamweaver	FrontPage 2000	PageMill 3.0	HTML-Kit 1.0	NetObjects Fusion 3 with TeamFusion
Forced syntax compliance	No	No	No	No	No	Yes	No	No	No	No
Browser-specific tags	No	Yes	No	Yes	Yes	Yes	No	No	No	No
Tag cues	Yes	Yes	Yes	Yes	No	Yes	No	No	No	No
Tag completion	No	Yes	Yes	Yes	No	Yes	Yes	No	Yes	No
Colored tags	No	Yes	Yes	Yes	Yes	Yes	Yes	Yes	Yes	No
Auto-detection of width and height for images	No	Yes	Yes	Yes	Yes	Yes	Yes	Yes	Yes	Yes
Internal browser	No	No	Yes	Yes	Yes	Yes	Yes	Yes	No	Yes
Define multiple internal browsers	No	No	No	Yes	Yes	Yes	Yes	Yes	No	No
Accurate internal browser	No	No	Yes	Yes	Yes	Yes	Yes	Yes	No	No
External browser required	Yes	Yes	No	No	No	No	No	No	Yes	Yes
JavaScript	Yes	Yes	Yes	Yes	Yes	Yes	Yes	Yes	Yes	Yes

Continued

Table 8-1 *(continued)*

	TextPad 4.2	Hot Dog Pro 6.0	HomeSite 4.5	HoTMetaL 6.0	CoffeeCup	Dream-weaver	FrontPage 2000	PageMill 3.0	HTML-Kit 1.0	NetObjects Fusion 3 with TeamFusion
ActiveX	No	No	Yes	Yes	No	Yes	Yes	Yes	Yes	Yes
Applets	No	Yes	Yes	Yes	No	Yes	Yes	Yes	Yes	Yes
ASP	No	Yes	Yes	Yes	No	Yes	Yes	No	No	Yes
Cold Fusion	Yes	No	Yes	No	No	Yes	No	No	No	No
CSS	Yes	Yes	Yes	Yes	Yes	Yes	Yes	No	Yes	Yes
Global find/ replace capability	Yes	Yes	Yes	Yes	Yes	Yes	Yes	Yes	Yes	Yes
Link checking	No	Yes	Yes	Yes	No	Yes	Yes	Yes	Yes	Yes
Link manager/ repair	No	Yes	No	Yes	No	Yes	Yes	Yes	Yes	Yes
Spell Checker	Yes	Yes	Yes	Yes	Yes	Yes	Yes	Yes	Yes	Yes
Site manager	No	Yes	No	Yes	Yes	Yes	Yes	Yes	Yes	Yes

Looking at HTML Editors

Now that you've examined the features HTML editors offer, take a look at some of the most popular programs. There's no such thing as a "best" HTML editor — but you should be able to find one just right for you.

TextPad 4.2.1

Available for Windows 3.1/95/98/2000/NT, this is the most basic of text editors that supports HTML. If you want to write your own HTML from the ground up, this is your program — but it's strictly no frills. Without any wizards, syntax checking, integrated FTP client, or site-management programs, you are truly on your own. But that's just where expert HTML coders want to be. In some of the highest-powered Web production workshops, most expert HTML coders are using the lowest-powered software. For example, the Windows Notepad utility is the program of choice for those who want to take the minimalist route to the max.

Note   What does TextPad offer that the Windows Notepad doesn't? For one thing, an integrated spell checker. That's a real benefit for professional Web publishing, in which spelling mistakes can't be tolerated. Also, you can create files larger than 32K, the current Notepad limit.

TextPad comes with several clip libraries, its lists of HTML tags or JavaScript properties. Unfortunately, when you select a tag from the clip library, you get every attribute for that tag, with the value of the attribute blank, or a question mark where you might want to insert a value (see Figure 8-5). This feature is confusing unless you know what you're doing — and what's worse, it enters a lot of code into your documents you don't really need. Still, TextPad is fast and stable, and it's a genuine improvement over non-HTML-savvy text editors.

To get your copy of TextPad, access the program's Web site at www.textpad.com. A shareware product, TextPad, at the time of this writing, costs $27 for the downloadable version and $15 for the floppy disks. It also requires licenses for multiple users; the cost for 5 users is $120, and goes up incrementally depending on the number of users.

HotDog Professional 6.0

The nicest thing about this program is that things work the way you expect them to work. Available for Windows 95/98/2000/NT, this impressive text-based HTML-development environment includes such features as page-building wizards, extensive customization, a channel definition wizard (see Figure 8-6), support for tables, frames, and style sheets, split-screen view of the HTML and the page concurrently, and the capability to use HTML 4 the way it was intended to be used. You can also implement ASP, JavaScript, and VBScript with this tool. HotDog Professional also uses something called *SuperToolz,* which is their marketing name for downloadable plug-ins, which are usually free. All the wizards are installed this way. This is a great feature if space is tight on your system.

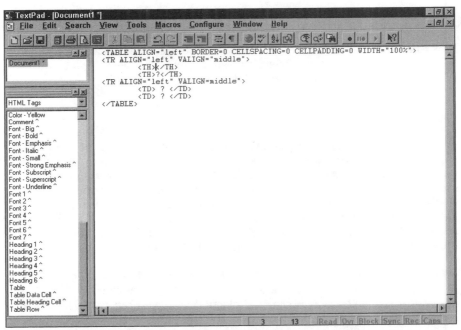

Figure 8-5: TextPad using the HTML-Forms clip library; notice the question marks for the <TABLE> tag.

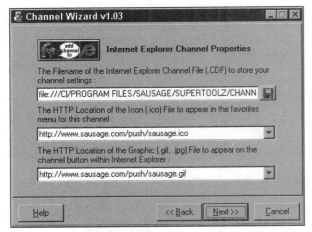

Figure 8-6: HotDog PRO makes creating a channel simple with a Channel Wizard.

Who fits the HotDog profile? Somebody who really wants to get into the nitty-gritty of actual HTML code, but doesn't want to hassle with tables, frames, forms, and other hard-to-code HTML elements. An additional benefit is the program's interactive split-screen browser, which dynamically displays your changes. This feature alone makes HotDog a real plus when you're learning HTML; you see the results of your changes immediately, without having to switch to your browser.

HotDog Professional sells for $99.95. You can purchase additional SuperToolz, all 17 of them for $99.95, such as Java applets that you can use without learning Java, or the Smartlinks SuperTool that adds the power of the LookSmart Search Engine onto your Web page. Check out the Web site at www.sausage.com/.

HomeSite 4.5

Perhaps the most full-featured of HTML tag-based editors, HomeSite started off as shareware. It complements Allaire's Cold Fusion Web-to-database engine very well. HomeSite is also the text editor for the PC version of Macromedia's Dreamweaver. Useful features include

✦ Powerful wizards — HTML structure, style sheets, tables, and forms

✦ An internal, accurate, user-definable browser

✦ Tag coloring, tag completion, and tag cues (an irresistible threesome)

✦ Extensive customization of interface, templates, and tags

✦ Integrated on-demand syntax checking

✦ An integrated FTP client, with browsing of FTP directories with the FTP and Site Deployment Wizard to easily deploy your site while creating a reusable, shareable deployment script

Who might enjoy using HomeSite? Someone who wants to see the HTML without having to endure the tedium of coding tables, form elements, and frames (see Figure 8-7). Also anyone who wants to use style sheets, but isn't familiar with all the properties that comprise them. The extensively customizable interface makes it user-friendly for you in a matter of minutes.

This invaluable program, which runs on Windows 95/98/2000/NT, is priced at $89 for the electronic download and $99 for the CD-ROM — what a deal! Once again, HomeSite utilizes licenses for extra copies of their software, so if you have multiple users your price goes up. HomeSite is available from Allaire at www.allaire.com.

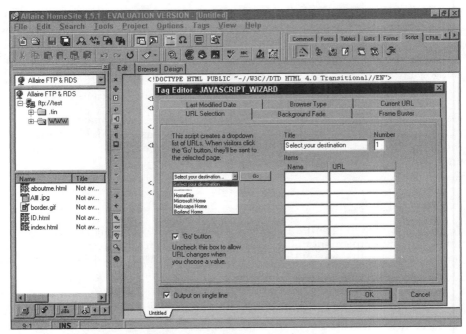

Figure 8-7: HomeSite 4.5 with the JavaScript wizard open

HoTMetaL PRO 6.0

The folks at SoftQuad must develop a lot of Web sites, because they seem to have thought of about everything. HoTMetaL PRO 6.0 for Windows 95/98/2000/NT includes nearly every type of wizard:

✦ ActiveX Wizard

✦ Database Import Wizard

✦ Dynamic Button Maker

✦ Form Wizard

✦ Frames Editor

✦ Integrated Site Management

✦ Site Wizard

✦ Style-sheets Wizard

✦ Table Wizard

The *tags-on view* is a great way to see your content without being overwhelmed by the HTML (see Figure 8-8). You can easily switch between WYSIWYG view, tags-on view, and HTML editing. Syntax checking, which defaults to continuous, can be set to on-demand.

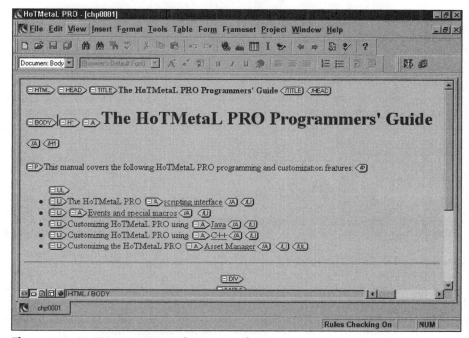

Figure 8-8: HoTMetaL PRO 6.0 in tags-on view

If you want the best of both worlds, WYSIWYG and text editing, HoTMetaL may be the way to go. HoTMetaL, the annoying capitalization aside, is available from the SoftQuad Web site at www.hotmetalpro.com for $129, or $59.95 for the upgrade.

CoffeeCup 8.2

CoffeeCup (see Figure 8-9) is being touted about as one of the new, great HTML editors. The CoffeeCup HTML Editor is fast, easy-to-use, and full of features. CoffeeCup has a split-screen preview for you to see your page change as you edit. Adding your pages to your Web site is just a right-mouse-click away.

Figure 8-9: The CoffeeCup HTML Editor

Following are some of the most important features CoffeeCup has to offer:

✦ Easily upload pages and images directly to your server.

✦ Edit your Web site by simply entering the URL.

✦ Editing is facilitated by a global search and replace function.

✦ Imagemap creation with the built-in Image Slicer.

✦ No need to create your own JavaScript, there are 100 ready-made scripts for you to use.

✦ Validate your code with Code Cleaner.

✦ Verify your spelling as you type.

✦ View your edits as you make them with the Split-Screen Live Preview Edit Mode.

Who will like CoffeeCup? People who like to muck around in their HTML code, as well as having fancy things, such as the split screen preview, or the snippets editor that enables you to insert custom code with ease. CoffeeCup 8.2 sells for $49 and is available from CoffeeCup at www.coffeecup.com.

Dreamweaver

This program is, indeed, a dream. You almost can't imagine a tool, system, or convention that isn't included in this incredible package. Dreamweaver was built with the HTML 4 model in mind and cleverly uses HomeSite 4.5 on the PC and BBEdit on the Mac as the text-editing programs for the WYSIWYG interface Macromedia provides. This results in a program that does everything it does well — whether on Windows 95/98/2000/NT, or the Mac. But what would you expect from Macromedia, the company that brings you Shockwave, Flash, Director, and Authorware, all multimedia development tools.

Dreamweaver has support for XML, JavaScript, and CSS. Dreamweaver 3 (see Figure 8-10) is a professional Web developer's program, as demonstrated by the price: $299 full featured, $129 if you're upgrading, but this is one spiffy program. It includes a library where you can store scripts, HTML tag combinations, images, imagemaps, or whatever you need for use in all the other pages in your site. Making a change to the library item automatically changes the item in all the pages where it appears, working like a server-side include.

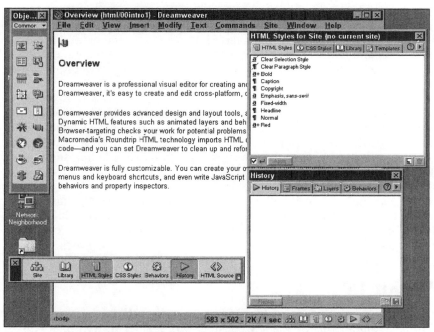

Figure 8-10: Dreamweaver may well be the ultimate Web development program.

To support animations and the Macromedia suite of programs (Director, Flash, Authorware, and Fireworks), Dreamweaver includes a timeline feature.

This program is one of only three of the programs reviewed here that includes useful group collaboration tools. Entire books are devoted to this package — and they should be. It is available from Macromedia (`www.macromedia.com`). Macromedia's site provides a downloadable 30-day trial of the software, although the downloadable version doesn't include BBEdit/HomeSite. Purchasing from the demo is as easy as clicking a button and entering your billing information.

FrontPage 2000

FrontPage 2000 gives you both WYSIWYG and text-based editing, on Windows 95/98/2000/NT or the Mac. You can use Dynamic HTML to animate, use CSS 2.0 to wrap or layer text and images, and get just the colors you want with enhanced color tools. In addition, FrontPage 2000 makes site management easy. FrontPage automatically fixes hyperlinks when files are renamed or moved, and 13 new management reports summarize the status of a site at a glance.

You can define multiple internal browsers, including Netscape Navigator! The getting started wizards are powerful, and the HTML they produce is legible. There are several useful tools, such as site management, link management, and project management — including the capability to assign tasks to project team members. The nicest part of all is that FrontPage 2000 relies on the HTML 4 Way of doing things, rather than tables, for attractive layout of pages.

FrontPage 2000 appeals to both the beginning and the professional Web developer. It has a steep learning curve, but once you know it, you'll be very productive. And if you use Microsoft Office, FrontPage 2000 makes creating a Web site easier than ever because it shares toolbars, menus, themes, background spell checking, and Format Painter with Microsoft Office.

FrontPage also includes plenty of interactive features, such as database interaction, animation tools, a JavaScript Wizard, and an ActiveX Wizard. FrontPage 2000 is available for $149, but the upgrade is $59.95, and available from Microsoft (`www.microsoft.com`).

HTML-Kit 1.0

HTML-Kit (see Figure 8-11) is designed to help HTML, XML, and script authors to edit, format, validate, preview, and publish Web pages. HTML authors of all experience levels will enjoy HTML-Kit. It can benefit beginners by pointing out errors and suggesting improvements to their code.

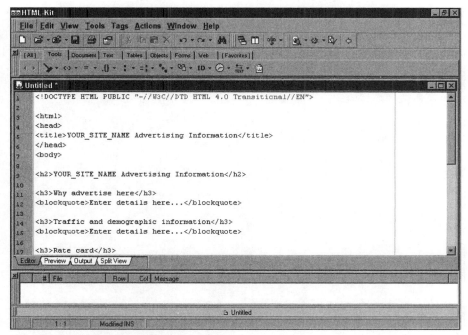

Figure 8-11: HTML-Kit in the Tools view

Some of the HTML-Kit features are as follows:

✦ Full-featured drag-and-drop enabled editor

✦ With syntax highlighter you can read code more easily by customizing colors and font styles.

✦ HTML-Kit also supports validation for HTML, XML, and CSS using W3C's HTML Tidy. Check out Chapter 24 for more information about this helpful feature.

Who would groove with the HTML-Kit program? Someone who wants a lot of capability from his or her software and doesn't want to spend any money. Yes, you read that right, the download is free, and works with Windows 95/98/2000/NT. You can try it out from Chami.com's Web site at www.chami.com/html-kit/.

PageMill 3.0

PageMill 3.0 (see Figure 8-12) is a big improvement over 2.0. You can place and preview Java applets and ActiveX controls (Windows only) directly in your PageMill pages. It includes an enhanced site/file manager that gives you a graphical view of your site. PageMill 3.0 also works seamlessly with Photoshop and Illustrator, two of the most commonly used image manipulation packages.

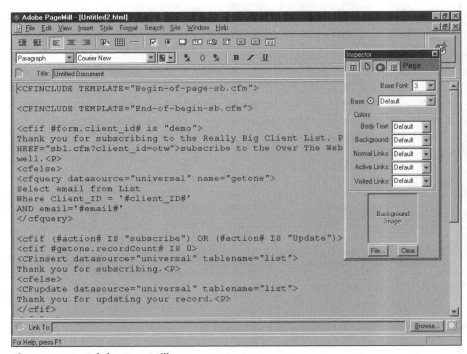

Figure 8-12: Adobe PageMill 3.0

NetObjects Fusion 5.0

NetObjects Fusion 5.0 (shown in Figure 8-13) is an excellent product. Fusion may be the most popular tool on the market for maintaining huge, distributed Web sites. There are many great new features that make using NetObjects Fusion 5.0 the best bet. You can

✦ Quickly plan and build an entire site, with a consistent theme and formatting.

✦ Manage, promote, and grow your e-business; there is a new online guide that shows you how to do this.

✦ Automatically create and update navigation and links, without writing any HTML code.

✦ Choose from dozens of professional, customizable SiteStyles or create your own, with drag-and-drop simplicity.

✦ Connect with databases for interactive Web applications.

Supported features are team collaboration tools, version control, a WYSIWYG editing environment, and a tag-based editing environment, the most intuitive drag-and-drop editing environment of all the tools reviewed.

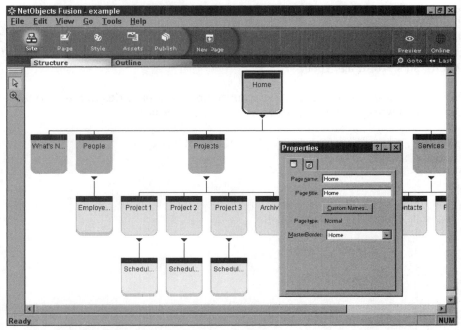

Figure 8-13: NetObjects Fusion with the Properties dialog box displayed — NetObjects Fusion is available for both the Mac and PC platforms for $299.95 or $99 for the upgrade.

From Here

Cross-Reference

Ready to dive into HTML 4? Flip to Chapter 12, which explores the fundamentals of HTML document architecture. You'll learn some important distinctions to help you grasp HTML more quickly.

Want to see some CSS now? Jump to Chapter 25.

With your HTML-development program in hand, you can proceed to develop your site's style and content. Before you jump ahead, though, take a moment to read about your Web server: what it does, what kind you have, and what you can make it do with server-side scripting, all in Chapter 11.

Summary

Before you can select the best Web page creation and editing program for you, you need to understand what features are available and which ones you need. Once you have your list of required features in hand, you can start to investigate the programs on the market. It is well worth your time to download and test a program before you purchase it so you know it works the way you expect it to work. All the programs profiled in this chapter have free evaluation software, except for Microsoft's FrontPage 2000.

Whatever program you select, you want to be sure it provides the functionality that makes you work as effectively and efficiently as possible.

✦   ✦   ✦

Writing for the Web

If you are not in the habit of writing, you may be a little intimidated by the idea of putting your thoughts into writing. Remember high school composition classes? Probably not, but that's okay. This chapter takes you through what you should know to communicate well in writing for digital, nonsequential reading.

If you are in the habit of writing, you may still need some guidance. Business, academic, or government writing doesn't always carry over to the Web with its passive voice — for example, *mistakes were made.* This chapter gives you guidelines you can apply to your writing style to make it more readable on your Web pages.

Designing for Quick Scanning

Most visitors who come to your page won't actually read all the text. You should expect this. Don't let it hurt your feelings. If you know people won't actually read much of your prose, then you can write with this in mind. So, if visitors don't read your pages, what do they do there? They scan them, looking for specific information.

Cross-Reference

Chapter 33 has a lot of information on design. You may want to jump there after you finish this chapter!

Can you make your pages easier to scan? Yes. Some of the design ideas discussed in Chapter 33 can help. What follows is a set of guidelines that overlaps with the design ideas from Chapter 33. Most of the design ideas of Chapter 33 relate to designing the shell pages. This chapter addresses what you actually put into your terminal pages, your Welcome Page, and, to some degree, your links pages (when they have prose).

Here are some basic guidelines to consider:

✦ **White space.** You've heard it before, you'll hear it again. White space draws the eye. Chapter 33 recommends that white space play prominently into your design. White space should also play prominently in your page layout. Separate paragraphs of text adequately with white space. Leave plenty of white space around headings and images.

✦ **Use lots of headings.** Headings are valuable to visitors because they give visitors the first clue they have found the right page and the information they need is contained on it.

✦ **Wrap text to create a visual flow**. You can do interesting things with text flow both around images and around white space (or what looks to be white space) that help make your point. When you add an image to your page, whether or not the text wraps around the image makes a difference in how people perceive it. Try it both ways (text wrapped around image and text not wrapped around image) and see which seems more effective for your application.

✦ **Keep paragraphs short.** This means several things. You have to limit the amount you say about any one thing and organize the material you include, and then you leave room for more white space. All these things are good for your visitors.

✦ **Use bulleted lists**. Bulleted lists are often the first place the eye goes. People remember items displayed in lists better than the same items comma-delimited in a paragraph. Why do you suppose this book uses so many bulleted lists?

✦ **Use numbered lists.** Especially when you are informing your reader of things that happen in a particular sequence, numbered lists are effective in drawing the eye. Try using the technique used in this book. Begin each list item with the short version in bold and then explain it further as part of the same list item. This makes for especially easy scanning.

✦ **Include graphics when appropriate.** You should consider removing unnecessary graphics from your design to make download times shorter. Graphics as part of your content (as opposed to part of your design) are another story. If a diagram is more effective at communicating your message than words, include it. Remember, different people learn differently. Some people would rather see the picture than read the text. Include both so you don't exclude anyone.

✦ **Use hypertext to define terms.** Take advantage of the power of hypertext. Define your terms either elsewhere in your same page or on another page. That a hypertext link is underlined and a different color than the rest of the text also draws the eye to the term. This helps readers by keeping the text shorter and making scanning easier.

Writing Concisely

You've done everything you can to make your site easy to scan. Visitors can find what they want. And what they want is in a short paragraph. But you can do more. Consider the following two paragraphs (underlined text represents hyperlinks):

> All Over the Web services make use of the latest security technologies, including Secure-sockets layer (SSL), which allows all transactions to be encrypted so that only you and the server know what you're sending, which should give you peace of mind to know that no one lurking on the Web can read your private information. Additionally, your own site visitors, who are just as concerned about the privacy and security of their own personal information, will feel more comfortable entering their own personal information into your guestbook when they see that your guestbook is administered by Over the Web.

Or

> Over the Web employs <u>SSL</u>, the latest security technology available, to guarantee all transactions with our <u>secure server</u> are indecipherable to hackers lurking on the Web. Your private information stays private.
> Visitors to your site, wisely concerned about their own privacy, will have confidence their personal data is in good hands when they see Over the Web administers your guestbook. And this gives them confidence in you.

Active verbs

Active verbs make your writing more interesting to read. Between "extensive customization is supported by Stay in Touch" and "Stay in Touch supports extensive customization," which reads better? The second example makes use of an active verb. The first example uses the passive voice, where the subject of the verb is either missing or an inanimate object. Take responsibility for the action. People don't speak in the passive voice — unless they're in politics and they've done something wrong — and you shouldn't write in it.

Active verbs also give you more of a sense of action. Consider the following examples:

Active verbs	Passive verbs
Pollution endangers the native wildlife	The native wildlife is endangered by pollution.
Our product performs calculations like nothing else on the market.	Calculations are performed by our product like nothing else on the market.
Your donation can save the life of a hungry child.	The life of a hungry child can be saved by your donation.

Active verbs are simply more compelling.

Subordination

Your sentence usually has a main point and then there may be some relevant, ancillary data, which is outside the main point. Without resorting to diagramming sentences (remember that from the 7th grade?), you should be able to find the main point by finding the verb, the subject of the verb, and the object of the verb. An example helps:

> A bomb, the third in as many years, damaged the Church of St. George in the Greek Orthodox Patriarchate in Istanbul and seriously injured one priest (he's still recovering).

What is the verb? What is the subject? What is the object of the verb? All the other words are part of the ancillary information. The verbs are (trick question) *damaged* and *injured*. The subject of both verbs is *a bomb*. The objects of the verbs are *the Church* and *one priest*. Everything else in the sentence is either part of a prepositional phrase, an appositive, or a parenthetical.

Subordination is the process of deciding what the main point is and moving the rest of the sentence either into another sentence or into a subordinate clause. Subordinate clauses often begin with that, which, or who.

Parentheticals

You've seen a lot of these in this book. In fact, one occurs in the last paragraph. A parenthetical is something you insert in parentheses. At least three good reasons exist to use parentheticals:

1. To give your opinion in a sentence that is otherwise fact.

2. To interject tangentially related information.

3. To include details about the preceding word.

Appositives

People use appositives when they talk:

> I ran into Chuck, that designer I told you about from the Neon Guild, today at the mall. He said he did have Windows NT server experience.

That designer I told you about from the Neon Guild is the appositive. Appositives directly follow the noun they modify; an appositive is preceded and followed by a comma.

Expletives

Even though writing for the Web can be quasi-conversational, expletives may be out of place, depending on your audience. Instead, use exclamations and italics to make a point:

This particular beta software is nowhere ready for production. After installing my operating system for the *third* time, all I could say was: *"what a complete waste of time!"*

Expletives may work in conversations in the movies, but they may bring down the quality of your Web pages immeasurably.

Sentence length

Given a choice, shorter sentences are better than longer ones. As much as possible, break up your sentences. If you must use long sentences at times, make sure the preceding and following sentences are short. See if you can break up your long sentence with lists or with subordination. Shorter sentences require less concen-tration to be understood. What you really want to avoid is sentences that are so long that they span several lines.

Write Vividly

Writing vividly involves selecting the most appropriate and powerful words and omitting any unnecessary words. If you think your vocabulary isn't that strong, get a thesaurus. Consider the following sentence. What can you do to clean it up, given the suggestions in this chapter?

This product manufactured by ABC is unlike any others on the market in that it removes spots from wool, cotton, and other natural fibers, melts ice even on the coldest days, protects your bathroom enamel from hard water marks caused by calcium and iron, and can be delivered directly to your door in one-gallon jugs overnight.

First, the comma-delimited list goes into a bullet list. Notice the last item isn't really a feature of the product, but information about distribution; that'll go into its own sentence. Also, *This product* isn't very vivid; use the product's name. *Unlike any others on the market* translates to unique. What does *in that* it add? Finally, *manufactured by ABC* should be moved into an appositive or into the sentence about distribution. So, we have:

Toxic-toner, manufactured by ABC,

- **removes spots** from cotton, wool, and other natural fibers
- **melts ice** even on the coldest days
- **protects** your bathroom enamel from hard water marks caused by calcium and iron

This unique product can be delivered overnight to your door; it is available in convenient one-gallon jugs.

Check Spelling and Proofreading

It seems so obvious, but you do need to edit your page. Just as you put your HTML through a validator, you need to put your text through a spelling checker. Then have it carefully reviewed by someone with a good command of the language to make sure all your verbs agree with your nouns, your references make sense, and that generally it is readable. It's difficult to edit your own material. You're familiar with what you meant to say, and you may gloss over errors by subconsciously filling in the blanks. Get someone else to go over your page after you've checked it yourself.

The editor you have been using up to this point, either SimpleText or Notepad, doesn't have a spelling checker. All the HTML-editors reviewed in Chapter 8 do have one. If you are serious about developing Web pages, you'll want to find an editor with a spelling checker. Start looking around the Web. Many pages have misspelled words. We wouldn't mention this problem if it didn't happen a lot!

From Here

Jump to Part III: "Developing Document Structure with HTML 4."

If you haven't already done so, see Chapter 8 and select your HTML editor.

Summary

Writing for the Web is different from most of the writing you do in other professions. You need to make sure the page can be easily scanned because most people looking at your pages are looking for something in particular. You can use white space, short paragraphs, lists, lots of headings, hypertext, and graphics to make your page more easily scanned. You also want to make sure your sentences are vividly written, using just the right words (but not too many). Finally, you want to take that extra minute or two after you think you are done writing your page to edit it carefully and run it through a spelling checker. Another set of eyes also helps. Embarrassing typos are completely avoidable.

✦　　✦　　✦

Considering Special Needs – Web Accessibility

Web accessibility allows those with visual or hearing impairment to access the same information available to others on the Web. But even though that's important, accessibility goes far beyond that purpose. New generations of devices with differing degrees of Web-browsing capability are becoming more and more common, and accessibility standards also ensure that Web pages degrade gracefully on machines that can't fully support all the page's features.

Accessible Design

Accessible design requires graceful transformation. Pages that transform gracefully are accessible to all regardless of any barriers such as physical disability and sensory challenges. In order for content to transform gracefully, it must provide a text equivalent for images and audio content, and must offer the same information to users who cannot see or hear. Visually impaired users can use screen-reader technology, but the contents of the site must be available as text in order for the screen reader to access the information. Similarly, hardware constraints cannot stand in the way of the data. A user who is unable to control a mouse or who uses a black-and-white screen should still have the full content available to them.

Making content understandable and navigable is the second part of accessible design. This requires clarity of language, and it also calls for site design that provides an easy and understandable way of traveling from page to page and back again. Image maps and menu bars may look spiffy, but they may be confusing to some users. Providing an alternative is good design, because users access-ing the page by alternate means may lose the context of the menus or image maps.

The accessibility guidelines (www.w3.org/TR/1999/WAI-WEBCONTENT-19990505/) describe three priority levels, as well as conformance standards. Level-1 priorities are those standards content developers *must* satisfy, or some groups will find it impossible to access the content. Level-2 priorities are standards that developers *should* adhere to, or some groups may find it difficult to access the site. Level-3 priorities are standards the developers *may* adhere to so they don't make it somewhat difficult for certain groups to access the Web documents.

Conformance to all level-1 priorities is considered conformance-level A. Adherence to all level-1 and -2 priorities is double-A conformance, while meeting all level-1, -2, and -3 guidelines is referred to as triple-A conformance.

Accessibility Guidelines

There are 14 accessibility guidelines. This section lists and provides a brief description of each.

1. **Provide equivalent alternatives to auditory and visual content.** Alternative content that provides the same information as the original audio or visual material should be provided to the user.

2. **Don't rely on color alone.** Many people have partial color-blindness, which means that some color combinations may be almost indecipherable to them. Color is best used as a means of emphasizing content; when certain combinations are used, or if insufficient contrast exists between the background and foreground colors, you have excluded a group of users from clear understanding of your Web material.

3. **Use markup and style sheets, and do so properly.** In this book we emphasize the importance of separating structure and content. In accessibility terms, misuse of markup may render content indecipherable to screen readers or other specialized software.

4. **Clarify natural language usage.** Content developers need to specify the natural language used on their pages. Braille devices and speech synthesizers can adjust to many languages, but only if it is properly designated.

5. **Create tables that transform gracefully.** Tables should not be used to lay out pages, or for any other purpose than to lay out information that is best described in tabular form. Tables are a challenge for many screen-reader programs.

6. **Ensure that pages featuring new technologies transform gracefully.** Developers using the latest technology on their pages should also ensure that the pages are accessible and navigable when the new features are turned off.

7. **Ensure user control of time-sensitive content changes.** Blinking, moving, or scrolling text may be challenging for users with certain cognitive or visual disabilities. Be certain that this type of content can be turned off.

8. **Ensure direct accessibility of embedded user interfaces.** If an embedded object has its own interface, be certain that alternative navigation controls are provided, such as those embedded in the browser itself.

9. **Design for device-independence.** Don't always assume your pages are being viewed on a traditional PC with a mouse. Consider users with mouth-sticks, those using voice commands, and others.

10. **Use interim solutions.** Older browsers and screen readers may not be able to support all new features. A commonly used Web design spawns a new browser window when the user selects a link, rather than opening the link in the current browser window. This may be confusing to a user accessing the page through a screen-reader program.

11. **Use W3C technologies and guidelines.** Whenever possible, use W3C guidelines and technologies. These guidelines typically provide accessibility alternatives. In contrast, some plug-ins and new technologies may not provide simple accessibility alternatives, which means you must provide the alternatives yourself.

12. **Provide context and orientation information.** Providing contextual references and grouping elements may be useful to users. What may appear clear to you may be almost indecipherable to a visually impaired user unless your grouping or layout is clarified.

13. **Provide clear navigation mechanisms.** Consistency in providing navigation devices—menu bars, text equivalent navigation tools, and the orientation and grouping information just discussed—assists users in navigating your site.

14. **Ensure that documents are clear and simple.** Providing easy-to-understand documents in a consistent manner page-to-page may be the most important of all the accessibility guidelines.

From Here

Proceed to Chapter 11 to learn about server options.

Jump to Chapter 49 and start using Frames.

Summary

You now know the most important considerations for ensuring that your Web content is accessible to the most users, and how to design your Web page so that access challenges you may not have considered can still be surmounted.

✦   ✦   ✦

Understanding Server Options

The longer you support and maintain a Web site, the more fancy things you want to do there. What kind of fancy things? You may include server variables, such as the date the page was last modified, the page's URL, or information stored in a database. Or, you may take information your visitors enter into your forms and use it to populate a database.

Before you can incorporate any of these variables, you need to understand the client-server model and processing options. This chapter gives you a solid understanding of what processing takes place where, what you must have installed to take advantage of server processing, what types of server processing software are available and how they work, and what you can take for granted on your server. This chapter also discusses peculiarities of both UNIX and NT servers.

The Client-Server Model

Lately, there's been a lot of press about the thin-client model. The *thin-client model* isn't a reference to a client of a modeling agency, but rather a reference to the idea of putting less computing power on the desktop and more on the server. Since the late 1980s, the debate has raged over where computer power should reside: on the desktop (thick client) or on the server (thin client).

Before the late 1980s, most people who did any computer processing had dumb terminals on their desktops, which were hooked up to some sort of a mainframe computer. The *dumb terminal* was only a screen, a keyboard, and a wire. The wire connected to the mainframe, where all the processing took place. The keyboard enabled you to enter data. The screen enabled you to see data. In the beginning, all the power resided at the hub, in a big, expensive mainframe computer. (See Figure 11-1 for an example.)

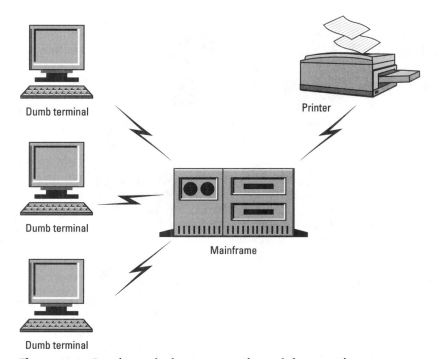

Figure 11-1: Dumb terminals connect to the mainframe at the center of the model

When personal computers (PCs) became affordable and useful software for PCs became available, businesses moved more processing from the center (the mainframe or server) to the periphery (the client). By the late 1990s, many offices had incredibly powerful computers on every desktop, far in excess of the power needed to do the kind of processing computer users were actually doing. This was the thick-client model, as shown in Figure 11-2. Because middle-sized servers have become so powerful for far less than the cost of a mainframe, the server has replaced the mainframe at the model's center.

The client-server model

The pendulum in business today is swinging back in the other direction to the idea of putting less power on the desktop and more on the Web server. Why? Several reasons:

✦ The growth of intranets, wherein many applications are delivered to the desktop via Web servers

✦ The continued need for shared files (and, thus, associated file servers)

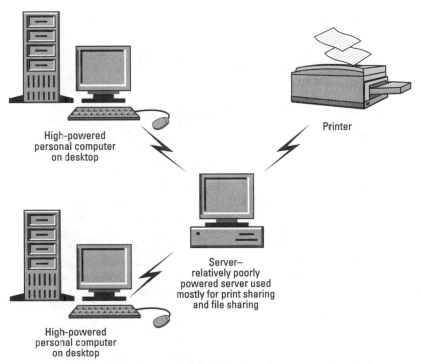

Figure 11-2: The thick-client model with a lot of power on the desktop

✦ The realization that for most office applications, desktops don't need the processing power of the latest, greatest personal computers

✦ The availability of client-server software engineered to run from a server

Processing: The crux of the issue

When you connect your computer to a server, where does the processing take place: on your desktop computer or on the server? That depends. When you request a Web page, if any processing is required other than serving the page, the processing usually takes place on the server. When you sign in to your Web server to publish your files (using the FTP client explained in Chapter 4), the processing takes place on your desktop computer.

Cleverly designed Web applications can move some of the processing burden from the server to the client. Remember, in most Web applications, as the Webmaster, you are paying for the cost of processing on the server, but not on the client. The client computer belongs to the person visiting your site. The way to get the most bang for your Web-page buck is to move any processing you can from *your* server to *the visitor's* client workstation.

Client Processing

So how do you take advantage of client processing? First you must understand what you can and can't do using client processing, as detailed in Table 11-1.

Table 11-1 Client Processing Capabilities and Restrictions	
What You Can Do	*What You Can't Do*
Validate data entry. If you have form fields on your page, you can make sure they contain the right kind of data before re-submitting them to the server. How does this save server processing? First, your server doesn't have to do the validation. Second, data will only be submitted once, when it is complete, saving your server the trouble of having to serve the same page (with error messages on it) multiple times to the same client.	**Serve a page.** You can't serve a page using client processing. You can load another page that has already been downloaded with the current page, which can be a clever technique, but at some point all the data you display must come from the server (except for data collected from the visitor and data collected from the client workstation).
Rearrange data on the page. This is new to HTML 4! If you are running a page that serves data from a database, you can save your server the trouble of having to serve the same data multiple times, sorted differently, by taking advantage of client-side processing. The Document Object Model and client-side scripting enable you to deliver all the data to the client one time and then give the client the option of seeing it different ways. Visitors don't need to know that instead of going out to your server every time they want to see the data rearranged, the processing takes place on their machine. This can take a real load off your server.	**Deliver data from a database.** The database has to reside on a server (either your own or another you have permission to read). The only way to get this data to the client is to deliver it from a server.
	Collect data into a database. You have to get the data from the client's workstation back to the server. Client processing can't do this. The chapter on external databases (Chapter 45) covers this in detail.
	Read data from the visitor's computer. With few exceptions, you can't use client-side scripting to collect information about visitors or data from their machines. This kind of privacy safeguard for the Web surfer has contributed to the popularity and acceptability of client-side scripting. Other less innocuous technologies, such as ActiveX controls and Java applets, have failed to catch on as fast because they didn't safeguard the client workstation as well.

What You Can Do	What You Can't Do
Date and time processing. Say you need to create a clock in a Web page. No good reason exists to run back to the server at set intervals when every client computer has a built-in clock. With client-side scripting, you can get at the local client variables, including the date and time, and process this data on the client side.	**Write data to a client workstation.** With the exception of cookies, which are covered later in this chapter, you can't write anything to your visitor's computer.
Measure visitor response. If you want to do any kind of testing of visitor response, you can administer the entire test in one or more pages, without returning to the server, until the test is complete. This includes dynamic testing, where the next question asked is based on the answer to the current question. For testing the time it takes for visitors to complete questions, nothing will be more accurate than client-side processing.	

So how do you take advantage of client-side processing? Whenever you need to validate forms data, rearrange data on a page, perform date and time processing, or measure visitor response, you include a client-side script that does this using client power, rather than server power.

Chapter 48 teaches you what you need to know about JavaScript, the most popular language for client-side processing, to do all these things.

Introducing Web Servers

What exactly is a Web server? A *Web server* is a patient program that sits on your server (that is, the physical machine dedicated to serving pages and performing other server functions) waiting to receive an HTTP request via TCP/IP. Helpful, huh?

Any server configured to handle communications via TCP/IP (the Internet's communications protocol) has ports. These aren't physical ports, like the serial port and parallel ports on the back of your computer, but they serve the same purpose. All HTTP requests come through port 80 unless the server has been configured differently. *Port 80* is the default Web server port. This is how your server, which may be a file server, an applications server, and an FTP server, in addition to being a Web server, keeps it all straight.

When an HTTP request comes through port 80 to the Web server, the Web server finds the page requested, checks the permissions of the client making the request, and, if the client has the appropriate permission, serves the page. Permission? Aren't all requests for pages anonymous? Not exactly. Figure 11-3 illustrates the request process.

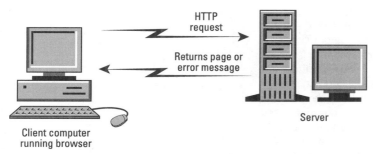

Figure 11-3: The client requests the page. Then the server evaluates the request and serves the page or an error message.

Permissions

Generally, HTTP requests are anonymous. What this really means is an account has been created on the Web server for HTTP requests. When a request comes through port 80, it is assumed to come from this account. Each file on the Web server has certain permissions associated with it. If the HTTP account (which may, in fact, be called *anonymous*) has adequate permission to read (or execute) that page, the Web server will serve that page.

All files and folders on a server have permissions associated with them. Whether or not you set them explicitly, they are there. Usually, when you create files on a server, they inherit the permissions of the directory in which you place them. The systems administrator usually sets the permissions for your directories. If you are having problems getting your page to load or seeing images on your page, have the systems administrator check the permissions on your files and directories to make sure they are, in fact, universally readable and executable.

NT: Hidden permission

What if you are sitting at a non-Windows-98/NT client? Then, if you try to get to a page that isn't accessible to the anonymous HTTP account, you either get an error message indicating you don't have permission to get to the page or a dialog box asking you to sign in.

Is this a good thing? It is a great thing for intranets! This means you don't have to rekey your ID and password into your browser every time you want to see a secure page. It can be a headache for Web server administrators because that much more security information must be monitored. For the Webmaster, it means more testing is required. You must test your pages from both Windows 98 and NT clients and others, signed in as someone with less authority than yourself.

Note NT servers handle permissions a little differently. Really, it's sort of sneaky. If you are sitting at a Windows 98 or Windows NT client and you request a page from a Windows NT Web server, you won't necessarily be making the request under the guise of the anonymous account set up for HTTP requests. In fact, your browser has sent your login ID and password (encrypted, of course) to the Web server with your request. If your ID is a valid ID on the Web server, then you are permitted to see any files on the server you have read (or executed). You are also able to see all the files the anonymous account is permitted to see.

Server Processing

What kinds of processing are best performed on the server? Any kind of processing or interaction with databases or any data stored on the server. How does it work? The visitor requests a page from the Web server. The Web server knows the page contains something it can't process and hands off the page to the appropriate auxiliary software for processing. The software that performs auxiliary processing, which sometimes comes installed with the Web server, converts the page into HTML and hands it back to the Web server. The Web server serves the page. Figure 11-4 illustrates this concept.

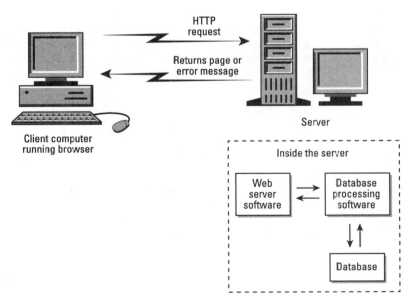

Figure 11-4: Server processing

What the Web server can't process

What can't the Web server process? Scripts, for one thing. Many proprietary flavors of server-side scripting exist. When a Web server comes across scripting that it recognizes isn't client-side scripting, it passes the page to the appropriate external software, which may be a middleware engine. Most often, pages with scripting not meant to be processed either by the client or by the server have different extensions. (Some you may have run across are in Table 11-2 later in this chapter.) Other times, the page has an extension of .html, but has a call to a script within the page. The Web server knows to hand this page to external software or a middleware engine (or has the processing capabilities built-in) when it comes to this code.

Middleware. Software that sits outside the Web server software, but on the same physical server, which performs specialized processing related to the Web, but also related to other technologies, such as databases.

Converting scripts to HTML

How does the middleware or external software produce an HTML page? The reason server-side processing is necessary is for a page to be able to pull data out of a database and present it on a page or to write data taken from a form to a database. Usually when you write a page using a scripting language, you indicate all records that meet certain criteria should be written into the HTML and served to the client. The middleware or external software goes out to the database (usually using ODBC standards), reads the database, and formats the data with HTML. Then it returns the page to the Web server. The Web server recognizes the page as containing only HTML and serves it to the client.

CGI script. The external software used to produce an HTML page is usually a Common Gateway Interface script written in C, C++, or Perl. The compilers for these scripts are usually free. The CGI script does the same thing as the middleware, but usually requires a higher level of technical proficiency to accomplish it.

The History of Middleware

Up until about 1995, a standard for software that performed auxiliary processing existed. It was called the *Common Gateway Interface* (CGI). Every type of server-side processing required the Webmaster to write a script in Perl, C, or C++. The script was saved with an extension of .cgi. When the Web server saw this extension, it read only the first line of the file and passed the script on to the appropriate compiler. Advantages to this system were: All three of these languages were commonly found on UNIX, most Web servers up until 1995 were UNIX based, and compilers for all three of these languages were in the public domain and likely to be found on your UNIX server.

The disadvantages were and still are as follows:

✦ All three of these languages are programming languages

✦ A single page of HTML may take pages of code to generate

✦ Making a change to the HTML on a page requires a programmer

✦ Hours of programming produce relatively modest results

Today, many people who use CGI programs either use pre-existing programs and don't make any programming changes to them, pay their ISPs to make programming changes, or are hardcore programmers.

Unfortunately, no standard exists in middleware. Quite a number of different types of systems are available to you as a Web developer to produce high-quality server-side processing. Most middleware revolves around interacting with a database. The advantages of using modern middleware include fast development time and the availability of rapid-application development (RAD) tools for many of these products. The disadvantage is cost. Most of them are commercial software. If you administer your own server, you can choose which one you like best. If you are already using an ISP with which you are happy, you will probably use one of the RAD tools it provides. Table 11-2 shows common extensions used to indicate that external processing is required.

Cross-Reference   Chapter 8 compares HTML-development tools, some of which are RAD tools for middleware.

Table 11-2 Extensions of Specific Languages	
Extension	**Language**
.cgi	Common Gateway Interface (usually means the entire page is written in Perl and the result of the Perl script is a page of HTML)
.asp	Active server pages (proprietary to Microsoft)
.qry	Query page (proprietary to Tango)
.cfm	Cold Fusion markup language (proprietary to Allaire)
.js	Server-side JavaScript (used by Netscape servers for server-side processing)
.jsp	Java server pages (proprietary to Sun)

Rapid application development (RAD) tools are productivity-enhancing if they permit

- ✦ drag-and-drop access to data sources
- ✦ uniform-style application across all pages in your site or project
- ✦ multifile search-and-replace
- ✦ spelling check
- ✦ looking up of HTML tags
- ✦ auto-tag insertion
- ✦ wizards

and all without creating messy code.

Built-in middleware

The most popular type of server-side script processing comes built-in to the Web server. Two of the most popular commercial Web servers — Microsoft Internet Information Server and Netscape servers — use this approach. Internet Information Server (IIS) supports active server pages internally; Netscape servers support server-side JavaScript.

Built-in server-side script processing makes processing scripts transparent. For the server administrator, there is no additional software to install and configure. For the Web page developer, once you know what Web server software is running, you know what type of scripting you can use and you know it will work (as shown in Figure 11-5).

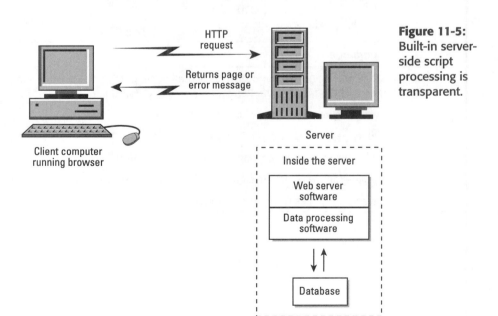

Figure 11-5:
Built-in server-side script processing is transparent.

Cold Fusion

Cold Fusion by Allaire is one product that greatly increases what your Web site can do without requiring any programming. Using a simple language, called *Cold Fusion Markup Language* (CFML), you can create powerful scripts you write right into your HTML pages. The Cold Fusion server returns the script's results right into your page.

Some of the cool things you can do are as follows:

✦ Schedule the generation of a page daily, hourly, or at whatever interval you choose.

✦ Pull content off other sites and parse it into your own format. (Get permission from the site owner before you try this.)

✦ Send mail to everyone in a database from a Web page based on criteria indicated on the form on the Web page.

✦ Insert records into a database. Update a database record. Read a database for records that meet certain criteria.

Cold Fusion is available for both NT and UNIX (Solaris) platforms. It works with ODBC-compliant databases. You can find out more from the Allaire Web site (www.allaire.com).

Stand-alone middleware

The alternative to built-in server-side script processing is stand-alone middleware. Why use stand-alone middleware? You may be running a Web server that doesn't include server-side scripting (other than CGI scripts). Another good reason exists. Some stand-alone middleware expands the processing power of your Web server to such a great extent, it is worth investing in another software program to get these extra benefits. What might these capabilities include? Sending e-mail from the Web site using data in a database, for one. See the following sidebar for more information.

Rapid application development

The difference between easy-to-write and pain-to-maintain scripts is often the existence of an effective rapid application development environment. What is this? Essentially *rapid application development* (RAD) is a software program that makes it easy for you to write scripts. Microsoft includes support for active server pages in FrontPage. Netscape has a visual development environment for JavaScript. Allaire has Cold Fusion Studio for easy creation of Cold Fusion scripts.

Cookies

Cookies are small text files written to visitors' computers when they visit certain sites. These files enable the site to recognize visitors upon returning. Sometimes visitors want to be recognized and sometimes they don't.

As a Web developer, you can use cookies to identify visitors to your site. What can you do with this information?

✦ You can keep track of returning visitors.

✦ You can count new visitors.

✦ You can store visitors' preferences so they see what they told you they'd like to see.

Before you make the decision to use cookies, think about what kind of processing you want to do with this information. Writing a cookie is no work at all. Using the cookie effectively requires a lot more work.

The Web is a stateless system. A Web server doesn't know whether the same person has come to the Welcome page 100 times in a day or whether 100 different people have come once. This is why hit counts are so inaccurate. Cookies can change the stateless nature of the Web. If you know what you are doing with cookies, you can begin to collect valuable information about visitors to your site.

Cookies can also be abused. Many sites place cookies on visitors' pages and then do nothing with the data they are able to collect. Don't set cookies just because you can. You also need to remember visitors to your site have the option not to accept your cookies. You must make your site accessible even to people who don't want your cookies or can't save the cookie file (such as users at library computers or school computers). Figure 11-6 shows a typical cookie file.

Secure Servers

If you want to collect private information about your visitors or conduct any type of commerce, you need to set up a secure server. The term secure server is actually a misnomer. What is really secure on a *secure server* is the transmission of information, but because secure server is the expression everyone else uses, this book also uses this terminology.

How does a secure server work? When you go to a secure Web page, you will notice the lock on your browser (either in the lower left-hand corner of your screen on Netscape — or on the bottom toward the right part of your screen in Internet Explorer) is locked. By default, your browser gives you a warning every time you go to (or leave) a secure page, but you can turn off those annoying warnings (you may have already done this).

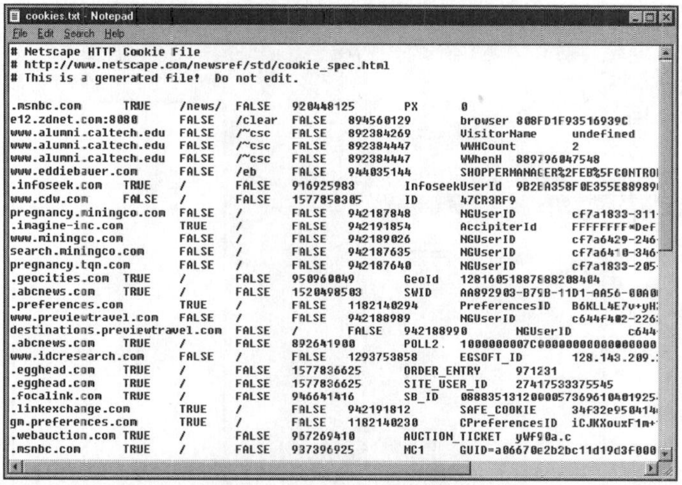

Figure 11-6: A cookie file

Normally, only pages that show you confidential information (such as the value of your mutual fund portfolio) or pages into which you enter confidential information (such as your credit card number) are secure. When this page was sent to your browser, it was sent encrypted. This means people with a lot of time on their hands who were sniffing packets on the Internet couldn't open your packets to read what was sent. When you enter information on a secure form, it is, likewise, sent encrypted back to the server. The term *secure server* says nothing about how tight the security is on the server itself.

A secure key is identical to a digital server certificate. The certificate provider, Verisign for example, assures end-users of whom they are communicating with.

Four steps are involved in setting up a secure server:

1. Get a secure key. The secure key is what your server uses to send encrypted data. You can get a secure key from Verisign (www.verisign.com).

2. Install the key on your Web server. Your server will have a key manager (as shown in Figure 11-7) or a flat file, where you install the key you purchase from the certification authority.

3. Publish your pages to the secure directory. Your systems administrator will be able to tell you where the secure directory is on your server. Any pages that need to be secure should be published to that directory.

4. Link to your secure pages using https:// instead of http://. When you link to pages in your secure directory, instead of using relative links, such as commerce/buynow.html, you need to use absolute links, such as https://www.sellingstuff.com/commerce/buynow.html. Notice this absolute link uses the https protocol rather than the http protocol.

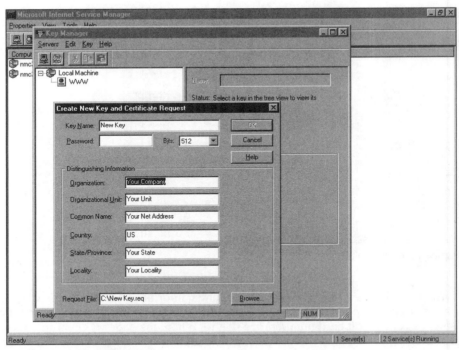

Figure 11-7: IIS Key Manager

Definition

Secure servers versus secure directories. Whether you will be required to publish all your secure pages in one directory or whether they can be anywhere on your server is really a policy issue. Just as with managing your media files, you may find placing all your secure pages (pages with which you communicate using the https protocol) in a single directory more convenient.

Looking at UNIX Servers

UNIX servers are the old warhorses of the Web server world. UNIX servers make reliable Web servers. The only drawback to UNIX Web servers is the environment isn't as graphical as it is with NT servers (or Mac servers, for that matter). More and more tools have become available to make publishing to a UNIX server more straightforward, such as the FTP clients shown in Chapter 4.

If you are publishing to a UNIX server, you must be aware of the following things:

✦ **Capitalization matters.** When you link from one page to another or when you publish a page, `MyPage.html`, `mypage.html`, `MYPAGE.html`, `MyPage.HTML`, and `mypage.Html` are all different pages.

✦ **Scripts traditionally are published to your CGI-bin directory.** Unless your systems administrator tells you otherwise, assume any executable pages (that is, pages that require server-side processing) should be stored in your CGI-bin directory. If you are using any canned Perl scripts, this is where you are likely to find them.

✦ **Permissions.** You need read, write, and execute permissions to your directories and your files. Your directories and files will also have to be set so everyone has read and execute permissions. You can check your permissions by using some FTP clients or by using Telnet, if you are authorized access to your files via Telnet.

Looking at Windows NT Servers

Windows NT servers are newer to the field, but offer their users many advantages. The biggest advantage is the interface looks just like the PC that is probably sitting on your desk. For Windows 95, Windows 98, and Windows NT users, you can drag-and-drop into a Windows NT server environment as easily as you can onto your own local hard drive. Another advantage of publishing to a Windows NT Web server is capitalization doesn't matter. Unless you *wanted* Mypage.html to be a different page from MyPage.html, this is a real advantage!

A downside of publishing to a Windows NT server is you can't check file and directory permissions remotely. This is a source of frustration for server administrators, as well. You must test thoroughly to be sure others can see your files and execute your scripts, because no one place exists where you can go to check your permissions. To make matters worse, if the permissions on a higher directory are too restrictive, you can't see a page even if the permissions for that directory and page are set appropriately. The only solution to this is to test, test, test!

From Here

Proceed to Part III to start laying the foundation of your Web pages.

Jump to Chapter 45 to begin accessing external databases

Summary

In this chapter you learned about some of the fancier things you can do with your Web server. First, you learned about the client-server model and how you can use client-side processing to reduce the load on your server. You also learned about

Web servers and permissions. Included were some tidbits about how you can use middleware to communicate with a database on your server.

You learned about how you can use cookies to do more sophisticated hit counting. Secure servers were also discussed, including the four steps you must take to implement a secure page on your site. Finally, you looked in-depth at UNIX and NT Web servers.

✦   ✦   ✦

Developing Document Structure with HTML 4

Understanding HTML 4 Document Architecture

This chapter is about building the basic infrastructure of your page. Later, you learn about making everything look nice, but here you'll lay the foundation to build upon.

What's New in HTML 4?

HTML 4 introduces a number of new elements. They fall into the categories of frame elements, forms elements, annotation elements, table elements, and CSS-facilitating elements. One stray new element doesn't conveniently fall into any category — the BDO element — which gives you the ability to change text direction for an inline element. If the standard text direction of your document is left-to-right and you want to override that to display one sentence of a language requiring right-to-left directionality, you would use the BDO element.

Frames

Even though you may have been using frames for two years or engaged in heated debates about whether frames are a good way to structure a site, frames have never been an official part of the HTML specification until now. The World Wide Web Consortium (W3C) has finally embraced frames or at least recognized frames by adding the FRAME, FRAMESET, NOFRAMES, and IFRAME elements to the HTML 4.0 specification.

Framesets are what you use to define the presence of frames on your page. The IFRAME element is truly new to HTML and is a fabulous way to introduce an element to your page that stays consistent across pages. Unfortunately, the IFRAME element is not yet supported in both the major browsers, but the IFRAME element may well replace the FRAME element, once it is well supported.

You can read more about the FRAMESET element, the FRAME element, and the IFRAME element in Chapter 22.

The IFRAME element is supported in Internet Explorer 3 and higher, but not in Netscape 4.7.

Forms

A number of new elements have been introduced into the HTML specification to make forms more intuitive to the site visitor. The OPTGROUP element enables you to group your form fields in such a way that the visitor to your site should be able to navigate them more easily. Using style sheets, you can use one background color for the personal information form fields and another background color for the order form fields. The LABEL element gives you the opportunity to label each group of fields to process back on your server or to increase clarity to the visitor. The BUTTON element increases your flexibility when creating submit-type buttons at the bottom of your form.

Annotation

There are literary conventions that aren't currently supported in browsers, even though they may be useful. These include the capability to indicate what part of a text has been deleted and what part of a text has been inserted (for example, in drafting a law) using the DEL and INS elements. Other annotation-type elements are the ABBR (abbreviation) element, the ACRONYM element, and the Q (quote) element. None of these last three elements are currently displayed in any special way by browsers.

If you read more about these three elements, you can clearly see how they could come in handy. Check out Chapter 17 where they are discussed in detail.

Tables

You might have thought there wasn't anything you could imagine that would make tables any more attractive to you as a Web developer, but the new HTML 4 elements for tables have something for everyone. Even though the rest of HTML 4 moves formatting into style sheets, CSS1 doesn't support table formatting well, so the new elements are all about improving and simplifying table presentation. They include the COLGROUP, THEAD, TBODY, TFOOT, and LEGEND elements.

Facilitating CSS

The last group of new elements helps make CSS possible. These elements are the OBJECT element, which is how you incorporate images, sounds, movies, animations, and other types of multimedia into your page, and the SPAN element, which helps you define an area to which you want to apply a style from your style sheet.

What's gone from HTML 4.0?

Very little. As with any language, a few things fall by the wayside but many new terms become accepted. The only three obsoleted elements were associated with changing the way the text looked on the page to make it use fixed-width font. The way to do this in HTML 4 is probably the way you've been doing it all along—with the PRE element. The ways not to do it are with the LISTING element, the PLAINTEXT element, or the XMP element. Also, there are deprecated elements and attributes.

Obsoleted. An obsoleted element is one that won't necessarily work in future versions of browsers. You should find ways to remove it from your pages now.

Deprecated. A deprecated element is one that will be obsoleted in the future. You can use it today without any negative consequences, but you might have to go through all your pages in a year or two to pull it when it gets obsoleted.

Components of HTML

This is probably a good time to review the basic building blocks of HTML. You learned them in Chapter 1, but that was a long time ago. To review, they are elements, attributes, and entities.

Elements

Elements are how you tell the browser what part of the page a certain segment of text is in your page. The browser isn't smart enough to know that if you leave a blank line in front of a few sentences of text and leave another blank line after the text, that is probably a paragraph. You tell it that is a paragraph by using the P element. If, instead, this text was a blockquote, you'd tell it using the BLOCKQUOTE element—and you'd be pleased the browser hadn't guessed wrong.

All the elements are listed in Appendix B.

Attributes

Attributes are how you dress up and customize your elements. Just about every element has at least two attributes. These are the id attribute and the class attribute. There are hundreds of other attributes, but each element only takes a few. Many of these they share in common. You'll soon find you remember which attributes go with which elements. HTML editors often provide a list of attributes for an element as part of tag hints.

You'll learn everything you want to know about the id attribute and the class attribute in Chapter 26. All the attributes are listed in Appendix C.

Entities

Entities enable you to display special characters on your page. Without entities, you can only display the characters you can type, minus the characters that have special meaning to HTML, such as less than (<), greater than (>), and ampersand (&). With entities, you can display the copyright symbol (©), the trademark symbol (™), the cent sign (¢), the symbols for other currencies (¥ yen, £ pound sterling), and hundreds of other characters, including letters and symbols from other alphabets.

All the entities are listed in Appendix D.

Block Versus Inline Elements

Elements fall into two categories: block and inline. *Block elements* can contain other block elements and can also contain inline elements. *Inline elements* can only contain other inline elements. Block elements have more to do with the structure of your page. Inline elements are more about emphasis. Consider Table 12-1.

Table 12-1	
Comparison of Block and Inline Elements	
Block elements	*Inline elements*
structure your document	add emphasis
define parts of your document	set a part of a block apart from the rest of the block
permit formatting	
take IDs and classes for purposes of style sheet formatting	
can contain other block elements	
can contain inline elements	

Examples of block elements are: P, HTML, BODY, and BLOCKQUOTE. Examples of inline elements are: B (bold), I (italics), Q (quote), and A (anchor).

Understanding Nesting

To make HTML work, you must learn to put block elements within other block elements and to put inline elements into other inline elements and into block elements. This process is called *nesting*. Consider the following nested list:

✦ This is the first bulleted item

✦ This is the second bulleted item

    • This is a numbered item

    • This is another numbered item

    • This is a third numbered item

✦ This is the third and final bulleted item

The following HTML will create the same thing:

```
<UL>
   <LI> This is the first bulleted item
   <LI> This is the second bulleted item
   <OL>
       <LI> This is a numbered item
       <LI> This is another numbered item
       <LI> This is a third numbered item
   </OL>
   <LI> This is the third and final bulleted item
</UL>
```

First, you should know—and you may already know—that the rules about nesting are not enforced by all browsers. What this means is if you break them, there might not be any visible penalty *today*. In the future, as more elements are introduced, nesting rules will have to be more strictly enforced. Now the rules:

1. **Close your elements in the reverse of the order you opened them.** If you have a paragraph in which you identify a book title, which you both bold and italicize, you must close the inner element before you close the outer element.

   In the following example, notice the B element is the last one opened and, therefore, is the first one closed. The P element, which is the only block-level element, is the first one opened; therefore, it is the last one closed.

   ```
   <P>One book I can highly recommend is Dostoyevsky's
   <I><B>Crime and Punishment</B></I></P>.
   ```

2. **Always close inline elements before you close the block element that contains them.** This is a subset of the previous rule. But the consequences of breaking it can be visible on your page. If you fail to close an inline element when you intend to, you could end up with bolded or italicized and bolded text on the rest of your page.

3. **Sometimes opening a new block automatically closes the previous open block.** You need to play this by ear, but there are times when beginning a new block element automatically ends the previous block element. One time this absolutely works is with paragraphs. You simply can't put a P element within another P element. Go ahead and try it. When your browser sees the second P element, it automatically closes the first one. However, you certainly can put a list within another list. Starting a second UL element doesn't close the previous UL element. You can also put a P element into a UL element, which doesn't close it either.

The HTML Element

The HTML element is the mother of all block-level elements. It contains the HEAD and the BODY. That said, it is optional, according to the HTML 4 specification, but older browsers will expect to see it. Your browser is smart enough to know—when it hits a HEAD element—that it is squarely in the middle of an HTML element. Putting it in is considered good form but no calamities will befall you if you leave it out (at least not any calamities related to the HTML element). The end tag is also optional.

HTML <HTML>

Start Tag:	Optional
Content:	HEAD
	BODY
End Tag:	Optional
Attributes:	Lang: language
	Dir: text direction
	Version: version (deprecated: should go on its own line)

```
<HTML>
<HEAD>
  <TITLE>This is the title</TITLE>
</HEAD>
<BODY>
        The body goes here.
</BODY>
</HTML>
```

The HEAD Element

Generally speaking, you'll want to include a HEAD element at the top of your document.

Head \<HEAD\>	
Start Tag:	Optional
Content:	TITLE: title
	BASE: base directory for relative references
	META: meta elements
	SCRIPT: script
	STYLE: style element for internal style sheets
	LINK: link to external style sheets
	OBJECT: object
End Tag:	Optional
Attributes:	Lang: language
	Dir: text direction
	Profile: URL of metadata

```
<HEAD>
    <TITLE>A really spiffy page</TITLE>
    <META name="creator" content="John Q. Public">
</HEAD>
```

Additional HEAD Elements

What else can you put into the HEAD? A TITLE element, a BASE element, a SCRIPT element, a STYLE element, a LINK element, and an OBJECT element. You remember the TITLE element from Chapter 3. You should have one, and only one, of those. You use the TITLE element to title your document; it also shows up in search engines. The TITLE element shows up in the top of the browser, above the menus.

Title \<TITLE\>	
Start Tag:	Required
Content:	Document title
End Tag:	Required

Attributes: lang: language code (see Appendix F for a complete list), if different from the language code specified in the

BODY element

dir: text direction, if different from that specified in the

BODY element

The BASE element is a clever device you can make use of whether or not you are using a frameset. If you are using a frameset, you can use the BASE element to tell all references contained in your page to open in the same frame in which the current page is open. (This will make more sense in Chapter 22.) If you are not using frames, the BASE element is a way to say: "start looking for all relative references from this point." This can be convenient if all your relative references (in images and in links) start from two directories below the current page. You can avoid having all your URLs begin with "../../". It also makes things easier if you have to move a page later. You can make the BASE element the directory where the page used to reside so you needn't recode all the links.

Base <BASE>

Start Tag: Required

Content: Forbidden

End Tag: Forbidden

Attributes: target: frame name where you want all links in this page to open

href: URL to use as base point for all relative references

If you want to have a script that is event-driven in your page, then you should use the SCRIPT element in your HEAD to include it. An *event-driven script* is one that only gets called when a certain event occurs. Events can be created by visitor actions, by the clock, or by other things you set up. The results of actions taken by the visitor—clicking a check box, for example—are the most common type of events.

Cross-Reference   You'll learn about JavaScript and writing scripts in Chapter 48.

Script <SCRIPT>

Start Tag: Required

Content: The script

End Tag: Required

Attributes: type: Scripting language; content type

If you want to include a style sheet within your page, which is *not* the recommended way, you can use a STYLE element to do this. The recommended way is to define the style sheet externally, in a text document with a .css extension, and link to it using the LINK element. The style sheet definition will look exactly the same, whether you define it in a STYLE element or in an external file linked to your document by the LINK element.

Style <STYLE>

Start Tag:	Required
Content:	Style sheet definition
End Tag:	Required
Attributes:	type: content type, just as with the SCRIPT element
	media: screen, print, and so forth (not actually implemented yet, but a good idea)

Link <LINK>

Start Tag:	Required
Content:	Forbidden
End Tag:	Forbidden
Attributes:	id, class, lang, dir, title, style: as defined elsewhere in this chapter
	events: see Chapter 48
	href: URL for linked resource, such as external style sheet
	hreflang: language code for linked resource
	type: content type of href
	rel: forward link types
	rev: reverse link types
	target: target frame information
	media: for rendering on media
	charset: character encoding of linked media

```
<LINK href="styles/css1.css" type="text/css">
```

The BODY Element

The BODY element is the block-level element that holds nearly everything that shows up in your browser window. It can contain all the other block elements, except for HEAD and HTML.

Body <BODY>

Start Tag:	Optional
Content:	Document title
End Tag:	Optional
Attributes:	onload, onunload: event, see Chapter 48
	background: URL for background image (deprecated)
	text: foreground color for text (deprecated)
	link: foreground color for link (deprecated)
	vlink: foreground color for visited link (deprecated)
	alink: foreground color for active link (deprecated)
	id, class: for style sheets
	lang, dir: language and direction, as previously explained
	title: title
	style: style information
	bgcolor: background color (deprecated)

Structure Versus Presentation, Again

You will notice this book often lists all those nasty legacy attributes from HTML 3.2 that affect presentation right in your HTML code. Again, you should try to avoid using them as much as possible. Even though you may now be convinced you can live without style sheets and that CSS is something too complicated for your simple site, when the time comes to maintain your pages and you have to wrestle with all those nasty presentation attributes, you will regret it.

The HTML 4 Way is to separate presentation from structure. If you are dying to get to the interior decorating and you are willing to wait to learn how to build the structure, jump to Chapter 25 and get it out of your system now. If you are willing to deny yourself the pleasure of designing for the nonce and to stick with learning and applying the fundamentals, you will be rewarded later.

Making Your HTML as Readable as Possible

When you create your HTML, you can make sense of it most easily if you use a few typographical conventions. Consider implementing the following guidelines in your files:

✦ Leave a blank line between block-level elements.

✦ Indent subordinate block-level elements.

✦ Indent any nested elements.

✦ Leave inline elements on the same line as the block in which they are contained.

✦ Format paragraphs as paragraphs (except the indent on the first line, which won't show up anyway).

✦ Format lists as lists.

✦ Keep each cell on a table in its own line.

This book scrupulously follows these guidelines because they make writing easy and maintaining easier. Most HTML editors also implement some sort of formatting of the HTML to make it easier to read.

 CSS has its own rules about readability. Read all about them in Chapter 26.

From Here

 Jump to Chapter 25 and get acquainted with style sheets.

Jump to Chapter 15 and learn about structuring text with block-level elements and lists.

Summary

This chapter gave you a thorough explanation about the nitty-gritty of page structure. If you've made it this far, you won't have any problems with HTML. Much of what this chapter covered you needn't know for your first page, but if you made it through Chapter 12 of a book this size, you're obviously serious about your HTML.

You know what's new in HTML 4 and what's gone altogether. You learned the difference between a block element and an inline element. You know about nesting.

You learned about the HTML element, the HEAD element — with the somewhat confusing META element and all its variations — and the other elements that can go in the head. You also learned the basics of the BODY element. Finally, you learned how to write your HTML so it will be readable and instantly make sense to you when you come back to it in six months.

✦   ✦   ✦

Specifying the HTML Version and Document Title

Including version information is very important to ensure that your HTML coding runs properly. This chapter explains why that is and how to write the version information. Also important to your Web page, and covered in this chapter, is the document title. Read on to learn why these two items are key to the success of your Web page.

Version Information

One part of your page isn't HTML at all — it's SGML. This is the first line of your file, which should contain version information. If you use an HTML editor, you will notice it may add the version information (or its best guess at the version information) to the beginning of your document. The version information tells the browser what set of rules to use when rendering the page. It won't recognize elements that aren't in the specification you use.

You can choose from three version statements in HTML 4:

1. **Strict.** This definition includes non-frames documents and none of the deprecated elements. If you choose to use this one, you must have extremely clean HTML.

```
<!DOCTYPE HTML PUBLIC "-//W3C//DTD HTML
4.01//EN"
"http://www.w3.org/TR/html4/strict.dtd">
```

2. **Transitional.** This definition includes deprecated elements (the way people used to write HTML) and all the new HTML elements, but no frames elements. This is the one to use if you don't think you can control yourself or if you have to use deprecated elements to support a large base of visitors who will come from older versions of browsers.

```
<!DOCTYPE HTML PUBLIC "-//W3C//DTD HTML 4.01
Transitional//EN" "http://www.w3.org/TR/html4/loose.dtd">
```

3. **Frames.** This definition is the one you need to use if you use any of the frames elements. It also includes all the elements in the transitional version. This is the most flexible and you should use it if you don't know what you might put into your page.

```
<!DOCTYPE HTML PUBLIC "-//W3C//DTD HTML 4.01 Frameset//EN"
"http://www.w3.org/TR/html4/frameset.dtd">
```

Document Title

The TITLE element is an important, and often overlooked, part of every document. Since the title you choose is displayed in the title bar of browsers accessing the document but not in the document itself, it needs to be short. However, it also needs to be descriptive, since it's the default shortcut name when that page is bookmarked.

The title is created with the TITLE element, as described below.

Title <TITLE>

Start Tag: Required

End Tag: Required

Content: Description of document, but no elements are permitted

Attributes: lang: add the desired language for the browser to read

dir: select a direction for text to be read. For example, Arabic reads right to left.

Since the title is used in indexing by Web engines and robots, it pays off to include substantive and descriptive terms in the title. It's a sign of incompleteness to see a Web page that has no title displayed, so be sure you take the time to include one.

From Here

Jump to Chapter 24 to learn how to test and validate your HTML.

Continue to Chapter 14 and learn about specifying metadata.

Summary

In this chapter, you learned how to include version information appropriate to the strictness of the HTML coding you've done. You also learned how to specify your document's title, and why it's an important element for your pages.

✦　　✦　　✦

Specifying Metadata

This chapter is about how search engines track and index your page. The META tags you include have a big influence on how likely your page will be found by people who are using search engines to find specific answers. There are some building blocks to cover, as well as a few tips and tricks that may help.

The META Element

Meta means *about*. This element is the place where you give information about your page. Search engines use the META element to help index your page. The problem with the current scheme of META elements is that no standard exists. This is about to change and a standard is being developed. Using META elements according to the new standard is highly recommended.

Meta <META>

Start Tag:	Required
Content:	Empty
End Tag:	Forbidden
Attributes:	http-equiv: http response header name
	name: metainformation name
	content: value associated with name
	scheme: select form of content usually used to provide helpful but noncritical information or to provide more context for the correct interpretation of metadata.
	lang: add the desired language for the browser to read.
	dir: select a direction for text to be read. For example, Arabic reads right to left.

Despite the fact that the META element is infinitely flexible, the way you use it is pretty straightforward. Here are some examples:

```
<META name="creator" content="Bill Karow">
<META name="publisher" content="IDG Books Worldwide">
<META name="description" content="really fabulous resource
about developing Web sites using all the cool new features of
HTML 4.0">
```

For the most part, when you use the META element, you assign a value to the name attribute and to the content attribute.

Name attributes

The Dublin Core Data Set (in Table 14-1) is the most widely accepted of the emerging standards, and you will be safe to draw the values of your name attributes from it. You certainly don't need to include all of these; they are optional. Also, if you need to include one more than once — say, there are multiple contributors — then you can repeat an element.

Table 14-1
The Dublin Core Data Set

Purpose	Value of name attribute	Explanation
Title	title	The title of the page.
Author or Creator	creator	The person or organization responsible for creating the page.
Subject and Keywords	subject	The subject of the page or keywords that describe the content of the page. As much as possible, you are encouraged to use controlled vocabularies and formal classification schemas (like the kind used by a library).
Description	description	A narrative description or abstract of the page.
Publisher	publisher	The publisher (your employer, your university, your publisher).
Other Contributor	contributor	Anyone who has contributed to the content of the page.
Date	date	The date of publication. Consider using YYYY-MM-DD. This is no place to get creative.

Purpose	*Value of name attribute*	Explanation
Resource Type	type	The type of page this is: novel, poem, personal page, and so on.
Format	format	Don't use this yet. A standard is under development.
Resource Identifier	identifier	A unique number you associate with the page so that no two documents at your URL have the same number.
Source	source	If your page was derived from a book, give the ISBN of the book. Otherwise, don't worry about this one.
Language	language	Language of the page. Use the 2-digit code, which can be found in Appendix F at the end of this book.
Relation	relation	This is an experimental attribute. If your page has a formal relationship with another page, this is where you can specify it.
Coverage	coverage	Perhaps to be used for geographical specification; they aren't sure yet.
Rights Management	rights	You can use this to link to a copyright notice or to specify your copyright statement.

Definition

ISBN. The International Standard Book Number is the unique 10-digit number assigned to a book by its publisher. For example, the ISBN of this book is 0-7645-3473-4. The number can usually be found on the back cover of a book or on the copyright page.

The http-equiv attribute

The previous name attributes are currently only good for search engines and people who want to view your source to see who else contributed to the creation of your fabulous page. The http-equiv attribute is something you can use instead of the name attribute that actually means something special to the browser that requested the page. The browser can use this data when displaying your page. A few examples are telling the browser when your content expires, the character set used in your page, and when to refresh the page:

```
<META http-equiv="expires" content="Mon, 23 Mar 1998 20:00:00
EST">
```

```
<META http-equiv="Content-Type" content="text/html;
charset=ISO-8859-5">
<META http-equiv="refresh"
content="10,http://www.mycompany.com/home.html">
```

In the last example, the refresh rate is in seconds. This is something you might use if you want to show a splash screen briefly and then have the browser automatically load the Welcome page.

Robots.txt

When a search-engine robot attempts to index a site, it looks for a file named robots.txt. The robots.txt standard is a very useful tool for both Webmasters and the people who run Web crawlers.

If the site `http://www.cyclingforum.com` is being indexed, the search engine looks for `http://www.cyclingforum.com/robots.txt`. This filename is case-sensitive, and must be lowercase. If the search-engine robot finds this document, it looks at it for instructions on what documents from that site, if any, it has permission to index. The robots.txt file can be written to disallow only certain search engines, or to protect specific directories from being indexed.

The following is a sample robots.txt file. The items beginning with a number sign (#) are for human viewing. You can say anything you like here, but I recommend something like the following:

```
# robots.txt file for http://yourdomain.com/
# e-mail webmaster@yourdomain.com for problems
# webmasters may change or alter this txt to fit your needs
User-agent: *
Disallow: /cgi-bin
Disallow: /images
Disallow: /logs
Disallow: contactus.html
```

The asterisk (*) indicates that the text to follow is for all search engines. See the list at the end of this chapter for specific robot names. The `Disallow:` command tells the robot not to index what follows. You can disallow entire folders or exact pages. Since Excite only accepts 25 pages per domain, you may want to use the `User-Agent` tag to make pages for specific search engines. `User-agent` is the name of the spider program.

In the robots.txt file, blank lines are permitted only between records. One `User-agent` field per record is allowed, though there can be as many user agent entries as needed, provided they are contained in separate records.

Save this text file in your top-level directory. It is the first page many search engines will seek and it is accepted by the major indexes. If you are using free space in someone else's directory (if you use AOL, for example) this will not work. Since there are so many pages inside the big services, most search engines ignore those sites. You should e-mail the various search engines asking to be indexed.

Some of the more common User-agents are:

✦ AltaVista — Scooter

✦ Excite — ArchitextSpider

✦ Infoseek — Infoseek Sidewinder

✦ Lycos — Lycos_Spider_(T-Rex)

From Here

**Cross-
Reference**

Jump to Chapter 25 and get acquainted with style sheets.

Proceed to Chapter 15 and learn about structuring text with block-level elements and lists.

Summary

This chapter gave you a thorough explanation of search engines and how they look at pages. You learned about the somewhat confusing META element and all its variations. Finally, you learned how to write your HTML so that you can control if and how it will be indexed by most Web search engines and robots.

✦   ✦   ✦

Structuring Lines and Paragraphs with Block-Level Elements

You are now squarely in the middle of building your Web page. The basic building blocks of a page are block-level elements. This chapter covers them all in detail. When you finish this chapter, you will have more than 50 percent of what you need to create most Web pages. This excludes your style sheet, which is covered in Part IV.

This chapter steps up the pace a bit. If you weren't serious, you wouldn't have gotten here, so to some degree, the material starts to become more challenging. Don't worry, though, if you don't understand something. Everything glossed over in this chapter (or included in an example for purposes of demonstrating a topic) is covered in-depth later in the book. Focus on picking up the main points of this chapter; any stray items that pop up in examples are explained later.

Introducing Block-Level Elements

Block-level elements are your page's building blocks. Most of your content will go into block-level elements (unless you use the HTML 3.2 Way of putting all your content into tables, which is highly discouraged). Block-level elements serve two purposes: They tell the browser what type of content is contained in the block and they enable you to define how that content is displayed in style sheets.

Dictating presentation

Another reason to use block-level elements is to define the layout of your page. Block-level elements are easily formatted using style sheets. Without getting into a long explanation of style sheet definitions, consider the following style sheet:

```
BODY {
        background: #FFFFFF;
        margin-left: .5in;
        margin-right: .5in;
}
BLOCKQUOTE {
        padding: .5in;
}
P {
        text-indent: .5in;
}
UL {
        margin-left: 1in;
}
LI {
        margin-left: .25in;
}
```

What does this say? It tells most of the block elements in your document how to format themselves. Why is this so great? Because it is all in one place! If you want to change your style, you can do it in a central location: in your style sheet. If you cheat and use the BLOCKQUOTE element for all your paragraphs, because you want a half-inch margin of white space on either side of the text, you won't have any good way to change your style — say, right-justify the entire page — without manually editing your HTML. And, if you want to add an actual blockquote to your page, you must nest BLOCKQUOTE elements.

Creating Paragraphs: The P Element

If your document contains prose, you'll probably want to include it in a paragraph. Do you think all documents contain text? They needn't. You can use graphics or lists effectively to communicate many messages. Creating a paragraph is easy. In the past, you might have used only a <P> tag at the end of each paragraph. This works, but it can produce unpredictable results with style sheets. If you plan to use style sheets, you should open and close all your paragraphs with the appropriate tags.

Paragraph <P>

Start Tag:	Required
Content:	Inline elements Text
End Tag:	Optional
Attributes:	id, class: used in conjunction with style sheets

lang, dir: indicate language and text direction; better specified in the BODY element unless this element is an exception to the rest of the page

title: title of this element

style: define style here to override the style sheet

align: alignment is deprecated; should be specified in style sheet

events: see Chapter 48

Controlling Line Breaks and Spacing

HTML offers you two easy ways to break up your page visually: creating white space and dividing your page with lines. Many good reasons exist to use both these techniques. Generally speaking, more white space is better than less. Take advantage of white space to attract the visitor's eye.

Breaking up your page

You can use the BR element to break a line wherever you want to, even in the middle of a word. The BR element is an inline element, so it doesn't interfere with your block-level element. You can use the BR element within a block or between blocks.

Break

Start Tag:	Required
Content:	Empty
End Tag:	Forbidden
Attributes:	id, class: used in conjunction with style sheets

title: title of this element

style: define style here to override the style sheet

clear: deprecated; used to indicate where floating objects are to appear following the break; use style sheets, instead

The other way to break up your page is with horizontal lines. The HR element is just as easy to use as the BR element.

Horizontal Rule <HR>

Start Tag: Required

Content: Empty

End Tag: Forbidden

Attributes: id, class: used in conjunction with style sheets

lang: instructs the target browser to apply language rules to the text. If you entered: <HTML lang="fr"> you would be telling the browser that French rules apply.

dir: text directionality. This becomes an issue with Arabic and Hebrew because they display right to left.

title: title of this element

style: define style here to override the style sheet

align: alignment is deprecated; use style sheets, instead

noshade: deprecated; indicates the line shouldn't have a shadow, which is the default; use style sheets instead

size: deprecated; used to define the height of the rule; use style sheets instead

width: deprecated; used to define the length of the rule across the page (default is 100 percent of the width of the page); use style sheets instead

events: see Chapter 48

Preventing a line break

At times, you want to keep your line from breaking in the wrong place. You can prevent a line from breaking where you don't want it to by using a nonbreaking space, which is an entity. To add a nonbreaking space, use   as in:

```
The delegates signed the Constitution in September 1787.
```

This forces September and 1787 to appear on the same line. Be sure not to leave any spaces between September, , and 1787.

Adding Headings

Headings are another easy way to break up your page. Notice how this book takes advantage of headings. They not only make it easier to read your page, but they make it easier for visitors to find what they need when they return to your page.

There are six levels of headings: H1, H2, H3, H4, H5, and H6. H1 is the most important; H6 is the least important. Use them in order of importance, not based on how they render in your browser. That's what style sheets are for.

Heading 1 <H1> through Heading 6 <H6>

Start Tag:	Required
Content:	Inline elements
End Tag:	Required
Attributes:	id, class: used in conjunction with style sheets
	lang, dir: indicate language and text direction; better specified in the BODY element unless this element is an exception to the rest of the page
	title: title of this element
	style: define style here to override the style sheet
	align: alignment is deprecated; should be specified in style sheet
	events: see Chapter 48

Creating Indented Quotations: The BLOCKQUOTE Element

The BLOCKQUOTE has been one of the most misused elements. It should be used to quote a long passage of text and, in the past, to create white space on both sides of your paragraph. Worse yet, people have used nested BLOCKQUOTE elements to get even *more* white space on their pages.

The BLOCKQUOTE element is great for quoting long passages of text. It has an attribute called cite, which, while not currently processed by browsers, could prospectively be used to link to the page where the quotation is found in its entirety.

Blockquote <BLOCKQUOTE>

Start Tag:	Required
Content:	Inline elements
End Tag:	Required
Attributes:	id, class: used in conjunction with style sheets
	lang, dir: indicate language and text direction; better specified in the BODY element unless this element is an exception to the rest of the page
	cite: URL of the quotation if taken from the Web

title: title of this element

style: define style here to override the style sheet

events: see Chapter 48

Adding Preformatted Text

Sometimes you want to show text, but you don't want the browser to have control over how it formats that text. You can force your browser to use a fixed-width font by implementing the PRE element. The browser also recognizes your end-of-line markers (when you hit return in your typing) to indicate the end of the line.

```
<P>The following is an example of how you use the PRE
element:</P>
<PRE>&lt;PRE&gt;Put the text you want to appear preformatted in
a PRE element.&lt;/PRE&gt;</PRE>
```

This will render as:

The following is an example of how you use the PRE element:

```
Put the text you want to appear preformatted in a PRE element.
```

Preformatted text <PRE>

Start Tag:	Required
Content:	Inline elements
End Tag:	Required
Attributes:	id, class: used in conjunction with style sheets
	lang, dir: indicate language and text direction; better specified in the BODY element unless this element is an exception to the rest of the page
	width: suggested width that the block of preformatted text should be; currently ignored by most browsers
	title: title of this element
	style: define style here to override the style sheet
	events: see Chapter 48

Grouping Block Elements: The DIV Element

Just to tantalize you, you're now going to learn about the DIV element. The DIV *element* is how you group block-level elements to format them with a style sheet. Normally, you only create a style for an element, but the DIV element gives you greater flexibility by enabling you to create a zone that includes multiple block elements. Those elements can be nested, in which case inheritance would come into play, or consecutive. Consider the following example.

You have two paragraphs of text and an unnumbered list you want to draw attention to by adding a border and giving it a different background color. Without the DIV element, there is no way to put a border around multiple blocks, short of putting them all into one big cell in a table (ugly and messy). With the DIV element, you would create the following:

```
<DIV class="special">
<P>The reasons for using the DIV element are numerous:</P>
<UL>
<LI> to group block-level elements
<LI> to put a border around multiple block-level elements
<LI> to change the background color of multiple block-level
elements
</UL>
<P>Isn't HTML 4 grand?</P>
</DIV>
```

Then you would create a style sheet definition, ideally in your externally defined style sheet, to tell the browser this DIV element should have a yellow background and a blue border.

```
DIV.special {
        background: #FFFF00;
        border-top: ridge;
        border-bottom: ridge;
        border-left: ridge;
        border-right: ridge;
        padding: 15pt.;
}
```

Division <DIV>

Start Tag: Required

Content: Blocks

                  Inline elements

End Tag: Required

Attributes: id, class: used in conjunction with style sheets

lang, dir: indicate language and text direction; better specified in the BODY element unless this element is an exception to the rest of the page

align: deprecated; use style sheets

title: title of this element

style: define style here to override the style sheet

events: see Chapter 48

From Here

Jump to Chapter 26 and start learning CSS syntax.

Move on to Chapter 23 to group elements with DIV and CLASS.

Proceed to Chapter 17 and master inline elements.

Summary

You learned a lot in this chapter: how to create all the basic block-level elements, how to nest elements, and how to create three kinds of lists. You also got a taste of what the DIV element can do for your layout.

You learned how to break text, how not to break text, and how to insert preformatted text. You are well on your way to having mastered the essentials of HTML 4.

✦   ✦   ✦

Creating Lists

Now we will continue where Chapter 15 left off and discuss creating lists. We'll continue to step up the pace a bit. From ordered lists to unordered lists, this chapter has what you need to get started.

Introducing Lists

Lists are absolutely essential to good Web page design. You need to break up your page into digestible chunks whenever you can. Too often, Web pages are long collections of paragraphs, which can get monotonous for the reader. If you've got material that lends itself to presentation in a list form, try it. You'll be surprised how much a simple list can make key points stand out, even if your content is best presented in paragraph form. By offering this type of summary in an eye-catching manner, you'll be able to convey the purpose of your text to grab the attention of the casual browser, and to let readers quickly determine if this material is what they're seeking.

Creating bulleted lists: The UL element

The list type you see most commonly is the bulleted list, also called the *unordered list*. You create a bulleted list using the UL element. Every list worth its salt also has list items. The list items are created with the LI element. In fact, a list created with the UL element with no LI elements within it isn't a list at all!

Unordered List <UL>

Start Tag:	Required
Content:	List items
End Tag:	Required
Attributes:	id, class: used in conjunction with style sheets

lang, dir: indicate language and text direction; better specified in the BODY element unless this element is an exception to the rest of the page

title: title of this element

style: define style here to override that in a style sheet

type: deprecated; indicates the bullet type; should be specified in style sheet

compact: deprecated; tells the browser to display the list in a more compact way; results vary by browser

events: see Chapter 48

Whether you are creating a bulleted list or a numbered list, you won't have anything in your list unless you use the LI element.

List Item <LI>

Start Tag:	Required
Content:	Inline elements
End Tag:	Optional
Attributes:	id, class: used in conjunction with style sheets

lang, dir: indicate language and text direction; better specified in the BODY element unless this element is an exception to the rest of the page

title: title of this element

compact: Boolean attribute renders the list in a more compact way. The interpretation of this attribute depends on the user agent.

style: define style here to override that in a style sheet

value: deprecated; used to tell the browser what number to associate with this list item (works only with numbered lists)

type: deprecated; indicates the bullet type; should be specified in style sheet; but even in a style sheet, you don't want to indicate the bullet type separately for each item in the list; this is better indicated in the list element

events: see Chapter 48

An example using UL follows:

```
Common symptoms of early pregnancy include:
<UL>
  <LI> nausea
  <LI> vomiting
  <LI> loss of appetite
  <LI> strange food cravings
  <LI> exhaustion
  <LI> mood swings
  <LI> crying for no reason
<UL>
```

Creating numbered lists: The OL element

The other popular kind of list is the *ordered list,* which you can create using the OL element. The OL element is every bit as easy to create as the UL element. Again, you need an LI element for each item on your list.

Ordered List <OL>

Start Tag:	Required
Content:	List items
End Tag:	Required
Attributes:	id, class: used in conjunction with style sheets

lang, dir: indicate language and text direction; better specified in the BODY element unless this element is an exception to the rest of the page

title: title of this element

style: define style here to override that in a style sheet

type: deprecated; indicates the numbering style; should be specified in style sheet

start: deprecated; tells the browser what number it should use to start the numbering; should be specified in style sheet

compact: deprecated; tells the browser to display the list in a more compact way; results vary by browser

events: see Chapter 48

An example using OL follows:

```
When you first get into your car, before you turn the key in
the ignition, be sure that
<OL>
  <LI> Your seat is adjusted properly
  <LI> Your seatbelt is fastened
  <LI> Your rearview mirror is adjusted properly
```

```
<LI> Your outside rearview mirror is adjusted properly
</OL>
```

Creating definition lists: The DL element

The definition list is used far less frequently than the other two kinds of lists and it has three parts: the definition list (DL), the definition term (DT), and the definition description (DD). The DL element works just like the OL and UL elements. The DT element works much the same way as the LI element. The DD element is different: It contains the term's actual definition. How this type of list renders depends on your browser.

Definition List <DL>

Start Tag:	Required
Content:	Definition terms Definition descriptions
End Tag:	Required
Attributes:	id, class: used in conjunction with style sheets
	lang, dir: indicate language and text direction; better specified in the BODY element unless this element is an exception to the rest of the page
	title: title of this element
	style: define style here to override that in a style sheet
	events: see Chapter 48

Definition Term <DT>

Start Tag:	Required
Content:	Inline elements
End Tag:	Optional
Attributes:	id, class: used in conjunction with style sheets
	lang, dir: indicate language and text direction; better specified in the BODY element unless this element is an exception to the rest of the page
	title: title of this element
	style: define style here to override that in a style sheet
	events: see Chapter 48

Definition Description <DD>

Start Tag:	Required
Content:	Inline elements

End Tag: Optional

Attributes: id, class: used in conjunction with style sheets

lang, dir: indicate language and text direction; better specified in the BODY element unless this element is an exception to the rest of the page

title: title of this element

style: define style here to override that in a style sheet

events: see Chapter 48

Because you don't see too many definition lists, an example is in order:

```
<DL>
  <DT>chop
  <DD>to cut into random-sized pieces
  <DT>grate
  <DD>to shred into small irregular strips
  <DT>dice
  <DD>to cut with a knife into regular-sized cubes
</DL>
```

Figure 16-1 shows how the text renders in Netscape.

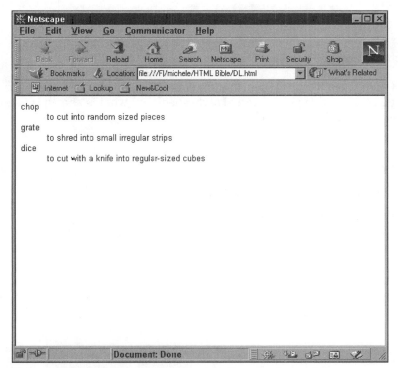

Figure 16-1: Definition list in Netscape Communicator 4.7

Cross-Reference You might want to use style sheets to make that look a little bit nicer. Check out Chapter 25 to learn more about CSS.

Nesting Block Elements

You might want to nest block-level elements occasionally, but in some conditions you can't. You can't nest P elements because the presence of the second start tag for the P element ends the previous P element. You can, however, nest lists. This is a great thing, too. You can also nest paragraphs within lists. Consider the following:

```
<P>Suggestions for adding flavor to your low-fat recipes.</P>
<UL>
<LI> Always invite a member of the onion family to every dish!
    <UL>
    <LI> white onions
    <LI> Vidalia onions (in season)
    <LI> shallots, finely chopped
    <LI> purple onions as a garnish
    <LI> green onions for crunch
    </UL>
<LI> Use only freshly ground pepper; invest in an attractive
pepper mill.
<LI> Sprinkle your plain vegetables with a small amount of
freshly grated parmesan cheese—so much flavor for so little
fat.
</UL>
```

Figure 16-2 shows how the text renders in Netscape.

You could, of course, spiff up the presentation of that subordinate list by using square bullets, as defined in your external style sheet, but what is shown is what renders in the absence of a style sheet.

From Here

Cross-Reference Jump to Chapter 26 and start learning CSS syntax.

Proceed to Chapter 17 and master inline elements.

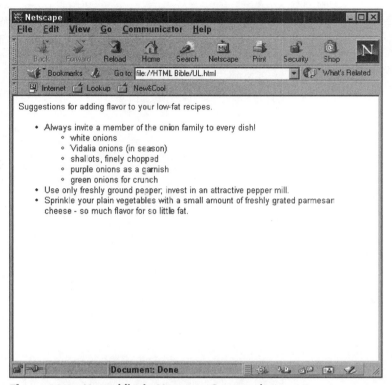

Figure 16-2: Nested list in Netscape Communicator 4.7

Summary

In this chapter, you learned how to create the three different types of lists. You also got a taste for nesting these elements to create a multilevel list. Lists are an often underutilized block-level element, and one that can help you convey you message more clearly. You are well on your way to having mastered the elements of HTML 4.

✦   ✦   ✦

Using Inline Elements and Special Characters

Inline elements enable you to specify the structure of your document further. They also enable you to add emphasis to specific words in a way style sheets can't. This chapter takes you through the details of inline elements and special characters. It includes information about using foreign languages, adding inline quotes, and using the SPAN element to change the presentation of a group of elements within a block.

Introducing Inline Elements

Inline elements are the parts of your document that fill the block elements. You may have a paragraph of text defined with the P element (a block-level element). Within the P element, you can define inline elements, such as quotes, book titles (to be italicized), words in a foreign language, words to which you'd like to draw attention (to be bolded), and special characters (such as a copyright symbol).

Inline elements give you the control to make these specific formatting changes within your block elements. Table 17-1 includes all inline elements.

Table 17-1
All Inline Elements

Element	Description	Deprecated	Logical or Physical
ABBR	abbreviated form		L
ACRONYM	instance of an acronym		L
B	bold		P
BIG	big		P
CITE	citation		L
CODE	computer code fragment		L
DEL	deleted text		L
DFN	instance definition		L
EM	emphasis		L
I	italics		P
INS	inserted text		L
KBD	text to be entered by the user		L
Q	quotation		L
S	strikeout	deprecated (use DEL)	P
SAMP	sample of code		L
SMALL	small		P
SPAN	container for grouping within a block element		
STRIKE	strikeout	deprecated (use DEL)	P
STRONG	strong		L
SUB	subscript		P
SUP	superscript		P
TT	teletype		P
U	underline	Deprecated (use DEL)	P
VAR	variable or program argument		L

All inline elements have a few things in common. They all require both start and end tags. They can all have other inline elements as part of their content. They can all be grouped for purposes of formatting with style sheets with the SPAN element.

Note You can nest inline elements. All nestings are not valid. For instance, nesting a CODE element within a CITE element gives you unpredictable results. Even more important with inline elements than with block elements is that you close the elements in the reverse order they were opened.

Logical Versus Physical Styles

There is more than one way to italicize text as it appears in your browser. You can use the straight-shootin' approach and use the I element, you can use the more indirect route and use the EM element, or you can use the CITE element because the phrase you want italicized is a book title. What is the difference? It depends on whether you are using italics for the sake of using italics or whether you are using italics to convey some other information.

This is a philosophical discussion, really. Purists, from the SGML school, believe all text formatting is associated with some deeper meaning. You don't bold because you want bold, you bold because you want the words you think should be bolded to come across as stronger than the rest of the text. As it turns out, most browsers render the STRONG element the same as the BOLD element.

It doesn't reflect poorly on you either way. You can make your own call as to whether you use the physical inline elements or the logical inline elements. Table 17-2 shows physical styles; Table 17-3 shows logical styles.

Table 17-2 **Physical Inline Elements**		
Element	*Description*	*Renders As*
B	bold	bold
I	italics	italics
S	strikeout	text with a line through it
SMALL	small	smaller than the regular font
STRIKE	strikeout	text with a line through it
SUB	subscript	text that falls below the baseline of the rest of the text
SUP	superscript	text whose baseline is above the baseline of the rest of the text
TT	teletype	fixed-width font
U	underline	underlined text (obsoleted: don't use this; it is too confusing because links are underlined)

Table 17-3
Logical Inline Elements

Element	Description	Renders As
ABBR	abbreviated form	nothing special
ACRONYM	acronym	nothing special
CITE	citation	italics (I)
CODE	code sample	fixed-width font (TT)
DEL	deleted text	text with a line through it (STRIKE or S); renders differently in IE and Netscape
DFN	definition	italics (I); renders differently in IE and Netscape
EM	emphasis	italics (I)
INS	inserted text	underlined (U); renders differently in IE and Netscape
KBD	code sample	fixed-width font (TT)
Q	quote	nothing special
SAMP	code sample	fixed-width font (TT)
STRONG	strong	bold (B)
VAR	program variable	italics (I)

Understanding Web Character Sets

The Web supports several character sets. This includes the standard English character set, the extended English character set (which includes all types of accents for the vowels, mathematical symbols, reference symbols, and Greek letters), and internationalization characters. To include characters from any of these character sets, select the appropriate entity from Appendix D.

Adding Special Characters

What if you need to insert the copyright symbol? Use an entity. Entities can be inserted into inline elements or block elements. Remember to use an ampersand (&) at the beginning of the entity and a semicolon (;) at the end. The most common special characters are included in Table 17-4. A complete list of entities is available in Appendix D.

Table 17-4
Common Special Character Entities

Character Notation	Hex Notation	Entity Created
nbsp		nonbreaking space
iexcl	&#161;	inverted exclamation mark
cent	&#162;	cent sign
pound	&#163;	pound sign
curren	&#164;	currency sign
yen	&#165;	yen sign
sect	&#167;	section sign
copy	&#169;	copyright sign
laquo	&#171;	left-pointing, double-angle quotation mark
not	&#172;	not sign
shy	&#173;	discretionary hyphen
reg	&#174;	registered trademark sign
deg	&#176;	degree sign
plusmn	&#177;	plus-or-minus sign
para	&#182;	paragraph sign
raquo	&#187;	right-pointing, double-angle quotation mark
frac14	&#188;	fraction one-quarter
frac12	&#189;	fraction one-half
frac34	&#190;	fraction three-quarters
iquest	&#191;	inverted question mark

Special Characters for Specific Jobs

If you are doing anything with math, you should be able to display the mathematical symbols. The most common of these are in Table 17-5.

Table 17-5
Common Mathematical Entities

Character Notation	Hex Notation	Entity Created
forall	&#8704;	for all
part	&#8706;	partial differential
exist	&#8707;	there exists
empty	&#8709;	empty set = null set = diameter
nabla	&#8711;	nabla = backward difference
isin	&#8712;	element of
notin	&#8713;	not an element of
Ni	&#8715;	contains as member
prod	&#8719;	n-ary product = product sign
sum	&#8721;	n-ary summation
minus	&#8722;	minus sign
lowast	&#8727;	asterisk operator
radic	&#8730;	square root = radical sign
prop	&#8733;	proportional to
infin	&#8734;	infinity
ang	&#8736;	angle
and	&#8743;	logical and = wedge
Or	&#8744;	logical or = vee
cap	&#8745;	intersection = cap
cup	&#8746;	union = cup
int	&#8747;	integral
there4	&#8756;	therefore
sim	&#8764;	tilde operator = varies with = similar to
cong	&#8773;	approximately equal to
asymp	&#8776;	almost equal to = asymptotic to
Ne	&#8800;	not equal to
equiv	&#8801;	identical to
Le	&#8804;	less than or equal to
ge	&#8805;	greater than or equal to

Character Notation	Hex Notation	Entity Created
sub	&#8834;	subset of
sup	&#8835;	superset of
nsub	&#8836;	not a subset of
sube	&#8838;	subset of or equal to
supe	&#8839;	superset of or equal to
oplus	&#8853;	circled plus = direct sum
otimes	&#8855;	circled times = vector product
perp	&#8869;	up tack = orthogonal to = perpendicular
sdot	&#8901;	dot operator
lceil	&#8968;	left ceiling
rceil	&#8969;	right ceiling
lfloor	&#8970;	left floor
rfloor	&#8971;	right floor
lang	&#9001;	left-pointing angle bracket
rang	&#9002;	right-pointing angle bracket

How about if you need special punctuation symbols? See Table 17-6 for the most common entities that represent punctuation.

Table 17-6
Common Punctuation Entities

Character Notation	Hex Notation	Entity Created
bull	&#8226;	bullet = black small circle
hellip	&#8230;	horizontal ellipsis = three-dot leader
prime	&#8242;	prime = minutes = feet
Prime	&#8243;	double prime = seconds = inches
oline	&#8254;	overline = spacing overscore
frasl	&#8260;	fraction slash

Handling Foreign Languages

What if you need to include text from other languages? Greek? French (with its accents)? Or even Chinese? The first thing you must do is to define the base language for your page. You can do this in the HTML element itself. Your HTML element would look like this:

```
<HTML lang="EN">
```

The value of the lang attribute should be a valid two-character language code. If you then have a paragraph with a different language as the base — say Spanish — then you could identify the base language for that paragraph by putting a lang attribute into the P element like this:

```
<P lang="SP">
```

Sometimes you simply want to include a sentence or a word in another language. The SPAN element is most appropriate for those times. A complete list of language codes is in Appendix F.

> **Note**
>
> There is a lot more to showing foreign languages that require a different alphabet on your page. If you have only a sentence or two to display, your best bet is probably to use an image of the text. If you have a considerable amount of text to display in a language other than English — say Japanese — which uses Kanjii and Katakana, your visitors must run a Japanese operating system because Japanese, Chinese, and other character-based languages use a double-byte character set, quite different from the single-byte character set (ASCII) used for English. For more information about this complex topic, visit www.samsung.co.kr. You may want to click on the English tab in the upper right corner.

You probably noticed in Chapter 15 that most of the block-level elements include both lang and dir attributes. These often need to work together. Some languages are actually read right to left. HTML accommodates the creation of pages using these languages by rendering in the direction you dictate. You still create the text in a left-to-right direction, but it is rendered right-to-left, if you indicate, thus

```
<BODY lang="CH" dir="rtl">
```

would give you a body with a base language of Chinese and a text direction of right to left. In Chapter 12, an element called BDO was introduced as a new element. This is the bidirectional algorithm override element. It enables you to override the base direction. The dir attribute is mandatory for the BDO element.

Bidirectional Algorithm Override `<BDO>`

Start Tag:	Required
Content:	Inline elements
End Tag:	Required
Attributes:	`dir`: Mandatory: `ltr` or `rtl`
	`id, class`: used in conjunction with style sheets
	`lang`: language
	`style`: for style sheets
	`title`: gives the element a title

Adding Quotes: The Q Element

The `Q` element is a prospective element. The `Q` element doesn't render as anything other than ordinary text, but it may someday in the future. The `Q` element is the inline equivalent of `BLOCKQUOTE` and takes the same attributes.

Quote `<Q>`

Start Tag:	Required
Content:	Inline elements
End Tag:	Required
Attributes:	`id, class`: used in conjunction with style sheets
	`lang, dir`: indicate language and text direction
	`cite`: URL of the quote if taken from the Web
	`title`: title of this element
	`style`: define style here to override that in a style sheet
	`events`: see Chapter 48

Grouping Inline Elements: The SPAN Element

The `SPAN` element is the inline equivalent of the `DIR` element. You can group any number of elements within a block-level element or between block-level elements by enclosing them in a `SPAN` element.

The SPAN element can then use an id or a class, as defined in a style sheet, to change the look of the elements it encompasses. Suppose you want to change the background to yellow for part of some text (to make it look like it is highlighted). You can use the SPAN element as follows:

```
<P>It is very important to proofread <SPAN class="highlight">
all your text </SPAN> carefully. You can find examples of <SPAN
class="highlight">common misspellings in Table A4.</SPAN> As
Strunk and White always say, <SPAN class="highlight"><Q>"You
should always find time to proofread."</Q> Spell checking
simply is not enough.</SPAN></P>
```

This text would render as follows. The yellow background text is shown as underlined.

```
It is important to proofread all your text carefully. You can
find examples of common misspellings in Table A4. As Strunk and
White always say, "You should always find time to proofread."
Spell checking simply is not enough.
```

And the style sheet would look like this:

```
SPAN.highlight {
            background: yellow}
```

From Here

Cross-Reference

Go to Chapter 26 and learn the CSS syntax.

Jump to Chapter 48 and learn about events and JavaScript.

Proceed to Chapter 18 and learn about hyperlinks.

Summary

This chapter covered the essentials of inline elements. You learned the difference between physical inline elements, which actually make the browser render in a certain way, and logical inline elements, which tell the browser what message you are trying to send with your text. You also learned about inline elements that currently don't render differently at all, such as ABBR, ACRONYM, and Q.

This chapter explained the use of entities in depth, including using them to display mathematical symbols, punctuation, and foreign languages. You learned about text language and direction. Finally, you learned about the SPAN element, which enables you to apply a style across inline elements.

✦   ✦   ✦

Adding Hyperlinks

Hyperlinks are what make your page really click! Without them you couldn't have a site (only a page), and the Web wouldn't be a Web at all. This chapter tells you everything you need to know about links — internal links, relative links, absolute links, FTP links — you name it.

When you complete this chapter, you will be able to create any kind of link you can find on the Web. You can even use an image on the CD-ROM at the back of this book to link from an image on your page to the IDG Books Worldwide page for this book.

Understanding Links

Links are what make the World Wide Web so interesting and so compelling. In the early days of the Web, a lot of people with pages didn't have much to say other than: "This is what I think is cool." What did they give you? A list of their favorite links. At one time, there were more links than pages.

Today, you have an amazing range of places to link. You can create your own *cool links* page, or you can be more discriminating and only link to other places within your own sites and your own strategic alliances.

How do links work? Basically what a link does is tell the browser to load a new URL using the HTTP protocol (or another protocol, but more on that later). It's that simple.

URLs Dissected

Why is it so important to stop and analyze the parts of a URL? It isn't just to slow you down and keep the good stuff for later in the book. You need to understand the parts of a URL if you want to create links. Depending on the type of link you are using, you need to include different parts of the URL. This may be dry, but hang in there. The rest of the chapter assumes you have read this part.

A *uniform resource locator* (URL) has several parts (see Figure 18-1). There is the protocol, say, http://. When you loaded a page locally in Chapter 3, what appeared in place of http:// was file://. That is because the file you were opening was a local file; no protocol was necessary.

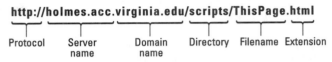

Figure 18-1: Anatomy of a URL

What comes next? The server name. There are two parts to the server name: the machine name and the domain name. If you have a domain with only one server, you've probably never given this any thought. Your server name is something like www.overtheweb.com. But if you are part of a large organization, like the University of Virginia, many, many servers exist within the virginia.edu domain. Each one has a different name: holmes.acc.virginia.edu, maewest.itc.virginia.edu, faraday.clas.virginia.edu.

Note   In addition to being able to have more than one server associated with one domain, you can have more than one domain reside on one physical server. An ISP may have hundreds of domains hosted from one physical server. How this is configured depends on the Web-server software running.

Following the server name comes the directory location on the server. This directory may be an actual directory, it may be a short name that maps to a longer directory name, or it may be a completely different name. For example, consider the following URL: http://watt.seas.virginia.edu/~bp/c34.html. The ~bp is the directory name. Does this mean there is a single directory directly under the root directory of watt.seas with the name ~bp? No. It means ~bp maps to some physical directory. This directory could be h1/users/bp/public_html or something even longer!

Finally, in the URL, you have the filename something.html. In fact, the extension on the file doesn't have to be .html. It should be appropriate for whatever type of file it is. If your file is an Active Server Pages (ASP) file, the extension would be .asp. If your URL is linking to a specific place on the current page or another page, you also need to include the anchor name of that place. If you don't include a valid anchor name, the page will load at the top. The anchor name begins with a pound sign (#).

Linking Local Pages with Relative File Names

The easiest kind of link to create is a link to a page in the same directory. Say you are currently working on a page you are going to publish as File1.html. You would like to link to another page you are going to publish into the same directory as File2.html. Here is all you need to create the link:

```
<A href="File2.html">Text that links</A>
```

Even though the browser always needs the fully qualified URL, it can figure out the rest of the URL from the current URL. All you need to provide is the file name. The browser assumes any information you leave out matches the information it used to get your current page. So if your visitor comes to your page at http://this. domain.org/greatstuff/tidbits/File1.html, his or her browser will turn your link of File2.html into http://this.domain.org/greatstuff/tidbits/ File2.html.

Qualifying the URL

How does this work? The browser looks to see what page it is already on and then removes only the file name from the existing URL, adds the new file name onto the end of the URL, and requests the page. Pretty smart, eh?

The A element

Without even taking particular note of it, you just learned the A element, which you may remember from Chapter 3. When you want to link to a page, or to another location within the same page, all you need is the A element with the href attribute. In fact, the A element has several attributes. The two you use most often are href and name. The href attribute gives the destination of the link; name names the anchor you are creating (more on that later).

Anchor <A>

Start Tag:	Required
Content:	Inline elements but no nesting of A elements
End Tag:	Required
Attributes:	id, class, lang, dir, title, style: previously defined
	href: destination for a link
	hreflang: language of the href attribute
	type: content type of the link; most commonly "text/html"
	rel: relationship in sequence of this hrefrev: relationship in sequence of this href

`charset`: character encoding of the link

`shape`, `coords`: for imagemaps, see Chapter 39

`target`: identifies which frame in a frameset gets loaded with the contents of the `hreftabindex`, `accesskey`: for accessibility

`name`: name of an anchor

Linking to Pages in Other Directories

Of course, you can't spend your life linking only to other files within the same directory on the same server. Sometimes you simply must link to pages in other directories. When you do this, you can go one of two directions: up or down. Up means you will be going to a directory further up the directory structure or at least down a different leg of the directory structure than you are in currently. Down means you will go to a subdirectory of the directory you are in currently. The following helps make this clear:

```
Root
history
American          European
revolution    20thcent  WWI  WWII
```

If you are working on a page in the `history/american/revolution` directory and you want to link to a page in the `20thcent` directory, you would take advantage of double dots (`..`) to go up a directory. This means if you are working on a page, the ultimate URL of which will be `http://this.domain.org/history/American/revolution/index.html`, and you want to link to a page in the `20thcent` directory, you would use the following `href` value:

```
<A href="../20thcent/index.html">Learn about the history of the
20th Century</A>
```

Be sure not to put a slash (/) before the double dots or it won't work. How would you point to a file called `index.html` in the `WWI` directory? Don't look ahead.

```
<A href="../../European/WWI/index.html">Learn about World War I
in Europe</A>
```

You can put as many sets of double dots as you need. However, at some point, it might be clearer just to use an absolute reference, which you learn about next.

Linking to External Pages

Relative references were covered in the last section. That is to say, all links were relative to the current page. When you link to pages outside your current server, you need to use absolute references. Absolute references do not depend on the location of the page that is linking to them. An *absolute reference* is simply a fully qualified URL. When you link to an external page, you use the URL as you would type it in the location window of your browser, if you wanted to open that page.

```
<A href= "http://my.domain.org/history/American/revolution/
index.html">Learn about the American Revolution</A>
```

In most browsers today, you don't actually need to type the protocol information (`http://`). If you simply type `my.domain.org/history/American/revolution`, you normally get the right page on your screen. Why? First, the browser assumes you are using the http protocol. Second, `index.html` (along with `default.html` or `home.html`) is one of the file names a server will serve if you don't tell it which page in a directory you want. Servers can be configured to serve any page as the default page; they frequently have a list and go down the list looking for the page defined as the default.

Tip   You can actually give your Web server a bit more information about your links to help them load faster. By putting a / at the end of a link, you tell the Web server the name is a *directory name*, and not a *filename*. This saves the Web server the trouble of looking for a file with that name. This will not work if your link is to a file name (`something.html`). In fact, it will result in a broken link.

In your absolute reference, however, you always need to give the protocol and the file name. So the following won't work:

```
<A href= "my.domain.org/history/American/revolution">Learn
about the American Revolution</A>
```

Because typing a URL incorrectly is so easy and then you end up with a broken link on your page, it is *highly recommended* you do bring up the page to which you want to link in your browser, copy the URL from the location window, and paste it into your HTML.

Linking to Locations on the Same Page

What if you have a long page, such as a FAQ, which by all the chunking rules you know you shouldn't break up into more than one page, perhaps because people will want to print it? How can you link to the middle of a page? You create a named anchor. A *named anchor* is simply a point on the page to which you can link directly.

```
<A name="Q21">Question 21</A>
```

The previous code creates a named anchor at Question 21. There are no rules about names, except they can't have spaces in them, so make up something you'll remember. Now if you want to link from somewhere else in the same page to Question 21, you use the following code:

```
<A href="#Q21">See also Question 21.</A>
```

If you want to link from somewhere else in another page in the same directory, you use the following code:

```
<A href="faq.html#Q21">See also Question 21 in the FAQ.</A>
```

You can, of course, link to a named anchor from pages in other directories or from pages on other servers. You should be able to figure out how to do this by now.

Chapter 22 explains frames and targets in detail.

Does capitalization matter when you are creating links? It depends. If you are publishing to an NT server, no. If you are publishing to a UNIX server, yes. It definitely matters when you are linking to pages on other sites, because you don't know on what kind of server they reside. The easiest way to keep your own links straight on your own site is to pick a system and stick with it. Use all lowercase filenames and you shouldn't have a problem.

Link to Pages from Images

One feature you see on many pages is linking from images. Sometimes you can click an image and hyperlink to another page or to another place on the same page. Linking from an image is simple. An image is on the CD-ROM in the back of this book that you can use for this. This image is called HTML4.gif. To place this image on your page and link from that image to the IDG Books Worldwide page for this book, include the following code:

```
<A href="http://164.109.153.102/product.asp?isbn=0764534734"><IMG
src="images/HTML4.gif"></A>
```

You just used the IMG element. The IMG element is covered in depth in Chapter 19. For now, just know you need to publish the image file from the CD to your images directory as binary (or raw data) for this to work.

How does this work? The image behaves exactly the same as text would as the content of an A element. On older browsers, you might see a blue box around the image to indicate it links. But you'll learn how to turn that off when you get to Chapter 26 about style sheets.

Linking to Non-Web Data

What if you want to link to a file for your visitors to download? You can do this using the same A element.

```
<A href="http://www.yourserver.com/pub/contract.doc"> Download
the latest version of our contract.</A>
```

This works as long as it is in the pub directory and it is a file called `contract.doc`. When a visitor clicks this link, the browser asks what to do with this file. Once the browser gets it downloaded, the visitor can open it with any program that will open a `.doc` file. It's a good idea to give visitors a choice of ways to get at any file you want to download and also to give them a choice of formats including `.rtf` (rich text format). Check with your systems administrator to make sure permissions are right for this to work.

Tip   Better yet, create the document and save it as a `.pdf` file (portable document format) using Adobe Acrobat. Then visitors can see the document with all its formatting right on the screen and print it to a printer without needing to have the right word processor installed.

The BASE Element

What if you want to have many links to a different directory on the same server or you have to move your page to another directory, breaking all your links? HTML helps you out here by offering the BASE element. The BASE element goes into the HEAD element. It is easy to use. It tells any visiting browsers they should act as if this page is located in the BASE URL location for purposes of all relative references. An example helps:

You have 20 links on your page to other pages in your site. Your current page is called `history/American/20thCentury/WWII/Pacific/thispage.html`. Your links are mostly to pages in the `history/European/WWII/Japan` directory. So most of your links look something like this:

```
<A href="../../../../European/WWII/Japan/page1.html"> Click
here.</A>
```

Now, for some reason, you have to move this page to the history/Asian directory. Does this mean you must go through and recode all your links? No. You can simply add the following BASE element to your page:

```
<BASE
url="http://this.domain.org/history/American/20thCentury/WWII/
Pacific/">
```

Now all your relative links originate from the correct directory. This solves this immediate problem, but what you might want to do in the first place is to make all your links relative to the history directory. Then your BASE element would look like this:

```
<BASE url="http://this.domain.org/history/">
```

And your link would look like this:

```
<A href="European/WWII/Japan/page1.html"> Click here.</A>
```

Using the BASE element can make maintenance of your site much easier in the long run.

Adding a mailto Link

Have you ever clicked someone's e-mail address at the bottom of a page and had a mail window open? This is done with a mailto link. If you do use a mailto link, you should also give your e-mail address so people with nasty old browsers, or the stand-alone version of Navigator, can still send you e-mail. Here's how it works:

```
Contact me at<A href="mailto:info@yourdomain.org">
info@yourdomain.org.</A>
```

Where info@yourdomain.org is your e-mail address.

Bonus: Create a Link Without Leaving Your Page

Isn't it risky to put links on your pages to other sites? Doesn't this mean you could be sending your visitors away, never to return? It is, indeed, risky, but you don't want to have a site without any links to the rest of the world. There is a way around this quandary. When you link to other locations, open up new windows! This means your own site is still there—it just ceases to be the active window.

```
<A href="http://other.site.com/relevant/index.html"
target="_blank">A strategic partner of ours</A>
```

The *target* attribute is set to _blank, which is a reserved target name. This attribute tells the browser to open a new, blank window the URL specified by the `href` attribute. You learn more about targets and reserved target names in Chapter 22, which is all about frames.

From Here

Jump to Chapter 22 to learn how to use frames in your Web page.

Proceed to Chapter 19 and start inserting graphics and other objects in your Web pages.

Summary

In this chapter, you learned how to create all kinds of links: links to pages in the same directory on the same server, links to pages in different directories on the same servers, and links to pages on different servers. You learned how to link images to pages. You also learned how to create a `mailto` link and how to open a new page when you link to an external page, so the visitors don't leave your page altogether.

✦　　✦　　✦

Inserting Graphics and Other Objects

What is a Web page without graphics? This chapter takes you through the basics of inserting graphics and multimedia effectively into your pages. The IMG and OBJECT elements enable you to insert images and other types of multimedia into your pages.

A Quick Introduction to Graphics File Formats

Image files come in many formats. Fortunately, the Web only supports three formats: JPEG (Joint Photographic Experts Group), GIF (Graphics Interface Format, pronounced *jiff* by the inventor of the format, and *gif,* as in gift, by everyone else), and PNG (Portable Network Graphic). Initially, the Web only supported GIF images for inline viewing and JPEG images for out-of-line viewing. Today, you can use all three formats in the middle of your page. The Web uses these three types of graphics files because each format supports some type of compression.

JPEG

JPEG compresses your image by removing redundant data. It maintains the complete color spectrum of your image. If you have a photo of yourself in front of a tree or a beautiful sunset, JPEG is a good compression choice. In the tree photo, the slightly inaccurate re-creation of the leaf pattern is of little consequence. Because JPEG preserves all the colors, your tree and sunset are as lovely as the original when compressed with JPEG.

GIF

GIF compresses your image by removing colors down to the 256-color palate. As a result, your GIF photo of a sunset probably has stripes (where one color ends and the next closest color begins), and your tree is also less vibrant. If you have an architectural drawing in which the straightness of the lines matters more than the background shade of sepia, then GIF is the proper format. Because this format handles line art skillfully, use GIFs to save text images.

PNG

PNG is the newest graphics file format supported on the Web. By using an exclusively designed algorithm, PNG provides the best overall quality. Only the newest browsers support PNG, however. If visitors view your page without the latest browser, they receive the broken-image graphic — unless you provide an alternate image.

Creating a graphic image

Many available software packages create graphics. Chapter 37 discusses your options for creating images and goes into greater detail about selecting the appropriate format.

Adding Inline Images with the IMG Element

Use the IMG element to add an image to your page simply. The IMG element includes everything you need in the start tag. IMG does not have content or end tags.

Image <IMG>

Start Tag: Required

Content: Empty

End Tag: Forbidden

Attributes: id, class: used in conjunction with style sheets

lang, dir: indicate language and text direction

src: URL of image

alt: short description; used for text-only browsers

longdesc: long description; used for text-only browsers

title: title of this element

style: define style here to override style sheet

usemap: URL of client-side image map

ismap: use server-side image map

height: height of image; use if overriding the actual image height

width: width of image; use if overriding the actual image width align, hspace, vspace, border: deprecated; should be specified in style sheet

events: see Chapter 48

The two most important (and required) attributes are src and alt. The src attribute specifies from where the image arrives. Even with an inline image, the image exists as a separate file, usually stored in your images directory. To support the shrinking number of text-only browsers, as well as the growing number of text-synthesizing browsers, include a useful alt attribute value. The alt attribute should contain a short, accurate description of the image's appearance. If you need a longer description, you should use the longdesc attribute.

Height and width serve two purposes. If you use an HTML editor to specify an image, the HTML editor automatically inserts the height and width attributes to facilitate quick page loading. In addition, if you want to load a small image and stretch it into a larger image, then use the height and width attributes.

Tip Don't try to stretch a GIF image. Use JPEGs and PNGs for stretching instead.

Usemap and ismap are associated with image maps. Image maps are images with clickable areas — actually hyperlinks — under the image. Image maps are discussed fully in Chapter 39.

The following examples show how to use the IMG element:

```
<IMG class="logo" src="images/logo.gif" alt="Really Big Company
Logo">
```

This code inserts an image called logo.gif into your page. If you hold your mouse over the image using Internet Explorer 3 and above, or Netscape Navigator 4 and above, the words Really Big Company Logo pop up. The formatting — padding, borders, alignment, and text wrapping — of the image depends on your style sheet and the definition of the IMG class logo.

```
<IMG class="wrapped" src="images/stretch-box.gif"
alt="Concentric boxes" height="200" width="200">
```

The preceding code inserts an image called stretch-box.gif. The original image is 16 × 16 pixels, while the stretched image will be 200 × 200 pixels. If successful, stretching an image is a great way to minimize the load time of your page. The formatting of the image on the page depends on how the IMG class "wrapped" is defined in your style sheet.

Multimedia

A growing number of inline and external multimedia formats work on the Web. Some multimedia files play in your browser without any special plug-ins, while others require plug-ins. Multimedia files can include video, sound, animation, VRML (Virtual Reality Modeling Language), QuickTime VR, and a number of other formats.

As the page designer, remember that visitors to your site may need special software to load your page properly. You should include links to any plug-ins required for your page. Some of the more common multimedia file formats follow:

Extension	Description
.mov	movie
.wav	sound
.qtvr	QuickTime VR
.wrl	Worlds 3D VRML
.midi	sound
.dcr	Shockwave
.pdf	portable document format (Adobe)

Adding Inline Multimedia with the OBJECT Element

With more formats and each requiring different information, adding multimedia is trickier than adding an image. Add multimedia to your page using the OBJECT element. Currently, most images are inserted into your page using the IMG element, but even images will eventually be inserted using the OBJECT element.

Object <OBJECT>

Start Tag:	Required
Content:	Alternate text
	Other OBJECT elements
	One or more PARAM elements, description of what should appear
End Tag:	Required

Attributes: id, class, lang, dir, events

declare: Boolean flag indicating the object is declared but should not be instantiated; if you use this attribute, you'll have to instantiate the object later with another OBJECT element

classid: URL of object's implementation; may be used either in conjunction with or instead of the data attribute, depending on the object

codebase: URL of base point for resolving relative references related to this object (specifically from the classid, data, and archive attributes)

codetype: content type of object specified in classid attribute in MIME format; saves time for a visitor downloading a content type that his or her browser can't render

data: URL of the object's data
type: MIME type of data specified in the data attribute; saves time for a visitor downloading a content type that his or her browser can't render

archive: list of URLs in space-delimited format that gives resources relative to the object's classid and data attributes; it may include the object's classid and data attributes; and the browser should preload the archive, which results in a quicker object load

standby: a message that the browser may show while loading the object

title: title of this element

style: define style here to override style sheet

usemap: URL of client-side image map

name: name for form submission

height: height of object; use if overriding the actual image height

width: width of object; use if overriding the actual image width

align, hspace, vspace, border: deprecated; should be speci hfgfied in style sheet

tabindex: tabbing order (for forms)

The OBJECT element can be very confusing. Fortunately, you will probably never need to use all attributes at the same time.

The OBJECT element can be nested into a sort of pecking order. Your browser uses the first instance of the nested OBJECT element that it supports. If you, as a Web developer, put the spiffiest items first, then the visitor sees the coolest multimedia that her browser can support without realizing she is missing any items, as shown in the upcoming example.

You want to include a model of a protein molecule for your cool chemistry site. The coolest model is the VRML version of the molecule, which is 3D and rotates and zooms at the visitor's discretion. Unfortunately, the visitor needs to have a computer that can handle 3D rendering and a VRML player installed. The next coolest way to show the model uses a QuickTime VR model of the molecule. This method enables the visitor to rotate the model without the ability to zoom and travel through the molecule. If the visitor can't even handle the QuickTime VR model, use an MPEG movie of the molecule bonding with another molecule. The last option is a GIF image of the molecule. For text-only browsers, settle for a short, text description of the molecule.

The following creates the nested OBJECT elements for this example:

```
<OBJECT classid="http://nmc.itc.virginia.edu/nlii/Grisham/
vrml/modelA1.wrl" codetype="application/wrl" height="250"
width="600">
   <OBJECT classid= "http://nmc.itc.virginia.edu/qtvr/atp_
synthase.qtvr" codetype="application/quicktime">
      <OBJECT data="synthase.mpeg" type="application/mpeg">
         <OBJECT data="atp_synthase.gif" type="image/gif">
            You are missing the ATP Synthase molecule.
         </OBJECT>
      </OBJECT>
   </OBJECT>
</OBJECT>
```

Tips on Using Images Effectively

Good Web designers often debate when and how to use images. The two major issues with regards to images on your page are download time and visual clutter. No hard and fast rules about using images exist, but the following guidelines help:

1. **Use the lowest color depth appropriate for your application.** Chapter 37 discusses this issue in greater depth. In simple terms, don't save your black-and-white image in 16.7 million colors. If your image uses only primary colors, save it with the least color-palette baggage to reduce download time tremendously.

2. **Use the smallest image appropriate.** What are you trying to communicate with the image? You need to have a certain level of detail in your image to make your point, but try to keep images small. Crop them tightly and leave the white space on the page using padding in the style sheet.

3. **Use text instead of a text image, if at all possible.** If the your font is widely available (meaning it comes installed with Windows 95/98/NT with a reasonable facsimile available on the Mac), then use text; if not, use an image of text. (See Figure 19-1.)

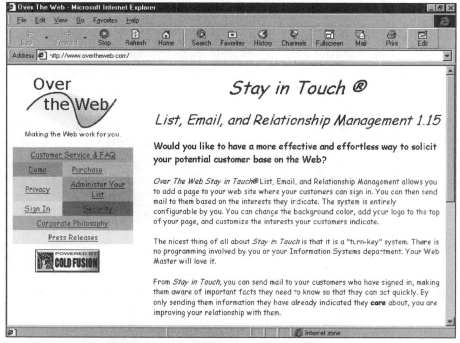

Figure 19-1: Using a text image is sometimes unavoidable.

4. **Keep images in the context of your page.** Make sure all your images contribute to the message of your page. Don't add images just because you like them. Avoid visual clutter by prioritizing the message of your page.

Providing Alternatives for Text-Only Browsers

Only a small fraction of Web surfers have text-only browsers. Should you bother to mark up your page to accommodate them? Probably not, but you should include alternatives for other reasons. The Americans with Disabilities Act (ADA) requires all government sites to be accessible to the visually impaired.

What does the term *speech-synthesizing browser* mean to you? If you only think of the visually impaired, broaden your horizon. The biggest growth in speech-synthesizing browsers will come in alternative browser locations, such as your car! Because of this growing segment of the browser market, you should include alternatives to images and multimedia for text-only browsers.

How can you make your Web page friendly to speech synthesizing?

+ **Use the alt attribute on every image.** Since speech-synthesizing browsers can't see your image, state your image contents.

+ **Use text as the content of your OBJECT element.** Speech-synthesizing browsers skip the OBJECT element but process the content — the equivalent of alt text.

+ **Never use the deprecated FONT element.** This element gives speech-synthesizing browsers fits. Use style sheets instead.

+ **Use images only when absolutely necessary.** Use text instead of an image of text if possible. The image of text can be anti-aliased, but your ears-only visitors hear silence instead of your lovely image of text.

From Here

Go to Chapter 37 and learn about creating graphics for the Web.

Jump to Chapters 40 through 43 and learn about creating multimedia for the Web, including sound, video, ActiveX controls, and Java.

Proceed to Chapter 20 to begin adding tables to your Web page..

Summary

This chapter taught you how to add images and multimedia to your pages. You learned the IMG element and the dreaded OBJECT element. The examples provided with the OBJECT element should clarify its use. Finally, you learned about using images on your page effectively and accommodating text-only browsers.

✦   ✦   ✦

Adding Tables

Although tables have their place in a Web page, they should not format text. This chapter focuses on using tables in their intended manner: to display tabular data. For most of the other elements covered in this book, style sheets provide formatting. The first version of cascading style sheets (CSS1) did not provide adequate support for tables, so for this purpose, the style-sheet model falls short. As we'll discuss in Chapter 25, the implementation of style sheets varies between browsers. Because style sheets supported by older browsers don't sufficiently support table formatting, tables may need to include formatting information in the table definition.

This chapter covers everything from creating a basic table to grouping cells or columns to spanning cells or columns, and contains the most complete explanation of tables created with all available HTML 4 elements. Chapter 30 discusses the implications of CSS1 and CSS2 on formatting tables.

Introducing the HTML Table Model

HTML 4 adds to the potential formatting of tables on your Web page. For the first time, you can group rows and columns for purposes of formatting. Even though you have to include formatting in your table definition under CSS1 (unlike in the rest of HTML 4), you can include it at the group level, rather than at the cell or row level — a truly powerful feature.

In addition, you can group columns. To understand this profound change, examine the HTML 3.2 table model. Tables are created from left to right, top to bottom. The following table is defined in this order: A1, A2, A3, A4, B1, B2, B3, B4, C1, C2, C3, D1, D2, D3.

A1	A2	A3	A4
B1	B2	B3	B4
C1	C2	C3	
D1	D2		D3

If all the cells in the fourth column (A4, B4, and D3) had the same background color, that formatting information would have to be defined three times, once in each cell definition. Grouping formatting for rows would be easier, because all the cells in a row are defined together, but if you wanted to define formatting for all the rows except the first row, you'd have to put the definitions into each row.

Using the COLGROUP element, you can group columns for formatting purposes. As a result, you can define all the cells in a column to look the same without inserting formatting information into each cell. This feature is especially useful in terms of maintenance. If you change the background color of your page from your style sheet and find that the background color of one column doesn't match, you can change the formatting information only for that COLGROUP and have it reflected in every COLGROUP table cell.

In addition, the following set of elements in HTML 4 affects the formatting of rows: THEAD, TFOOT, and TBODY. You can define one or more rows as the THEAD, one or more rows as the TFOOT, and the remaining rows take on the TBODY formatting.

Defining the Table

Create a table in HTML with the TABLE element. As with the UL, OL, and DL elements, however, this element alone won't achieve your desired results. You have to define table data in your table to see anything on your page.

Table <TABLE>

Start Tag:	Required
Content:	CAPTION
	COL
	COLGROUP
	THEAD
	TFOOT
	TBODY
	TR, TD
End Tag:	Required

Attributes: id, class, lang, dir, events, style, text

align: deprecated; use style sheets

cellpadding: the amount of white space between the contents of a cell and its border

cellspacing: the amount of white space between cells and between cells and the outside borders of the table

border: the width in pixels of the frame around the table

frame: the side, if any, of the border of the table that is visible (see following choices)

rules: the rules, if any, that appear between cells (see following choices)

width: width of the table either in pixels or as a percentage of the window

summary: purpose of this table for speech-synthesizing browsers

The frame attribute takes one of the following values:

✦ **void.** No sides. This is the default value.

✦ **above.** The top side only.

✦ **below.** The bottom side only.

✦ **hsides.** The top and bottom sides only.

✦ **vsides.** The left and right sides only.

✦ **lhs.** The left-hand side only.

✦ **rhs.** The right-hand side only.

✦ **border or box.** All four sides.

The rules attribute takes one of the following values:

✦ **none.** No rules. This is the default value.

✦ **groups.** Rules appear between row groups and column groups only.

✦ **rows.** Rules appear between rows only.

✦ **cols.** Rules appear between columns only.

✦ **all.** Rules appear between all rows and columns.

The following examples combine these interesting formatting options:

Row 1

Row 2

Row 3

frame="lhs", rules="rows"

Column 1	Column 2	Column 3

frame="above", rules="cols"

Column 1	Column 2	Column 3	Column 4	Column 5	Column 6

frame="void", rules="groups"

Adding Table Data

All data in a table goes into cells. A cell is created with the TD element or the TH element. Before you start defining cells, first set up rows into which the browser puts the cells. If you don't define rows to hold your cells, each cell will be its own row — meaning your table will be exactly one column wide. Create a row with the TR element.

Table Row <TR>

Start Tag:	Required
Content:	TD
	TH
End Tag:	Optional
Attributes:	id, class, lang, dir, events, title, style
	align: right, left, center, justify, char (these are not deprecated)

valign: top, middle, bottom, baseline (these are not deprecated)

char: indicate the character used for character alignment: default is decimal point

charoff: character offset from left when using character alignment

The TR element can contain both cell data and cell headers. To differentiate the two items, the cell headers are formatted in bold by your browser. To define the formatting for your header cells yourself, use the class attribute and define a class for your headers in your style sheet.

Table Data <TD>

Start Tag:	Required
Content:	Cell data
End Tag:	Optional
Attributes:	id, class, lang, dir, events, title, style

align: right, left, center, justify, char (these are not deprecated)

valign: top, middle, bottom, baseline (these are not deprecated)

colspan: number of columns this cell spans (defaults to 1)

rowspan: number of rows this cell spans (defaults to 1)

abbr: abbreviated version of the cell's content

axis: a comma-delimited list of category names; used for associating each cell with a category in speech-synthesizing browsers

headers: ID that associates a header cell with table data; can be used for speech-synthesizing browsers, for grouping columns, or for style sheets

nowrap: deprecated; avoid wrapping text within this cell; can make cells very wide

char: indicate the character to be used for character alignment; default is decimal point

charoff: character offset from left when using character alignment

bgcolor: deprecated; background color for this cell

width: deprecated; width of cell in pixels

height: deprecated; height of cell in pixels

Table Heading `<TH>`

Start Tag:	Required
Content:	Cell heading
End Tag:	Optional
Attributes:	`id`, `class`, `lang`, `dir`, `events`, `title`, `style`

`align`: right, left, center, justify, char (these are not deprecated)

`valign`: top, middle, bottom, baseline (these are not deprecated)

`colspan`: number of columns this cell spans (defaults to 1)

`rowspan`: number of rows this cell spans (defaults to 1)

`abbr`: abbreviated version of the cell's content

`axis`: a comma-delimited list of category names; used for associating each cell with a category in speech-synthesizing browsers

`headers`: ID that associates a header cell with table data; can be used for speech-synthesizing browsers, for grouping columns, or for style sheets

`scope`: scope covered by header cell; valid values are row, column, rowgroup, colgroup

`nowrap`: deprecated; don't wrap text within this cell

`width`: deprecated; width of cell in pixels

`height`: deprecated; height of cell in pixels

After all the preceding definitions, you may be rethinking putting a table into your page to display tabular data. Don't get discouraged. The following simple example shows how to include a table on your page:

```
<TABLE border="1" frame="border" rules="all">
  <TR>
      <TH>
      <TH>Grams of Fat
      <TH>Grams of Protein
  <TR>
      <TH>Graham Crackers
      <TD align="center">1
      <TD align="center">0
  <TR>
      <TH>Raspberry Yogurt
      <TD align="center">2
      <TD align="center">9
  <TR>
      <TH>Turkey Breast
      <TD align="center">1
```

```
      <TD align="center">6
</TABLE>
```

This example generates a table that looks roughly like the following:

	Grams of Fat	Grams of Protein
Graham Crackers	1	0
Raspberry Yogurt	2	9
Turkey Breast	1	6

In reality, the borders crowd the text more than in this illustration. You can, of course, include cellpadding to keep the table from looking crowded, but this feature complicates the simple example.

The next example adds a few more features. This example uses the align attribute with the value set to "char," and the default alignment character is the decimal place. Internet Explorer 5.5 and Netscape 4.7 do not support character alignment, but this feature should be included in future versions. If you want to change the alignment character, add the char attribute and set it to the character you want to align.

```
<TABLE cellspacing="2" cellpadding="2" border="1" frame="box"
rules="cols">
<TR align="center">
   <TD>
   <TH>Chicago
   <TH>Washington, DC
   <TH>New York
   <TH>Charlottesville
<TR>
   <TH align="center">Breakfast
   <TD align="char">12.95
   <TD align="char">9.95
   <TD align="char">15.95
   <TD align="char">4.95
<TR>
   <TH align="center">Lunch
   <TD align="char">13.50
   <TD align="char">9.50
   <TD align="char">16.00
   <TD align="char">6.50
<TR>
   <TH align="center">Dinner
   <TD align="char">35.00
```

```
     <TD align="char">26.00
     <TD align="char">55.00
     <TD align="char">18.00
   <TR>
     <TH align="center">Transportation
     <TD align="char">12.00
     <TD align="char">15.00
     <TD align="char">22.00
     <TD align="char">9.00
   <TR>
     <TH align="center">Entertainment
     <TD align="char">45.00
     <TD align="char">45.00
     <TD align="char">75.00
     <TD align="char">20.00
   <TR>
     <TH align="center">Total
     <TD align="char">118.45
     <TD align="char">105.45
     <TD align="char">183.95
     <TD align="char">58.45
   </TABLE>
```

Figure 20-1 shows how the text renders in Netscape.

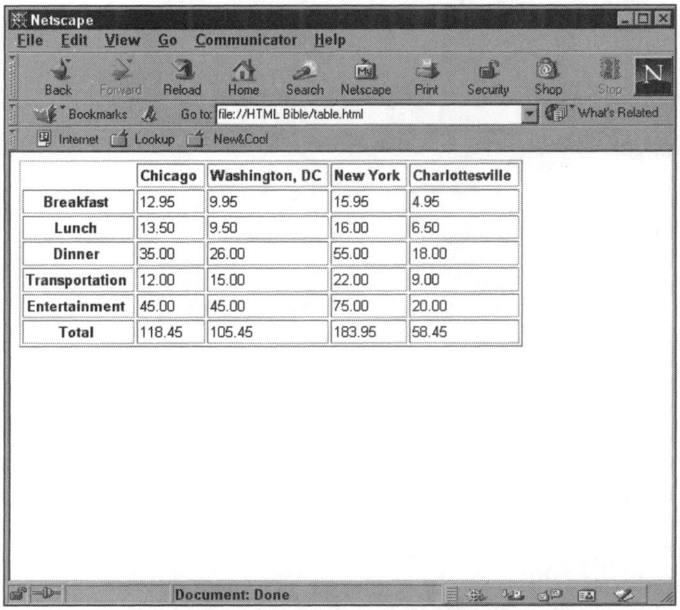

Figure 20-1: Bordered Table in Netscape Communicator 4.7

Grouping Rows

HTML 4 enables you to group rows using the THEAD, TFOOT, and TBODY elements. When you create a table, you commonly have a header row (with cell headings), a number of rows with data, and then a footer row with totals, as in the preceding example.

If you use the THEAD, TFOOT, and TBODY elements, you must use every element, even if you don't need the entire set. Although you must use them, you can leave them empty. The order in which they should appear is THEAD, TFOOT, and TBODY. Why in this particular order? The browser needs to be able to load both the header and the footer information before it loads the body, which could be hundreds of rows. Down the road, you will be able to fit the entire table in one screen with the body scrolling, or the browser automatically putting a header and a footer on each page, when it prints a long table.

Table Header <THEAD>

Start Tag:	Required
Content:	TR
End Tag:	Optional
Attributes:	id, class, lang, dir, events, title, style, char, charoff

align: right, left, center, justify, char (these are not deprecated)

valign: top, middle, bottom, baseline (these are not deprecated)

char: specifies a single character within a text fragment to act as an alignment axis. The default value for this attribute is the decimal point character for the current language as set by lang.

charoff: specifies the offset to the first occurrence of the alignment character on each line.

Table Footer <TFOOT>

Start Tag:	Required
Content:	TR
End Tag:	Optional
Attributes:	id, class, lang, dir, events, title, style, char, charoff

char: specifies a single character within a text fragment to act as an alignment axis. The default value for this attribute is the decimal point character for the current language as set by lang.

charoff: specifies the offset to the first occurrence of the alignment character on each line.

align: right, left, center, justify, char (these are not deprecated)

valign: top, middle, bottom, baseline (these are not deprecated)

Table Body <TBODY>

Start Tag:	Required
Content:	TR
End Tag:	Optional
Attributes:	id, class, lang, dir, events, title, style, char, charoff

char: specifies a single character within a text fragment to act as an alignment axis. The default value for this attribute is the decimal point character for the current language as set by lang.

charoff: specifies the offset to the first occurrence of the alignment character on each line.

align: right, left, center, justify, char (these are not deprecated)

valign: top, middle, bottom, baseline (these are not deprecated)

These three elements improve the appearance of the code from the preceding costs-and-cities table. The table renders as follows in Internet Explorer 4 and newer, but won't work properly in any version of Netscape; Netscape doesn't support these elements yet.

```
<TABLE cellspacing="2" cellpadding="2" border="1" frames="box"
rules="cols">
<THEAD align="center" class="table_header1">
<TR align="center">
  <TD>
        <TH>Chicago
        <TH>Washington, DC
        <TH>New York
        <TH>Charlottesville
<TFOOT align="char" class="table_footer1">
<TR>
  <TH align="center">Total
        <TD>118.45
        <TD>105.45
        <TD>183.95
        <TD>58.45
<TBODY align="char" class="table_body1">
<TR>
        <TH align="center">Breakfast
        <TD>12.95
        <TD>9.95
        <TD>15.95
        <TD>4.95
<TR>
        <TH align="center">Lunch
```

```
                <TD>13.50
                <TD>9.50
                <TD>16.00
                <TD>6.50
        <TR>
                <TH align="center">Dinner
                <TD>35.00
                <TD>26.00
                <TD>55.00
                <TD>18.00
        <TR>
                <TH align="center">Transportation
                <TD>12.00
                <TD>15.00
                <TD>22.00
                <TD>9.00
        <TR>
                <TH align="center">Entertainment
                <TD>45.00
                <TD>45.00
                <TD>75.00
                <TD>20.00
    </TABLE>
```

Figure 20-2 shows how the text renders in IE 5.0.

Several items in the preceding table definition may not have been clear in the first costs-and-cities-table example. First, notice the align attributes. These attributes are the only version of align that are not deprecated, because the text cannot be formatted in any other way within a cell. In addition, the first costs-and-cities table contains more instances of the align attribute. Grouping the rows enables you to move the align="char" attribute-value pair from each TD element to the TBODY element. Because the TH elements for each row still have an align="center" attribute-value pair, this condition overrides the align attribute definition in the TBODY element. The headings should be centered, rather than decimal-aligned.

All three of the new elements in this example have defined classes. As a result, classes must be defined in the style sheets for these elements. The classes are called table_header1, table_footer1, and table_body1, respectively.

The align attribute appears in the preceding examples with a value of "char." What does this mean? The "char" value causes alignment over a set character. The default is the decimal. You can change the default by using an additional attribute called char. If you have a set of cells that all have slashes (/), and you want to align the cells by the slash, use the following code:

```
align="char" char="/"
```

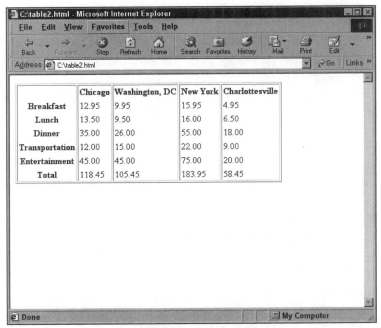

Figure 20-2: Bordered Table in IE 5.0

You can further customize the alignment of the cell values by using the `charoff` attribute with a length (the number of pixels by which to offset the alignment), as in the following example:

```
align="char" char="/" charoff="15"
```

Netscape Navigator and Internet Explorer do not currently support these uncommon usages.

Defining Columns

Where do you define a column? Until now, you haven't defined any columns. The browser calculates the number of columns based on the number of cells defined in a row. If you put more cells into one row than into other rows, the results can be unpredictable. The two major browsers do not fully support each column element.

Browsers prefer an up-front definition of the columns. You can perform this task with the `COL` element.

Column `<COL>`

Start Tag: Required

Content:	TR
End Tag:	Forbidden
Attributes:	id, class, lang, dir, events, title, style, char, charoff

span: number of columns affected by COL attributes

char: specifies a single character within a text fragment to act as an alignment axis. The default value for this attribute is the decimal point character for the current language as set by lang.

charoff: specifies the offset to the first occurrence of the alignment character on each line.

width: column width

align: right, left, center, justify, char (these are not deprecated)

valign: top, middle, bottom, baseline (these are not deprecated)

For example, suppose you want to define a table with five columns of 100 pixels each. Use the following COL element at the top of your table definition before you start defining rows or row groups:

```
<COL span="5" width="100">
```

If those five columns don't share the same width, use the following code:

```
<COL width="15%">
<COL width="25%">
<COL span="3" width="20%">
```

If you want the browser to set the widths, use either of the following code examples:

```
<COL width="0*" span="5">
```

or

```
<COL span="5">
```

Grouping Columns

You may need to use the COLGROUP element, which can be used with or without the COL element.

Column group	**<COLGROUP>**
Start Tag:	Required
Content:	TR
End Tag:	Optional

Attributes:	id, class, lang, dir, events, title, style, char, charoff

span: number of columns included in group

char: specifies a single character within a text fragment to act as an alignment axis. The default value for this attribute is the decimal point character for the current language as set by lang.

charoff: specifies the offset to the first occurrence of the alignment character on each line.

width: column width

align: right, left, center, justify, char (these are not deprecated)

valign: top, middle, bottom, baseline (these are not deprecated)

If you define all a group's columns in the same manner, use the COLGROUP to both group columns and define them as in the following code. This example creates a table with six columns, with the first three in one group, the next two in another group, and the last one in a third group.

```
<COLGROUP span="3" style="group1">
<COLGROUP span="2" style="group2">
<COLGROUP span="1" style="group3">
```

If the first group has three columns of different widths, use the following code:

```
<COLGROUP span="3" style="group1">
  <COL width="75">
  <COL width="150">
  <COL width="100">
<COLGROUP span="2" style="group2">
<COLGROUP span="1" style="group3">
```

When you define the rest of your table, the fourth column will be formatted using style group2 without further instructions. The browser determines the fourth column in each row and applies the appropriate style.

Spanning Rows and Columns

Spanning rows and columns is easy, but neither major Version-4 browsers fully support all of these elements. To span columns, simply add an attribute called colspan to any cell you want to span more than one column. Because the default is one, set the value of colspan to any number greater than one to create a cell that is the specified number of columns wide.

To span rows, use the `rowspan` attribute, which works in the same way as `colspan`. Keep an eye on the arrangement of your cells, though. In the following representation, only one cell should be defined in both the first and third rows for a proper result.

	Chicago	Washington, DC	New York	Charlottesville
Breakfast	12.95	9.95	15.95	4.95
Lunch	13.50	9.50	16.00	6.50
Dinner	35.00	26.00	55.00	18.00
Transportation	12.00	15.00	22.00	9.00
Entertainment	45.00	45.00	75.00	20.00
Total	118.45	105.45	183.95	58.45

```
<TABLE border="1" frame="box" rules="all" cellspacing="2"
cellpadding="2">
<TR>
  <TD colspan="3">A1
<TR>
  <TD>B1
  <TD>B2
  <TD rowspan="2">B3
<TR>
  <TD colspan="2">C1
</TABLE>
```

Adding Finishing Touches to a Table

You can add two more elements to the table: a caption, created with the `CAPTION` element, and a summary, created with the `summary` attribute. Both features ease the comprehension of a table by speech-synthesizing browsers.

The `CAPTION` element must be defined immediately following the `TABLE` element start tag. The element's rendering depends on the particular browser.

Caption `<CAPTION>`

Start Tag:	Required
Content:	Caption to be displayed
End Tag:	Required
Attributes:	`id`, `class`, `lang`, `dir`, `events`, `title`, `style` `align`: **deprecated; use style sheets**

The `summary` attribute should be used as follows:

```
<TABLE summary="This table reflects the costs of living for a
day in major U.S. cities. It includes the costs of eating out
for breakfast, lunch, and dinner, the cost of transportation by
taxi, and the cost of entertainment in each city. Finally, it
shows totals for each city in the bottom row.">
<CAPTION>Daily Expenses for Travelers in Major U.S.
Cities</CAPTION>
```

Nesting Tables

Tables may be nested to produce interesting effects, such as the following example:

A1		
B1	B2	B3
C1		

Because the `TABLE` element must have an end tag, no particular tricks exist for nesting tables. You may include a table within another table's cell or another table's row.

From Here

Jump to Chapter 33 to learn about formatting your page with CSS.

Proceed to Chapter 21 and learn creating forms and inserting scripts.

Summary

This chapter taught you everything you could possibly want to know about tables in HTML 4. You first discovered the table model in HTML. You also learned how to include defining tables as containers and defining rows and cells within tables.

You also learned how to nest tables and add features to improve table rendering by speech-synthesizing browsers. To make your tables more interesting, you learned how to specify column groups and row groups. To format your data more effectively, you learned how to span rows and columns.

✦   ✦   ✦

Creating Forms and Inserting Scripts

The face of the Web changed dramatically when Web forms became possible. Unfortunately, forms haven't changed much since then. This chapter teaches you about all the basic controls forms can include. It covers how form processing works, what your choices are, and what you can do with the data you collect.

In addition to all the existing form fields you've seen before, HTML 4 introduces a few new form-related elements, including the feature that enables you to link a field to the caption for that field. This chapter discusses all these new elements with examples.

Introducing Forms

Forms are a way of collecting information from your site visitors. What you collect, how you collect it, and how you process it vary from site to site and from application to application.

How does it work?

1. You place data-entry fields on your Web page. These can include text fields, radio buttons, checkboxes, text area fields (for more extensive data entry), and other buttons, such as submit and reset buttons.

2. Your site visitors fill in the fields from their own computers and click a button.

3. The information typed by the visitors is sent over the Internet to your server.

4. Your server takes action on the data.

5. Ideally, you provide your visitors with a screen confirming you have received the data and that some action will be taken.

You can do fancier things, such as sending a confirming message by e-mail, sending yourself a notice that someone is using your form, or entering the data submitted by the visitor into a database.

Understanding Form Processing

Before you start designing your form, consider what you want to do with the data you will be collecting. What can you do with the data you collect from a form? All options fall into one of three categories:

1. Saving the data for further processing

2. Returning information to the visitor

3. Taking other action (such as financial transactions)

Saving the data for further processing

You might want to do this if you require people to register for your site or if you want to collect names for a mailing list. You could store the data in a database to verify the visitor is registered before giving access on subsequent visits. You might run a raffle on your page with a prize randomly awarded to people who sign in to your site. You might require people to sign in before they download your free software or newsletter. In any case, you need to collect certain data and store it on your server — either in a database or in an ASCII file.

Returning information to the visitor

You could perform processing based on the data. For example, you might search through a book list to find books that match the visitor's list of favorite types of literature. If the processing doesn't require any input from the server, then this processing is better performed using client-side processing. If, however, your processing requires access to data that resides on the server, such as a card catalog, a site index, or an inventory database, then you can use the data provided by the visitor to perform server-side processing against existing data.

This is probably the most common and acceptable use of forms on the Web. People aren't as likely to question or refuse providing information when they can get something in return, such as information they are seeking. You need to be reason able with what kind of information you require your visitors to enter. Most people will not give you a social security number or credit card information unless they are purchasing something.

Taking other action

If someone comes to your site to purchase something, that visitor expects to provide certain types of information, including personal information, payment information, and shipping information. One of the processing decisions you must make is whether you will collect and retain the payment information on the server or whether you will send the information offline to a place where it is less vulnerable to hackers. In either case, you'll collect information using a form or a series of forms, and all your site visitor normally receives back is confirmation the purchase was completed.

Inserting the FORM

There are two parts to the form: The first is the FORM element and the second is the fields or controls that accept data. Without a FORM element, your form may appear to look fine when you test it, but it will never work.

Form <FORM>

Start Tag:	Required
Content:	Inline elements
	Form field elements
End Tag:	Required
Attributes:	id, class, lang, title, style: previously defined
	action: the URL of the script for processing the data or a mailto address if the action is just to mail the data
	accept_charsets: list of supported character sets
	dir: direction of text
	name: name of form for scripting
	accept: list of MIME types for file upload
	isindex: single-line text input control
	method: how the data is to be sent to the script
	enctype: what types of files will be accepted if one or more of form fields accept file uploads
	target: the target name of the frame within the frameset, if your script is a frameset
	events: see Chapter 48

The two attributes you see used most frequently are action and method.

```
<FORM method="dosomething.cfm" action="post">
... form fields here ...
</FORM>
```

Action

The action attribute tells the form where to send the data it collects. Without an action, your data won't be sent anywhere. Ideally, your action will be the URL of a file containing a script that does something with the data or the URL of a page containing server-side processing.

If you start sniffing through other people's HTML (using View Source in your browser, or Page Source in Netscape 4.x), you will notice that a lot of action attributes don't call scripts. What they do instead is send e-mail, using the mailto: method. How does this work? Instead of a URL, you specify mailto: followed by your e-mail address. This instructs your browser to send this data to your e-mail address.

Is this a good thing? It depends. It's easy to do. You can have a "functional" form on your Web page in minutes. But does this really do you any good? Not if you expect a high volume of traffic to your site. If a lot of people use your form, you may soon be inundated by data you don't have the capacity to process. If you expect only a few people to complete your form each week, then you may have time to process this data manually.

The bottom line is you should have a real script to process your data if you expect to do anything serious with your form.

Method

The method attribute indicates how you want the data to be sent. Your choices are "get" and "post." When you use the "get" method, you send the data as part of the URL. You are limited to 100 characters with the "get" method. This means that if your form data might approach 100 characters, and one text area could exceed 100 characters if you don't set it up properly, then you cannot use the "get" method.

With the "post" method, no limits exist on the number of characters you can send. Also, the values of all the input fields aren't displayed on the browser's location line, the way they are with the "get" method. Generally speaking, "post" is the preferred method of sending form data to a script.

Note   Have you ever noticed when you do a search on a search engine that the URL in your location window gets very long with strange codes? This is because search engines use `method="get"` (for example, `http://www.lycos.com/srch/ ?loc=searchbox&ss=957455750%7C2&query=HTML+parameters`).

Adding Controls

Controls are the generic name for all the form fields you can add to your page — the second necessary component of the form. You can add nine types of controls; they do everything from enabling a person completing your form to enter text, to accepting yes or no answers from that person, to enabling that person to choose one or more items from a list you provide. Controls also define the buttons your visitor needs in order to submit data.

You need to know what type of data your form needs to collect before you create controls. Table 21-1 shows what controls can help you collect values for each type of data.

Table 21-1
List of Controls by Type of Data Desired

Type of Data to Be Collected	What Will Be Displayed on the Form	Control to Use	Value String Returned to Script
text data to be processed or evaluated	text entry field, the size of which is defined using the `size` attribute	`INPUT type= "text" name= "text1"`	`text1="the text entered"`
text data (as lengthy comments)	a large text area field for data entry, the size of which is defined using the `rows` and `cols` attributes	`TEXTAREA name= "textarea1"`	`textarea1="very long text string. May include punctuation."`
text data that needs to be protected from view, such as password data	text entry field, but characters typed appear as either asterisks or dots	`INPUT type= "password" name= "password1"`	`password1= "visible text"`

Continued

What's a Boolean Attribute?

This is in case there are those of you out there who still can't figure out what the heck a Boolean attribute is, as mentioned in the check attribute. The term Boolean comes from George Boole, whose claim to fame is a form of symbolic logic, later christened Boolean algebra, in which there are only two ultimate values — true or false.

Another form of Boolean logic uses punctuation and prepositions (the words AND, OR, NOT, and sometimes NEAR as operators, and occasionally quotation marks or brackets) to narrow a search. For example, when performing a search on flax, linen generally appears.

There is a visual representation of Boolean search attributes at: http://adam.ac.uk/ info/boolean.html#bool.

Radio button

This is similar to a checkbox, in that the site visitor can't make up the value of the field. But unlike the checkbox, a set of radio buttons enable you to give the visitor a choice. Radio buttons are created in sets. When one button of a set is checked, then the other buttons in that set can't be checked. A good example of this is payment information: either you are paying by Visa, Mastercard, or American Express. Radio buttons are perfectly suited to collect this type of data.

You create a set of radio buttons by assigning the same name attribute to all the buttons. Then, so you know which button was associated with which value, you assign a unique value to the value attribute of each radio button. For three buttons in a set, the skeletal HTML might look like this:

```
Which of the three colors in the United States flag is your
favorite?<BR>
<RADIO name="flag" value="red" checked> red
<RADIO name="flag" value="white"> white
<RADIO name="flag" value="blue"> blue
```

In the previous example, the button next to the word "red" is checked. One of the three values will be sent with the field name *flag* to the script. The site visitor cannot leave this field blank.

You may also want to include the alt, disabled, tabindex, and accesskey attributes, which are defined in the previous "Checkbox" section.

File

You can let site visitors upload files to your server, such as images or resumes, using the file value of the type attribute. This is actually a bit trickier than the other types of the INPUT element because you must be sure to include the enctype attribute for the FORM element or it won't work. The accept attribute of the INPUT element limits the MIME types your server accepts. Telling people what types of files they can upload is a good idea; then they won't get unhelpful messages from the server and think your form is broken.

Uploading files with the INPUT element doesn't work with all servers. Check with your system administrator to see whether it will work on your server, but it generally works with NT servers.

Uploading files is easy for visitors if they are using any of the earlier version browsers, except for Internet Explorer 3. IE 3 has a bug and won't display the Browse button next to the text entry field. This means visitors must type in the exact path name of the file on their computers for the upload to work. Of course, you can download a patch from the Microsoft site, but this is little solace to a visitor who can't figure out how to use your form.

The following HTML shows the essentials for creating a form that accepts files for uploads. In this example, the Web page is for an employment agency. It only accepts resumes in Microsoft Word format. The get method will not work with file uploads.

```
<FORM action="upload-resume.cgi" method="post" enctype=
"multipart/form-data">
Upload your resume by finding it on your local hard drive,
using the Browse button below. Remember that your resume must
be in Microsoft Word format, with a file extension of .doc.<BR>
Full name as it appears on the resume: <INPUT type="text"
name="full_name" size="30" maxlength="50"><BR>
Social security number: <INPUT type="text" name="ssn" size="15"
maxlength="11"><BR>
Resume file: <INPUT type="file" name="resume" size="30" accept=
"application/msword"><BR>
<INPUT type="submit" value="Send Your Resume Now!">
<INPUT type="reset" value="Reset Form">
</FORM>
```

Notice in the previous form, no special action is required to create the Browse button for the file upload. The browser creates this automatically when it sees the input type is file.

Hidden

What is the point of putting a hidden form field on your page? After all, who can fill in a field if it's hidden? Actually, a *hidden field* isn't really a form field, but a way to pass data from one page to another. For many reasons, you may want to pass data from one page of your site to another. For example, you may have already asked for information on a previous page that you don't want to ask for again. By using a hidden field, you can pass that data into your script without the visitor knowing. You might also include a hidden field to ensure the script is really receiving data from your form, rather than from another page (for example, someone trying to break into your system). Or, if a script is multipurpose, you might include a hidden field to tell the script which action you want it to take.

Your basic hidden field looks like this:

```
<INPUT type="hidden" name="this_page" value="page1.html">
```

The hidden field doesn't show up on your page at all. You would have to view the source for the page to know the field is exists. Also, the hidden field must be placed between the FORM element's begin and end tags or the field won't be sent with the rest of the data.

Submit or reset

Input types of submit or reset create buttons that either submit the form data to the action attribute of the FORM element, or reset all the fields to the values you assigned using the value attributes.

You can specify what text appears in your button by setting the value attribute. The following code shows three different ways to create a submit button that says "Purchase!" on it. The GIF file, called *purchase-image.gif,* contains an image that says "Purchase!"

```
<INPUT type="submit" value="Purchase!">
<INPUT type="image" src="images/purchase-image.gif"
alt="Purchase!">
<BUTTON type="submit">Purchase!<IMG src="images/purchase-
image.gif" alt="Purchase!"></BUTTON>
```

Image

The *image value* of the type attribute enables you to create a submit button that uses an image for the button. This can be more visually appealing, but it can also be more confusing. People are used to buttons on the Web looking a certain way. Unless you make your image look like a button, you risk having people complete your form and then not understand how to submit the data.

Creating an image button is easy:

```
<INPUT type="image" src="images/accept.gif" alt="Accept">
```

Button

The button value of the type attribute is yet another way to create a button on your page. In case you lost count, this is the fourth way to do this using the INPUT element. The *button value* of the type attribute is a way to execute client-side scripts, rather than the standard submit or reset actions of the other buttons.

Client-side scripts usually use JavaScript or VBScript. One type of button you might want to include checks to make sure a password meets your criteria. By including a button labeled "Check Password" next to two password entry fields, you can perform this type of verification on the client's machine even before you send the data across the network.

The following HTML shows how you might do this. The JavaScript in this example is called TestPasswords(). It confirms that the passwords in both password fields match each other and are of a certain length, don't use the same letter repeatedly, and a few other things. If the password doesn't pass these tests, a message is returned to the visitor with instructions on which rules weren't met.

```
<FORM action="password-change.cfm" method="post">
Enter your old password here: <INPUT type="password" name="old-
password" size="12" maxlength="12"><BR>
Enter your new password here: <INPUT type="password" name="new-
pwd1" size="12" maxlength="12"><BR>
Please re-enter your new password: <INPUT type="password"
name="new-pwd2" size="12" maxlength="12"><BR>
<INPUT type="button" value="Check new passwords" onclick=
"TestPasswords()">
<INPUT type="reset">
<INPUT type="submit" value="Submit passwords for change">
</FORM>
```

BUTTON Element

To add a bit more confusion to the whole discussion of buttons, in addition to the four ways you can create buttons using the INPUT element, the W3C has created the BUTTON element. The BUTTON element is supposed to give you more flexibility in creating buttons. It is hoped the browsers will implement the BUTTON element in such a way that both text buttons and image buttons actually recess when clicked, the way most menu buttons do in normal desktop applications.

Button <BUTTON>	
Start Tag:	Required
Content:	Inline elements
End Tag:	Required
Attributes:	id, class, lang, dir, title, style: previously defined name: name to be associated with the data sent to the script (optional)
	value: value sent to the script (optional)
	type: submit, reset, or button
	disabled: for use with JavaScript and the Document Object Model

`tabindex`: a number assigning the tabbing order through the form

`accesskey`: shortcut key to access button for accessibility purposes

`events`: see Chapter 48

Why would you ever use the `BUTTON` element when you can create buttons in four other ways, including buttons with images on them? The `BUTTON` element is far more flexible than any of the other ways of creating buttons. Additionally, the `INPUT` element's variations of buttons doesn't actually depress on the page the way people expect buttons to depress when they are clicked. HTML 4 specifies browsers should support the `BUTTON` element by having a button take action when it is clicked.

The `BUTTON` element has several attributes, but you rarely need more than the type attribute. Defining a button with the `BUTTON` element is different from defining a button with the `INPUT` element because the `BUTTON` element takes content. It also requires an end tag. You include an image as the button in the `BUTTON` element by including the `IMG` element between the start tag and the end tag. You should also include text in the content so that if for some reason the image doesn't load, text is available to indicate what the button does.

Two examples of buttons created with the `BUTTON` element follow:

```
<BUTTON type="submit">Click here to submit!<IMG
src="images/submit.gif"></BUTTON>
<BUTTON type="button" onclick="ValidateForm()">Validate form
before submitting</BUTTON>
```

SELECT, OPTION, and OPTGROUP Elements

The standard drop-down list, known in HTML as the *select list,* is created with the `SELECT` element and the `OPTION` element. HTML 4 introduces the `OPTGROUP` element, which enables you to group `OPTION` elements so your standard drop-down list looks more like a directory listing than like the drop-down lists you are used to seeing, with a single, long listing of all the options.

Figure 21-1 shows two types of select lists. The first is the standard select list with a drop-down box. You can select one item from a list that can be as long as you wish. The second shows a select list that actually looks like a scrollable list. Notice eight lines are visible. In this list, you can choose more than one from the eight items. As of publication, none of the major browsers supported the `OPTGROUP` element, so you have to see how this is supported on your own desktop.

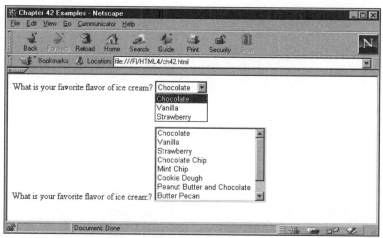

Figure 21-1: Two different types of select lists

SELECT element

The SELECT element is the structure in which you build a select list. A select list should have a name, but doesn't generally demand any of the other attributes available to it. A SELECT element must have at least one OPTION element.

Select <SELECT>

Start Tag:	Required
Content:	OPTGROUP, OPTION: elements text
End Tag:	Required
Attributes:	id, class, lang, dir, title, style: previously defined
	name: name associated with the value or values returned to the script
	size: if this is to be a scrollable list instead of a drop-down list, you must specify the number of rows to be visible with the size attribute
	multiple: Boolean value that indicates more than one value may be selected; must be used in conjunction with the size attribute
	disabled: for use with JavaScript and the DOM
	tabindex: indicates tabbing order in form; a number
	events: see Chapter 48

Two examples of the SELECT element in action appear later in this section.

OPTION element

For each item on the select list you want your visitors to be able to select, you need an instance of the OPTION element.

Option <OPTION>

Start Tag:	Required
Content:	Text
End Tag:	Optional
Attributes:	id, class, lang, dir, title, style: previously defined
	selected: indicates the drop-down list or scrollable list will begin with this item in focus or highlighted
	disabled: for use with JavaScript and the DOM
	label: to be sent as the value of this selection; should be used if the contents of the OPTION element are too long to be useful for processing
	value: the initial value of the choice; normally the same as the contents of the OPTION element

The OPTION element is straightforward. For each item you want in your drop-down list, you create an OPTION element. In the example in Figure 21-1, the following HTML was used to create the drop-down list.

```
What is your favorite flavor of ice cream?
<SELECT name="test1">
   <OPTION>Chocolate
   <OPTION>Vanilla
   <OPTION>Strawberry
</SELECT>
```

Using attributes

If one of the flavors had been called "Very Berry Razzamatazz Strawberry" and you didn't want to send all this information to the script, you use the following OPTION element (in addition to the previous ones).

```
<OPTION label="Strawberry">Very Berry Razzamatazz Strawberry
```

If you don't include a label attribute, the contents of the OPTION element will be sent as the value selected. Notice that even though an end tag is optional, it isn't generally used.

If you wanted the select list to start off with the word *Vanilla* in view, instead of just having the first OPTION element in the list in view, you could have used the selected attribute.

```
<OPTION selected>Vanilla
```

OPTGROUP element

The OPTGROUP, once it is fully implemented, will make select lists much more powerful and flexible. The OPTGROUP is intended to work like the drop-down menus you see at the top of most applications. It is a way of organizing your select lists.

Option Group <OPTGROUP>

Start Tag:	Required
Content:	OPTION elements
End Tag:	Required
Attributes:	id, class, lang, dir, title, style: previously defined
	disabled: for use with JavaScript and the DOM
	label: to appear in the select list as the title of this group

HTML 4 does not allow for nested OPTGROUP elements, but it won't be surprising to see the major browsers implement it anyway. Currently, none of the major browsers implement the OPTGROUP element.

Unlike the OPTION element, where the label attribute is optional and is used only if the contents of the element are too long to send and process, the label attribute on the OPTGROUP element is necessary if you want the group heading to appear in the list. Also, unlike the OPTION element, the visitor can't select the label of the OPTGROUP as the value to send to the script. The OPTGROUP only leads to a list of options. All the selectable options must be in OPTION elements.

For example, if you wanted to create a select list with the following groups:

"What is your favorite frozen dessert?"

Ice Cream

Chocolate
Vanilla
Strawberry
Chocolate Chip
Mint Chip
Cookie Dough
Peanut Butter and Chocolate

Sorbet

Raspberry
Lemon
Lime

Frozen Yogurt

Vanilla
Chocolate
Peanut Butter
Raspberry

The HTML would be:

```
What is your favorite frozen dessert?
<SELECT name="test3" multiple size="8">
   <OPTGROUP label="Ice Cream">
        <OPTION>Chocolate
        <OPTION>Vanilla
        <OPTION>Strawberry
        <OPTION>Chocolate Chip
        <OPTION>Mint Chip
        <OPTION>Cookie Dough
        <OPTION>Peanut Butter and Chocolate
   </OPTGROUP>
   <OPTGROUP label="Sorbet">
        <OPTION>Raspberry
        <OPTION>Lemon
        <OPTION>Lime
   </OPTGROUP>
   <OPTGROUP label="Frozen Yogurt">
        <OPTION>Vanilla
        <OPTION>Chocolate
        <OPTION>Peanut Butter
        <OPTION>Raspberry
   </OPTGROUP>
</SELECT>
```

TEXTAREA Element

The TEXTAREA element is a way to accept free-form text from your visitors. If you want to accept suggestions or other types of lengthy text, this is the control to use.

Text Area <TEXTAREA>

Start Tag: Required

Content: Initial text to appear in TEXTAREA

End Tag: Required

Attributes: id, class, lang, dir, title, style: previously defined

name: name associated with the value or values returned to the script

rows: number of rows of text permitted

cols: number of columns of text visible

disabled: for use with JavaScript and the DOM

readonly: shows contents of TEXTAREA element, but doesn't allow editing tabindex: number indicating tab order in form

accesskey: shortcut key for accessibility

events: see Chapter 48

Text areas are easy to create. To define one that has 4 visible rows that are 60 columns wide, with the initial text "Enter your comments here," you would use the following HTML:

```
<TEXTAREA name="comments1" rows="4" cols="60">Enter your
comments here.</TEXTAREA>
```

LABEL Element

The LABEL element enables you to attach text to the control. When you create most form controls, such as text fields, select lists, or checkboxes, there is some text, such as a question, that isn't attached in any way to the actual control that answers that question.

Why would you want to attach text to a control? So site visitors can click the text, as well as the control (such as a tiny checkbox). The text associated with a control may not be immediately adjacent to a control—when using tables for formatting, for example, associating text with a control is a little bit tricky.

Label <LABEL>	
Start Tag:	Required
Content:	Text
End Tag:	Required
Attributes:	id, class, lang, dir, title, style: previously defined
	for: indicates the ID value of the control with which it is associated
	accesskey: shortcut key for accessibility
	events: see Chapter 48

The LABEL element (not to be confused with the label attribute of the OPTION and OPTGROUP elements) is attached to the text you want associated with a control. Here are the steps involved in assigning text to a control:

1. Use the id attribute of the form control to assign an ID to the form field.

2. Place the text you want associated with the form control within a LABEL element.

3. Assign the for attribute of the LABEL element to match the value of the id in the form control.

Here is a relatively complex example using tables for formatting a form.

```
<FORM action="do-something.cgi" method="post">
<TABLE>
<TR>
<TD align="right"><LABEL for="fname">Please enter your first
name</LABEL>
<TD><INPUT type="text" name="first_name" id="fname">
<TR>
<TD align="right"><LABEL for="lname">Please enter your last
name</LABEL>
<TD><INPUT type="text" name="last_name" id="lname">
<TR>
<TD align="right"><LABEL for="spam">May we sell your personal
data to spammers?</LABEL>
<TD><INPUT type="checkbox" name="spam" value="yes" id="spam">
<TR>
<TD align="right"><LABEL for="comments">Please enter any
comments you have about our site</LABEL>
<TD><TEXTAREA name="comments" id="comments" rows="4"
columns="40">Enter your comments here</TEXTAREA>
<TR>
<TD><INPUT type="submit" value="Send this now">
<INPUT type="reset" value="Clear">
</TABLE>
</FORM>
```

Notice that the id and the name can be the same, but that isn't always necessary.

FIELDSET and LEGEND Elements

The FIELDSET and LEGEND elements work together. The FIELDSET is strictly a structural element; its presence or absence doesn't affect the rendering of your page. The LEGEND element is an added convenience for visitors "seeing" your Web page with their ears.

Fieldset <FIELDSET>

Start Tag:	Required
Content:	LEGEND element elements
End Tag:	Required
Attributes:	id, class, lang, dir, title, style: previously defined

Legend `<LEGEND>`

Start Tag:	Required
Content:	Text of the legend
End Tag:	Required
Attributes:	`id`, `class`, `lang`, `dir`, `title`, `style`: previously defined
	`accesskey`: shortcut key for accessibility

Neither of these elements would be difficult to implement. The `FIELDSET` element should surround related fields so they are grouped. The `LEGEND` element immediately follows the `FIELDSET` element with a descriptive title for the `FIELDSET`.

Form Processing Options

Today, more options for processing your data are on the server than this book can cover. Just a few of the options available to you include:

✦ **Common Gateway Interface Scripts (CGI scripts).** This is the oldest type of server-side processing. You can write your program/script in Perl or C, or by using a shell script. This is still the most common type of script running on UNIX servers.

✦ **Server-side JavaScript.** JavaScript is a widely known scripting language. It can, in fact, be used for full-scale, object-oriented programs. Netscape has introduced servers that include server-side JavaScript processing.

✦ **Server-side Java.** Java has almost caught up with the hype associated with it when it was first introduced. You can use Java on your server to perform many form-processing functions. If you know Java, and if your Web server supports server-side Java (Microsoft Internet Information Server [IIS] does not), then this is a good option. If you don't know Java, much easier ways exist to accomplish server-side processing of forms.

✦ **Cold Fusion.** Cold Fusion, by Allaire, is the easiest way to add server-side processing to your pages. In only minutes, you can have a form on your page that collects data into a database and sends out confirmation mail. New features are constantly being added to this product to make it even more useful.

✦ **Active Server Pages (ASP).** ASP was created by Microsoft, and can be created using JavaScript, PERL, and C++, but true ASP is done using VBScript. Your server must be running the Microsoft IIS operating system, version 3.0 or higher, and then implementing ASP on your site is simple. Front Page 98, the Microsoft Web authoring tool, makes this even easier.

Dealing with Form Data

What is the best way to handle form data? With a script or program. Ideally, you will know how you are planning to use each piece of data you request before you request it. Then, you will have a program or script in place that acts on the data when you first publish your form.

When you create your form, you need to give some thought to how each piece of returned data will be used. If you don't plan to look at or respond to comments, don't ask for them. You will probably find that if you have multiple-word responses to questions in select lists, working with shortened versions of these responses using the label attribute in the OPTION element will be easier, as shown here:

```
<OPTION label="girl colors">Red, pink, fuchsia, yellow, or
orange
```

Where the question might have been: "In what colors do you prefer to dress your daughter?"

If you make use of checkboxes or radio buttons, remember that a value is only sent when the checkbox or radio button is checked. This means even from a long set of checkboxes, it is possible that no values will be returned. Your script must be able to deal with the absence of data.

What if you don't know how to write a script, but you still want to collect data? You can use a mailto: script.

Mailto:

With your e-mail address as the action of the script, mailto: sends the field names (as set by you in the name attributes) and their values to you via e-mail. The problem with this technique is, while you have the data, you don't have the data in any particularly useful form. All that is returned to you is a list with each line containing a field name and the value entered for that field.

```
last_name = Miller
first_name = John
email = miller@somewhere.org
color = blue
flavor = Mint Chip
music = Meatloaf
```

Even worse than having the data returned in a difficult-to-process format, the mailto: script doesn't always return the fields in the order they were completed.

For these reasons, `mailto:` should be used only when you really do plan for the data to go no further than your mailbox.

From Here

Jump to Chapter 45 and learn about accessing external databases.

Proceed to Chapter 22 and learn about using frames

Summary

Forms enable you to take input from your site visitor for processing on your server. If you want to add a site search, sell anything, or take a survey, you must learn how to put form fields on your page. A lot of flexibility exists in creating forms. Also, HTML 4 specifies some new elements, which give you more control over buttons and enable you to group your fields. And more accessibility features are in HTML 4, such as the `tabindex` attribute and the `accesskey` attribute.

The most important thing to know about forms is that you must have plans for processing your data; otherwise you are wasting your visitors' time in collecting data. Before you put up a form, be sure you have plans to use the data wisely.

✦   ✦   ✦

Creating Frames

Frames are an exciting, though controversial, way to enhance the navigational possibilities of your page. Frames give you an interesting kind of control over the layout of your site because parts of your page can remain static, while other parts change. This chapter explains how frames work, why they are controversial, and how best to use them. Finally, at the end of this chapter is a section about a newcomer to frames, the inline frame, which adds frames to your site in a way that doesn't carry all the liabilities of traditional frames.

Introducing Frames

Frames are a way of dividing your browser window so it can hold more than one logical page. When you create a framed site, the page has a URL, and then each frame within the page has its own URL. Because each frame within a framed site has its own URL, you can load other pages into only a part of your browser, keeping the rest of your frames static.

Figure 22-1 shows one way of dividing your site using frames. This is a common way. At the top, in the banner, you put the site name, logo, ads, and so on. In the lower-left frame, the navigational tools (buttons, a table, or text) are placed. Finally, the content goes in the main frame. The content can change, but banner and navigational tools frames stay the same.

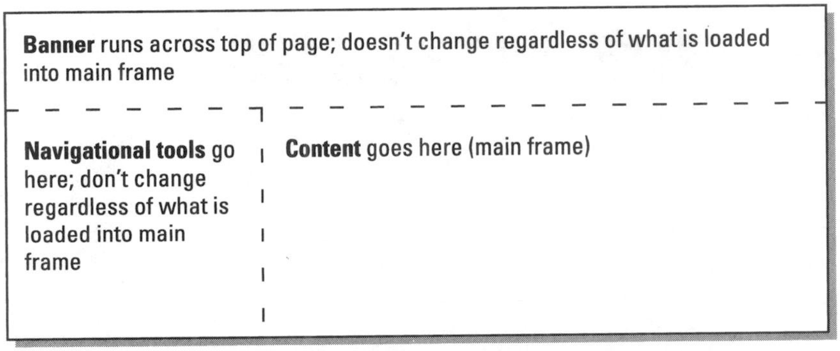

Figure 22-1: Sample layout for a framed site

Developing the Master Frame Document

So how does the browser know it needs to load more than one URL and where to put each one? You create a master frame document. Instead of a BODY element, you create a FRAMESET element or, as in the previous example, nested FRAMESET elements.

The master frame document is a standard HTML document, but there is no BODY element. Instead, there is a HEAD (and you should include all the usual HEAD information, including META elements and a TITLE element), and a FRAMESET element. The FRAMESET element is defined as follows:

Frameset <FRAMESET>

Start Tag:	Required
Content:	FRAMESET, FRAME, and NOFRAMES elements
End Tag:	Required
Attributes:	id, class, title, style: defined previously

rows: used to indicate the widths of the rows in order from top to bottom; the default is 100%, meaning one row; you can specify the widths in pixels, a percentage of the browser window, or relative width

cols: used to indicate the widths of the columns in order from left to right; the default is 100%, meaning one column; you can specify the widths in pixels, a percentage of the canvas, or relative width

events: defined in Chapter 48

Rows only

If you define only rows, you will have a framed document that looks like Figure 22-2.

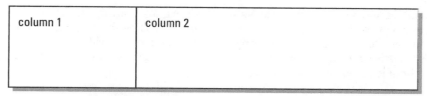

Figure 22-2: A framed page with two rows

The widths of the rows in Figure 22-2 would be determined by the values you specify in the rows attribute. The following FRAMESET shows using a percentage to indicate the size (pixels and relative sizes are discussed in the "Columns Only" section).

```
<FRAMESET rows="15%, 85%">
</FRAMESET>
```

Columns only

Or, you might want to define a framed document with only columns, as in Figure 22-3.

Figure 22-3: A framed page with two columns

The widths of the columns in Figure 22-3 would be determined by the values you specify in the cols attribute. The following FRAMESET might have created Figure 22-3. The number 200 indicates the number of pixels (which might be dictated by the width of a graphic you are including in that column). The asterisk (*) tells the browser to use the rest of the space for the second column.

```
<FRAMESET cols="200, *">
</FRAMESET>
```

Both rows and columns

If you define both rows and columns, you end up with a grid-like framed document. Figure 22-4 is one example of a framed document with both rows and columns.

Figure 22-4: A framed document with both rows and columns

Figure 22-4 might have been created with the following HTML:

```
<FRAMESET cols="200, *" rows="1*, 5*">
</FRAMESET>
```

In the previous definition, the first column will be 200 pixels wide, regardless of how wide the page is. The second column will be the rest of the page. The first row will be one part of the height of the page; the second column will be five parts of the height of the page. The browser will calculate that the page must be divided into six parts and assigned to the rows in that proportion. The 1*, and 5* mean 1 part and 5 parts, respectively.

Relative versus Absolute widths and heights. You can define cols and rows using both relative and absolute measurements. If you use absolute measurements, you need to know exactly how many pixels you want for the width or height. If you use relative measurement, you specify the percentage or the proportion of the browser window you want the frame to fill.

A warning is in order about using absolute values for frame widths. If you specify an absolute column width and visitors to your site don't have their browser in full-screen mode, they might only see the left-hand column and not even realize a right-hand column (or more than one) exists. If possible, use relative values for column widths and row heights.

Nested FRAMESETs

What if you want to create a framed document, like the example in Figure 22-1? After all, that is probably the most common model on the Web today. Use nested FRAMESETs. The outer FRAMESET will define the rows. The inner FRAMESET divides the second row into two columns.

```
<FRAMESET rows="20%, 80%">
        ... FRAME element for first row ...
        <FRAMESET cols="25%, 75%">
            ... FRAME element for first column ...
            ... FRAME element for second column ...
        </FRAMESET>
</FRAMESET>
```

Targets

The browser needs to know three things. First, how much space you want it to allo-cate for each of your frames. You have already told it this with the FRAMESET ele-ment. Second, how you want to refer to each of those frames: as target names. And third, how to populate each of those frames initially.

With the FRAME element, one of the attributes is name. With the name, you specify how you want to refer to the frame. This is called the *target name* of the frame. You can direct other links into this target. For example, if you have navigational tools in one frame, you can have the destination of those links load into your main frame by specifying the target attribute on the A element.

Consider the following master frame document:

```
<HTML>
<HEAD>
  <TITLE>This is the title of my site</TITLE>
  ... lots of META elements here ...
</HEAD>
<FRAMESET rows="200, *">
  <!-- creates first row as banner -->
  <FRAME name="banner" src="banner1.html">
  <FRAMESET cols="25%, 75%">
      <!-- creates column on left for navigational tools -->
      <FRAME name="navigate" src="navigational-tools.html">
      <!-- creates main frame for content -->
      <FRAME name="main" src="home.html">
  </FRAMESET>
</FRAMESET>
</HTML>
```

Now, look at a possible version of navigational-tools.html, the file containing the navigation buttons (in this case text) and the links. Notice how the A element for each of the links includes a target attribute directing the results of the link to load into the main frame.

```
<HTML>
<HEAD>
  ... TITLE and META elements here ...
</HEAD>
```

```
<BODY>
  <A href="products.html" target="main">Products and
Solutions</A>
  <A href="custsvc.html" target="main">Customer Service</A>
  <A href="white.html" target="main">White Papers</A>
  <A href="jobs.html" target="main">Job Postings</A>
</BODY>
</HTML>
```

You must start your `target` names with letters. After that, you can use any of the regular, acceptable characters. Some `target` names begin with underscore (_). These are the reserved `target` names HTML makes available to help you with your frames. Using reserved names gives you a way to reference your frames relatively. Even if you change the `target` names of your frames, the reserved names still work.

✦ **blank.** This causes the results of the link to be loaded into a new browser window. Unless the document referred to by the src attribute is a master frame document, the new page won't use frames.

✦ **self.** This causes the results of the link to be loaded into the same frame as the A element, which created the link. In the previous example, you would use the _self target for links you have within the main frame.

✦ **parent.** This causes the results of the link to be loaded into the FRAMESET parent of the current frame. If there is no FRAMESET parent, the results of the link are loaded into the same frame.

✦ **top.** This causes the results of the link to be loaded into the full browser window, canceling frames. When would you want to use this? If you have a "back to home" link on the bottom of your main screen, you'd want it to point to the master frame document with a target of _top. This way, you wouldn't end up with the problem of unintentionally nested frames.

Creating FRAMEs

Finally, having told the browser how much space to allocate for each frame and having given each frame a name, you need to tell the browser what to put into each frame. You do this with the FRAME element. You've already seen the FRAME element at work.

Frame `<FRAME>`

Start Tag: Required

Content: Empty

End Tag: Forbidden

Attributes: id, class, title, style

name: used to indicate the name to be associated with this frame (the target name)

src: used to specify what should initially be loaded into this frame

longdesc: specifies a link to a longer frame description using the title attribute, and may be particularly useful for nonvisual user agents.

frameborder: tells browser to draw a border around this frame (1, the default value), or not to draw a border (0); if the adjoining frame has a frameborder, it will appear between the unbordered frame and the bordered frame

marginwidth: width of margin in pixels (margin between frame contents and borders on sides)

marginheight: height of margin in pixels (margin between frame contents and borders on top and bottom)

noresize: Boolean attribute (meaning if you want to indicate noresize, you just include the attribute without a value) that tells the browser this frame is not resizable by the visitor

scrolling: There are three values for this attribute: yes, no, and auto. Choose no if you know the contents of the frame will always fit into the frame (say you have column width and row height set in pixels to fit the image in the frame). Choose yes if you want there always to be a scroll bar on the side of this frame. Choose auto if you want the browser only to display a scroll bar if the content doesn't fit into the frame.

You must define a FRAME element for each frame you want to create. The FRAMESET element tells the browser how many frames and how much space to give them. The FRAME element names each frame and gives it an initial value.

When defining FRAMEs, you can specify URLs using either relative or absolute file names. Just as with any other reference element (A or IMG), you can specify both local and remote file names. It is probably better to refer to local file names with relative file names. Remote file names require fully qualified URLs.

Enhancing Navigability

Frames are a great way to ensure that visitors always have navigational tools right on the screen where they can see them. Right? Not necessarily. One thing you should be cautious about is creating a page you plan to use only in the main frame, when a search engine might index it as a stand-alone page. Why is this a problem?

Because when visitors come to that page from a search engine, they have no way to get to the rest of your site. Does this mean you need to put navigational tools on every page? Not necessarily. What you should have on every page is a link back to the front page of your site. That link must have a target of _top to work properly.

If you don't include a target of _top, you will have a problem with your site self-nesting when anyone clicks that link if the main page is actually part of the framed site.

If your site looks like Figure 22-5, and someone clicks the [Go to Home Page] link you rightly have at the bottom of every page, but you forget the target="_top" attribute-value pair in your link, visitors get the results shown in Figure 22-6.

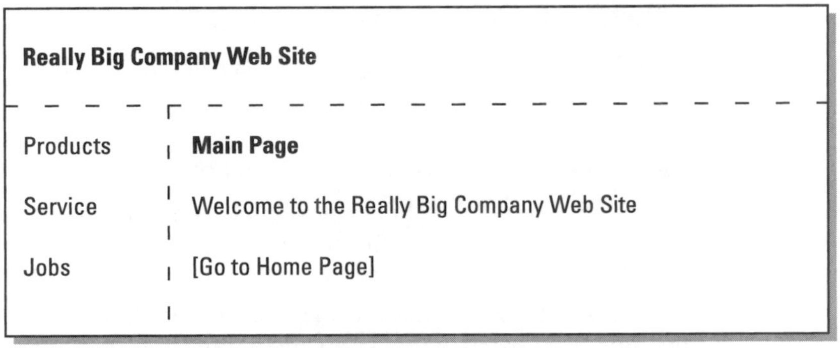

Really Big Company Web Site

Products | **Main Page**

Service | Welcome to the Really Big Company Web Site

Jobs | [Go to Home Page]

Figure 22-5: Your framed site

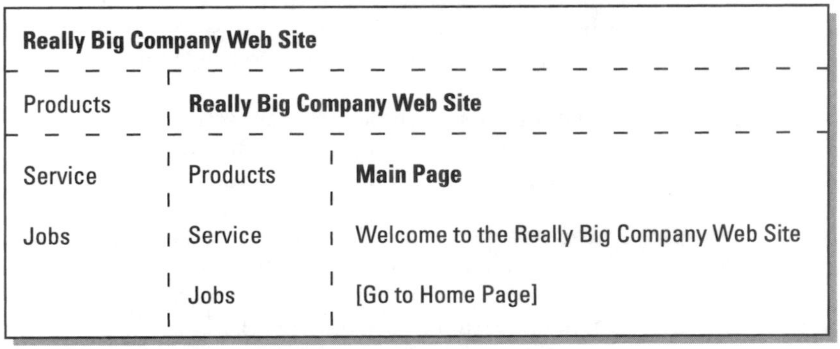

Really Big Company Web Site

Products | **Really Big Company Web Site**

Service | Products | **Main Page**

Jobs | Service | Welcome to the Really Big Company Web Site

Jobs | [Go to Home Page]

Figure 22-6: Your framed site with unintentional nesting

NOFRAMES

You can place one more element in your FRAMESET element. This is the NOFRAMES element. The NOFRAMES element is one you should include in the outermost FRAMESET, after you have defined all your other FRAMESETs and FRAMEs. NOFRAMES contains the page you want your visitors to get if their browsers don't support frames, or if their browsers support frames but are configured not to display frames. It could be as simple as a message telling them to upgrade their browsers or enable frames to see your site properly.

Note If you do use the NOFRAMES element, and you should, be sure the text you include is something you wouldn't mind seeing on a Search Engine Results page. Search engines are notorious for using this text as your synopsis when indexing a site. This won't help attract visitors to your site.

```
<NOFRAMES>
Over the Web provides robust, turn-key modules for your
professional Web site.  The Over the Web site is only
accessible with a frames-capable browser. Please upgrade your
browser at one of the following locations:<BR>
<UL>
<LI><A href="http://www.netscape.com/">Netscape
Communications</A>
<LI><A href="http://www.microsoft.com/ie">Microsoft</A>
<LI><A href="http://www.aol.com">America Online</A>
</UL>
</NOFRAMES>
```

More likely, it will be the front page for the scaled-down version of your site that doesn't require frames. It's up to you to decide if the expense is justified to maintain a non-frames version of your site.

No frames <NOFRAMES>

Start Tag:	Required
Content:	HTML for non-frames page
End Tag:	Required
Attributes:	id, class, title, style, lang, dir

Adding Inline Frames (IFRAMEs)

Inline frames give you the best of both worlds. They provide many of the benefits of frames without the disadvantage of having navigation in more than one frame. Inline frames do not look like frames at all. No border separates an inline frame from the rest of the page. Inline frames also do not have the capability of independent scrolling.

An inline frame is like a server-side include. You refer to the HTML file you want to appear in the inline frame, and when the page is rendered, it appears as if the inline frame were part of the main HTML document.

Definition

Server-side include. A *server-side include* is a clever way to reuse HTML. If all your pages take advantage of the same header and footer, you can put the header HTML and the footer HTML into separate HTML files and *call* them from all your documents. The syntax of using a server-side include varies from Web server to Web server, so check with your systems administrator if you want to use these. When the page is rendered in the browser, the server-side include HTML (the HTML in the separate file) appears in the main HTML document as if it were typed there. The advantage of using a server-side include is that you can change only the HTML in the server-side include and have it reflected on every page that calls the server-side include.

The principal disadvantage of using inline frames is they are not well supported by the browsers in use. Inline frames are a recent addition to the HTML elements. Currently, only Internet Explorer 4 and newer browsers support inline frames. Inline frames and <IFRAME> are identical. Browsers that don't support IFRAME, or have IFRAME support turned off, will display everything contained between the <IFRAME> tag and the ending </IFRAME> tag in the current window. Those browsers with IFRAME support will link to the SRC attribute for the URL of the page to display in the inline frame, and ignore text contained in the IFRAME tags.

Inline <INLINE>

Start Tag: Required

Content: Empty

End Tag: Required

Attributes: id, class, title, style, longdesc

name: name of this element; useful for scripting

src: required; the URL of the page you want inserted into the inline frame

frameborder: defaults to "1"; set to "0" if you don't want a border

marginwidth: width of margin in pixels for both sides

marginheight: height of margin in pixels for top and bottom

scrolling: yes, no, or auto; you only need to worry about this if you set the height and width to be smaller than the known contents of the URL

height: height of the inline frame in pixels

width: width of the inline frame in pixels

align: deprecated; used to specify alignment on the page

From Here

Jump to Chapter 33 to learn about CSS positioning options.

Proceed to Chapter 23 to learn more about grouping elements with DIV and SPAN.

Summary

In this chapter you learned about frames. You learned how framed documents work — with a master frame document, targets, and frames. You learned how to define horizontal frames, vertical frames, or some combination of both. This chapter also discussed how your screen gets divided: using absolute measurements, per-centages, or fractions of the screen. You learned about naming your frames, directing the results of links into specific frames (targets), and reserved target names. This chapter also covered how to define the initial values of your frames.

One of the controversial aspects of frames is that all browsers don't support them. Using the NOFRAMES element, you learned how you can make this problem transparent to your site visitors. Finally, you learned about inline frames and how they help you get around some of the drawbacks of using traditional frames.

✦ ✦ ✦

Grouping Elements with DIV and SPAN

This chapter discusses DIV and SPAN. In Chapters 15 and 17 you learned how to group block-level and inline elements with DIV and SPAN. In Chapter 25 you learn more about defining classes within style sheets. Here you get in-depth coverage of DIV, SPAN, and CLASS.

What Is CLASS?

Classes enable you to assign a name to a group of formatting declarations. This enables you to create a specific class, such as intro, and reuse it several times without retyping. Class is an attribute of DIV, SPAN, and other elements. For example, if you always want your first paragraphs to have the same appearance on your Web page, you can define a paragraph intro style:

```
<HTML>
<HEAD>
<STYLE TYPE="text/css">
<!--
        P.intro {background:lime}
-->
</STYLE>
</HEAD>
```

You can then reference the style:

```
</HEAD>
<BODY>
```

```
<P CLASS=intro> This is the first sentence of this simple
example. Here is the first supporting sentence. This is the
second supporting sentence. </P>
<P> This is the next paragraph. It's not introductory so it
doesn't use the class. </P>
</BODY>
</HTML>
```

The output of this example (see Figure 23-1) displays the first paragraph with a lime background. The class makes changing the appearance of the intro paragraphs easy because you only need to change the definition of the class in one place, not within each intro paragraph.

Figure 23-1: The results of the previous example in Netscape

 Tip   Classes may be assigned anywhere a declaration can be used, such as where block and inline elements are defined using the DIV and SPAN elements.

Introducing DIV

DIV stands for *logical DIVision*. This tag is often used to divide a Web page into sections. Each section has its own style. The DIV element is used to mark up divisions in a document. DIV is called a block-level element because you use it to affect a complete block of text. It can enclose headers, paragraphs, tables and other block-level elements, and any combination of these elements. Therefore you can, for example, use the DIV element to mark up both headers and paragraphs at the same time.

Tip   DIV tags are ideal for dividing your Web pages into themes (thematic sections).

As part of the DIV element, you include either declarations or a class name to define the appearance of the elements contained in your DIV block.

Introducing SPAN

If you only want to apply styles to a few words or letters, you use the SPAN element. You can think of the SPAN element as spanning a few words or characters. You would use the SPAN element in the same way as the DIV element, except that you use the word SPAN instead of the word DIV.

Note   You use DIV and SPAN instead of applying a style directly to an element when you wish to apply the style to more than one element or less than one element, respectively.

As part of the SPAN element, you include either declarations or a class name to define the appearance of the words or characters contained in your SPAN block.

Here is an example of DIV, SPAN, and CLASS at work:

```
<HTML>
<HEAD>
<STYLE TYPE="text/css">
<!--
        SPAN.big {color:green; background:black; font:20pt
Helvetica}
-->
</STYLE>
</HEAD>

<BODY>
<P STYLE="color:red; background:black; font:14pt Helvetica">
You can apply styles to a single paragraph. This paragraph
displays with red lettering on a black background. The font is
14-point Helvetica. It gets its style attributes from the
declarations after STYLE=.</P>
<P STYLE="color:red; background:black; font:14pt Helvetica"> To
start another paragraph of the same style without using a class
you need to repeat all of the declarations.</P>
```

```
<DIV STYLE="color:yellow; background:black; font:14pt
Helvetica">
<P> This paragraph appears in yellow lettering on a black
background. The font is 14-point Helvetica.</P>
This text is also inside of the DIV block, so it displays in
yellow on black 14-point Helvetica too.
</DIV>
This text displays normally, except for the words <SPAN CLASS=
big>big</SPAN> and <SPAN CLASS=big>green</SPAN>, which are
within two SPAN blocks that use the class big. The class big
specifies that the words big and green display as green
20-point Helvetica on a black background.
</BODY>
</HTML>
```

In the DIV STYLE example block, the first two sentences display in a Web browser as text highlighted in black, with a text color of yellow and a font size of 14.

From Here

 Jump to Chapter 25 to start learning about Cascading Style Sheets.

Turn to Chapter 24 to start testing and validating your HTML.

Summary

In this chapter you learned the basics of CLASS, DIV, and SPAN. Now you can apply separate formatting declarations from characters to even multiple paragraphs.

✦   ✦   ✦

Testing and Validating Your HTML

With the structure of your page in place, you need to make sure it runs on all browsers. This chapter tells you how to make sure that your HTML is valid and renders properly. You will also discover common HTML mistakes, how to test your HTML, and how to validate your HTML on the Web using free software.

Watch for These Common HTML Mistakes

If you manage to avoid these common HTML mistakes, you have completed 80 percent of the steps needed for a valid HTML page. The most common HTML mistakes are

+ **Failing to complete a tag.** Do all your elements have the necessary end tags? This element is particularly important for inline elements, such as bold and italics.

+ **Failing to include a forward slash (/) in an end tag.** You may think you included an end tag, but the browser may see another start tag instead. Your browser isn't smart enough to figure out that the second occurrence of <B> in your paragraph should have been </B>.

+ **Failing to close a comment.** If you fail to close a comment, everything after the comment's start tag disappears from your screen.

+ **Improper nesting of tags.** This element won't always be a problem, but as more elements are added to HTML, browsers will get pickier. From now on, only publish pages with proper nesting so you won't have to fix those pages later.

✦ **Missing end quotation marks.** This mistake is tough to catch. If you don't close your quotation marks carefully, your browser thinks that the URL is another element.

Testing Your HTML

Check your HTML as you go by using an HTML editor that uses tag coloring. If you can see the color of your tags, you can tell whether you have completed all your tags and comments. After getting comfortable with a tag-coloring HTML editor, you will find it invaluable.

Cross-Reference   Chapter 8 introduced several HTML editors.

To test your HTML code, load your page into your browser. Just because your page looks great in your browser doesn't mean it looks great in every browser, however. Testing your HTML requires adherence to some guidelines. If you publish your page for access by anyone with any kind of browser from any platform, you want make sure it works properly for each configuration. Start with the checklist in Table 24-1.

Table 24-1
Guidelines for Testing Your HTML

Test from the most recent version of:
❏ Netscape Navigator
❏ Internet Explorer
❏ The AOL browser

Test from the previous version of:
❏ Netscape Navigator
❏ Internet Explorer
❏ The AOL browser

Test from all platforms:
❏ Windows 95/98/00/NT
❏ Windows 3.1
❏ Mac O/S
❏ UNIX platforms

Test with screen resolution set to:
❑ 640×480
❑ 800×600
❑ 1024×768

If your server is Windows NT/2000, test from a machine in which you are logged on as another user, so that the security information is not passed through.

Why You Should Validate

Because you can't catch everything and your page's appearance will vary in different browsers, you should also validate your HTML.

What is validating?

Validating submits your HTML to rules-checking. You can validate your HTML with software residing on your computer or the Web. When you validate your HTML, the validator returns listings of all the places in your page where your HTML does not comply to its rules. Many validators are available; if you build lots of pages, you'll probably want to purchase one that sits on your desktop. If you own an HTML editor, it may come with its own internal validator.

Definition

Validating. Checking your HTML with software to identify where you have failed to close tags, improperly nested tags, and broken other syntax rules that may affect how your page renders; also sometimes making sure that your site complies with the specifications for speech-synthesizing sites.

Why validate?

Although you create your page carefully, you should expect some mistakes to occur. HTML validating can help you

1. Find blatant HTML errors (such as the errors listed in the section, "Watch for These Common HTML Mistakes," found earlier in this chapter). Validating also finds misspellings in tags or attributes.

2. Find out whether your page complies with your rules.

3. Find out if any parts of your page are difficult to render in speech-synthesizing browsers or Braille browsers.

4. Find out whether your page works with all major browsers.

Validating Your HTML

Many free validation services are available on the Web. Some of these free validators check your HTML syntax, while other support HTML 4.0's hexadecimal character references. One site where you can immediately validate your HTML, instead of downloading a Perl script, is the W3C's validator (see Figure 24-1). Although the service is a bit verbose, it not only points out problems with your HTML but also suggests corrections (such as entity numbers).

You can find the W3C's validator on their Web site at http://validator.w3.org/.

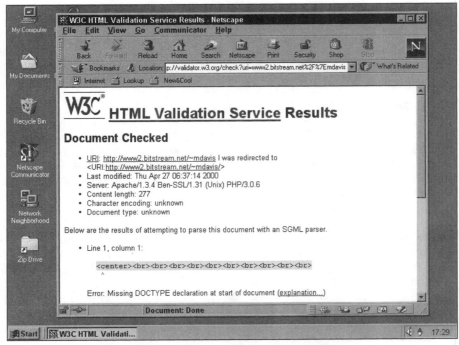

Figure 24-1: The W3C HTML validator gives helpful, if verbose, results.

What should you expect from HTML validation? (Validation may be built into your HTML editor, so you may not have to go too far to find out whether your code is compliant.) The following list describes some expected services:

✦ A list of errors in your HTML

✦ A list of any open quotes without closure

✦ A list of nesting problems (usually listed as warnings, not as errors)

✦ A list of any place you used characters instead of entities (such as putting a >
in your document)

Validating Your CSS

When you use a Cascading Style Sheet, there is less room for error in your plain
HTML code. There doesn't seem to be much difference between validating your CSS
and validating your Web page.

Why would you want to validate your CSS? Well, mostly for the same reasons you
would validate your Web page. If you don't validate your CSS code, you run the risk
of your page not displaying as you intend on different browsers. There are com-
plaints about bugs in browsers, when in reality the problem is probably caused by
an incorrect CSS syntax that another browser accommodates, despite being incorrect. Internet Explorer is particularly forgiving when it comes to invalid style sheets.
If you usually test your Web pages with IE, you might get some surprises when you
view the page in another browser that supports CSS.

The most common example is leaving units off values. For example the following
rule is invalid CSS. Browsers should ignore it.

```
H1 {margin-left: 12}
```

This specifies that the left margin for <H1> elements should be 12, but 12 what? It
isn't specified; thus, this is invalid, and should be ignored. Netscape ignores it, but
Internet Explorer eagerly treats this as 12 pixels. Often HTML writers consider
Netscape buggy, when in fact it is behaving correctly by following the standard.

Short of knowing the specification, how can we ensure that our style sheets are
valid? Validate them! There are a couple of ways to validate your CSS pages. There
are downloadable validators, which run on your computer; validators built in to
HTML editors; and finally, online validators that allow you to enter your URL, or
paste your page into them.

There are two popular online validators that will help ensure that your CSS is valid,
and will warn you about problems. Just as in validating your HTML, the W3C Web
page is invaluable. The two validators can be found at

✦ http://jigsaw.w3.org/css-validator/

✦ http://htmlhelp.org/tools/csscheck/

To use these sites, go to the page and enter the URL you want validated.

Different ways of validating your CSS

There are three levels of validation: strict, loose, and frameset. The strict variant excludes all presentational markup (such as <font> elements), while loose (or transitional), includes these elements. Frameset does what its name implies, which is including support for frames.

You should always try for strict validation. Then you'll be ready for future iterations of HTML. Depending on the validator you use, the approach is slightly different.

First, you need a way of telling the validator which DTD you are validating against. You do this by adding a link above the head of your HTML document. Examples follow for the three levels.

Strict

```
<!DOCTYPE HTML PUBLIC "-//W3C//DTD HTML 4.01//EN" "http://www.
w3.org/TR/html4/strict.dtd">
```

Loose

```
<!DOCTYPE HTML PUBLIC "-//W3C//DTD HTML 4.01 Transitional//EN"
"http://www.w3.org/TR/html4/loose.dtd">
```

Frameset

```
<!DOCTYPE HTML PUBLIC "-//W3C//DTD HTML 4.01 Frameset//EN"
"http://www.w3.org/TR/html4/frameset.dtd">
```

Use the strict DTD if your page contains no presentational markup, and the frameset DTD if your pages has frames; otherwise go ahead and use the loose DTD. But, as recommended above, for the most accurate validation, the strict level should be used most of the time.

After you enter the DTD information in your HTML page, you can copy your page and go to http://htmlhelp.org/tools/validator/. Paste your code into the validator and it will return errors and/or warnings if they are found.

Assessing Usability

You have a beautifully designed page that now — thanks to the time you took to validate the HTML — complies with the DTD. But how long does it take to download? Will it work on every browser? How will speech-synthesizing browsers handle it?

Part of the impetus of the HTML 4 push for moving formatting out of the page is to increase the distribution of Web sites to nontraditional browsers, such as speech-synthesizing browsers and Braille browsers.

A wonderful service available on the Web, called Bobby (www.cast.org/bobby/), reviews your HTML just like a validator. Instead of returning a list of errors, however, it returns a list of places where you can make changes to your page to increase its usability by nontraditional browsers (see Figure 24-2). Bobby can also point out any rendering problems for your page in different browsers. Finally, Bobby calculates your page's download time along with other download statistics.

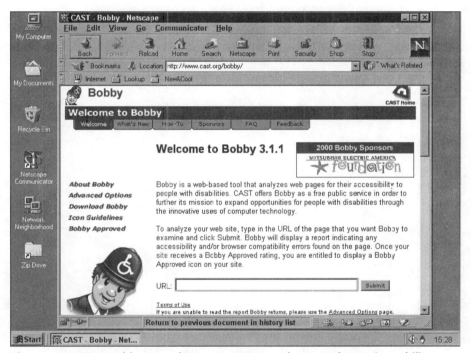

Figure 24-2: Use Bobby to evaluate your HTML and your Web page's usability.

From Here

Cross-Reference Jump to Chapter 44 to learn about delivering content via push technologies.

Proceed to Chapter 25 and dive into Cascading Style Sheets (CSS).

Summary

This chapter covered the fundamentals of testing and validating your HTML. You learned about resources for validating your HTML on the Web. You learned the most common HTML mistakes, how to check and test your HTML, and why you should validate. You also learned about assessing the usability of your HTML with the Bobby service.

✦   ✦   ✦

Enhancing Presentation with Cascading Style Sheets

Introducing Cascading Style Sheets

Perhaps the most exciting part of HTML 4 is its complete support for cascading style sheets. Style sheets completely change the model of HTML for the better. This chapter explains why you need style sheets (even if you are still a little bit afraid of them) and what they can do. It also explains the cascading model of the style sheets and your choices for creating style information to associate with your page. You also get to see a few more examples of the basic meat-and-potatoes kind of style sheet you will get used to creating or modifying. Finally, you learn about browser-compatibility issues related to style sheets.

Why Style Sheets Are Needed

The earlier chapters in this book alluded to all the great things style sheets can do so many times that, if you haven't flipped to this chapter to read ahead at least once, it's safe to say you are a disciplined individual. Once you understand why you need style sheets, you'll be hard-pressed to believe you ever lived without them.

On the Web, there is a lot of hype about a lot of things. Rarely does any product or technology live up to the hype it engenders. *Cascading style sheets* (CSS) are one of those rare technologies.

HTML 3.2, with all its built-in formatting elements and attributes, made it a nightmare to create pages and even worse to maintain them. Web developers managing sites with hundreds or even thousands of pages had to face this problem daily.

Style sheets directly address the problem of formatting information cluttering up your pages. With style sheets, all formatting information moves from the HTML document to a style sheet (a text file with a .css extension). Any page that wants to use that format simply links to the style sheet. Any changes made to the master style sheet are automatically reflected in all pages that link to the style sheet. Now that is real power!

What Style Sheets Can Do

Style sheets can change the look of any element on your page. Element by element, you can define the way you want things to look in a style sheet. Your paragraphs will all take on the formatting you associate with the P element in your style sheet. If you want to define more than one look for an element, you can create classes of an element and assign the classes to the elements when you define them in the pages.

Say you have two types of paragraphs in your pages: normal and newspaper. The normal paragraphs should use a half-inch indent on the first line and leave quarter-inch of white space (padding) above them. The newspaper paragraphs should indent a quarter inch on the first line and leave two inches of white space on both the right and left sides. Style sheets can accomplish this easily. You, as the developer, simply define a regular P element in your style sheet to match the formatting you want your normal text paragraphs to have. Then you define another P.newspaper element (that is a P element with a class of newspaper) with the formatting you want your newspaper paragraphs to have. Whenever you come to a normal text paragraph, you use the regular P element. When you come to a newspaper paragraph, you use the P element with the class (an attribute) specified as "newspaper." What could be easier?

Grouping elements

Remember in Chapters 16 and 17, when you learned about grouping elements with the DIV (for block elements) and the SPAN (for inline elements) elements? Style sheets can also do something HTML 3.2 can't do, even with all those ugly, deprecated presentation elements. If you wanted to group two paragraphs, give them a background color in common, but different from the rest of the page, and put a nice thick border around them, you'd have to use tables in the way tables were never intended to be used. With style sheets, you can define a DIV class in your style sheet, and by including the paragraphs in the DIV element with the class set to whatever you called it in your style sheet, all this formatting will appear on your page. If you ever want to change the background color for that class of the DIV element, you can do this one time in one place, in your style sheet, and the changes will be reflected everywhere you used that DIV class.

Site face-lift

If nothing else you've read about style sheets thus far impresses you, this will. Imagine giving your site a complete face-lift in a morning. This might not sound impressive if your site is still only a handful of pages, but if your site has matured into the dozens, hundreds, or thousands of pages that many Webmasters have to maintain, this is truly revolutionary.

With style sheets, all the formatting information resides in one place. If you change the definitions in that one place, you can affect literally thousands of pages — however many link to the style sheet — in one fell swoop.

One day visitors come to your site and find a white background, left-justified text, blue headings, black text in Times Roman font. The next day they find a light blue background with the embossed logo of your company subtly woven into the background, navy headings in Verdana font, dark grey text in Verdana font, and the entire page is fully justified! That'll grab them!

Delegating page assembly without sacrificing design control

Wouldn't you love to implement a distributed team model to facilitate Web development in your organization? After all, the information you use in the pages comes from all over the organization. Why not just have them put all the material into Web pages directly? Before style sheets, about a million good reasons existed. Every which way a person can design a Web page is another reason not to let people who aren't part of the Web design team assemble their own pages. Who knows what they would look like?

But with style sheets, if you can train people to use the H1–H6 elements and to markup their paragraphs with the P element, then most of the work can be done by a distributed team of people who are not necessarily Web designers. You can go in later, check their work, and add any tables. Most important of all, if they link to your style sheet, even if they don't do things exactly as you would have, their pages will look pretty much like the rest of the site.

The Cascading Model

So, what is this cascading business about? The cascading model depends on the idea that you can specify style sheets at more than one level. The lowest-level style sheet takes precedence. For example, say your company has a corporate style sheet, called corporate.css. Your department might have its own style sheet called hr.css. Finally, you might want to create a specific style for a class of the DIV element, right in the HTML document. You could even define styles at the element level in the BODY of your page, but that isn't included in this example. How does this work?

In your HTML HEAD element, you would create a link to the corporate style sheet, then another link to the department style sheet. Following those, also in the HEAD element, you would define a style for the DIV element, using the STYLE element. Now, say the corporate style sheet had the following styles defined (to name a few):

✦ background tan

✦ text color brown

✦ font face Helvetica

✦ H1 is 22pt, H2 is 18pt, H3 is 16pt

Say the department had the following style defined (to name one):

✦ H2 is 20pt, H3 is 18pt, H4 is 16pt

And in the STYLE element in the HEAD element of your page, you define a DIV element with a class of highlight with a background of white and text color of black, with a black border.

What would show up in your document? Everything from the corporate style sheet that is not also defined in the department style sheet, and everything in the department style sheet that is not defined in the STYLE element, and everything in the STYLE element that is not defined at the element level. The result would be:

✦ background tan

✦ text color brown

✦ font face Helvetica

✦ H2 is 20pt, H3 is 18pt, H4 is 16pt

✦ DIV class of highlight with a background color of white, text color of black, with a black border

Style Sheet Examples

Even though you may find a style sheet definition intimidating at first, don't fret; lots of great tools are available to help you create a syntactically correct style sheet. Refer to Chapter 8 for a list. A number of Web-based resources also exist for creating style sheets. Unlike pages, you won't be creating a lot of style sheets. You'll create one you like, use it for the majority of your pages, and modify it occasionally.

If worse comes to worse, you could always start with one of the style sheets on the CD-ROM and modify it to meet your needs.

Here is an example style sheet. Explanations of things to notice are listed after the entire style sheet definition. Your style sheet doesn't need to contain all these rules (definitions of all these elements). You might just define a style for the body (one rule) and be content with the way your browser renders everything else.

```
BODY {
        font-family: "Book Antiqua", "Times New Roman", serif;
        color: #0C0040;
        background: #FFFF9F;
        padding: 1in;
}
A:LINK {
        color: #FF00FF;
}
A:VISITED {
        color: #808080;
}
BLOCKQUOTE {
        margin-left: 1in;
        margin-right: 1in;
}
HR {
        height: 2pt;
}
P {
        text-indent: .5in;
}
P.double {
        text-indent: .5in;
        line-height: 24pt;
}
SPAN.highlight {
        color: #000080;
        background: #FFFF00;
}
```

The only difficult part about creating a style sheet is remembering the property names. For example, to indent a paragraph a half inch, you need to know that the property is `text-indent`, not `paragraph-indent`, or `indent-text`. If you can find a reasonably priced tool you like for creating style sheets (the previous one took advantage of the style sheet wizard in HomeSite 4.0), then you don't have to worry about the syntax; you can put your energy into creating the style sheet you want.

In the previous example, notice each element name (called a *selector* in style sheets) is followed by a curly brace ({), and then comes a property followed by a colon, and then a value (called a *declaration*). With attributes, the syntax is

```
attribute = "value"
```

With style sheets, the syntax for a declaration is

```
property: value;
```

or

```
property: value, value, value;
```

Notice no quotes are around the value of the property in the style sheet (unless a single value with more than one word in it, such as a font). Don't worry about learning all these rules right now. You get a more thorough explanation in the next chapter. Right now you should notice that for each element, you can define several different formatting features. The last two elements on the list also have class definitions: `P.double` and `SPAN.highlight`. Those would be used in your document as follows:

```
<P class="double">
```

and

```
<SPAN class="highlight">
```

What does this style sheet do?

1. It formats all the `BODY` elements with a light yellow (#000040) background and dark gray (#FFFF9F) text using a font of Book Antiqua or, if that font is not available, Times New Roman or, if that is not available, any serif font, and it sets padding on the page of one inch.

2. It formats not-yet-visited links (`A:LINK`) to fuchsia (#FF00FF).

3. It formats visited links (`A:VISITED`) to gray (#808080).

4. It formats blockquotes to have one-inch left and right margins, which the browser would add to the one-inch padding already defined in the `BODY` element.

5. It formats all horizontal rules to be two pixels tall.

6. It gives paragraphs a half-inch indentation on the first line.

7. It creates a paragraph class called double (`P.double`), which has the same half-inch indentation on the first line, but also includes double-spacing of text (line height: 24pt).

8. It also creates a `SPAN` class called highlight (`SPAN.highlight`), which will have a text color of navy blue (#000080) and a background color of bright yellow (#FFFF00).

Browser Compatibility Issues

What about actually using style sheets in browsers? Is all this stuff supported? Unfortunately, no. Internet Explorer 5 does the best job of implementing style sheets. Netscape 4.x is significantly less supportive of style sheets, but does support many features of style sheets. Internet Explorer 3 and 4 also do a respectable job of supporting style sheets.

What does this mean for you? If you are creating pages for an intranet and you know people using your pages will have IE 5, or Navigator 4, then you can test your pages on the platform you know people will be using, and only use the styles supported on that platform. However, if you are creating pages for the Internet, where you can't predict what kind of browser visitors will be using, you have three choices, recapped from Chapter 2:

✦ Don't use style sheets. Continue to design your pages with the deprecated HTML 3.2 elements and attributes and look forward to the day when browsers that support style sheets are more widely used.

✦ Maintain two versions of your site. Believe it or not, this is what many large, high-profile sites do. In Chapter 48, you will learn how to test to see which browser a visitor is using so that you can automatically load the appropriate version of the page.

✦ Use style sheets and to heck with the luddites who haven't upgraded. They will, after all, be able to see your site; they just won't get the same design look that they should.

From Here

Cross-Reference

Jump to Chapter 48 and learn about using JavaScript to test to see which version of which browser a visitor is using.

Proceed to Chapter 26 and learn the syntax of style sheets.

Summary

In this chapter you learned just why style sheets are so valuable. You learned what they can do that couldn't previously be done. You learned about the cascading model. You got a chance to analyze an example of a style sheet. You also learned enough about browser compatibility issues to understand that making a decision about using style sheets requires some analysis.

✦   ✦   ✦

```
        }
        A:visited {
                color: blue;
        }
        A:active {
                color: green;
        }
        A.special:link {
                color: #FF33FF;   /* fuchsia */
        }
```

This style sheet has four rules. The first three define the colors of unvisited links, visited links, and active links. The last one will only be used when the class is specified as special; it specifies the color of unvisited links.

Defining IDs

You won't use IDs nearly as often as you use classes, but it's nice to know they are there if you need them. *IDs* are like classes, except they are not necessarily associated with elements. Isn't this contrary to the HTML 4 Way? Yes, but it's there if you need it. IDs are defined as follows:

```
        #wide {
                letter-spacing: .4em;
        }
```

And used as follows:

```
        <H1 id="wide">This is a wide heading</H1>
        <P id="wide">This is a paragraph of widely spaced text.</P>
```

As you can see, the ID wide can be used with any element. It is recommended you use classes rather than IDs.

Grouping Elements with DIV and SPAN

In Chapters 16 and 17, you learned about using the DIV and SPAN elements to group block-level elements and inline elements, respectively. Now you can finally see how this works with style sheets. Consider the following style-sheet rules:

```
        DIV.important {
                background: red;
                font: bold 14pt/18pt Helvetica;
        }
```

```
SPAN.incidental {
        font: normal 8pt/8pt Helvetica;
background: gray;
}
```

You can use them as follows:

```
<DIV class="important"><P>This is one very important
paragraph.</P>
<TABLE>
...table contents...
</TABLE>
<P>This is another important paragraph.</P></DIV>
<P>This is somewhat important. <SPAN class="incidental">And
this is really incidental.</SPAN> But you might want to
remember this fact.</P>
```

This creates two paragraphs with a table between them that have a background color of red and 14pt bold Helvetica text. Following this mess is another paragraph with formatting inherited from the BODY element, but the middle sentence has gray 8 pt Helvetica text.

Comments in Style Sheets

Adding comments to your style sheets, just as you add comments to your HTML pages, is not a bad idea. Comments are defined in your style sheet using a different convention than in your HTML pages. Look back to the sample code for the pseudo-classes style sheet. Notice next to the hexadecimal value #FF33FF, there is the following:

```
/* fuchsia */
```

That is a comment in CSS. Adding a comment is little trouble when you create the style sheet; it is a lot more work to go back and remember what you meant when you defined the style sheet. If you use comments nowhere else, use them when you use hexadecimal notation for colors.

Comments are created with a /* preceding them and a */ following them.

From Here

Jump to Chapter 33 to learn about CSS positioning options

Proceed to Chapter 27 and begin adding styles to your Web page.

Summary

In this chapter you learned about the basics of CSS. You learned the vocabulary, the conventions, and differences between CSS and HTML syntax. You learned about defining properties, grouping properties, and defining properties using shortcuts. You learned about the CSS box model and about inheritance from containers to elements. You also learned about classes, pseudo-classes, and IDs. Finally, you learned about using the DIV and SPAN elements to group elements so they can all take advantage of the same formatting.

✦   ✦   ✦

Adding Styles to Your Web Pages

Now that you know why you should use a style sheet
and how to write a style sheet, you need to know how
to include style sheets in your page. This document takes you
through the three options you have for adding styles to your
page. With the cascading approach, you can actually use all
three at the same time, but you probably don't want to do
this, as you learn in this chapter.

Using an External Style Sheet

The preferred way to include styles in your page is to use an
external style sheet. This is the only way to take advantage of
all the benefits you have read about relating to using style
sheets. If you use an external style sheet, then all your style
information for all your pages is stored in one central place.
If you want to give your site a face-lift, it's as easy as changing
the external style sheet.

To use an external style sheet, simply create your style sheet
and save it with a .css extension. Then link to it from the HEAD
of your page using the LINK element. The following list is not
the complete specification for the LINK element. The LINK
element is used for other unrelated functions, which only
confuse this use.

**Cross-
Reference** For the complete specification of the LINK element, refer
to Chapter 12.

Adding Inline Styles

Reasons may exist why you would want to add style information directly at the element level. You may have noticed that nearly every element introduced in this book has had a `style` attribute. This attribute is used to define element-specific style information. The `style` attribute is used as follows:

```
<P style="text-indent: 1in; color: blue;">This paragraph has a
one inch indentation--twice the normal paragraph indentation--
on the first line and is rendered with blue text.</P>
```

Notice you don't need a selector (P) in the `style` attribute because you are only defining a rule for this instance of the element. You do need double quotes around the rules, as with any attribute value, and each descriptor does need to be followed by a semicolon.

The use of the `style` attribute is preferred to the use of the `FONT` element, which is deprecated in HTML 4, but the `style` attribute is still not the ideal. Whenever possible, you should try to determine what formatting you need before you get to the element that needs special formatting and define a class for that element in your style sheet. The previous example could have been written instead as:

```
<P class="deep-blue">This paragraph has a one inch indentation--
twice the normal paragraph indentation--on the first line and is
rendered with blue text.</P>
```

A rule would have to be in your style sheet as well:

```
P.deep-blue {
    text-indent: 1in;
    color: blue;
}
```

Either example renders the same in the browser. Either one enables your page to be rendered easily in speech-synthesizing browsers. Both are vastly preferable to the HTML 3.2 method of using a clear GIF to indent the paragraph and then using the `FONT` element to change the text color to blue.

Using a Standardized Style Sheet

If after all these style sheets examples, you still don't feel comfortable writing your own style sheet, don't despair. Many standard style sheets are available. Most people get started writing HTML by copying pages with features they like and modifying the code to meet their needs. Most people who write Perl use this

Adding Styles to Your Web Pages

Now that you know why you should use a style sheet and how to write a style sheet, you need to know how to include style sheets in your page. This document takes you through the three options you have for adding styles to your page. With the cascading approach, you can actually use all three at the same time, but you probably don't want to do this, as you learn in this chapter.

Using an External Style Sheet

The preferred way to include styles in your page is to use an external style sheet. This is the only way to take advantage of all the benefits you have read about relating to using style sheets. If you use an external style sheet, then all your style information for all your pages is stored in one central place. If you want to give your site a face-lift, it's as easy as changing the external style sheet.

To use an external style sheet, simply create your style sheet and save it with a .css extension. Then link to it from the HEAD of your page using the LINK element. The following list is not the complete specification for the LINK element. The LINK element is used for other unrelated functions, which only confuse this use.

Cross-Reference For the complete specification of the LINK element, refer to Chapter 12.

Link `<LINK>`

Start Tag:	Required
Content:	Empty
End Tag:	Forbidden
Attributes:	`id`, `class`, `lang`, `dir`, `title`, `style`, `events`

`href`: URL of style sheet

`hreflang`: language of document specified in `href` attribute

`type`: MIME type of document specified in `href` attribute, usually "text/css"

Here is an example of the `LINK` element used to link to an external style sheet called `may2000.css` that exists in the styles subdirectory:

```
<HEAD>
<LINK href="styles/may2000.css" type="text/css">
</HEAD>
```

The `LINK` element, whether it is used for linking to an external style sheet or for some other purpose, must be located in the `HEAD` element.

Using a STYLE Element within the HEAD

If you are unhappy with any pre-existing style sheet or you don't want to store your styles in a separate style sheet for whatever reason, then you can store your complete style sheet in the `HEAD` element directly. How does this work? You put the rules (the statements that tell the browser how to render each element) directly into a `STYLE` element in the `HEAD`. As you can imagine, this could make your `HEAD` quite long.

The `STYLE` element has the following specification:

Style `<STYLE>`

Start Tag:	Required
Content:	Rules
End Tag:	Required
Attributes:	`lang`, `dir`

`type`: MIME type, usually "text/css"

`media`: types of medium for which this style sheet is relevant; defaults to "screen"; must be a keyword or comma-delimited list of media keywords from list (see following valid list)

`title`: title of style information

The valid media types are as follows:

✦ **screen.** For computer screens.

✦ **tty.** For fixed-width terminal displays.

✦ **tv.** For televisions.

✦ **projection.** For projectors.

✦ **handheld.** For handheld devices.

✦ **print.** For print.

✦ **braille.** For braille-tactile feedback devices.

✦ **aural.** For speech synthesizers.

✦ **all.** For all devices.

The STYLE element is used as follows:

```
<HEAD>
<STYLE>
  BODY {
        color: black;
        background: white;
        padding-left: 1in;
        padding-right: 1in;
  }
  H1 {
        font: bold 24pt/30pt black;
  }
  P {
        text-indent: .5in;
  }
  A:link {
        color: blue;
  }
  A:visited {
        color: red;
  }
  A:active {
        color: yellow;
  }
  BLOCKQUOTE {
        margin-left: 1in;
        margin-right: 1in;
  }
</STYLE>
</HEAD>
```

Adding Inline Styles

Reasons may exist why you would want to add style information directly at the element level. You may have noticed that nearly every element introduced in this book has had a `style` attribute. This attribute is used to define element-specific style information. The `style` attribute is used as follows:

```
<P style="text-indent: 1in; color: blue;">This paragraph has a
one inch indentation--twice the normal paragraph indentation--
on the first line and is rendered with blue text.</P>
```

Notice you don't need a selector (P) in the `style` attribute because you are only defining a rule for this instance of the element. You do need double quotes around the rules, as with any attribute value, and each descriptor does need to be followed by a semicolon.

The use of the `style` attribute is preferred to the use of the FONT element, which is deprecated in HTML 4, but the `style` attribute is still not the ideal. Whenever possible, you should try to determine what formatting you need before you get to the element that needs special formatting and define a class for that element in your style sheet. The previous example could have been written instead as:

```
<P class="deep-blue">This paragraph has a one inch indentation--
twice the normal paragraph indentation--on the first line and is
rendered with blue text.</P>
```

A rule would have to be in your style sheet as well:

```
P.deep-blue {
    text-indent: 1in;
    color: blue;
}
```

Either example renders the same in the browser. Either one enables your page to be rendered easily in speech-synthesizing browsers. Both are vastly preferable to the HTML 3.2 method of using a clear GIF to indent the paragraph and then using the FONT element to change the text color to blue.

Using a Standardized Style Sheet

If after all these style sheets examples, you still don't feel comfortable writing your own style sheet, don't despair. Many standard style sheets are available. Most people get started writing HTML by copying pages with features they like and modifying the code to meet their needs. Most people who write Perl use this technique; most people who write JavaScript got started this way. Finding a style sheet you like and modifying it to meet your needs is no disgrace.

On the CD-ROM

To help make it easier, the CD-ROM in the back of this book has several standard style sheets on it. Pick one that comes close to approximating the look you want and customize it to make it your own.

You might find your organization has its own style sheet, which you are expected to use. If this is the case, the powers that control the style sheet might not let you create special classes to accommodate your formatting needs. Fortunately, CSS has a way to help you get around any limitations this might present. Consider the following HTML, which refers to a corporate style sheet. It doesn't even matter what is in the style sheet for your purposes because you are required to use it and you are not allowed to change it.

```
<HTML>
<HEAD>
<LINK href="style/corporate.css" type="text/css">
</HEAD>

<BODY>

<H1>A heading</H1>

<P>This paragraph looks just the way they want it to look.</P>

<P>But I sure wish I could make this one look different.</P>

</BODY>
</HTML>
```

You can see the frustration you would encounter because you can't change the formatting of the second paragraph using the corporate style sheet you are provided. Given what you've learned in this chapter, you know two ways to get around this limitation. The first is to create a STYLE element in the HEAD element and create a class for the second paragraph.

```
<HTML>
<HEAD>
<LINK href="style/corporate.css" type="text/css">
<STYLE>
  P.different {
       color: blue;
       font-size: 14pt;
  }
</STYLE>
</HEAD>
```

```
<BODY>

<H1>A heading</H1>

<P>This paragraph looks just the way they want it to look.</P>

<P class="different">I'm so pleased that I can make this one
look different.</P>

</BODY>
</HTML>
```

The other way you learned is to put the style information directly into a `style` attribute in the `P` element.

```
<HTML>
<HEAD>
<LINK href="style/corporate.css" type="text/css">
</HEAD>

<BODY>

<H1>A heading</H1>

<P>This paragraph looks just the way they want it to look.</P>

<P style="color: blue; font-size: 14pt;">I'm so pleased that I
can make this one look different.</P>

</BODY>
</HTML>
```

For the previous example, where the customization you want to affect in formatting is minimal and only affects one element, either of the two methods of accomplishing this would be fine. Neither one substantially clutters your HTML. The first one is probably better, but the difference is minuscule. However, there is one other way to take control of the look of your page at a micro level when you are forced to use a style sheet over which you have no control. This is to create another external style sheet and link to it in the HEAD following the link to the standard style sheet. If, however, you want to create classes or change formatting for multiple elements, you probably want to move this formatting to your own style sheet, as shown in the following:

```
<HEAD>
<LINK href="style/corporate.css" type="text/css">
<LINK href="style/mine.css" type="text/css">
</HEAD>
<BODY>
<H1>A heading</H1>
```

```
<P>This paragraph looks just the way they want it to look.</P>

<P class="different">I'm so pleased that I can make this one
look different.</P>

</BCDY>
</HTML>
```

You can actually include as many links to external style sheets as you need. Does the order matter? You bet! Because of the cascading rules discussed in the last chapter, the last style sheet specified can override all previous style sheets specified. If you are supposed to use a standard style sheet created by someone else, then you want to be careful not to override any of those styles. As with all style definitions, the lowest-level style defined has the highest priority. Conversely, the higher a style is defined, the lower the priority.

Mixing the Approaches: An Example

The following example of combining style definitions should help make the concept of cascading style sheets and the use of classes, IDs, and inline style definitions clear. This is a long example, but it is one to which you can refer later if you have questions about your own implementation of style sheets.

```
Corporate.css
  BODY {
       color: black;
       background: white;
       padding-left: 1in;
       padding-right: 1in;
  }
  H1 {
       font: bold 24pt/30pt black;
  }
  P {
       text-indent: .5in;
  }
  A:link {
       color: blue;
  }
  A:visited {
       color: red;
  }
  A:active {
       color: yellow;
  }
  BLOCKQUOTE {
       margin-left: 1in;
```

```
        margin-right: 1in;
    }
```

mine.css
```
  SPAN.special {
      color: red;
  }

  #wide {
      letter-spacing: .5em;
  }
  HR {
      width: 3pt;
      color: red;
  }
```

The two external style sheets used in this example are defined previously. They are called `corporate.css` and `mine.css`. The HTML page is defined in the following:

```
<HTML>
<HEAD>
<LINK href="corporate.css" rel="stylesheet" type="text/css">
<LINK href="mine.css" rel="stylesheet" type="text/css">
<STYLE>
  H1#wide {
      line-height: 40pt;
  }
</STYLE>
</HEAD>
<BODY>
<H1 ID="wide">A page with <SPAN class="special">special</SPAN>
formatting</H1>
<P>This paragraph contains <SPAN id="wide">some rather widely-
spaced text.</SPAN></P>
<HR style="color: black">
<HR>
<P>This paragraph is normal, but you can <A href="weird.html">
link</A> to weird stuff from here.</P>
</BODY>
</HTML>
```

In the previous example, many conflicting instructions exist in the form of style information for the browser. How will it render?

The first H1 has an ID of wide. If you look at `mine.css`, you can see an ID of wide is defined that affects letter spacing. But this won't be used. Why? Because another ID of wide specific to the H1 element is defined in the STYLE element and that ID affects line height. Notice the H1 element also has a SPAN element with a class of special that affects one word. The special class is defined in `mine.css` and isn't overridden anywhere further down, so the word special, within the SPAN element, will be rendered as red.

The first paragraph also uses the SPAN element with an ID of wide. How will this render? It will use the ID wide defined in mine.css, because it isn't affected by the H1 element defined in the STYLE element.

The first HR element will render in black, because the style attribute is defined right there and will override the HR definition in mine.css. It will render with the width provided in mine.css, since the new definition doesn't specify the width. How about the second HR definition? Will it inherit the color of the previous HR element? No. It will render just as mine.css defines it because no style information overrides the style information in mine.css.

Finally, in the last paragraph, which doesn't have any style references, there is a link. How will the link render? Until the link is visited, it will render in blue as defined by A:link in corporate.css. Once it is visited, it will render in red, and when it is active, it will render in yellow. Nothing special must be done to the HTML to take advantage of the three pseudo-elements related to the A element.

From Here

Cross-Reference

Jump to Chapter 33 and learn about absolute positioning in CSS.

Proceed to Chapter 28 and learn about adding colors and backgrounds to your pages.

Summary

In this chapter you got a crash course in using CSS in your page. You learned how to link to an external style sheet. You learned about using the STYLE element and you learned about using inline style definitions. You learned about using a standardized style sheet and how you can get around any limitations related to this. If you persevered, you also learned how cascading rules affect the implementation of styles in your page in a thorough example.

✦   ✦   ✦

Adding Colors and Backgrounds

The HTML 4 Way gives you lots of ways to change the colors on your screen. You can change text colors, background colors, and background images for everything on the page, or on an element-by-element basis. This chapter explains how your screen renders colors and why no two monitors look alike. It also discusses color palettes — the color information an image sends — including a color-safe palette that renders properly on both PCs and Macs. Next, you learn about color compatibility and why it's wise to choose your colors and stick with them. You learn how to define a background color and text colors. Finally, you learn how to add a background graphic and to specify whether it repeats.

How Your Monitor Creates Color

Computers use the RGB system to create colors. Don't be put off by another acronym; RGB stands for *Red-Green-Blue*. Basically, the computer can generate only red, green, or blue light. When it generates all three together, at full power, it produces white. When it generates none of them, it produces black. This is contrary to the way that artists think about color. White is usually the absence of color in art — but on your computer screen, white is what you get when you mix all the other colors together.

All information on your computer is passed in the form of binary data — a long string of ones and zeros — which is not a very useful way to convey information to people. A shorthand for the ones and zeros, *hexadecimal* (or *hex*) notation, offers people a way to discuss this information. The hexadecimal system assigns each digit a value between 0 and 15. The decimal system, the way we're used to counting, takes two digits to convey the numbers 10, 11, 12, 13, 14, and 15; hex substitutes letters for those six numbers. So, this is how you count from 0 to 15 in hex: 0, 1, 2, 3, 4, 5, 6, 7, 8, 9, *A, B, C, D, E, F.* If you want to count to 16, it's like going from 9 to 10 in the decimal system; to go from 15 to 16 in the hex system, you introduce a new digit. That's where it gets confusing. If 15 is *F,* then you write 16 as 10 (pronounced "one-zero," *not ten*) in hex.

You frequently see numbers in hex like FF33A0. That might look like a foreign language, but it's far easier to work with than 111111110011001110100000, which translates to the same thing! Here's the good news: You won't have to do math in hex to add colors to your page.

Introducing Color Codes

The computer projects color based on the intensity of red, green, and blue you tell it to provide. You tell it what intensity to provide by using *color codes* written in the hex system; you have already seen colors in this book defined in hex. In HTML, when you specify a color in hex, you need to precede the color code with a pound sign (#). Here are some easy ones: #000000 (no red, no green, no blue) is black; #FFFFFF (full-power red, full-power green, full-power blue) is white. Are you getting the hang of this? How about #FF0000? Red. #008000? Green. #0000FF? Blue.

Using English

At this point, there's more good news: You needn't use color codes to define your colors. All the colors in the previous section actually have English names that HTML recognizes. The problem with using English color names is only 16 of them are guaranteed to work. They are listed in Table 28-1.

<table>
<tr><td colspan="2" align="center">Table 28-1
English Names for Colors</td></tr>
<tr><td>*Color Name*</td><td>*Hex Value*</td></tr>
<tr><td>Black</td><td>#000000</td></tr>
<tr><td>Green</td><td>#008000</td></tr>
<tr><td>Silver</td><td>#C0C0C0</td></tr>
<tr><td>Lime</td><td>#00FF00</td></tr>
<tr><td>Gray</td><td>#808080</td></tr>
</table>

Color Name	Hex Value
Olive	#808000
White	#FFFFFF
Yellow	#FFFF00
Maroon	#800000
Navy	#000080
Red	#FF0000
Blue	#0000FF
Purple	#800080
Teal	#008080
Fuchsia	#FF00FF
Aqua	#00FFFF

Monitor-to-monitor variations

Have you ever noticed that a screen image you're used to seeing one way on your monitor renders in slightly different colors on another monitor? The reason is no absolute red exists in the computer world. There isn't even an absolute white. Depending on the tubes in your monitor, how old it is, how it is adjusted, and a few other things, white may be white, pinkish white, bluish white, greenish white, or just plain gray. Your eyes adjust to what they know ought to be white, but if you hold a white piece of paper up next to your monitor, you will see your monitor's idea of white probably isn't true white.

What does this mean to you as a designer? It means that although you want to select your colors carefully, you don't have control over how they render. You want to test them extensively on a number of different monitors — not just the same brand of monitor on ten different desks, although there will be a difference — but even on other platforms and brands of monitors.

Chapter 37 takes you through an explanation of bit depth that you may want to review before you select the colors for your site.

Color Palettes

Remember opening that box of 64 crayons as a child? That was a color palette of 64. It didn't seem limiting at the time. You had blue, green-blue, blue-green, green, and 60 other colors to choose from. If you had to limit yourself to a 64-color palette for your Web site, though, you'd be terribly frustrated. Fortunately, nearly everyone who visits your site with a browser that supports more than text is also likely to have a color monitor that supports at least 256 colors. Where does that number 256 come from? In the hex system, 100 (one-zero-zero) translates into 256 in the decimal system.

When you send information (such as a background image or information about the text color), you want to save time by using the palette on the visitor's system whenever possible, rather than sending another palette across the Web to the visitor's system. All computers have built-in color palettes — how convenient! — the only problem is that color palettes are not the same on all systems. A 256-color palette is available on both Macs and PCs, but only 216 of the colors are the same on both platforms. If you plan to use the built-in color palette on your visitors' computers, make sure your site is using a *color-safe* palette.

Tip   You can find the color-safe palette on the Web at `www.lynda.com/hex.html`, courtesy of Lynda Weinman.

Color-Compatibility Considerations

When you choose the colors for your background, background images, text color, and headings colors, you want to be sure that you are selecting them all from the same palette. If you select colors across palettes, there are two problems. The first is you need to send more palette information over the Web than necessary, slowing your page's download time. The second is your colors might not match. Not every shade of blue goes with every shade of green. By keeping your color selection within a single palette, you are sure to avoid the problem of clashing shades, where some of your colors are considered warm, while others are considered cool.

Defining a Background Color

You are finally ready to start defining colors for your page. You saw in the previous chapters that you can define colors in your style sheet. You can define a background color for each element on your page, but unless you are doing that for some instructional purpose, you probably don't want to do that. Under normal circumstances, you define a background color for your BODY element and just let inheritance do its job so that every other element on the page ends up with the same background color.

By including a declaration like the one here in your style sheet, you can set the background color for any element:

```
background-color: #00AAAA;              /* light aqua */
```

The important thing to remember is that the property is called *background-color*. If you are used to defining the background color directly in the BODY element, you are used to an attribute name of bgcolor.

Changing Default Text Colors

You can use style sheets to set text colors, as well. The property name to remember is *color*. By setting the color property for the BODY, all other elements will inherit that color. You can, of course, change the color of the text for any element by including the color property in a declaration like the one in the following, in that element's style-sheet rule.

```
color: #FF33FF;          /* a loud shade of fuchsia */
```

You have already seen how text colors for links can be changed: You use the pseudo-elements related to the A element. In the style sheet that follows, the link color for links that have not yet been visited is yellow. The color for links that have been visited is gray; the color of the active link is blue. It sounds awful, but it wouldn't look bad if the background color were very dark.

```
A:link {
      color: yellow;
}
A:visited {
      color: gray;
}
A:active {
      color: blue;
}
```

Adding a Background Graphic

HTML 4 does a great favor for Web visitors by helping Web designers curb their natural desire for flash. For the first time, you can add a background graphic to your page that does not tile. The default is for all background images to tile. This means any image you assign to be your background image automatically repeats itself until the screen is covered. This may or may not have been what you intended. If you aren't careful, the results can be horrendous.

Clever Web designers have always taken advantage of the tiling effect by specifying graphics that tile well, or tile invisibly, such as a marble effect, or clouds. An effect that can be stunning is creating a logo or the name of your company in a nice font and then using a graphics package—such as Photoshop—to emboss the image and then subduing the colors and letting that tile.

Adding a background image is a cinch in CSS:

```
BODY {
        background-color: white;
        background-image: url(../images/background.gif);
        background-repeat: no-repeat;
        background-attachment: scroll;
        background-position: top center;
}
```

A few things to note about these five background properties:

✦ **background-color.** This property determines the background color for your page. You want to make sure that the background color you select matches your background image color, if you have one.

✦ **background-image.** This property contains the URL of the background image. Notice that the URL is specified within parentheses with the keyword url preceding the parenthesis. This is how URLs are specified in CSS. You haven't seen this convention yet in this book.

✦ **background-repeat.** This property determines whether to repeat (that is, tile) the background image. Your choices are repeat (tile the way you are used to seeing background images tile), repeat-x (tile horizontally only), repeat-y (tile vertically only), or no-repeat.

✦ **background-attachment.** This property enables you to specify whether the background image moves with the text (that is, scrolls) or stays in one position relative to the page (remains fixed).

✦ **background-position.** You can specify two values for this property with a space between them: vertical position and horizontal position. You can specify them in terms of a percentage of the page, the distance on the page, or a keyword. All of the following are valid:

```
background-position: 10% 10%;
```
```
background-position: 1cm 3in;
```
```
background-position: top center;
```
```
background-position: 30% center;
```

As with font definitions, you can define background properties together in one property called background. The background property is defined by this code:

```
background: background-color background-image background-repeat
background-attachment background-position
```

In the following valid examples of the background property, notice background-position is actually two values; a complete list of all the background properties is actually six values long. As with all shortcuts, you needn't include all the values.

```
background: white url(../images/logo-faded.gif) no-repeat
scroll center center;
background: url(../images/logo-faded.gif) 2cm center;
background: url(../images/logo-faded.gif) repeat-x fixed
10% center;
```

From Here

Jump to Chapter 37 and learn about bit depth in colors.

Proceed to Chapter 29 and learn about formatting paragraphs.

Summary

In this chapter, you learned about how your computer creates colors from zeros and ones. You learned a little bit about the hexadecimal system and how you can use it to define colors. You also learned about palettes and where to find system-safe palettes. Finally, you learned how to apply all this information to define a background color, text colors, and a background image that doesn't tile.

✦   ✦   ✦

Formatting Paragraphs

In this chapter, you learn about formatting paragraphs with the *box formatting model*. This CSS feature formats block-level elements of a document, including paragraphs. You learn about indenting text, controlling alignment, specifying line spacing, and controlling lists. You also learn how to add rules and borders.

Reviewing the CSS Box Formatting Model

You may recall the CSS box formatting model from Chapter 26: After a block-level object is rendered, the browser uses information in the style sheet to determine how to format around the box in which the object is rendered.

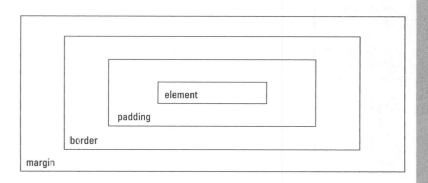

Padding summary

Padding—the white space between the element itself and the border (if there is one)—takes on the background color assigned to the element. These five properties are related to padding:

✦ `padding-top`

✦ `padding-right`

✦ `padding-bottom`

✦ `padding-left`

✦ `padding`

The first four take either a valid length or a percentage of the canvas. The fifth property, `padding`, is the shortcut for the first four. It can take between one and four values. It assumes that the values you provide are for the top, right, bottom, and left, in that order.

Margins summary

Margins take on the background color of the parent element—the container in which this block-level element is defined. For example, if the element being defined is a paragraph, the parent element might be the `BODY` element. Suppose two items are vertically aligned on the page, each with its own margin defined; for the top element, the margin would be the `margin-bottom` element, for the bottom element, it would be `margin-top`; the browser renders the two elements with a margin between them that equals the larger of these two margins, not the sum of the margins. For elements aligned horizontally, the browser renders each element with its own margin; it does not collapse the two margins into the greater of the two.

Five properties specify not only the margins, but also the white space between the border of the element (if it has one) and the margin of the next element. These properties are as follows:

✦ `margin-top`

✦ `margin-right`

✦ `margin-bottom`

✦ `margin-left`

✦ `margin`

The margin properties work exactly the same as the padding properties.

Units of length

To define padding or margins, first you need to know what units you can use to define them. Many properties in CSS take lengths in both *relative units* and *absolute units*. The relative units are as follows:

- ✦ **em** — the height of the element's font
- ✦ **ex** — the height of the letter x
- ✦ **px** — pixels, which are measurable on the canvas

The absolute units are as follows:

- ✦ **in** — inches
- ✦ **cm** — centimeters
- ✦ **mm** — millimeters
- ✦ **pt** — points; 72 points to an inch
- ✦ **pc** — picas; 12 points to a pica

Adding Indentations

Another way to format your paragraph is to indent the first line of text, or outdent the first line of text. *Outdenting*, also known as creating a hanging indent, is when the first line of text hangs out into the margin and subsequent lines of text begin further in. You can define text indenting using the text-indent property as follows:

```
text-indent: .5in;
text-indent: 2cm;
text-indent: -8em;
```

Controlling Alignment

You might also want to control what is normally called text justification. CSS calls it *alignment*. Text alignment can be set to left, which is the default; center;, right;, or justify, which is full alignment.

The property is called text-align. Here are some examples:

```
text-align: left;
text-align: center;
text-align: justify;
```

Choosing Line Height

By default, your browser renders your font size with one pixel above the tallest letter and one pixel below the lowest-reaching letter. So, if you specify you want the font-size to be 12pt, the browser assumes line spacing should be 14pt. You can, however, change that by using a greater `line-height` to spread out your text on the page.

The following example creates a paragraph with standard indentation and very tight line spacing:

```
P {
   font-size: medium;
   line-height: 12pt;
}
```

Controlling Lists with Styles

You can use most of the properties listed earlier in this chapter to format your lists as well. Each list item is formatted as its own block-level element, which means you can assign that element its own padding, borders, and margins. You can specify what bullets look like for unordered lists, the numbering system used for ordered lists, and (if you prefer) the image to be used as a bullet point. You can also specify whether the bullets are outdented (which is probably the way you're used to seeing them in lists), or flush with the left margin; if your text direction is right-to-left, your bullets can be flush with the right margin.

List style type

For ordered lists (`OL`), which typically have a number or a letter next to each list item, you can choose from among these types of list style:

- ✦ **decimal.** 1, 2, 3, 4, 5, and so on
- ✦ **lower-roman.** i, ii, iii, iv, v, and so on
- ✦ **upper-roman.** I, II, III, IV, V, and so on
- ✦ **lower-alpha.** a, b, c, d, e, and so on
- ✦ **upper-alpha.** A, B, C, D, E, and so on

For unordered lists, which typically have some shape of bullet next to each list item, you can choose between

- ✦ **disc.** standard solid circle

✦ **circle.** empty circle

✦ **square.** solid square

Some examples follow:

```
OL {
list-style-type: lower-alpha;    /* a, b, c, etc. */
}
UL {
        list-style-type: circle;
}
```

List style image

CSS enables you to specify an image instead of a disc, circle, or square for the bullet in unordered lists; you identify the image by its URL. The property is named list-style-image. If the browser can't find the URL of the image you have selected, it uses the style type you specified in the list-style-type property.

```
UL {
        list-style-type: square;
        list-style-image: url(../images/blue-box.gif);
}
```

List style position

The following example shows regular formatting of lists.

✦ Outside list item 1

 has bullet outside the margin of subsequent lines

✦ Outside list item 2

 has bullet outside the margin of subsequent lines

This is how you specify it:

```
UL {
        list-style: outside;
}
```

The next example shows compact formatting of lists:

✦ Inside list item 1

has flush subsequent lines

✦ Inside list item 2

has flush subsequent lines

You can specify compact formatting by using the CSS property called list-style. The code looks like this:

```
UL {
        list-style: inside;
}
```

Notice the property is associated with the UL element and not with the LI elements.

List style shorthand

As with many CSS property groups, you can use the list-style property to group your list formatting. The list-style property takes three values: the value of the list-style-type property, the value of the list-style-position property, and the value of the list-style-image property. The possible values of the three don't conflict; you can specify only one value—or any three values—and it will work. An example follows:

```
UL {
        list-style: square outside url(../images/blue-box.gif);
}
OL {
        list-style: decimal inside;
}
```

Adding Borders

Borders are a great way to break up your page and to draw attention to something important. CSS offers you superior flexibility when you specify which (if any) rules and borders you want to include with your box-formatted elements. You can choose border-width properties, a border-color property, a border-style property, and a variety of shorthand notations to define borders.

Border width

You can use five properties to define the width of the border. They are border-top-width, border-right-width, border-bottom-width, border-left-width, and border-width. CSS is nothing if not predictable. You can specify any of the first four or you can use the fifth one to specify up to all four of the widths in shorthand, just as with the margin and padding properties.

If you specify one value for the border-width property, all four sides will be that width. If you specify two values for the border-width property, the top and bottom are assigned the first value, and the sides are assigned the second value. If you specify three values (and this is completely unintuitive), the top is assigned the first value, the sides are assigned the second value, and the bottom is assigned the third value.

In addition to specifying a valid length (using one of the measurements listed earlier), you can also use one of three keywords to instruct the browser to render your border width: thin, medium, and thick. The default is medium. An example of such a border rendering follows:

```
border-width: thin;         /* all 4 sides will be thin */
border-width: medium thick; /* top, bottom medium, sides
thick */
border-width: 4px thin 2px; /* top 4px, sides thin, bottom
2px */
border-width: 3mm 4mm 2mm 1mm; /* top, right, bottom, left, in
that order */
```

Border color

The border-color property takes up to four values; it works exactly like the border-width property. You can specify border color for all four sides at once or for each side individually. The property is called border-color. Here is what it looks like in action:

```
border-color: #FF0000;        /* makes all four borders
red */
border-color: red blue red blue; /* makes top and bottom
borders red, sides blue */
border-color: yellow black;   /* makes top and bottom
yellow, sides black */
```

Border style

The border-style property tells the browser what kind of border to use. As with the border-width property, you can specify one to four values. Netscape 4.7 supports more styles then Internet Expolorer 5.0. Your choices are as follows:

◆ **none.** No border; overrides border-width specification.

◆ **dotted.** Border is a dotted line.

◆ **dashed.** Border is a dashed line.

◆ **solid.** Border is a solid line (the default).

✦ **double.** Border is a double line. The border-width value specifies the total width of both lines and the white space between them.

✦ **groove.** Border is a 3D groove of the color assigned in border-color property.

✦ **ridge.** Border is a 3D ridge of the color assigned in border-color property.

✦ **inset.** Border is a 3D inset of the color assigned in border-color property.

✦ **outset.** Border is a 3D outset of the color assigned in border-color property.

```
border-style: solid none;       /* makes top and bottom solid,
none on sides */
border-style: ridge;            /* ridge on all four sides */
border-style: dotted dashed solid   /* top dotted, sides
dashed, bottom solid */
border-style: solid dotted double dashed    /* top, right,
bottom, left in that order */
```

Shorthand techniques

CSS provides several techniques for creating shorthand definitions related to borders. Four properties—border-top, border-right, border-bottom, and border-left—can be used to specify values for width, style, and color, in that order. A brief example follows:

```
border-top: thick dashed blue;
border-bottom: thick dashed red;
```

A border property can be used to set values for width, style, and color—but only if you want to assign the same values to all four sides, as in the following example:

```
border: thin solid black;       /* all four sides will be thin,
solid, and black */
border: 6px double yellow;      /* all four sides will be 6px,
double, and yellow */
```

From Here

Cross-Reference

Jump to Chapter 33 and learn about using CSS for absolute positioning.

Proceed to Chapter 30 and learn about CSS and tables.

Summary

In this chapter, you reviewed the CSS box-formatting model. You learned more about specifying margins and padding for paragraphs. You learned the units of measurement to use when specifying many CSS property values. You also learned about including paragraph indentation, paragraph alignment, and the property that specifies line spacing. You learned about formatting lists, either with the bullet outdented or flush with the text. Finally, you learned about specifying borders for your block-level elements.

✦   ✦   ✦

Formatting Tables

In this chapter, you learn about using CSS to format tables. As you read in Chapter 20, CSS1 does not provide as many ways to affect formatting of tables as it does formatting of other elements. Fortunately, the W3C has remedied this problem with CSS2. As always, the transition isn't seamless, because not all browsers fully support CSS2. This chapter incorporates both CSS1 and CSS2 to show you how to format every aspect of your HTML table.

Controlling Table Alignment

CSS provides the align property to enable you to specify table alignment. The align property for tables works exactly as it does for aligning paragraphs or any other block-level element. You can choose to align the table on the left, in the center, on the right, or fully justified across the canvas. Look at the code for an example. You can specify the align property for the TABLE selector, for a class of the TABLE selector, or for an ID that affects the TABLE element.

```
TABLE {
        text-align: center;
}
TABLE.right-leaning {
        text-align: right;
}
TABLE#full {
        text-align: justify;
}
```

Setting Horizontal Cell Alignment

You can specify horizontal cell alignment in four places: at the cell level, at the row level, at the column level, or at the row group level.

At the cell level

Specifying alignment at the cell level is easy. Include the align attribute in the TD element. The problem with this is you could end up defining this attribute in every single cell. If you can define this attribute at a higher level, this can save you a lot of typing and reduce the chance of introducing errors into your TABLE definition.

```
<TABLE>
  <TR>
        <TH align="center">Vacation Location
        <TH align="center">Avg. Temp.
        <TH align="center">Package Deal
  <TR>
        <TD align="left">Ireland
        <TD align="char" char="&deg;">68&deg;
        <TD align="char" char=".">$799.95
  <TR>
        <TD align="left">Greek Islands
        <TD align="char" char="&deg;">84&deg;
        <TD align="char" char=".">$649.95
  <TR>
        <TD align="left">Cancun
        <TD align="char" char="&deg;">85&deg;
        <TD align="char" char=".">$729.99
</TABLE>
```

Using CSS, you can move some of this formatting into classes. There is no character alignment in CSS, so some formatting would have to remain in the HTML. The style sheet would look like this:

```
TD.left {
        align: left;
}
TH.center {
        align: center;
}
```

And the HTML would look like this:

```
<TABLE>
  <TR>
        <TH class="center">Vacation Location
```

```
        <TH class="center">Avg. Temp.
        <TH class="center">Package Deal
    <TR>
        <TD class="left">Ireland
        <TD align="char" char="&deg;">68&deg;
        <TD align="char" char=".">$799.95
    <TR>
        <TD class="left">Greek Islands
        <TD align="char" char="&deg;">84&deg;
        <TD align="char" char=".">$649.95
    <TR>
        <TD class="left">Cancun
        <TD align="char" char="&deg;">85&deg;
        <TD align="char" char=".">$729.99
</TABLE>
```

At the row level

As you can see in the previous example, defining alignment at the cell level is impractical — especially for the first row, where every cell has the same class. Moving alignment to the row level makes more sense. The style sheet would now look like this:

```
TD.left {
        text-align: left;
}
TR.center TH.center {
        text-align: center;
}
```

And the HTML would look like this:

```
<TABLE>
   <TR class="center">
        <TH>Vacation Location
        <TH>Avg. Temp.
        <TH>Package Deal
    <TR>
        <TD align="left">Ireland
        <TD align="char" char="&deg;">68&deg;
        <TD align="char" char=".">$799.95
    <TR>
        <TD align="left">Greek Islands
        <TD align="char" char="&deg;">84&deg;
        <TD align="char" char=".">$649.95
    <TR>
        <TD align="left">Cancun
        <TD align="char" char="&deg;">85&deg;
        <TD align="char" char=".">$729.99
</TABLE>
```

Notice the alignment for the first row was moved from the cell level to the row level. Already, the HTML looks better.

At the column level

Unfortunately, none of the other rows lend themselves to moving the alignment attribute to the row level. But all of them share column formatting. They all have a left column with left alignment; a center column with character alignment that lines up on the degree sign (°), defined using the ° entity; and a right column with character alignment that lines up on the decimal point.

To take advantage of column-level alignment, you have to define columns. The previous example doesn't define columns, but the following example does. All the alignment formatting for rows after the first row is moved to the column level. The style sheet needs to be modified to look like this:

```
COL.left TD.left {
        text-align: left;
}
TR.center TH.center {
        text-align: center;
}
```

Because there is no character alignment in CSS, the formatting for the second and third columns would still need to be specified in the HTML.

```
<TABLE>
  <COL class="left">
  <COL align="char" char="&deg;">
  <COL align="char" char=".">
  <TR align="center">
        <TH>Vacation Location
        <TH>Avg. Temp.
        <TH>Package Deal
  <TR>
        <TD>Ireland
        <TD>68&deg;
        <TD>$799.95
  <TR>
        <TD>Greek Islands
        <TD>84&deg;
        <TD>$649.95
  <TR>
        <TD>Cancun
        <TD>85&deg;
        <TD>$729.99
</TABLE>
```

first row would be affected by the alignment formatting defined at
el, the row-level alignment overrides the column-level formatting, so
Even th the first row will have center alignment. Finally, the HTML looks like
the ou probably wouldn't mind maintaining.
a

e row group level or column group level

revious example doesn't lend itself to the use of the THEAD, TFOOT, TBODY, or
GROUP elements to specify alignment, but you can specify alignment at either
e row group level or the column group level.

```
COLGROUP.center {
        text-align: center;
}
TBODY.right {
        text-align: right;
}
```

Setting Vertical Cell Alignment

New to CSS2 is the vertical-align property. You can specify vertical alignment
(called *valign* in HTML 3.2) in your style sheet to apply to TD elements. See the code
example for how to implement the TD elements.

```
TD.mid {
        vertical-align: middle;
}
```

You may use a keyword or specify a percentage value. The keywords are as follows

✦ **top.** Sets the top of the cell to align with the top of the row in which the cell
   defined.

✦ **middle.** Sets the middle of the cell to align with the middle of the row in
   the cell is defined.

✦ **bottom.** Sets the bottom of the cell to align with the bottom of the row
   which the cell is defined.

✦ **baseline.** This is a relative specification. The baseline of the row is
   line of the top line of the text in the row. The baseline of the top li
   in the row depends on the font sizes used in each of the cells. Th
   determines the baseline of the first row of text and aligns the ba
   text in this cell with the baseline of the row.

✦ **sub.** This subscripts the cell.

✦ **super.** This superscripts the cell.

✦ **text-top.** Aligns the top of the cell with the top of the font of t.
that row.

✦ **text-bottom.** Aligns the bottom of the cell with the bottom of the f..t in
lowest text in that row.

Specifying Table and Cell Widths

You can specify widths for both the table and individual cells. With cell specifications, specify width at the column level or at the cell level. For both cells and
tables, you can either specify widths as absolute values or as relative values.

Absolute values

Before you decide to specify your table width using absolute values, be sure you
know how each cell will render. Otherwise, you could end up with cells that aren't
wide enough to hold an entire word. Tables don't do a good job of breaking words
at the syllable or hyphenating your words when you specify too small a width for
cells. In fact, if you specify an absolute value for cell height and an absolute value
for cell width, your cell might be too small to display all your text. In this case, the
text might spill over into the next cell, crossing rules!

ocabulary

sestablishmentarianis

ify absolute widths, you are specifying them in pixels. A screen can
e; 800 pixels wide; or 1,024 pixels wide (even more for super-high-
), but the browser will not always be set to fill the entire screen.
redicting how wide the browser window will be. The attribute
th is the width attribute.

="2">

set to 200 pixels wide, the first column is 100
columns are each 50 pixels wide. Normally
h and COL width absolutely.

Relative values

Whenever possible, you want to use relative values to specify table width. You can specify the table width as a percentage of the screen.

```
<TABLE width="40%">
  ... rest of table...
</TABLE>
```

You can also specify relative cell widths within a table for which you have specified an absolute width. The example in the previous section about absolute widths would probably be better defined as follows:

```
<TABLE width="200">
  <COL width="50%">
  <COL width="25%" span="2">
  ... rest of table...
</TABLE>
```

Another way to define cell widths is to use the 0* value. The 0* value is the way you instruct the browser to use the minimum width necessary to construct a table.

```
<TABLE>
  <COL width="0*">
  <COL width="100" span="2">
  ... rest of table...
</TABLE>
```

Specifying width in style sheets

You can also use style sheets to specify widths. The property is called width. The last two examples could be reworked, using style sheets, into the following code:

```
<TABLE class="this-one">
  <COL ID="half">
  <COL ID="quarter" span="2">
  ... rest of table...
</TABLE>
<TABLE>
  <COL class="min">
  <COL class="this-one" span="2">
  ... rest of table...
</TABLE>
```

The style sheet for these two tables would look like this:

```
TABLE.this-one {
        width: 200;
```

```
        }
#half {
            width: 50%;
        }
#quarter {
            width: 25%;
        }
COL.min {
            width: 0*;
        }
COL.this-one {
            width: 100;
        }
```

Adding Cell Spacing

You can specify cell spacing within a table. The property is called *cell spacing* (cell spacing as an attribute of the TABLE element). *Cell spacing* is the space between the border on the inside of one cell and the border on the inside of the next cell or the outside border of the table. When you define borders, borders are actually around each cell, and a separate border is around the entire table. If the borders are thin and there is no cell spacing, it will look like it is one line that surrounds the cells and attaches to the border around the table. The more cell spacing you define, the clearer it will be that these are separate lines.

The previous table has no cell spacing.

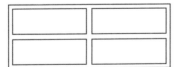

The previous table has cell spacing. The spacing attribute is defined as part of the TABLE element as follows:

```
<TABLE cellspacing="3">
```

Or, as part of a style sheet:

```
TABLE {
        cellspacing: 3
}
```

New to CSS2, you can specify different values for horizontal space between cells and for vertical space between cells. The first value supplied to the cellspacing property is for horizontal cell spacing; the second is for vertical cell spacing. If you provide only one, it applies to both kinds of cell spacing.

Also new to CSS2, you can collapse borders, removing the cell spacing altogether. This makes your table look more like the way a table appears in a word-processing document. The property is called border-collapse. This applies only to table elements: TABLE, COLGROUP, COL, THEAD, TFOOT, TBODY, TR, TH, and TD.

```
TABLE {
        border-collapse: collapse;
}
```

The default value of border-collapse is *separate*. You can choose between the keywords *collapse* and *separate*.

Defining Cell Padding

Cell padding is the white space between the contents of a cell and the borders of a cell. Cell padding can be defined at the TABLE level, the column group or column level, the row group or row level, or the cell level. By default, browsers render tables without any cell padding. This tends to make the widest element in each cell look crowded.

The property is the same padding property used to define padding for any block-level element that takes advantage of the box formatting model.

```
TABLE {
        padding: 1em;
}
```

Even if you specify an absolute width for a table or a cell, the padding attribute has an effect. If you specify an absolute width and padding, the browser will make the width of the cell in which the contents appear smaller, allowing room for the padding.

Using Colors in Tables

Within a table, you can assign color to several elements. These elements include the borders, the rules, the background color, and the text color. You can specify all these things as the same for a table or you can specify different colors for every rule, border, cell text color, and cell background color. The properties are the same as for the rest of CSS: `color`, `background-color`, and the variations on the `border/border-color` **property.**

```
COLGROUP {
        border: thin solid black;
        background-color: white;
        color: black;
}
COLGROUP.highlight {
        border-left: thick solid blue;
        background-color: yellow;
        color: navy;
}
```

Defining Rules and Borders

By default, tables in HTML have a border-width set to zero. This means all rules and borders are turned off. If you take the small action of setting border-width to 1, you will suddenly have both borders and rules.

Rules are the lines between cells. The capability to define these independently of the border, which is the line around the table, is new to HTML 4. The three attributes for defining borders are: `rules`, `frame`, and `border`. The border attribute defines the width of the frame and rules; the value must be defined as a valid measurement using the units listed in Chapter 29.

The `frame` attribute takes a keyword value; valid values are as follows:

- ✦ **void.** No borders are displayed on the table; this is the default value.
- ✦ **above.** Only a top border is displayed.
- ✦ **below.** Only the bottom border is displayed.
- ✦ **hsides.** The top and bottom borders are displayed.
- ✦ **vsides.** The right and left borders are displayed.
- ✦ **lhs.** Only the left-hand side border is displayed.
- ✦ **rhs.** Only the right-hand side border is displayed.
- ✦ **box.** All four sides are displayed.
- ✦ **border.** All four sides are displayed.

The `rules` attribute also takes a keyword value. The `rules` attribute specifies internal lines. Valid values for the `rules` attribute are as follows:

✦ **none.** No rules are displayed. This is the default value.

✦ **group.** Rules are displayed only between groups.

✦ **rows.** Rules are displayed between rows.

✦ **cols.** Rules are displayed between columns.

✦ **all.** Rules are displayed between all cells.

From Here

Jump to Chapter 33 and learn about CSS absolute-positioning tricks.

Proceed to Chapter 31 to learn about using CSS to define fonts.

Summary

Using a combination of CSS1, CSS2, and HTML 4, you can define the formatting of your tables. Controlling table alignment, horizontal alignment of cell contents in your cells, and vertical alignment of cell contents in your rows is relatively straightforward. In this chapter, you learned about specifying table and cell widths as both relative and absolute values. You also learned about cell spacing, cell padding, defining rules and borders, and defining colors in tables.

✦   ✦   ✦

Adding Fonts

CSS gives you incredible flexibility in defining fonts for your pages. You can specify multiple font faces, sizes for each element, the width between letters, and the spacing between words. You can even add interesting typographical effects, such as all caps on the first line (which many magazines and newspapers use), and a first letter that spans multiple lines. This chapter explains how to create all these effects using CSS.

Introducing Fonts

Most people think of fonts as letters. Fonts are really the representation of letters with *glyphs* (pictures). The letters a, b, and c can look very different in Arial, Times New Roman, and Lucida Console. Even though the letters are the same, the glyphs are different.

Font families

The two major font families are *serif* and *sans serif*. Serif fonts include little decorations on the edges of letters. The most common serif font is Times Roman or Times New Roman, depending on your platform. Sans serif (meaning without serif) fonts are much plainer. As you can see in Figure 31-1, Arial and Lucida Console are sans serif fonts.

When you send text over the Internet, normally you send only your choices of the letters that make up the text. The recipient's browser renders your text by using whatever font face and size its owner has configured it to use. Until recently, you couldn't send the choice of font — and you certainly couldn't send the actual font. With CSS, Web authors have increasing control over font choice.

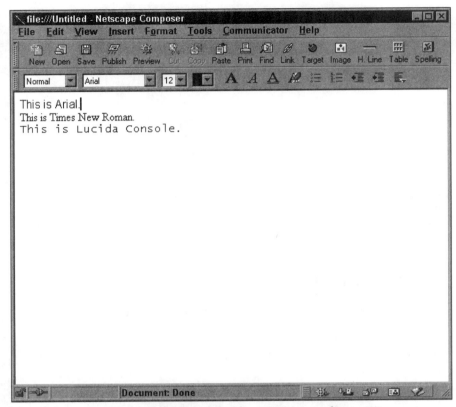

Figure 31-1: Sample fonts displayed in Netscape Communicator 4.7

One reason text renders so quickly in your browser is that nothing more than choices of letters — not the actual glyphs — are sent to your computer. With CSS, the Web developer now has four possible choices:

✦ Send text without specifying a font

✦ Send text that specifies which font the browser should use (usually as a list of choices in case the first choice isn't present)

✦ Rely on CSS2's support for intelligent matching or font synthesis, if the specified font is unavailable on the target computer — if supported by the browser

✦ Send the text with the URL of a *downloadable* font (which requires specialized software)

Fonts versus the image of fonts

Most Web developers who want to include fonts other than those commonly available create their text as graphics and send graphics instead of text. This approach can substantially slow down the load time of their pages. On the upside, it does guarantee that anyone with a graphics-capable browser will see the font the same way. If you want to show a small amount of a foreign language, using an image of text is probably the best way to go; your visitors need not load a special font set or run any particular operating system.

Using Local Fonts

If you decided you don't want to be stuck using the default font on the system — and you don't want to play games with creating images of text instead of sending the text — then you may want to take advantage of the CSS capability that specifies which local fonts the system ought to use. Because you can't know which fonts are installed on the browser — and you can't even know whether the browser is a PC, a Mac, or something else (unless you are developing for an intranet) — CSS gives you the option of specifying a list of fonts from which the browser can select. It will use the first listed font that matches one currently installed. To be even more thorough, after specifying each specific font name you would prefer the browser to use, you can specify font family names; doing so ensures that if none of your specified fonts is present, the browser selects something that at least looks similar.

Font-Selection Considerations

There are two major factors to consider when selecting the fonts for your page. The first relates to aesthetics:

✦ Do the fonts on the page work together?

✦ How many different fonts work on one page?

✦ Should you mix serif and sans serif fonts?

The second factor relates directly to whether the browser can re-create the page as you initially conceived it.

The aesthetics of font selection

Different fonts connote different qualities. Do you want the artistic sweep of a cursive font such as Brush Script? Do you want the clean lines of a sans serif font such as Helvetica? There are good reasons to use just about any font, but you'll want to make sure the font you select helps convey your message, rather than getting in the way of it.

Consider whether to use the same font for headings as you do for paragraph text. Serif fonts such as Times Roman (which have little hooks on the ends of the letters) are easier to read. Sans serif fonts such as Helvetica are cleaner looking and leave more white space. For these reasons, many people choose to use serif fonts for paragraph text and sans serif text for headings. You can use more than one font family in your document, but normally it's wise to avoid using more than two font families in one document. Too many font families can contribute to a cluttered or disorganized look.

Availability of local fonts

Even if you can create the perfect page, with just the right fonts, on your local system, what can you do to ensure that the browser renders your page as you would like it to be rendered? You can send a list of fonts you would like the browser to use, and the browser will use the first one in your list that it has. You aren't limited in how many you can list. If the default browser font would be noticeably worse, you would be well advised to list every font that would work well.

Controlling Font Selection

You can use the font-family property to indicate which font you want the browser to use. You can identify specific fonts, font families (serif, sans serif, cursive, fantasy, monospace), or both. If you list both, include the font families at the end so the browser will look for the most precise match before it uses a generic font family.

```
P {
        font-family: "Bookman Antiqua", Georgia, "Times New
Roman", "Times Roman", Times, serif;
}
```

The rule just given tells the browser the paragraph text should be rendered with Bookman Antiqua font; if that is not available, Georgia; if Georgia is not available, Times New Roman; if Times New Roman is not available, Times Roman; if Times Roman is not available, Times — or, if none of those fonts are available, any serif font. Note, any font name with more than one word in it should be contained in double quotes.

Tip Internet Explorer does a pretty good job of handling font families. It does provide a script font when you specify cursive, but it gives you the same font for fantasy as for sans serif. Netscape gives you sans serif for both cursive and fantasy font families. However, if you specify "Comic Sans MS" font (which is part of the fantasy family), it will work on both Netscape and Internet Explorer. The moral of the story: Specify the exact font you want used; don't rely on font families.

Choosing Font Sizes

You can set the font size with the font-size property. Setting the font size is useful because you can be sure the browser will lay out headings as you want them to appear. Normally, H6 elements render the same as regular paragraph text. You can change this and give greater importance to H6 elements by increasing the font size, changing the font style, or increasing the line height.

The font-size property takes a value in points (pt):

```
H6 {
        font-size: 14pt;
}
```

Using Condensed and Expanded Fonts

You can condense and expand fonts both horizontally — by compressing or spreading out the letters or the words — and vertically — by decreasing or increasing the white space between lines, using CSS. Table 31-1 shows each type of property at work.

	Table 31-1	
Expanding and Condensing Lines, Words, and Letter Spacing		
Type of Spacing	*CSS*	*Example*
Expanding letter spacing	P.wide {letter-spacing: .5pt; }	This is an example of increased letter spacing.
Condensing letter spacing	P.narrow {letter-spacing: -.8pt; }	This is an example of decreased letter spacing.

Continued

Table 31-1 *(continued)*

Type of Spacing	*CSS*	*Example*
Condensing space between rows	`P.crowded { line-height: 10pt; }`	This is an example of decreased line height; notice the lines really crowd each other.
Expanding space between rows	`P.speaking-slowly { line-height: 18pt; }`	This is an example of increased line height; notice the lines are a bit more spread out.
Expanding space between words	`P.speaking-slowly { word-spacing: 1em; }`	This is an example of expanded word spacing.

Condensing and expanding horizontally

To condense or expand fonts horizontally (meaning the letters appear closer to each other than they normally would), use the letter-spacing property to add to the default value of space between letters.

```
H1 {
      letter-spacing: .2em;
}
```

In the preceding example, the letter spacing will be increased by 0.2em for `H1` elements.

```
P.legal {
      letter-spacing: -.2em;
}
```

In the preceding example, the letter spacing will be decreased by 0.2em for `P` elements with a class of *legal*.

You can also expand or condense fonts by increasing or decreasing the white space between words. The property for this is called *word spacing*. It works like letter spacing, which adds to the default amount of white space between words.

```
P.spread-out {
      letter-spacing: .2em;
      word-spacing: .5em;
}
```

The previous example creates a class called *spread out,* in which there is an extra 0.2em of space between letters and an extra 0.5em of space between words.

Tip

If you spread out letters, you probably want to spread out words as well, or it might not be clear where one word ends and the next one begins.

Condensing and expanding vertically

Condensing or expanding text on the page vertically — that is, leaving more or less white space between lines — is easily accomplished with the line-height property. By default, line height is two pixels greater than font-size. For example, if you have a 12pt font for your paragraph text, the browser will automatically render the text with 14pt line height — 12 points for the letter and one blank point to provide blank space at both the top and bottom of the letter. If you want to condense the line height, you can do so by specifying a line height less than 2 points greater than the font size. If you want to increase the white space between lines, increase the line height to more than two points greater than the font size.

```
P {
        font-size: 12pt;
        line-height: 14pt;
}
P.double {
        font-size: 12pt;
        line-height: 24pt;
}
P.smooshed {
        font-size: 12pt;
        line-height: 12pt;
}
```

For clarity in this example, the font size is repeated for each class, but it needn't be repeated. The double class double-spaces the 12pt text. The smooshed class leaves no white space between lines.

Adding Small Caps and Other Decorations

You can do two very cool things with CSS. They take advantage of the pseudo-elements called first-line and first-letter. You learned about pseudo-classes in Chapter 26; pseudo-classes are related to the A element. The descriptors for these classes (A:link, A:visited, A:active) can be assigned their own values to further customize the look of linked text.

Changing the first line

Pseudo-elements relate to the typographical layout of your page. The property called first-line enables you to simulate newspapers and magazines, which often apply a different typographical effect to the first line of text in a paragraph (all caps, for example).

```
P.first:first-line {
        font-style: small-caps;
}
```

When you have this rule in your style sheet, you can use the following HTML:

```
<P class="first">In Chicago today, it was announced that people
with more money live in nicer neighborhoods.</P>
```

This approach would render text similar to the following example in your browser:

IN CHICAGO TODAY, IT WAS ANNOUNCED
that people with more money live in
nicer neighborhoods.

Changing the first letter

The property called first-letter enables you to create text with a first letter that extends below the first line. For example, in many magazines, the first letter of the first paragraph in an article is two lines high.

```
P.drop-cap:first-letter {
        font-size: 36pt;
        float: left;
}
```

With this rule in your style sheet, you can use the following HTML:

```
<P class="drop-cap">In Chicago today, it was announced that
people with more money live in nicer neighborhoods.</P>
```

In a browser that supports this feature (which currently excludes both Netscape 4 and Internet Explorer 4), the code just given renders like this:

In Chicago today, it was announced
that people with more money live
in nicer neighborhoods.

From Here

 Proceed to Chapter 32 and explore the essentials of Web page design.

Refer back to Chapter 22 to review frames.

Summary

In this chapter, you learned about specifying the fonts you want used with your Web page. You also learned that fonts are really pictures of letters called *glyphs*. This chapter discussed the factors you should consider when selecting fonts and the number of font faces you probably don't want to exceed. You learned to specify font size and font spacing (both horizontally and vertically), and you learned to add very cool text decorations, such as all caps on the first line, or a first letter that spans several rows.

✦　　✦　　✦

Lay It Out Like the Pros

◆ ◆ ◆ ◆

Essentials of Web Page Design

Are you ready to design a page? How you design your page is a *tactical decision*, which this chapter covers.

Your page design must be focused to contribute the feelings you want your visitors to have about your site. It needs to incorporate consistency, predictability, navigability, and a clear purpose with visual appeal and interactivity. When you finish this chapter, you'll be ready to start designing your content.

What's in a Page?

The first thing you must do is decide what you want to communicate in each page. As you break your text into separate thoughts, a process referred to as chunking, the result will be a number of pages. Each page will contribute in some way to the overall goal of your site, either directly or indirectly.

Figure 32-1 shows a diagram of a listing page.

What needs to be in a page? Generally, you want all your pages to have certain items. These include the following:

+ The name of the organization or person publishing the page. Remember, with search engines indexing your site, someone can jump into the middle of your site. If you don't say who you are on every page, visitors may not know.

+ A way to get to your Welcome page. This follows from the previous one. Don't assume everyone coming to your site is coming through the front door.

Figure 32-1: A detail from the fully developed Over the Web site map

Other optional elements include the following:

✦ Your logo

✦ How to contact you

✦ A navigation bar or navigation buttons

✦ A link to a table of contents

✦ A link to a site search page

✦ A link to a site map

✦ A drop-down list of places to go

✦ Content, if a terminal page

✦ Links to a group of pages, if a links page

Focusing on Your Message

Now that you have a page-size morsel of information, you should have an idea of what the message of that page is. If you don't know, consider how it fits into the site. If you don't think it contributes to the overall goals of the site in some way, drop it.

Everything you put on your page should contribute in some way to communicating your message. One of the secrets of creating consistent, easily navigated, visually appealing, compelling sites is to limit the amount of content on each page.

Keeping it to the point (your left brain)

Your message needs to be short and sweet. If you find you have too many different things to communicate in your page, take one of three actions:

1. **Unless your page is a *terminal page*, you can group related material and link to it.** Be careful about adding too many layers of linking pages, though. Whenever possible, group your links so even though the list of links might be long, your visitors can still find what they want relatively easily. The nicest way to do this is by using dynamic HTML, which is discussed in Part VII. The next best thing is to give a list of the groups of links on your page at the top of your page and then use internal links (remember learning about them in Chapter 3?) to jump within your page to the group of links associated with the short list.

2. **Decide what is important and forget about the rest.** You keep reading this, don't you? Simply too much information is on most sites. Unnecessary information does not help your visitor understand your message. Unnecessary information just clutters.

3. **Break your material into more than one page.** We put this last because if you've broken your material into separate thoughts (chunking) and you still think you have too much to put into one page, then you probably have material that isn't well suited to hypertext. Or, you have material that will be printed, and your visitors will appreciate you not breaking up your material if they plan to print it.

Definition

Terminal page. A terminal page is a page whose primary function is to provide content, rather than to provide links. This is what your visitors came for: content. Your site is composed of a Welcome page, linking pages, and terminal pages. You can visualize the Welcome page as the root of a tree, the linking pages as the trunk and branches, and the terminal page as the leaves.

Go with the feeling (your right brain)

What kinds of thoughts and feelings do you want to convey with your page? What adjectives do you want people to use when they describe your site? Your page design will evoke certain feelings in your visitor, even if you don't want it to do this. What kinds of feelings do you get from each of the following?

✦ White background with black text, Helvetica font

✦ Cream background with brown text, brush script font

✦ Cool gray background with burgundy and black lines breaking up the black text, font that looks like printing

✦ Tan background, forest green text, mustard-colored lines and accents

Your colors, accents, graphics, and text style and size can all contribute to your message. They make an impression on your visitors whether or not you intend them to do so. Don't take shortcuts here.

When to ask for help

If, after reading through this chapter, you decide you are simply not a *designer,* and many of us are not, then hire someone to provide just the *look* of the page. You can do everything else with the HTML; your designer can just create the style sheet and the graphics. This is too important to take shortcuts.

How do you find a good designer? Surf the Web. If you find a site that rings your bell, write to the Webmaster and find out who designed it. Designers each have their own looks. Find a designer who has the look you want. Professional designers often leave their signatures on the site, as an artist signs a painting. Look for this. Explain that you will create the site and all you are looking for is the design work. It won't cost that much. The labor-intensive part is creating and maintaining the HTML.

Note   One respected professional Web designer, Tamra Heathershaw-Hart, had this to say about the costs of creating versus maintaining a Web site: "I've found that for most 20-page sites, graphic design (and the management of getting the design) takes 50 percent of the cost. Another 30 percent is HTML and production, and 20 percent is for content creation. Because graphics are so subjective (unlike a typo), there's a lot of overhead in the graphics production process. It also usually takes 4–6 weeks to get a design from first meeting to HTML comps -- producing the pages is quick once that's all done."

Lead me not into temptation

It's easy to get distracted from the message of your page when you start thinking about graphics, fonts, colors, animations, and so forth. You need to balance these competing interests. The HTML 4 Way helps relieve you of this temptation. You can actually separate your right-brain work (design) from your left-brain work (content and structure) by using style sheets.

To help you stay focused, settle on your design and *move on.* Commit to a design and don't go back and fiddle with it. You can easily change the style sheet later, but you will have more work if you change the basic design. The best way to avoid the constant temptation to add nice-looking things to your site is to divide the work of your site between two people or teams. This way the person responsible for the content won't get off track. And, most important, the site will be finished — at least for a moment! Later in this chapter, we give some attention to the myth of Web site completeness. You will be relieved to know you aren't the only one who feels like your site is never done.

The Shell Game

Is there any good way to assure consistence, predictability, and easy navigation from all the pages of a site? You bet! Use a shell. Your page has basically three types of pages:

1. A Welcome page

2. Links pages

3. Terminal pages

Each of these three types of pages requires a slightly different design. Page shells — or templates — provide the consistency you need.

The word *shell* is more accurate than the word *template* because templates traditionally have formatting information in them. Because The HTML 4 Way pulls all this formatting out, what is left is a shell of a page. Look at the three screen captures, shown in Figures 32-2, 32-3, and 32-4. They show the page design for each of the three types of pages for this site. Wouldn't it be easy to create a great-looking site if you could insert your content into shells that looked like this?

Figure 32-2: This Welcome page isn't really a shell, because there will only be one, but it is consistent with the design of the rest of the site.

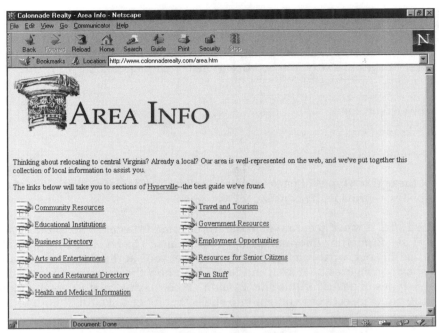

Figure 32-3: Links pages share the look of the Welcome page.

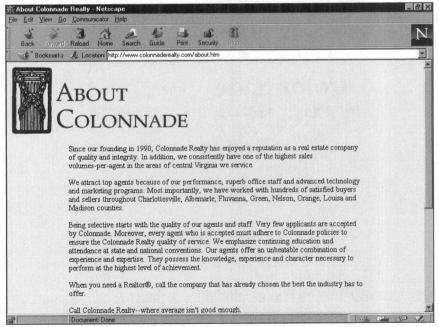

Figure 32-4: Terminal pages carry out the same design theme.

Consistency

You want to make sure your entire site has the same look. Not just in the big picture, but in the details. Fortunately, style sheets can help you here. You can assure that all your paragraphs have the same level of indentation and the same amount of white space above and below them.

As a Webmaster, you do have to make sure everyone developing content for your site understands when to use the paragraph element and when to use the blockquote element. Veteran Web developers have had to use a lot of tricks in the past to get paragraphs to look nice; one of these tricks was using the blockquote element to format paragraphs. This is a habit you should help them break.

Figure 32-5 illustrates the problem of distinguishing one from the other.

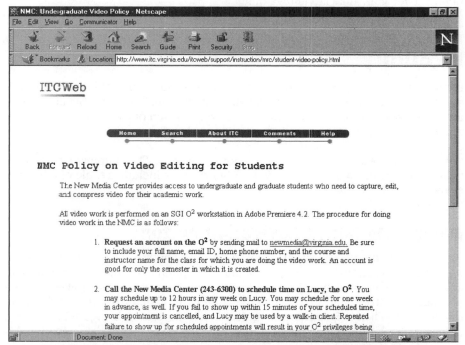

Figure 32-5: Are these paragraphs or blockquotes? You'd have to view the source to find out.

Applying a style sheet to a page with paragraphs formatted with the blockquote element can have unpredictable and unattractive results.

Predictability

No one really likes surprises. Elements of your page should behave the way visitors expect. Don't format text in blue with an underline, because it will look the way visitors expect links to look, but won't link. Don't create button-looking designs with text in your graphic unless your graphic is also an imagemap. On the other side of the coin, don't format your links to be the same color as your other text or visitors won't know to click them. Also, while subtlety is nice, don't make the buttons on your imagemaps so subtle that no one would think to click them.

The Web is a fabulous platform and is unique among platforms because your visitors don't have to learn to use a new interface to view your material. In the olden days, before the Web, every software program had its own interface. This meant users of the software had to learn new interfaces every time they wanted to use new software. With the Web, if you give users what they expect, the interface is a nonissue for you. Take advantage of it.

Navigability

Because this is the tactics chapter, this is where you need to think about how you are going to implement them within your page design. Earlier in this chapter, some attention was devoted to navigational controls. Which ones should you use? How much screen real estate should you devote to them?

You certainly need to use *some* navigational controls. The simplest kind to use is a navigation bar or navigation buttons. Other options include a table of contents, site searching, and site maps.

Navigation bar or navigation buttons

The simplest kind of navigational tool to use is the *navigation bar*. A navigation bar can be either text, text in a table, or an imagemap. The navigation bar should appear on every page in the same place or places. Many sites use frames to keep the navigation bar or buttons stationary while the content and links move into and out of a different frame. The navigation bar with text in a table, shown in Figure 32-6, is in a different frame from the content on the right. Figure 32-7 shows a navigational bar used with an image map.

Jump to Chapter 22 for a refresher on the pros and cons of using frames.

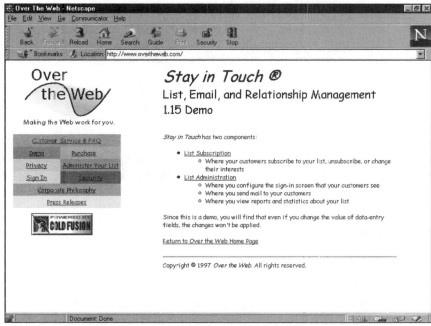

Figure 32-6: Over the Web uses a navigation bar with text in a table.

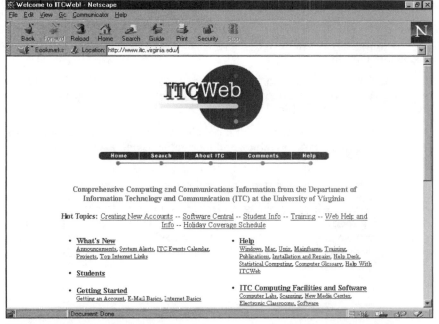

Figure 32-7: The University of Virginia uses a navigation bar with an imagemap.

Definition

Frames. Frames are a way to have two different HTML files open at the same time in the browser. You can divide your browser page either vertically, horizontally, or both. Frames keep your visitor grounded because only part of the browser gets updated most of the time, which leads to faster page loading.

You are likely to see text navigation bars on the *text-only* version of a site, but you can certainly put them on all versions of the site. They look like this:

```
[Home][Support][Service][Sales][Contact Us][Feedback]
```

Each item within the square brackets is a hyperlink to that area of the site. A text navigation bar should go on its own line and should appear in the same place on every page.

Table of contents

Having a table of contents (TOC) only one click away can be a lifesaver for your visitor. This can also save you valuable screen real estate as a designer. A site map and a TOC should contain basically the same information, but a TOC is usually text-based, whereas a site map is usually graphical. You can implement a TOC in two ways — the easy way and the elegant way.

Text-only sites

Should you create a text-only version of your site? Yes. Every site should have a text-only version to allow maximum access even to people whose Internet connections involve cups and a string. Is that realistic? No.

If you have the resources to maintain a text-only site, great. But for most Webmasters, who are struggling just to keep the primary Web site up-to-date and keep up with emerging technologies, it is simply not realistic.

Why maintain a text-only site? Faster access for people with slow Internet connections who have never heard of turning off the graphics, and for people using Lynx browsers, who can't see graphics.

Why not maintain a text-only site? Time, energy, and expense.

What alternative do you have to providing a text-only site? You can do several things to increase downloading speed and they are all discussed later in this chapter. In addition, there are things that will make a page heavily dependent on graphics useful to a visitor who arrives with image loading turned off. Watch for the `alt` attribute to elements throughout this book.

The easy way

Even if you choose to implement the TOC the elegant way, you still need to implement it the easy way for people who have old browsers. In the easy way, every page in your site has a button or part of the navigation bar that links to a separate page where the TOC resides.

If the TOC is large, then you want to have all the major headings near the top of the page with links to the details later in the same page. If you can, try to keep the short list at the top of the page only one screen long.

If the TOC is not that long, just list all the pages. You probably want to have the names of the pages in the TOC correspond with the titles of the pages. You certainly want every page name in the TOC to link to the corresponding page in your site.

If the page names, or if only a few page names, aren't adequately descriptive, include a brief description under those page names. Use the brief description only if it increases clarity; you needn't do it for every single page.

The elegant way

Using JavaScript and the Document Object Model, collectively known as dynamic HTML, you can create an incredibly rich, interactive table of contents that can make your site look like a million dollars. Of course, this only works on browsers that support HTML 4, but you can use another line or two of JavaScript to check to see what browser your visitor is running and implement the easy way for those who can't see your work of art in dynamic HTML.

Definition

Document Object Model (DOM). A set of rules that, when implemented by browsers, give you, the designer, incredible access to the elements on your Web page. Formerly, if you wanted to have JavaScript change the color of your text, you had to reload your page; with the DOM the change to text color can happen when the user clicks a radio button or a check box. You can create dynamic forms, where the next field on the screen appears in response to the information entered in the previous field. The DOM empowers the designer enormously and saves the visitor from page reloads and multiple screens. This is so exciting and important, Part VII is devoted to it.

Site map

Site maps can be useful, and Chapter 36 has in-depth coverage of them. You want to be careful how much detail you include in your site map, which should be an imagemap, as well. If you include too much detail either it will take a long time to load, because the graphics file will be enormous, or the text will be tiny and difficult to read, or both.

Site mapping tools

There are site mapping tools and there are site mapping tools. Most often when one hears about site mapping, it is about mapping the site from a Webmaster's perspective: Do all the links work? Where are the files physically located? This is not the kind of site map a visitor to a site needs. In addition, tools that map sites for purposes of site management rarely produce Web-quality digital images that make sense to the visitor. Two different approaches you can take to create a site map for the Web visitor are demonstrated by Microsoft Organization Chart and Dynamic Diagrams' MAPA Service.

On the low end is Microsoft Organization Chart. This is an easy tool to use to create attractive site maps, but you have to do all the work yourself. If you have PowerPoint installed on your computer, then you already have it. Whenever you change your site, you must remember to update your site map published with the new version. This product only works for small sites. The amount of energy required to maintain the site map for sites developed by the team would soon outstrip the economy of the initial software price.

On the high end is Dynamic Diagrams' MAPA Service. This is written in Java and lets your Web site map itself. Because it is a service, there is no software to purchase, upgrade, or install. You always get the most recent version of the product. MAPA creates a 3D animated map, a Java applet, that runs on the Java-enabled browsers of your visitors. The MAPA service is priced based on the size of your site. You pay a monthly fee for either daily or weekly mappings. The price is so low that if your site is over 100 pages, you shouldn't even consider creating and maintaining the site map yourself. The applet it creates is so smooth and well designed, it solves all your navigation problems. Definitely look at it at http://www.dynamicdiagrams.com.

Site search

Some sites include a search field on every page; some link to a search page. If your audience is sophisticated enough to know how to use the search field and you can spare the space on your page, then go ahead and put the search field on every page. If your audience is likely not to be too technically sophisticated or you want to give them more information about searching, then link to a separate page for entering search terms. In either case, you need either a separate page or a separate frame for search results. On the back end, you need to be sure your server has a search and index program running or your visitor's search will never return any results.

Site drop-down list

This is a clever item to add to your arsenal of navigational tools. Using a drop-down list, you can give your visitors the power to link anywhere on your list with just one click. The list can be as long as you want. The drop-down list (called a *select list* in HTML) takes up little screen real estate, so it is a double value.

> **Tip** Make sure your visitors understand the drop-down list is another navigational tool. Otherwise, the value is wasted. Visitors to your site — especially inexperienced users — may need a little direction.

Visual Appeal

Beautiful pages are not that plentiful on the Web. What do people find beautiful on a page? The same things that are beautiful on a brochure: clean lines, smooth shapes, and complementary colors. In 1765, Edmund Burke, the English political philosopher, wrote *A Philosophical Enquiry into the Origin of Our Ideas of the Sublime and Beautiful.* This short book (less than 200 pages) about what we find beautiful is as accurate today as any book you can find on creating graphics for electronic delivery. Nothing has changed. Beauty is timeless.

You are receiving a lot of design suggestions in this chapter. You might be wondering how you can fit all these things into just one page and *still* have room for the content or the links. Try to incorporate as many guidelines as possible into your page. The page shown in Figure 32-2 meets every test of good design in this chapter and it looks like it isn't even trying. Good design is like that. Great athletes make their feats look effortless; good design works the same way. At the end of this chapter is a checklist you can use to make sure your pages have the essentials of good design for the Web.

Interactivity

Your visitors expect almost every page to have some level of interactivity. For links pages and the Welcome page, this is easy. That is really all they do. For content pages, however, visitors also expect to be able to interact with your site. You can include interactivity by using hyperlinks and imagemaps to link both within and outside of the site. You can use dynamic HTML to have interactivity within your page. Forms are another way to provide interactivity.

Speed

How much should you worry about speed? Worry may be too strong a word. Even though bandwidth is getting cheaper and more available, don't make the mistake of believing everyone accessing your page is on a T1 line (with fast access). You still should be considerate about the amount of data you expect them to download to see your page. Even though this book talks about *visitors to your site,* in fact, your site is *delivered to* the desktops of the people who request it in their browsers.

When you design your pages with huge graphics — background images that fill the screen, large image maps, graphical representations of text rather than text — you are telling your visitors you don't respect their time. Is this the message you want to send?

The facts about Internet connections

T1, T3, dial-up, 56K, cable modem: what does it all mean in plain English? T1 and T3 are types of Internet connections used by those users willing to pay more for the faster connection—typically businesses, universities, and probably by your ISP, if you have one. The backbone of the Internet is T3. T1 transfers data at 1.5 Mbps. T3 communicates at between 3 Mbps and 45 Mbps (something you want to ask your ISP about if it claims to have a T3 line). When you have a dial-up connection to the Internet, your modem communicates with your ISP's modem at the speed of the slower modem. So even if you have a 56K modem, if your ISP has 28.8 lines, you communicate at 28.8. Some technologies, such as 56K modems and cable modems, use asymmetrical communication, which means download *from the Internet* is at one speed and upload *to the Internet* is at another speed. Download may approach the promised speed, but upload won't. This chart should help. It assumes the other end of the connection is at least as fast.

Type of Connection	Download	Upload
28.8K modem	28.8K	28.8K
56K modem	50K	33.6K
cable modem (varied by modem)	400K	100K
T1	1MG	1MG
T3	10MG	10MG

Of course, there is no guarantee you will ever communicate at the ceiling speed, which is what the table shows, but for purposes of calculation, you must assume something. An overloaded Web server could cut download speed by a factor of ten or more. The chart doesn't define *K*, which is 1,000 bytes per second or 1,000 characters per second, but what really matters is you see the relationship between the different connection speeds. If a page takes a moment to download for you when you are connected via a T1, it will take a long time to load for your visitors, who, you should assume, are probably at a slower connection speed.

Design Guidelines

Good page design is a skill. If you know absolutely nothing about page layout and design, it'll show. If you are attempting to design a site for commercial use, it's probably best to hire a professional. You can learn it yourself, but you must expend some intensive time and effort. For those of you insistent upon doing page layout yourselves, here are ten things to remember:

1. Think of the underlying design as a *hanger*. Once you figure out what the basic design is, everything else *hangs* off it. If you don't have the hanger, you're going to be struggling with each element and it's going to drive you insane.

Look at Figure 32-2 again. The designer, Debra Weiss of drw Design (http://www.cstone.net/~debra/drwdesign), had this to say about it:

"I was struggling over the look and feel of this site for quite some time. I wanted it to look elegant, but I didn't want the design to get in the way of the functionality. Then, it struck me. When I was visiting the Colonnade offices, I remembered noticing several framed prints of Greek architectural drawings of temples and columns and admiring them. I was able to locate some wonderful digital artwork of this type—floorplans, pillars, columns, and colonnades. This concept became the hanger. Each section of the site has a different column that represents it. One of the page backgrounds is a screened-back floor plan. The headline font is Palatino, a classical font. The navigational icons are teeny column tops. The design just snapped into place."

2. Decide on an underlying grid structure and don't deviate. Look at any magazine or publication. Analyze how the text and graphics are aligned. Is it a one-, two-, three-, or four-column grid? For consistency, use the same number of pixels for horizontal spacing between text and images—at least 5 pixels.

3. Use real typographical marks. This is a subtlety, but it makes a subconscious impression on the reader. Most Web browsers display quotation marks like this: "hello." You want this: "hello." While not all browsers support these entities yet, ideally you can insert real typographical quotation marks using entities as follows:

```
"        =        &ldquo;
"        =        &rdquo;

'        =        &lsaquo;
'        =        &rsaquo;
```

4. Decide on your color palette, and stick with it. If your colors are navy, burgundy, and cream, don't make your links green.

5. Anti-alias your display fonts. The mark of a professional site can sometimes be as simple as the look of the fonts.

6. Be target-aware. Many sites make the mistake of providing hundreds of links to other sites. It's hard enough to get people to come to your site—why send them away? If you link to other sites, use the target =_blank attribute-value pair to open the link in a new window. This way, visitors can return to your site easily. Opening links in a separate window also solves anomalies that occur when your site has frames and you link to a site that also has frames.

7. People read from left to right and from top to bottom. This seems obvious, but inexperienced designers seem to have trouble remembering this. Put your most important elements at the top left of the page. If you don't grab the reader's attention there, you're never going to get them to read more.

8. Think carefully about bells and whistles. Animations, marquees, DHTML, and so forth are all great, *when used in moderation*. Don't pull all your tricks out of the bag and plop them all on one page. If your content isn't good enough to stand alone, rethink it.

9. Use different font styles sparingly. A good rule of thumb is to pick two font families at the most. Use one for your headlines and subheads. Use the other for body copy.

10. Look at your site using the worst conditions possible. Get a copy of Netscape 2.0. Set your display to 600×480, 256 colors. Set your modem down to 14.4 or 28.8 and look at your site. Every page. If you can't stand it, redesign until it's acceptable. If your page looks great under the worst conditions, it'll shine under the best ones.

Does this mean you have to sacrifice design to keep pages loading quickly? Not necessarily. The important thing is you don't add gratuitous graphics if you can avoid it. If you need slow-to-load features on your site—as an example, Java applets can be very slow to load—then you want to do what you can to have them load without making the visitor wait for them. Just ignore this whole section if you are designing for an intranet where every visitor to your pages will have a reliably fast connection. There are environments where you don't have to worry about these things. For the rest of us: things can be done to speed the delivery time of your pages. But first you need to understand what slows the loading of your page.

Slow modems and large graphics are the biggest offenders. Because you can't control the modem speed of your visitor, you have to do what you can on your end to make sure your page won't take an unreasonably long time to download. The only control you have is to control the size of graphics on your page. By using intelligent compression on your images and by using multiple small images with white space around them (rather than one large image), you can reduce the size of the files your visitor has to download, thus reducing the download time.

Cross-Reference   Chapter 37 explains all these concepts and more.

Without getting a Ph.D. in Digital Art, the following guidelines can help you make intelligent decisions about how to show you respect the time of your visitors:

1. Reduce the number of graphics files on your pages. Simple enough. Decide what you need (element-wise) on your page and see how you can convey the information you want to convey without using graphics. Two no-brainers: Don't use custom bullets in a bulleted (unnumbered list), or if you feel you absolutely *must* use custom bullets, use only one bullet graphic for every bullet in your site; and don't create custom Go or Submit buttons.

2. Reduce the size of graphics files. You can do this two ways: reduce the dimensions of the file (height and width) before you publish it, or reduce the bit depth of the images (the amount of color information the file carries). You can also use a trick under certain circumstances to load a tiny file and show a full-sized file. If what you want to do is show some pattern of colors, create the file as a tiny version of the image you want and use the height and width attributes of the object element or the image element (whichever you prefer) to *stretch* the file to the dimensions you want.

Tip

Check out GIF Wizard at www.gifwizard.com. This is a Web-based utility that analyzes and shrinks your GIFs and JPGs.

GIF or JPG? For additional information, check out the collection of excellent articles on the Microsoft Site Builder site at http://msdn.microsoft.com/workshop/design/color/default.asp.

3. Don't use a background image. Or, if you absolutely must, then use a tiny background image that tiles well. See Figure 32-8.

Cross-Reference

Chapter 28 discusses the use of background images at length.

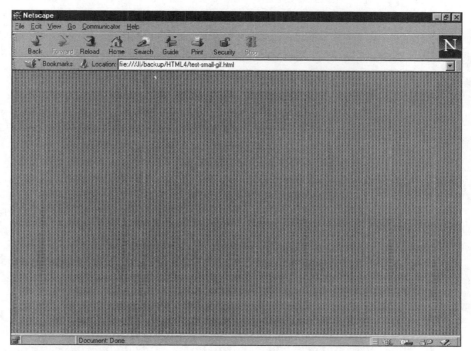

Figure 32-8: The background image on this page is a 6×6-pixel file.

4. Use text when you can use text. What a concept! Next time you have your word processor open, if you use Windows 95, Windows NT, or higher, click the list of fonts available to you. Unless you installed some fancy fonts package, you have the base install of fonts. These same fonts are available to everyone else on the Web who is browsing from either Windows 95 or Windows NT (your results will vary on a Mac or on UNIX). Is this huge list so limiting, you have to re-create text in a graphics package and load it as an image? Get real!

Tip   You can create nice bullets using symbol fonts, such as Wingdings. To figure out what keystrokes to use to insert into your file, use the Windows Character Map, found under Accessories. If you don't have this installed, you should. Don't do this if you expect a significant number of visitors to come to your page from Macs. Macs don't have Wingdings as an installed font and what they see will be unpredictable.

Effective Use of White Space

White space has the most remarkable effect on a page's design. It improves it immeasurably. When you are designing, make sure you allow plenty of it. When you have a lot of white space, you can include the same information (sure, the page will be longer) without creating the feeling of frenzy and chaos that permeates the Web. White space is relaxing. White space doesn't have to be white. If your background is pale powder blue, then your *white space* is really *blue space*.

Definition   **White space.** Uncluttered space on the page. Margins around text and images is white space.

You can use white space to draw attention to a title, a heading, or even a list. Why do you suppose a bulleted list draws your eye? White space contributes to the effect. When in doubt, use white space to break up your design.

Optimum Page Length

Forget about the idea that your entire page needs to fit into one screen without scrolling. What you really must do is to make sure what you do see looks complete. How can you tell how much will fit into a screen? Don't assume all your visitors are running their browsers the way you are. The following section on testing walks you through all the ways you need to test your design to make sure visitors see what looks like a complete page.

More important than the page length is the page content. You don't want to break up your content into annoyingly small bites just to have everything fit into one screen. Frames can help you maintain the sense of completeness so even if visitors have to scroll, they won't lose their grounding.

What you want to avoid at all costs is horizontal scrolling. Do not make your visitors pan across your page to see your content. If you design your pages with a width of 550–600 pixels, you avoid this.

Future Expandability

You mean there'll be more? Definitely. Assume your site will never go away. It will continue to grow. Paying close attention to the site architecture and site organization, as we'll cover in Chapter 36, and to navigational controls as previously described, takes you 80 percent of the way toward having an infinitely expandable site. Creating effective page shells and applying them with discipline takes you the rest of the way.

Designing an Effective Welcome Page

However you decide to organize your site and the content on the pages within your site, you need a Welcome page. The *Welcome page* is the first place visitors see when they come through the front door of your site. As discussed previously, some visitors will come to your site through other doors.

What should you have on a Welcome page? Just enough. Look again at Figure 32-2, because a picture really is worth a thousand words. Just enough to convey a sense about who put up the site. Just enough to get you heading in the direction of the content.

Splash Screens

What about splash screens? *Splash screens* are pages that appear before the Welcome page. They can also be called *entry tunnels*. Usually all they do is enable you to pass through to the Welcome page. There is just one link on a splash screen and it takes you to the Welcome page.

The theory behind the splash screen is you have the visitors' complete attention and you can use this moment to create one strong impression (whether this impression is that you have a great logo or graphic artist or you are wasting their time with slow-loading graphics is hard to say). If you are going to use a splash screen, which is of arguable value — how much attention is the loss of goodwill worth? — then at least look around the Web and find some nice ones. Make sure your splash screen fits into one screen on all browsers at all screen resolutions; this is no time to scroll.

Testing

The importance of testing your page design cannot be emphasized enough. Look at it in all browsers on all platforms at all screen resolutions you can possibly conceive of your visitors using. Subtle differences exist between browsers and you can't assume things will look the same. If you are one who spends weeks at the paint store trying to find just the right shade of paint for your room, then you will waste a lot of time playing with colors in your design only to learn that what looks like a beautiful, rich burgundy on one screen is brown on another and purple on yet another.

 Tip Looking for information about the Web-safe palette? An excellent article is at http://msdn.microsoft.com/workshop/design/color/safety.asp.

The Myth of Completeness

Never, never, never say *under construction*. The entire Web is under construction. If it is complete enough to publish, publish it; otherwise, don't. In the process of writing this book, dozens of professional Web developers were contacted for permission to use their materials in the figures throughout these pages. Probably half of them said something about how the screen captures shouldn't be taken until they had fixed just one more thing they didn't like. You will never be entirely satisfied with your page. You will always want to do more. If it is so embarrassing you have to tell people it is under construction, then you probably shouldn't publish it yet.

Along the same lines, don't be afraid to retire pages. Don't leave old junk up there if it is no longer attractive or accurate. Run link-checking software right away to make sure all your links still work. Because others will retire their own pages occasionally, you'll want to run link-checking software regularly to be sure your external links aren't broken either.

From Here

 Cross-Reference Jump to Part VII and learn about the most exciting thing going on with the Web: Dynamic HTML.

Jump to Chapter 37 and get an intensive course in graphics.

Summary

Page design requires balancing visual appeal against speed, consistency, predictability, easy navigation, and a host of other things. Getting distracted is easy when you are involved in the design process. Remember, this is just a step on the way to publishing your site. If you continually change your design, you'll never get your site published. The HTML 4 Way supports the separation of content from presentation that can help keep you focused. Finally, test, test, test your design to make sure all visitors, no matter where they come from, have a positive experience on your site.

✦　　✦　　✦

Understanding CSS Positioning Options

I n the last few chapters of Part IV, you learned much of what you need to know to use CSS. In this chapter, you learn about positioning options available to you in CSS. This chapter focuses on the five properties that give you complete control over how your elements are positioned on the page. The positioning properties — display, float, clear, position, and z-index — give you the power to position your text and graphics relatively, absolutely, or using some combination of the two.

The display Property

The display property is one you already take for granted. All elements have a display property. You can use the default display property or set your own. You can also use the display property to make elements appear and disappear on your page. Dynamic HTML, which is just JavaScript and CSS with the Document Object Model, takes advantage of the display property to have objects appear and disappear without reloading the page.

There are 17 valid values for the display property:

> ◆ **block.** All block elements have a default display value of block. You can make an inline element behave like a block element by setting the value of the display property to block.

> ◆ **inline.** All inline elements have a default display value of inline. You can, of course, change this.

✦ **list-item.** List items are sort of a hybrid between block elements and inline elements. You probably noticed the chapter that discusses lists beats around the bush on what type of element lists and list items are. A list item is treated as a block element with an added list-item marker.

✦ **compact.** This value creates either block or inline boxes, depending on the context of its use. Properties apply to run-in and compact boxes based on their final status (inline or block level).

✦ **marker.** This value declares generated content before or after a marker box. This value should only be used with :before and :after pseudo-elements that are attached to block-level elements. In other cases, this value is interpreted as inline.

✦ **none.** An element with a display value set to none does not render on the page. The border, if there is any around the element, is not rendered either. The element doesn't take up any space on the page; thus, it doesn't affect the layout of any other elements. Finally, any child elements of the element whose display value is set to none are not rendered (they inherit this display value), *even if* their own display values are explicitly set to something other than none.

Cross-Reference Chapter 48, which covers JavaScript, explains why you might set the display property to none.

✦ **table, inline-table, table-row-group, table-column, table-column-group, table-header-group, table-footer-group, table-row, table-cell, and table-caption.** These values cause an element to behave like a table element (subject to table restrictions).

✦ **run-in.** No elements have a default value of run-in. Setting the display value of an element to run-in has this effect: If the following element is not of type block, is floating, or is positioned absolutely, the run-in element renders as a block element. Otherwise, the run-in element renders as if it were part of the following element, which means inline with the following element. This doesn't work in Version 5 or earlier browsers.

```
H6.run-in {

        display: run-in;
        font-variant: bold;
        }
H6:after.run-in {
        content: ". ";
        }
```

```
<H6 class="run-in">Run-in.</H6>

<P>No elements have a default value of run-in. Setting the
display value of an element to run-in has the effect you see
in this example.</P>
```

The previous example, using the style sheet rules immediately preceding it, renders as follows:

Run-in. No elements have a default value of run-in. Setting the display value of an element to run-in has the effect you see in this example.

The float Property

It is not unusual to want to arrange your page so that one or more elements, most commonly images, appear next to (rather than above or below) other elements. The following HTML and CSS create the effect you see in Figure 33-1:

```
IMG.icon {
        padding: 20px;
        float: left;
}

<HTML>
<HEAD>
  <LINK rel="stylesheet" type="text/css" href="ch33.css">
  <TITLE>Chapter 33 Examples</TITLE>
</HEAD>

<BODY>
<H1>Chapter 33 Examples</H1>

<IMG class="icon" src="fir.gif">

<P>It is common to want to have images appear on the same line
as your text. In this example, the float property of the IMG
class icon is set to "left" to achieve this effect. More text
is required in this example so that you can see that the text
continues to wrap around the image. This is that additional
text that is required. By now, the example should have enough
text to make the point. Just in case, another sentence will
provide additional text for purposes of making this point. This
will be the last sentence. OK, maybe just one more, but I mean
it this time.</P>

</BODY>
</HTML>
```

The float property has three values: left, right, and none. Setting the value of the float property to none (the default value) results in the element not floating at all. In the previous example, the page would instead be rendered as seen in Figure 33-2.

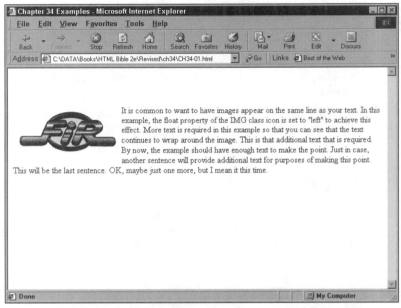

Figure 33-1: Using the float property to wrap text around an image

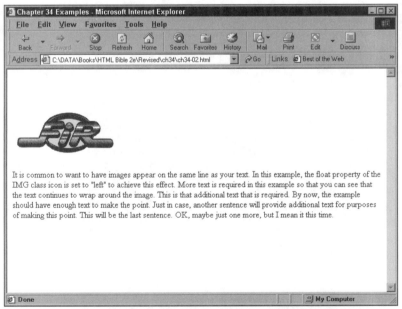

Figure 33-2: Setting the float property to none results in no floating

The clear Property

The clear property works in conjunction with the float property. While the float property is applied to the object you want to wrap around, the clear property is applied to the object you want to do the wrapping. The default value for the clear property is *none*. This means both the right and the left sides of the element are allowed to have a floating object next to them.

In the following example, there are two icon classes. One positions an image as floating to the left of the nonfloating element. The other positions an image as floating to the right of the nonfloating element: in this case, the P element. Notice that both the images must appear *before* the nonfloating element. If they don't, the nonfloating element only wraps around the first image and the second image appears on a line by itself after the nonfloating element.

```
IMG.icon {
       padding: 20px;
       float: left;
}
IMG.icon2 {
       padding: 20px;
       float: right;
}
P {
       clear: none;
}

<BODY>
<H1>Chapter 33 Examples</H1>
<IMG class="icon" src="../public_html/itclogo.gif">
<IMG class="icon2" src="../public_html/itclogo.gif">

<P>It is common to want to have images appear on the same line
as your text. In this example, the float property of the IMG
class icon is set to "left" to achieve this effect. More text
is required in this example so that you can see that the text
continues to wrap around the image. This is that additional
text that is required. By now, the example should have enough
text to make the point. Just in case, another sentence will
provide additional text for purposes of making this point. This
will be the last sentence. OK, maybe just one more, but I mean
it this time.</P>

</BODY>
```

The results of the preceding example can be seen in Figures 33-3 and 33-4. The same example is shown in both Netscape and Internet Explorer so you can see that both browsers render the same thing slightly differently. Specifically, Internet Explorer seems not to respect the padding property. Netscape graduates the text around the image.

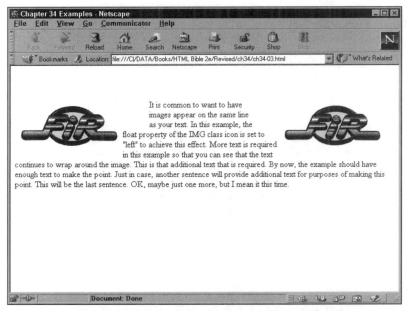

Figure 33-3: Using the float and the clear properties together (in Netscape)

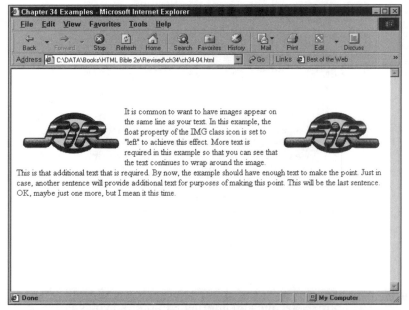

Figure 33-4: Using the float and the clear properties together (in Internet Explorer)

In Figure 33-5, the clear property of the nonfloating element (P) is set to left. This prevents anything from floating to the left of the P element. In this example, however, because both images (being the same image) are the same height, the second image (with a class of icon2) floats to the right on the page, parallel to the first image.

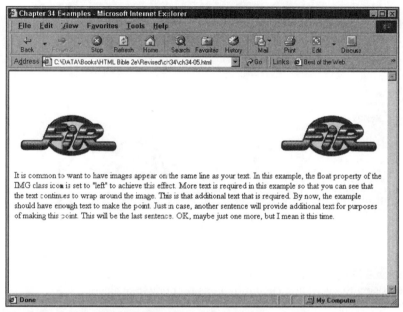

Figure 33-5: Floating with the clear property set to left

The results in Figure 33-5 are not exactly what were intended. If what was wanted was for the second image to float to the right of the text and the first image to be positioned above the text, then the float property of the first image must also be turned off (set to none, commented out, or deleted from the style sheet). The resultant style sheet would look like this:

```
IMG.icon {
        padding: 20px;
        /* float: left; */
}

IMG.icon2 {
        padding: 20px;
        float: right;
}

P {
        clear: left;
}
```

And the results of this style sheet, with the HTML previously given, can be seen in Figure 33-6.

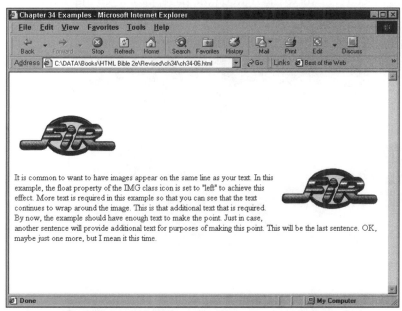

Figure 33-6: Using the float and clear properties properly to achieve desired results

The position Property

The fourth of the five properties you can use to control positioning with CSS is the position property. The position property takes one of three values:

✦ **normal.** This is the default value. Normal position simply means the rules you have learned thus far about CSS apply to your element, and it renders in a position based on the values you assign to it and the values of the previous normal elements.

✦ **relative.** This means relative to the position the element would have if it were defined as a statically positioned element. All children elements are positioned with this new relative position as their starting point. When positioning elements with the relative position, overlaying or obscuring other elements is possible.

✦ **absolute.** When you define an element as absolutely positioned, it is not included in the calculations used to position other elements on the page. The element is simply put where you tell it to be put. All children elements of this element are positioned relatively to this absolute position. When using absolute positioning, it is possible to overlay or obscure other elements.

The z-index Property

The z-index property is a wonderful addition to CSS. It enables you to position elements in the third dimension: depth.

Why would you want to position elements with the z-index property?

✦ To layer graphics (each of which are links), to save space, or to create an interesting visual effect

✦ To layer text over an image

✦ To hide graphics for use later, using JavaScript, when you can simply change the z-index of an object and have it magically appear

Understanding Relative Positioning

In CSS, relative positioning has two possible meanings. Most Web designers think of relative positioning as when they position an element using the float property (formerly the valign and align attributes) or by changing the margins or padding on an element to scoot it one way or another. Generally speaking, *relative positioning* is positioning the element using any means other than absolute positioning. All the properties you have learned about CSS in this chapter and in previous chapters have been about relative positioning, which CSS2 now confusingly calls *static positioning*.

To make matters more interesting, CSS introduced the position property, which you can set to *relative*. This enables you to move an element by some offset from the position at which it would have been positioned if you had allowed the browser to position it using all the previous properties you defined for it and for preceding elements.

To unconvolute the previous sentence, these are the plain-English steps the browser goes through to position an element not defined as absolutely positioned:

1. Calculate the internal size of the box associated with each element

2. Calculate the size of each element's box, including padding, borders, and margins

3. Calculate the position of each element's box on the page based on the amount of space taken up by each previous box

If you choose to set the value of the position property to *relative,* then the browser takes a fourth step to calculate the element's position. After calculating the starting point for that box, the browser uses the relative offset you have indicated to calculate a new position, relative to that starting point.

Understanding Absolute Positioning

When you position an element with absolute positioning, the browser only takes the first two steps previously listed. After it has calculated the size of the box, it renders that box exactly where you tell it. You risk overlaying other elements, if you are not careful, but it can be used to create stunning layout effects.

Combining Relative and Absolute Positioning

You can combine relative and absolute positioning in CSS, but you must do so thoughtfully or you will end up with your text running over your graphics, or your graphics overlaying your text.

The easiest way to combine relative and absolute positioning is to define the first element on your page — say, an image of known dimensions — as absolutely positioned near the top-left of the page, or wherever you want it positioned, and then to define the rest of your page as being relative to that offset (the dimensions of the absolutely positioned element).

Other options for combining relative and absolute positioning include positioning an element to the right or left of the body of your page and limiting the width of the rest of the elements in your page by using the width attribute.

You learn more specific applications of both relative and absolute positioning in Chapter 35.

From Here

Jump to Chapter 47 and learn about the Document Object Model (DOM), which is essential to dynamic HTML.

Proceed to Chapter 34 to learn about positioning and sizing graphics.

Summary

In this chapter you learned advanced CSS. You learned the five essential layout properties: `display`, `float`, `clear`, `position`, and `z-index`. You learned how relative positioning differs from static positioning and how they both differ from absolute positioning. You also learned how to combine relative and absolute positioning.

✦   ✦   ✦

Positioning Graphics and Text

In this chapter, you learn more tricks to give you control over your page's layout using CSS and HTML together. Specifically, you learn how to have an image appear in the location of your choice. This chapter explains how to position your text where you want it to appear and how to wrap your text around floating graphics. Many examples help jog your own creativity.

Specifying Image Location

In the previous chapters, you learned enough CSS to specify where on the page an image should be located. In fact, you learned more than one way to do this.

Using frames

One way to ensure that your image ends up where you want it is to use frames. Consider placing an image in the upper right-hand corner of the screen. If you use frames, you can be sure the graphic will never move.

Your HTML might look like this:

```
<FRAMESET rows="200, *">
  <FRAMESET cols="*, 200">
      <FRAME name="banner" src="banner.html"
frameborder="0">
      <FRAME src="image.gif" scrolling="no"
frameborder="0">
  </FRAMESET>
  <FRAME name="main" src="home.html">
</FRAMESET>
```

In the preceding example, your image, called image.gif, should be exactly 200×200 pixels. By setting the scrolling attribute to *no,* you are assured that a scroll bar won't be to the right of your image. By setting the frameborder attribute to zero for both the columns in the first row of the page, you are assured a border won't be around the banner or around the image next to the banner.

Using CSS with absolute positioning

Another way to specify an image's position is to use the CSS position property with a value of absolute. You can use this method to position one or more graphics on the page. The problem with this technique is that it requires careful planning to make sure the elements positioned as static (or relative) don't run over your absolutely positioned element — in this case, an image. You can also use absolute positioning to position subtle graphics in a case where you want the text run right across the images.

Consider the following CSS:

```
IMG.no1 {
        position: absolute;
        top: 200;
        right: auto;
        bottom: auto;
        left: 350;
}
IMG.no2 {
        position: absolute;
        top: 800;
        right: auto;
        bottom: auto;
        left: 350;
}
```

Both images have absolute positioning from the top-left of the browser window. All images that use either of the two classes no1, and no2, will take their positioning from the class. The resulting page looks like Figure 34-1. Notice you only see one image. Because the absolute position of the second image (no2) is 800 pixels down the page and the viewable area is less than that, the second image is only visible when you scroll down the page.

Using CSS with relative positioning

Figure 34-2 uses relative positioning to place the image to the left of the text.

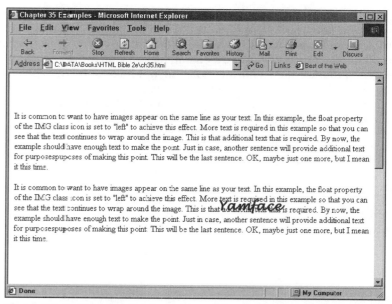

Figure 34-1: This absolutely positioned image has text overlaying the image.

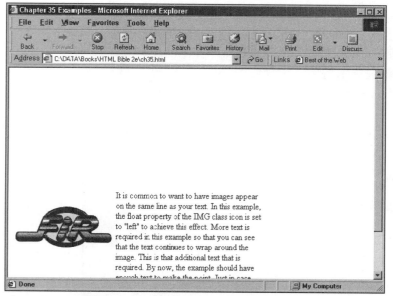

Figure 34-2: Relative positioning places the image to the left of the body of text.

Look at the following style sheet and notice the BODY element is formatted with a 200-pixel left-hand border. This leaves room to relatively position the image next to the text. What about all that white space above the paragraph? This is because when you use relative positioning for one element, all subsequent elements are positioned based on that element's normal position, not its new, relative position. What does this mean? It means the browser leaves space for the image *above* the paragraph of text, even though the image is positioned *next to* the paragraph of text. If you have multiple paragraphs, this could be ugly.

```
P.thisone {
        position: normal;
}
IMG.relative {
        position: relative;
        left: -190;
        top: 150;
}
BODY {
        margin-left: 200;
}
```

Using CSS to float the image

If the float property had been used instead, the result would have been Figure 34-3.

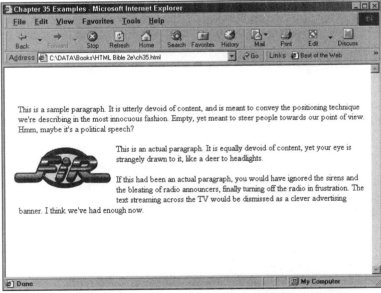

Figure 34-3: The float property wraps the text around the image.

Notice the text wraps around the image, rather than giving you a clean left margin. Either look has its place, depending on what you desire. The CSS for Figure 34-3 follows:

```
IMG.icon {
        float: left;
}
P {
        margin-left: 15px;
}
```

Defining Text Positions

How can you put text where you want it? You have several formatting choices. You can format your text by modifying the padding and margin of the text element itself, as in Figure 34-4.

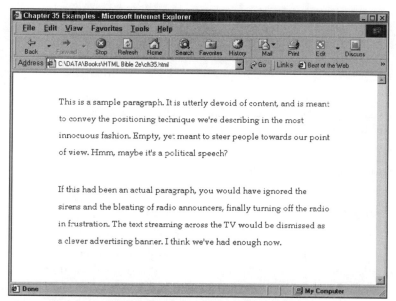

Figure 34-4: Text formatted with margins and padding

The CSS that follows was used to create the simple effects you see in Figure 34-4:

```
P {
        margin-top: 1cm;
        line-height: 200%;
        font-family: "Book Antiqua";
        padding: 0 2cm;
}
```

Changing the BODY element

Another option you have for formatting your page — so the text appears where you want it — is to change the formatting of the BODY element. Figure 34-5 uses BODY element formatting.

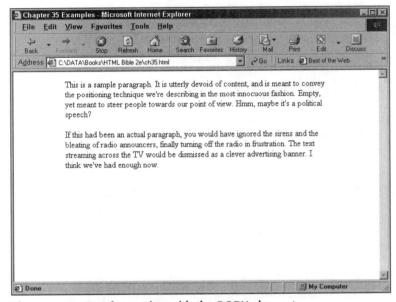

Figure 34-5: Text formatting with the BODY element

Figure 34-5 was created with the following CSS:

```
BODY {
        margin-left: 1in;
}
```

If you wanted to add page decorations to the left margin, you could put it in the one-inch, left-hand margin. Or, you could put an absolutely positioned graphic, with a negative horizontal position, in that space.

Positioning text with relative positioning

You might need to pull text out of the body of the page for some reason. Figure 34-6 uses relative positioning to pull a paragraph of text out of the body of the page and draw attention to it.

The following CSS was used to create Figure 34-6:

```
BODY {
        margin-right: 1.5in;
}
P.pull {

        position: relative;
        padding: 1em 1em 1em 3em;
        left: 150px;
        top: auto;

        border-left: red .25cm solid;
        border-top: red 1px solid;
        border-bottom: red 1px solid;
}
```

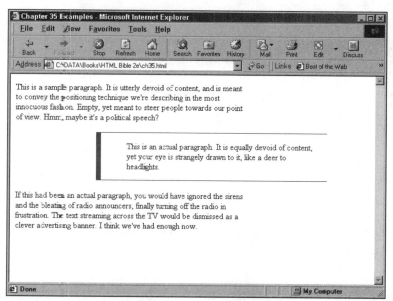

Figure 34-6: Text formatted with relative positioning

Floating an Image Next to Text

In Figure 34-7, you can see the same boring text and the same boring images are rearranged, so the text floats around the image, first to the right of the image and then to the left.

The CSS used to create this effect follows:

```
IMG.left {
        float: left;
        margin-left: 1.5cm;
        margin-right: 10pt;
}
IMG.right {
        float: right;
        margin-right: 1.5cm;
        margin-left: 10pt;
}
```

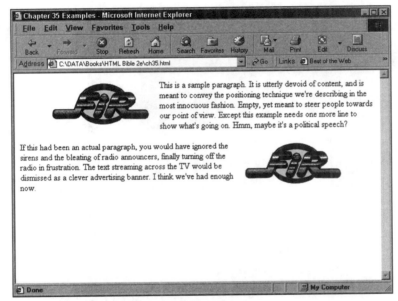

Figure 34-7: Text floating around images

The float property is not perfectly implemented in either Internet Explorer 5 or Netscape 4.7. Generally, Internet Explorer supports more of the CSS properties. Some combinations of properties give strange and unpredictable results, so you need to test your work carefully.

Floating both the text and the image

Figure 34-8 is the result of applying the float property to both the P elements and the IMG elements. In Internet Explorer, this combination has no visible effect and the result looks exactly the same as Figure 34-7, where the float property is only applied to the IMG element. As you can see, Netscape does not handle this combination well.

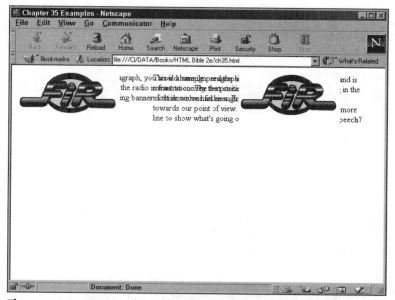

Figure 34-8: Netscape has problems with the float property being applied to both the P element and the IMG element.

Floating only the text

Neither browser wants to have the float property assigned to the text. Both browsers want to have the float property assigned to the IMG element. The result of applying the float element to the text element (in this case, the P element) varies by browser, but is equally unappealing in both browsers, as can be seen in Figures 34-9 and 34-10.

The order of the HTML matters

If you use the same CSS that was effective in Figure 34-7, but change the HTML so the IMG element appear *after* both P elements, then you get different and unsatisfactory results, as you can see in Figures 34-11 and 34-12.

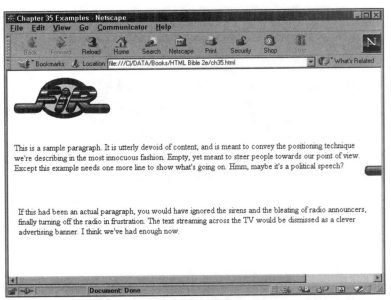

Figure 34-9: Netscape can't handle floating when the float property is applied to the text, rather than to the IMG element.

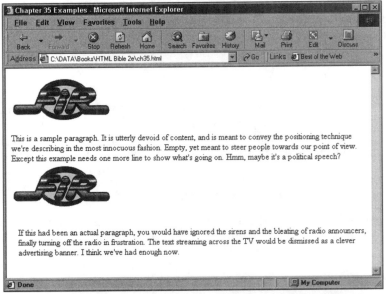

Figure 34-10: Internet Explorer doesn't even try to float anything when the float property is applied to the text, rather than to the image.

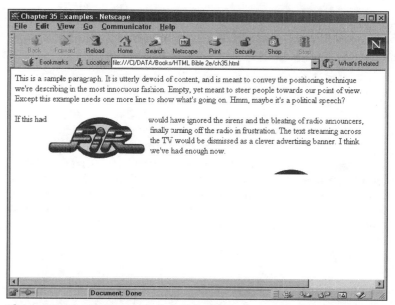

Figure 34-11: Netscape chokes if the IMG element is listed in your HTML after the P element.

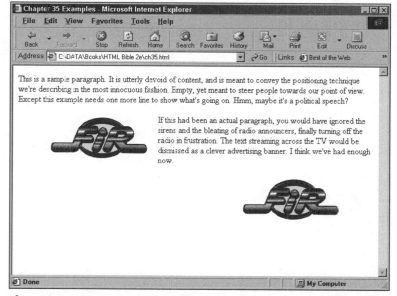

Figure 34-12: Internet Explorer doesn't seem to understand that the IMG element should float next to the preceding P element, even when the IMG element will be floating to the right of the P element.

From Here

 Jump to Chapter 37 and learn how to create still graphics for the Web.

Proceed to Chapter 35 and learn more cool CSS positioning tips and tricks.

Summary

In this chapter, you learned how to position text and graphics using a variety of techniques, including frames, the position property, the float property, changing margins and padding of text blocks, and changing margins of the BODY element. You also learned some of the implementation shortcomings of the two leading browsers: Internet Explorer 5 and Netscape 4.7.

✦   ✦   ✦

Cool CSS Positioning Tips and Tricks

In this chapter, you see more CSS positioning tricks. Specifically, you learn how to lay out your page in ways that simply weren't possible before CSS. You learn how to create newspaper columns. You see how (finally!) you can superimpose text over graphics to title your image or to annotate your image. You also learn how to create pull quotes. This chapter assumes you have read (and understood) all previous chapters about CSS.

Creating Columns of Text

You can use CSS to create columns of text. For a brief moment in time, one draft of the CSS2 specification included a property for real newspaper columns. It enabled you to create text columns that dynamically resized themselves to fit on the page. It decided how much of the text should go in the first column and how much should go in subsequent columns, so each column was the same length. Unfortunately, this property (called columns), along with a host of related properties that permitted customization of columns, has been dropped from the CSS2 specification. It is being considered, under the catchy name *Multi-column layout in CSS,* for inclusion in CSS3, the next version of CSS, which is still in working draft on a component-by-component basis.

Fortunately, you can still create columns of text with CSS, but you simply must do more of the work yourself. To create columns of text, use the DIV element (you will recall this is used to format and group multiple block-level elements). You also need most of the following properties in your style sheet:

✦ **width.** This property tells the browser how wide to make each column. You can use a percentage or a value. Generally, using a percentage is safer, in case the browser window isn't open in full-screen mode.

✦ **float.** This property puts the text column either on the right or the left. Even though the only official values available to you for this property are right, left, or none, Internet Explorer does support a center value for this property.

✦ **border.** If you want to put a border between your columns of text, you can use one or more of the border properties to do this.

✦ **margin.** You might need either margins or padding to format your text columns to your satisfaction.

✦ **padding.** Padding can help provide white space between the column of text and the border, if you use one.

✦ **text-align.** You can use the text-align property to fully justify your text, so neither the left nor the right edge of the text is jagged. If you want the text to look like newspaper text, you definitely want to set text-align to justify.

Figure 35-1 shows two sample columns created using CSS.

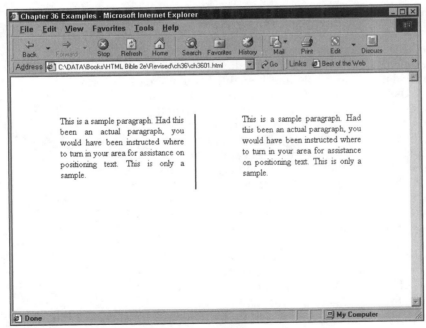

Figure 35-1: Creating text columns with CSS

The HTML used to create these columns is simple:

```
<BODY>
<H1>Chapter 35 Examples</H1>
<DIV class="left"><P>This is a sample paragraph. Had this been
an actual paragraph, you would have been instructed where to
turn in your area for assistance on positioning text. This is
only a sample.<P></DIV>
<DIV class="right"><P>This is a sample paragraph. Had this been
an actual paragraph, you would have been instructed where to
turn in your area for assistance on positioning text. This is
only a sample.<P></DIV>
</BODY>
```

The CSS used to create the columns is a bit more interesting:

```
DIV.left {
        width: 40%;
        text-align: Justify;
        float: left;
        padding-right: 0.3in;
        border-right: solid thin;
        margin-left: 1cm;
}
DIV.right {
        width: 40%;
        text-align: Justify;
        float: right;
        padding-left: 0.25in;
        margin-right: 1cm;
}
```

Notice only the left column has a border. You could just as easily have put the border on the left-hand side of the right column. In either case, you must be careful not to use the margin property to create white space on the side on which you have the border. Use padding on that side instead (remember, the border is drawn between the margin and the padding).

Netscape 4.7 doesn't support this implementation of the float property.

Superimposing Text and Graphics

The z-index property, mentioned briefly in Chapter 33, is just the ticket for layering text and graphics, only text, or only graphics. In Figure 35-2, the z-index property is used to superimpose text — in this case, a caption on an image.

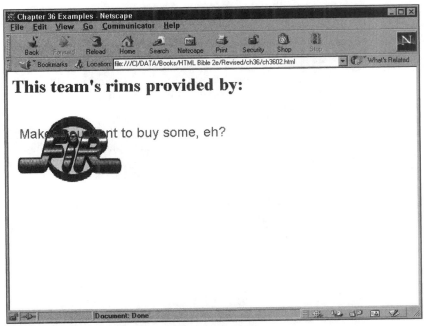

Figure 35-2: Text superimposed on a graphic

Again, the HTML is simple:

```
<BODY>
<H1>This Team's rims provided by: </H1>
<img class="under" src="fir.gif" width=200 height=150 alt="FiR
logo" border="0">
<P class="over">Makes you want to buy some, eh?</P>
</BODY>
```

The CSS uses the z-index property, which layers the element with the lower
z-index value on top of elements with higher z-index values.

```
IMG.under {
        position: absolute;
        top: 10;
        left: 20;
        z-index: 300;
}
P.over {
        position: absolute;
        z-index: 100;
        font-size: 18pt;
```

```
        font-family: sans-serif;
        top: 100;
        left: 20;
        color: Fuchsia;
}
```

The z-index property is not implemented in Internet Explorer 5.

Creating Pull Quotes

Not much has been written about creating pull quotes, but they can be an attractive addition to your Web page. *Pull quotes* can draw attention to a few key words or sentences that summarize a thought, thus giving the visitor a quick idea of the point of the page. This is especially important if a lot of text is on the page. Web visitors have become used to gleaning the message of the page from a combination of things, of which text is only a small part. Some visitors won't sit still to read an entire page of text unless you can grab them with a snappy quote. Pull quotes can do this for you.

Figure 35-3 shows an effective use of columns and pull quotes together.

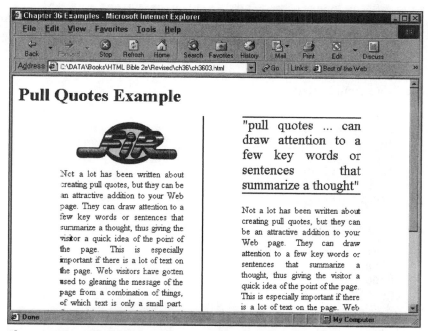

Figure 35-3: Pull quotes used in combination with columns

The HTML, as you've become used to seeing, is simple:

```
<BODY>
<H1>Pull Quotes Example</H1>
<DIV class="left"><IMG class="icon" src="fir.gif">
<P>Not a lot has been written about creating pull quotes, but
they can be an attractive addition to your Web page. They can
draw attention to a few key words or sentences that summarize a
thought, thus giving the visitor a quick idea of the point of
the page. This is especially important if there is a lot of
text on the page. Web visitors have gotten used to gleaning the
message of the page from a combination of things, of which text
is only a small part. Some visitors won't sit still to read an
entire page of text unless you can grab them with a snappy
quote. Pull quotes can do that for you.</P></DIV>
<DIV class="right">
<P class="pull">"pull quotes ... can draw attention to a few
key words or sentences that summarize a thought"</P>
<P>Not a lot has been written about creating pull quotes, but
they can be an attractive addition to your Web page. They can
draw attention to a few key words or sentences that summarize a
thought, thus giving the visitor a quick idea of the point of
the page. This is especially important if there is a lot of
text on the page. Web visitors have gotten used to gleaning the
message of the page from a combination of things, of which text
is only a small part. Some visitors won't sit still to read an
entire page of text unless you can grab them with a snappy
quote. Pull quotes can do that for you.</P></DIV>
</BODY>
```

The CSS is more complicated:

```
DIV.left {
        width: 35%;
        text-align: Justify;
        float: left;
        padding-right: 0.2in;
        border-right: solid thin;
        margin-left: 1cm;
}
DIV.right {
        width: 45%;
        text-align: Justify;
        float: right;
        padding-left: 0.3in;
        margin-right: 1cm;
}
IMG.icon {
        float: left;
        margin-left: .2in;
        margin-right: .2in;
}
P.pull {
```

```
        font: 18pt Helvetica blue;
        border-top: thin blue solid;
        border-bottom: thin blue solid;
    }
```

The DIV.left and DIV.right rules should look familiar. The IMG.icon rule also has nothing new. Notice the CSS for the pull class of the P element doesn't use any advanced CSS properties. Notice, too, the float value of the DIV.left rule is *left*. Also notice the float property of the IMG.icon rule is *left*. Because the DIV element contains the IMG element (in the previous HTML), this means you can float an element within another floated element.

None of this works in Netscape 4.7, due to its lack of support for the float element. Figure 35-4 shows how Netscape handles this example.

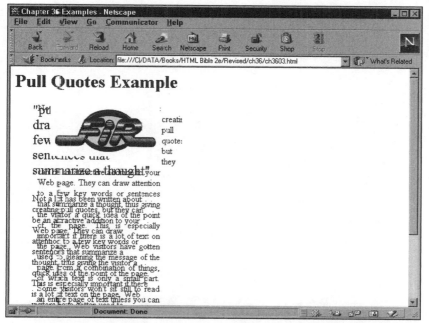

Figure 35-4: Netscape's lack of support for the float property leaves this page unintelligible.

From Here

Cross-Reference

Go to Chapter 39 to learn to design Imagemaps.

Jump to Chapter 47 for an introduction to Dynamic HTML.

Proceed to Chapter 37 and begin creating still graphics for the Web.

Summary

This chapter has given you some ideas of the interesting ways you can use the CSS properties you learned in the previous chapters. It introduced layering of text and graphics with the z-index property. It showed you how to create text columns with the width and float properties. It also demonstrated how to create pull quotes to draw attention to a phrase or sentence from a body of text. You are now fully armed to write CSS. Part VI shows you how to add sensory excitement and interactivity.

✦   ✦   ✦

Structuring Multipage Sites

Now it's time to move from defining the message of your site to the delivery of that message on Web pages. In this chapter, we discuss the variety of choices you have to implement a multipage site and the pros and cons of each choice. We talk about the pitfalls to avoid when creating multipage sites. This chapter discusses the types of organization and the architectures available to you when you build a multipage site. Navigation also figures prominently in this chapter. If you are going to have more than one page in your site, you need to have a logical, intuitive, consistent way for your visitors to get around it. Finally, we discuss maintaining your site.

Possibilities and Problems of Multipage Sites

Most Web sites are implemented across multiple pages. Isn't that the great thing about the Web? You can break up your content by type and group it together, so if visitors to your site only want to know how to order spare parts for the exercise equipment you manufacture, they needn't read through all your marketing literature and the entire service manual.

Good and bad things exist about breaking your content into multiple pages: both for you, as the Webmaster, and for your visitors. First, let's look at the pros and cons for your visitors (because those should receive greater weight in your calculus).

The Pros of multipage sites for your visitors

Your visitors can (theoretically) find what they want without having to read through everything on your site. It is a great feeling to go to a site with a clear idea of what you want and to find it within two or three clicks, even when you have never been to that site before. Visitors will return to such a site often.

A site is richer with multiple pages. There is more content to choose from. A well-done multipage site gives visitors the choice of knowing a little or a lot about the topic in which they are interested.

All the information visitors need is there. While visitors certainly don't want all the information at once, they may eventually want all the information. One of the nice things about the Web is supposed to be that you don't have to wait on hold to get answers.

The Cons of multipage sites for your visitors

Navigation can be confusing. What may be obviously clear directions to you may not even be noticed by visitors, especially first-time visitors. Sometimes subtle imagemaps (graphics with hot spots that, when clicked, take you somewhere else, just like hypertext), which may be obvious to the designer, may not be at all obvious to visitors. This is something you can avoid with good design. Figures 36-1 and 36-2 show two Web sites, one with subtle navigational tools and one with very clear navigational tools.

 Definition

Imagemap. An *imagemap* is an image with clickable regions. Each clickable region acts as a hyperlink. Plenty of free or cheap software exists to help you convert an image into an imagemap. This tool is built in to many HTML editors.

 Cross-Reference

For an in-depth examination of imagemaps, including instructions for creating one, see Chapter 39.

Loading time can become a problem with multipage sites. If visitors have to wait for big, cumbersome graphics to load for each page, they may well get impatient. Fortunately, technical and design solutions exist to help avoid this problem, which we discuss later.

Printing can be more complicated. If the content you have split into multiple pages is something you imagine people may want to print, and they have to go to more than one page to print the entire thing, then dividing the content into multiple pages is a hassle for your visitors.

Of less import, but certainly worth mentioning, are the pros and cons of developing a multipage Web site to you, the Webmaster.

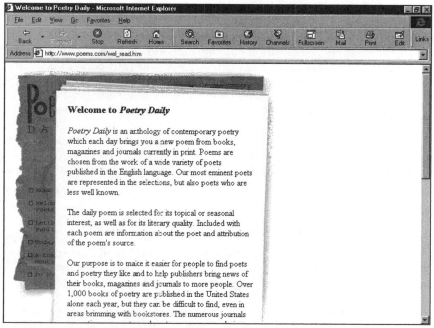

Figure 36-1: Can you find the navigational tools on this site? Perhaps too subtle. © Poetry Daily.

Figure 36-2: How about on this site? Much more obvious, don't you think?

The Pros of developing a multipage site

You can break up your content into manageable pieces. For most sites, this is going to be necessary. The question you must answer through the rest of this chapter is: How do I break up the content? Breaking up your content is great if a team is developing your site. Each Web page is stored in a separate file, so if you had several people writing to the same file, you'd have a mess. Dividing the work among the team members is much easier when the site is also divided.

Updating your content is easier. Different pages require different update frequencies. Much of the site you should be able to leave alone for months at a time (the "Contacting Us" page, for example), which leaves you more time to update the pages that do need work.

The Cons of developing a multipage site

If you aren't focused on your message and your visitors' needs, you could end up breaking content unnecessarily. This is a major inconvenience for your visitors, who won't know intuitively where to go to find what they need.

Maintenance of multipage sites requires more organization. You are going to have more files to monitor. Especially if you are working with a team, you need to have good organizational skills and even tools that facilitate organization to make sure nothing falls between the cracks and you don't have two people overlaying each other's work.

 Cross-Reference   Chapter 8 has detailed information about team and site management tools.

Dividing the Site

How do you divide your content? Included in this question is *how much* do you divide your content? The tricky part is deciding how to break up your content and how to indicate to your visitors that the content you have available *is* available. This is one of the two main questions you want to have answered by the end of this chapter. The other main question is: How do you provide navigation around your site? First, we address dividing your content.

You can divide your content in three ways, assuming it needs to be divided at all. These are as follows:

✦ By origination of content

✦ By type of content

✦ By visitor type

By origination of content

If your organization is large enough to have multiple departments, then you may think of dividing your content by where the content comes from or the functional group that owns that content. In this approach, your Web site organization reflects your organizational chart to some degree. Figure 36-3 shows an example of an organizational chart.

Over the Web Organization Chart

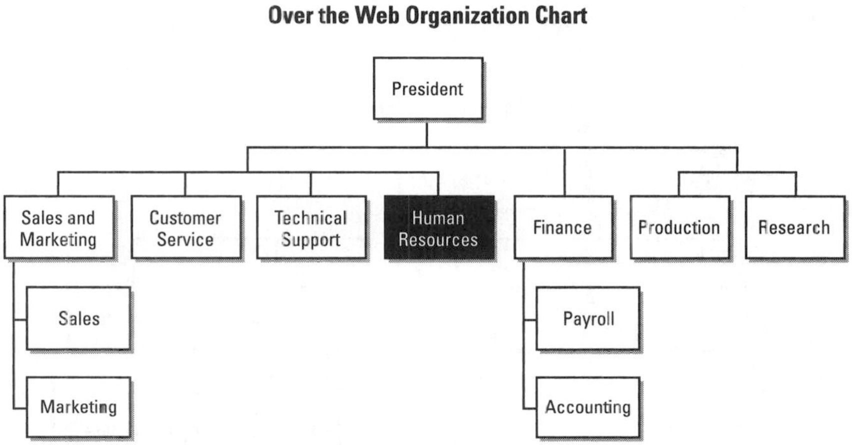

Figure 36-3: An organizational chart

It may make sense to divide the site by functional unit. In the case of Over the Web, the Web site may be organized as shown in Figure 36-4. Just because only one box exists for an item (say, product listings) doesn't mean there is only one page; it's just easier to represent it that way for this example.

Links, which simply aren't apparent in this type of site map, would be across the chart. For example, "Contacting us" may merit its own link on the highest level; you'd indisputably want to link to it from at least the "Online shopping" page (in case visitors have questions before they order), the Press page, and the Job listings page. This is also true with "Information about upcoming versions," which is listed under Research; marketing would certainly want to link to that.

Dividing your site by where the content originates is not a bad way to go, but read through the other two systems before you commit to it. For large organizations, this may be the only way to manage your content reasonably. If you use links effectively, this type of organization can appear intuitive and seamless. If you use links poorly, or if communication between departments (or Web builders in different departments) is poor, it can look like the right hand doesn't know what the left hand is doing.

By type of content

Another way to organize your site is by type of content. This organizational scheme often results in a similar site map to the previous system of site organization, by functional unit of your organization. The difference in breaking up your content by type is that you are less interested in where the information for the content comes from than what type of information it is. For example (from the preceding example), the finance department is the place where strategic alliances are brokered. They are the ones who make these arrangements, but who would think to look there? Figure 36-5 reflects this new information.

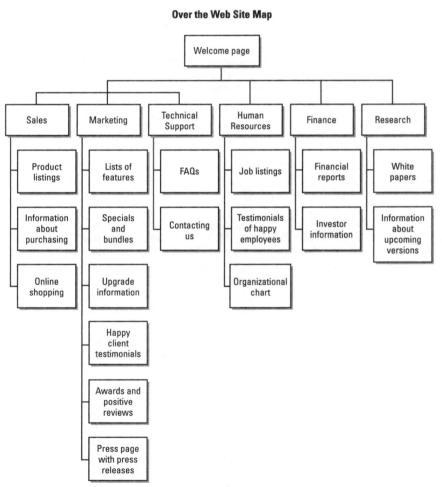

Figure 36-4: A site map based on the preceding organizational chart

Even if the marketing department has a link to the Finance page or the Strategic alliances page, you have to wonder if that is adequate prominence for this information. If the marketing department isn't involved in arranging these alliances, then they probably won't be enthusiastic about promoting them; heck, they may not even be aware of them!

Another obvious place to question the logic of the site organization, shown in Figure 36-5, is in the separation of sales from marketing. Wouldn't it make sense that a features list would be something you'd want to see on the way from Product listings to Online shopping?

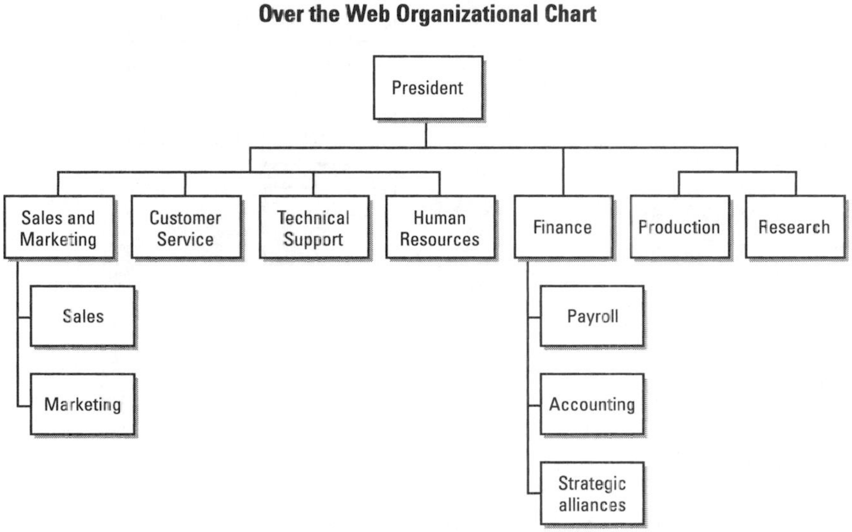

Over the Web Organizational Chart

Figure 36-5: This organizational chart reflects that the finance department negotiates strategic alliances.

If this site were now to be organized by type of information, instead of origin of information, then Figure 36-6 reflects what the site map would look like.

By visitor type

Another way to organize your site is by your visitors' interests. Remember them? We always come back to them eventually and so will you. Can you break your visitors into groups? Say, members and nonmembers? That's too easy. Here are some other examples: end users, programmers, and other interested parties; doctors and patients; activists and citizens; clients, potential clients, and others. Whatever division you come up with, *others* will always be the last group in the list. This is simply the nature of the Web. You can't predict who is going to show up on your site.

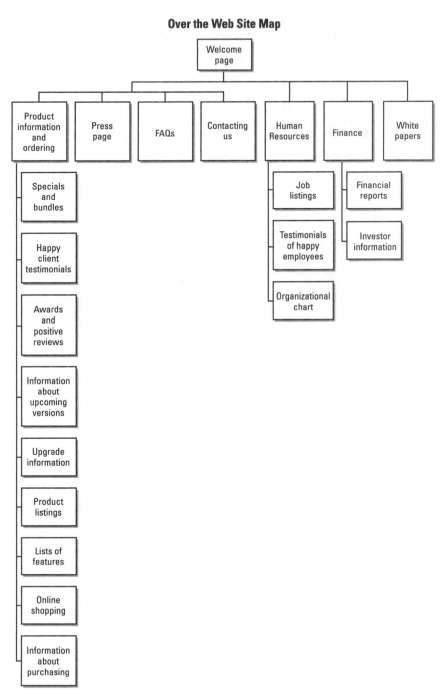

Figure 36-6: Organization by type of content

To continue with this example, Over the Web has decided to consider breaking up their site by visitor type. They have broken their visitors into the following groups: customers (or people who are interested in becoming customers), the press, job hunters, investors, programmers, and others. Because knowing what *others* want to see is impossible, they won't have their own pages. Figure 36-7 shows an attempt at reorganizing the site along these lines.

Dividing Content

How much information goes on a page? Even if you have determined which of the previous models suits your site best, you still may need to break up content within each section as well. Within what we represented as the Press page in the preceding example, will everything go on one page or will there be multiple pages? How do you decide?

Some of the factors you need to consider are as follows:

✦ What information do visitors need to see at once? Don't think in terms of the length of the material; think in terms of the use of the material. How do you anticipate the information being used? Most of the time, these decisions are between having one longish page and breaking the same material into multiple pages. If you think most of the people who come to the first part of your material will proceed in a linear manner through the material, then save them the trouble and put all the material on one page.

✦ Will visitors be printing this information? If you want your visitors to be happy with their experience of visiting your site, don't annoy them by dividing information they may want to print. Sure, some people print everything and you can't plan around them, but some pages just lend themselves to printing. One example of this is a review of a book or a software package. Another is instructions. Who would want to print only half a set of instructions?

✦ As you provide the information visitors need, are there points where visitors may want to go more than one place? If yes, then stop the page and give the visitor choices of places to go. If no, then continue the page.

✦ What about the notion your visitors should never have to scroll? This is a crazy idea. Sure, you want the screen that visitors see to look complete, but this doesn't mean every time you have enough text to fill a screen, you should force the visitor to click and wait to link to what is really only a continuation of the same material. User Interface Engineering (http://world.std.com/~uieweb) did a study that showed visitors don't mind scrolling to get to the information they are seeking.

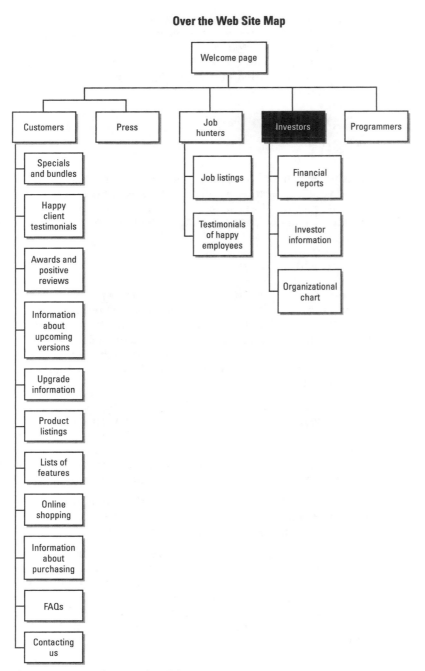

Figure 36-7: A site map by visitor type

Site Architecture

We've already touched on site architecture, but it deserves more attention. What is the architecture of your site going to be? Because we are confined to a two-dimensional space, the previous site maps all look hierarchical. That is simply the easiest way to represent a site. In fact, a site map may look more like the one represented in Figure 36-8.

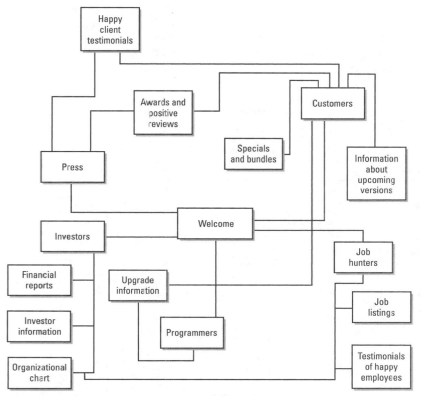

Figure 36-8: Mapping your site in a nonhierarchical way is messy.

Site architecture has to do with the way that pages link to each other. On one extreme, there is a linear site architecture, where you torture your visitors by forcing them to click a link to get to another page, where there still are no choices. On the other extreme, there is the completely anarchical architecture, where pages link to each other without any structure behind the links — call it *stream-of-consciousness* architecture. In the middle, you have hierarchical sites. We discuss all three of these in the following sections.

Linear architecture: The forced march

Hypertext is supposed to give readers the control to decide what they want to learn about next and when they want to know more. Only a control freak would work in this freedom-loving medium and then try to deny visitors their rights as Web surfers. People don't especially like to sit through presentations. When you arrange your site with linear architecture, this is what you force your visitors to do.

Linear architecture assumes that pretty much everyone wants to see pretty much everything. There are times when linear architecture may be appropriate for a portion of your site. Suppose you have a site that, among other things, has a virtual museum exhibit. In most museum exhibits, the material is arranged in a particular order for a particular reason. How might the site map look for this kind of architecture? See Figure 36-9.

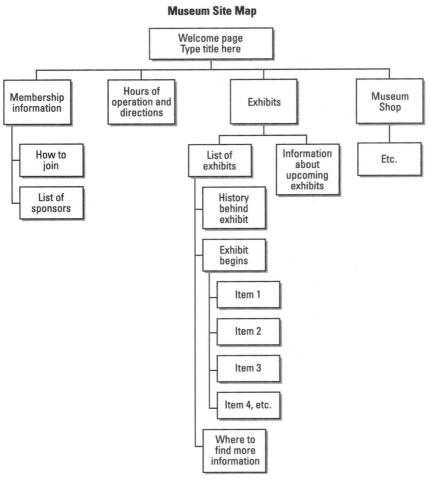

Figure 36-9: Site map including a linear section

The key to using linear architecture is to not apply it to the entire site. Certain areas of a site may lend themselves to a linear approach, but it is inconceivable that the entire site should be a forced march. Other times you may need to use a linear architecture are when giving quizzes (a quiz to determine whether you are left-brained or right-brained) and when giving a virtual tour (of the Blue Ridge Mountains on Scenic Drive in Virginia).

Hierarchical architecture

Hierarchical architecture depends on the idea of grouping content by some criteria, and then providing a list of the members of the group. Each item in a group can also be a group, but you can get carried away with this if you are not careful. Eventually, your visitors want to come to something other than a list of items. They want to come to real content. Real content is something more substantive than a list of places to go (unless your site is a transit site and then this doesn't apply). Most sites use a hierarchical architecture for the framework. All the previous examples use a hierarchical architecture.

Hierarchical architecture is a useful way to organize your site. It is relatively easy to map and to divide a hierarchical site for team development and maintenance. Best of all, visitors understand the idea of a hierarchical site, where each subsequent page has a greater level of detail until, eventually, they find the material they were seeking.

Avoid extreme devotion to hierarchy

Slavish adherence to hierarchical architecture can be a problem. Visitors should not have to click more than two or three times to get to a page where it is clear to them they are at least in the neighborhood of the material they need.

What makes you have a positive experience on a site? Your perception. If you *feel* like you can find the information you want — based on the navigational controls visible to you on the Welcome Page or your previous visits to this site — and within two or three clicks you get to the neighborhood where you believe the information should be and then two clicks later, you find it, you have a positive experience with that site. You don't feel like you wasted your time (or worse yet, that *they* wasted your time). If you keep coming to lists that either don't have the level of detail you need or a vocabulary you recognize, then you get frustrated and leave.

Visitors shouldn't have to click four or five times to feel they are finally in the right area. Isn't this why site searches are so popular? When you go to a site where you don't know if they have what you want, you click Search on the Welcome page. On the Search page, you type your keywords and click Find. Then you see the list of pages. That was two clicks. Your keywords may have been overly broad and your search may not have been effective, but, within two clicks, you feel you can find what you came to find or you learn the site doesn't have what you were looking for and you go elsewhere.

Visitors failing to find what they want on a site, by the way, is not a disaster. Your visitors can have a positive experience on your site even if they don't find what they want, as long as they quickly realize they aren't going to find it, and they are confident they aren't missing it only because of the site's organization. When your visitors begin to think, "It must be here somewhere, I just can't find it," click around your site for 20 minutes looking for it, and then finally leave, this has not been a positive experience!

Anarchy

Sound emancipating? Forget it. Anarchy only works for really small sites. An *anarchical hierarchy* (a contradiction in terms?) is based on the idea that organization isn't necessary and visitors only want to wander through the site, not looking for anything in particular. They can click any link they find, but no guarantee exists they can ever get back to a page they visited, unless they click the back button the correct number of times.

This feeling of groundlessness that anarchy creates is not positive for visitors. They aren't familiar with this feeling and it assumes visitors have nothing better to do than wander aimlessly around your site. It may work if your audience consists of college students with free Internet access and a need to avoid studying, but unless you are really clever with this approach, it will fail and so will your site.

A seamless web

How, then, do you create the feeling that your site is a seamless web of related content, the page visitors want is only a click or two away, and visitors will be able to find this content again? You need to find the right combination of the various architectures for your content and you need good, consistent navigational tools.

The following rules will help:

✦ **Have a search option on your site.** This requires that your site be indexed. Software that indexes sites is included with many Web servers (especially NT Web servers). Unfortunately, installing indexing software on UNIX servers is a bit of a trial. If you have an internal server, ask your systems administrator about this option. If you have an ISP, ask them. Especially as your site grows, your visitors will benefit greatly from the ability to search your site. Being able to search if you keep archival information on your site is also useful. Often archival information is only available by search (it is not linked into the current material on your site).

✦ **Have navigational controls in the same place on every page.** We discuss this further in the next section. It is that important.

✦ **Don't be afraid to link across divisions.** Linking from a page full of highly technical information about your product to a page of job listings in your company makes perfect sense if your company needs people who are highly technical. Information about contacting your company (including the mailing address) should be available from lots of places; don't expect visitors to remember they can get to it from your Welcome Page. Remember: Links are free; your visitors' time is not. Because of all these links across different areas, having your files organized according to some formal system (as discussed in Chapter 4) is especially important if you have a team working on your site. Otherwise, your team members may rearrange their own files, not realizing they just broke all your links.

✦ **Select an architecture and be consistent.** Visitors want to know what to expect. Whichever architecture you select, be consistent and make it obvious to visitors. They don't want to learn different site navigation on each page.

Providing Navigational Aids

Now it's time to think about visitors again. We won't let you forget them for a while. Whichever architecture you select, your job is to make getting around your site easy for visitors. They need to know how to get to what they seek, how to get back to the Welcome page, and how to find what they seek on subsequent visits.

You can use several tools to make the process of navigating around your site as painless as possible for your visitor. Let's start with the ideal: In the ideal world, your site would be able to read visitors' minds (or read some sort of configuration file their browsers provide) to give them a Welcome page that showed exactly what they were seeking. You can't do this today, but no technical reason exists why you couldn't do it (if not the mind-reading part, at least the configuration file part) in a few years.

More realistically, you can provide some or all of the following devices to make navigation intuitive and easy for your visitors:

✦ **Table of contents.** Easy enough, right? Using client-side scripting techniques (you learn about these later, and they are only available in HTML 4), you can even make your table of contents *expand and retract*. This means if visitors click a section heading, they see a listing of the contents of that section, right onscreen, without going elsewhere. If they click a different section heading, the details of the first section they clicked retracts and the new section expands. What a great way to give your visitors the information they need, conserve screen real estate (more on this later), and avoid making users bounce all over the place!

✦ **Search function.** We talked about this previously. It isn't much extra work to index your site and provide for searching. You can find plenty of free or inexpensive tools to do this if your Web server doesn't include site indexing. You want to make certain the search is available from every page. Remember: Links are free.

✦ **Site Map.** This one is a little bit trickier to implement. You need to think about a way to show — graphically — where things are on your site. This is done most elegantly with JavaScript, but it can be difficult.

✦ **Consistently placed navigational bar or buttons.** Of all of these devices, this is the easiest to implement. Nearly every decent site has navigational buttons or bars. Visitors expect them to stay in the same place from one screen to another. Don't surprise them.

✦ **Drop-down list of places to go.** This is a great way to save page real estate. You can include an enormous list of places to go, or a short one, and it takes up the same amount of space: one line the width of the widest entry in your list. You can use this approach for links to sections of your site or for links to your product information.

Maintaining a Multipage Site

You need to start thinking about many maintenance issues. A reasonably comprehensive list follows:

✦ **Schedule face-lifts to the site.** While we haven't talked about the look of your site yet, you need to make certain you update your look periodically. You don't want to change it just because you discovered a new font you like, but you may want to change it when your organization makes changes to marketing literature. You'll also want to change your site to take advantage of the latest technologies and looks being used by other cool people on the Web.

✦ **Run link-checking software on a regular schedule.** If your site has more than a dozen pages, you'll want to take advantage of link-checking software (see Figure 36-10). This product tests out every link in your site and reports back with a list of broken links. Acquiring this software, learning it, and running it on a regular schedule is worth your peace of mind.

✦ **Test your site daily or find an agent to do it and to notify you if it is down.** If your site is hosted elsewhere and you don't have reason to visit your site daily, how will you know whether you are up and running or dead in the water? A number of ways exist to check your site and to make sure it is up. The easiest, but least reliable, is to go to it yourself. Remember, every time an agent checks to see whether your site is up, it counts as a hit!

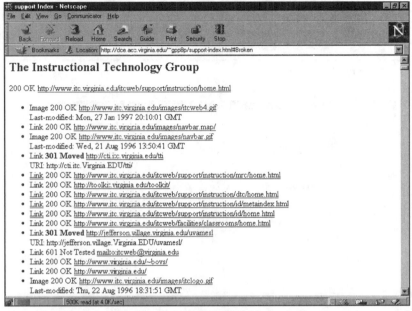

Figure 36-10: A report from link-checking software

✦ **Keep your index up-to-date so the search is always accurate.** If you are going to index your site to provide a search function, then you must be sure you have the index function running at some regular interval so your search function is always up to date. The index for a site with constant changes shouldn't be maintained manually because it's a hassle. Figure 36-11 shows Cold Fusion's Verity Indexing, an automatic way to index a dynamic site.

✦ **Review and revise your content on a scheduled basis so it always sounds fresh.** Don't take this for granted. Lots of Webmasters publish content and forget about it. Even a month after you have published a page, you may have forgotten the details of what it says. Set aside time to review all your content on a regular basis. Is it any wonder maintaining a Web site is so expensive?

✦ **Keep your competitors' or alliances' information up-to-date.** Providing a comparison chart with features of your product and your competitors' products is not generally frowned upon, but it is bad form for your information about your competitors' products to be out-of-date. People will wonder what other information is incorrect. If you are going to include information about your competitors' products, keep it up!

Figure 36-11: Cold Fusion's Verity Indexing

Bonus: Maintaining a Really Large Web Site

You may be getting in really deep. If you are or you think you may eventually be responsible for maintaining a thousand-page Web site, then you need to start thinking about two things: how will you manage the information and how will you manage the people who do the work? Some practices you may want to implement are as follows:

1. Create a Central Web Team. This team will be working on the Web site full-time.

2. Have all design decisions, all procedural changes, and all organizational decisions originate with the Central Web Team. You need to set a precedent right away that every page can't be unique. HTML 4 supports your decision to control the look of the site by providing you with style sheets. Create your style sheets at this level.

3. Have content originate with distributed Web developers who are closer to the content. These are basically loaners to the Central Web Team. We'll call them the *Distributed Web Team*.

4. Have meetings of both groups together. You need to keep the Distributed Web Team informed about new policies you institute, any changes to servers or accounts, and procedures you implement. You also want to be respectful of their time because you aren't their real boss and you want them to want to do the work for you.

5. Use e-mail to notify the Distributed Web Team of changes to the look and to procedures. Create a mailing list to notify the Distributed Web Team of changes. Consider having a mailing list where they can ask each other questions and help each other.

6. Have written procedures and standards for publishing a page for the Distributed Web Team. Tell them enough, but don't tell them more than they need to know. These are people who have other responsibilities. If you make the Web maintenance part of their jobs too big of a pain (with too much mail and too many meetings), then they will put it off and avoid you. Include information about linking to style sheets in your written instructions, with an example — or better yet, give them a copy of this book.

7. Organize accounts and permissions on your Web server so people can't accidentally delete or overlay each other's files. What files are called, where they go, and how they get there must be part of your written procedures. Publish your written procedures to a page on your Intranet so people can check on things without bothering you and so new members of the Distributed Web Team can get up to speed quickly.

8. Follow the procedures yourself that you impose on the Distributed Web Team. No cheating. You won't exactly inspire the trust and enthusiasm of the Distributed Web Team if you don't have to follow the rules yourself.

From Here

 Jump to Chapter 32 for a refresher on the essentials of Web page design.

Refer to Chapter 8 and find the HTML editor that's right for you.

Proceed to Chapter 37 to learn about creating still graphics for the Web.

Summary

We covered a lot of ground in this chapter. You learned the pros and cons of developing a multipage site, effective ways to organize your site for easy navigation, and intelligent ways to break up your content into pages. You also learned about site architecture: good and bad ways to use hierarchy, as well as times when you may want to mix in linear architecture into your hierarchy.

You learned about the basics of navigational aids to make the journey through your Web site easy and intuitive for your visitors. We also covered the basics of site maintenance for most sites and, as a bonus, for really big sites.

✦   ✦   ✦

Adding Sensory Excitement and Interactivity

Creating Still Graphics for the Web

You have been working with images for about 400 pages now. In this chapter, you learn how to *create* images. You learn about your choices for file formats. You also learn about color depth (bit depth) and what you can do — between file format selection and bit-depth reduction — to shrink the size of your file so it downloads quickly. This chapter also shows you how to create graphics using two popular tools, how to capture graphics you like from elsewhere, how to create image previews, and how to create transparent GIFs.

Understanding Graphics File Formats

Web browsers support — to some degree — three graphics file formats: GIF, JPEG, and PNG. All three of these graphics file formats use some form of compression to store your image.

Why compression?

Uncompressed images can be large. Consider Table 37-1, which compares image dimensions, number of colors, and file size for some sample uncompressed images.

As you can see, with file sizes like this, you would have to limit yourself to mighty tiny images, or two-color, such as black and white, images. Or, you could compress the files.

Table 37-1
Uncompressed Image File Size Comparison by
Image Dimensions and Number of Colors

Dimensions (in Inches)	Colors	File size
1×1	2	9K
1×1	256	9K
1×1	16.7 million	18K
2×2	2	16K
2×2	256	24K
2×2	16.7 million	63K
3×3	2	16K
3×3	256	49K
3×3	16.7 million	139K

Figures 37-1 to 37-9 show these images with compression. Even though these are only black and white images, to look good, they still require a lot of shades of gray.

Figure 37-1: This 1×1-inch image uses only two colors: black and white

Figure 37-2: The same 1 × 1-inch image using 256 colors: all shades of gray

Figure 37-3: The same 1 × 1-inch image using 16.7 million colors

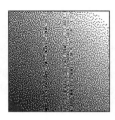

Figure 37-4: This 2×2-inch image uses only two colors: black and white

Figure 37-5: The same 2×2-inch image using 256 colors — obviously a big improvement

Figure 37-6: The same 2×2-inch image using 16.7 million colors; notice there is no color striping as in the previous image

Figure 37-7: This 3×3-inch image uses two colors

Figure 37-8: The same 3×3-inch image using 256 colors

Compression options

When you implement file compression, you either have to throw away some information about the image or find a way to store the existing information about the image in a more intelligent manner. GIF files throw away some color information. JPEG files throw away some information about the image itself. PNG files store the information using a more intelligent algorithm.

GIF

GIF was the earliest format in use in inline images on the Web. Version 1 browsers could open GIF images inline, but required that JPEG images be opened out-of-line. GIF uses a compression scheme — called *LZW compression* — that predates Compu Serve, even though you might see it called CompuServe GIF. CompuServe implemented LZW compression, thinking it was in the public sphere and then found out it was proprietary. A lot of lawyers sorted it out.

Figure 37-9: The same 3 × 3-inch image using 16.7 million colors, which looks nicest, but makes too large of a file size

How does GIF work? Simply, GIF indexes images to an 8-bit palette. The system palette is 256 colors. Before you can save your file in GIF format, the utility you are using simply makes its best guess at mapping all your colors to one of the 256 colors in an 8-bit palette.

Is a reduction in color depth a problem? That depends. GIF uses dithering to achieve colors between two colors on the palette. Even with dithering, however, GIF images of a sunset have stripes of color, where a smooth gradation would be more natural. GIF images also tend to have more cartoonish colors because flesh tones aren't part of the palette. A GIF image of a drawing, say, of a checkerboard, however, will look just fine.

Cross-Reference See Chapter 38 for a lesson in creating animated GIFs. Transparent GIFs are discussed at the end of this chapter.

Definition **System Palette.** The system palette is the 256 colors your monitor is able to display if you set your video board only to show 256 colors. These colors differ from a PC to a Mac.

JPEG

JPEG takes a different approach. JPEG, in case you are curious, stands for the *Joint Photographic Experts Group,* the name of the group that created the standard. With JPEG, you get to keep all your colors, but you don't get to keep all the data about the image. What kinds of images lend themselves to being compressed with JPEG? A tree. If you take a photo of a pine tree, the acorns are in specific places, but when the image is compressed and decompressed (opened on your Web page), the computer has to approximate where those acorns went, because it had to throw away some of the data. Is this a problem? Not with most photos of most pine trees. Faces also take well to JPEG because the colors are all there; faces in GIF can look unnatural because of the color loss.

Every generation 3 and higher browser can handle inline JPEGs. JPEGs are also ideal for showing gradient filled graphics (when the color changes gradually from one color to another). The same graphic would suffer enormously under the GIF compression because all those in-between colors wouldn't be there.

What suffers under JPEG compression? Text, schematic drawings, and any line art. Of course, with JPEG, you can select the level of compression (usually either as a percentage or as Maximum, High, Medium, or Low). You generally want to use the maximum compression level your image can handle without losing image quality. You won't know how much compression your image can handle without loss until you try it at different levels of compression.

PNG

The *Portable Network Graphics,* or PNG format, was developed exclusively for the Web and is in the public domain. The PNG format takes advantage of a clever way of storing the information about the image so you don't lose color and you don't lose image quality; it is a lossless format. The only drawback is, because the standard is so new, only fourth-generation and later browsers support PNG graphics. Eventually, PNG will replace GIFs for many color-rich still image files. Only GIFs can support animation and transparency.

Definition

Lossy versus lossless. File formats that implement compression schemes that discard information about the image are called *lossy* file formats. Both GIF, which discards color information, and JPEG, which discards image information, are lossy file formats. File formats that don't discard any information about an image are called *lossless.* PNG is a lossless compression scheme.

Understanding Color Depth

In the computer world, everything is black or white, on or off. Computers operate in the base two system, so when creating colors, your choices of colors are base two numbers. A *bit* is a representation of on or off (1 or 0). One-bit color uses a two-color palette (2^1). Two-bit color uses a four-color palette (2^2). Eight-bit color uses a 256-color palette (2^8). Thirty-two-bit color uses a 16.7-million-color palette (2^{32}).

Definition

Browser-safe color palette. Between the two system palettes, there are 216 colors in common. This is called the *216-browser-safe palette.* By limiting your graphics to colors from this palette, you can be sure the browser won't have to guess or dither to achieve the color you want.

You might be thinking: *Two colors: that's not so bad. An artist can do a lot with two colors; think of the ways you can blend them.* Unfortunately, this isn't how computers work. When you select a color palette, you get only the colors in that palette, not any blends of colors in that palette.

When you create an image, you want to balance the quality of the image against the file size of the image. When you send an image file over the Internet to a Web page, you send either information about the palette or you send the actual palette. With GIF files, you send a color look-up table (CLUT) with the image. With JPEG files, you send a palette. As you can imagine, this makes the files considerably larger.

Enhancing Downloading Speed

The bandwidth conservation society was created to help with these problems. You can find their useful Web site at `www.infohiway.com/faster/index.html`. What can you do to ensure your pages download quickly? There are a few things:

✦ Limit image file sizes.

✦ Limit the number of images.

✦ Reuse images as much as possible so images can be loaded from cache.

✦ Use frames so only part of the browser windows need to reload.

✦ Use text rather than images, where possible; see Figure 37-10 for an example of changing the colors of cells in a table to approximate a graphic image.

Image file sizes

You can limit image file sizes

✦ by using the maximum compression your image will take

✦ by using the smallest bit-depth your image can stand

✦ by minimizing the dimensions of your image on the page

Test your pages at 640×480, 800×600, and 1024×768 to see how they will look to different visitors. Often an image that renders well at 1024×768 and doesn't dominate the page may look huge and overbearing at 640×480.

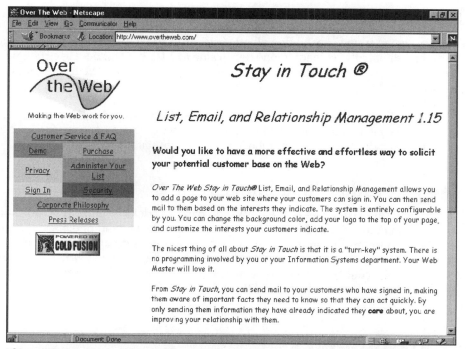

Figure 37-10: Use a table with text instead of a graphic to create visually appealing navigational tools.

Number of images

How many images is the right number? You may be surprised to learn that sometimes very small images with white space between them load faster than one large image.

Take advantage of white space to contribute to your images. You can use two intelligent techniques to get more image for the byte. By changing the background color to match the background color of your images, you can keep your images smaller. By anti-aliasing the text against that background to blend the edges into the background color, you can achieve the look of one large graphic with multiple small — and fast to load — images.

Reuse images

Reusing images is as simple as having a single graphic for "home" on all your pages. Have a single bullet graphic (if you can't stand to use the standard bullet) for every bullet on every page. Why does this help your pages load faster? Your browser checks to see whether an image it needs is already in cache and loads the image from cache, if it can. This reduces the number of bytes that actually needs to be downloaded.

Use frames

How can using frames speed download time? After the initial frameset loads, the browser will usually be loading one new frame at a time. Also, because the images are probably part of the banner and/or the navigational tools, the frame that does reload is less likely to be image-intensive.

Tip By putting all or most of the images into one of your frames and the mostly text-based content into your main frame, you can save visitors from having to load the images more than once. After the initial load, subsequent loads will be faster.

Use text rather than images

You've read this elsewhere in the book. You can use tricks to make text look somewhat like an image. Consider Figure 37-10, for example. Instead of using a graphic with boxes and buttons in the left frame (this is a frameset page) for navigation, it uses a table with each cell assigned a different background color. You can assign each cell a different text color. You can even assign each cell a different font, if that would contribute to the message of the navigational tools.

Creating Graphics

If you want to create top-notch graphics, the tool of choice among professionals is Adobe Photoshop, available for the Mac, the PC, and the SGI computer (see Figure 37-11). Freeware and shareware software programs also are available that perform subsets of the functions performed by Photoshop. Photoshop LE, the lite version, ships with many scanners.

Essential functions

What should your graphics package be able to do? For existing images, such as photographs, you want to sharpen, blur, and perform some special effects on the image (for example, posterize, swirl, and mosaic). For images you create on the screen, you want to create your own custom palette (so you can send as few colors as you need). You also need some basic artist tools, such as a paintbrush, a pencil, a spray can, and a magnifying glass for magnifying part of the image to see it better.

Regardless of whether the image is made by hand or based on a photograph or clipart, you need the following capabilities:

✦ to reduce the bit-depth of any image you want to save as GIF

✦ to index the color of the image so you can save the image to GIF

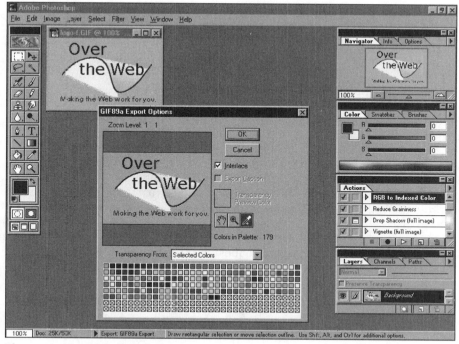

Figure 37-11: Adobe Photoshop

- ✦ to save the image as an interlaced GIF
- ✦ to save the image as a transparent GIF
- ✦ to save the image as a PNG file
- ✦ to save the image as a progressive JPEG, which is discussed at the end of this chapter

Definition

Progressive JPEG. Progressive JPEGs are a nice addition to a Web page. They work the same as interlaced GIFs. Before the entire image has been downloaded, you can begin to see the image. Then the images slowly come into focus.

Free alternatives

If you aren't ready to commit to a $500 software package to get all these great functions, you can work with a number of small, free software packages and services that do many of the things previously listed for you. On the Web, you can find sites that turn your TIF file into a GIF, or make your GIF an interlaced GIF. The trade-off is the time. Finding, learning, and using a variety of small packages to solve all your imaging needs obviously takes longer than learning one package and using it on your desktop.

Capturing Graphics

What about taking graphics you like from another site? This is generally not an okay thing to do. Unless you have explicit permission from the creator of the images — say, you are taking graphics from a site that makes free images available or you have written permission from the owner of the site — you are essentially stealing the images from the legitimate owner. Images are intellectual property and are protected by copyright laws. Most people won't take you to court, but you are still a thief.

Just because an image is on a Web page doesn't mean it is in the public domain. Yes, it gets downloaded onto your own computer (into cache), and, yes, your browser gives you the ability to save the image as a local file (using the right mouse button or prolonged clicking on a Mac), but it still doesn't mean you own the image or the right to use the image. If you see something you like on another page, write to the page owner and ask if he or she owns the image and if you can use it. Chances are, the owner will be flattered by your request. Be sure that person owns the image or permission won't mean anything (if the image was stolen from somewhere else).

Progressive JPEGs and Interlaced GIFs

Once upon a time on the Web, you had to wait for an image to finish loading before you knew what it was. Today, you can save your files using the progressive JPEG format or the interlaced GIF format and watch the image come into focus as it loads.

The advantage to this approach is a visitor to your site knows roughly what an image is before the entire image has downloaded. If download times are long, say, due to a poor Internet connection, the visitor to the site can actually take a link off the page before the image has finished loading without having missed anything.

Finally, these two image formats are good because the visitor participates in the download time. Instead of waiting for the page to download — sitting idly by — the visitor waits for the page to download while watching the images become clearer. This is more of a reward for waiting — and less of a sense of waiting — for the visitor.

The sense of "coming into focus" that these types of images provide is the result of the way the images are stored. Progressive JPEGs and interlaced GIFs download only every eighth line at first, then every fourth line, then every second line, and then, finally, the odd-numbered lines. The result is the image goes from blurry to focused.

You create a progressive JPEG or an interlaced GIF by saving it into this format. In Photoshop, when you save a file as a GIF file, it asks you whether you want the file to be normal or interlaced (see Figure 37-12). Freeware packages are also available that convert your regular JPEGs and GIFs into progressive JPEGs and interlaced GIFs.

Figure 37-12: Adobe Photoshop asks you whether you want your GIF file to have rows interlaced or normal.

Using Transparent GIFs

Transparent GIFs are a wonderful invention that enable your image to blend into your background or to float over your page. The effect of a transparent GIF on a page can be magical. By setting the page background color to the same color as the outline of the image or to one of the colors of the image, transparent GIFs can contribute a light, airy look to a page.

Transparent GIFs enable you to choose one or more colors that will not appear. Whatever color you set as the transparent color, depending on how you do it, will be transparent when rendered in the browser. This can result in the cut-out parts of letters also being clear — say, the hole in the middle of an *O*. The danger to this effect is if you have a part of your image that should be white — say, the whites of a cartoon character's eyes, and you set the transparent color to white and put the image on a yellow background — then the cartoon character will look like he has jaundice or hepatitis (yellow whites to his eyes).

From Here

 Jump to Chapter 41 and learn how to add video to your Web pages.

You can learn to create animated graphics by jumping to Chapter38

Summary

In this chapter, you learned most of what you should know to use images in your pages. You learned about the compression choices you have for images. You learned about color palettes and bit depth. This chapter also discussed clever tricks for increasing the download speed of your page, such as using frames and reusing images.

You learned a few things about creating graphics and the tools you can use to do this. You also were warned about copyright issues related to using graphics from other people's sites. You learned about progressive JPEGs and interlaced GIFs, about transparent GIFs, and about tools for creating these interesting types of images.

✦   ✦   ✦

Creating Animated Graphics for the Web

C reating an animated image for the Web is incredibly simple. Those banner ads you see with animation are both simple to create and relatively small to load, compared to old-fashioned animations. This chapter takes you through what you need to know to create animated GIFs (the most popular type of animation on the Web). It also discusses other options you have for more sophisticated animations.

Introducing Animated GIFs

Animated GIFs are an easy way to add motion to your Web page without any programming, using only the simplest of tools. Animated GIFs are like slide shows. The steps involved are simple:

1. Plan the animation.

2. Create the individual frames of the slides in your favorite image creation tool.

3. String your images together into a long "filmstrip" using a GIF animation tool.

4. Modify the animated GIF properties, such as palette information, number of times you want the images to loop (once, 20 times, or continuously), and image size.

5. Export your animated GIF from the animation tool to a .GIF file.

6. Add your animation to your HTML using the IMAGE element.

Planning Your Animation

As with anything else, planning is essential to creating effective animated GIFs. Suppose you wanted to animate a stick figure jumping up into the air, and then landing and doing a flip. Because you want this to be a loop, you also need to get the stick figure back to the starting point gracefully, so the loop can begin again.

How many images do you need? Figure 38-1 is the starting point.

Figure 38-1: This is the starting point for stick-art animation.

Then the figure must squat to get some momentum for a big jump. Figures 38-2 and 38-3 capture the squat and the jump.

Figure 38-2: The stick figure squats.

Figure 38-3: The stick figure jumps.

How should the stick figure land? The easiest thing would be to land the stick figure back in the squat from which it started and use this as the beginning motion for the big flip. Figure 38-2 can be reused for the landing position. This means it is time for the flipping figures. Figures 38-4 and 38-5 show the flip.

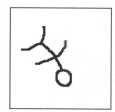

Figure 38-4: The stick figure begins its flip.

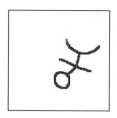

Figure 38-5: The stick figure continues its flip.

Again, the stick figure needs to land. Fortunately, the squatting figure can be reused, by just moving the squatting character over to the right in your image editor. The standing figure (Figure 38-1) can also be moved to the right in your image editor to make the stick figure stand where it should have landed. The two figures created are shown in Figures 38-6 and 38-7.

Figure 38-6: The stick figure lands.

Figure 38-7: The stick figure completes its flip.

If an animated GIF weren't a loop, the animation would end there. But because the character needs to get back to the beginning, another squat and the two flipping frames, in reverse order, of course, will return it to the beginning.

Creating the Animation

Creating the animation requires a bit of artistic talent and a lot of imagination. Just as when you were a child and you created flip books of animation, each image should be only a slight variation of the previous image. You want to be careful not to use too much motion in your animation because the size of the file grows as the number of still images in your animation grows. By limiting the dimensions of the images and the bit-depth, however, you can help limit the size of the file.

Note   Your animated GIF has *frames*. Within each frame there can be one or more *images*. You can create interesting effects by changing the size of the image in the frame to make it appear to be getting closer or farther away.

You want to follow some guidelines when creating your animations:

✦ Keep all frames the same size.

✦ Keep colors to a minimum.

✦ Limit the amount of motion from one image to the next.

✦ Limit the number of frames.

As with anything else, you need to plan your animation carefully so the effect you desire is achieved in a reasonable number of images. When you export the animation from the animation tool, you can specify the file to be a vertical row of images or a horizontal row of images. The effect can be different depending on which direction you choose.

Because the previous example uses simple stick figures, creating the animation is pretty fast.

Using a GIF Animation Editor

Plenty of useful GIF animation editors are available. You can do a search on the Web to find the most recent tools available. At one site, you can create your own animated GIF banner with text of your choice.

An easy and relatively inexpensive tool is Gamani's GIF Movie Gear (see Figure 38-8). It is $30 shareware available from www.gamani.com. It takes care of all the settings you might want to manipulate, without requiring you to learn anything technical about animated GIFs. Everything takes place in well-documented dialog boxes.

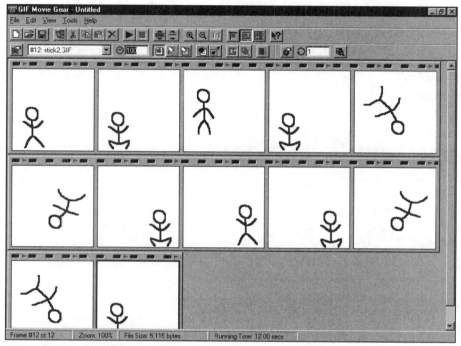

Figure 38-8: GIF Movie Gear makes creating animated GIFs easy.

You can find a 30-day version of GIF Movie Gear 2.63 on the CD-ROM in the back of this book.

In Figure 38-8, the animated GIF uses the seven still frames shown in Figures 38-1 to 38-7. Some of them are reused, which saves time in creating the images. The film-strip is created as a horizontal strip because the action of the animation is mostly horizontal. It could have been just as easily set as a vertical strip.

You can do everything from optimizing the palette to sizing the frames to setting the number of loops using GIF Movie Gear. You can preview your animated GIF right in Movie Gear. When you are satisfied, you can export the file to a .GIF file for use in your Web pages.

Including an Animated GIF on Your Page

Including an animated GIF on your page is just like including any other GIF on a page. You use the IMG element. The following HTML is all you need to include the GIF, which is included on the CD-ROM:

```
<IMG src="patrice.gif" width="144" height="144" alt="stick
figure acrobatics">
```

You could also make this animated GIF a link to another page by including the IMG element within an A element.

Testing Your Animation

As with everything else on your page, you want to test your animation from your browser and from a variety of other browsers, to make sure it works as you expect. You also want to run your page through Bobby, which is discussed in Chapter 24, to make sure the download time for your page with the animation is reasonable. Finally, you want to be sure to use the alt attribute of the IMG element so visitors looking at your page with a browser that doesn't support animated GIFs know what they are missing.

More Animation Options

You can use other techniques to add animation to your page. Some of your options include

✦ Shockwave/Flash

✦ Movies

✦ Java applets

✦ ActiveX controls

Shockwave/Flash

Shockwave and Flash are a proprietary animation system owned by Macromedia. To create a shockwave or a flash file, you need to use either Authorware or Director. To play a shockwave or a flash file, your site visitors need to have a special plug-in loaded.

Chapter 42 discusses Shockwave and Flash in more detail.

Movies

Another way to add motion to your page is to add a movie. The problem with most movie files is they tend to be considerably larger than animated GIF files. This means they take a lot of time to download—although you can do things to get them to start playing before they complete the download—and they take up a lot of space on your server. Movies will run in most browsers without any additional plug-ins.

 Chapter 41 discusses video in more detail.

Java applets

If you are comfortable with programming, you might find Java to your liking. With Java, you can create more than just simple animations. Generally, when you work with Java, you work with a dataset and some actions on a dataset. The previous stick figure animation wouldn't be well-suited to a Java animation. Java files tend to be small, but sometimes run slowly. Additionally, the visitor to your site must have a Java-enabled browser.

 Chapter 43 discusses Java Applets in more detail.

ActiveX controls

ActiveX controls can give you lots of interesting animation effects without a lot of work. The only real work involved is locating them. Plenty of ActiveX controls are available (free or for a small fee). Once you find them, you include the reference to them in your HTML and visitors to your site—if their browsers can handle it—can see your interesting animation effects with relatively little work. The downside of ActiveX controls is they install software directly on the visitor's computer. Cautious visitors won't give your page permission to install the control.

 Chapter 42 discusses ActiveX controls in more detail.

From Here

 Jump to Chapter 41 and learn about creating video for the Web.

Jump to Chapter 42 and learn about plug-ins you can use to spice up your Web page.

Proceed to Chapter 39 and learn about designing and implementing imagemaps.

Summary

In this chapter you learned how to create animated GIFs for your page. You need a basic image editor (anything that can create an image and save it as a GIF), a GIF animation editor, and some imagination. The most important thing is planning your animation well, so it works as you expect. You also learned about alternatives for adding animation and motion to your page.

✦   ✦   ✦

Designing and Implementing Imagemaps

Imagemaps are images with clickable regions under them. An imagemap can be a wonderful way to make a visually appealing page interactive. Or, it can be slow-to-load and confusing, if not done properly. This chapter helps you to do it right. You learn about both server-side and client-side imagemaps. You also learn about the tools you can use for creating imagemaps. Finally, you learn about testing your imagemaps and adding alternative text to increase their effectiveness.

Introducing Imagemaps

Imagemaps work by having an image with defined regions under the image. Each of those regions is associated with a link just as with the other linking elements, such as LINK and A. The browser or the server calculates the regions under the image based on the shape associated with each region, the dimensions of the region, and the anchor point of the region, which is where the region starts — usually from the upper left-hand corner of the image.

Imagemaps can be effective ways of communicating information without excessive reliance on text, possibly making a site accessible to people for whom English is a foreign language or to small children. This theory breaks down if your site design includes any destination pages that rely on text in English, which almost all sites do. In any case, you can use a large site map for a single transit page, but you risk incurring the ire of your visitors if you put too many large, slow-to-load imagemaps on your site.

Imagemap Design

An imagemap can be a valuable addition to your site or it can be an annoyance to your site visitor. How do you know which? You can review some questions to see if your application of an imagemap is likely to elicit favorable responses or to anger visitors.

1. **Did you keep the imagemap size to a minimum?** You might be thinking you want your initial imagemap to fill a screen. What size screen? You certainly want to design for a 640×480 screen, to keep the image size down and to guarantee everyone can see the whole image. Even if your image is well compressed, you are still talking about a large image. Why not use one or more smaller images with some white space between them and plenty of white space around the margins of the page?

2. **Can you navigate around your site another way, other than the imagemap?** You definitely want to make sure another way exists. The simplest and least glamorous way is to enclose the names of the pages you are linking to within square brackets [like this].

3. **Can people with their browsers set *not* to load images still navigate through your site?** This relates to the previous question. In the worst case, you will have visitors to your site who don't see any of your images. Can they navigate?

4. **Is it obvious what the *hot* regions of your imagemaps link to?** Think of the average sign for a ladies room in a nice grocery store. It usually has the word *women* (wanting not to offend women who aren't ladies?), an illustration of a wheelchair, and an illustration of a baby in a diaper. What does this tell you? Previously the sign also had a stick figure with a skirt on, but that went the way of the word *ladies*. Those illustrations tell you the bathroom is wheelchair-accessible and it has a changing station for babies. These signs are as clear as can be. The images that are part of the hot regions of your imagemaps need to be just as clear. If you have any doubt that your hot regions accurately and adequately convey their destinations, do user testing. Find people who aren't part of the Web design group, who aren't necessarily experts on your product line, and watch them click around. Can they find what they want right away?

5. **Is there `alt` text for each hot region?** The `alt` attribute should be populated for each region so if visitors have any doubt where a link goes, they can place their cursors over the region and read the `alt` text.

Server-Side Versus Client-Side Imagemaps

Imagemaps can either run on the browser or on the server. They look identical, regardless of where the processing takes place. In the earlier days of the Web, when most Web pages were published by systems administrators or UNIX gurus, server-side imagemaps were the thing to do. Today, when most pages are published by clients of ISPs, server-side imagemaps are a nightmare for systems administrators. The preferred method of delivering an imagemap is with a client-side imagemap.

Server-side imagemaps usually require root permission to write to files shared by everyone on the server. You can see why that mode doesn't scale well. Server-side imagemaps also put some processing that can be delegated to the visitor's computer back on the server. This doesn't fit the model of distributed computing most systems administrators are pursuing.

Client-side imagemaps are easy to create and plenty of free or inexpensive tools can help you create them. The information the browser needs is all included in the HTML or in a separate file referred to by the HTML. The imagemapping tool creates this for you based on the regions you draw on the image.

 Cross-Reference Some of the HTML editors reviewed in Chapter 8 have imagemapping tools built into them.

Developing Graphics for Imagemaps

What kinds of images lend themselves to becoming imagemaps? You can use any kind of image, with any shape of hot regions, but the more complex the shapes of your regions, the more work you must do mapping the image. The important thing is the regions give site visitors a clear idea of where they are linking to.

There is an application of imagemaps you might not have considered. Some sites use narrow toolbars with links to the essential pages on their sites. Figure 39-1 is an example of such a toolbar.

The toolbar in Figure 39-1 is small and attractive. It fits conveniently between the heading of a page or the banner of a page, if there is one, and the content. The toolbar can also be placed at the bottom of the page, to facilitate navigation.

Figure 39-1: This is a toolbar as an imagemap.

Using an Imagemap Editor

Plenty of inexpensive imagemapping tools are available. One nice one is Mapedit, by Boutell.Com. This is shareware that can be downloaded as a 30-day trial version and as of this writing can be purchased for $25. It runs on just about every platform including Windows 95/98/NT, Mac, and UNIX varieties.

Figure 39-2 shows Mapedit in use.

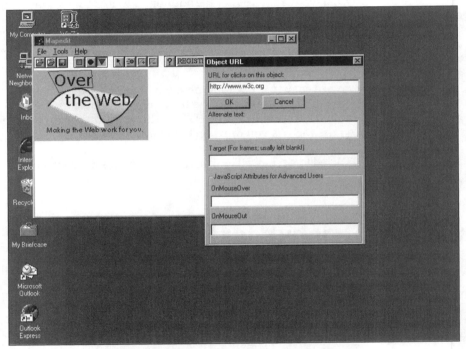

Figure 39-2: Mapedit creates clickable regions under your images.

Definition

The major drawback to the way Mapedit works is it only opens .htm, .html, and .asp files, even though plenty of other file extensions might actually be Web pages (such as .cfm, .cgi, and so forth). If a lot of your Web pages have an extension other than .html, .htm, or .asp, you will want to find a different imagemapping program.

With Mapedit, you define regions right on top of your image using either a circle drawing object, a rectangle drawing object, or a free-form drawing tool. For each region you define, you have a dialog box that requests the URL for the link, alt text for a text description of the link destination, and a target name, if the destination of the link is supposed to populate a frame.

The MAP Element

Essential to creating an imagemap are the MAP element and the AREA element. The MAP element tells the imagemap, "this is where information about clickable regions begins."

Map <MAP>

Start Tag: Required

Content: AREA elements

End Tag: Required

Attributes: title, id, class, style, lang, dir

name: required; contains name associated with the usemap attribute of the IMG element

alt: alternate text

The AREA Element

The AREA element defines the regions within the imagemap that link to other pages.

Area <AREA>

Start Tag: Required

Content: Empty

End Tag: Forbidden

Attributes: id, class, lang, dir: defined elsewhere

shape: "rect"; some browsers support other shapes. but this is the only one in the HTML 4.01 spec

coords: coordinates that define the beginning point of the shape and the dimensions of the shape

href: URL of the link

nohref: Boolean attribute that indicates there is no link

tabindex, accesskey: see Chapter 21

accesskey: accessibility key character

onfocus: the element got the focus

onblur: the element lost the focus

alt: alternate text (recommended)

events: see Chapter 48

The Anatomy of an Imagemap

For the toolbar image in Figure 39-1, the HTML looks like this:

```
<A HREF="http://www.itc.virginia.edu/images/navbar.map/">
<IMG width="436" height="52" border=0
src="http://www.itc.virginia.edu/images/navbar.gif"
ismap usemap="#navbar" alt="ITCWeb" ></A>
<MAP name="navbar">
<AREA shape="rect" coords="2,11,77,43" href=" http://www.itc.
virginia.edu/home.html"
alt="ITCWeb Home">

<AREA shape="rect" coords="162,12,260,43"
href=" http://www.itc.virginia.edu/org/"
alt="ITC Organization">

</MAP>
```

You should recognize some of the elements. To begin with, an A element is at the very top. Within this is the IMG element for the graphic used, which is the same one you see in Figure 39-1. There is also an ismap attribute, which is Boolean (meaning if it is present, it is on; otherwise it is off), which indicates this is the image for an imagemap. The next attribute, usemap, gives the URL of the map to be used. You've seen the pound sign (#) before. It indicates the map to be used is located within the current document. It could just as easily have given a file name or any other valid URL. Finally, there is the alt attribute, which you definitely want to use.

Adding Alternate Text

As you have just read, it is important to include text in the alt attribute, describing where each of your links leads. This isn't the place to give the URL; this isn't useful. This is the place to give a short text description of what will be found at that page.

Where should you include alternate text? In the AREA element for each link and again in the IMG element. The IMG element's alt text will be shown whenever the cursor is positioned at a point that isn't part of one of the hot regions. If the cursor is over a hot region, the alt text for that AREA element will be displayed.

From Here

Cross-Reference

Go to Chapter 42 and learn about incorporating plug-ins.

Jump to Chapter 43 and learn about adding Java applets.

Proceed to Chapter 40 and learn about producing and adding sounds.

Summary

In this chapter, you learned all about imagemaps. The most important thing about imagemaps isn't where the hot regions are; it's what the image contains to direct visitors to the correct links. This chapter gave you some guidelines for designing imagemaps. It also explained how to design graphics to meet these guidelines. You learned about client-side imagemaps, server-side imagemaps, and why systems administrators much prefer you use client-side imagemaps. You learned about using an imagemap editor and about the importance of adding alternate text. Finally, you learned about the MAP and AREA elements and the anatomy of an imagemap.

✦   ✦   ✦

Producing and Adding Sounds

Adding sounds to your Web pages is not particularly difficult. There are advantages to adding sound to your pages, but equally good reasons exist not to put sound in your pages. This chapter talks about how digital audio works, what sound formats work on the Web, how audio compression works, how streaming audio differs from regular audio, how to obtain and record sound files, how to use sound editing software, and, finally, how to add sound to your page with the OBJECT element and the EMBED element.

Understanding Digital Audio

Digital audio tries to represent sound, which is inherently analog (being a wave), with ones and zeros. When you digitize sound waves, you take samples of the wave at certain intervals. Just as you select the quality of images you scan by setting the resolution, you can select the precision of the sound captured by setting the bit-depth of the sound file. Eight-bit sound divides the spectrum into 256 levels. Sixteen-bit sound gives you 65,536 levels. There is also 32-bit sound, but it does not run over the Web and it is not highly accessible to client workstations because so few truly 32-bit sound cards exist.

The quality of sound your computer produces is dependent on five things:

1. The quality of equipment used to record the sound
2. The bit-depth of the recorded sound
3. The frequency of sampling (sample rate)
4. Whether the sound is recorded in mono or stereo (the number of channels)
5. The quality of equipment in the machine playing the sound back

As with images and other types of multimedia files, the quality has to be balanced against the file size. You want to deliver the maximum quality sound for the minimum file size. Compression can help to some degree.

Recording equipment

Several factors figure into the quality of the sound you record. One is the recording environment. If you are going to record voice, you'll want to record in a room with good acoustics. You also need to be sure the bit-depth of the recording equipment is at least as high as the bit-depth at which you are recording. A smart system won't even let you *try* to record 16-bit stereo sound on an 8-bit mono system.

Recording bit-depth

The *bit-depth* of the sound recording indicates how precisely the sound that occurs at the moment of sampling is recorded. As with color palettes, the number of sounds you can choose from is limited to the palette you select. For 8-bit sounds, the sampled sound will be one of 256. For 16-bit sound, the sampled sound will be one of 65,536 sounds. Table 40-1 shows bit-depth and sample rates for common types of digitized sound.

Table 40-1 Sample Rates and Bit-Depth for Common Types of Digitized Sound				
Quality	Sample Rate (kHz)	Bits per Sample	Mono/Stereo	Uncompressed Data Rate (Kbps)
Telephone	8	8	Mono	8
AM Radio	11.025	8	Mono	11.0
FM Radio	22.050	16	Stereo	88.2
CD	44.1	16	Stereo	176.4
DAT	48	16	Stereo	192.0

Sample rate

Sample rates are measured in kilohertz (kHz). The more frequently you sample sound, the higher the sample rate, and the more your digitized sound will match the original sound. Of course, the more frequently you sample, the more information you have to store, resulting in a larger file size.

Mono versus stereo

The difference between mono and stereo is the number of sound channels in the file. For stereo, there is exactly twice as much data. Why does twice as much data exist? Because you are sending two channels of information: one for the left speaker and one for the right speaker.

Do you want to use stereo sound? This depends on two things: file size and likely equipment of the end user. Do you expect site visitors to have stereo playback equipment? If not, it doesn't matter. The real question is whether the sound you are delivering is audio for its own sake, in which the sound quality really matters, or whether the sound is part of something bigger, in which case, mono is probably fine.

Playback equipment

All this business about bit depth, sample rates, and mono versus stereo don't mean much if the people trying to play back your sound have old or low-quality sound cards. If people playing back your sound don't have a 16-bit sound card, they can't possibly play back all 65,536 sounds in the 16-bit spectrum. Their computers will automatically choose the next closest sound from the 256 sounds in the 8-bit spectrum. Bad speakers and a slow processor — that can't re-create the sound at the proper sample rate — can also result in inferior sound quality.

Introducing Sound File Formats

Four sound formats frequently used on the Web include the following:

✦ **.WAV** is the original Windows file format. Although it used to be proprietary to Windows, you can actually play it now under any of the newer browsers, even on a Mac or on UNIX.

✦ **.AIF** (or .AIFF) stands for Audio Interchange File Format. This common audio file format is also cross-platform, but doesn't take advantage of any compression.

✦ **.AU** is the original Sun standard; it enables you to make tiny sound files.

✦ **.MPEG** and MPEG Audio Layer 3 (.MP3) are part of the MPEG2 standard. With it, you can create small files while maintaining a pretty high sound quality. It is nonproprietary. You can achieve compression rates of 1:10 or 1:12 with CD-quality sound. On the downside, it does require a special player. A streamworks player will play streamed files. A lot of record companies are using the MPEG format because you can put CD-quality files on the Web. You also need special software to compress your audio files into .MP3 format.

Other ways exist to put sound on the Web, including Shockwave, RealAudio, and QuickTime, but they are proprietary. They require plug-in software (as does .MP3, although it is nonproprietary), which can inconvenience your site visitors enough that they might not bother to get the plug-in or to try to hear the audio files you put so much time into creating.

Introducing Streaming Audio

Streaming audio has caught on so well that now everyone wants to call their product *streaming*. Consequently, two possible things are meant by the term *streaming audio*. Both kinds of streaming audio enable the visitor to your site to begin hearing the audio file before it finishes downloading, which is the usual way you listen to audio files on the Web.

The first involves a special server that delivers the audio over the Web using a proprietary protocol (not HTTP) to get it to the desktop. It also requires a special plug-in for the browser. The most popular streaming audio server on the market is the RealAudio server. You can learn more about it and about the technology in general at the RealAudio Web site at www.realaudio.com.

The other kind of streaming audio does take advantage of the HTTP protocol, so for lack of a better name, it is called *HTTP Streaming*.

Streaming audio is a big improvement over traditional audio, because the sound file can begin to play before it has completed downloading. Normally, a sound file won't begin playing until the entire file has downloaded. This was part of the reason for the initial impatience with audio on the Web.

How does streaming audio work? When you save a file for streaming, all the basic file format information is front-loaded in the file. This means the first things the browser computer receives about the audio file is enough information to begin playing immediately. In a nonstreaming file, the audio file information is spread out along the length of the file, so the receiving computer can't begin to play the file until the entire file is downloaded.

If you are going to use either kind of streaming audio, you might also have to make changes to the MIME type on your server. Check with your systems administrator to see if your server can handle the MIME type you will be using.

Obtaining Sound Files

You can legally obtain public domain digital music at some sites, but many of the sources you might consider using can get you into trouble with lawyers. You may not obtain sound files by capturing music off your favorite CDs, the radio, or cassettes. You may obtain sound files by recording your own musical works or your own voice, or by purchasing licensed production music or sound effects.

Will you get caught if you use music you obtain illegally or you even own legally, but you distribute illegally (and this is what you are doing when you publish music, even music from recordings you've purchased) on the Web? Probably. There are Web agents — software programs that crawl around the Web looking for sound files belonging to different recording companies — and these agents have been successful at locating illegally distributed music being published by even the most harmless organizations.

Being hassled by a big-name law firm in New York City with a cease-and-desist order is only half the trouble. If you are using music because you think it adds something spicy to your site — say, the theme music from *Mission Impossible* — it will be obvious to visitors to your site, unless your site appears affiliated with the movie in some way, that you have stolen the music and are using it illegally. Does this make your site look professional? No.

Recording Sound Files

If you choose to use a professional sound-editing tool, such as Sound Edit 16, you can record directly into that. Or, you can use whatever sound-recording software comes installed with your sound card. You do need a sound card and an input jack or CD-ROM. Because you know you shouldn't record music off your CD, you won't actually be using any music from your CD collection, but you might be using *clip sounds,* which are like clip art in that you can reuse them if you purchase the CD on which they are distributed.

Figure 40-1 shows the screen for Sound Edit 16 when you are recording sound. You can set the sample rate, the bit-depth, and mono versus stereo. The controls for record, stop, pause, and so forth should look familiar, if you have ever played a CD on your computer.

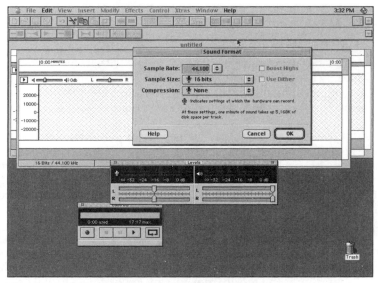

Figure 40-1: Recording sound with Sound Edit 16

Editing Sound Files and Adding Filters

Sound-editing software, unlike image-editing software, isn't usually cheap or free. One free package runs on the Mac, called SoundHack, which does a respectable job. One of the more reasonably-priced packages is Sound Edit 16, by Macromedia. What can you do with your sound files? You can add noise, remove noise, and add filters to create effects such as if you were singing the national anthem in a football stadium (or in space!).

Sound Edit 16 makes it easy to add special effects to your sound files. Just as easy is removing loud breath sounds from a voice recording and adding pauses. Figure 40-2 shows one of the filters you can apply in Sound Edit 16.

Compressing Sound Files

Once you have made all the trade-off decisions about your audio files, bit depth, sample rate, and mono versus stereo, you can still use compression to reduce the file size. Many compression schemes are available. Probably the two seen most often are MPEG Audio Layer 3 (also known as MP3) and RealAudio.

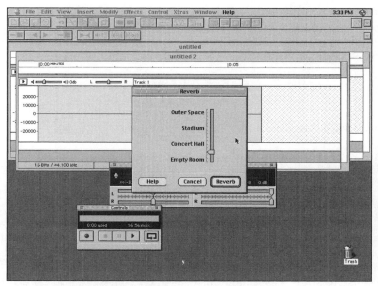

Figure 40-2: Adding effects with Sound Edit 16

RealAudio is proprietary, but is widely used and the compression tool is free, as is the plug-in. MP3 is not proprietary. The MPEG standard is probably the future of free audio on the Web. Their Web site (www.mpeg.org) is a treasure trove of information about audio compression and video compression, along with tools for delivering both on the Web.

Other compression standards exist, but they are not as compatible across platforms and your site visitors might have trouble playing the files back.

Adding Sound Files to Your Page

You have two choices for adding sound to your page with HTML: You can add inline sound, which starts to play as soon as your page loads, or you can add out-of-line sound that plays as a result of some action on the part of the visitor.

Inline sound

The official HTML 4 specification indicates that inline sound should be created with the OBJECT element, but as of publication of this book, the OBJECT element did not work to deliver sound in any of the major browsers. You can add inline sound using the EMBED element (which is deprecated, but works with all major browsers), with the value of the src attribute being the URL for the sound file. You'll also want to use the loop attribute to indicate how many times to play the sound in the background. If you want the sound to play ad nauseam, you can set the value of loop to *infinite* (which should probably be *ad nauseum* to make it clear to Web authors that this is the effect of playing a loop of sound an infinite number of times).

```
<EMBED src="media/sound/annoying-beep.mpeg" loop="infinite"
autostart="true">
```

Or, the official way, with the OBJECT element:

```
<OBJECT data="media/sound/annoying-beep.mpeg"
type="application/mpeg">This is an annoying beep.</OBJECT>
```

Out-of-line sound

The alternative to inline sound is the preferred method of delivering sound, which is delivering sound only when the visitor to your page requests it. Many record stores on the Web let you play snippets from songs on albums they are selling. It wouldn't make sense to show a list of albums (based on your selection criteria) and then start playing snippets from all the songs from all the albums in a row. Out-of-line sound gives the visitor to your site the option to listen to your audio file or to browse in silence.

Adding out-of-line sound to your page is as simple as using the A element and pointing to the sound file with the href attribute.

```
<A href="media/sound/elvis-impersonation.wav" alt="me singing
Blue Christmas with the stadium filter">Listen to me singing
Blue Christmas at the Meadowlands</A>
```

From Here

Jump to Chapter 42 and learn about plug-ins and ActiveX controls.

Proceed to Chapter 41 to learn how to create video and add it to your page.

Summary

In this chapter you learned how digital audio works, what the variables are that make for a better or a worse recording, and why even the best recording may play back poorly on a visitor's computer. You learned about sound file formats and why streaming audio is a good idea. You also endured a stern lecture about why you shouldn't use unauthorized sound files, even if you think you can get away with it.

This chapter discussed Sound Edit 16, which you can use both to record and edit the sound, along with adding effects and filters. As with most multimedia objects, you must understand quality decisions, sample rate, and bit depth to deliver the best quality sound for the smallest file size to your site visitors. Finally, you learned about your two options for adding sound to your Web page, and why out-of-line is probably the better approach.

✦　　✦　　✦

Producing and Adding Video

Digital video has made tremendous strides in the last five years. This is a complex science that doesn't lend itself to a thorough explanation in one short chapter. While this chapter introduces you to the fundamentals of digital video, the list of what it doesn't cover is almost as long as the list of what it does cover. This chapter defines the terms you will come across in making buying decisions about video hardware and software. More important, this chapter is full of references to other more comprehensive sources, most notably, magazines that include up-to-the-minute reviews of hardware and software.

The short version is if you are serious about putting high-quality video on your Web site, you must either devote a tremendous amount of time and a lot of money to the under-taking or you should hire a company dedicated to video compression to take your edited analog video and convert it into a Web-ready format. If you simply want to produce the kind of video — small frame size and choppy — you see on most Web pages, this chapter gets you started nicely. In any case, you need to know the vocabulary and the anatomy of digital video.

Introduction to Digital Video

Video is by nature an analog product. Converting analog video into ones and zeros has always been fraught with challenges. With still images, you have a similar problem: how to store colors and shapes as ones and zeros in as little space as possible, while retaining as clear a copy of the original image as possible. With video you have the added dimension of movement.

With film, motion is created by showing a series of still images in rapid succession. The more images in a given time interval, the more fluid the motion. If you start with clear still images and add fluid motion, you have top-quality video or film.

When digitizing video, you have to consider the size of the frame and the number of colors (2 if just black and white, 256, or even 1.7 million), as in capturing still images. Just as with film, you also have to decide how many still images will be seen in a given interval of time. With digital video, you also must think about compression of the images and the motion. That compression can take two forms: compression within each frame or compression between frames.

Expectations

If you spend a lot of time on the Web, your expectations are probably pretty humble. You'll settle for postage-stamp-size video that plays relatively smoothly. This is what most sites deliver today. Fortunately, the current state of video compression and delivery can help you deliver better video than this. A number of excellent products are available for desktop computing to help you produce results at better than the postage-stamp level for a consumer's budget. The resources listed at the end of this chapter point you to the state-of-the-art technology.

Garbage in, garbage out

As with many other components, with video, the quality of the digital video you produce is highly correlated with the quality of the analog with which you have to begin. While you can take high-quality analog video and still produce junk in digital form, you can't take bad analog video and produce clear, sharp digital video.

The Anatomy of Digital Video

Digital video takes advantage of the best of imaging technologies and a thing or two from audio technologies. Digital video, at its most basic level, is a collection of still images that are sequenced. Intelligent compression schemes exist that you can apply to allow the video to be compressed both within each frame and between frames.

The problem with digital video has always been the compression versus file size trade-off. If the file is too big, the computer trying to play the file will be unable to play the frames at the rate they were intended to play. If the file is compressed too much, the computer won't have the power to decompress in real time, producing the same playback problem.

Regardless of how you compress video files, capturing and editing video can require huge wedges of disk space for even the shortest snippet of video. Video capture, editing, and compression require special hardware and software not often found on regular desktop computers.

Three factors dictate video quality: frame rate, frame size, and compression technology. Compression technologies are discussed in their own section later in this chapter.

Frame rate

The *frame rate* is measured in frames per second. Full-motion video is considered 30 frames per second (fps). Films are 29.75 fps. Most video shown over the Web plays at 15 fps. The more frames you show per second, the larger the file you need to send, but the smoother the motion.

Frame size

The *frame size* is measured in pixels and indicates the amount of screen space your movie will fill. Common frame sizes are 80×60, 160×120, 176×144, 240×180, 320×240, and 352×288. Video delivered over the Web is rarely 640×480 or full-screen because the file sizes become prohibitive. This kind of video is usually reserved for CD-ROMs or DVD.

Introducing Video File Formats

Few video formats work on the Web. These include the following:

✦ **.MOV.** This is the original movie format of the Web. It isn't owned by anyone and it doesn't require any special plug-ins to play it back. On the downside, it also doesn't use good compression, so file sizes can be large.

✦ **.QT.** The QuickTime architecture is owned by Apple computers. Playback requires a special plug-in, which you probably already have on your Mac, but you have to download on your PC.

✦ **.MPG.** MPEG, the standard set by the Motion Picture Experts' Group, is probably the best, nonproprietary standard available for video on the Web. Compressing your video as MPG will take a while, but the results can be pretty impressive.

Introducing Streaming Video

Streaming video works just like streaming audio. When you compress video normally, the video file contains all the movie information, frame by frame, for the entire movie in order. In parallel with this information is information about the file: the file type, the file size, and compression information. The problem with normal video compression is that, for the browser to begin to play the movie, it has to receive all the information about the file first.

Streaming video moves all the information about the file to the front of the file. This means the first information the browser receives is the information it needs to get the computer ready to play a movie. Once the actual movie starts to download, the browser is ready to start playing the movie as it arrives. Obviously, if the file is too big or if the frame rate can't be met by the download speed, then the movie won't play back properly. Used properly, however, streaming video can be a valuable addition to your Web site.

Video Compression Schemes

Essentially two kinds of video compression exist: intraframe and interframe. *Intraframe compression* takes advantage of the kind of compression used with images. It compresses each frame as well as it can. *Interframe compression* actually compresses between frames. The amount of *guessing* you let the computer do between frames affects how smoothly the video plays back. This also affects the size of the file. Obviously, if you can drop half the frames and still have a decent video, your file size will be much smaller.

Capturing Analog Video

Capturing analog video requires some playback device, such as a VCR if your source video is on VHS tape, or a camcorder if your source video was recorded that way. Capturing analog video also requires video in jacks on the video board of your computer. You may need to purchase a special video-capture board for your computer, although more and more video cards are coming with video-capture capability. The video-capture board will likely take S-video, an 8-pin mini DIN connector, or an RCA phono jack.

Capturing digital video is something of an art. Depending on the software you use, you have to adjust from 2 to about 30 settings in the software. You also want to make sure your disk is defragmented or, better yet, that you have a separate hard drive you can reformat between each session of video capture. Capturing video can take up a lot of hard drive space. Sometimes you'll want 30 frames from one part of a tape and then another 30 from another part. Finding the exact starting and ending frames can require capturing far more video and then editing it.

Editing Digital Video

Editing digital video is definitely the fun part. One relatively easy-to-use software package is Adobe Premiere, available for both Macintosh and Windows. When editing, you can add interesting (or annoying) transitions from one frame to the next. Figure 41-1 shows a list of transitions.

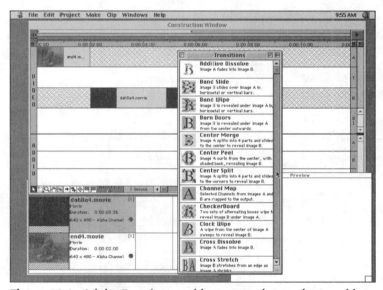

Figure 41-1: Adobe Premiere enables you to choose the transitions.

Another feature you want your video-editing software to have is titling capabilities. You might want to add scrolling credits at the end or a title at the beginning. Figure 41-2 shows the movie being titled in Premiere.

Finally, when you are done with your editing, you kick off the compression process (see Figure 41-3) and go home for the night. Frequently the compression will take overnight. The length of time it takes depends on the power of your computer, the type of compression, the length of the video, and the frame rate.

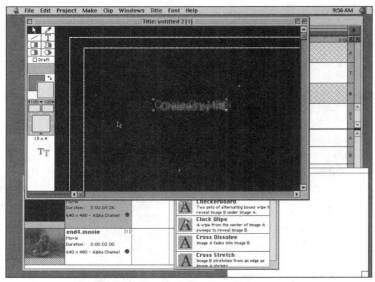

Figure 41-2: Titling with Premiere

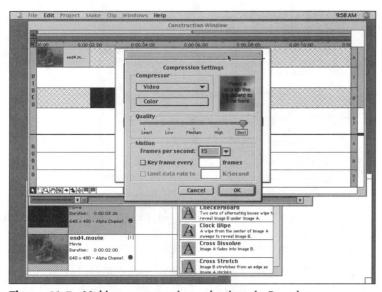

Figure 41-3: Making compression selections in Premiere

Adding Video Files to Your Page

Video is usually added as out-of-line video, meaning to see the video, the site visitor must take an action. However, you can create inline video, which is added with the OBJECT element. The OBJECT element is discussed in depth in the next chapter. Out-of-line video is added with the familiar A element. Examples for both follow:

Inline movies

```
<OBJECT data="media/movies/cool.mpeg"
type="application/mpeg">Sorry you can't see this movie. It is
pretty cool.
</OBJECT>
```

Out-of-line movies

```
<A href="media/movies/cool.mpeg" alt="Very cool movie">Click
here to see a cool movie</A>
```

Invaluable Resources

AV Video Multimedia Producer (www.kipinet.com/av_mmp/index.html) is available by subscription or on newsstands.

Digital Video (www.dv.com) is available by subscription or on newsstands.

Videography (www.videography.com) is available by subscription or on newsstands.

Advanced Imaging (www.advancedimagingmag.com) is available by subscription.

From Here

Cross-Reference

Go to Chapter 43 to learn how to add Java applets.

Proceed to Chapter 42 to begin incorporating plug-ins and ActiveX controls.

Summary

In this chapter you learned how digital movies work, what parameters contribute to the quality and size of movie files, and how video compression works. You learned about capturing and editing video and about including video in your Web sites. Many alternative ways to create video on your page require plug-ins. These are discussed in Chapter 42.

✦   ✦   ✦

Incorporating Plug-Ins and ActiveX Controls

Plug-ins offer you the ability to add many diverse types of media to your Web pages. Many of the desktop software packages you may use daily have plug-ins that enable the results of your work to be seen on the Web. Far too many types of plug-ins exist for this chapter to list all of them.

Netscape was first on the scene with plug-ins. ActiveX controls are Microsoft's answer to plug-ins. ActiveX controls, while they run under Netscape as well, were designed to add functionality to Internet Explorer 3 and higher. Just like plug-ins, before visitors to your site can use an ActiveX control on your Web page, they must download it.

What kind of functionality can ActiveX controls add to your page? Nearly any kind you can imagine and program. ActiveX controls are written in regular programming languages, using one of the Microsoft Software Development Kits (SDKs). Many ActiveX controls are available at no cost. Others can be licensed from the developers. Many resources are on the Web for finding both these kinds of controls. If you still can't find the one you want, you can write one yourself.

Reviewing the OBJECT Element

The OBJECT element is one of the most versatile elements in HTML. You can use it to include inline graphics, audio, video, Java applets, and plug-ins in your page. Even though it has many attributes, you rarely need more than a few for any instance of the element. Because this book aims to be comprehensive, you can find the complete OBJECT element definition in Chapter 19.

The main attributes you need in order to include inline plug-ins with the OBJECT element are data and type. For example, to include an inline VRML model, you would use the following HTML:

```
<OBJECT data="media/3D/music.wrl" type="world/wrl">
Too bad you don't have a VRML plug-in. You can find one at <A
href=" http://home.netscape.com/plugins/3d_and_animation.html"
alt="Netscape plug-in download center">the Netscape plug-in
download center</A>.
</OBJECT>
```

Visitors to your site would have to have a plug-in that recognized the MIME type "world/wrl."

How Plug-Ins Work

It's like magic. You download a plug-in and you install it. Then you come across a page with an application requiring that plug-in and voilà! Your browser runs that application just as if that functionality was built into the browser. How does the browser know which plug-in to use?

The answer is MIME types. Your computer has a list of MIME types it recognizes. Where does this list come from? Every time you install a software package, your computer adds this MIME type to the list. It uses this same list to assign a special icon to a file when you look at a file listing.

In Netscape, you can define a new MIME type manually, by going into Edit ➪ Preferences ➪ Applications. In Figure 42-1, you see a list of MIME types. A MIME type consists of the file extension (so the computer knows which files to associate with this MIME type on a PC or on UNIX), the category of file (audio, video, application, image, and so forth), and the application that should be used to open the file. For Macs, there aren't any file extensions.

In Internet Explorer, you actually set the MIME types and define new MIME types in the operating system, from any file listing (see Figure 42-2). If you go into an Explorer window (right-mouse click the Start button and choose Explore), and then select View ➪ Options and click the File Types tab, you see a list of valid MIME types for your computer.

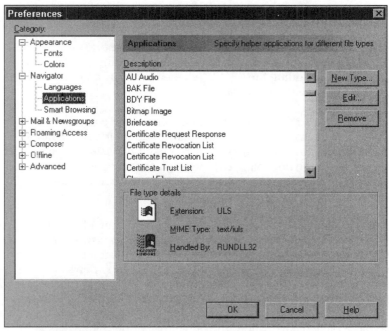

Figure 42-1: Setting MIME types manually in Netscape

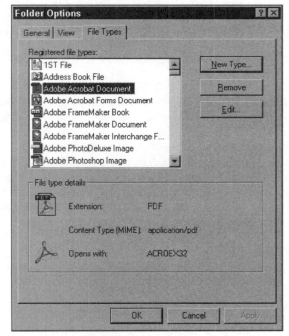

Figure 42-2: Setting MIME types manually for
Internet Explorer

Plug-In Pluses and Minuses

Plug-ins can be a rich addition to your site. They add interesting visual stimuli and are relatively quick to develop. As you read previously, adding an inline plug-in to your page is as simple as adding the OBJECT element. Adding an out-of-line plug-in to your page uses the familiar A element.

Plug-ins can do so much, so easily, why would a Web author want to avoid them at all? The major drawback to plug-ins is that visitors to your site might decide not to download the plug-in and would miss whatever exciting visual/aural stimuli you prepared for them. If a large portion of the message on your page is contained in a file requiring a plug-in, then you risk failing to communicate that message to much of your audience.

Plug-ins are best used in intranets, where you have some control over (or at least a knowledge of) the setup of each of the computers likely to visit your page. The other relatively safe environment in which to use a plug-in is on a site where the same information is offered in another format, say, text. Many news sites rely primarily on text to convey their messages, but offer video or audio to supplement the message of the text.

You want to avoid a page design where the only element on the page is your plug-in. This annoys people who don't have the plug-in, especially if you haven't provided enough information to convince them that they should go to the trouble of getting the plug-in and installing it. Make sure to provide a direct link to the site providing the plug-in, so people don't have to search for the plug-in.

Adding Plug-Ins

Plug-ins can be divided into several categories: 3D and animation plug-ins, audio and video plug-ins, discipline-specific plug-ins, business plug-ins, image viewers, and presentation plug-ins. Often, the effects achieved with plug-ins can be achieved equally well with either JavaScript or Java. The drawback to using programming, specifically Java, is that the development time is much longer than simply using a plug-in. Frequently you must purchase additional software to implement a plug-in. Sometimes, your systems administrator must make changes to the server to accommodate new MIME types, because the Web server must also be familiar with the MIME type.

3D and animation plug-ins

If you want to take advantage of vector graphics or 3D models, you need a plug-in for now. Future versions of browsers undoubtedly will include support for vector graphics but, even then, not all visitors to your site will have the latest browser.

Cosmo Worlds and World View

The most popular 3D plug-in is the one that has been around the longest: Cosmo Worlds by SGI. This runs on PCs or UNIX. If you want to display 3D models on a Mac, you can use World View by Intervista. The nonproprietary standard you can use to create 3D models is VRML. Creating sophisticated 3D models without some sort of tool is difficult and time consuming. Cosmo Create, also by SGI, is the most powerful tool for creating 3D models in VRML, the most commonly used 3D modeling language on the Web.

Shockwave and Flash

Shockwave and Flash are plug-ins by Macromedia. Not surprisingly, these plug-ins support files created by Macromedia's own products: Director, Authorware, and Flash (see Figure 42-3). You can create impressive interactive animations and applications with Authorware and Director. Flash creates vector graphics.

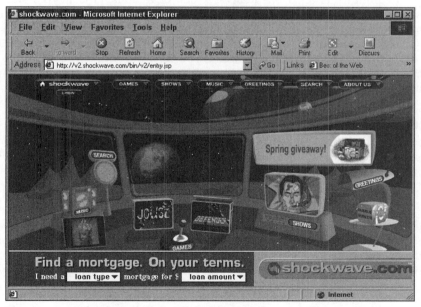

Figure 42-3: Shockwave plays Director and Authorware files.

Why would you want to use Flash as a plug-in when you can create graphics that display inline without any plug-ins? Vector graphics are an efficient way to deliver graphics to the Web.

In Depth   Vector graphics files are small because, instead of a file containing the image, the file contains only the equations that create the images (remember geometry class?). Also, the graphics created by the equations are infinitely scalable without any loss of quality. Expect to see much more of vector graphics on the Web as Version 5 browsers support this format for inline graphics.

Audio and video plug-ins

Both audio and video can be played by the Version 3 and 4 browsers without any special plug-ins. If you want to use fancier video or audio tools, however, including real-time streaming video or audio that takes advantage of a special server, you need a special plug-in. The other reason to use a plug-in is to show QuickTimeVR movies, which can be an effective way to show an object in 3D or to navigate around a space.

RealPlayer

RealPlayer by RealNetworks, Inc. kills two birds with one stone. If you are using either the RealAudio server or the RealVideo server, RealPlayer is all your site visitors need. Either of these technologies, while relatively expensive to implement, result in excellent image/sound quality delivered in real-time without those pesky download delays. Another advantage to this technology is the browser computer reuses cache when downloading the files. This means the entire video or audio file doesn't reside on the visitor's computer at any given time, saving the visitor precious hard drive space.

NetShow

NetShow is another streaming video application. NetShow is seen more commonly on sites designed to use the full suite of elements only available to Internet Explorer. NetShow does nearly as nice a job as RealPlayer. The NetShow server is available at no cost from Microsoft.

QuickTimeVR

QuickTimeVR is a video application that competes with both video products and 3D modeling products. QuickTime is the original video technology used on Macs. QuickTimeVR can be effective at showing an object from any perspective. Say you are creating an exhibit of products and you want people to move the objects so they can look at the objects from all sides. How would you do this? You might create a movie of the object as you move it (or move around it, depending on its size), but how fast should you move? What if visitors want to linger at a certain perspective? QuickTimeVR solves all this by creating a cylinder of images, woven together so viewers can turn the cylinder, looking at any angle, and then move the object so they can look at any other angle. The same can be done with panoramas: QuickTimeVR can create a seamless view of the Grand Canyon from the middle. In addition to giving viewers control over the speed of the "movie" and the navigation, QuickTimeVR creates relatively small files — compared to real movies — so this is a winner from every perspective.

Discipline-specific plug-ins

For some fields, such as chemistry, incredibly powerful plug-ins enable you to express an idea or equation with such brevity, you just can't avoid using plug-ins. If your discipline is something other than chemistry, look and see if there isn't some plug-in to make your life easier before you embark on a Java program to solve your display problems.

Chime by Chemscape is one of these plug-ins. You might not need to represent molecules, but if you did, this would be the product to use. Go to www.mdli.com to download the tool.

Business plug-ins

Probably the single most popular plug-in in use on the Web is the Acrobat Reader, which displays Portable Document Format (PDF) files. *PDF* is Adobe's own format for saving formatted files for printing. Who uses PDF files on the Web? The IRS for one. Nearly any tax form you could possibly want is available on the IRS Web site (www.irs.gov). The beauty of PDF is that the file can be printed the way it was intended. If you take a form and re-create it on the Web (in HTML), you can't be sure where page breaks will fall. If you take a form and create a PDF file with it, then everyone who opens it can print it to look exactly the same.

To create PDF files, you need to purchase one of the Adobe products that creates PDF files. Adobe Acrobat ($249 as of this writing) is the basic package you need if you want to publish documents in PDF format. Figure 42-4 is an example of what a PDF file would look like on your screen. If you already use Adobe Illustrator to create documents, you can export directly from Illustrator into the PDF format. For most documents, which you create in your favorite word processor or scan in using optical character recognition (OCR), you need Acrobat. Using the Acrobat Writer, you can "print" any document to PDF format. If you have a document in postscript format, Distiller converts it into PDF. You can even edit a file you have converted into PDF format using Adobe Exchange.

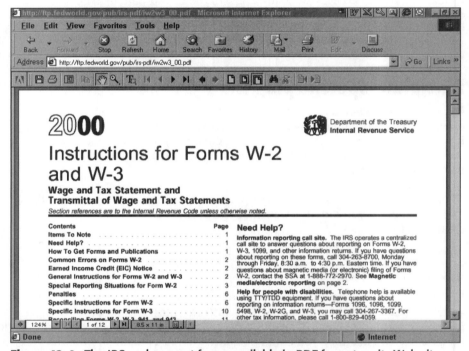

Figure 42-4: The IRS makes most forms available in PDF format on its Web site.

Testing Your Plug-In

As with everything else you publish on your Web site, you should test your plug-ins extensively. You want to test them from multiple platforms, using Internet Explorer, Netscape, and AOL. In fact, you probably want to test your plug-in from a computer that doesn't already have the plug-in installed. This way, you can go through the process many of your site visitors will go through:

1. **Arrive at your page and get notification you need a plug-in.**

2. **Follow the link on your page to get the plug-in.** This link should open a new window so the visitor doesn't lose your page.

 Tip   Use an A element to link with the value of the `target` attribute set to "blank" to open a new window for the plug-in page.

3. **Download and install the plug-in.** Does it require restarting the browser? You want to know this so you can tell the visitor to bookmark your page before quitting the browser. You might also want to tell the visitor on your page how long a download takes and what is involved in installation.

4. **Play the plug-in on your page.** Does it require reloading the page? You should mention this somewhere.

Configuring Your Server

For some plug-ins, the server needs some special information. For the Chime plug-in, for example, the server must be notified some special MIME types exist. When you use a plug-in, be sure you have read all the documentation on the plug-in site, so you know if any changes must be made to your server. The odd thing about these server changes is, if you had played the same plug-in from a CD on your desktop, you wouldn't need any new MIME types. No good rule exists about when you will need to have your systems administrator make MIME type changes to your server. You have to read the documentation and do some testing yourself to see if your plug-ins will play from your server.

Introducing ActiveX

ActiveX is Microsoft's solution for letting Web developers add their own functionality to Internet Explorer. *ActiveX* is a marketing name for a set of technologies based on the Component Object Model (COM). ActiveX controls run under Netscape as well, but they require a Netscape ActiveX control to do so. Programmers, writing in traditional second-generation languages, such as C, C++, Visual Basic, and Java, can write ActiveX controls. By taking advantage of existing Object Linking and Embedding (OLE) architecture, ActiveX controls are smaller than regular programs or Java Applets, and they are optimized for download and execution. In addition, they register themselves on the client computer.

Unlike pages with plug-ins, pages with ActiveX control initiate the download of the ActiveX control. The beauty of this approach is that visitors to the page don't need to know anything about anything. They can simply accept or refuse the download.

Licensing for ActiveX controls can be complicated. Some ActiveX controls are freely distributable. Some require licensing from the author. In these cases, you must get a license file to place on your server so the ActiveX control will run properly. Of course, if you write your own, you needn't worry about licensing issues.

ActiveX Pluses and Minuses

ActiveX has its advantages over plug-ins. The biggest advantage is to the site visitor. Visitors to the site needn't know anything to accept the ActiveX control. All they need to do is click the word *Accept* to have the ActiveX control download.

ActiveX controls exist that don't support specific commercial technologies. The vast majority of Netscape plug-ins were written — like the Acrobat Reader and RealPlayer — to facilitate distribution of proprietary media standards over the Internet. ActiveX controls tend to focus more on performing a specific task (running a clock, displaying a calendar, showing a stock ticker) than on delivering technologies.

One downside of ActiveX controls is, while ActiveX controls aren't necessarily difficult to implement, they are more complicated to implement than a plug-in. Another disadvantage of ActiveX controls, which is the same as the disadvantage of plug-ins, is that people can choose not to accept the download of the plug-in. When this happens, your page might have a big hole in it or it might not function properly.

Mac Support

The biggest minus to ActiveX controls is they don't run on Macs. If you are building an application for the Internet or, more specifically, for education, this is an insuperable obstacle to using ActiveX controls. You can do something to get around this major hole in ActiveX design. See the section "Getting Around the Mac Problem" later in this chapter.

Understanding the ActiveX Security Model

How safe is it to use ActiveX controls? That depends. The ActiveX security model relies on the goodwill of the ActiveX control programmer. ActiveX controls are inherently dangerous. The ActiveX security model enables the programmer to have full and free control of your computer. This makes ActiveX controls powerful. They can read, write, and edit files. This also makes ActiveX controls potentially *very* dangerous. Because ActiveX controls have unrestrained access to your computer, no limit exists to the damage they can do. There is no logging of the actions ActiveX controls take, so there is no way later to trace which controls, if any, caused system problems you are having.

The Microsoft answer to the cavalier approach ActiveX controls take to security is that all controls will be digitally signed by the distributor, and you, as the site visitor, have the power to accept or refuse controls, based on whether you trust the distributor. Is this enough? No. What if the programmer, whom you trust, accidentally leaves a security hole on your system and another site you go to knows about this and takes advantage of it? Once you accept an ActiveX control, it gets installed on your system and stays there. Any site you subsequently visit can use this control, even if you never granted it explicit permission to do so.

What does all this mean to you as a Web developer? It means you should be careful about using other ActiveX controls you come across—even if you think they're perfectly safe—because you may unwittingly contribute to problems on your visitors' computers. It also helps you understand why so many people who come to your site choose not to accept your controls. Visitors need to look after the integrity of their own computers.

When can this security model be a good thing? If you are developing for an intranet, you can write ActiveX controls that perform powerful actions on client computers, without having to install that software manually on every computer. Be sure to test your controls carefully, especially if they affect the file system at all.

Finding ActiveX Controls

Chances are, you'll start your foray into using ActiveX controls by using ones others have written. Lots of places exist on the Web where you can find sources of controls. Some of these controls have licensing costs associated with them, but you can find out about this when you identify the controls you want to use.

Dozens of sites consider themselves resources for ActiveX controls. One place to start is the Browser Watch site (http://browserwatch.internet.com/activex.html). Although you may find 20 sites that list controls, you will find they all list basically the same controls. Browser Watch does a nice job of directing you to the control without numbing your senses with visual clutter and advertising in the process.

In Depth   **Publicizing your own controls.** If you find no one has written the control you need and you are brave enough to take this on yourself, you might want to have your own control listed on these sites. Each site has its own form for submitting your ActiveX control information.

Incorporating ActiveX Controls

Once you identify the ActiveX control you want, you insert it with the OBJECT element. Even though over a dozen attributes exist for the OBJECT element, most of the time you only need four of them. You also need an indeterminate number of PARAM elements.

```
<OBJECT id="Calendar1" width=372 height=279
 classid="CLSID:8E27C92B-1264-101C-8A2F-040224009C02">
  <PARAM name="_Version" value="458752">
  <PARAM name="_ExtentX" value="9843">
  <PARAM name="_ExtentY" value="7382">
  <PARAM name="_StockProps" value="1">
  <PARAM name="BackColor" value="12632256">
  <PARAM name="Year" value="2000">
  <PARAM name="Month" value="3">
  <PARAM name="Day" value="9">
</OBJECT>
```

In the previous example, which inserts the calendar ActiveX control into your Web page, only four attributes of the OBJECT element are needed.

```
<OBJECT id="ShockwaveFlash1" width="192" height="192"
 classid="CLSID:D27CDB6E-AE6D-11CF-96B8-444553540000">
  <PARAM name="Movie" value="">
  <PARAM name="Src" value="">
  <PARAM name="WMode" value="Window">
  <PARAM name="Play" value="-1">
  <PARAM name="Loop" value="-1">
  <PARAM name="Quality" value="AutoLow">
  <PARAM name="SAlign" value="">
  <PARAM name="Menu" value="-1">
  <PARAM name="Base" value="">
  <PARAM name="Scale" value="ShowAll">
  <PARAM name="DeviceFont" value="0">
  <PARAM name="EmbedMovie" value="0">
  <PARAM name="BGColor" value="">
</OBJECT>
```

In the previous example, which inserts the Shockwave ActiveX control, again only four attributes are needed.

> **Tip**
>
> **The** classid **attribute**. Where do you get that long, nasty classid attribute? You get this information, which is the unique identifier for that ActiveX control, from the owner of the control. Depending on the licensing of the control, you can sometimes copy the source of a control you find on a page you like. If licensing restrictions exist, then this approach won't work and the control won't run on your page.

Defining Options (Parameters)

How many parameters do you need for an ActiveX control? This depends on the control. For some controls, no parameters exist. For others, there can be ten or more. You can find out about the parameters you have to set wherever you find out about the control.

How do you set parameters? With the PARAM element.

Parameter <PARAM>

Start Tag:	Required
Content:	Empty
End Tag:	Forbidden
Attributes:	id: document-wide unique ID; optional
	name: name of the parameter; defined by the ActiveX control
	value: value associated with the parameter specified by the name attribute
	valuetype: how to interpret the value: data or ref or object; data is the default, ref indicates the value is a URL, object indicates the ID of another object defined in this page
	type: MIME type of parameter

Getting Around the Mac Problem

The easiest thing you can do is to nest OBJECT elements. Place the OBJECT you most want your visitors to use in the outermost OBJECT element. Then, after your PARAM elements, place the next OBJECT element you would want them to use. Finally, within your last choice OBJECT element, you can include alternate text explaining what they are missing.

```
<OBJECT id="ShockwaveFlash1" width=192 height=192
  classid="CLSID:D27CD36E-AE6D-11CF-96B8-444553540000">
  <PARAM name="Movie" value="mymovie.dcr">
```

```
<PARAM name="Src" value="">
<PARAM name="WMode" value="Window">
<PARAM name="Play" value="-1">
<PARAM name="Loop" value="-1">
<PARAM name="Quality" value="AutoLow">
<PARAM name="SAlign" value="">
<PARAM name="Menu" value="-1">
<PARAM name="Base" value="">
<PARAM name="Scale" value="ShowAll">
<PARAM name="DeviceFont" value="0">
<PARAM name="EmbedMovie" value="0">
<PARAM name="BGColor" value="">
 <OBJECT name="veryshocked.dcr"
type="application/futuresplash"
This is a very nice Shockwave animation. You should consider
downloading the plug-in for this at <A
href="http://www.macromedia.com" alt="Macromedia">the
Macromedia site</A>.
 </OBJECT>
</OBJECT>
```

Testing Your Control

In every chapter, when this book discusses testing your work, you hear you need to test from more than one browser. This is extra important when using ActiveX controls because they weren't really designed to run in Netscape. ActiveX controls also aren't natively supported in AOL or in Internet Explorer browsers prior to Version 2. To test your control, start by testing your control from a computer that doesn't already have the control installed. This is the only way to check and make sure the control downloads and installs itself properly. You also want to test your control on multiple PC operating systems to make sure it works properly. Because ActiveX doesn't run on Macs reliably, you needn't worry about testing it on a Mac, but you will want to include alternate text between your OBJECT begin and end tags explaining what the viewer is missing.

From Here

Cross-
Reference

Jump to Chapter 48 and learn about another way to make your pages interactive — with JavaScript.

Proceed to Chapter 43 and learn about Java applets.

Summary

In this chapter you learned about some of the powerful effects you can add with plug-ins. This chapter discussed how they work, using MIME types, and how you include them in your Web page, using the OBJECT element. You also learned about the pros and cons of using plug-ins and why you should include the same information in an alternate form for people who don't bother to go out and get the plug-ins. You learned about some of the hottest plug-ins on the Web today, how to test your plug-ins, and a bit about configuring your server for plug-ins that require the server to know about its MIME type.

In this chapter you also learned about the pros and cons of ActiveX controls. You learned how they differ from plug-ins and how the security model (or lack thereof) works. You also learned ActiveX controls aren't your best choice if you anticipate any of the visitors to your site might be using Macs. This chapter gave you resources for finding ActiveX controls on the Web and for publicizing your own, if you choose to write any yourself. Finally, you learned how the OBJECT element and PARAM element are used to define an ActiveX control within your Web page. Testing an ActiveX control is similar to testing a plug-in.

✦   ✦   ✦

Adding Java Applets

Java! What technology has produced more hype than Java? Is it merited? Will it really change the face of computing? This chapter won't cover much about that, but it can help you understand what Java applets can do for your Web page today. It explains how Java differs from plug-ins and ActiveX controls, the other ways of adding extra functionality to your Web page. You learn about the Java security model, which is much stricter than the ActiveX or plug-in security model. You also learn how to insert a Java applet into your page.

Introducing Java

Java is a way to add additional functionality to your browser. Because it downloads within the browser page and doesn't operate outside of the browser's operating space, it doesn't require permission from the page visitor before it can run. Visitors can set their browsers not to accept any Java applets, but this isn't all that common. As long as visitors to your page have a Java-enabled browser and the patience to wait for the applet to start, they will get your Java applet.

Java is a nonproprietary software standard developed by Sun Microsystems. Java is an open standard, intended to take the best of C++ and simplify it — stripping out the most convoluted parts, such as memory management, which Java handles automatically. Java is fully supported in both Microsoft Internet Explorer and Netscape Navigator.

Java is an *object-oriented programming language.* Note two things about this catch phrase: First, *object-oriented* means a program is designed around the data. This only means something if you understand the old way of programming — procedure-oriented programming — where the program was designed around what it did, not around the data. Second, Java is a *programming language*. Java is not for the faint-hearted. If you are not a programmer, this probably isn't how you want to begin. JavaScript, which is completely unrelated to Java, is a better starting point for aspiring programmers.

Two kinds of Java actually exist: server-side Java and client-side Java. This chapter only discusses client-side Java, which is inserted into your page as an applet. Server-side Java enables your page to talk to a database or to perform advanced server functions. Server-side Java doesn't have all the constraints on what it can and can't do that client-side Java has. Server-side Java uses the full power of the Java programming language.

Java Pluses and Minuses

Why would anyone want to use Java? Java is a safe way to add limited functionality to your browser. Java uses a much tighter security model, so people are less worried about damage to their computers. Consequently, more people have their browsers set to accept Java applets than have their browsers set to accept (or are willing to accept) ActiveX controls.

So, what can Java do? It can read the local file system, meaning it can show you the contents of a local file, and it can perform animations. Java can create new windows within the existing browser, and it can perform certain actions based on the position of the mouse.

The biggest drawback to using Java applets is you have to write a program. The beauty of the Web and the reason it has grown so fast is that creating Web pages doesn't require any special programming skills or training. Anyone can write HTML, as this book shows. Java applets return to the programming model of delivering functionality. When you program, you have to test thoroughly to make sure there aren't any unintended consequences from your actions. With HTML, most of the mistakes you can make are immediately visible and easily corrected.

Programming Java is time consuming and requires special skills. It is often faster to find a plug-in or ActiveX control to do the same thing or to find a way to provide comparable functionality without programming.

The Java virtual machine

Why else might you not want to use Java? Speed, or lack thereof. Java is a clever programming language, but this cleverness results in decreased performance in a network environment. Java is designed to run on any platform. When you compile Java (as you normally do with any programming language), instead of being compiled into machine language, which is specific to the platform on which you are compiling, Java is compiled into byte-code, which is generic and platform-independent.

That byte-code is what is sent over the network to your browser. Your browser has a virtual machine built into it that compiles the byte-code into machine language before it runs. The time saved by the programmer in writing the code only once and having it run on every platform is spent by everyone who ever tries to run the program on his or her own virtual machine.

The Just-In-Time compiler

Virtual machines, through the use of Just-In-Time compilers, are getting faster. Perhaps as desktop machines get faster you won't notice the time it takes to run the byte-code through the virtual machine to get the machine code, but today it is slow. Some of your site visitors will get impatient and stop the download, not understanding why it takes so long.

Understanding the Java Security Model

The Java security model is much safer for the casual Web visitor. While the ActiveX security model and the plug-in security model rely on the intelligence of the user and the goodwill and competence of the programmer, the Java security model relies on the sandbox.

Everything that takes place within a Java applet takes place within a sandbox that constrains the Java applet. The Java applet can't act on anything outside of this sandbox in any permanent way. What can a Java applet do?

✦ Access the CPU.

✦ Work within the limited space the browser uses.

✦ Read input from the mouse or keyboard when the mouse has clicked within the applet window.

✦ Work within the browser's windowing system.

✦ Create new windows within the browser.

Where can even this tight security fail the user? If the sandbox security is not implemented properly by the browser developers, then the Java applet could presumably take advantage of any security hole they created.

Overall, the Java security model is much tighter than the ActiveX security model. ActiveX can write to your file system, potentially corrupting essential system files. Java can't touch your file system. Java can view your file system, but can't make any changes to it.

Java Development Tools

Many Java development tools are on the market. Two with wide popularity for good reasons are Microsoft's Visual J++ (see Figure 43-1) and Visual Cafe for Java by Symantec (see Figure 43-2).

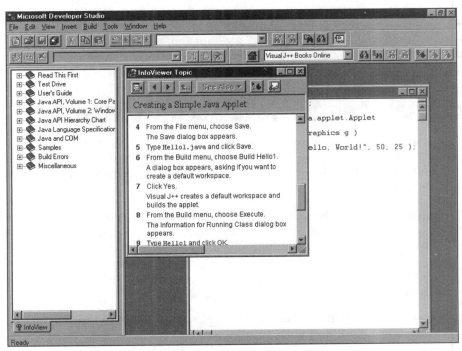

Figure 43-1: Visual J++ by Microsoft

Microsoft's Visual J++ isn't completely compatible with Netscape. Sun Microsystems writes the Java standard. Microsoft's standard isn't completely compatible with Sun's standard. To make matters worse, Netscape is behind on the Java standard, meaning Netscape 4 requires a patch to run the 1.1 Version of Java.

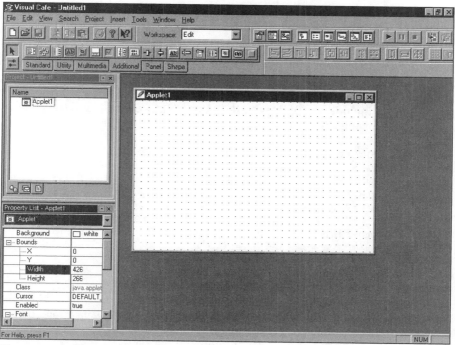

Figure 43-2: Visual Cafe for Java by Symantec

If you do anything that is more than a basic applet, you must choose which browser it runs on, because the two major browsers are so incompatible. Also, for anything more than the basic sandbox application, you need to get a digital signature (which gives you more control over the system, like an ActiveX control) from Verisign. If you want digital signatures for both Microsoft and Netscape, you have to buy both separately. Then you have to get the digital signature tool from either Netscape or Microsoft (each is application-specific).

Java SDK

You can get the software development kit (SDK) at www.javasoft.com. It has all the libraries, instructions, and Java tools that work on the command line. The JavaSoft site is the place to go for information about writing Java and adding Java applets to your pages.

Incorporating Java Applets

Not surprisingly, Java applets can be included in your Web page with the OBJECT element (defined in its entirety in Chapter 19). Before HTML 4, Java applets were routinely inserted with the APPLET element, but that is deprecated in HTML 4. Because the OBJECT element doesn't work with every browser, this chapter gives you examples of how to include an applet with both the APPLET element and the OBJECT element. The following code demonstrates how to use the APPLET element.

```
<APPLET code=graph.class width=760 height=470>
<PARAM name= "title" value = "Hanes-Woolf Kinetics">
<PARAM name="xLabel" value = "[S]">
<PARAM name="yLabel" value = "[S]/v">
<PARAM name="xUnits" value = "mM">
<PARAM name="yUnits" value = "sec/micro-mole">
<PARAM name="imageName" value = "hw.gif">
<PARAM name="scaleX" value = ".2">
<PARAM name="scaleY" value = ".01">
<PARAM name="quadrants" value = "2">
</APPLET>
```

You only need a few attributes of the OBJECT element for your Java applet definitions, as shown in the following code. Implementing an applet with the OBJECT element isn't supported yet in either Netscape 4.7 or Internet Explorer 5.

```
<OBJECT
classid="http://nmc.itc.virginia.edu/nlii/grisham/kinetics/hw/
graph.class" width=760 height=470 type="application/java-
archive">
<PARAM name = "title" value = "Hanes-Woolf Kinetics">
<PARAM name = "xLabel" value = "[S]">
<PARAM name = "yLabel" value = "[S]/v">
<PARAM name = "xUnits" value = "mM">
<PARAM name = "yUnits" value = "sec/micro-mole">
<PARAM name = "imageName" value = "hw.gif">
<PARAM name = "scaleX" value = ".2">
<PARAM name = "scaleY" value = ".01">
<PARAM name = "quadrants" value = "2">
</OBJECT>
```

Defining Options (Parameters)

As with ActiveX controls, Java applets take parameters in the PARAM element. Important to note is the PARAM names must exactly match what the Java applet is looking for. The values assigned to these names must also be of the correct type.

See Chapter 42 for a more thorough explanation of how the PARAM element works.

Testing Your Applet

You must test your Java applet on both your local workstation (before you include it on your page) and on your Web page. The best place to do your first round of testing is in the Java development tool you use.

When you are confident your Java applet does what you want it to do, you can upload it to your server. Your Java applet must reside in a directory with execute permissions. Most of your pages only require read permission, but because the Java applet is executable code, your directory also must permit execution. If your applet won't run at all, check with your systems administrator to see whether you have execute permissions on that directory.

As with everything else on your pages, you should test your Java applet from a variety of platforms, from more than one browser. If any unusual behavior occurs in any of these environments, you should warn visitors and refer them to a configuration that works. Not every implementation of Java on every platform works consistently.

Introducing Server-Side Java

What can you do with server-side Java? Server-side Java enables your Web pages to interact with your Web server. Pretty much anything you can do with CGI (Common Gateway Interface) scripts, Perl, or server-side JavaScript, you can do with server-side Java. Using the JDBC (Java database connector), you can have your Web page communicate with a database, returning dynamic pages based on the information entered. You can also create and read files on the server.

If you already know Java, this may be a way to perform server functions, such as those discussed in Chapter 21. Many of the back-end tools you can purchase for your server, including some that perform database access, are written in Java.

From Here

Go to Chapter 45 to learn about accessing external databases.

Jump to Chapter 48, which provides an introduction to JavaScript.

Review how to create forms in Chapter 21.

Summary

Java applets can add functionality to your pages. They generally adhere to a tight security model that doesn't permit them to do any damage to your machine. Signed applets can be given (by you) permissions to act on your machine like ActiveX controls. Unfortunately, Java isn't yet truly cross-platform; applets you write to run under Internet Explorer won't necessarily work under Netscape. Chapter 45 discusses how you can access external databases with your form data. Server-side Java is one technology that enables you to do this.

✦　　✦　　✦

Creating Subscriptions with the Channel Definition Format

CHAPTER

44

Push technology was going to revolutionize the way people used the Web. Despite the hype, push technology never materialized as promised. One of the problems with early push technology was that no standard existed. If you wanted to use push technology—which is better entitled *smart pull*—you had to get a client that supported it and then the server from which you wanted to pull also had to support it. Or, you could use an agent to search the Web for you, pulling down new pages that met your criteria. Either way was cumbersome and nonstandard.

The *Channel Definition Format* (CDF) is an attempt by Micro soft to standardize the world of push technology. Some push vendors have signed up to support the standard, but Netcape has not. Netscape promotes its own proprietary subscription format, which this book does not discuss at length.

Introducing Push Options

What is push technology? *Push* (also known as *server-push/client-pull*) *technology* is the idea that citizens of the Web can define their interests on their own computers in some sort of channel client. Then that client can go out to the Web at regular intervals and download only the material of interest to Web citizens. This idea was good, but it hasn't been implemented with much success.

What push has come to mean in actuality is the same citizens of the Web (sometimes called *Webizens* or *Netizens*) subscribing to channels that interest them. At regular intervals, the client software can go only to those channel sites and download the latest updates to pages.

Nothing new

The truth about push technology is nothing new is there. Push uses the HTTP protocol to get pages off a server (or multiple servers). The difference between push and other means of getting at Web pages is that with push, you set up some preferences up-front (or as you go) and the pages are *pre-cached* (a fancy expression for downloaded) to your client during low-use times. You don't have to wait for the download; it happens in the background.

Two kinds of push technology exist — those using keywords and those using subscriptions. With *keywords,* you define what keywords you want included, just as if you were at a search engine page performing a regular search. The client that sits on your computer communicates during nonpeak hours with a central server, which has agents crawling and indexing the Web. Your client queries that server for any new pages it has found during the last period you defined in your search criteria (day, week, month, whatever). It returns the page descriptions and URLs of all the pages matching your criteria, just like a search engine. Then you can scroll through the pages it returns and load any that sound interesting into your browser. As you can see, there isn't much being *pushed* in this scenario.

The second kind of push technology uses channels.

Channels

Here the television analogy is appropriate. *Channels* are Web destinations to which you can subscribe. Why would you subscribe? So a site's contents can be pre-cached onto your desktop during nonpeak hours (when the Web won't keep your unattended computer waiting). What can a channel include? Anything that goes into a Web page can be part of a channel. A channel is simply a preloaded bookmark. If you do take advantage of channels, you'll find when you go to a channel to which you subscribed, it loads instantly. Why? Because it is loading from cache memory.

If you want to follow all the late-breaking developments at Netscape and you visit their site daily to find out anyway, why not subscribe to the Netscape channel? This way, when you do visit their site, it loads instantly.

What is the downside of channels? If you subscribe to too many, your cache could become dangerously large. When you subscribe to a channel, you are prompted with a setting for the cache size you are willing to allow this channel to occupy. The default (on Netcaster) is 1MB. If you subscribe to 30 channels and each one uses up 30MB of cache, you could quickly have a lot of garbage on your machine.

Marketing with Push

From a Web developer's perspective, you want to know how you can get your page before as many of the right people as possible. Unfortunately, the first kind of push technology doesn't facilitate your marketing efforts any more than does a search engine. Changing your content — at least a little bit every day — helps your page appear in more results lists, but pretty much every page on the Web using the META elements successfully has the same chances of being found.

Using channels, however, can help you set your site off from the rest. Most Web sites don't take advantage of channels and subscriptions. Consequently, those that do — mostly sports, entertainment, and news sites — set themselves apart.

You can be especially successful in getting your visitors to subscribe if you meet the following criteria:

✦ Give your visitors a compelling reason to download and install a Version 4 or higher browser, so the client software is built into the browser.

✦ Host a newsgroup or chat room on your site that is both relevant to the rest of your site and engages visitors.

✦ Keep your content current.

✦ Link to other sites with current content.

Introducing Channel Definition Format

The closest thing to a standard for channel definition is the Channel Definition Format (CDF), which has been proposed by Microsoft. CDF certainly has the potential to be the most successful solution to the different, proprietary approaches to delivering push content because it is based on the XML standard discussed in Chapter 6. The XML standard is the W3C's proposal for making the Web more extensible (that's where the *X* comes from in XML: *eXtensible Markup Language*).

Don't expect the CDF to be roundly endorsed by any governing body — this doesn't happen too often on the Web — but you can develop your own channels with it. The CDF is easy to use and up and working in Internet Explorer 4 and higher. Best of all, some Web-development tools (notably HotDog Pro) have channel wizards, which take you through the creation of the Channel Definition File (.cdf file).

The Channel definition has three parts: the channel, the items, and the schedule. All this information goes into the .cdf file.

CDF (XML) syntax

The CDF is based on XML. This means, even though CDF has elements and attributes, like HTML, it won't look exactly the same. In CDF, each element is contained in angle brackets (<>) but, instead of having a start tag and an end tag, there is only one tag, with a slash (/) right before the close to the angle brackets. An example helps to clarify this:

```
<LOGO HREF="http://www.overtheweb.com/images/wave.ico"
STYLE="icon" />
```

The previous is the tag for the LOGO element. There are two attributes: href and style.

The CHANNEL element is an HTML element that contains the actual channel definition as its content. Within the CHANNEL element, you want to include — as a minimum — the two graphics that are part of your channel: a title and an abstract.

Images

If your channel definition has nothing else, it must have two graphics:

1. A 16×16-pixel icon, stored in a .ICO file (referred to as an *icon*)
2. A 32 × 80-pixel graphic image, stored as a .GIF file or a .JPEG file (an *image*)

You can also have an optional wide image, which is 32 × 194 pixels, and is also either a .GIF or .JPEG. This last type of image is referred to as *image-wide*.

Images are included in your channel using the LOGO element, which is defined using XML syntax. The LOGO element has two attributes: href, which gives the URL of the image, and style, which can be one of three values: icon, image, or image-wide.

```
<LOGO href="http://www.somesite.com/images/pict1.ico"
style="icon" />
<LOGO href="http://www.somesite.com/images/pict2.gif"
style="image" />
<LOGO href="http://www.somesite.com/images/big-pict.gif"
style="image-wide" />
```

Title

Your channel's title is included in a regular old HTML TITLE element:

```
<TITLE>Sample Channel Created for Chapter 44</TITLE>
```

Abstract

Your channel's abstract is included in an HTML ABSTRACT element:

```
<ABSTRACT>This channel will give you the examples that you need
to create a channel, as described in Chapter 44 of the HTML 4
Bible.</ABSTRACT>
```

Scheduling pre-caching of your channel

The CDF offers an HTML element called SCHEDULE, which you can use to indicate the frequency with which your page is updated. This information tells the client workstation how frequently to check the server to see whether the content has changed. The SCHEDULE element has three attributes: startdate, stopdate, and timezone. The content of the SCHEDULE element is a series of XML elements: INTERVALTIME, EARLIESTTIME, and LATESTTIME. You needn't use them all. Only use the ones you need.

Both the date attributes take a date in the format of YYYY-MM-DDTHH:mm, where YYYY is the four-digit year, MM is the two-digit month, DD is the two-digit day, T is the letter "T" indicating the time formatting is beginning, HH is the two-digit hour, and, finally, mm is the two-digit minute.

```
<SCHEDULE startdate="2000-04-01T14:00"></SCHEDULE>
```

In the preceding example, the schedule would be good starting on April 1, 2000, at 2 p.m. It would not have an end date.

For the timezone attribute, the time zone is indicated relative to Greenwich Mean Time. Thus, Eastern Standard Time is +5. To add this to the previous example:

```
<SCHEDULE startdate="2000-04-01T14:00"
TIMEZONE="+5"></SCHEDULE>
```

The XML elements, INTERVALTIME, EARLIESTTIME, and LATESTTIME all take one or more of the following interval attributes: day, hour, and min.

To complete the previous example:

```
<SCHEDULE startdate="2000-04-01T14:00" TIMEZONE="+6">
  <INTERVALTIME day="7" />
  <EARLIESTTIME hour="4" min="30" />
  <LATESTTIME hour="8" min="30" />
</SCHEDULE>
```

Items

Items are hierarchical nodes within the channel. Items are also where the content that belongs to your subscription is defined. One channel can have multiple items within it. You can define items to make the channel more easily navigable for subscribers. For example, you can define a channel that points to your home page and then have items that point to technical resources, customer service, a chat room, and so forth.

The other thing you can do with items is to specify the number of levels the client should pre-cache (meaning the number of levels of links to follow), and the usage of the channel. The usage can be either Channel or ScreenSaver.

```
<ITEM href="http://www.somesite.com/images/screensaver.html"
level="1">
  <USAGE value="ScreenSaver"></USAGE>
</ITEM>
```

You can specify as many items as you need. In the previous example, the item is a screensaver.

Creating a subscription doesn't require the detail given in the previous example. A subscription can be as simple as:

```
<CHANNEL href="http://www.mychannel.com" level="3">
  <LOGO href="http://www.mychannel.com/images/logo.ico"
image="icon" />
  <LOGO href="http://www.mychannel.com/images/pict1.gif"
image="image" />
  <TITLE>This is the title</TITLE>
  <ABSTRACT>This is the abstract</ABSTRACT>
  <SCHEDULE starttime="2000-05-20" timezone="+6">
  <INTERVALTIME day="7" />
  </SCHEDULE>
  <ITEM href="http://www.mychannel.com" level="1">
  <USAGE value="ScreenSaver"></USAGE>
  </ITEM>
</CHANNEL>
```

Subscribing to a Channel

What does it mean to subscribe to a channel? The word *subscribe* isn't as apt as the word *channel* in the television analogy. In fact, subscribing to a channel involves no more than having your client copy the .cdf file so it knows where to get the pages that constitute the channel and the frequency information found in the SCHEDULE element. In Internet Explorer 4 and higher, you can do this by selecting "Add to Favorites" from the Favorites menu.

From a developer's perspective, you want to create a button on your subscription information page. This page should explain what is involved in subscribing to anyone who is thinking of subscribing. The page should explain how frequently you update the site, the advantages of subscribing, and the technical requirements to subscribe. In the case of the previous CDF example, subscribers must have Internet Explorer 4 or higher as their browser.

To create the subscription, create an image on which the visitor can click and then place that image within an anchor element that refers to your .cdf file.

```
<A href="mychannel.cdf" alt="Subscribe to this channel"><IMG
src="images/subscribe.gif"></A>
```

From Here

 Jump to Chapter 48 and learn about JavaScript.

Proceed to Chapter 45 to find out how to access external databases.

Summary

Channels can be a great service to visitors to your site. If you have content that is updated regularly and your visitors want to be apprised of the changes to your site on a regular basis, then your site is ripe for subscriptions. Creating a channel is relatively simple. One standard (if you can call it that) is the Channel Definition Format, which is simply a text file stored in a .cdf file.

To create a .cdf file, you must learn a bit of XML syntax. Because most of the channel definition is comprised of HTML elements, however, it will look familiar to you.

✦   ✦   ✦

Accessing External Databases

T he Web-to-database interface is the best thing to happen to the Web since inline graphics. So many ways exist to connect your Web page to a database that this chapter can't begin to discuss all the options available today. Instead, this chapter discusses how the Web-to-database interface works, what software types are available for this interface, and how they work. Finally, the chapter focuses on four of the technologies that work well.

Understanding Databases

Databases have been around for a long time. Properly used, databases are an efficient way to store data so redundancy is removed. On UNIX, most databases are text files with indexes. This chapter should be of particular interest to you if your organization already has data in a database.

Regardless of how much data is in your database, the most important things you should know about that data is how to get at it (meaning the unique keys to the data) and how to modify it (again using the unique keys).

Tables

A database is made up of *tables*. Tables hold *rows* of data. Rows of data in a database are similar to rows of data in a spreadsheet. Tables also have *fields*. Each field in a database is similar to a column of data in a spreadsheet. If one field is for e-mail addresses, then for every row of data, either an e-mail address will be in that field or it will be blank. Tables are related to each other with keys.

Keys

A *key* is a value associated with one row in a table. Usually, a key is unique, meaning a key can only be associated with one row. A social security number would be a unique key. While a last name could be used as a key, it would not always be a unique key. Frequently, a database assigns its own unique value to each row to ensure that all keys are, indeed, unique.

Relationships

So far, nothing about databases makes them any more powerful than spreadsheets. It is the relationships you can create between tables that makes them powerful. A *normalized* database consists of multiple tables related to each other by keys so the same data isn't stored more than once, such as name and address information.

Common databases

The most common enterprise databases are Oracle, Sybase, and SQL server. The most common desktop database is Microsoft Access.

 Enterprise Database. An *enterprise database* is one that resides on a server and can be accessed from multiple clients and multiple applications, concurrently.

 Desktop Database. A *desktop database* is one that resides on the user's desktop. It is only intended for use by an individual or from the Web, depending on the interface, for a low volume of transactions.

ODBC

Databases can talk to each other and to Web servers using the Open Database Connectivity Standard (ODBC). *ODBC* is a set of rules databases agree to obey. Most databases, and software that interacts with databases, know this language and can communicate with each other using this language. You needn't worry about how it works; you only need to know whether your database is ODBC-compliant and whether your Web server or database-to-Web engine is ODBC-compliant. If they both are, then you have the tools you need to start building a Web-to-database interface.

If your database or your database-to-Web engine are not ODBC-compliant (such as File Maker Pro), then you must use the proprietary system this database has available for communicating with the Web. In the case of File Maker Pro, there is one. Not every non-ODBC-compliant database makes such a tool available. Even if your non-ODBC-compliant database has a way to get data to and from the Web, it will probably not be a scalable, enterprising solution. The most robust solutions — the ones that can handle the most traffic — tend to be ODBC-compliant.

The Web-to-Database Interface

To understand how the Web-to-database interface works, it helps to review how data is normally delivered to a client workstation, in a browser, via the Web (using the HTTP protocol, to be specific). Figure 45-1 shows the client workstation (on the left) requesting a page (using the HTTP protocol) from a Web server (on the right). The Web server receives the request and, if it can find the page requested and if the client workstation meets any security restrictions that may exist on the page, the server delivers the page to the client workstation (using the HTTP protocol).

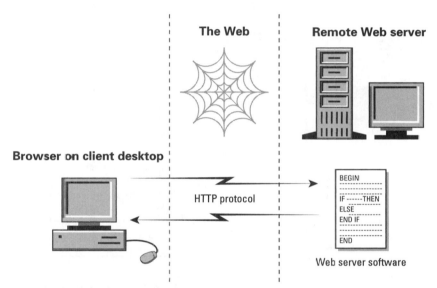

Figure 45-1: Delivering a page with no database interaction

Requesting data

When database interaction is required, a few more steps need to take place on the server. Figure 45-2 shows the client workstation (on the left) requesting a page (using the HTTP protocol) from a Web server (on the right). In this case, the page has a file extension of something other than .HTML (or .HTM), indicating to the Web server that some special type of action is required. The Web server determines whether it can handle the processing by itself or whether it needs to pass this page onto another software package. How does it know whether to pass on the page and where to pass the page? By checking the MIME type of the page requested.

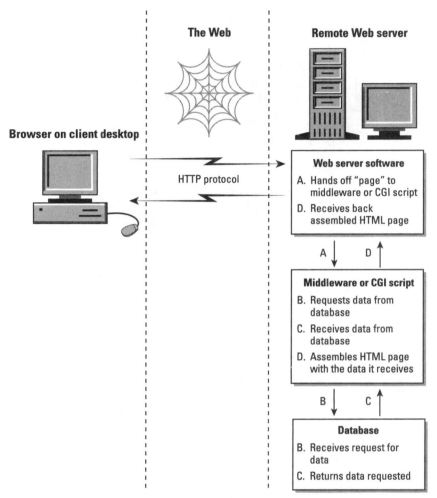

Figure 45-2: Delivering a page with database interaction

Communicating with the database

If the MIME type of the page requested is not supported by the Web server software, the page is handed off to the appropriate application, referred to as the Web-to-Database Engine, based on the MIME type. This application communicates with the database (usually in ODBC) to perform one of three actions:

1. **Search for data.** From the Web page, the visitor can indicate search criteria and only receive back data that matches those criteria.

2. **Add new data to the database.** From the Web page, the visitor can enter new data that will be added to the database.

3. Modify existing data in the database. From the Web page, the visitor can modify existing data — say, updating his address or phone number, or changing the inventory by making a purchase.

If the MIME type of the page requested is supported by the Web server, then it processes the request and communicates with the database directly. The choice of actions will still be one from the preceding list.

Returning results

Finally, the Web-to-Database Engine has the results of its communications with the database and can format those results into HTML, which is easily understood by the Web server (again, this can all take place within the Web-server software, if the Web-server software supports the MIME type of the page requested). The Web server delivers the results of the action on the database to the client workstation.

Conclusions from the Web-to-database interaction

Important to note about this entire transaction are the following points:

✦ The workstation doesn't perform any extra processing.

✦ The Web server, or the combination of the Web server and Web-to-Database Engine, communicates transparently with the database.

✦ The database can actually reside on a different computer than the Web server and Web-to-Database Engine.

That last observation is the most salient. You can leave your database wherever it normally resides and communicate with that database — via ODBC — across a network. This enormously expands your options for Web-to-database interaction.

Note   A significant performance penalty can occur when the Web server software resides on a different physical machine from the database. You must do extensive testing before implementing this approach. One way around this slow-down is to copy (nightly or more often, if necessary) the data from the remotely located database to a mirror copy of the database located on your Web-server machine. How well this actually works depends on the location of the database, the size of the database, and the processing power of both machines.

Options for Accessing Database Data

Now that you understand how the interface between the Web server and the database works, you should understand what kind of choices you have for delivering this service on your own Web server. Because the Web-server side of the processing has three components — the Web server, the Web-to-Database Engine, and the database—you can purchase three different combinations of products to meet these needs.

1. Three stand-alone components: stand-alone Web server, stand-alone Web-to-Database Engine, and stand-alone database

2. Dual-purpose Web server and stand-alone database

3. Stand-alone Web server and dual-purpose database

Three stand-alone components

Using three stand-alone components gives you the greatest flexibility in creating your applications. Chances are, your Web server has already been selected for you and is running on your server. For most people, this is half the equation in selecting complementary products. The other half of the equation is the database, which you probably already have in place, populated with your business data. This leaves you with the decision of which solution to use to connect your Web server to your database.

If your database is ODBC-compliant, then the hands-down best middleware on the market is Cold Fusion, by Allaire (www.allaire.com). Using Cold Fusion, you can script interaction with the database right in your Web pages. The scripting language is Cold Fusion Markup Language (CFML) and looks like HTML. The Cold Fusion Web-to-Database Engine processes the CFML tags and returns the data from the database to the Web server, as in Figure 45-2.

Cold Fusion is available in both a workgroup edition, which works with desktop databases, such as Fox Pro and Access, and an Enterprise version, which works with enterprise databases such as Oracle, Sybase, Paradox, and SQL Server. Cold Fusion for Workgroups runs on Windows NT/2000 Server. Cold Fusion Enterprise Edition runs on both Windows NT/2000 Server and UNIX servers.

Dual-purpose Web server and stand-alone database

When would you want to use a dual-purpose Web server? When it is free and already installed on your Web server. Microsoft Internet Information Server (IIS) supports Active Server Pages (.ASP files), which can be processed right in the IIS Web server.

When would you want to use a stand-alone Web server (that is, not use the built-in functionality of the Web server to process some form of database-interaction pages)? When you want to perform more actions than the freeware/middleware included with the Web server will provide.

One function you might want to perform from your database-interaction script is to send a confirmation message to the visitor's e-mail account, confirming certain action has been taken. With IIS, you can't do this without purchasing additional

COM objects, so your free solution is no longer free. With Cold Fusion, which you must purchase up-front, it is included.

Other dual-purpose Web servers include the Netscape Enterprise servers, which process server-side JavaScript, and O'Reilly servers, which process server-side Java, VBScript, JScript, Perl, or Python. If you decide to use either of those technologies, you won't have to purchase separate middleware. Whichever direction you take, you want to make sure the middleware you select is compatible with your database.

Stand-alone Web server and dual-purpose database

Why would you want to use a dual-purpose database that doubles as middleware? When it is built into your database. Netiva is one company that offers such a product. File Maker Pro is another such product. Netiva, unlike most other dual-purpose databases, can handle enterprise-level traffic. Most of the other dual-purpose databases are designed for low volume.

External Database Access without Programming

Today, many ways exist to perform basic interactions with a database without programming. Using FrontPage 2000, Microsoft's Web-development tool, you can create interactive Web pages with Access without programming. If your back-end database is File Maker Pro, Claris HomePage communicates directly with it, in a seamless, drag-and-drop environment. Regardless of the back-end database, as long as it is ODBC-compliant, you can use Tango, which is both the middleware and the editor, to create data-based Web pages without programming.

Only a few of the products on the market meet these needs. The market is quite crowded now. In the next few years, it could winnow down to the few best-of-breed products. For this reason, you want to make sure you select your products carefully.

External Database Access with SQL

To get the maximum flexibility when interacting with your database, you want to get your hands on the code and do the programming or the scripting yourself. Most middleware uses SQL, the structured query language for communicating with a database—not to be confused with the Microsoft product by the same name.

The problem with SQL is it is not standard. Whichever database you select will have its own slight variation on SQL, which you must learn to get data into or out of the database. To perform three tasks on your data, you can use statements similar to the following ones, where the data source name (the ODBC name for the database) is *Inventory;* the field names are *Partno, Description, Quantity,* and *Cost;* and the unique key is *Partno:*

✦ **Search for data.**

```
Select * from Inventory
  Where Description = '%description%'
```

✦ **Add new data to the database.**

```
Insert into Inventory (Partno, Description, Quantity, Cost)
  Values ('Partno', 'Description', Quantity, Cost)
```

✦ **Modify existing data in the database.**

```
Update Inventory
  Set Description = 'Description'
        Quantity = 'Quantity'
        Cost = 'Cost'
  Where Partno = 'Partno'
```

From Here

Jump to Chapter 48 to learn about JavaScript.

Proceed to Chapter 46 and begin incorporating discussion groups and chats.

Summary

Communicating with a database can be a bit of a hurdle to set up, but nothing enriches your Web pages like access to current, real-time data your visitors want to see. Creating static Web pages that reflect database data accurately is impossible, so if you want your visitors to get at your real-time database data, you must take the time to get this up and running. Once you are operational, the maintenance costs of these products are negligible.

Before you purchase products to get your Web server to communicate with your database, you want to see if your Web server includes middleware and if this middleware is adequate to meet your needs. You also want to confirm that your database can handle the volume of traffic you expect your site to receive.

Once you select your tools, you can determine whether you will be satisfied creating your data-based Web pages with nonprogramming tools or whether you should get your hands dirty with SQL.

✦   ✦   ✦

Building a Community: Incorporating Discussion Groups and Chat

Before a World Wide Web existed, clever individuals had already figured out how to congregate in a virtual space for discussion and socializing. These places were called *newsgroups*. They still exist today as part of the Usenet system. You can use this same concept — of enabling people on your site to talk to each other in a structured setting, or a real-time version of this concept — to develop a virtual community on your page.

When you put a threaded discussion group into your Web page, you won't use any of the Usenet newsgroups that already exist. Instead, you'll create a threaded discussion group. This chapter explains how you can use threaded discussion groups and real-time chatting to make your site interactive and vital.

Introducing Threaded Discussion Groups and Chat

Newsgroups are like bulletin boards. You can post messages that anyone else in the world can read, and then anyone can respond to your messages either on the bulletin board or by e-mail. Over 28,000 newsgroups are on the Web today that are part of the Usenet system. They have names like `comp.lang.java.beans` and `misc.kids.pregnancy`. Both major browsers have newsreaders built into them (in Netscape Communicator, it's called *Netscape Newsgroup,* while in Internet Explorer, it is called *Outlook Express*).

When you post a message on a newsgroup, if that message doesn't directly relate to what others have been talking about (although it should be related to the broad topic of the group), that is called a new *thread.* Most people want to read newsgroups by threads. This way, they can read the messages only in the threads that interest them.

Threaded discussion group. A *threaded discussion group* is like a newsgroup except it runs off your Web server, instead of running as part of the Usenet. Your visitors don't need any special software to participate in your threaded discussion group (also referred to as a *forum*).

Chatting is the real-time equivalent of newsgroups. Unlike newsgroups, where messages get posted to a virtual bulletin board for anyone to see, with *chat rooms,* the message is addressed to someone else in the room and scrolls off the screen in a short time. In chat rooms, anyone else in the room can see what you are saying, even if it is addressed to one specific person. While threaded discussion groups usually maintain the messages for a few days to a few weeks, chat discussions go away within minutes.

Applications of threaded discussion groups

Why would you want to add a newsgroup to your page? For many reasons. By creating a newsgroup, you can have a place where people can come and discuss your product or service, or tangentially related topics. The newsgroup you add to your page won't be a Usenet newsgroup (such as `misc.legal.computing`), but a threaded discussion group of your own creation.

What you do when you create a threaded discussion group on your site is create a community on your site. You give visitors a reason to return. They know information might change daily, even if you aren't the one changing the information. You enable your visitors to contribute to the content of your site.

Applications of chat rooms

Chat rooms are better suited to highly subjective, emotional discussions with strangers than to sorting out the facts in a clear, rational way. Thus, you are more likely to see chat rooms on political or news sites, where everyone is entitled to an opinion and no one cares who's right.

The MSNBC news site uses chat rooms to hash out breaking political stories. Discussions can be heated, so if you want to maintain a semblance of control over the discussions on your site, be advised to stick to threaded discussion groups, where you can even pull threads that wander far afield.

Adding Threaded Discussion Groups to a Web Page

Adding a threaded discussion group to your Web page requires special software. The software interacts with either a database, where messages posted are stored, or a flat file, with an index. You can write your own threaded discussion group or purchase an off-the-shelf product. Forums, by Allaire, is one product that can add a threaded discussion group to your site. Check with your systems administrator to see if Forums, or some other software that provides threaded discussion groups, already exists on your server. Each package is different but, generally, you should be able to modify the following settings to customize the interface so the discussion group page matches the rest of your site:

✦ Background color or graphics

✦ Button color or graphics

✦ Fonts

In addition, you want to administer the discussion group, so if someone begins a thread that bashes your site or your product — as opposed to asking questions — you can pull that thread or, at least, pull those messages. Here are some settings you want to make:

✦ Number of threads permitted

✦ Number of discussion groups permitted (so you can have more than one newsgroup — perhaps one for each product you produce)

✦ Ability to moderate the threads and pull inappropriate threads or messages

✦ Password protection for administrative privileges

Adding Chat to a Web Page

Several products are on the market that enable you to add chat rooms to your Web page. In most cases, chat rooms require more client-side processing than do discussion groups. Discussion groups are entirely server-based activities. Chat rooms are usually Java based. This means they rely on your visitors to have Java-compatible browsers.

Text chat

The usual kind of chat room is text based. Each person creates a nickname before entering the chat room, and that nickname precedes all the comments made by that person. When you want to say something, you type your comment in and press Enter. Immediately, that comment appears in the chat window of everyone who is "in" the chat room. Other people, of course, are talking concurrently. By the time you finish answering a comment made by someone else, that comment may have scrolled off the screen.

Visual chat

With graphical chat-room software, when you sign in, you select an avatar that represents you in the room. You can be a beautiful woman or Pinocchio. When you enter the room, you see the avatars of everyone else in the room with their names under them. When you speak (which is done the same way as in the text chat), your dialogue may appear in a bubble over your head or in a scrolling text box, as with a text chat. In either case, the dialogue disappears in a short time.

 Definition

Avatar. An *avatar* is a graphical representation chosen by the user as a representation of him- or herself. It can be an animal, person, or any object of the user's choice.

When you first enter a chat room, it takes a moment to get your bearings, figure out what everyone is talking about, and decide who makes any sense to you. Some people live in chat rooms and spend all their time there inciting riots. You want to avoid those people. You also want to avoid attracting those people to your site.

Creating Community

One way to create a loyal following of visitors who return to your site with regularity is to create a sense of community. Adding discussion groups and chat rooms to your site are the tactical methods of creating community, but you need to think back to the strategic goals of attracting a crowd.

Will people come to your Web site because you have fancy features like a discussion group or a chat room? Probably not. Heck, the Web is full of fun places to waste time. You need to find a way to set your site apart because of something visitors can only get from your threaded discussion group or chat room.

Your first thought may be that people will come to your site to talk about your products, but this may be a bit optimistic. Look at the Gund site (www.gund.com). The discussion group there is about collecting teddy bears (and other stuffed animals). Gund happens to make teddy bears, but they don't limit discussion on their site to their own creatures. The Gund site is a general meeting place for collectors of stuffed critters.

What can you offer?

What can you offer from a discussion group or chat room? In the case of Allaire, all free customer support is offered only on their forum. This certainly attracts a crowd. They make sure every question is answered in short order. They also offer an archive of old questions for searching, if you don't feel bold enough to post your own question or you don't want to look stupid.

Can you offer a service that is only available from a threaded discussion group or chat room? Some of the parenting sites on the Web have chat rooms and threaded discussion groups where parents ask questions of other parents. How to get their children to sleep through the night? Which brand of stroller is best? How to get the kids to stop fighting? Parents flock to sites where they can share their concerns and get their questions answered quickly by both experts and peers.

A big-name columnist

Perhaps you have a celebrity who could publish a column on your site, such as Danny Goodman, author of *JavaScript Bible* (IDG Books Worldwide, 1999), who publishes the JavaScript Apostle column on the Netscape site. People know of Goodman, own his books, and visit the Netscape DevEdge site to see what he has to say about late-breaking technologies.

Celebrities can attract people to your site because people already feel they "know" them. Visitors come to learn more about their area of expertise and to get closer to them.

Talk with a professional

Perhaps you can offer a certain number of hours a week when a professional in your field will be online taking questions. Whether your field is cooking, car repair, quilting, or oncology, people will be delighted to have a chance to get their questions answered by a real professional.

This type of discussion doesn't lend itself to a chat room, but by taking submitted questions and answering them in real-time, publishing the answers right to the Web site, you can create a vibrancy and interactivity that people will return for again and again.

Beyond Chat and Threaded Discussion Groups

Another way to create a community on your site is to offer resources that are hard to find elsewhere. Many people make the mistake of offering links to resources rather than offering the actual resources. When you offer links to resources, you give people a reason to leave your site. When you offer resources, you give people a reason to come to your site and stay. A threaded discussion group can be a resource — for example, if visitors can actually get samples of code, get answers as to why their specific problems are happening and how to fix them, and get these answers and solutions in a timely manner, then you have offered a real resource and these visitors will return.

An expert in the field, who can give tips on how to use your technology in ways others hadn't considered, can be a valuable resource. A regular column that keeps visitors to your site apprised of how new developments in technology will affect your products and services is certainly a valuable resource.

What kind of services can you offer that attracts your visitors? Perhaps you can create instructions for doing slightly less than your product does at little or no cost. This way, when your visitors are ready to buy or need the extra features your product offers, they will already feel favorably disposed because of the free resources you have offered. One resource — nearly pervasive among software developers — is offering a lite version of the software at no charge.

From Here

 Proceed to Chapter 47 to learn other ways of enhancing your site.

Summary

Creating a community on your Web site is an excellent way to develop a dedicated following of site visitors. Creating a community is not particularly difficult but, unfortunately, few sites take advantage of this avenue of increased traffic.

Web site development is frequently left to the techies who know how to do fancy things with technical tools. They get bogged down in the tactical side of assembling a Web site without giving much thought to the strategy of creating community as a means of developing a loyal following. Threaded discussion groups and chat rooms can help enhance traffic on your site, but only if you are truly offering the visitors something they can't get otherwise. Celebrity columnists and area professionals can help create a vibrant community on your site.

✦   ✦   ✦

Using
Cross-Browser
Dynamic HTML

◆ ◆ ◆ ◆

◆ ◆ ◆ ◆

Introducing Dynamic HTML and the Document Object Model

✦ ✦ ✦ ✦

In This Chapter

What is Dynamic HTML?

The Document Object Model (DOM)

Implementing the DOM

DOM properties

✦ ✦ ✦ ✦

Once upon a time, if you wanted to interact with the user of a Web page, there were two options. First, you could stand over their shoulder and talk to them while they were browsing. This was very personal, but difficult if more than one person browsed your page at a time, or if the person happened to be in a faraway place such as Turkmenistan or Argentina.

The other option was to run your own Web server, write your own server-side scripts in a language such as Perl, and depend on the user having a reasonably fast connection to handle the network traffic required to handle the updates to the user's page. Because each page was essentially static, it required the server to send pages that prompted the user's browser to ask for a new page, which the server would generate and send back to the user.

Although the second method required far less travel than the first, it was still inaccessible for many people who did not have the programming knowledge required to work with server-side scripting, or were short of cash to hire someone who did. Then, Netscape introduced JavaScript and made it possible to add scripting directly to a Web page, which ran directly on the user's browser without any additional help from the server. A new era was born. In this book, a new section begins.

This section is an introduction to Dynamic HTML (DHTML) — one of the most interesting and rewarding ways to manipulate a Web page. DHTML provides exciting and creative ways for developers and HTML authors to bring their pages to life. While this section is not an all-encompassing tutorial on DHTML, it gives you a taste of what's possible with a little work and imagination.

Note   Lots of information is available from the leading browser companies. Check out the developer sites at Netscape (`http://developer.netscape.com`) and Microsoft (`http://msdn.microsoft.com`).

What Is Dynamic HTML?

Like an interactive page, Dynamic HTML can be a bit of a moving target. It's a technology and idea that's evolved since Netscape first introduced JavaScript in Navigator 2. But we all need a starting place, so let's break the term apart.

First, there's *dynamic*. In DHTML, *dynamic* means that the page is subject to change at any time. More specifically, this change does not require any interaction with a server — everything happens on the client side (the browser), so it's quick and doesn't depend on a fast connection or an optimized server.

Then there's HTML — this book is dedicated to building pages with HTML, so you've got a pretty good idea what it's all about. At the heart of HTML is the ability to define a page's structure so that a browser knows how to interpret the page for the user. Traditional HTML is static — you load the page and it's done. It just sits there like a good dog ready for you to read or move on to another page.

Putting the two together means we have a method of manipulating the structure of a Web page without getting the server involved beyond loading the initial page. What does this mean? This means suddenly you can do things on your Web page you couldn't do before, such as

✦ Redraw a page without reloading

✦ Move images and text around the page without using a movie or animation (see Figure 47-1)

✦ Create dynamic forms that automatically ask the next question based on the answers to the previous questions

✦ Create a dynamic table of contents (see Figure 47-2)

✦ Show and hide levels of detail based on visitor actions without reloading the page

✦ Change the color of text or an image as the cursor moves over it

Figure 47-1: Words gyrate and circle on this Netscape page thanks to scripting harnessing the power of the DOM. This page uses layers to move text without using an animated GIF or other bulky graphic files.

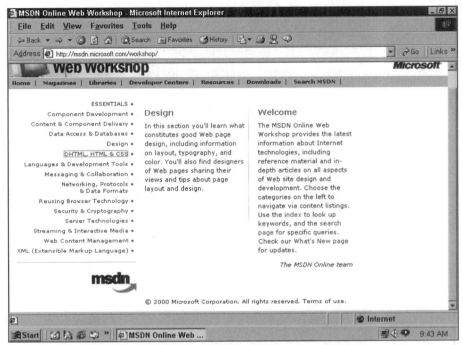

Figure 47-2: Menus appear and disappear as the mouse hovers over the words, which act as a table of contents on the left-hand side of this Microsoft page. This page uses the DOM to detect mouse position and display hidden layers.

In DHTML, the instructions for all of these features become a part of your Web page. All of the instructions are executed without the page being reloaded from a server. They go a long way toward converting a Web page into a true application.

However, none of the exciting things you can do with your page can be done without learning a scripting language. Because JavaScript is the most widely implemented and the most widely used, this book uses JavaScript for its examples. JavaScript is covered in more detail in the next chapter, although you'll begin to see how it looks in this chapter.

Cross-Reference   For lots of examples and in-depth knowledge of JavaScript, be sure to check out the *JavaScript Bible* by Danny Goodman from IDG Books Worldwide, Inc.

The ability to address and change tags and their content utilizes the Document Object Model (DOM). As browsers have evolved, virtually every element on a Web page is now reflected in the DOM and is exposed to change or observation.

Foundation for Change: The Document Object Model

DHTML needs a way to look at the document. In static HTML, the page is loaded, interpreted, displayed, and that's it. It's simply a set of instructions on how the page should appear.

In DHTML, the elements are related to each other through the use of the Document Object Model (DOM). As each element is loaded, it is placed in a stack with similar elements with a note as to where it is in relation to other documents. In this way, it keeps track of everything on the page — in essence creating a mini-database reflecting the page's structure and content.

Without the DOM, the Web would never be more than a series of static magazine pages. Sure, some pages would look pretty sexy with plug-ins like Shockwave, animated GIF images, or pages created using a real-time database. But, essentially, everything you would ever see on a page would be the same, regardless of how you interact with the page. With the DOM, the Web becomes an application on your desktop. Using the DOM, every Web page can be a functional software application that responds to the actions of the user, including typing information in form fields, moving a mouse over words and images, and clicking.

The DOM makes all of this possible by creating a structured way to access elements in a document in an orderly fashion. It relates each element to its neighbors through the use of parent-child-sibling relationships. The DOM is not a new set of tags or attributes to learn, because the DOM's job is to work within existing document formats, including HTML and XML.

The DOM standard is maintained by the World Wide Web Consortium, or W3C (www.w3c.org), which works hard to create universal recommendations that aren't application- or vendor-specific (see Figure 47-3). The DOM as described by the W3C is language- and browser- independent. This is a step forward from the first implementation of a DOM, which was created and interpreted solely in context of Netscape Navigator 2.0, where the DOM was tied directly to JavaScript. The DOM created by the W3C lays the groundwork for how a document's properties are accessed, but not the structure or method.

Note

All the information you would ever want on the DOM is located at the W3C's Web site (www.w3c.org/DOM). This includes history, current status and future plans for the DOM, and the current DOM recommendations and drafts.

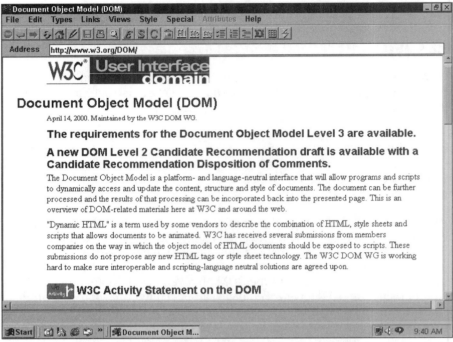

Figure 47-3: The World Wide Web Consortium officially maintains the standards for the Document Object Model, and posts the most current revisions on its Web site.

How is the DOM implemented?

The DOM by itself doesn't do anything, but it does provide a way to address any object on your page. In previous chapters, each *thing* on your page was referred to as an *element*. Now, with the Document Object Model, suddenly everything becomes an *object*. What's the difference? Not much. An element is something you define for display only. In the DOM, the element becomes an object to act upon.

Typically, the browser creates a document-specific DOM from the elements on a Web page. A scripting language (usually JavaScript) is then used to interact with the user and environment to manipulate the page's appearance or behavior. In the DOM, every object can be referred to either by name or by its relationship to other objects on the page. You may have noticed that nearly every element in the HTML 4.01 specification has name as one of its attributes. You can use this attribute to assign a name that won't be of any use anywhere except in the script, using the DOM.

Every element in HTML has an associated object name in the DOM, which enables you to refer to objects by relationship. Most of these names are obvious, but not always, because not all object names are the same on all browsers, and not all object properties work on all browsers. This is not as bad as it sounds, because browser developers are making progress in implementing standards from the W3C.

Note

Sometimes people write HTML pages leaving out what seem to be critical elements, such as HTML, HEAD, and BODY. Under DOM rules, the corresponding objects for these missing elements are automatically created because their existence is assumed. Otherwise, there would be no document object from which to refer to all the other objects on the page.

Cross-browser compatibility and the DOM

The DOM as recommended by the W3C is currently only available in fifth-generation browsers. Other browsers support a less complete DOM, which means that not all features of the DOM are available (access to all events, recognition of all user events, and so on).

This complicates your life. You'll need to create your scripts that interact with the DOM very carefully, and employ a lot of error checking, object detection, and browser sniffing to make sure you create stable, dependable scripts that don't crash the user's browser. This is especially true if you are trying to maintain backward compatibility.

Cross-Reference

See Chapter 48 for a way to look for specific DOM features on a browser, and a method to determine which browser is in use for exclusionary methods of writing DHTML.

In a nutshell, there's really no such thing as cross-browser compatibility. In the next chapter, you'll see a method for detecting which parts of the DOM are supported on a given browser before the code is executed. This is a good way to implement backward compatibility. The other option is to do what accessibility purists really don't like — write your DHTML pages to run only on browsers that are fully compatible with the W3C DOM, and skip execution on all others.

Cross-Reference

A comprehensive reference guide to DOM objects is available at the MSDN Online Web Workshop site (http://msdn.microsoft.com/workshop/). Netscape includes additional information and links to the DOM (http://developer.netscape.com/tech/dom/).

The structure of the DOM

Relationships between objects in the DOM are patterned after relationships between family members. An object can have a parent, a child or children, and one or more siblings. Sibling objects share a parent. The Adam and Eve of this family is the *document* object. The document object has no parent, and the list is defined as follows:

```
<OL name="this-list">
<LI name="first-child">
<LI name="second-child">
```

```
<OL name="third-child">
    <LI name="first-grandchild">
    <LI name="second-grandchild">
</OL>
</OL>
```

In the preceding HTML snippet, *this-list* is a child of the document. The list items *first-child*, *second-child*, and *third-child* are all children of *this-list* and siblings to each other. The nested list items *first-grandchild* and *second-grandchild* are children of *third-child*.

All objects within a document are referenced by what type of object they are and what occurrence of this type of object they are, beginning with 0 for the first occurrence. For example, if this-list was the first list on the page, it would be ordered list 0. The second-child would be list item 1 of ordered list 0.

Referring to objects in the DOM is relatively simple. If you have a named object, you can refer to it as itself. Consider the following HTML, which defines the object:

```
<IMG src="images/volcano.gif" name="volcano">
```

In the JavaScript example below, you can easily refer to the image object named above.

```
<SCRIPT language="javascript">
objImg = volcano;
</SCRIPT>
```

If the element definition had omitted the name attribute — for whatever reason — the HTML would look instead, like this:

```
<IMG src="images/volcano.gif">
```

As the page author, you can still refer to the image using a relative method of addressing. The relative method selects the image based on its position within other images in the document. In this example, if the object previously defined is the first instance of an image on the page, then the JavaScript definition would look like this:

```
objImg = document.image[0];
```

In the implementation of the DOM, numbering systems begin at zero, so the first instance of an object is 0, the second is 1, and so on.

In addition to being able to refer to an object by name using the DOM, you can also determine or *set* the value of attributes of the element by getting at an object's *properties*. Every object has properties. With few exceptions, the object's properties parallel the object's attributes. This even includes, for example, formatting attributes such as the `align` attribute, which is deprecated in most elements (tables being one case where there are no alternatives, because CSS doesn't support table formatting well). Properties are available for deprecated attributes.

Other DOM objects

In addition to querying the value of a property, you can also change the value of the property. This is the power of the DOM. After a page has been loaded, you can change the value of an element's attributes by changing the object's properties. Using the `style` property and subproperties of the `style` property, you can change anything about the look of an element you can set with CSS, the DOM, and the `style` attribute. Style becomes a DOM object:

✦ `style.color` changes the color of the object.

✦ `style.textDecoration` changes the text to be underlined, overlined, struck-through (line-through), or to blink.

✦ `style.fontFamily` changes the font of the text.

✦ `style.fontSize` changes the size of the text.

As you may recall learning in Part IV of this book, CSS elements have a display attribute. The three common values are `""` (empty value), `"none"` (meaning not visible and taking up no space on the page), and `"hidden"` (meaning not visible, but taking up space on the page anyway). If you want to set an object as invisible and not to take up any space on the page—in other words, to disappear as if it had never been there—after the page has been loaded, usually as the result of an event, you can use the following JavaScript code:

```
document.all.image(0).display = "none";
```

Notice the property name is tacked onto the end of the object name. In this case, the object is being referred to by relationship. From the object name, you can tell this is the first image on the page. The next example refers to the object by name.

```
objImg.display = "none";
```

The object was named *objImg*, but you can't tell what kind of object it is from the JavaScript alone. Whatever kind of object it is, it will be rendered invisible and the rest of the page will be redrawn, so this invisible object doesn't take up any space on the page as a result of this JavaScript.

In addition to showing or hiding objects, you can change almost every property CSS can affect. The fastest way to apply style qualities to an object is to define a style within the HEAD element and to apply the entire style by name. In the following example, you can see the STYLE element in the HEAD, and then the JavaScript you would use to set the style of an object to a different value.

```
<HEAD>
<STYLE>
  beginning {
color: black;
font-family: Helvetica;
font-size: 12pt;
}
alternate {
color: red;
font-family: Helvetica;
font-size: 14pt;
}
</STYLE>
<!-- and later on in the document, in the JavaScript, you could
use the following code -->
document.all.div(4).style = alternate;
<!-- more JavaScript would follow, then the rest of the rest of
the page definition -->
```

Notice the DOM object is assigned directly to the name of the style.

DOM event model

To enable interactive documents, the DOM includes an event model to enable it to respond to a wide range of user actions and changes in page status. In previous implemented versions of the DOM, events have been tied to specific objects. For example, hyperlinks and buttons were the only objects that could detect mouse clicks. You could detect the mouse moving over a hyperlink, but not over a heading. A key part of the W3C DOM is that *all* objects recognize *all* events. This will be a good thing, once it's implemented, enabling you to turn a Web page into a feature-rich graphical user interface.

Another feature of the DOM is called *event bubbling*. When implemented, this feature can pass off event handling for an object to the object's parent. For example, clicking on a form button is initially handled by the event handler for that element. With event bubbling, further handling can then be passed off to the form to which the element belongs. If needed, further handling can then be passed up to the document or other parent structure.

From Here

Cross-Reference If you're interested in learning more about JavaScript, go to Chapter 48 for more in-depth information.

Jump to Chapter 49 to experiment with creating cross-browser DHTML.

Summary

The DOM is the greatest thing to hit the Web since forms. It adds a whole new dimension of functionality to Web sites. Together with CSS (especially the capability to place objects in all three dimensions) and JavaScript, the DOM can literally make your page dance. Thanks to the DOM, every element of your page is completely addressable. In addition, the DOM demands that every browser redraw the page dynamically, meaning if you change the definition of an element after the page has been rendered, the browser will redraw the page without having to reload the page from the server.

You can address objects on your page either by name — if they have names and you know them — or by relationship (the child of my parent's third sibling). The exciting thing about the DOM is you take actions on objects by changing their properties; it is this simple. Properties correspond almost identically to attributes in the HTML definition of the object.

Unfortunately, the conclusion to this chapter of the DOM is not as rosy as it should be. Microsoft and Netscape still haven't implemented the DOM the same way. In fact, before a DOM existed, there were just two browser developers trying to offer some level of scripting to their developers. Microsoft goes beyond what the DOM demands while Netscape falls short. Everyone hopes that someday all popular browsers will fully (and identically) support the DOM.

✦ ✦ ✦

Cross-Browser Basics with JavaScript

The previous chapter looked at the Document Object Model. A pertinent detail of the DOM is that we need a way to look at it and manipulate it within the context of a Web page. This is where we need JavaScript — a Web-page-based scripting language.

JavaScript: The Dynamic in DHTML

JavaScript is the language of choice for the vast majority of DHTML pages. It is supported by the two major browsers (Internet Explorer and Navigator), along with other flavors including StarOffice (www.staroffice.com) and Opera (www.opera.com). JavaScript is a relatively simple and powerful language, and is in broad enough use to make it the de facto standard for Web scripting languages.

Note   VBScript is an extension of Visual Basic created by Microsoft as a competitor to JavaScript. However, Microsoft's efforts were not as widely accepted, because JavaScript was introduced to the Web developer world first. As a result, Microsoft has added complete support for JavaScript (calling it *Jscript*) to Internet Explorer, in addition to VBScript.

However, using JavaScript to create DHTML Web pages does have a drawback. As long as there is more than one browser, there will be more than one way of doing things. Different developers will keep up with industry standards and recommendations at different rates. The result is a mess for the lowly Web author who wants to do fun and exciting things with a Web page, but doesn't want to limit their site to only those with the latest and greatest browser. What's a poor soul to do?

In this chapter, we'll show you the basics of JavaScript, and also include some techniques for working around the inconsistencies of the world while still delivering a combination of scripts and DOM that will work for (almost) everyone.

JavaScript is an object-oriented scripting language. With JavaScript, you can manipulate many variables and objects on your page. With JavaScript and the DOM, you can change the value of all the properties of all the objects on your page. Because the DOM requires browsers to redraw pages in response to events, JavaScript becomes far more powerful with the DOM.

Note   It's easy to confuse Java and JavaScript — after all, they appear to be closely related. Although JavaScript bases its syntax and structure on Java, the two languages are quite independent of each other and serve completely different purposes. Java is the product of Sun Microsystems, which created it as a cross-platform, object-oriented programming language. JavaScript is a product of Netscape, which developed it to enable Web developers to add programming functionality to Web pages.

JavaScript is the most widely used scripting language on the Web. Originally developed by Netscape, JavaScript has now grown beyond the realm of anything Netscape can control and is supported natively by all the major browsers. When used with the Document Object Model (DOM), you can use JavaScript to animate, display, or hide any part of your page, validate forms, and interact in other ways with the end user.

Note   A standardized version of JavaScript is defined by European Computer Manufacturers Association (www.ecma.ch), which calls their language *ECMAScript*. Netscape turned JavaScript over to ECMA in an attempt to stabilize the language and make it more widely accessible to other developers. This has not prevented Netscape or Microsoft from continuing to make their own innovations and changes outside the standards created by ECMA.

When combined with the DOM, you can do many things with JavaScript on a Web page, such as

✦ **Create a real-time clock with a working second hand.** A DOM-compliant browser redraws the part of the page that has changed without the need for the page to reload.

✦ **Create a dynamic form displaying relevant fields, based on information already provided.** For example, if a visitor answers yes to an insurance form question about whether any family members have died before age 55, then a set of questions about which relatives and how they died would appear. If the answer is a no, then the next question to appear might ask whether the visitor uses tobacco or illegal drugs. This helps to avoid such techniques as "If no, skip to question 13."

✦ **Reward certain screen interactions, such as answering a series of trivia questions correctly, by providing a congratulatory animation.** The JavaScript can both evaluate the results of the quiz and animate a still image (or a series of images) without reloading the page and without requiring additional actions by the visitor, such as clicking a "see results" button.

✦ **Sort the results of a database table based on the sort order requested by the visitor without additional server requests.** Once receiving the information from the server, the client can sort the data in useful ways utilizing JavaScript and the DOM.

Note This chapter is a very brief introduction to JavaScript. For the full story, plus lots of examples and expert advice, check out Danny Goodman's *JavaScript Bible* (IDG Books Worldwide, Inc.).

Even with all JavaScript can do, it has limitations. JavaScript is limited to its own sandbox within the browser. JavaScript cannot manipulate files on the client computer, including creating, writing, or deleting any system files. JavaScript also cannot execute any operations outside of the browser, including launching an installer or initiating a download.

These limitations may seem like a handicap for developers, but they help to safeguard site visitors. Right now, few Web citizens fear JavaScript because of the limitations built into it — it is not perceived as a security threat. This is unlike Java and ActiveX. Many visitors have disabled the capability for their browsers to accept any of those technologies, for fear of rogue programs. JavaScript would do well to avoid any similar security scare. If the price for this is some modest limitations, then it is probably worth the price.

Adding scripts with the SCRIPT element

Now that you have an idea what JavaScript can do, you must understand how to insert your JavaScript into your page. HTML offers the SCRIPT element. If you want the script to be event-driven, include the SCRIPT element in the HEAD. If you want the script to execute when the page first loads, include the script in the BODY element. You can have both types of scripts.

The basic syntax is the same as any other HTML:

```
<SCRIPT language="javascript">
/* script goes here */
</SCRIPT>
```

Most scripts tend to be placed directly in the Web page, but you have one other option. If your script is long or if it uses functions you want other scripts to use, you can put your script into an external text file and link to it with the SCRIPT element's `src` attribute, as shown in the following code. For JavaScript scripts, the file extension is usually JS.

```
<SCRIPT language="javascript" src="/javascript/lib_date.js">
/* Perhaps a comment on why the external script is needed */
</SCRIPT>
```

Although the most popular browsers (Navigator, Internet Explorer, Opera, and StarOffice) are JavaScript-capable, other browsers still do not support it for a variety of reasons. As a responsible developer, you should hide your scripts from non-JavaScript browsers by commenting out the contents of your script. A browser ignores any tags it doesn't recognize, so the JavaScript-challenged browser will see the <SCRIPT> tag and ignore it, and then it will see a big, long comment (that actually contains your script) that it will ignore, and finally it will come to the </SCRIPT> tag and ignore that.

```
<SCRIPT language="javascript">
<!-- Hide script from incompatible browsers
...script here...
// finish hiding script -->
</SCRIPT>
```

The JavaScript-capable browser, on the other hand, won't be fazed by HTML comments. It will ignore the opening HTML comment tag by accepted language convention, and then process the rest of the contents as JavaScript. When it gets to the bottom, it sees a JavaScript comment marker (//), and ignores that line, which includes the closing half of the HTML comment tag.

JavaScript execution

When does JavaScript script execute? That depends on where the script is and how it's written. If a script has some effect on the initial display of the page, it should run before the page is loaded. If a script needs to be ready to run when a certain condition is met on the page, it needs to appear before the place on the page that will encounter the event. If a script needs to run in the course of loading the page, then it needs to be included in the page itself.

```
<HEAD>
<SCRIPT language="javascript">
function currentTime() {
   var timeStr = ""; //declare an empty string
now = Time();
timeStr = now.getHours() + ":";
timeStr = now.getMinutes();
return timeStr;
}
</SCRIPT>
```

```
<TITLE>My Home Page</TITLE>
</HEAD>
<BODY>
<!-- rest of document here -->
```

This snippet declares a function called currentTime in the head of the document, but it doesn't execute yet. But, once the page is loaded, any hyperlink, form, or other page feature that wants to use currentTime can, because it was declared before the page was loaded. If the script was placed at the bottom of the document, then the entire page would have to be loaded before the function was available, which could create problems if the user or page tries to invoke the function before it's ready.

Tip

JavaScript is an *interpreted* language, which means it is evaluated and executed line by line. Because the JavaScript interpreter is moving through the scripts sequentially, you need to make sure that functions and other routines are declared *before* they're needed.

The choice of when the script executes is yours. If you want the script to execute when the page is finished loading, you can place it as the last script on the page, or put it in the head of the document with a reference to it in the <BODY> tag.

```
<BODY onload="runScript()">
```

Your document can include as many scripts as you want or need in the head and body of the document, depending only on the patience of the end user to wait for the download.

As we delve deeper into JavaScript, you need to know a few important rules, which you may have noticed in the examples so far.

First, JavaScript is case-sensitive. This means the following three statements refer to three completely different variables:

```
Rose = 4;
rose = 5;
ROSE = 6:
```

In the preceding three lines of code, a Rose is not a rose is not a ROSE — there are three distinct variables with three distinct values. If you're not careful, this can cause a real programming headache. Be sure to follow logical, predictable naming conventions so you're not left tracking insidious spelling errors in your code.

Next, virtually all JavaScript lines need to end with a semicolon. Some of your lines of code will be more than one line. You can format your lines however you want, inserting line breaks wherever it is convenient so your code is easy to read.

Remember to put a semicolon at the end of each line; then the browser knows when the line ends.

Events, event handlers, properties, functions, methods, and DOM properties and methods use special capitalization. You've already seen this unusual capitalization system. The first letter of the first word is in lowercase and then each subsequent word has the first letter capitalized, such as `onMouseOver`, `ifValid`, and `isIndexOf`.

Variables in JavaScript are like variables in any other programming or scripting language. Variables in JavaScript are simply containers for holding data. If you want to store data temporarily, or until you can move it into a container that gets displayed on the page somewhere, you create a variable. Unlike some programming languages, you don't have to define your variables before you use them. The first time the variable name appears, the script recognizes this as a new variable and assigns a type to it (integer, number, character, and so on) based on the value you give it. The type of variable is not fixed — it can be text one moment and an integer the next, depending on its usage.

Here's the quick run-down of JavaScript syntax "gotchas":

✦ Variable names are case-sensitive.

✦ Variable names must begin with an alphabetic character or an underscore. Subsequent characters in the name can be alphabetic, numeric, or underscore (notice hyphens aren't allowed).

✦ Variables cannot be JavaScript keywords.

✦ Variables can be any length, but your fingers will get tired of typing 32-character variable names. Make names long enough to be meaningful, but short enough to type accurately.

Event handling in JavaScript

You have seen the word *events* thrown around a lot in this part of the book so far. You'll remember that an *event* is any action taken by the visitor sitting at the browser. An event can also be caused by the browser, such as when the page finishes loading. Every movement of the mouse, every click of the mouse, every keystroke can generate an event. As a developer, you must decide what kinds of actions you want to take based on events. Acting on events requires `event handlers`, which are discussed later on in this chapter.

Table 48-1 shows the major scriptable events.

Table 48-1
Scriptable Events

Event	Trigger
Load	This event is triggered when the page is loaded.
Unload	This event is triggered when the page is unloaded (usually when another page is called).
mouseOver	This event is triggered when the mouse goes over an object on the page.
mouseOut	This event is triggered when the mouse is no longer over an object it was formerly over.
mouseDown	This event is triggered when a visitor clicks (only the downstroke of the mouse button) on an object.
mouseUp	This event is triggered when visitors release the mouse button they have depressed. Most systems handle only the mouseUp event, rather than both mouseDown and mouseUp, or only mouseDown. If visitors start to click (triggering a mouseDown), and then move the mouse off of the object (triggering a mouseOut), and then release the button (triggering a mouseUp), then normally visitors don't want any action taken.
click	This event is triggered when visitors both click and release an object.
dblClick	This event is rarely used in Web pages because Web pages rely on single clicks, but you can capture and act on a double-click, as well.
keyPress	This event is triggered when a keyboard key is depressed and released.
keyDown	This event is triggered when a keyboard key is depressed.
keyUp	This event is triggered when a keyboard key is released.
Focus	This event is triggered only in forms, when the cursor moves to highlight a field (either by tabbing to that field, by using a mouse to place the cursor at that field, or by using an access key to bring the focus to that field).
Blur	This event is triggered only in forms when the cursor is moved away from a field that was formerly in focus.
Submit	This event is only triggered in forms when the object clicked is a BUTTON element with a type of "submit" or an INPUT element with a type of "submit."
Reset	This event is only triggered in forms when the object clicked is a BUTTON element with a type of "reset" or an INPUT element with a type of "reset."
Change	This event is only triggered in forms when the contents of the object in focus are changed and then the focus leaves this object. In other words, if an input field has today's date in it and the visitor changes the date and tabs to another field or clicks another field, then the change event is triggered.

As a developer, you must know what events you can detect. Then you need to think about what events you need to trap and how you want your page to behave, based on those events.

As you can see, events are happening every time visitors move their mouse across your page, even if they never click anything. Think of all the mouseOver events this might generate. However, the browser only pays attention to the ones you tell it to notice. It does this by looking for event handlers. Event handlers are attributes you can include in the definitions of your HTML elements.

```
<INPUT type="submit" value="Buy Now!" onSubmit="return
ifValid(this.form)">
```

In the preceding code, the submit button executes the JavaScript function ifValid() before submitting the form. If the ifValid() function validates all the data, then it returns *true* and the form is submitted using the action attribute of the FORM element. If the function returns *false,* then the function should return some useful information as to why (which you must include in the function), and the form is not submitted.

```
<INPUT type="checkbox" name="Family_History" value="yes"
onClick="determineFamilyHistory()">
```

If the check box defined in the preceding code is clicked, regardless of whether the check box is clicked to be selected or clicked to be deselected, a function called determineFamilyHistory() is called. This function can then reevaluate the appearance of the page or other form fields based on the new value of the checkbox.

Table 48-2 shows all the event handlers, what event they trap, and the valid elements you use them with.

Table 48-2 Event Handlers		
Event Handler	**Triggered on . . .**	**Valid Elements**
OnLoad	page finished loading	BODY, FRAMESET
OnUnload	page unloading (or another page loading into the same window or frame)	BODY, FRAMESET
OnMouseOver	mouse being over an object	ALL
OnMouseOut	mouse being moved off of an object	ALL
OnMouseDown	mouse being depressed	ALL

Event Handler	Triggered on . . .	Valid Elements
OnMouseUp	mouse being released	ALL
OnClick	mouse being depressed and released	ALL
OnDblClick	mouse being clicked twice	ALL
OnKeyPress	keyboard key being depressed and released	ALL
OnKeyDown	keyboard key being depressed	ALL
OnKeyUp	keyboard key being released	ALL
OnFocus	form field being highlighted either by tabbing, by an access key, or by clicking in the field	INPUT, SELECT, BUTTON, TEXTAREA
OnBlur	form field losing the focus by tabbing out of the field, by an access key, or by clicking another form field	INPUT, SELECT, BUTTON, TEXTAREA
OnSubmit	submit button being clicked or pressed	INPUT, BUTTON
OnReset	reset button being clicked	INPUT, BUTTON
OnChange	the value of any field being changed and then that field losing focus	INPUT, SELECT, TEXTAREA

Properties, methods, and functions

Properties in JavaScript work the same as properties in the DOM. Because the DOM properties are being evaluated in JavaScript, you really can't tell them apart when working through a script. Most properties can be either viewed or changed. Some properties can only be viewed.

You access properties in JavaScript by appending the property name to the object name. For example, if you have a check box called box1, you might take some action based on whether it is selected. In this case, the object name is box1 and the property name is checked.

```
if (box1.checked) {
take some action
}
```

Another property you will use often is the length property. It applies to any object that can be enumerated, such as form elements, strings, arrays, and so on. For example, radio buttons usually occur in sets (one name is associated with multiple buttons, only one of which can be checked at one time). If you want to check to see which button is checked, you might want to loop through all the buttons. Even if you don't know how many buttons there are, you can loop through the list by checking each button from the 0th to the last in the list (the last in the list is the value of the object.length property). In this example, buttonSet is the name of the radio button set.

```
for (var i = 0; i < buttonSet.length; i++) {
  take some action
}
```

One of the properties that makes the DOM useful in manipulating the appearance of the page is the display property (a part of CSS). In the following example, the display property is set to none when box1 is checked.

```
if (box1.checked) {
document.all.form[0].button[3].display == "none"
}
```

What if you want to force an event? Sometimes, you don't want to wait for a visitor to click a button, especially if only one field is in the form. Event-based methods are a way to force events or perform actions with or without user interaction.

Not all methods work with all elements, but the methods available to you are the same as the events listed previously. A method is always followed by parentheses, because a method takes an action on something. For example, focus(box1) brings focus to whatever object is called box1.

How do you call a method? From anywhere in a script or from an event handler in your element definition. One example of each follows:

```
if (box1.checked) {
focus(document.all.testform.newname)
}

<INPUT type="checkbox"
onClick="focus(document.all.testform.newname)">
```

Notice in both examples, the method simply acts on whatever is in the parentheses. Generally, methods are used only in forms, and the objects of the methods (what they act on) are also in forms. Using the focus() method is a good way to move the visitor to the correct next field for data entry.

Most of what you want to do with JavaScript, you write yourself in functions. *Functions* act on some data, so function names are also followed by parentheses. *Methods* are the freebie actions you can take in JavaScript without doing any real work. Everything else you need your scripts to do requires the sweat of your own brow.

Functions are the JavaScript workhorses. Because JavaScript is an event-driven language, most of your functions will be called either by event handlers or by other functions. In earlier examples, you've seen events call functions from within the Web page, such as the following:

```
<BODY onload="initializeForms()">
```

This calls a function named `initializeForms` which should be defined in the document's head. The definition for this function would look something like this:

```
function initializeForms() {
  //Function activity here
}
```

This function will only run when its name is invoked from within an event handler or when it's called from a script or other function. It will not run spontaneously by itself. In addition to any manipulation of the DOM or other objects inside the function, it can also return a value.

```
function initializeForms() {
  //Function does work, and sets a flag called successful
if (successful) {
        return 1;
} else {
  return 0;
}
}
```

In this case, if the form was completed as expected, it would return a 1 (which is evaluated as a logical true); otherwise it ends with a 0 (logical false). You can use this feature to ensure a function did what was expected, or you can use it to return other values in a calculator-type format.

```
function circleCircum(radius) {
  circumference = 2 * Math.PI * radius;
  return circumference;
}
```

Passing data from the page to the script

For example, you have a form with two questions, Q1 and Q2; what form fields will be used in the HTML to accept the answers to the questions posed in Q1 and Q2 is not clear. Check boxes will not work because, if the answer to both questions is "no," then neither will be checked, no visitor action will be taken, no events will be created, and the form fields for accepting the names will never appear. The two working options are radio buttons, with both Q1 and Q2 having two buttons: One each for "yes" and "no," and a select list with two options, "yes" and "no."

Either of these choices requires data be passed from the page to the script. Notice all the functions in the previous example have those parentheses following them? Well, this is where you put the data you want to pass. On the HTML definition, you put the data you want to send; on the JavaScript side, you put what you want to call the data when you receive it. This sounds simple enough, but how can you put data the visitor hasn't yet entered into the function name to send it from the page to the script? Obviously, you can't. JavaScript has a way of getting around this: it is called this.

This

No, this isn't one of those "Who's On First" routines. JavaScript enables you to send the contents of a form field, after it is entered, or if any action is taken on the field by the visitor, by using the reserved word this. What this sends is the value of only that field. If you need to send the contents of the entire form, say, from the onSubmit event handler to validate data before you submit it, you can say this.form. So, if you want to send the value of Q1 radio buttons to the script, you could use the following HTML:

```
Q1. Are the twins both boys: <BR>
<INPUT type="radio" name="bothBoys" onClick="form(this)"> Yes
<BR>
<INPUT type="radio" name="bothBoys" onClick="form(this)"> No
<BR>
```

If you want to validate an entire form when the submit button is clicked, you could use the following HTML:

```
<INPUT type="submit" value="Send Now!" onSubmit="validateAll
(this.form)">
```

This submit button would submit the names and values of all the form fields to a function of your own creation called validateAll.

What the script sees

Sending the value of the bothBoys radio button in the previous example is the same as telling the script to use the value of the object document.form[0]. bothBoys. You can see that using this property name in every reference in this script could get cumbersome fast. Instead, when you send the value of bothBoys using the reserved word this, you can choose what you want to call the field within the script.

Being able to call the field whatever you want is important. Notice the showBoy1() function is called by two other functions. If showBoy1() acted on data, rather than just displaying (or rather unhiding) form fields, then you would have to create two different versions of the same function, one to act on each specific object. This wouldn't be at all efficient. Instead, you can create a variable to hold the value of the object you are processing in the script until you return it to the page.

```
function bothBoys ( boys2 ) {
  if (boys2 = "yes") {
      document.all.bothGirls.display = "none";
      showBoy1 ();
      showBoy2 ();
  }
}
```

Notice in the function definition line, you are told whatever data comes into the bothBoys function will be called boys2 while it is inside the function. JavaScript simply creates a container of the type of the data sent to it. In this example, the variable boys2 is only referred to once. Even so, it is far more convenient to refer to the value of boys2 than to refer to the entire object name.

Sending form data

When you send the entire contents of a form to a script to be validated, you will be grateful for the reserved word this. Here is an example of a possible validateAll() function for a short form.

```
function validateAll (myform) {
  validText(myform.first_name);
  validText(myform.last_name);
  validEmail(myform.email);
  validPhone(myform.phone);
}
```

Without the this reserved word, your script would be far more verbose and prone to error.

Testing and debugging JavaScript

As you'll see when trying some of the examples in this chapter and during your own experimentation, you can't avoid testing and debugging JavaScript. When you load a page with JavaScript, the first thing the browser does is review the script for syntax. Anything it doesn't like, it tells you about — right then and there. Then, as you try to execute the script, it finds *and reports* every error along the way.

JavaScript is interpreted, rather than compiled. This means, instead of giving you a single, long listing of errors, it tells you about errors as it finds them — one annoying pop-up box at a time. Even after you figure out what all your errors are and fix them to your satisfaction, a good idea is to try clicking fields in an order that doesn't make sense, to be sure things work as they should even when visitors do unexpected things.

Cross-Browser JavaScript

Making truly cross-browser Dynamic HTML with JavaScript begins with cross-browser HTML. If your Web page breaks on old browsers without scripting, it's certainly not going to work when you start adding in JavaScript. Solid, clean, validated HTML code is the first step in any DHTML venture.

Tip   Looking for a place to start in validating? Check out the source of the standards—the World Wide Web Consortium. They have a useful validation service at `http://validator.w3.org/`.

Having a technically perfect page ensures that the DOM for your page will be valid. This in turn means it will behave in a predictable fashion when it is evaluated and manipulated with your scripting.

However, there is another wrinkle. JavaScript was introduced with Netscape Navigator 2.0, next appearing in Internet Explorer 3.0. Each subsequent browser and implementation of JavaScript has been different in some form from competitors and predecessors. How do you implement new features without breaking old browsers? Read on.

Surveying the Browser Environment

There are two schools of thought on determining which part of a script to run in a given environment. The first is to detect the platform, browser, and version of the host, using properties of the `navigator` object. Table 48-3 summarizes the properties of the navigator object that enable you to determine information about the user's system.

Table 48-3
Key Properties of the Navigator Object for Detecting a User's Environment

Navigator Object Properties	*Determines*
appVersion	Current version of the user's browser
appName	Name of the user's browser
platform	Operating system type
plug-ins	An object that includes an array of plug-ins or ActiveX controls currently configured for the browser

Following this school of thought means keeping track of every version of every potential browser, the different features and implementations between versions, and if it has different capabilities on different platforms. The following script, when executed on a JavaScript-compatible browser, will display all of the properties of the navigator object known to the browser.

```
<SCRIPT language="javascript">
function showProperties () {
   document.write("<H1>Properties of Navigator</H1>");
   document.write("<HR>");
   var displayline;
   var obj = navigator;
   var name = "navigator";
   for (var prop in obj) {
         displayline = name + "." + prop + " = " + obj[prop];
         document.write(displayline + "<BR>");
   }
}
</SCRIPT>
```

Figures 48-1 and 48-2 show the results on Netscape Navigator 6 and StarOffice 5.1, so you can get a feel for how the results differ between browsers.

Figure 48-1: The properties of the browser and user's platform as displayed by Navigator 6

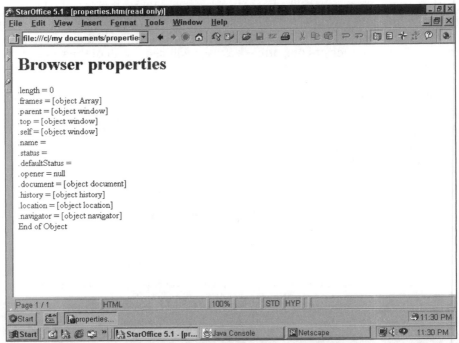

Figure 48-2: The properties of the browser and platform as exhibited by StarOffice 5.1

Cross-Reference

The people at Netscape have developed a comprehensive script for determining the browser type, version, and platform for applications that depend on specific browsers. It can be found at `http://developer.netscape.com/docs/examples/javascript/browser_type.html`. You'll still need to know the compatibilities and inconsistencies of each browser to take advantage of this. And this script doesn't allow for every instance of every browser. For example, it doesn't detect the JavaScript enabled in Sun's StarOffice application.

Sound like a nightmare? It is. Those who have remained sane in the JavaScript programming business gave this approach up a long time ago. As a sole solution, it continues to grow ever more unwieldy and unworkable given the pace of development in the browser market since 1995.

The second school of thought believes it is better to use browser detection in conjunction with object detection. Object detection can get you into the ballpark quicker, and browser detection can help fine-tune idiosyncrasies as needed.

Object detection in JavaScript

Object detection is hard to beat given the variety of browsers since Navigator 2.0, and the various legacy Document Object Models that are in existence. Object detection works by detecting which features (practically always related to an object in some form) a browser can support based on which objects JavaScript can see.

The nice feature to this method is that it provides for forward compatibility. If Netscape integrates a new object in their version of JavaScript that's not supported by Internet Explorer, then object detection will prevent the Internet Explorer user from errors generated by the unknown object. But, if Microsoft chooses to implement the new object in its next release, the feature will be enabled next time it encounters the script.

An example of object detection can be found in the following script, which determines if a browser supports the image object (not supported in early JavaScript implementations). Here's how object detection is used:

```
if (document.images) {  // if an "images" document exists
        // do something with images
}
```

If this script ran on a Navigator 2.0, the object `document.images` would be undefined and return a 0 when evaluated (interpreted as a logical *false*). This makes the `if` statement false, so it doesn't execute the statements within it.

If this script ran on Internet Explorer 4.0, `document.images` would return an object (inherently non-zero), which would be interpreted as a logical *true*. The interior of the `if` statement would run.

All of the code that depends on the image object is contained within the `if` statement that first detects if the object exists. The basic syntax of object detection is this:

```
if (name of object you want to use) {
  code which requires the object
}
```

Once you know if the object exists, you can work with it as much as you need to. This simple method will work whether you're working with math functions, images, style sheets, frames, or layers.

If Navigator suddenly starts supporting Internet Explorer's objects (or vice versa) the script will automatically "adapt" without recoding. For example, you can create a pointer to CSS layers using this method:

```
var ptrLayer;
//layerName is set to the name of the desired layer
```

```
if (document.layers) layerPointer = document.layers[layerName];
if (document.all) layerPointer = document.all[layerName].style;
```

Now you have a handle that you can use to manipulate the various CSS properties of the layer. You may have to do additional testing for specific features to ensure complete compatibility, but most of the work is done at this point. To continue to perfect the use of object detection, you'll need to know which objects you're dealing with.

When it comes to DHTML, you'll want to concentrate most on `document.layers` and `document.all`. The former essentially tells you that you're working with a Navigator DOM implementation, and the latter tells you you're working with an Internet Explorer DOM. You may want to include a test case so that if neither is true, then the browser will bypass code intended for more current browsers.

From Here

 Cross-Reference To learn more about Java Applets, go to Chapter 43.

Summary

JavaScript is the muscle in Dynamic HTML. It provides a way to examine and manipulate the DOM of its host browser, and perform other general programming functions.

As its name implies, JavaScript is a scripting language. As such, it is interpreted line by line during execution rather than being compiled into one file and executed like a traditional program. It is interpreted in the context of its environment. In this section, that means a browser.

While JavaScript has a lot of power to work within the confines of a browser, it is limited to activities within a Web page. It is not allowed to perform other actions in the user's computing environment, including accessing files, printers, or other resources on their local computer.

JavaScript is a programming language. This chapter has only given a taste of its syntax and how it works. As you work more with DHTML, you'll need to learn more about JavaScript. There are many books on the market, in addition to a plethora of online resources.

✦   ✦   ✦

Frames, Layers, and the Shell Game

The DOM and JavaScript make it possible for the contents of a browser page to resemble closely the interactivity and responsiveness of any other application on your desktop. When you see a file listing on your desktop, you can show or hide the files and folders within a given directory. Text can move about on the screen without the use of animated GIF files or specialized plug-ins and applets. With the DOM and JavaScript, you can simulate these types of dynamic responses to user interaction or create spontaneous behavior.

Defining Hidden Text

JavaScript is a powerful language. JavaScript enables you to define HTML elements right from the script, even if you don't define those elements in your HTML body. This probably isn't the way you want to do things, however. Why not?

- ♦ Writing the page takes longer
- ♦ Maintaining the page is more difficult
- ♦ Testing the page is more difficult

An easier way to create hidden text is to include anything you want hidden right in your HTML and then to define it with a style of display: none.

```
<DIV CLASS="leveltwo" STYLE="display:none">
<H1>Defining Hidden Text</H1>
<H2>Bringing hidden text into view</H2>
<H2>Designing an interactive table of contents
</H2>
<H2>Dynamically modifying styles</H2>
</DIV>
```

In this example, these four lines of H1 text will not appear until the display property is set to something other than *none*.

Bringing hidden text into view

To make your hidden text display, all you do is turn the display property of the DIV element that contains your hidden text to "visible" or "" (empty quotes). The following JavaScript turns the previous hidden text into visible text or visible text into hidden text. In the first line, an if statement tests to see whether the element is visible. If the text is visible (style.display==""), then JavaScript makes the text invisible. If the text is invisible (style.display=="none"), then JavaScript sets the text to be visible.

```
if (thisChild.style.display == "" ) {
thisChild.style.display = "none"; }
else {
thisChild.style.display = ""; }
```

Note that *thisChild* is the variable name assigned to the H2 entries listed in the preceding example.

Designing an interactive table of contents

In the following example, the table of contents dynamically shows and hides section headings from Chapter 48 and this chapter. Figures 49-1 and 49-2 show examples of the table of contents fully collapsed and fully revealed.

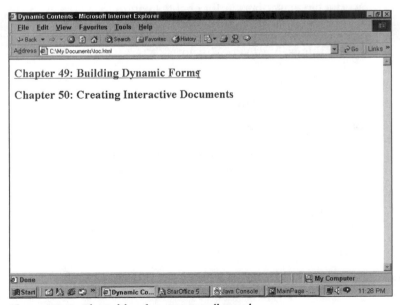

Figure 49-1: The table of contents collapsed

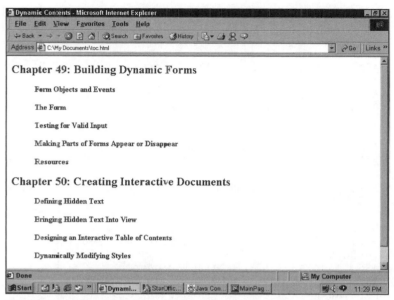

Figure 49-2: The table of contents with all text visible

The HTML used to accomplish the results shown in the preceding figures is as follows:

```
<HTML>
<HEAD>
<TITLE>Dynamic Contents</TITLE>
<STYLE TYPE="text/css">
  H1 {
color: blue;
font-size:18pt;
}
  H2 {
color: black;
font-size: 12pt;
}
  DIV.leveltwo {
margin-left: 0.5in;
}
</STYLE>
<SCRIPT Language="JavaScript">
<!--
... script goes here ...
-->
</SCRIPT>
</HEAD>
<BODY>
<DIV class="levelone" STYLE="position:absolute; width:550">
```

```
<DIV> <!-- although this DIV has no apparent purpose, it needs
to be here -->
<H1 onMouseOver="onLevelOne( this );"
  onMouseOut="notOnLevelOne( this );"
  onClick="hideContents( this );">Chapter 49: Building Dynamic
Forms</H1>
  <DIV CLASS="leveltwo" STYLE="display:none">
      <H2>Form Objects and Events</H2>
      <H2>The Form</H2>
      <H2>Testing for Valid Input</H2>
      <H2>Making Parts of Forms Appear or Disappear</H2>
      <H2>Resources</H2>
  </DIV>
</DIV> <!-- close for DIV with no apparent purpose -->
<DIV> <!-- DIV with no apparent purpose -->
<H1 onMouseOver="onLevelOne( this );"
  onMouseOut="notOnLevelOne( this );"
  onClick="hideContents( this );">Chapter 50: Creating
Interactive Documents</H1>
  <DIV CLASS="leveltwo" STYLE="display:none">
      <H2>Defining Hidden Text</H2>
      <H2>Bringing Hidden Text Into View</H2>
      <H2>Designing an Interactive Table of Contents</H2>
      <H2>Dynamically Modifying Styles</H2>
      <H2>The Script</H2>
  </DIV>
</DIV> <!-- close for DIV with no apparent purpose -->
</DIV> <!-- close for levelone DIV -->
</BODY>
</HTML>
```

Note these few things about the preceding HTML:

✦ The styles are defined right in the HEAD, rather than in a separate style sheet.

✦ The script is missing. Because this requires its own explanation, it will be outlined later in this chapter.

✦ Everything is contained in DIV elements. You can pretty much divide the page into a series of nested DIV elements. This is important to the way formatting works, as well as in the way text is made to appear and disappear. In fact, if you strip out all the rest of the content, you have the following sets of DIV elements:

```
<DIV class="levelone">

<DIV>

        <DIV class="leveltwo">

        </DIV>

    </DIV>
```

```
<DIV>
      <DIV class="leveltwo">
      </DIV>
</DIV>
</DIV>
```

✦ Some of the DIVs have no apparent purpose. We want to give you a good explanation for why they are needed, but we can't. This script simply won't work properly without them.

✦ The H1 elements have three event handlers on them: onMouseOver(), onMouseOut(), and onClick(). The first event handler, onMouseOver(), enables your script to do something when the mouse is over the contents of the H1 element — in this case, change the text color. The second event handler, onMouseOut(), enables your script to do something when the mouse is no longer over the contents of the H1 element — in this case, return to the original text color. The final event handler, onClick(), is the one you are most used to seeing. It actually calls the function that shows or hides the contents.

✦ This example includes the actual text that will show and hide. It would be more common actually to pull the text to be used in this table of contents from an external file or database. Exactly how you would do this depends on the technology you are using, which would be specific to your Web server.

Dynamically modifying styles

The presence of the onMouseOver() and onMouseOut() event handlers in the previous HTML suggest we can make changes to the contents of those elements or to other elements on the page based on where the mouse is. In fact, what we do in this example is change the color and decoration of the text in the H1 elements. Of course, you could change anything about the styles of the H1 elements.

The style definition of the H1 element is as follows:

```
H1 {
color: blue;
font-size:18pt;
}
```

Changing the value of the color property to red and adding a text decoration of underline is easily accomplished in JavaScript:

```
function onLevelOne( el ){
  el.style.color = "red";
  el.style.textDecoration = "underline";
  return;
}
```

Changing the style back to the original style is just as simple:

```
function notOnLevelOne( el ){
  el.style.color = "blue";
  el.style.textDecoration = "none";
  return;
}
```

The script

Finally, here is the entire JavaScript you need to include in the SCRIPT element in the previous HTML. Most of it should look familiar.

```
function onLevelOne( el ){
  el.style.color = "red";
  el.style.textDecoration = "underline";
  return;
}
function notOnLevelOne( el ){
  el.style.color = "blue";
  el.style.textDecoration = "none";
  return;
}
function hideContents( el ){
  var elParent = el.parentElement;
  var childrenCount = elParent.children.length;
  var thisChild = 0;
  for( i = 0; i<childrenCount; i++ ){
      thisChild = elParent.children(i);
      if (thisChild != el ){
          if (thisChild.style.display == "" )
              thisChild.style.display = "none";
          else
              thisChild.style.display = "";
      }
  }
  return;
}
```

The only function that should look unfamiliar to you is hideContents(). This function loops through all the children of the element that calls it (this means it loops through all the DIV elements nested within the DIV element of the element that calls it) and changes the display property for each one.

As mentioned in the previous two chapters, JavaScript and the implementation of the DOM vary for Microsoft Internet Explorer and Netscape Navigator. This example only works properly in Internet Explorer 4 and higher.

Moving Layers

We've played with hiding and displaying layers. Now let's see about moving one around on the screen. Microsoft includes a script on the DHTML section of their Web Workshop (under Positioning) called glide.html. This script shows how to move a layer across a page using JavaScript and the Microsoft DOM. The script can be found at http://msdn.microsoft.com/workshop/Author/dhtml/dhtml.asp

```
<HTML>
<HEAD><TITLE>Glide the DIV</TITLE>
<SCRIPT LANGUAGE="javascript">
var action;
function StartGlide() {
    Banner.style.pixelLeft = document.body.offsetWidth;
    Banner.style.visibility = "visible";
    action = window.setInterval("Glide()",50);
}
function Glide() {
    document.all.Banner.style.pixelLeft -= 10;
    if (Banner.style.pixelLeft<=0) {
        Banner.style.pixelLeft=0;
        window.clearInterval(action);
    }
}
</SCRIPT>
</HEAD>
<STYLE type="text/css">
DIV {
visibility:hidden;
position:absolute;
top:0;
left:0
}
</STYLE>
<BODY onload="StartGlide()">
<P>With dynamic positioning, you can move elements and their
content anywhere in the document even after the document has
loaded!
<DIV ID="Banner">Welcome to Dynamic HTML!</DIV>
</BODY>
</HTML>
```

This page works exactly as designed — but only on Internet Explorer (see Figure 49-3). On other JavaScript-enabled browsers that don't share the Microsoft DOM, the script does nothing or generates errors for the user (see Figures 49-4 and 49-5). Simply being inoperable is okay for the majority of users. Causing errors is to be avoided at all costs.

Figure 49-3: Glide.html, as created by Microsoft, works well on Internet Explorer.

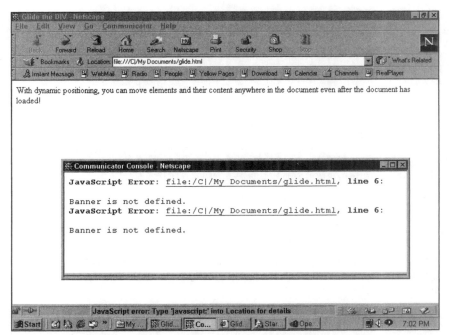

Figure 49-4: The same script creates errors in other browsers such as Netscape Navigator 4.5.

Figure 49-5: Other JavaScript-aware applications also break.

Creating cross-browser HTML

We need to work on making this script cross-browser compatible. We'll start with the HTML, which seems to put the page in reverse order. To make the elements stand out, we'll make the last line into an H1 heading. All of the style information is also a little unnecessary, so we'll remove it and place an inline style attribute for absolute positioning.

Tip   Absolute positioning is required for dynamic placement of objects on a page.

```
<BODY onload="StartGlide()">
<DIV id=Banner style="position:absolute">
<H1>Welcome to Dynamic HTML!</H1>
</DIV>
<P style="position:absolute;top:50">With dynamic positioning,
you can move elements and their content anywhere in the
document even after the document has loaded!
</BODY>
```

Now, we need to go to work on the scripts. We'll add a variable declaration called divBanner to the top of the script declaration. This is the object that will be used to represent the layer during execution. It needs to be global to the script, so we place it outside both function declarations.

DOM object detection

The new `divBanner` variable becomes very important as we take a look at the opening lines of code for script declaration.

```
if (document.all) {
divBanner = document.all.Banner.style; //Line 10
} else if (document.layers) {
divBanner = document.Banner;
} else {
return;
}
```

Here's where we start detecting the environment to see what kind of browser we're working with. The Microsoft DOM includes objects from the body of the document under `document.all`. The first line checks for the existence of this object, and if it exists, assigns `divBanner` to the value of the object. In essence, this creates another handle we can use to manipulate the banner. The trailing `style` object is used by the Microsoft DOM as a prefix to the various style attributes of the object. Because all we'll be manipulating with this object is its style, we add it, also.

If the `document.all` object isn't valid, chances are we're working in a Netscape-compatible environment. Netscape doesn't use the `all` or `style` objects. It just appends the name of the object to `document`.

These are the only two current valid document objects to represent `Banner`. If neither of these shoes fit, then we should exit the function before doing anything else. All script execution will end at this point if neither of the DOM objects were detected.

Setting the initial position

Next, we need to determine where the right side of the screen is so we can position the left side of the banner at its starting point. Again, the Netscape and Microsoft DOMs differ on how to do this, so we use JavaScript's conditional assignment feature, checking to see which value is valid.

```
//                    if the document.body object exists...
divBanner.left = (document.body) ?
document.body.offsetWidth : window.innerWidth;
// use the MS DOM                otherwise, use the NS DOM
```

Once this line executes, the left side of the banner is placed at the far left of the screen (out of sight). The next line sets the wheels in motion.

```
action = window.setInterval("Glide()",50);
```

The `action` object becomes a metronome that executes the `Glide` function every 50 milliseconds until it's stopped.

Moving the object

There's one last bit of detail to take care of. In the two DOMs, there are two methods for moving objects. The Microsoft way is to decrement the *pixelLeft* property, while Netscape uses a method called *moveBy*. We check for the existence of the *body* object to determine if we're in a Microsoft browser, and if not, we use the Netscape method.

```
if (document.body) {
  divBanner.pixelLeft -= 10;
} else {
  divBanner.moveBy(-10,0);
}
```

As the last action, we see if we've reached the left side of the window yet. If so, then the action object is disengaged and script execution stops. This new version of the script is only eight lines longer than the original. It still accomplishes the same purpose on Internet Explorer (see Figure 49-6), but now it also works on Netscape Navigator (see Figure 49-7), and it doesn't break StarOffice (see Figure 49-8).

Figure 49-6: Glide-crossbrowse.html still works as intended on Internet Explorer.

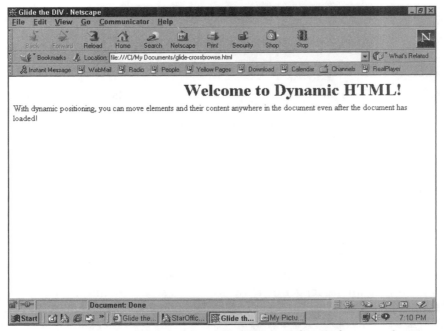

Figure 49-7: The same script, with object detection, also works on Navigator.

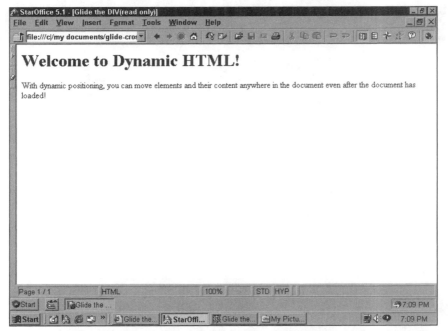

Figure 49-8: Although the dynamic movement doesn't happen, the page still displays in its final intended form without errors on StarOffice.

```
<HTML>
<HEAD>
<TITLE>Glide the DIV</TITLE>
<SCRIPT LANGUAGE="javascript">
var action;
var divBanner;
function StartGlide() {
    if (document.all) {
  divBanner = document.all.Banner.style;
    } else if (document.layers) {
  divBanner = document.Banner;
    } else {
  return;
    }
    divBanner.left = (document.body) ?
document.body.offsetWidth : window.innerWidth;
    divBanner.visibility = "visible";
    action = window.setInterval("Glide()",50);
}
function Glide() {
    if (document.body) {
  divBanner.pixelLeft -= 10;
    } else {
  divBanner.moveBy(-10,0);
    }
    if ((divBanner.left<=0) || (divBanner.pixelLeft<=0)) {
        divBanner.left=0;
        window.clearInterval(action);
    }
}
</SCRIPT>
</HEAD>
<BODY onload="StartGlide()">
<SPAN id=Banner style="position:absolute">
<H1>Welcome to Dynamic HTML!</H1>
</SPAN>
<P style="position:absolute;top:50">With dynamic positioning,
you can move elements and their content anywhere in the
document even after the document has loaded!
</BODY>
```

Tip   Macromedia Dreamweaver is a fine software tool for creating DHTML effects, such as moving text. The code Dreamweaver creates for events and moving elements is cross-browser compatible. If you're going to be doing a lot with DHTML, Dreamweaver is the tool to have.

From Here

Cross-Reference   Want to change styles with DHTML? Move ahead to Chapter 50.

Summary

In this chapter, you saw a simple example of a collapsible table of contents, along with a cross-browser version of moving text. Some of the properties should have looked familiar to you, but you saw them used in new ways. The complete working examples in this chapter can be used as a jumping-off point for your own dynamic Web pages.

With all this exposure to JavaScript, you are well-armed to make your pages dance. If you want to script your pages to the hilt, though, be well-advised to consult the resources on the Web for additional techniques and pitfalls waiting for you. Scripting exclusively for one browser may be easier, but your efforts will go unappreciated by a great many viewers.

✦   ✦   ✦

Doing Windows with JavaScript

With the predominance of Microsoft products in the marketplace, the word *Windows* has become synonymous with *Microsoft Windows Operating System*. But here in the world of the Web, it's not the only definition. In this chapter, we talk about browser windows. Everything that happens on a Web page happens in context to a browser window.

This chapter shows you how to control the activity within a window and then create and control new windows from there. And you'll see a powerful feature—windows that can talk to each other.

What's a Window?

Browsers use windows to display content. Some pages tell the browser to create new windows for additional content. You've probably seen this in e-commerce sites that ask you to fill out surveys about service, in pop-up advertising on some search engines, and in sites that open a new window when you click on links outside their domain (see Figure 50-1).

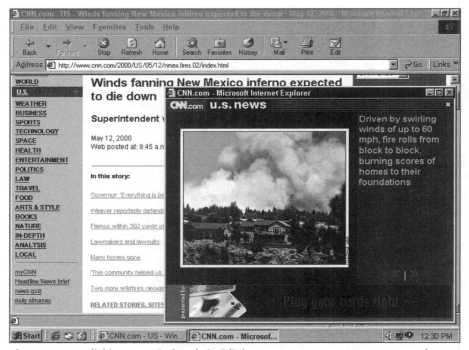

Figure 50-1: Clicking on a "related site" link on **www.cnn.com** opens a new browser window.

Everything that happens on a Web page—dynamic or not—takes place in a window. Using JavaScript and DHTML, you can create your own new windows in any size you want, with any control elements you want, and with any content you want. You can also have these windows communicate with one another.

Window Workings

The browser window is referred to in JavaScript with the `window` object. This refers to the current window with the active page. You can use this object to change the contents of the window by loading a new page, utilizing the `location` property.

```
<SCRIPT language="javascript">
window.location = "http://www.idgbooks.com";
</SCRIPT>
```

When the script runs, the contents of the window change from whatever they are currently to the location specified in the string assigned to `window.location` — in this case, the IDG Books Worldwide site.

Of course, at this point the script isn't very useful. It happens automatically before the user has a chance to do anything about it. We could add it to an `if` statement to load the IDG page if another condition is met.

```
<SCRIPT language="javascript">
if ( idgInfo ) {
window.location = "http://www.idgbooks.com";
}
</SCRIPT>
```

If the value of `idgInfo` is non-zero, then the current window loads `http://www.idgbooks.com`, just as if the user had clicked on a hyperlink with that URL as its *href*, or if they had typed the URL into the address field of the browser directly.

With this key concept under your belt, let's create a new window from the existing one.

Opening Windows

JavaScript can create and control more than one window as easily as it controls one. How does this happen? Take a look at the following code snippet:

```
<SCRIPT language="JavaScript">
var winNew;
function openNew() {
winNew = window.open('http://www.idgbooks.com', 'newWindow')
}
</SCRIPT>
<!-- other HTML here -->
<A href= "javascript:openNew()">Open a Window</A>
```

Clicking on the hyperlink opens a new window with a new file (see Figure 50-2).

As you can see, this window looks different from a "normal" browser window. This happens with the `window.open` method. Table 50-1 lists one key property of this method — file name. This identifies the name of a file or URL to open into the new window. Without this property, the browser would open a blank window without content.

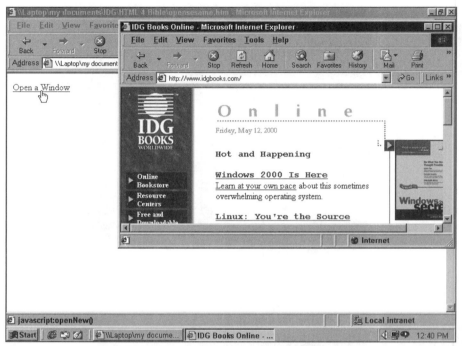

Figure 50-2: A new window is opened when a JavaScript function runs to create it.

Table 50-1 Window.open() Properties	
Property	**Definition**
File name	URL of a file to be displayed in the window
Target name	A name for the new window to use in the `target` attribute of hyperlink tags
Window features	A list of features and display characteristics for the new window, separated by commas and enclosed together in one set of quotation marks

Special-Purpose Windows

As you've seen in the previous section, one purpose of a new window is to provide users a method to view pages that are not a part of your Web site, without losing them from your site. The easiest way to do this is to provide a complete browser to the user. This is essentially the same as selecting File ➪ New Browser Window (or the equivalent) from your Web browser.

But, what if you just wanted to show a series of images? What if you wanted the user to enter a place where it was necessary for them to only click on hyperlinks to navigate, and not use any forward, back, or address-bar features of the browser?

By using the window features options of the window.open() method, you can include all or none of the basic features of a browser window

You can control any of the properties of the window when it's created — absence or presence of toolbars, scrollbars, statusbars, and menus; width and height; and the ability to resize the window. See Table 50-2 for a summary of these properties.

Table 50-2
Window Properties

Property	Value type	Controls
width	number	Width of the window (in pixels).
height	number	Height of the window (in pixels).
toolbar	yes/no	Include a standard browser toolbar (forward, back, refresh, home, and so on).
menubar	yes/no	Include a standard browser menubar (file, edit, view, tools, and so on). Display the browser statusbar (hyperlink location, security status, page-loading information).
scrollbars	yes/no	Include vertical and horizontal scrollbars as needed to display larger pages.
resizable	yes/no	Include the ability for the user to resize the window.

All or any combination of the properties in Table 50-2 can be included in the third value of the window.open() method. For example, to open a new window with the page index.html called *IndexWindow,* and with scrollbars and a statusbar but no menu or toolbar, you would use a line like this:

```
Window.open("index.html", "IndexWindow", "toolbar=no,
menubar=no, status=yes, scrollbars=yes")
```

Note that the properties controlling the appearance and features of the window are separated by commas within *one* set of quotation marks.

 Tip Specifying the Windows features results in a strange side effect in JavaScript. If just one feature is listed, such as toolbar=yes, all other features are set to *no* by default. If you want to specifically exclude one feature but include the others, you'll need to include all the features with a *yes.*

Windows by remote

You can only exert a limited amount of control over a window just by using the `target` attribute of the `anchor` tag. By giving a name to the window using the second property of the `window.open()` method, you can direct hyperlinks to load pages in the new window. But, beyond directing hyperlinks, your ability to do things within the new window is limited.

Using JavaScript, however, you have an option to maintain a "handle" on the created window.

```
<SCRIPT language = "javascript">
var winLinks = null;
function go ( url ) {
   winLinks = window.open("", "links", "width=150,height=200");
   winLinks.location.href = url;
   if (winLinks.opener == null) {
         winLinks.opener = window; }
}
</SCRIPT>
```

What's happening here? First, we created a new JavaScript variable called `winLinks`. This is a null, nondescript variable initially. It has a name, but no value. Then, a value is assigned to `winLinks`—a value that happens to be a new window object sized 150×200 pixels. Note that it doesn't have a location yet (the first property of `window.open()` is blank).

After the window object is created, it is assigned a location using the window's `location.href` property. But notice that we're not using the `window` object name anymore. Now we're using the name of the window object we created, called `winLinks`. Because we created it as a window object, it has all the same properties and methods as the traditional object `window` that represents the current window, including the *href* property used to change its contents.

The last `if` line may be a bit confusing. What is the `opener` property? This is created to make sure the remote window knows about its parent. The parent that "opened" the new window is called the *opener*. You can include JavaScript code in the child window, which refers back to its parent, so that the child can direct the parent to open, close, or load new locations, as shown in the next snippet.

```
<SCRIPT language = "javascript">
function goThere ( url ) {
   if (url) {
         window.opener.location.href = url;
   }
}
</SCRIPT>
```

```
<H3>News links</H3>
<A href="javascript:goThere('http://www.cnn.com')">
CNN OnLine</A><BR>
<A href="javascript:goThere('http://www.abcnews.com')">
ABC News</A><BR>
<A href="javascript:goThere('http://www.cnet.com')">
C|net</A><BR>
```

Closing windows

The methods for closing windows are even more simple than opening the window in the first place. Closing the current active window uses the close method of the window object.

```
window.close();
```

This is easy enough. Now, let's work on closing some remote windows. One of the things I find annoying with some Internet sites are the extra windows (usually with advertising) that pop up during browsing. Even more annoying is the fact that most site developers don't bother to close any of these windows when you leave the site. You're left with a lot of extra windows eating up system resources.

While you can just leave closing the windows to the user, it's also a simple matter to close the window when you're done with it. Remember the earlier script to create a remote window by creating a window object:

```
<SCRIPT language = "javascript">
var winLinks = null;
function go ( url ) {
  winLinks = window.open("", "links", "width=150,height=200");
  winLinks.location.href = url;
  if (winLinks.opener == null) {
        winLinks.opener = window; }
}
</SCRIPT>
```

In this script, winLinks is an object that represents the remote window. Using this object, we can control the remote window in virtually any way, including closing it.

```
winLinks.close();
```

This closes the remote window just as if the user had selected File ➪ Close or clicked on the close button.

Summary

In HTML and JavaScript, a window is a place where Web pages are displayed. A new window is created in a browser either by selecting File ➪ New Window or by selecting a hyperlink with an external target.

JavaScript recognizes and supports the new windows in a variety of ways. First, it's possible to create a new window from the current window by using the `window` object with the `open` method. Invoking `window.open()` creates a new blank browser window. By adding additional options to the `open` method, it's possible to do much more:

✦ `window.open("url")` opens a new window and loads the specified page or URL

✦ `window.open("url", "name")` opens a new window, loads the specified URL, and assigns it a name that can be used with the `target` attribute in a hyperlink.

✦ `window.open("url", "name", "window features")` opens a new window, loads the specified URL, gives it a name, and determines the use or behavior of one or more window features, such as toolbars, window size, scrollbars, and so on.

By assigning the results of the `window.open` operation to an object, it's possible to control the new window from the originating page.

```
newWindow = window.open();
```

Properties of the object can be used to change the new window, such as the `location` property to load a new URL. Within the new window, a special object called `window.opener` lets the remote window refer back to and control the calling window in the same fashion. In this way, the two windows can interact with one another.

When it's time to close a window, use the `close` method of the appropriate window object. For example, `window.close()` closes the current window, while `newWindow.close()` would close a remote window called *newWindow*.

✦　　✦　　✦

HTML 4 Data Types

Case sensitivity of a particular attribute value can be described in one of five ways:

- ✦ **CS** — The value is case sensitive, or in other words, upper- and lowercase letters are interpreted differently.

- ✦ **CI** — The value is case-insensitive, so upper- and lowercase letters are treated identically.

- ✦ **CN** — The value's case can't be changed, such as a number or other non-alphabetic character.

- ✦ **CA** — The attribute or element gives the case information.

- ✦ **CT** — You must check the type definition for information on case sensitivity for this particular value.

URIs

URIs include URLs, and are case sensitive.

Colors

See Appendix G.

Lengths

Attributes can have length values described in one of three ways:

- ✦ **Pixels** — A number that refers to a specific number of pixels on the screen

- ✦ **Length** — Expressed either in pixels or a percentage of available screen space

◆ **MultiLength** — When multiple elements are competing for space, it is allocated first by pixel and percentage lengths, and then the remaining space is divided by relative length values, which are integers assigned to relative lengths.

Content types (MIME types)

Content type specifies in what form a linked resource is available. Examples include `text/html` and `video/mpeg`.

Language codes

Language codes identify the natural language spoken or written by a specific group of people.

Cross-Reference   See Appendix F for a complete language code list.

Character encodings

Character encoding defines how streams of data are converted to character sets, and is an integral part of HTML data transmission.

Link types

Link types are used by authors to convey a variety of information to user agents. Examples include `alternate` and `stylesheet`.

Media descriptors

Media descriptors are recognized methods of sharing data. Examples include `tty`, `tv`, `print`, and `braille`.

Script data

Script data is passed along by the user agent as data to the script engine, rather than interpeted as HTML data.

Style sheet data

Style sheet data is data that refers to a specific style sheet for data-formatting purposes, and should not be interpreted by the user agent as HTML data.

Frame target names

Frame target names must begin with an alphabetic character, with the following reserved exceptions:

_blank

_parent

_self

_top

✦   ✦   ✦

HTML 4 Elements Reference

This appendix provides a reference guide to all the elements and attributes defined in the HTML 4.01 strict, transitional, and frameset flavors. Deprecated elements and attributes are noted. Deprecated attributes and elements are outdated by newer constructs, mostly by style sheets. Deprecated elements may also become obsolete in future versions of HTML, however user agents should continue to support deprecated elements for reasons of backward compatibility. Style sheets should be used to achieve stylistic and formatting effects instead of the older HTML presentational attributes.

Optional attributes are not required. If you do not specify a value, these attributes will take on the default or previously defined value.

Attributes labeled scripts enable authors to create dynamic Web pages that react while users fill them out; however, when it says script next to an attribute this does not imply a specific scripting language, like JavaScript, or Visual Basic.

The difference between elements and attributes is that element names are written in uppercase letters (BODY, for example), whereas attribute names are written in lowercase letters (lang, and onmouseover, for example). In HTML, element and attribute names are case insensitive. See Appendix C for an explanation of attributes and their permissible values.

Note Intrinsic events are defined at the end of this appendix.

A

PURPOSE	Inserts a hyperlink
TYPE	Inline
NESTED WITHIN	BODY
START TAG	Required
END TAG	Required
CONTENT	Contains inline elements and text
ATTRIBUTES	id = "name" (OPTIONAL)
	type = "content" (OPTIONAL)
	name = "link end" (OPTIONAL)
	class = "name" (OPTIONAL)
	style = "style" (OPTIONAL)
	title = "name" (OPTIONAL)
	lang = "language" (OPTIONAL)
	dir = (rtl, ltr) (OPTIONAL)
	accesskey = "character" (OPTIONAL)
	shape = "image maps" (OPTIONAL)
	coords = "image maps" (OPTIONAL)
	charset = "charset" (OPTIONAL)
	href = "url" (OPTIONAL)
	hreflang = "langcode" (OPTIONAL)
	rel = "link-type" (OPTIONAL)
	rev = "link-type" (OPTIONAL)
	tabindex = "number" (OPTIONAL)
	target = "(_blank, _self, _parent, _top, or name)" (OPTIONAL)
	onclick = "script" (OPTIONAL)
	ondblclick = "script" (OPTIONAL)
	onkeydown = "script" (OPTIONAL)
	onkeypress = "script" (OPTIONAL)
	onkeyup = "script" (OPTIONAL)
	onmousedown = "script" (OPTIONAL)
	onmousemove = "script" (OPTIONAL)
	onmouseover = "script" (OPTIONAL)
	onmouseout = "script" (OPTIONAL)
	onmouseup = "script" (OPTIONAL)
	onblur = "script" (OPTIONAL)
	onfocus = "script" (OPTIONAL)
EXAMPLE	`<A href = "http://www.yahoo.com">` `Yahoo!</A>`
TIP	Make sure you surround the URL with quotation marks.

ABBR

PURPOSE	Indicates an abbreviation
TYPE	Inline
NESTED WITHIN	Any `block` element
START TAG	Required
END TAG	Required
CONTENT	Text
ATTRIBUTES	id = "name" (OPTIONAL)
	class = "name" (OPTIONAL)
	style = "style" (OPTIONAL)
	title = "name" (OPTIONAL)
	lang = "language" (OPTIONAL)
	dir = (rtl, ltr) (OPTIONAL)
	onclick = "script" (OPTIONAL)
	ondblclick = "script" (OPTIONAL)
	onkeydown = "script" (OPTIONAL)
	onkeypress = "script" (OPTIONAL)
	onkeyup = "script" (OPTIONAL)
	onmouseover = "script" (OPTIONAL)
	onmouseout = "script" (OPTIONAL)
	onmousedown = "script" (OPTIONAL)
	onmousemove = "script" (OPTIONAL)
	onmouseup = "script" (OPTIONAL)
EXAMPLE	`<ABBR title = "Incorporated">Inc.</ABBR>`
TIP	Use the `title` attribute so users can see what the spelled-out version of the abbreviation looks like.

ACRONYM

PURPOSE	Indicates an acronym
TYPE	Inline
NESTED WITHIN	Any `BLOCK` element
START TAG	Required
END TAG	Required
CONTENT	Text
ATTRIBUTES	id = "name" (OPTIONAL)
	class = "name" (OPTIONAL)
	style = "style" (OPTIONAL)
	title = "name" (OPTIONAL)
	lang = "language" (OPTIONAL)

dir = (rtl, ltr) (OPTIONAL)
onclick = "script" (OPTIONAL)
ondblclick = "script" (OPTIONAL)
onkeydown = "script" (OPTIONAL)
onkeypress = "script" (OPTIONAL)
onkeyup = "script" (OPTIONAL)
onmouseover = "script" (OPTIONAL)
onmouseout = "script" (OPTIONAL)
onmousedown = "script" (OPTIONAL)
onmousemove = "script" (OPTIONAL)
onmouseup = "script" (OPTIONAL)

EXAMPLE   `<ACRONYM = "World Wide Web">WWW</ACRONYM>`

TIP   Use the `title` attribute so users can see what the spelled-out version of the acronym looks like.

ADDRESS

PURPOSE   Provides information about the author

TYPE   Inline

NESTED WITHIN   Any `BLOCK` element

START TAG   Required

END TAG   Required

CONTENT   Text

ATTRIBUTES   id = "name" (OPTIONAL)
class = "name" (OPTIONAL)
style = "style" (OPTIONAL)
title = "name" (OPTIONAL)
lang = "language" (OPTIONAL)
dir = (rtl, ltr) (OPTIONAL)
onclick = "script" (OPTIONAL)
ondblclick = "script" (OPTIONAL)
onkeydown = "script" (OPTIONAL)
onkeypress = "script" (OPTIONAL)
onkeyup = "script" (OPTIONAL)
onmouseover = "script" (OPTIONAL)
onmouseout = "script" (OPTIONAL)
onmousedown = "script" (OPTIONAL)
onmousemove = "script" (OPTIONAL)
onmouseup = "script" (OPTIONAL)

EXAMPLE   `<ADDRESS>John Doe (<A
HREF="mailto:jd@bogus.org>
jd@bogus.org</A>)</ADDRESS>`

TIP   Place this element at the bottom of your page to indicate who's responsible for its maintenance. Use a mailto URL (as shown) to incorporate a clickable e-mail link. Usually rendered in italics.

APPLET (Deprecated)

PURPOSE	Incorporates a Java applet
TYPE	Inline
NESTED WITHIN	BODY element
START TAG	Required
END TAG	Required
CONTENT	None
ATTRIBUTES	id = "name" (OPTIONAL)
	class = "name" (OPTIONAL)
	style = "style" (OPTIONAL)
	title = "name" (OPTIONAL)
	archive = "CDATA" (OPTIONAL)
	code = "CDATA" (REQUIRED)
	codebase = "url" (OPTIONAL)
	object = "CDATA" (OPTIONAL)
	alt = "text" (OPTIONAL)
	name = "CDATA" (OPTIONAL)
	width = "length" (REQUIRED)
	height = "length" (REQUIRED)
	align = "(top, middle, bottom, left, right)"
	hspace = "pixels"
	vspace = "pixels"

EXAMPLE

```
<APPLET code = "tic-tac-toe.class" width="500
height = "500">Play tic-tac-toe!</APPLET>
```

TIP   To conform to the strict flavor of HTML 4, use the OBJECT element instead.

AREA

PURPOSE	Defines regions in a client-side imagemap
TYPE	Inline
NESTED WITHIN	MAP element
START TAG	Required
END TAG	Forbidden

CONTENT	Empty
ATTRIBUTES	id = "name" (OPTIONAL) class = "name" (OPTIONAL) lang = "language" (OPTIONAL) dir = (rtl, ltr) (OPTIONAL) style = "style" (OPTIONAL) title = "name" (OPTIONAL) shape = "(rect, circle, poly, default)" (OPTIONAL) coords = "comma-separated list of lengths" (OPTIONAL) href = "url" (OPTIONAL) nohref (OPTIONAL) alt = "text" (REQUIRED) tabindex = "number" (OPTIONAL) accesskey = "character" (OPTIONAL) onclick = "script" (OPTIONAL) ondblclick = "script" (OPTIONAL) onkeydown = "script" (OPTIONAL) onkeypress = "script" (OPTIONAL) onkeyup = "script" (OPTIONAL) onmousedown = "script" (OPTIONAL) onmouseover = "script" (OPTIONAL) onmouseout = "script" (OPTIONAL) onmousemove = "script" (OPTIONAL) onmouseup = "script" (OPTIONAL) onblur = "script" (OPTIONAL) onfocus = "script" (OPTIONAL)

EXAMPLE

```
<MAP name = "mymap">
<AREA href = "page1.html"
     alt = "Page 1"
     shape = "circle"
     coords = "184,200,60"
</AREA>
</MAP>
```

TIP　The code for client-side imagemaps is generated by imagemap editors.

B

PURPOSE	Bold emphasis
TYPE	Inline
NESTED WITHIN	Any BLOCK element
START TAG	Required

END TAG	Required
CONTENT	Text
ATTRIBUTES	id = "name" (OPTIONAL)
	class = "name" (OPTIONAL)
	lang = "language" (OPTIONAL)
	dir = (rtl, ltr) (OPTIONAL)
	style = "style" (OPTIONAL)
	title = "name" (OPTIONAL)
	onclick = "script" (OPTIONAL)
	ondblclick = "script" (OPTIONAL)
	onkeydown = "script" (OPTIONAL)
	onkeypress = "script" (OPTIONAL)
	onkeyup = "script" (OPTIONAL)
	onmouseover = "script" (OPTIONAL)
	onmouseout = "script" (OPTIONAL)
	onmousedown = "script" (OPTIONAL)
	onmousemove = "script" (OPTIONAL)
	onmouseup = "script" (OPTIONAL)
EXAMPLE	`<B>Text in bold</B>`
TIP	Be careful to close this element properly.

BASE

PURPOSE	Specifies an absolute URL to use as the basis for resolving relative URLs in your document
TYPE	inline
NESTED WITHIN	HEAD element
START TAG	Required
END TAG	Forbidden
CONTENT	Empty
ATTRIBUTES	href = "url"
	target = "(_blank, self, parent, top, or frame name)"
EXAMPLE	`<BASE = "www.myserver.org/myhome/">`
TIP	Always use relative URLs within your document and specify the base with this element. You can then move your document easily by making one change (to the BASE element).

BASEFONT (Deprecated)

PURPOSE	Sets the default font, font size, and color for the entire document
TYPE	Inline
NESTED WITHIN	BODY
START TAG	Required
END TAG	Forbidden
CONTENT	Empty
ATTRIBUTES	id = "name" (OPTIONAL) size = "CDATA" (OPTIONAL) color = "color" (OPTIONAL) face = "CDATA" (OPTIONAL) class = "name" (OPTIONAL) lang = "language" (OPTIONAL) dir = (rtl, ltr) (OPTIONAL) style = "style" (OPTIONAL) title = "name" (OPTIONAL)
EXAMPLE	`<BASEFONT face = "Helvetica" color = "silver" size = "4">`
TIP	You can change the font locally using the FONT element.

BDO

PURPOSE	Overrides the default text direction
TYPE	Inline
NESTED WITHIN	Any BLOCK element
START TAG	Required
END TAG	Required
CONTENT	Text
ATTRIBUTES	id = "name" (OPTIONAL) class = "name" (OPTIONAL) style = "style" (OPTIONAL) title = "name" (OPTIONAL) lang = "language" (OPTIONAL) dir = (rtl, ltr) (REQUIRED)
EXAMPLE	`<BDO dir = "ltr">Here's some English amidst a language requiring right-to-left presentation.</BDO>`
TIP	You can set the whole document's text direction using the dir attribute in the HTML element.

BIG

PURPOSE	Displays text in a large font
TYPE	Inline
NESTED WITHIN	Any BLOCK element
START TAG	Required
END TAG	Required
CONTENT	Text
ATTRIBUTES	id = "name" (OPTIONAL)
	class = "name" (OPTIONAL)
	style = "style" (OPTIONAL)
	title = "name" (OPTIONAL)
	lang = "language" (OPTIONAL)
	dir = (rtl, ltr) (OPTIONAL)
	onclick = "script" (OPTIONAL)
	ondblclick = "script" (OPTIONAL)
	onkeydown = "script" (OPTIONAL)
	onkeypress = "script" (OPTIONAL)
	onkeyup = "script" (OPTIONAL)
	onmousedown = "script" (OPTIONAL)
	onmousemove = "script" (OPTIONAL)
	onmouseup = "script" (OPTIONAL)
	onmouseover = "script" (OPTIONAL)
	onmouseout = "script" (OPTIONAL)
EXAMPLE	`<BIG>Text in a large font</BIG>`
TIP	Be careful to close this element properly.

BLOCKQUOTE

PURPOSE	Indents an extended quotation
TYPE	Block
NESTED WITHIN	BODY element
START TAG	Required
END TAG	Required
CONTENT	Text
ATTRIBUTES	id = "name" (OPTIONAL)
	class = "name" (OPTIONAL)
	style = "style" (OPTIONAL)
	title = "name" (OPTIONAL)
	lang = "language" (OPTIONAL)
	dir = (rtl, ltr) (OPTIONAL)
	cite = "url" (OPTIONAL)

onclick = "script" (OPTIONAL)
ondblclick = "script" (OPTIONAL)
onkeydown = "script" (OPTIONAL)
onkeypress = "script" (OPTIONAL)
onkeyup = "script" (OPTIONAL)
onmousedown = "script" (OPTIONAL)
onmousemove = "script" (OPTIONAL)
onmouseup = "script" (OPTIONAL)
onmouseover = "script" (OPTIONAL)
onmouseout = "script" (OPTIONAL)

EXAMPLE   `<BLOCKQUOTE>Here's a long quotation.`
`</BLOCKQUOTE>`

TIP   You can use the Q element for inline quotations.

BODY

PURPOSE   Provides a container for all the text and elements that appear onscreen within the browser window

TYPE   Block

NESTED WITHIN   HTML element

START TAG   Optional

END TAG   Optional

CONTENT   Block elements

ATTRIBUTES   Strict DTD:
id = "name" (OPTIONAL)
class = "name" (OPTIONAL)
style = "CSS style definition" (OPTIONAL)
title = "name" (OPTIONAL)
lang = "language code" (OPTIONAL)
dir = (rtl, ltr) (OPTIONAL)

Transitional DTD (deprecated)
background = "url" (OPTIONAL)
text = "color" (OPTIONAL)
link = "color" (OPTIONAL)
vlink = "color" (OPTIONAL)
alink = "color" (OPTIONAL)
onclick = "script" (OPTIONAL)
ondblclick = "script" (OPTIONAL)
onkeydown = "script" (OPTIONAL)
onkeypress = "script" (OPTIONAL)
onkeyup = "script" (OPTIONAL)
onmousedown = "script" (OPTIONAL)
onmousemove = "script" (OPTIONAL)
onmouseup = "script" (OPTIONAL)

onload = "script" (OPTIONAL)
onunload = "script" (OPTIONAL)
onmouseover = "script" (OPTIONAL)
onmouseout = "script" (OPTIONAL)

NOTE	Although the BODY tags are optional, you shouldn't omit them.

EXAMPLE	`<BODY>`
	`<H1>Sailing the Southern Chesapeake Bay</H1>`
	`</BODY>`

TIP	Use substantive title words to increase chance of detection by Web search engines.

BR

PURPOSE	Inserts a line break at the element's position
TYPE	Inline
NESTED WITHIN	BODY
START TAG	Required
END TAG	Forbidden
CONTENT	Empty (no content permitted)
ATTRIBUTES	Strict DTD: id = "name" (OPTIONAL) class = "name" (OPTIONAL) style = "style" (OPTIONAL) title = "name" (OPTIONAL) Transitional DTD: clear = "(none, left, right, all)"
EXAMPLE	`I will put a line break  ` `here.`
DON'T FORGET	Enter blank lines with ` `, not `<P>`.

BUTTON

PURPOSE	Creates a button with definable text on the button face
TYPE	Inline
NESTED WITHIN	FORM element
START TAG	Required
END TAG	Required
CONTENT	Text (displayed on button face)

ATTRIBUTES	id = "name" (OPTIONAL)
	class = "name" (OPTIONAL)
	style = "style" (OPTIONAL)
	title = "name" (OPTIONAL)
	lang = "language" (OPTIONAL)
	dir = (rtl, ltr) (OPTIONAL)
	name = "CDATA" (OPTIONAL)
	value = "CDATA" (OPTIONAL)
	type = "(button, submit, reset)" (OPTIONAL)
	disabled (OPTIONAL)
	tabindex = "number" (OPTIONAL)
	accesskey = "character" (OPTIONAL)
	onclick = "script" (OPTIONAL)
	ondblclick = "script" (OPTIONAL)
	onkeydown = "script" (OPTIONAL)
	onkeypress = "script" (OPTIONAL)
	onkeyup = "script" (OPTIONAL)
	onmousedown = "script" (OPTIONAL)
	onmousemove = "script" (OPTIONAL)
	onmouseup = "script" (OPTIONAL)
	onblur = "script" (OPTIONAL)
	onfocus = "script" (OPTIONAL)
	onmouseover = "script" (OPTIONAL)
	onmouseout = "script" (OPTIONAL)
EXAMPLE	`<BUTTON type = "submit" name = "submit">Send It!</BUTTON>`
TIP	If you want to specify the text on the button face, use this element instead of `INPUT`.

CAPTION

PURPOSE	Creates a caption for a table
TYPE	Inline
NESTED WITHIN	`TABLE` element
START TAG	Required
END TAG	Required
CONTENT	Text
ATTRIBUTES	Strict DTD:
	id = "name" (OPTIONAL)
	class = "name" (OPTIONAL)
	style = "style" (OPTIONAL)
	title = "name" (OPTIONAL)

lang = "language" (OPTIONAL)
dir = (rtl, ltr) (OPTIONAL)
onclick = "script" (OPTIONAL)
ondblclick = "script" (OPTIONAL)
onkeydown = "script" (OPTIONAL)
onkeypress = "script" (OPTIONAL)
onkeyup = "script" (OPTIONAL)
onmousedown = "script" (OPTIONAL)
onmousemove = "script" (OPTIONAL)
onmouseup = "script" (OPTIONAL)
onmouseover = "script" (OPTIONAL)
onmouseout = "script" (OPTIONAL)

Transitional DTD:
align = "(top, bottom, left, right)"

EXAMPLE
`<CAPTION>Table 19.3 Expected vs. Actual Values</CAPTION>`

TIP
You must use this immediately after the TABLE element's start tag. You can specify only one caption per table.

CENTER (Deprecated)

PURPOSE   Centers the text enclosed within the tags

TYPE   Inline

NESTED WITHIN   Any BLOCK element

START TAG   Required

END TAG   Required

CONTENT   Text

ATTRIBUTES   id = "name" (OPTIONAL)
class = "name" (OPTIONAL)
style = "style" (OPTIONAL)
title = "name" (OPTIONAL)
lang = "language" (OPTIONAL)
dir = (rtl, ltr) (OPTIONAL)
onclick = "script" (OPTIONAL)
ondblclick = "script" (OPTIONAL)
onkeydown = "script" (OPTIONAL)
onkeypress = "script" (OPTIONAL)
onkeyup = "script" (OPTIONAL)
onmousedown = "script" (OPTIONAL)
onmousemove = "script" (OPTIONAL)
onmouseup = "script" (OPTIONAL)

onmouseover = "script" (OPTIONAL)
onmouseout = "script" (OPTIONAL)

EXAMPLE	`<CENTER>This text is centered.</CENTER>`
TIP	Use `DIV align = "center"` instead, or style sheets.

CITE

PURPOSE	Marks a cited work
TYPE	Inline
NESTED WITHIN	Any `BLOCK` element
START TAG	Required
END TAG	Required
CONTENT	Text
ATTRIBUTES	id = "name" (OPTIONAL)
	class = "name" (OPTIONAL)
	style = "style" (OPTIONAL)
	title = "name" (OPTIONAL)
	lang = "language" (OPTIONAL)
	dir = (rtl, ltr) (OPTIONAL)
	onclick = "script" (OPTIONAL)
	ondblclick = "script" (OPTIONAL)
	onkeydown = "script" (OPTIONAL)
	onkeypress = "script" (OPTIONAL)
	onkeyup = "script" (OPTIONAL)
	onmousedown = "script" (OPTIONAL)
	onmousemove = "script" (OPTIONAL)
	onmouseup = "script" (OPTIONAL)
	onmouseover = "script" (OPTIONAL)
	onmouseout = "script" (OPTIONAL)
EXAMPLE	`<CITE>Leaves of Grass</CITE> by Walt Whitman`
TIP	Usually rendered in italics.

CODE

PURPOSE	Identifies text as computer code
TYPE	Inline
NESTED WITHIN	Any `BLOCK` element
START TAG	Required
END TAG	Required
CONTENT	Text

ATTRIBUTES   id = "name" (OPTIONAL)
class = "name" (OPTIONAL)
style = "style" (OPTIONAL)
title = "name" (OPTIONAL)
lang = "language" (OPTIONAL)
dir = (rtl, ltr) (OPTIONAL)
onclick = "script" (OPTIONAL)
ondblclick = "script" (OPTIONAL)
onkeydown = "script" (OPTIONAL)
onkeypress = "script" (OPTIONAL)
onkeyup = "script" (OPTIONAL)
onmousedown = "script" (OPTIONAL)
onmousemove = "script" (OPTIONAL)
onmouseup = "script" (OPTIONAL)
onmouseover = "script" (OPTIONAL)
onmouseout = "script" (OPTIONAL)

EXAMPLE   `<CODE>dowhile book-done = "no"</CODE>`

TIP   Usually rendered in a monospace font and indistinguishable from KBD, SAMP, TT, and VAR.

COL

PURPOSE   Identifies individual columns so you can assign attributes to them

TYPE   Block

NESTED WITHIN   COLGROUP element

START TAG   Required

END TAG   Forbidden

CONTENT   Empty

ATTRIBUTES   id = "name" (OPTIONAL)
class = "name" (OPTIONAL)
style = "style" (OPTIONAL)
title = "name" (OPTIONAL)
lang = "language" (OPTIONAL)
dir = (rtl, ltr) (OPTIONAL)
span = "number" (OPTIONAL)
width = "lengths" (OPTIONAL)
cellhalign = "horizontal alignment" (OPTIONAL)
cellvalign = "vertical alignment" (OPTIONAL)
align = "cell alignment" (OPTIONAL)
char = cell alignment (OPTIONAL)
charoff = cell alignment (OPTIONAL)
valign = cell alignment (OPTIONAL)
onclick = "script" (OPTIONAL)
ondblclick = "script" (OPTIONAL)

onkeydown = "script" (OPTIONAL)
onkeypress = "script" (OPTIONAL)
onkeyup = "script" (OPTIONAL)
onmousedown = "script" (OPTIONAL)
onmousemove = "script" (OPTIONAL)
onmouseup = "script" (OPTIONAL)
onmouseover = "script" (OPTIONAL)
onmouseout = "script" (OPTIONAL)

EXAMPLE   `<COL width = 20 span = 3>`

TIP   This is an empty element that contains attributes only. To create columns, specify TD elements within a TR element.

COLGROUP

PURPOSE   Groups columns and sets default alignments

TYPE   Inline

NESTED WITHIN   TABLE element

START TAG   Required

END TAG   Required

CONTENT   Empty

ATTRIBUTES   id = "name" (OPTIONAL)
class = "name" (OPTIONAL)
style = "style" (OPTIONAL)
title = "name" (OPTIONAL)
lang = "language" (OPTIONAL)
dir = (rtl, ltr) (OPTIONAL)
span = "number" (OPTIONAL>
width = "lengths" (OPTIONAL)
align = "(left, center, right, justify, char)"
char = "character"
charoff = "length"
valign = "(top, middle, bottom, baseline)"
onclick = "script" (OPTIONAL)
ondblclick = "script" (OPTIONAL)
onkeydown = "script" (OPTIONAL)
onkeypress = "script" (OPTIONAL)
onkeyup = "script" (OPTIONAL)
onmousedown = "script" (OPTIONAL)
onmousemove = "script" (OPTIONAL)
onmouseup = "script" (OPTIONAL)
onmouseover = "script" (OPTIONAL)
onmouseout = "script" (OPTIONAL)

EXAMPLE   `<COLGROUP width = 20 span = 3>`

TIP   This is an empty element that contains attributes only. To create columns, specify `TD` elements within a `TR` element. To define the attributes of individual columns and override `COLGROUP`, use `COL`.

DD

PURPOSE   Identifies a definition in a definition list

TYPE   Block

NESTED WITHIN   `DL` element

START TAG   Required

END TAG   Optional

CONTENT   Text and inline elements

ATTRIBUTES   id = "name" (OPTIONAL)
                 class = "name" (OPTIONAL)
                 style = "style" (OPTIONAL)
                 title = "name" (OPTIONAL)
                 lang = "language" (OPTIONAL)
                 dir = (rtl, ltr) (OPTIONAL)
                 onclick = "script" (OPTIONAL)
                 ondblclick = "script" (OPTIONAL)
                 onkeydown = "script" (OPTIONAL)
                 onkeypress = "script" (OPTIONAL)
                 onkeyup = "script" (OPTIONAL)
                 onmousedown = "script" (OPTIONAL)
                 onmousemove = "script" (OPTIONAL)
                 onmouseup = "script" (OPTIONAL)
                 onmouseover = "script" (OPTIONAL)
                 onmouseout = "script" (OPTIONAL)

EXAMPLE   `<DD>Here is the definition of the term.</DD>`

TIP   Use `DD` within a `DL` list. For the term, use `DT`.

DEL

PURPOSE   Indicates deleted text in a legal or political document

TYPE   Inline

NESTED WITHIN   Any `BLOCK` element

START TAG   Required

END TAG   Required

CONTENT	Text and inline elements (no block elements permitted)
ATTRIBUTES	id = "name" (OPTIONAL) class = "name" (OPTIONAL) style = "style" (OPTIONAL) title = "name" (OPTIONAL) lang = "language" (OPTIONAL) dir = (rtl, ltr) (OPTIONAL) cite = "url" (OPTIONAL) datetime = "YYYYMMDD" onclick = "script" (OPTIONAL) ondblclick = "script" (OPTIONAL) onkeydown = "script" (OPTIONAL) onkeypress = "script" (OPTIONAL) onkeyup = "script" (OPTIONAL) onmousedown = "script" (OPTIONAL) onmousemove = "script" (OPTIONAL) onmouseup = "script" (OPTIONAL) onmouseover = "script" (OPTIONAL) onmouseout = "script" (OPTIONAL)
EXAMPLE	`We can support <DEL>10</DEL><INS>12</INS>` `positions.`
TIP	Use `INS` to show what's inserted in place of the deleted text.

DFN

PURPOSE	Indicates the defining instance of a term
TYPE	Inline
NESTED WITHIN	Any `BLOCK` element
START TAG	Required
END TAG	Required
CONTENT	Text
ATTRIBUTES	id = "name" (OPTIONAL) class = "name" (OPTIONAL) style = "style" (OPTIONAL) title = "name" (OPTIONAL) lang = "language" (OPTIONAL) dir = (rtl, ltr) (OPTIONAL) onclick = "script" (OPTIONAL) ondblclick = "script" (OPTIONAL) onkeydown = "script" (OPTIONAL) onkeypress = "script" (OPTIONAL)

	onkeyup = "script" (OPTIONAL)
	onmousedown = "script" (OPTIONAL)
	onmousemove = "script" (OPTIONAL)
	onmouseup = "script" (OPTIONAL)
	onmouseover = "script" (OPTIONAL)
	onmouseout = "script" (OPTIONAL)
EXAMPLE	`<DFN>anime</DFN>` refers to a distinctive Japanese tradition of cartoon animation.
TIP	Use DL, DD, and DT for a definition list.

DIR (Deprecated)

PURPOSE	This element was originally intended for multicolumn directory listings, but browsers render it as an unordered list (UL)
TYPE	block
NESTED WITHIN	BODY
START TAG	Required
END TAG	Required
CONTENT	Text and inline elements
ATTRIBUTES	id = "name" (OPTIONAL)
	class = "name" (OPTIONAL)
	style = "style" (OPTIONAL)
	title = "name" (OPTIONAL)
	lang = "language" (OPTIONAL)
	dir = (rtl, ltr) (OPTIONAL)
	onclick = "script" (OPTIONAL)
	ondblclick = "script" (OPTIONAL)
	onkeydown = "script" (OPTIONAL)
	onkeypress = "script" (OPTIONAL)
	onkeyup = "script" (OPTIONAL)
	onmousedown = "script" (OPTIONAL)
	onmousemove = "script" (OPTIONAL)
	onmouseup = "script" (OPTIONAL)
	onmouseover = "script" (OPTIONAL)
	onmouseout = "script" (OPTIONAL)

EXAMPLE

```
<DIR>
<LI>Item 1
<LI>Item 2
<LI>Item 3
</DIR>
```

TIP   Use UL instead.

DIV

PURPOSE	Provides a means for grouping elements and assigning attributes to the group
TYPE	Block
NESTED WITHIN	BODY
START TAG	Required
END TAG	Required
CONTENT	Block elements
ATTRIBUTES	id = "name" (OPTIONAL) class = "name" (OPTIONAL) style = "style" (OPTIONAL) title = "name" (OPTIONAL) lang = "language" (OPTIONAL) dir = (rtl, ltr) (OPTIONAL) onclick = "script" (OPTIONAL) ondblclick = "script" (OPTIONAL) onkeydown = "script" (OPTIONAL) onkeypress = "script" (OPTIONAL) onkeyup = "script" (OPTIONAL) onmousedown = "script" (OPTIONAL) onmousemove = "script" (OPTIONAL) onmouseup = "script" (OPTIONAL) onmouseover = "script" (OPTIONAL) onmouseout = "script" (OPTIONAL)

EXAMPLE	`<DIV>`
	`<H1>Heading</H1>`
	`<P>Paragraph 1</P>`
	`</DIV>`

TIP	Use SPAN to group inline elements. Note, browsers generally place a line break before a DIV element, but impose no other presentation attributes.

DL

PURPOSE	Creates a definition list
TYPE	Block
NESTED WITHIN	DL element
START TAG	Required
END TAG	Required
CONTENT	Text and inline elements

ATTRIBUTES	id = "name" (OPTIONAL)
	class = "name" (OPTIONAL)
	style = "style" (OPTIONAL)
	title = "name" (OPTIONAL)
	lang = "language" (OPTIONAL)
	dir = (rtl, ltr) (OPTIONAL)
	onclick = "script" (OPTIONAL)
	ondblclick = "script" (OPTIONAL)
	onkeydown = "script" (OPTIONAL)
	onkeypress = "script" (OPTIONAL)
	onkeyup = "script" (OPTIONAL)
	onmousedown = "script" (OPTIONAL)
	onmousemove = "script" (OPTIONAL)
	onmouseup = "script" (OPTIONAL)
	onmouseover = "script" (OPTIONAL)
	onmouseout = "script" (OPTIONAL)

EXAMPLE

```
<DL>
<DT>term 1
<DD>definition of term 1
</DL>
```

TIP   Use DT within a DL list. Use DD for the definition.

DT

PURPOSE	In a definition list, identifies a defined term
TYPE	Block
NESTED WITHIN	DL element
START TAG	Required
END TAG	Optional
CONTENT	Text and inline elements
ATTRIBUTES	id = "name" (OPTIONAL)
	class = "name" (OPTIONAL)
	style = "style" (OPTIONAL)
	title = "name" (OPTIONAL)
	lang = "language" (OPTIONAL)
	dir = (rtl, ltr) (OPTIONAL)
	onclick = "script" (OPTIONAL)
	ondblclick = "script" (OPTIONAL)
	onkeydown = "script" (OPTIONAL)
	onkeypress = "script" (OPTIONAL)
	onkeyup = "script" (OPTIONAL)
	onmousedown = "script" (OPTIONAL)
	onmousemove = "script" (OPTIONAL)

onmouseup = "script" (OPTIONAL)
onmouseover = "script" (OPTIONAL)
onmouseout = "script" (OPTIONAL)

EXAMPLE	`<DT>antidisestablishmentarianism</DT>`
TIP	Use `DT` within a `DL` list. Use `DD` for the definition.

EM

PURPOSE	Marks text for emphasis
TYPE	Inline
NESTED WITHIN	Any `BLOCK` element
START TAG	Required
END TAG	Required
CONTENT	Text
ATTRIBUTES	id = "name" (OPTIONAL)
	class = "name" (OPTIONAL)
	style = "style" (OPTIONAL)
	title = "name" (OPTIONAL)
	lang = "language" (OPTIONAL)
	dir = (rtl, ltr) (OPTIONAL)
	onclick = "script" (OPTIONAL)
	ondblclick = "script" (OPTIONAL)
	onkeydown = "script" (OPTIONAL)
	onkeypress = "script" (OPTIONAL)
	onkeyup = "script" (OPTIONAL)
	onmousedown = "script" (OPTIONAL)
	onmousemove = "script" (OPTIONAL)
	onmouseup = "script" (OPTIONAL)
	onmouseover = "script" (OPTIONAL)
	onmouseout = "script" (OPTIONAL)
	onmouseover = "script" (OPTIONAL)
	onmouseout = "script" (OPTIONAL)
EXAMPLE	`Do this <EM>right now</EM>.`
TIP	Usually rendered in italics.

FIELDSET

PURPOSE	In a form, groups thematically related elements
TYPE	Block
NESTED WITHIN	`BODY` element
START TAG	Required

END TAG	Required
CONTENT	Contains HTML elements and text
ATTRIBUTES	Strict DTD:

id = "name" (OPTIONAL)
class = "name" (OPTIONAL)
style = "CSS style definition" (OPTIONAL)
title = "name" (OPTIONAL)
lang = "language code" (OPTIONAL)
dir = (rtl, ltr) (OPTIONAL)
onclick = "script" (OPTIONAL)
ondblclick = "script" (OPTIONAL)
onkeydown = "script" (OPTIONAL)
onkeypress = "script" (OPTIONAL)
onkeyup = "script" (OPTIONAL)
onmousedown = "script" (OPTIONAL)
onmousemove = "script" (OPTIONAL)
onmouseup = "script" (OPTIONAL)
onmouseover = "script" (OPTIONAL)
onmouseout = "script" (OPTIONAL)

EXAMPLE

```
<FORM>
<FIELDSET>
   <LEGEND>Title of Subsection of Form</LEGEND>
   <INPUT>
   <INPUT>
   <INPUT>
</FIELDSET>
</FORM>
```

TIP Use LEGEND to provide a title for the group.

FONT (Deprecated)

PURPOSE	Defines presentation styles for fonts
TYPE	Inline
NESTED WITHIN	Any BLOCK element
START TAG	Required
END TAG	Required
CONTENT	Text and other inline elements
ATTRIBUTES	id = "name" (OPTIONAL)

class = "name" (OPTIONAL)
style = "style" (OPTIONAL)
title = "name" (OPTIONAL)
lang = "language" (OPTIONAL)

dir = (rtl, ltr) (OPTIONAL)
size = "CDATA " (OPTIONAL)
color = "color" (OPTIONAL)
face = "CDATA" (OPTIONAL)

EXAMPLE   `<FONT face = "Times Roman" size = "5">`

TIP   Define font presentation styles with style sheets.

FORM

PURPOSE   Creates a form for user input

TYPE   Block

NESTED WITHIN   `BODY`

START TAG   Required

END TAG   Required

CONTENT   `INPUT` and `SELECT` elements; text

ATTRIBUTES   id = "name" (OPTIONAL)
class = "name" (OPTIONAL)
style = "style" (OPTIONAL)
title = "name" (OPTIONAL)
lang = "language" (OPTIONAL)
dir = (rtl, ltr) (OPTIONAL)
action = "url" (REQUIRED)
method = "(get, post)" (default = "get") (OPTIONAL)
enctype = "MIME type" (OPTIONAL)
target = "frame" (OPTIONAL)
name= "name" (OPTIONAL)
accept-charset = "charset" (OPTIONAL)
accept = "MIME type" (OPTIONAL)
onclick = "script" (OPTIONAL)
ondblclick = "script" (OPTIONAL)
onkeydown = "script" (OPTIONAL)
onkeypress = "script" (OPTIONAL)
onkeyup = "script" (OPTIONAL)
onmousedown = "script" (OPTIONAL)
onmousemove = "script" (OPTIONAL)
onmouseup = "script" (OPTIONAL)
onsubmit = "script" (OPTIONAL)
onreset = "script" (OPTIONAL)
onmouseover = "script" (OPTIONAL)
onmouseout = "script" (OPTIONAL)

EXAMPLE	`<FORM action = "script.cgi">`
	`<INPUT type = "text" size = "60" >`
	`</FORM>`

TIP	Forms don't do anything unless the output is directed to a program that can decode and process the submitted information.

FRAME

PURPOSE	Specifies the content and appearance of text loaded into a single frame
TYPE	Inline
NESTED WITHIN	FRAMESET
START TAG	Required
END TAG	Forbidden
CONTENT	Empty
ATTRIBUTES	id = "name" (OPTIONAL) class = "name" (OPTIONAL) style = "style" (OPTIONAL) title = "name" (OPTIONAL) src = "url" (OPTIONAL) longdesc = "url" (OPTIONAL) name = "CDATA" (OPTIONAL) frameborder = "(1, 0)" (OPTIONAL) marginwidth = "pixels" (OPTIONAL) marginheight = "pixels" (OPTIONAL) noresize (OPTIONAL) scrolling = "(yes, no, auto)" (OPTIONAL)

EXAMPLE	`<FRAMESET cols = "15%, *">`
	`<FRAME src = "navaids.htm">`
	`<FRAME src = "page1.htm">`
	`</FRAMESET>`

TIP	Don't use a BODY element on a page containing frame elements or the frames won't work.

FRAMESET

PURPOSE	Defines frame sizes and positions in a framed document
TYPE	N/A
NESTED WITHIN	HTML

START TAG	Required
END TAG	Required
CONTENT	FRAME elements
ATTRIBUTES	id = "name" (OPTIONAL) class = "name" (OPTIONAL) style = "style" (OPTIONAL) title = "name" (OPTIONAL) rows = "comma-separated list of lengths" (OPTIONAL) cols = "comma-separated list of lengths" (OPTIONAL) onload = "script" (OPTIONAL) onunload = "script" (OPTIONAL)

EXAMPLE	`<FRAMESET cols = "15%, *">`
	`<FRAME src = "navaids.htm">`
	`<FRAME src = "page1.htm">`
	`</FRAMESET>`

TIP	Don't use a BODY element on a page containing frame elements or the frames won't work.

H1 through H6

PURPOSE	Marks the enclosed text as a heading, ranging from most prominent (H1) to least prominent (H6)
TYPE	Block
NESTED WITHIN	BODY element
START TAG	Required
END TAG	Required
CONTENT	Contains HTML elements and text
ATTRIBUTES	Strict DTD: id = "name" (OPTIONAL) class = "name" (OPTIONAL) style = "CSS style definition" (OPTIONAL) title = "name" (OPTIONAL) lang = "language code" (OPTIONAL) dir = (rtl, ltr) (OPTIONAL) onclick = "script" (OPTIONAL) ondblclick = "script" (OPTIONAL) onkeydown = "script" (OPTIONAL) onkeypress = "script" (OPTIONAL) onkeyup = "script" (OPTIONAL) onmousedown = "script" (OPTIONAL) onmousemove = "script" (OPTIONAL)

onmouseup = "script" (OPTIONAL)
onmouseover = "script" (OPTIONAL)
onmouseout = "script" (OPTIONAL)

Transitional DTD:
align = "left, center, right, justify" (OPTIONAL)

EXAMPLE   `<H1>This is a major heading</H1>`

TIP   The H1 element appears to be the document's title, so it's
               wise to use it for this purpose. Note, heading levels H4
               through H6 are rarely used.

HEAD

PURPOSE   Demarcates an area containing elements describing the
               document's contents, including the TITLE

NESTED WITHIN HTML element

START TAG   Optional

END TAG   Optional

CONTENT   Can contain the SCRIPT, STYLE, META, LINK, OBJECT,
               TITLE, and BASE elements

ATTRIBUTES   profile = "url" (OPTIONAL)
               lang = "language-code" (OPTIONAL)
               dir = (ltr, rtl) (OPTIONAL)

EXAMPLE   `<HEAD>`
               `<TITLE>Sailing the Southern Chesapeake Bay`
               `</TITLE>`
               `</HEAD>`

TIP   The most important function of the HEAD element is to pro-
               vide a home for the TITLE element.

HTML

PURPOSE   Demarcates the portion of the document containing HTML

NESTED WITHIN None (encloses all other elements)

START TAG   Optional

END TAG   Optional

CONTENT   Contains HTML elements and text

ATTRIBUTES: lang = "language-code" (OPTIONAL)
               dir = (ltr, rtl) (OPTIONAL)

EXAMPLE:	`<HTML>`
	`[all other elements]`
	`</HTML>`

TIP	Although these tags are optional, it's good form to include them.

HR

PURPOSE	Inserts a horizontal rule
TYPE	Inline
NESTED WITHIN	Any `BLOCK` element
START TAG	Required
END TAG	Forbidden
CONTENT	Text and inline elements (no block elements permitted)
ATTRIBUTES	Strict DTD: id = "name" (OPTIONAL) class = "name" (OPTIONAL) style = "style" (OPTIONAL) title = "name" (OPTIONAL) lang = "language" (OPTIONAL) dir = (rtl, ltr) (OPTIONAL) Transitional DTD (deprecated): align = "(left, center, right)" (OPTIONAL) noshade (OPTIONAL) size = "pixels" (OPTIONAL) width = "length" (OPTIONAL) onclick = "script" (OPTIONAL) ondblclick = "script" (OPTIONAL) onkeydown = "script" (OPTIONAL) onkeypress = "script" (OPTIONAL) onkeyup = "script" (OPTIONAL) onmousedown = "script" (OPTIONAL) onmousemove = "script" (OPTIONAL) onmouseup = "script" (OPTIONAL) onmouseover = "script" (OPTIONAL) onmouseout = "script" (OPTIONAL)

EXAMPLE	`<P>A paragraph</P>`
	`<HR>`
	`<P>Another paragraph</P>`

TIP	Use style sheets to assign presentation attributes to rules.

I

PURPOSE	Italic emphasis
TYPE	Inline
NESTED WITHIN	Any BLOCK element
START TAG	Required
END TAG	Required
CONTENT	Text
ATTRIBUTES	id = "name" (OPTIONAL)
	class = "name" (OPTIONAL)
	style = "style" (OPTIONAL)
	title = "name" (OPTIONAL)
	lang = "language" (OPTIONAL)
	dir = (rtl, ltr) (OPTIONAL)
	onclick = "script" (OPTIONAL)
	ondblclick = "script" (OPTIONAL)
	onkeydown = "script" (OPTIONAL)
	onkeypress = "script" (OPTIONAL)
	onkeyup = "script" (OPTIONAL)
	onmousedown = "script" (OPTIONAL)
	onmousemove = "script" (OPTIONAL)
	onmouseup = "script" (OPTIONAL)
	onmouseover = "script" (OPTIONAL)
	onmouseout = "script" (OPTIONAL)
EXAMPLE	`<I>Text in italics</I>`
TIP	Be careful to close this element properly.

IFRAME

PURPOSE	Creates an inline subwindow in which you can insert another document
TYPE	Inline
NESTED WITHIN	Any BLOCK element
START TAG	Required
END TAG	Required
CONTENT	Text and inline elements (no BLOCK elements permitted)
ATTRIBUTES	height = "length" (OPTIONAL)
	width = "length" (OPTIONAL)
	id = "name" (OPTIONAL)

class = "name" (OPTIONAL)
style = "style" (OPTIONAL)
title = "name" (OPTIONAL)
longdesc = "url" (OPTIONAL)
name = "CDATA" (OPTIONAL)
src = "url" (OPTIONAL)
frameborder = "(1,0)" (OPTIONAL)
marginwidth = "pixels" (OPTIONAL)
marginheight = "pixels" (OPTIONAL)
scrolling = "(yes, no, auto)" (OPTIONAL)
align = "(top, middle, bottom, left, right") (OPTIONAL)

EXAMPLE

```
<IFRAME src = "insert.html" width = 200 height
= 300 scrolling = "yes" frameborder = "0">Your
browser doesn't support inline frames. However,
you can visit the <A href = "insert.html">
document </A> that would have been shown here.
```

TIP

Place text to be viewed by browsers that don't support inline frames between the tags. Given the inconsistent implementation of IFRAME, be sure to preview your page in both IFRAME compliant and noncompliant browsers.

IMG

PURPOSE   Inserts a graphic at the tag's location

TYPE   Inline

NESTED WITHIN   BODY

START TAG   Required

END TAG   Forbidden

CONTENT   Empty

ATTRIBUTES   Strict DTD:
                   id = "name" (OPTIONAL)
                   class = "name" (OPTIONAL)
                   style = "style" (OPTIONAL)
                   title = "name" (OPTIONAL)
                   src = "url" (REQUIRED)
                   alt = "CDATA" (REQUIRED)
                   longdesc = "url" (OPTIONAL)
                   usemap = "url" (OPTIONAL)
                   ismap = "ismap" (OPTIONAL)
                   onclick = "script" (OPTIONAL)
                   ondblclick = "script" (OPTIONAL)
                   onkeydown = "script" (OPTIONAL)
                   onkeypress = "script" (OPTIONAL)
                   onkeyup = "script" (OPTIONAL)

onmousedown = "script" (OPTIONAL)
onmousemove = "script" (OPTIONAL)
onmouseup = "script" (OPTIONAL)
onmouseover = "script" (OPTIONAL)
onmouseout = "script" (OPTIONAL)
Name = "CDATA" (OPTIONAL)

Transitional DTD (deprecated):
width = "length" (OPTIONAL)
height = "length" (OPTIONAL)
vspace = "length" (OPTIONAL)
hspace = "length" (OPTIONAL)
lang = "language" (OPTIONAL)
dir = (rtl, ltr) (OPTIONAL)
border = "pixels" (OPTIONAL)
align = "(bottom, middle, top, left, right)" (OPTIONAL)

EXAMPLE

```
<IMG source = "picture.gif" alt = "A picture of
my sailboat.">
```

INPUT

PURPOSE	Accepts user input within a form
TYPE	Inline
NESTED WITHIN	FORM
START TAG	Required
END TAG	Forbidden
CONTENT	Empty
ATTRIBUTES	id = "name" (OPTIONAL)

class = "name" (OPTIONAL)
style = "style" (OPTIONAL)
title = "name" (OPTIONAL)
lang = "language" (OPTIONAL)
dir = (rtl, ltr) (OPTIONAL)
accept = "MIME type" (OPTIONAL)
ismap = "ismap" (OPTIONAL)
type = "(text, password, checkbox, radio, submit, reset,
   file, hidden, image, button)" (REQUIRED)
name = "CDATA" (OPTIONAL)
value = "CDATA" (OPTIONAL)
checked (OPTIONAL)
disabled (OPTIONAL)
readonly (OPTIONAL)
size = "CDATA" (OPTIONAL)
maxlength = "number" (OPTIONAL)
src = "url" (OPTIONAL)

alt = "CDATA" (OPTIONAL)
usemap = "url" (OPTIONAL)
tabindex = "number" (OPTIONAL)
accesskey = "character" (OPTIONAL)

Transitional DTD (deprecated):
align = "(left, center, right)" (OPTIONAL)
onclick = "script" (OPTIONAL)
ondblclick = "script" (OPTIONAL)
onkeydown = "script" (OPTIONAL)
onkeypress = "script" (OPTIONAL)
onkeyup = "script" (OPTIONAL)
onmousedown = "script" (OPTIONAL)
onmousemove = "script" (OPTIONAL)
onmouseup = "script" (OPTIONAL)
onblur = "script" (OPTIONAL)
onfocus = "script" (OPTIONAL)
onchange = "script" (OPTIONAL)
onselect = "script" (OPTIONAL)
onmouseover = "script" (OPTIONAL)
onmouseout = "script" (OPTIONAL)

EXAMPLE	`<INPUT type = "text" size = "60" >`
TIP	Many of the attributes have specific meanings for a given input type. For example, in a text input box, the `size` attribute governs the length of the box displayed on-screen.

INS

PURPOSE	Indicates inserted text in a legal or political document
TYPE	Inline
NESTED WITHIN	Any `BLOCK` element
START TAG	Required
END TAG	Required
CONTENT	Text and inline elements (no `BLOCK` elements permitted)
ATTRIBUTES	id = "name" (OPTIONAL) class = "name" (OPTIONAL) style = "style" (OPTIONAL) title = "name" (OPTIONAL) lang = "language" (OPTIONAL) dir = (rtl, ltr) (OPTIONAL) cite = "url" (OPTIONAL) datetime = "YYYYMMDD" (OPTIONAL) onclick = "script" (OPTIONAL) ondblclick = "script" (OPTIONAL)

onkeydown = "script" (OPTIONAL)
onkeypress = "script" (OPTIONAL)
onkeyup = "script" (OPTIONAL)
onmousedown = "script" (OPTIONAL)
onmousemove = "script" (OPTIONAL)
onmouseup = "script" (OPTIONAL)
onmouseover = "script" (OPTIONAL)
onmouseout = "script" (OPTIONAL)

EXAMPLE	We can support `<DEL>10</DEL><INS>12</INS>` positions.
TIP	Use `DEL` to show what's deleted.

ISINDEX (Deprecated)

PURPOSE	Creates a single-line text input control for server-enabled searches
TYPE	Inline
NESTED WITHIN	Any `BLOCK` element
START TAG	Required
END TAG	Forbidden
CONTENT	Empty
ATTRIBUTES	id = "name" (OPTIONAL) class = "name" (OPTIONAL) style = "style" (OPTIONAL) title = "name" (OPTIONAL) lang = "language" (OPTIONAL) dir = (rtl, ltr) (OPTIONAL) prompt = "text"(OPTIONAL)
EXAMPLE	`<ISINDEX prompt = "Enter your search terms here">`
TIP	Use form elements instead.

KBD

PURPOSE	Displays text to be entered by the user as input
TYPE	Inline
NESTED WITHIN	Any `BLOCK` element
START TAG	Required
END TAG	Required
CONTENT	Text

ATTRIBUTES	id = "name" (OPTIONAL)
	class = "name" (OPTIONAL)
	style = "style" (OPTIONAL)
	title = "name" (OPTIONAL)
	lang = "language" (OPTIONAL)
	dir = (rtl, ltr) (OPTIONAL)
	onclick = "script" (OPTIONAL)
	ondblclick = "script" (OPTIONAL)
	onkeydown = "script" (OPTIONAL)
	onkeypress = "script" (OPTIONAL)
	onkeyup = "script" (OPTIONAL)
	onmousedown = "script" (OPTIONAL)
	onmousemove = "script" (OPTIONAL)
	onmouseup = "script" (OPTIONAL)
	onmouseover = "script" (OPTIONAL)
	onmouseout = "script" (OPTIONAL)
EXAMPLE	In the user name text box, type `<KBD>anonymous</KBD>`.
TIP	Usually rendered in a monospace font and indistinguishable from `CODE`, `SAMP`, `TT`, and `VAR`.

LABEL

PURPOSE	Associates text with a control so when the user passes the mouse pointer over the control, the focus (selection) passes to the associated control
TYPE	Inline
NESTED WITHIN	`FORM`
START TAG	Required
END TAG	Required
CONTENT	Text and Input controls
ATTRIBUTES	id = "name" (OPTIONAL)
	class = "name" (OPTIONAL)
	style = "style" (OPTIONAL)
	title = "name" (OPTIONAL)
	lang = "language" (OPTIONAL)
	dir = (rtl, ltr) (OPTIONAL)
	for = "id of another element" (OPTIONAL)
	accesskey = "character" (OPTIONAL)
	onclick = "script" (OPTIONAL)
	ondblclick = "script" (OPTIONAL)
	onkeydown = "script" (OPTIONAL)
	onkeypress = "script" (OPTIONAL)
	onkeyup = "script" (OPTIONAL)

onmousedown = "script" (OPTIONAL)
onmousemove = "script" (OPTIONAL)
onmouseup = "script" (OPTIONAL)
onblur = "script" (OPTIONAL)
onfocus = "script" (OPTIONAL)
onmouseover = "script" (OPTIONAL)
onmouseout = "script" (OPTIONAL)

EXAMPLE

```
<LABEL>Please type the date (DD/MM/YYYY).
<INPUT type = "text">
</LABEL>
```

TIP

In a table, use the for attribute to specify the ID of the associated control.

LEGEND

PURPOSE

In a form, provides a title for a thematically related group of elements established with the LEGEND element

TYPE

Inline

NESTED WITHIN

LEGEND element

START TAG

Required

END TAG

Required

CONTENT

Contains HTML elements and text

ATTRIBUTES

Strict DTD:
id = "name" (OPTIONAL)
class = "name" (OPTIONAL)
style = "CSS style definition" (OPTIONAL)
title = "name" (OPTIONAL)
lang = "language code" (OPTIONAL)
dir = (rtl, ltr) (OPTIONAL)
accesskey = "character" (OPTIONAL)
onclick = "script" (OPTIONAL)
ondblclick = "script" (OPTIONAL)
onkeydown = "script" (OPTIONAL)
onkeypress = "script" (OPTIONAL)
onkeyup = "script" (OPTIONAL)
onmousedown = "script" (OPTIONAL)
onmousemove = "script" (OPTIONAL)
onmouseup = "script" (OPTIONAL)
onmouseover = "script" (OPTIONAL)
onmouseout = "script" (OPTIONAL)

Transitional DTD:
align = "top, bottom, left, right" (OPTIONAL)

EXAMPLE	`<FORM>`
	`<FIELDSET>`
	`    <LEGEND>Title of Subsection of Form</`
	`LEGEND>`
	`    <INPUT>`
	`    <INPUT>`
	`    <INPUT>`
	`</FIELDSET>`
	`</FORM>`

TIP	Use `LEGEND` within a `FIELDSET` element.

LI

TYPE	Block
PURPOSE	Defines an item in a list
NESTED WITHIN	`UL, OL, DIR, MENU`
START TAG	Required
END TAG	Optional
CONTENT	`LI` elements for each line of list
ATTRIBUTES	Strict DTD: id = "name" (OPTIONAL) class = "name" (OPTIONAL) style = "style" (OPTIONAL) title = "name" (OPTIONAL) lang = "language" (OPTIONAL) dir = (rtl, ltr) (OPTIONAL) onclick = "script" (OPTIONAL) ondblclick = "script" (OPTIONAL) onkeydown = "script" (OPTIONAL) onkeypress = "script" (OPTIONAL) onkeyup = "script" (OPTIONAL) onmousedown = "script" (OPTIONAL) onmousemove = "script" (OPTIONAL) onmouseup = "script" (OPTIONAL) onmouseover = "script" (OPTIONAL) onmouseout = "script" (OPTIONAL) Transitional DTD (deprecated): type = "(disc, square, circle)" (OPTIONAL) value = "(number)" (OPTIONAL) compact = "(boolean)" (OPTIONAL)

EXAMPLE	`<UL>`
	`<LI>`Here's the first item in the list.
	`<LI>`Here's the second item in the list.
	`<LI>`Here's the third item in the list.
	`</UL>`

TIP	The end tag is optional.

LINK

PURPOSE	Defines the relationship between two linked documents
TYPE	Block
NESTED WITHIN	HEAD element
START TAG	Required
END TAG	Forbidden
CONTENT	Empty
ATTRIBUTES	id = "name" (OPTIONAL) class = "name" (OPTIONAL) style = "CSS style definition" (OPTIONAL) title = "name" (OPTIONAL) lang = "language code" (OPTIONAL) dir = (rtl, ltr) (OPTIONAL) charset = "character set" (OPTIONAL) href = "url" (OPTIONAL) hreflang = "language code" (OPTIONAL) type = "MIMEtype" (OPTIONAL) target = "(_blank, _self, _parent, _top, or frame name)" (Optional) rel = "(alternate, stylesheet, start, next, prev, contents, index, glossary, copyright, chapter, section, subsection, appendix, help, bookmark)" (OPTIONAL) rev = "(alternate, stylesheet, start, next, prev, contents, index, glossary, copyright, chapter, section, subsection, appendix, help, bookmark)" (OPTIONAL) media = "(screen, tty, tv, projection, handheld, print, braille, aural, all)" (OPTIONAL) onclick = "script" (OPTIONAL) ondblclick = "script" (OPTIONAL) onkeydown = "script" (OPTIONAL) onkeypress = "script" (OPTIONAL) onkeyup = "script" (OPTIONAL) onmousedown = "script" (OPTIONAL) onmousemove = "script" (OPTIONAL) onmouseup = "script" (OPTIONAL) onmouseover = "script" (OPTIONAL) onmouseout = "script" (OPTIONAL)

EXAMPLE	`<LINK rel = "stylesheet" type = "text/css">`
TIP	The various forward and backward link types aren't recognized by most browsers.

MAP

PURPOSE	Creates a client-side imagemap
TYPE	Inline
NESTED WITHIN	`BODY`
START TAG	Required
END TAG	Required
CONTENT	AREA or A elements with text
ATTRIBUTES	id = "name" (OPTIONAL) class = "name" (OPTIONAL) style = "style" (OPTIONAL) title = "name" (OPTIONAL) lang = "language" (OPTIONAL) dir = (rtl, ltr) (OPTIONAL) name = "CDATA" onclick = "script" (OPTIONAL) ondblclick = "script" (OPTIONAL) onkeydown = "script" (OPTIONAL) onkeypress = "script" (OPTIONAL) onkeyup = "script" (OPTIONAL) onmousedown = "script" (OPTIONAL) onmousemove = "script" (OPTIONAL) onmouseup = "script" (OPTIONAL) onmouseover = "script" (OPTIONAL) onmouseout = "script" (OPTIONAL)

EXAMPLE	`<MAP name = "navigation">`
	`<AREA href = "page1.html shape = "rect" coords = "0,0, 118, 28">`
	`<AREA href = "page2.html" shape = rect coords = "184, 0, 276, 28">`
	`</MAP>`

TIP	Define the map with `AREA`.

MENU (Deprecated)

PURPOSE	Creates a single-column menu list
TYPE	Block

NESTED WITHIN	BODY
START TAG	Required
END TAG	Required
CONTENT	LI elements, inline elements, and text
ATTRIBUTES	id = "name" (OPTIONAL) class = "name" (OPTIONAL) style = "style" (OPTIONAL) title = "name" (OPTIONAL) lang = "language" (OPTIONAL) dir = (rtl, ltr) (OPTIONAL)
	Transitional DTD (deprecated): compact = "(boolean)" (OPTIONAL) onclick = "script" (OPTIONAL) ondblclick = "script" (OPTIONAL) onkeydown = "script" (OPTIONAL) onkeypress = "script" (OPTIONAL) onkeyup = "script" (OPTIONAL) onmousedown = "script" (OPTIONAL) onmousemove = "script" (OPTIONAL) onmouseup = "script" (OPTIONAL) onmouseover = "script" (OPTIONAL) onmouseout = "script" (OPTIONAL)

EXAMPLE	`<MENU>`
	`<LI>Item 1`
	`<LI>Item 2`
	`<LI>Item 3`
	`</MENU>`

TIP	Use UL instead.

META

PURPOSE	Sets properties of a document (for example: author, expiration date, a list of key words, and so on)
TYPE	N/A
NESTED WITHIN	BODY
START TAG	Required
END TAG	Forbidden
CONTENT	Empty

ATTRIBUTES	lang = "language" (OPTIONAL) dir = (rtl, ltr) (OPTIONAL) http-equiv = "text" (OPTIONAL) name = "text" (OPTIONAL) content = "CDATA" (OPTIONAL) scheme = "CDATA" (OPTIONAL)
EXAMPLE	`<META name = "keywords" content = "Chesapeake Bay, cruising, sailing, marinas">`
TIP	A number of content description schemes are under development, but most browsers don't yet recognize them.

NOFRAMES

PURPOSE	Displays text for browsers incapable of displaying frames
TYPE	Block
NESTED WITHIN	BODY
START TAG	Required
END TAG	Optional
CONTENT	Block elements, inline elements, and text
ATTRIBUTES	id = "name" (OPTIONAL) class = "name" (OPTIONAL) style = "style" (OPTIONAL) title = "name" (OPTIONAL) lang = "language" (OPTIONAL) dir = (rtl, ltr) (OPTIONAL) onclick = "script" (OPTIONAL) ondblclick = "script" (OPTIONAL) onkeydown = "script" (OPTIONAL) onkeypress = "script" (OPTIONAL) onkeyup = "script" (OPTIONAL) onmousedown = "script" (OPTIONAL) onmousemove = "script" (OPTIONAL) onmouseup = "script" (OPTIONAL) onmouseover = "script" (OPTIONAL) onmouseout = "script" (OPTIONAL)
EXAMPLE	`<NOFRAMES>Your browser doesn't handle frames. Sorry!</NOFRAMES>`
TIP	Be sure to include this element when you create a main frames page. Include links to the pages that would have been displayed by a forms-capable browser.

NOSCRIPT

PURPOSE	Displays text for browsers that don't support scripting
TYPE	Block
NESTED WITHIN	BODY
START TAG	Required
END TAG	Required
CONTENT	Block elements, inline elements, and text
ATTRIBUTES	id = "name" (OPTIONAL) class = "name" (OPTIONAL) style = "style" (OPTIONAL) title = "name" (OPTIONAL) lang = "language" (OPTIONAL) dir = (rtl, ltr) (OPTIONAL)
EXAMPLE	`<NOSCRIPT>Your browser doesn't handle scripts. Sorry!</NOSCRIPT>`
TIP	Be sure to include this element when you add a script to your document. Explain what the script does.

OBJECT

PURPOSE	Inserts a type of data not natively supported by the browser, such as a Java applet, script, or font data. For images, use IMG.
TYPE	Block
NESTED WITHIN	BODY
START TAG	Required
END TAG	Required
CONTENT	Contains inline elements and text; cannot contain block elements
ATTRIBUTES:	id = "name" (OPTIONAL) class = "name" (OPTIONAL) style = "style" (OPTIONAL) title = "name" (OPTIONAL) lang = "language" (OPTIONAL) dir = (rtl, ltr) (OPTIONAL) tabindex = "number" (OPTIONAL) classid = "url" (OPTIONAL) codebase = "url" (OPTIONAL)

declare (OPTIONAL)
data = "url" (OPTIONAL)
type = "MIME type" (OPTIONAL)
codetype = "MIMEtype" (OPTIONAL)
archive = "url" (OPTIONAL)
standby = "text" (OPTIONAL)
height = "length" (OPTIONAL)
width = "length" (OPTIONAL)
usemap = "url" (OPTIONAL)
name = "CDATA" (OPTIONAL)
tabindex = "number" (OPTIONAL)
border = "pixels" (OPTIONAL)
hspace = "length" (OPTIONAL)
vspace = "length" (OPTIONAL)
align = "(bottom, middle, top, left, right)" (OPTIONAL)
onclick = "script" (OPTIONAL)
ondblclick = "script" (OPTIONAL)
onkeydown = "script" (OPTIONAL)
onkeypress = "script" (OPTIONAL)
onkeyup = "script" (OPTIONAL)
onmousedown = "script" (OPTIONAL)
onmousemove = "script" (OPTIONAL)
onmouseup = "script" (OPTIONAL)
onmouseover = "script" (OPTIONAL)
onmouseout = "script" (OPTIONAL)

EXAMPLE

```
<OBJECT classid = = "stupid.applet.class">
<PARAM name = "whirl" value = "incessantly">
Your browser doesn't support Java.
</OBJECT>
```

TIP

Between the tags, place text that will appear only in browsers that don't support the data type.

OL

PURPOSE   Creates a numbered list

TYPE   Block

NESTED WITHIN   BODY

START TAG   Required

END TAG   Required

CONTENT   LI elements

ATTRIBUTES	Strict DTD:
	id = "name" (OPTIONAL)
	class = "name" (OPTIONAL)
	style = "style" (OPTIONAL)
	title = "name" (OPTIONAL)
	lang = "language" (OPTIONAL)
	dir = (rtl, ltr) (OPTIONAL)
	onclick = "script" (OPTIONAL)
	ondblclick = "script" (OPTIONAL)
	onkeydown = "script" (OPTIONAL)
	onkeypress = "script" (OPTIONAL)
	onkeyup = "script" (OPTIONAL)
	onmousedown = "script" (OPTIONAL)
	onmousemove = "script" (OPTIONAL)
	onmouseup = "script" (OPTIONAL)
	onmouseover = "script" (OPTIONAL)
	onmouseout = "script" (OPTIONAL)

Transitional DTD (deprecated):
type = "(disc, square, or circle)" (OPTIONAL)
start = "number" (OPTIONAL)
value = "number" (OPTIONAL)
compact = "(boolean)" (OPTIONAL)

EXAMPLE	`<OL>`
	`<LI>Item 1`
	`<LI>Item 2`
	`</OL>`

TIP	Define the list style with style sheets.

OPTGROUP

PURPOSE	In a form, defines a group of items in a drop-down menu created with `SELECT`.
TYPE	Inline
NESTED WITHIN	`FORM`
START TAG	Required
END TAG	Required
CONTENT	Text
ATTRIBUTES	id = "name" (OPTIONAL)
	class = "name" (OPTIONAL)
	style = "style" (OPTIONAL)
	title = "name" (OPTIONAL)

lang = "language" (OPTIONAL)
dir = (rtl, ltr) (OPTIONAL)
disabled (OPTIONAL)
label = "text" (REQUIRED)
onclick = "script" (OPTIONAL)
ondblclick = "script" (OPTIONAL)
onkeydown = "script" (OPTIONAL)
onkeypress = "script" (OPTIONAL)
onkeyup = "script" (OPTIONAL)
onmousedown = "script" (OPTIONAL)
onmousemove = "script" (OPTIONAL)
onmouseup = "script" (OPTIONAL)
onmouseover = "script" (OPTIONAL)
onmouseout = "script" (OPTIONAL)

EXAMPLE

```
<SELECT name = "hull-length">
<OPTGROUP label = "Hull Length">
    <OPTION selected value = "34'">34'
    <OPTION>36'
    <OPTION>40'
</OPTGROUP>
<OPTGROUP label = "Year">
    <OPTION selected value = "1988">1988
    <OPTION>1989
    <OPTION>1990>
</OPTGROUP>
</SELECT>
```

TIP   Define the items to appear in the menu by using OPTGROUP
             and OPTION.

OPTION

PURPOSE   In a form, defines an item in a drop-down menu created
                 with SELECT

TYPE   Inline

NESTED WITHIN   FORM

START TAG   Required

END TAG   Optional

CONTENT   Text

ATTRIBUTES   id = "name" (OPTIONAL)
                 class = "name" (OPTIONAL)
                 style = "style" (OPTIONAL)
                 title = "name" (OPTIONAL)

lang = "language" (OPTIONAL)
dir = (rtl, ltr) (OPTIONAL)
selected (OPTIONAL)
disabled (OPTIONAL)
label = "text" (OPTIONAL)
value = "CDATA" (OPTIONAL)
onclick = "script" (OPTIONAL)
ondblclick = "script" (OPTIONAL)
onkeydown = "script" (OPTIONAL)
onkeypress = "script" (OPTIONAL)
onkeyup = "script" (OPTIONAL)
onmousedown = "script" (OPTIONAL)
onmousemove = "script" (OPTIONAL)
onmouseup = "script" (OPTIONAL)
onmouseover = "script" (OPTIONAL)
onmouseout = "script" (OPTIONAL)

EXAMPLE

```
<SELECT name = "hull-length">
<OPTGROUP label = "Hull Length">
    <OPTION selected value = "34'">34'
    <OPTION>36'
    <OPTION>40'
</OPTGROUP>
<OPTGROUP label = "Year">
    <OPTION selected value = "1988">1988
    <OPTION>1989
    <OPTION>1990>
</OPTGROUP>
</SELECT>
```

TIP

Define the items to appear in the menu by using OPTGROUP and OPTION.

P

PURPOSE

Defines a paragraph of body text (generally with a blank line above the paragraph)

TYPE

Block

NESTED WITHIN

BODY

START TAG

Required

END TAG

Optional

CONTENT

Contains inline elements and text — cannot contain block elements

ATTRIBUTES	Strict DTD: id = "name" (OPTIONAL) class = "name" (OPTIONAL) style = "style" (OPTIONAL) title = "name" (OPTIONAL) lang = "language" (OPTIONAL) dir = (rtl, ltr) (OPTIONAL) onclick = "script" (OPTIONAL) ondblclick = "script" (OPTIONAL) onkeydown = "script" (OPTIONAL) onkeypress = "script" (OPTIONAL) onkeyup = "script" (OPTIONAL) onmousedown = "script" (OPTIONAL) onmousemove = "script" (OPTIONAL) onmouseup = "script" (OPTIONAL) onmouseover = "script" (OPTIONAL) onmouseout = "script" (OPTIONAL)
	Transitional DTD: align = "(left, center, right, justify)" (OPTIONAL)
EXAMPLE	`<P>This is a text paragraph</P>`
TIP	For good form, begin each paragraph with `<P>` and close with `</P>`. Do not use `<P>` to enter blank lines.

PARAM

PURPOSE	Defines run-time settings for an object
TYPE	Inline
NESTED WITHIN	`OBJECT`
START TAG	Required
END TAG	Forbidden
CONTENT	Empty
ATTRIBUTES:	id = "name" (REQUIRED) name = "CDATA" (OPTIONAL) value = "CDATA" (OPTIONAL) valuetype = "(data, ref, or object)" (OPTIONAL) type = "MIME type" (OPTIONAL)

EXAMPLE	`<OBJECT classid = = "stupid.applet.class">`
	`<PARAM name = "whirl" value = "incessantly">`
	`Your browser doesn't support Java.`
	`</OBJECT>`

TIP	Check the applet's documentation to find out how to set the run-time settings (parameters).

PRE

TYPE	Inline
PURPOSE	Preserves spaces and line breaks as they are typed
NESTED WITHIN	BODY
START TAG	Required
END TAG	Required
CONTENT	Contains HTML elements and text (but see the following note)
ATTRIBUTES	width = "number" (OPTIONAL)
	id = "name" (OPTIONAL)
	class = "name" (OPTIONAL)
	style = "style" (OPTIONAL)
	title = "name" (OPTIONAL)
	lang = "language" (OPTIONAL)
	dir = (rtl, ltr) (OPTIONAL)
	onclick = "script" (OPTIONAL)
	ondblclick = "script" (OPTIONAL)
	onkeydown = "script" (OPTIONAL)
	onkeypress = "script" (OPTIONAL)
	onkeyup = "script" (OPTIONAL)
	onmousedown = "script" (OPTIONAL)
	onmousemove = "script" (OPTIONAL)
	onmouseup = "script" (OPTIONAL)
	onmouseover = "script" (OPTIONAL)
	onmouseout = "script" (OPTIONAL)
NOTE	You can't use IMG, OBJECT, BIG, SMALL, SUB, or SUP within a PRE element.

EXAMPLE	`<PRE>`
	`This`
	`text      will      preserve      its`
	`bizarre`
	`    spacing</PRE>`

TIP	To align characters correctly, consider using a monospace font.

Q

PURPOSE	Marks an inline quotation
TYPE	Inline
NESTED WITHIN	Any BLOCK element
START TAG	Required

END TAG	Required
CONTENT	Text
ATTRIBUTES	id = "name" (OPTIONAL)
	class = "name" (OPTIONAL)
	style = "style" (OPTIONAL)
	title = "name" (OPTIONAL)
	lang = "language" (OPTIONAL)
	dir = (rtl, ltr) (OPTIONAL)
	cite = "url" (OPTIONAL)
	onclick = "script" (OPTIONAL)
	ondblclick = "script" (OPTIONAL)
	onkeydown = "script" (OPTIONAL)
	onkeypress = "script" (OPTIONAL)
	onkeyup = "script" (OPTIONAL)
	onmousedown = "script" (OPTIONAL)
	onmousemove = "script" (OPTIONAL)
	onmouseup = "script" (OPTIONAL)
	onmouseover = "script" (OPTIONAL)
	onmouseout = "script" (OPTIONAL)
EXAMPLE	`<Q cite = "source.html">Here's a quotation.</Q>`
TIP	You can use the `BLOCKQUOTE` element for longer (indented) quotations. If you use `Q`, don't use quotation marks. They're supplied by the browser in a way that's sensitive to the document's language code.

S (Deprecated)

PURPOSE	Displays text in strikethrough font
TYPE	Inline
NESTED WITHIN	Any `BLOCK` element
START TAG	Required
END TAG	Required
CONTENT	Text
ATTRIBUTES	id = "name" (OPTIONAL)
	class = "name" (OPTIONAL)
	style = "style" (OPTIONAL)
	title = "name" (OPTIONAL)
	lang = "language" (OPTIONAL)
	dir = (rtl, ltr) (OPTIONAL)
	onclick = "script" (OPTIONAL)

ondblclick = "script" (OPTIONAL)
onkeydown = "script" (OPTIONAL)
onkeypress = "script" (OPTIONAL)
onkeyup = "script" (OPTIONAL)
onmousedown = "script" (OPTIONAL)
onmousemove = "script" (OPTIONAL)
onmouseup = "script" (OPTIONAL)
onmouseover = "script" (OPTIONAL)
onmouseout = "script" (OPTIONAL)

EXAMPLE

`<S>Text in a strikethrough font</S>`

TIP

Be careful to close this element properly.

SAMP

PURPOSE

Identifies computer output

TYPE

Inline

NESTED WITHIN

Any BLOCK element

START TAG

Required

END TAG

Required

CONTENT

Text

ATTRIBUTES

id = "name" (OPTIONAL)
class = "name" (OPTIONAL)
style = "style" (OPTIONAL)
title = "name" (OPTIONAL)
lang = "language" (OPTIONAL)
dir = (rtl, ltr) (OPTIONAL)
onclick = "script" (OPTIONAL)
ondblclick = "script" (OPTIONAL)
onkeydown = "script" (OPTIONAL)
onkeypress = "script" (OPTIONAL)
onkeyup = "script" (OPTIONAL)
onmousedown = "script" (OPTIONAL)
onmousemove = "script" (OPTIONAL)
onmouseup = "script" (OPTIONAL)
onmouseover = "script" (OPTIONAL)
onmouseout = "script" (OPTIONAL)

EXAMPLE

`Wait until you see <SAMP>fatal error</SAMP> on the screen; then panic.`

TIP

Usually rendered in a monospace font.

SCRIPT

PURPOSE	Contains a script
TYPE	Inline
NESTED WITHIN	BODY
START TAG	Required
END TAG	Required
CONTENT	A script in a language, such as JavaScript.
ATTRIBUTES:	Strict DTD: type = "MIME type" (REQUIRED) charset = "character set" (OPTIONAL) src = "url" (OPTIONAL) defer = "script" (OPTIONAL) Transitional DTD (deprecated): language = "scripting language" (OPTIONAL)

EXAMPLE	`<SCRIPT type = "text/javascript">`
	`<!—hide your script within HTML`
	`comment tags -->`
	`</SCRIPT>`

TIP	Hide your script within comment tags so it won't be displayed by older browsers.

SELECT

PURPOSE	In a form, creates a drop-down menu
TYPE	Inline
NESTED WITHIN	FORM
START TAG	Required
END TAG	Required
CONTENT	OPTGROUP or OPTION elements
ATTRIBUTES	id = "name" (OPTIONAL) class = "name" (OPTIONAL) style = "style" (OPTIONAL) title = "name" (OPTIONAL) lang = "language" (OPTIONAL) dir = (rtl, ltr) (OPTIONAL) name = "CDATA" (OPTIONAL) size = "number" (OPTIONAL) multiple (OPTIONAL) disabled (OPTIONAL)

tabindex = "number" (OPTIONAL)
onclick = "script" (OPTIONAL)
ondblclick = "script" (OPTIONAL)
onkeydown = "script" (OPTIONAL)
onkeypress = "script" (OPTIONAL)
onkeyup = "script" (OPTIONAL)
onmousedown = "script" (OPTIONAL)
onmousemove = "script" (OPTIONAL)
onmouseup = "script" (OPTIONAL)
onblur = "script" (OPTIONAL)
onfocus = "script" (OPTIONAL)
onchange = "script" (OPTIONAL)
onmouseover = "script" (OPTIONAL)
onmouseout = "script" (OPTIONAL)

EXAMPLE

```
<SELECT name = "hull-length">
<OPTGROUP label = "Hull Length">
    <OPTION selected value = "34'">34'
    <OPTION>36'
    <OPTION>40'
</OPTGROUP>
<OPTGROUP label = "Year">
    <OPTION selected value = "1988">1988
    <OPTION>1989
    <OPTION>1990
</OPTGROUP>
</SELECT>
```

TIP

Define the items to appear in the menu by using OPTGROUP and OPTION.

SMALL

PURPOSE   Displays text in a small font size

TYPE   Inline

NESTED WITHIN   Any BLOCK element

START TAG   Required

END TAG   Required

CONTENT   Text

ATTRIBUTES   id = "name" (OPTIONAL)
                 class = "name" (OPTIONAL)
                 style = "style" (OPTIONAL)
                 title = "name" (OPTIONAL)
                 lang = "language" (OPTIONAL)
                 dir = (rtl, ltr) (OPTIONAL)

onclick = "script" (OPTIONAL)
ondblclick = "script" (OPTIONAL)
onkeydown = "script" (OPTIONAL)
onkeypress = "script" (OPTIONAL)
onkeyup = "script" (OPTIONAL)
onmousedown = "script" (OPTIONAL)
onmousemove = "script" (OPTIONAL)
onmouseup = "script" (OPTIONAL)
onmouseover = "script" (OPTIONAL)
onmouseout = "script" (OPTIONAL)

EXAMPLE
`<SMALL>Use as directed. Call physician if con-
dition persists.</SMALL>`

TIP
You can use the `BIG` element to render text in a large size.

SPAN

PURPOSE
Encloses text within a generic inline element that you can define with style sheets

TYPE
Inline

NESTED WITHIN
Any `BLOCK` element

START TAG
Required

END TAG
Required

CONTENT
Block elements

ATTRIBUTES
id = "name" (OPTIONAL)
class = "name" (OPTIONAL)
style = "style" (OPTIONAL)
title = "name" (OPTIONAL)
lang = "language" (OPTIONAL)
dir = (rtl, ltr) (OPTIONAL)
onclick = "script" (OPTIONAL)
ondblclick = "script" (OPTIONAL)
onkeydown = "script" (OPTIONAL)
onkeypress = "script" (OPTIONAL)
onkeyup = "script" (OPTIONAL)
onmousedown = "script" (OPTIONAL)
onmousemove = "script" (OPTIONAL)
onmouseup = "script" (OPTIONAL)
onmouseover = "script" (OPTIONAL)
onmouseout = "script" (OPTIONAL)

EXAMPLE
`<SPAN class = "bibliography">Book Title</SPAN>`

TIP
Use `DIV` to group and define block elements.

STRIKE (Deprecated)

PURPOSE	Displays text in strikethrough font
TYPE	Inline
NESTED WITHIN	Any BLOCK element
START TAG	Required
END TAG	Required
CONTENT	Text
ATTRIBUTES	id = "name" (OPTIONAL)
	class = "name" (OPTIONAL)
	style = "style" (OPTIONAL)
	title = "name" (OPTIONAL)
	lang = "language" (OPTIONAL)
	dir = (rtl, ltr) (OPTIONAL)
	onclick = "script" (OPTIONAL)
	ondblclick = "script" (OPTIONAL)
	onkeydown = "script" (OPTIONAL)
	onkeypress = "script" (OPTIONAL)
	onkeyup = "script" (OPTIONAL)
	onmousedown = "script" (OPTIONAL)
	onmousemove = "script" (OPTIONAL)
	onmouseup = "script" (OPTIONAL)
EXAMPLE	`<STRIKE>Text in a strikethrough font</STRIKE>`
TIP	Be careful to close this element properly.

STRONG

PURPOSE	Marks text for emphasis
TYPE	Inline
NESTED WITHIN	Any BLOCK element
START TAG	Required
END TAG	Required
CONTENT	Text
ATTRIBUTES	id = "name" (OPTIONAL)
	class = "name" (OPTIONAL)
	style = "style" (OPTIONAL)
	title = "name" (OPTIONAL)
	lang = "language" (OPTIONAL)
	dir = (rtl, ltr) (OPTIONAL)

onclick = "script" (OPTIONAL)
ondblclick = "script" (OPTIONAL)
onkeydown = "script" (OPTIONAL)
onkeypress = "script" (OPTIONAL)
onkeyup = "script" (OPTIONAL)
onmousedown = "script" (OPTIONAL)
onmousemove = "script" (OPTIONAL)
onmouseup = "script" (OPTIONAL)
onmouseover = "script" (OPTIONAL)
onmouseout = "script" (OPTIONAL)

EXAMPLE   Do this <STRONG>right now</STRONG>.

TIP   Usually rendered in boldface.

STYLE

TYPE   Inline

PURPOSE   Defines the style to be associated with an HTML element
                  throughout the document

NESTED WITHIN   HEAD

START TAG   Required

END TAG   Required

CONTENT   CDATA (style sheet)

ATTRIBUTES   type = "CDATA" (REQUIRED)
                  media = "screen, tty, tv, projection, handheld, print, braille,
                      aural, all" (OPTIONAL)
                  lang = "language" (OPTIONAL)
                  dir = (rtl, ltr) (OPTIONAL)

EXAMPLE   <STYLE type = "text/css">
                  H1 {text-align: center; font-family: Helvetica;
                  color: red; font-style: italic}
                  </STYLE>

TIP   Define the type as text/css.

SUB

PURPOSE   Marks text as subscript

TYPE   Inline

NESTED WITHIN   Any BLOCK element

START TAG   Required

END TAG	Required
CONTENT	Text
ATTRIBUTES	id = "name" (OPTIONAL) class = "name" (OPTIONAL) style = "style" (OPTIONAL) title = "name" (OPTIONAL) lang = "language" (OPTIONAL) dir = (rtl, ltr) (OPTIONAL)
	onclick = "script" (OPTIONAL) ondblclick = "script" (OPTIONAL) onkeydown = "script" (OPTIONAL) onkeypress = "script" (OPTIONAL) onkeyup = "script" (OPTIONAL) onmousedown = "script" (OPTIONAL) onmousemove = "script" (OPTIONAL) onmouseup = "script" (OPTIONAL) onmouseover = "script" (OPTIONAL) onmouseout = "script" (OPTIONAL)
EXAMPLE	Display in `<SUB>subscript</SUB>`.
TIP	Be careful to close this element properly.

SUP

PURPOSE	Marks text as superscript
TYPE	Inline
NESTED WITHIN	Any `BLOCK` element
START TAG	Required
END TAG	Required
CONTENT	Text
ATTRIBUTES	id = "name" (OPTIONAL) class = "name" (OPTIONAL) style = "style" (OPTIONAL) title = "name" (OPTIONAL) lang = "language" (OPTIONAL) dir = (rtl, ltr) (OPTIONAL)
	onclick = "script" (OPTIONAL) ondblclick = "script" (OPTIONAL) onkeydown = "script" (OPTIONAL) onkeypress = "script" (OPTIONAL) onkeyup = "script" (OPTIONAL)

onmousedown = "script" (OPTIONAL)
onmousemove = "script" (OPTIONAL)
onmouseup = "script" (OPTIONAL)
onmouseover = "script" (OPTIONAL)
onmouseout = "script" (OPTIONAL)

EXAMPLE	Display in `<SUP>`superscript`</SUP>`.
TIP	Be careful to close this element properly.

TABLE

PURPOSE	Creates a table
TYPE	Inline
NESTED WITHIN	`COLGROUP` element
START TAG	Required
END TAG	Required
CONTENT	Table tags and text
ATTRIBUTES	Strict DTD:

id = "name" (OPTIONAL)
class = "name" (OPTIONAL)
style = "style" (OPTIONAL)
title = "name" (OPTIONAL)
lang = "language" (OPTIONAL)
dir = (rtl, ltr) (OPTIONAL)
summary = "text" (OPTIONAL)
width = "length" (OPTIONAL)
border = "pixels" (OPTIONAL)
frame = "(void, above, below, hsides, lhs, rhs, vsides, box, border)" (OPTIONAL)
rules = "(none, groups, rows, cols, all)" (OPTIONAL)
cellspacing = "length" (OPTIONAL)
cellpadding = "length" (OPTIONAL)
bgcolor = "color" (OPTIONAL)
onclick = "script" (OPTIONAL)
ondblclick = "script" (OPTIONAL)
onkeydown = "script" (OPTIONAL)
onkeypress = "script" (OPTIONAL)
onkeyup = "script" (OPTIONAL)
onmousedown = "script" (OPTIONAL)
onmousemove = "script" (OPTIONAL)
onmouseup = "script" (OPTIONAL)
onmouseover = "script" (OPTIONAL)
onmouseout = "script" (OPTIONAL)

Transitional DTD (deprecated):
align = "(left, center, right)" (OPTIONAL)

EXAMPLE

```
<TABLE>
<TR>
    <TD>Cell 1
    <TD>Cell 2
</TR>
</TABLE>
```

TIP

Use the summary attribute to specify a brief summary of the table for people using nongraphical browsers.

TBODY

PURPOSE

Creates a table body that scrolls within a fixed table header (see THEAD) and table footer (TFOOT)

TYPE

Inline

NESTED WITHIN

TABLE element

START TAG

Optional

END TAG

Optional

CONTENT

Table tags and text

ATTRIBUTES

id = "name" (OPTIONAL)
class = "name" (OPTIONAL)
style = "style" (OPTIONAL)
title = "name" (OPTIONAL)
lang = "language" (OPTIONAL)
dir = (rtl, ltr) (OPTIONAL)
align = "(left, center, right, justify, char)" (OPTIONAL)
char = "character" (OPTIONAL)
charoff = "length" (OPTIONAL)
valign = "(top, middle, bottom, baseline)" (OPTIONAL)
onclick = "script" (OPTIONAL)
ondblclick = "script" (OPTIONAL)
onkeydown = "script" (OPTIONAL)
onkeypress = "script" (OPTIONAL)
onkeyup = "script" (OPTIONAL)
onmousedown = "script" (OPTIONAL)
onmousemove = "script" (OPTIONAL)
onmouseup = "script" (OPTIONAL)
onmouseover = "script" (OPTIONAL)
onmouseout = "script" (OPTIONAL)

| EXAMPLE | ```
THEAD>
      <TR>
            <TH>Header 1
            <TH>Header 2
      </TR>
</THEAD>
<TBODY>
      <TR>
            <TD>Item 1
            <TD>Item 2
      </TR>
</TBODY>
``` |
|---|---|
| TIP | Note, THEAD must contain the same number of columns as the table body and THEAD. TFOOT must appear before TBODY. |

TD

PURPOSE	Creates a table cell
TYPE	Inline
NESTED WITHIN	TR element
START TAG	Required
END TAG	Optional
CONTENT	Table tags and text
ATTRIBUTES	Strict DTD: id = "name" (OPTIONAL) class = "name" (OPTIONAL) style = "style" (OPTIONAL) title = "name" (OPTIONAL) lang = "language" (OPTIONAL) dir = (rtl, ltr) (OPTIONAL) abbr = "header abbreviation" (OPTIONAL) axis = "text" (OPTIONAL) headers = "ID list" (OPTIONAL) scope = "(row, col, rowgroup, colgroup)" (OPTIONAL) rowspan = "number" (OPTIONAL) colspan = "number" (OPTIONAL) align = "(left, center, right, justify, char)" (OPTIONAL) char = "character" (OPTIONAL) charoff = "length" (OPTIONAL) valign = "(top, middle, bottom, baseline)" (OPTIONAL) bgcolor = "color" (OPTIONAL)
```

Transitional DTD (deprecated):
nowrap (OPTIONAL)
width = "length" (OPTIONAL)
height = "length" (OPTIONAL)
onclick = "script" (OPTIONAL)
ondblclick = "script" (OPTIONAL)
onkeydown = "script" (OPTIONAL)
onkeypress = "script" (OPTIONAL)
onkeyup = "script" (OPTIONAL)
onmousedown = "script" (OPTIONAL)
onmousemove = "script" (OPTIONAL)
onmouseup = "script" (OPTIONAL)
onmouseover = "script" (OPTIONAL)
onmouseout = "script" (OPTIONAL)

EXAMPLE

```
<TR>
    <TD>Cell 1
    <TD>Cell 2
</TR>
```

TIP   You can omit the end tag.

TEXTAREA

PURPOSE   In a form, creates a multiline text entry box

TYPE   Block

NESTED WITHIN   FORM

START TAG   Required

END TAG   Required

CONTENT   Text

ATTRIBUTES   id = "name" (OPTIONAL)
class = "name" (OPTIONAL)
style = "style" (OPTIONAL)
title = "name" (OPTIONAL)
lang = "language" (OPTIONAL)
dir = (rtl, ltr) (OPTIONAL)
name = "CDATA" (OPTIONAL)
rows = "number" (REQUIRED)
cols = "number" (REQUIRED)
disabled (OPTIONAL)
readonly (OPTIONAL)
tabindex = "number" (OPTIONAL)
accesskey = "character" (OPTIONAL)
onclick = "script" (OPTIONAL)

onddblclick = "script" (OPTIONAL)
onkeydown = "script" (OPTIONAL)
onkeypress = "script" (OPTIONAL)
onkeyup = "script" (OPTIONAL)
onmousedown = "script" (OPTIONAL)
onmousemove = "script" (OPTIONAL)
onmouseup = "script" (OPTIONAL)
onblur = "script" (OPTIONAL)
onfocus = "script" (OPTIONAL)
onchange = "script" (OPTIONAL)
onselect = "script" (OPTIONAL)
onmouseover = "script" (OPTIONAL)
onmouseout = "script" (OPTIONAL)

EXAMPLE

```
<TEXTAREA rows = "16 cols = "65" name =
"comments">
</TEXAREA>
```

TIP

Use `<INPUT type = "text">` to create a one-line text box.

TFOOT

PURPOSE

Creates a table footer that conforming browsers will prevent from scrolling

TYPE

Inline

NESTED WITHIN

TR element

START TAG

Required

END TAG

Optional

CONTENT

Table tags and text

ATTRIBUTES

id = "name" (OPTIONAL)
class = "name" (OPTIONAL)
style = "style" (OPTIONAL)
title = "name" (OPTIONAL)
lang = "language" (OPTIONAL)
dir = (rtl, ltr) (OPTIONAL)
align = "(left, center, right, justify, char)" (OPTIONAL)
char = "character" (OPTIONAL)
charoff = "length" (OPTIONAL)
valign = "(top, middle, bottom, baseline)" (OPTIONAL)

onclick = "script" (OPTIONAL)
ondblclick = "script" (OPTIONAL)
onkeydown = "script" (OPTIONAL)
onkeypress = "script" (OPTIONAL)

	onkeyup = "script" (OPTIONAL) onmousedown = "script" (OPTIONAL) onmousemove = "script" (OPTIONAL) onmouseup = "script" (OPTIONAL) onmouseover = "script" (OPTIONAL) onmouseout = "script" (OPTIONAL)
EXAMPLE	

```
<TFOOT>
     <TR>
             <TH>Header 1
             <TH>Header 2
     </TR>
</THEAD>
<TBODY
     <TR>
             <TD>Item 1
             <TD>Item 2
     </TR>
</TBODY>
```

TIP	Note, THEAD must contain the same number of columns as the table body and THEAD. TFOOT must appear before TBODY.

TH

PURPOSE	Creates a table header cell
TYPE	Inline
NESTED WITHIN	TR element
START TAG	Required
END TAG	Optional
CONTENT	Table tags and text
ATTRIBUTES	Strict DTD: id = "name" (OPTIONAL) class = "name" (OPTIONAL) style = "style" (OPTIONAL) title = "name" (OPTIONAL) lang = "language" (OPTIONAL) dir = (rtl, ltr) (OPTIONAL) abbr = "header abbreviation" (OPTIONAL) axis = "text" (OPTIONAL) headers = "ID list" (OPTIONAL) scope = "(row, col, rowgroup, colgroup)" (OPTIONAL) rowspan = "number" (OPTIONAL)

colspan = "number" (OPTIONAL)
align = "(left, center, right, justify, char)" (OPTIONAL)
char = "character" (OPTIONAL)
charoff = "length" (OPTIONAL)
valign = "(top, middle, bottom, baseline)" (OPTIONAL)
bgcolor = "color" (OPTIONAL)

Transitional DTD (deprecated):
nowrap (OPTIONAL)
width = "length" (OPTIONAL)
height = "length" (OPTIONAL)

EXAMPLE

```
<TR>
    <TH>Header 1
    <TH>Header 2
</TR>
<TR>
    <TD>Item 1
    <TD>Item 2
</TR>
```

TIP   You can omit the end tag. Most browsers render the
                contents of header cells in bold.

THEAD

PURPOSE   Creates a table header that conforming browsers will pre-
                    vent from scrolling

TYPE   Inline

NESTED WITHIN   TR element

START TAG   Required

END TAG   Optional

CONTENT   Table tags and text

ATTRIBUTES   id = "name" (OPTIONAL)
                    class = "name" (OPTIONAL)
                    style = "style" (OPTIONAL)
                    title = "name" (OPTIONAL)
                    lang = "language" (OPTIONAL)
                    dir = (rtl, ltr) (OPTIONAL)
                    align = "(left, center, right, justify, char)" (OPTIONAL)
                    char = "character" (OPTIONAL)
                    charoff = "length" (OPTIONAL)
                    valign = "(top, middle, bottom, baseline)" (OPTIONAL)
                    onclick = "script" (OPTIONAL)

ondblclick = "script" (OPTIONAL)
onkeydown = "script" (OPTIONAL)
onkeypress = "script" (OPTIONAL)
onkeyup = "script" (OPTIONAL)
onmousedown = "script" (OPTIONAL)
onmousemove = "script" (OPTIONAL)
onmouseup = "script" (OPTIONAL)
onmouseover = "script" (OPTIONAL)
onmouseout = "script" (OPTIONAL)

EXAMPLE

```
<THEAD>
    <TR>
            <TH>Header 1
            <TH>Header 2
    </TR>
</THEAD>
<TBODY
    <TR>
            <TD>Item 1
            <TD>Item 2
    </TR>
</TBODY>
```

TIP   Note, THEAD must contain the same number of columns as the table body and TFOOT.

TITLE

PURPOSE   Enables you to specify title text that appears on the browser's title bar (but not in the document itself)

NESTED WITHIN   HEAD element

START TAG   Required

END TAG   Required

CONTENT   CDATA; entities are permitted but no elements

ATTRIBUTES   lang = "language" (OPTIONAL)
dir = (rtl, ltr) (OPTIONAL)

NOTE   All other elements are excluded. You can't add character formatting (such as boldface) or any other presentation within the TITLE element.

EXAMPLE   `<TITLE>Sailing the Southern Chesapeake Bay </TITLE>`

TIP   Use substantive title words to increase chance of detection by Web search engines.

TR

PURPOSE	Creates a table row
TYPE	Inline
NESTED WITHIN	TABLE element
START TAG	Required
END TAG	Optional
CONTENT	Table tags and text
ATTRIBUTES	id = "name" (OPTIONAL)
	class = "name" (OPTIONAL)
	style = "style" (OPTIONAL)
	title = "name" (OPTIONAL)
	lang = "language" (OPTIONAL)
	dir = (rtl, ltr) (OPTIONAL)
	align = "(left, center, right, justify, char)" (OPTIONAL)
	char = "character" (OPTIONAL)
	charoff = "length" (OPTIONAL)
	valign = "(top, middle, bottom, baseline)" (OPTIONAL)
	onclick = "script" (OPTIONAL)
	ondblclick = "script" (OPTIONAL)
	onkeydown = "script" (OPTIONAL)
	onkeypress = "script" (OPTIONAL)
	onkeyup = "script" (OPTIONAL)
	onmousedown = "script" (OPTIONAL)
	onmousemove = "script" (OPTIONAL)
	onmouseup = "script" (OPTIONAL)
	onmouseover = "script" (OPTIONAL)
	onmouseout = "script" (OPTIONAL)

EXAMPLE

```
<TR>
    <TD>Cell 1
    <TD>Cell 2
</TR>
```

TIP	You can omit the end tag.

TT

PURPOSE	Displays text in a monospace font
TYPE	Inline
NESTED WITHIN	Any BLOCK element
START TAG	Required
END TAG	Required

CONTENT	Text
ATTRIBUTES	id = "name" (OPTIONAL)
	class = "name" (OPTIONAL)
	style = "style" (OPTIONAL)
	title = "name" (OPTIONAL)
	lang = "language" (OPTIONAL)
	dir = (rtl, ltr) (OPTIONAL)
	onclick = "script" (OPTIONAL)
	ondblclick = "script" (OPTIONAL)
	onkeydown = "script" (OPTIONAL)
	onkeypress = "script" (OPTIONAL)
	onkeyup = "script" (OPTIONAL)
	onmousedown = "script" (OPTIONAL)
	onmousemove = "script" (OPTIONAL)
	onmouseup = "script" (OPTIONAL)
	onmouseover = "script" (OPTIONAL)
	onmouseout = "script" (OPTIONAL)
EXAMPLE	`<TT>Text in a large font</TT>`
TIP	Usually rendered in a monospace font and indistinguishable from `CODE`, `KBD`, `SAMP`, and `VAR`.

U (Deprecated)

PURPOSE	Displays text with underlining
TYPE	Inline
NESTED WITHIN	Any `BLOCK` element
START TAG	Required
END TAG	Required
CONTENT	Text
ATTRIBUTES	id = "name" (OPTIONAL)
	class = "name" (OPTIONAL)
	style = "style" (OPTIONAL)
	title = "name" (OPTIONAL)
	lang = "language" (OPTIONAL)
	dir = (rtl, ltr) (OPTIONAL)
	onclick = "script" (OPTIONAL)
	ondblclick = "script" (OPTIONAL)
	onkeydown = "script" (OPTIONAL)
	onkeypress = "script" (OPTIONAL)
	onkeyup = "script" (OPTIONAL)
	onmousedown = "script" (OPTIONAL)
	onmousemove = "script" (OPTIONAL)

onmouseup = "script" (OPTIONAL)
onmouseover = "script" (OPTIONAL)
onmouseout = "script" (OPTIONAL)

EXAMPLE	`<U>Underlined</U>`
TIP	Avoid this element. Users may confuse underlined text with hyperlinks.

UL

PURPOSE	Creates a numbered list
TYPE	Block
NESTED WITHIN	`BODY`
START TAG	Required
END TAG	Required
CONTENT	`LI` elements
ATTRIBUTES	Strict DTD: id = "name" (OPTIONAL) class = "name" (OPTIONAL) style = "style" (OPTIONAL) title = "name" (OPTIONAL) lang = "language" (OPTIONAL) dir = (rtl, ltr) (OPTIONAL) onclick = "script" (OPTIONAL) ondblclick = "script" (OPTIONAL) onkeydown = "script" (OPTIONAL) onkeypress = "script" (OPTIONAL) onkeyup = "script" (OPTIONAL) onmousedown = "script" (OPTIONAL) onmousemove = "script" (OPTIONAL) onmouseup = "script" (OPTIONAL) onmouseover = "script" (OPTIONAL) onmouseout = "script" (OPTIONAL) Transitional DTD (deprecated): type = "(disc, square, or circle)" (OPTIONAL) start = "number" (OPTIONAL) value = "number" (OPTIONAL)

EXAMPLE	`<UL>`
	    `<LI>Item 1`
	    `<LI>Item 2`
	`</UL>`

TIP	Define the list style with style sheets.

VAR

PURPOSE	Marks text as a variable in a computer program
TYPE	Inline
NESTED WITHIN	Any BLOCK element
START TAG	Required
END TAG	Required
CONTENT	Text
ATTRIBUTES	id = "name" (OPTIONAL) class = "name" (OPTIONAL) style = "style" (OPTIONAL) title = "name" (OPTIONAL) lang = "language" (OPTIONAL) dir = (rtl, ltr) (OPTIONAL) onclick = "script" (OPTIONAL) ondblclick = "script" (OPTIONAL) onkeydown = "script" (OPTIONAL) onkeypress = "script" (OPTIONAL) onkeyup = "script" (OPTIONAL) onmousedown = "script" (OPTIONAL) onmousemove = "script" (OPTIONAL) onmouseup = "script" (OPTIONAL) onmouseover = "script" (OPTIONAL) onmouseout = "script" (OPTIONAL)
EXAMPLE	`<VAR>x = "19"</VAR>`
TIP	Usually rendered in a monospace font and indistinguishable from CODE, SAMP, and TT.

Intrinsic Events

Each of the following intrinsic events takes a value that is a script. The script is executed whenever the event occurs for that element. The syntax of script data depends on the scripting language, and is not dependent on one particular language over another.

onload	The onload event occurs when the user agent finishes loading a window or all frames within a FRAMESET.
onunload	The onunload event occurs when the user agent removes a document from a window or frame.

onclick	The onclick event occurs when the pointing device button is clicked over an element.
ondblclick	The ondblclick event occurs when the pointing device button is double clicked over an element.
onmousedown	The onmousedown event occurs when the pointing device button is pressed over an element.
onmouseup	The onmouseup event occurs when the pointing device button is released over an element.
onmouseover	The onmouseover event occurs when the pointing device is moved onto an element.
onmousemove	The onmousemove event occurs when the pointing device is moved while it is over an element.
onmouseout	The onmouseout event occurs when the pointing device is moved away from an element.
onfocus	The onfocus event occurs when an element receives focus by either pointing the mouse or tabbing navigation.
onblur	The onblur event occurs when an element loses focus by either pointing the mouse or by tabbing navigation.
onkeypress	The onkeypress event occurs when a key is pressed and released over an element.
onkeydown	The onkeydown event occurs when a key is pressed down over an element.
onkeyup	The onkeyup event occurs when a key is released over an element.
onsubmit	The onsubmit event occurs when a form is submitted.
onreset	The onreset event occurs when a form is reset.
onselect	The onselect event occurs when a user selects some text in a text field.
onchange	The onchange event occurs when a control loses the input focus and its value is modified since regaining focus.

It is possible to associate a script with one or more events that occur as a result of user interaction though a user agent.

Control elements respond to certain intrinsic events. Some control elements that support intrinsic events are INPUT, SELECT, BUTTON, TEXTAREA, and LABEL. These elements, when placed outside of a form, may be used to enhance the graphical user interface of a document.

For example, someone writing an HTML page may want to include a button outside of a form that, when pressed, tells the server to process but sends no other data. The typical form-submission button-press is accompanied by form data.

Some elements do not support intrinsic events. Typically these are elements that refer to the document instead of the document content. For example, the META element does not support intrinsic elements since it doesn't actually render anything on the user agent's page.

The following example demonstrates the interaction between user interface actions and the script.

```
<INPUT NAME="userID" onblur="validID(this.value)">
```

The text field *userID* is required in the example above. The user navigating out of the field triggers the onblur event. When this event occurs, the JavaScript function validID is called. This function validates the value of the userID field:

✦   ✦   ✦

HTML 4
Attributes
Reference

Attribute	Used in	Valid Value	Purpose
abbr	TD, TH	text	abbreviation for header cell
accept-charset	FORM	character set	list of supported code character sets
accept	INPUT	MIME types	list of MIME types for file upload
accesskey	A, AREA, BUTTON, INPUT, LABEL, LEGEND, TEXTAREA	character	character to press to bring focus to element
action	FORM	URL	form handler program
align	CAPTION	top, bottom, left, right	alignment relative to table
align	APPLET, IFRAME, IMG, INPUT, OBJECT	top, middle, bottom, left, right	vertical or horizontal alignment
align	LEGEND	top, bottom, left, right	relative to fieldset
align	TABLE	left, center, right	relative to window
align	HR	left, center, right	
align	DIV, H1, H2, H3, H4, H5, H6, P	left, center, right, justify	text alignment
align	COL, COLGROUP, TBODY, TD, TFOOT, TH, THEAD, TR	left, center, right, justify, char	table alignment
alink	BODY	color	color of selected links
alt	APPLET	text	text description
alt	AREA, IMG	text	text description
alt	INPUT	CDATA	text description
archive	OBJECT	URL	space-separated archive list
archive	APPLET	CDATA	comma-separated archive list
axis	TD, TH	CDATA	groups of related headers
BACKGROUND	BODY	URL	image for document background
bgcolor	TABLE	color	background cell color

Attribute	Used in	Valid Value	Purpose
bgcolor	TR	color	background row color
bgcolor	TD, TH	color	background cell color
bgcolor	BODY	color	document background color
border	IMG, OBJECT	pixels	link border width
border	TABLE	pixels	controls frame width around table
cellpadding	TABLE	length	spacing within cells
cellspacing	TABLE	length	spacing between cells
char	COL, COLGROUP, TBODY, TD, TFOOT, TH, THEAD, TR	character	alignment character
charoff	COL, COLGROUP, TBODY, TD, TFOOT, TH, THEAD, TR	length	offset for alignment character
charset	A, LINK, SCRIPT	character set code	code for character set of linked resource
checked	INPUT	checked	Boolean value for radio buttons and check boxes
cite	BLOCKQUCTE, Q	URL	source document
cite	DEL, INS	URL	info on reason for deletion or insertion
class	All elements except BASE, BASEFONT, HEAD, HTML, META, PARAM, SCRIPT, STYLE, TITLE	CDATA	space-separated list of class names
CLASSID	OBJECT	URL	location of code
clear	BR	left, all, right, none	control of text flow next to floated object
code	APPLET	CDATA	location of code
codebase	OBJECT	URL	base URL for object
codebase	APPLET	URL	base URL for applet
codetype	OBJECT	MIME type	MIME type of code
color	BASEFONT, FONT	color	text color

Continued

Attribute	Used in	Valid Value	Purpose
cols	FRAMESET	lengths in comma-separated list	list of lengths
cols	TEXTAREA	number	width of text box
colspan	TD, TH	number	number of cols spanned by cell
compact	DIR, MENU DL, OL, UL	compact	smaller list size
content	META	CDATA	type of content
coords	A, AREA	lengths in comma-separated list	coordinates of imagemap areas
data	OBJECT	URL	reference to object's data
datetime	DEL, INS	YYYY-MM-DD Thh:mm:ssTZD	date, time, and time zone in ISO format
declare	OBJECT	declare	declare but don't run
defer	SCRIPT	defer	optionally run later
dir	All elements except APPLET, BASE, BASEFONT, BDO, BR, FRAME, FRAMESET, IFRAME, PARAM, SCRIPT	ltr, rtl	text direction
dir	BDO	ltr, rtl	text direction
disabled	BUTTON, INPUT, OPTGROUP, OPTION, SELECT, TEXTAREA	disabled	Boolean value to disable this option
enctype	FORM	MIME type	encoding type
face	BASEFONT, FONT	CDATA	comma-separated list of font names
for	LABEL	ID name	matches field ID value
frame	TABLE	void, above, below, hsides, lhs, rhs, vsides, box, border	part to display
frameborder	FRAME, IFRAME	1, 0	borders on or off
headers	TD, TH	ID names	space-separated list of IDs for header cell

Attribute	Used in	Valid Value	Purpose
height	IFRAME	length	frame height
height	IMG, OBJECT	length	override height
height	APPLET	length	initial height
height	TD, TH	length	height for cell
href	A, AREA, LINK	URL	URL for linked resource
href	BASE	URL	base URL
hreflang	A, LINK	language code	language code
hspace	APPLET, IMG, OBJECT	pixels	horizontal gutter
http-equiv	META	text	HTTP response header name
id	All elements except BASE, HEAD, HTML, META, SCRIPT, STYLE, TITLE	ID name	document-wide unique ID
ismap	IMG, INPUT	ismap	use server-side imagemap
label	OPTION, OPTGROUP	text	for use in hierarchical drop-down menus
lang	All elements except APPLET, BASE, BASEFONT, BR, FRAME, FRAMESET, IFRAME, PARAM SCRIPT	language code	specifies language
language	SCRIPT	CDATA	script language name
link	BODY	color	color of links
longdesc	IMG, FRAME, IFRAME	URL	link to long description
marginheight	FRAME, IFRAME	pixels	margin height
marginwidth	FRAME, IFRAME	pixels	margin width
maxlength	INPUT	number	max chars for text fields

Continued

Attribute	Used in	Valid Value	Purpose
media	STYLE, LINK	screen, tty, tv, projection, handheld, print, braille, aural, all	media type
method	FORM	get, post	HTTP method used to submit the form
multiple	SELECT	multiple	Boolean value to enable multiple selections in drop-down list
name	BUTTON, FORM, IMG, TEXTAREA	CDATA	names input object
name	APPLET	CDATA	enables applets to find each other
name	SELECT	CDATA	names the field
name	FRAME, IFRAME	CDATA	name of target frame
name	A	CDATA	name of destination
name	INPUT, OBJECT	CDATA	name of form field
name	MAP	CDATA	name of map
name	PARAM	CDATA	name of applet parameter
name	META	text	name of metainformation field
nohref	AREA	nohref	Boolean value to set region to no action
noresize	FRAME	noresize	deny frame resize
noshade	HR	noshade	Boolean value to turn off 3D effects
nowrap	TD, TH	nowrap	Boolean value to turn off word wrap
object	APPLET	CDATA	serialized applet file
onblur	A, AREA, BUTTON, INPUT, LABEL, SELECT, TEXTAREA	script	event: loss of focus on element (pointer moved away)
onchange	INPUT, SELECT, TEXTAREA	script	event: value changed

Attribute	Used in	Valid Value	Purpose
onclick	All elements except APPLET, BASE, BASEFONT, BDO, BR, FONT, FRAME, FRAMESET, HEAD, HTML, IFRAME, ISINDEX, META, PARAM, SCRIPT, STYLE, TITLE	script	event: mouse click on element
ondblclick	All elements except APPLET, BASE, BASEFONT, BDO, BR, FONT, FRAME, FRAMESET, HEAD, HTML, IFRAME, ISINDEX, META, PARAM, SCRIPT, STYLE, TITLE	script	event: double-click element
onfocus	A, AREA, BUTTON, INPUT, LABEL, SELECT, TEXTAREA	script	event: element selected (receives focus)
onkeydown	All elements except APPLET, BASE, BASEFONT, BDO, BR, FONT, FRAME, FRAMESET, HEAD, HTML, IFRAME, ISINDEX, META, PARAM, SCRIPT, STYLE, TITLE	script	event: key pressed
onkeypress	All elements except APPLET, BASE, BASEFONT, BDO, BR, FONT, FRAME, FRAMESET, HEAD, HTML, IFRAME, ISINDEX, META, PARAM, SCRIPT, STYLE, TITLE	script	event: key pressed and released

Continued

Attribute	Used in	Valid Value	Purpose
onkeyup	**All elements except** APPLET, BASE, BASEFONT, BDO, BR, FONT, FRAME, FRAMESET, HEAD, HTML, IFRAME, ISINDEX, META, PARAM, SCRIPT, STYLE, TITLE	script	event: key released
onload	FRAMESET	script	all frames loaded
onload	BODY	script	document loaded
onmousedown	**All elements except** APPLET, BASE, BASEFONT, BDO, BR, FONT, FRAME, FRAMESET, HEAD, HTML, IFRAME, ISINDEX, META, PARAM, SCRIPT, STYLE, TITLE	script	event: mouse button depressed
onmousemove	**All elements except** APPLET, BASE, BASEFONT, BDO, BR, FONT, FRAME, FRAMESET, HEAD, HTML, IFRAME, ISINDEX, META, PARAM, SCRIPT, STYLE, TITLE	script	event: mouse pointer moved
onmouseout	**All elements except** APPLET, BASE, BASEFONT, BDO, BR, FONT, FRAME, FRAMESET, HEAD, HTML, IFRAME, ISINDEX, META, PARAM, SCRIPT, STYLE, TITLE	script	event: mouse pointer moved away from element

Attribute	Used in	Valid Value	Purpose
onmcuseover	**All elements except** APPLET, BASE, BASEFONT, BDO, BR, FONT, FRAME, FRAMESET, HEAD, HTML, IFRAME, ISINDEX, META, PARAM, SCRIPT, STYLE, TITLE	script	event: mouse pointer moved over element
onmouseup	**All elements except** APPLET, BASE, BASEFONT, BDO, BR, FONT, FRAME, FRAMESET, HEAD, HTML, IFRAME, ISINDEX, META, PARAM, SCRIPT, STYLE, TITLE	script	event: mouse button released
onreset	FORM	script	event: form reset
onselect	INPUT, TEXTAREA	script	event: text selected
onsubmit	FORM	script	event: form submitted
onunload	FRAMESET	script	event: frames removed
onunload	BODY	script	event: document removed
profile	HEAD	URL	explanation of metainformation
prompt	ISINDEX	text	prompt message
readonly	TEXTAREA, INPUT	readonly	user cannot modify
rel	A, LINK	alternate, stylesheet, start, next, prev, contents, index, glossary, copyright, chapter, section, subsection, appendix, help, bookmark	forward link types

Continued

Attribute	Used in	Valid Value	Purpose
rev	A, LINK	alternate, stylesheet, start, next, prev, contents, index, glossary, copyright, chapter, section, subsection, appendix, help, bookmark	reverse link types
rows	FRAMESET	lengths	comma-separated list of lengths
rows	TEXTAREA	number	height (in lines) of text entry area
rowspan	TD, TH	number	rows spanned by cell
rules	COLS, ROWS, TABLE	none, groups	rulings between rows and cols
scheme	META	CDATA	form of content
scope	TD, TH	row, col, rowgroup, colgroup	location of headers
scrolling	FRAME, IFRAME	yes, no, auto	scrollbar in frame
selected	OPTION	selected	Boolean value to set selected option in drop-down list box
shape	A, AREA	rect, circle, poly, default	set imagemap area shape
size	HR	pixels	size of rule
size	FONT	CDATA	relative font size
size	INPUT	CDATA	varies by field
size	BASEFONT	CDATA	base font size
size	SELECT	number	rows visible
span	COL	number	number of columns modified by attributes
span	COLGROUP	number	number of columns in group
src	SCRIPT	URL	location of external script
src	INPUT	URL	location of image

Attribute	Used in	Valid Value	Purpose
src	FRAME, IFRAME	URL	location of frame content
src	IMG	URL	location of image
standby	OBJECT	text	message to show while loading
start	OL	number	starting number
style	All elements except BASE, BASEFONT, HEAD, HTML, META, PARAM, SCRIPT, STYLE, TITLE	style definition	inline style definition
summary	TABLE	text	for speech output
tabindex	A, AREA, BUTTON, INPUT, OBJECT, SELECT, TEXTAREA	number	position in tab order
target	A, AREA, BASE, FORM, LINK	target name or _blank, _self, _top, _parent	display in frame
text	BODY	color	default text color
title	STYLE	text	title
title	All elements except BASE, BASEFONT, HEAD, HTML, META, PARAM, SCRIPT, TITLE	text	text to display in tool tip
type	A, LINK OBJECT, PARAM, SCRIPT, STYLE	MIME type	content type of data
type	INPUT	text, password, checkbox, radio, submit, reset, file, hidden, image, button	type of input control
type	LI, UL	disc, square, circle	bullet style
type	OL	1, a, A, i, I	number style

Continued

Attribute	Used in	Valid Value	Purpose
type	BUTTON	button, submit, reset	type of button
usemap	IMG, INPUT, OBJECT	URL	client-side imagemap
valign	COL, COLGROUP, TBODY, TD, TFOOT, TH, THEAD, TR	top, middle, bottom, baseline	vertical alignment
value	INPUT PAIR, OPTION	CDATA	default content of form control
value	PARAM	CDATA	value of parameter
value	BUTTON	CDATA	sent to server when submitted
value	LI	number	reset sequence number
valuetype	PARAM, OBJECT	DATA, REF	type of data
version	HTML	CDATA	HTML version
vlink	BODY	color	color of visited links
vspace	APPLET, IMG, OBJECT	pixels	size of vertical gutter
width	HR	length	width of rule
width	IFRAME	length	frame width
width	IMG, OBJECT	length	override width
width	TABLE	length	table width
width	APPLET	length	initial width of applet
width	COL, COLGROUP	space-separated list of lengths	width of columns
width	TD, TH	length	cell width
width	PRE	number	line length

✦   ✦   ✦

HTML 4 Character Entities Reference

Character Appearance	Character Name	Entity	Code Mnemonic
&	ampersand	&#38;	&amp;
«	angle quotation mark, left	&#171;	&laquo;
»	angle quotation mark, right	&#187;	&raquo;
¦	broken vertical bar	&#166;	&brvbar;
Á	capital A, acute accent	&#193;	&Aacute;
Â	capital A, circumflex accent	&#194;	&Acirc;
Ä	capital A, dieresis or umlaut mark	&#196;	&Auml;
À	capital A, grave accent	&#192;	&Agrave;
Å	capital A, ring	&#197;	&Aring;
Ã	capital A, tilde	&#195;	&Atilde;
Æ	capital AE diphthong (ligature)	&#198;	&AElig;

Continued

Character Appearance	Character Name	Entity	Code Mnemonic
Ç	capital C, cedilla	&#199;	&Ccedil;
É	capital E, acute accent	&#201;	&Eacute;
Ê	capital E, circumflex accent	&#202;	&Ecirc;
Ë	capital E, dieresis or umlaut mark	&#203;	&Euml;
È	capital E, grave accent	&#200;	&Egrave;
Ð	capital Eth, Icelandic	&#208;	&ETH;
Í	capital I, acute accent	&#205;	&Iacute;
Î	capital I, circumflex accent	&#206;	&Icirc;
Ï	capital I, dieresis or umlaut mark	&#207;	&Iuml;
Ì	capital I, grave accent	&#204;	&Igrave;
Ñ	capital N, tilde	&#209;	&Ntilde;
Ó	capital O, acute accent	&#211;	&Oacute;
Ô	capital O, circumflex accent	&#212;	&Ocirc;
Ö	capital O, dieresis or umlaut mark	&#214;	&Ouml;
Ò	capital O, grave accent	&#210;	&Ograve;
Ø	capital O, slash	&#216;	&Oslash;
Õ	capital O, tilde	&#213;	&Otilde;
Þ	capital THORN, Icelandic	&#222;	&THORN;
Ú	capital U, acute accent	&#218;	&Uacute;
Û	capital U, circumflex accent	&#219;	&Ucirc;
Ü	capital U, dieresis or umlaut mark	&#220;	&Uuml;
Ù	capital U, grave accent	&#217;	&Ugrave;
Ý	capital Y, acute accent	&#221;	&Yacute;
¢	cent sign	&#162;	&cent;
®	circled R registered sign	&#174;	&reg;
©	copyright sign	&#169;	&copy;
¤	currency sign	&#164;	&curren;
°	degree sign	&#176;	&deg;
÷	division sign	&#247;	&divide;
ª	feminine ordinal indicator	&#170;	&ordf;
½	fraction 1/2	&#189;	&frac12;

Character Appearance	Character Name	Entity	Code Mnemonic
¼	fraction 1/4	&#188;	&frac14;
¾	fraction 3/4	&#190;	&frac34;
>	greater-than sign	&#61;	&gt;
¡	inverted exclamation mark	&#161;	&iexcl;
¿	inverted question mark	&#191;	&iquest;
<	less-than sign	&#60;	&lt;
º	masculine ordinal indicator	&#186;	&ordm;
µ	micro sign	&#181;	&micro;
·	middle dot	&#183;	&middot;
×	multiplication sign	&#215;	&times;
¬	negation sign	&#172;	&not;
	nonbreaking space		
¶	paragraph sign	&#182;	&para;
±	plus-or-minus sign	&#177;	&plusmn;
£	pound sign	&#163;	&pound;
"	quotation mark	&#34;	&quot;
§	section sign	&#167;	&sect;
á	small a, acute accent	&#225;	&aacute;
â	small a, circumflex accent	&#226;	&acirc;
ä	small a, dieresis or umlaut mark	&#228;	&auml;
à	small a, grave accent	&#224;	&agrave;
å	small a, ring	&#229;	&aring;
ã	small a, tilde	&#227;	&atilde;
æ	small ae diphthong (ligature)	&#230;	&aelig;
ç	small c, cedilla	&#231;	&ccedil;
é	small e, acute accent	&#233;	&eacute;
ê	small e, circumflex accent	&#234;	&ecirc;
ë	small e, dieresis or umlaut mark	&#235;	&euml;
è	small e, grave accent	&#232;	&egrave;

Continued

Character Appearance	Character Name	Entity	Code Mnemonic
ð	small eth, Icelandic	&#240;	&eth;
í	small i, acute accent	&#237;	&iacute;
î	small i, circumflex accent	&#238;	&icirc;
ï	small i, dieresis or umlaut mark	&#239;	&iuml;
ì	small i, grave accent	&#236;	&igrave;
ñ	small n, tilde	&#241;	&ntilde;
ó	small o, acute accent	&#243;	&oacute;
ô	small o, circumflex accent	&#244;	&ocirc;
ö	small o, dieresis or umlaut mark	&#246;	&ouml;
ò	small o, grave accent	&#242;	&ograve;
ø	small o, slash	&#248;	&oslash;
õ	small o, tilde	&#245;	&otilde;
ß	small sharp s, German (sz ligature)	&#223;	&szlig;
þ	small thorn, Icelandic	&#254;	&thorn;
ú	small u, acute accent	&#250;	&uacute;
û	small u, circumflex accent	&#251;	&ucirc;
ü	small u, dieresis or umlaut mark	&#252;	&uuml;
ù	small u, grave accent	&#249;	&ugrave;
ý	small y, acute accent	&#253;	&yacute;
ÿ	small y, dieresis or umlaut mark	&#255;	&yuml;
-	soft hyphen	&#173;	&shy;
´	spacing acute	&#180;	&acute;
¸	spacing cedilla	&#184;	&cedil;
¨	spacing diaresis	&#168;	&uml;
¯	spacing macron	&#175;	&macr;
¹	superscript 1	&#185;	&sup1;
²	superscript 2	&#178;	&sup2;
³	superscript 3	&#179;	&sup3;
¥	yen sign	&#165;	&yen;

◆   ◆   ◆

Cascading Style Sheets Reference

Backgrounds and Color

color

PURPOSE	Specifies the foreground color of an element.
INHERITED	Yes
VALUES	Color code or mnemonic
DEFAULT	Defined by browser
USED IN	All elements
SUPPORT	MSIE 3.0/Win95: Yes
	MSIE 4.0/Win95: Yes
	MSIE 5.0/Win98: Yes
	NN 4.0/Win95: Yes
	NN 4.7/Win98: Yes
	MSIE 3.0/Mac OS: Yes
	MSIE 4.0/Mac OS: Yes
	NN 4.0/Mac OS: Yes
EXAMPLE	`{color: #C0C0C0}` or `{color: red}`
TIP	You can specify values using color codes or color mnemonics.

background

PURPOSE	Provides a shorthand method for grouping background properties.

INHERITED   Yes

VALUES   You can specify any of the values used for background-color, background-image, background-repeat, background-attachment, or background-position.

DEFAULT   Not defined

USED IN   All elements

SUPPORT   MSIE 3.0/Win95: Yes

MSIE 4.0/Win95: Yes

MSIE 5.0/Win98: Yes

NN 4.0/Win95: Yes

NN 4.7/Win98: Yes

MSIE 3.0/Mac OS: Yes

MSIE 4.0/Mac OS: Yes

NN 4.0/Mac OS: Yes

EXAMPLE   `{background: url("picture.gif") repeat fixed}`

TIP   This is a handy way to set background properties without much typing. Note, some browsers may not support all the background properties.

background-color

PURPOSE   Specifies the background color of an element.

INHERITED   Yes

VALUES   Color code or mnemonic

DEFAULT   Defined by browser

USED IN   All elements

SUPPORT   MSIE 3.0/Win95:Yes

MSIE 4.0/Win95: Yes

MSIE 5.0/Win98: Yes

NN 4.0/Win95: Yes

NN 4.7/Win98: Yes

MSIE 3.0/Mac OS: No

MSIE 4.0/Mac OS: Yes

NN 4.0/Mac OS: Yes

EXAMPLE	{background color: #C0C0C0} or {background color: red}
TIP	You can specify values using color codes or color mnemonics.

background-image

PURPOSE	Inserts a graphic in an element's background.
INHERITED	Yes
VALUES	Color code or mnemonic
DEFAULT	Defined by browser
USED IN	All elements
SUPPORT	MSIE 3.0/Win95: Yes
	MSIE 4.0/Win95: Yes
	MSIE 5.0/Win98: Yes
	NN 4.0/Win95: Yes
	NN 4.7/Win98: Yes
	MSIE 3.0/Mac OS: No
	MSIE 4.0/Mac OS: Yes
	NN 4.0/Mac OS: Yes
EXAMPLE	{background-image: url("picture.gif")}
TIP	Note the syntax for including URLs; it differs from the way you include URLs in HTML statements. Use caution with this property; current implementations are buggy.

background-repeat

PURPOSE	Specifies how a background image is repeated.
INHERITED	Yes
VALUES	repeat, repeat-x, repeat-y, or no-repeat. Repeat repeats the image both horizontally and vertically. Repeat-x repeats the image horizontally, while repeat-y repeats the image vertically.
DEFAULT	repeat
USED IN	All elements

SUPPORT	MSIE 3.0/Win95: No
	MSIE 4.0/Win95: Yes
	MSIE 5.0/Win98: Yes
	NN 4.0/Win95: Yes
	NN 4.7/Win98: Yes
	MSIE 3.0/Mac OS: No
	MSIE 4.0/Mac OS: Yes
	NN 4.0/Mac OS: Yes
EXAMPLE	`{background-repeat: repeat-x}`
TIP	If a browser doesn't recognize this property, it will ignore the property.

background-attachment

PURPOSE	Determines whether the background image scrolls with the content or remains fixed.
INHERITED	Yes
VALUES	Scroll or fixed
DEFAULT	Defined by browser
USED IN	All elements
SUPPORT	MSIE 3.0/Win95: No
	MSIE 4.0/Win95: Yes
	MSIE 5.0/Win98: Yes
	NN 4.0/Win95: No
	NN 4.7/Win98: No
	MSIE 3.0/Mac OS: No
	MSIE 4.0/Mac OS: Yes
	NN 4.0/Mac OS: No
EXAMPLE	`{background-attachment: fixed}`
TIP	This property isn't widely supported, but it isn't risky to use; if a browser doesn't recognize it, it scrolls the image with the text. This property isn't supported by Netscape Navigator 4.

background-position

PURPOSE	Specifies the position of the background graphic within an element.
INHERITED	Yes
VALUES	You can specify the position in several different ways. The easiest way uses keywords (top left, top center, right top, left center, center, right center, bottom left, bottom center, and bottom right). You can also type two percentages to express the distance from the left and the distance from the top, respectively; 50 percent 100 percent is the same as bottom center. You can also type measurements for an absolute position from the left and top, respectively (see the examples).
DEFAULT	Defined by browser
USED IN	All elements
SUPPORT	MSIE 3.0/Win95: No
	MSIE 4.0/Win95: Yes
	MSIE 5.0/Win98: Yes
	NN 4.0/Win95: No
	NN 4.7/Win98: No
	MSIE 3.0/Mac OS: No
	MSIE 4.0/Mac OS: No
	NN 4.0/Mac OS: No
EXAMPLE	`{background-position: top center}{background-position: 50% 0%}{background position: 48pt 60pt}`
TIP	This property is not supported by Netscape Navigator 4.

Box Properties

border

PURPOSE	Provides a shorthand means of specifying all types of properties for all borders.
INHERITED	No
VALUES	Specify any value used in the border color or border width properties.

DEFAULT	0
USED IN	Replaced and block-level elements
SUPPORT	MSIE 3.0/Win95: No
	MSIE 4.0/Win95: Yes
	MSIE 5.0/Win98: Yes
	NN 4.0/Win95: Yes
	NN 4.7/Win98: Yes
	MSIE 3.0/Mac OS: No
	MSIE 4.0/Mac OS: Yes
	NN 4.0/Mac OS: Yes
EXAMPLE	`{border: 1pt blue}`
TIP	If you type just one measurement, it applies to all four borders.

border-color

PURPOSE	Provides a shorthand means of specifying color settings for all borders.
INHERITED	No
VALUES	Specify colors for the top, right, bottom, and left borders, in that order. If you specify only one value, it applies to all four sides.
DEFAULT	Not defined
USED IN	Replaced and block-level elements
SUPPORT	MSIE 3.0/Win95: Yes
	MSIE 4.0/Win95: Yes
	MSIE 5.0/Win98: Yes
	NN 4.0/Win95: Yes
	NN 4.7/Win98: Yes
	MSIE 3.0/Mac OS: Yes
	MSIE 4.0/Mac OS: Yes
	NN 4.0/Mac OS: Yes
EXAMPLE	`{border-color: red}`
TIP	If you specify just one value, it applies to all four margins.

border-bottom-color

PURPOSE	Specifies the color of the box's bottom border.
INHERITED	No
VALUES	Specify a color code or mnemonic.
DEFAULT	Value of the color property for the current element
USED IN	Replaced and block-level elements
SUPPORT	MSIE 3.0/Win95: No
	MSIE 4.0/Win95: Yes
	MSIE 5.0/Win98: Yes
	NN 4.0/Win95: Yes
	NN 4.7/Win98: Yes
	MSIE 3.0/Mac OS: No
	MSIE 4.0/Mac OS: Yes
	NN 4.0/Mac OS: Yes
EXAMPLE	`{border-bottom-color: silver}`
TIP	You can use the border property to set the border properties for all four sides at once.

border-left-color

PURPOSE	Specifies the color of the box's left border.
INHERITED	No
VALUES	Specify a color code or mnemonic.
DEFAULT	Value of the color property for the current element
USED IN	Replaced and block-level elements
SUPPORT	MSIE 3.0/Win95: No
	MSIE 4.0/Win95: Yes
	MSIE 5.0/Win98: Yes
	NN 4.0/Win95: Yes
	NN 4.7/Win98: Yes
	MSIE 3.0/Mac OS: No
	MSIE 4.0/Mac OS: Yes
	NN 4.0/Mac OS: Yes

EXAMPLE   {border-left-color: red}

TIP   You can use the border property to set the border properties for all four sides at once.

border-right-color

PURPOSE   Specifies the width of the box's right border.

INHERITED   No

VALUES   Specify a color code or mnemonic.

DEFAULT   Value of the color property for the current element

USED IN   Replaced and block-level elements

SUPPORT   MSIE 3.0/Win95: No

MSIE 4.0/Win95: Yes

MSIE 5.0/Win98: Yes

NN 4.0/Win95: Yes

NN 4.7/Win98: Yes

MSIE 3.0/Mac OS: No

MSIE 4.0/Mac OS: Yes

NN 4.0/Mac OS: Yes

EXAMPLE   {border-right-color: red}

TIP   You can use the border property to set the border properties for all four sides at once.

border-top-color

PURPOSE   Specifies the color of the box's top border.

INHERITED   No

VALUES   Specify a color code or mnemonic.

DEFAULT   Value of the color property for the current element

USED IN   Replaced and block-level elements

SUPPORT   MSIE 3.0/Win95: No

MSIE 4.0/Win95: Yes

MSIE 5.0/Win98: Yes

NN 4.0/Win95: Yes

NN 4.7/Win98: Yes

	MSIE 3.0/Mac OS: No
	MSIE 4.0/Mac OS: Yes
	NN 4.0/Mac OS: Yes
EXAMPLE	{border-top-color: blue}
TIP	You can use the border property to set the border properties for all four sides at once.

border-style

PURPOSE	Provides a shorthand means of specifying color settings for all borders.
INHERITED	No
VALUES	Specify styles for the top, right, bottom, and left borders, in that order. If you specify only one value, it applies to all four sides. You can choose from none, dotted, dashed, solid, double, groove, ridge, inset, and outset.
DEFAULT	Not defined
USED IN	Replaced and block-level elements
SUPPORT	MSIE 3.0/Win95: Yes
	MSIE 4.0/Win95: Yes
	MSIE 5.0/Win98: Yes
	NN 4.0/Win95: Yes
	NN 4.7/Win98: Yes
	MSIE 3.0/Mac OS: Yes
	MSIE 4.0/Mac OS: Yes
	NN 4.0/Mac OS: Yes
EXAMPLE	{border-style: double}
TIP	If you specify just one value, it applies to all four margins.

border-bottom-style

PURPOSE	Specifies the color of the box's bottom border.
INHERITED	No
VALUES	none, dotted, dashed, hidden, solid, double, groove, ridge, inset, outset.
DEFAULT	Value of the color property for the current element

USED IN	Replaced and block-level elements
SUPPORT	MSIE 3.0/Win95: No
	MSIE 4.0/Win95: Yes
	MSIE 5.0/Win98: Yes
	NN 4.0/Win95: Yes
	NN 4.7/Win98: Yes
	MSIE 3.0/Mac OS: No
	MSIE 4.0/Mac OS: Yes
	NN 4.0/Mac OS: Yes
EXAMPLE	`{border-bottom-style: dashed}`
TIP	You can use the border property to set the border properties for all four sides at once. This property isn't supported by Netscape Navigator 4; you must use the same properties for all four borders. Note that neither Netscape Navigator nor Microsoft Internet Explorer support dashed or dotted border styles.

border-left-style

PURPOSE	Specifies the color of the box's left border.
INHERITED	No
VALUES	none, dotted, dashed, hidden, solid, double, groove, ridge, inset, outset.
DEFAULT	Value of the color property for the current element
USED IN	Replaced and block-level elements
SUPPORT	MSIE 3.0/Win95: No
	MSIE 4.0/Win95: Yes
	MSIE 5.0/Win98: Yes
	NN 4.0/Win95: Yes
	NN 4.7/Win98: Yes
	MSIE 3.0/Mac OS: No
	MSIE 4.0/Mac OS: Yes
	NN 4.0/Mac OS: Yes
EXAMPLE	`{border-left-style: groove}`

TIP | You can use the border property to set the border properties for all four sides at once.

border-right-style

PURPOSE	Specifies the width of the box's right border.
INHERITED	No
VALUES	none, dotted, dashed, hidden, solid, double, groove, ridge, inset, outset.
DEFAULT	Value of the color property for the current element
USED IN	Replaced and block-level elements
SUPPORT	MSIE 3.0/Win95: No
	MSIE 4.0/Win95: Yes
	MSIE 5.0/Win98: Yes
	NN 4.0/Win95: Yes
	NN 4.7/Win98: Yes
	MSIE 3.0/Mac OS: No
	MSIE 4.0/Mac OS: Yes
	NN 4.0/Mac OS: Yes
EXAMPLE	{border-right-style: inset}
TIP	You can use the border property to set the border properties for all four sides at once.

border-top-style

PURPOSE	Specifies the color of the box's top border.
INHERITED	No
VALUES	none, dotted, dashed, solid, hidden, double, groove, ridge, inset, outset.
DEFAULT	Value of the color property for the current element
USED IN	Replaced and block-level elements
SUPPORT	MSIE 3.0/Win95: No
	MSIE 4.0/Win95: Yes
	MSIE 5.0/Win98: Yes

NN 4.0/Win95: Yes

NN 4.7/Win98: Yes

MSIE 3.0/Mac OS: No

MSIE 4.0/Mac OS: Yes

NN 4.0/Mac OS: Yes

| EXAMPLE | `{border-top-style: groove}` |
| TIP | You can use the border property to set the border properties for all four sides at once. |

border-width

PURPOSE	Provides a shorthand means of specifying width settings for all borders.
INHERITED	No
VALUES	Specify lengths for the top, right, bottom, and left borders, in that order. If you specify only one value, it applies to all four sides.
DEFAULT	Not defined
USED IN	Replaced and block-level elements
SUPPORT	MSIE 3.0/Win95: Yes
	MSIE 4.0/Win95: Yes
	MSIE 5.0/Win98: Yes
	NN 4.0/Win95: No
	NN 4.7/Win98: No
	MSIE 3.0/Mac OS: Yes
	MSIE 4.0/Mac OS: Yes
	NN 4.0/Mac OS: Yes
EXAMPLE	`{border-width: 1pt}`
TIP	If you specify just one value, it applies to all four margins.

border-bottom-width

PURPOSE	Specifies the width of the box's bottom border.
INHERITED	No
VALUES	Specify thin, medium, or thick, or type a length.

DEFAULT	0
USED IN	Replaced and block-level elements
SUPPORT	MSIE 3.0/Win95: No
	MSIE 4.0/Win95: Yes
	MSIE 5.0/Win98: Yes
	NN 4.0/Win95: No
	NN 4.7/Win98: No
	MSIE 3.0/Mac OS: No
	MSIE 4.0/Mac OS: Yes
	NN 4.0/Mac OS: Yes
EXAMPLE	`{border-bottcm-width: 0.5in}`
TIP	You can use the border property to set the border properties for all four sides at once. This property isn't supported by Netscape Navigator 4; you must use the same properties for all four borders.

border-left-width

PURPOSE	Specifies the width of the box's left border.
INHERITED	No
VALUES	Specify thin, medium, or thick, or type a length.
DEFAULT	0
USED IN	Replaced and block-level elements
SUPPORT	MSIE 3.0/Win95: No
	MSIE 4.0/Win95: Yes
	MSIE 5.0/Win98: Yes
	NN 4.0/Win95: No
	NN 4.7/Win98: No
	MSIE 3.0/Mac OS: No
	MSIE 4.0/Mac OS: Yes
	NN 4.0/Mac OS: Yes
EXAMPLE	`{border-left-width: 0.5in}`
TIP	You can use the border property to set the border properties for all four sides at once. This property isn't supported by Netscape Navigator 4; you must use the same properties for all four borders.

border-right-width

PURPOSE	Specifies the width of the box's right border.
INHERITED	No
VALUES	Specify thin, medium, or thick, or type a length.
DEFAULT	0
USED IN	Replaced and block-level elements
SUPPORT	MSIE 3.0/Win95: No
	MSIE 4.0/Win95: Yes
	MSIE 5.0/Win98: Yes
	NN 4.0/Win95: No
	NN 4.7/Win98: No
	MSIE 3.0/Mac OS: No
	MSIE 4.0/Mac OS: Yes
	NN 4.0/Mac OS: Yes
EXAMPLE	`{border-right-width: 0.5in}`
TIP	You can use the border property to set the border properties for all four sides at once. This property isn't supported by Netscape Navigator 4; you must use the same properties for all four borders.

border-top-width

PURPOSE	Specifies the width of the box's top border.
INHERITED	No
VALUES	Specify thin, medium, or thick, or type a length.
DEFAULT	0
USED IN	Replaced and block-level elements
SUPPORT	MSIE 3.0/Win95: No
	MSIE 4.0/Win95: Yes
	MSIE 5.0/Win98: Yes
	NN 4.0/Win95: No
	NN 4.7/Win98: No

MSIE 3.0/Mac OS: No

MSIE 4.0/Mac OS: Yes

NN 4.0/Mac OS: Yes

EXAMPLE `{border-top-width: 0.5in}`

TIP You can use the border property to set the border properties for all four sides at once. This property isn't supported by Netscape Navigator 4; you must use the same properties for all four borders.

height

PURPOSE Specifies the height of an element.

INHERITED No

VALUES Specify a length or a percentage of the containing block, or auto.

DEFAULT auto

USED IN Replaced and block-level elements

SUPPORT MSIE 3.0/Win95: Yes

MSIE 4.0/Win95: Yes

MSIE 5.0/Win98: Yes

NN 4.0/Win95: Yes

NN 4.7/Win98: Yes

MSIE 3.0/Mac OS: Yes

MSIE 4.0/Mac OS: Yes

NN 4.0/Mac OS: Yes

EXAMPLE `{height: 50%}`

TIP If the height is set to auto, the height is determined by the intrinsic height of the element.

margin

PURPOSE Provides a shorthand means of specifying settings for all margins.

INHERITED No

VALUES Specify lengths for the top, right, bottom, and left margins, in that order. If you specify only one value, it applies to all four sides.

DEFAULT	Not defined
USED IN	Replaced and block-level elements
SUPPORT	MSIE 3.0/Win95: Yes
	MSIE 4.0/Win95: Yes
	MSIE 5.0/Win98: Yes
	NN 4.0/Win95: No
	NN 4.7/Win98: No
	MSIE 3.0/Mac OS: Yes
	MSIE 4.0/Mac OS: Yes
	NN 4.0/Mac OS: Yes
EXAMPLE	{margin: 0.5in}
TIP	If you specify just one value, it applies to all four margins.

margin-bottom

PURPOSE	Specifies the width of the box's bottom margin.
INHERITED	No
VALUES	Specify a length or a percentage of the containing block, or auto.
DEFAULT	0
USED IN	Replaced and block-level elements
SUPPORT	MSIE 3.0/Win95: Yes
	MSIE 4.0/Win95: Yes
	MSIE 5.0/Win98: Yes
	NN 4.0/Win95: No
	NN 4.7/Win98: No
	MSIE 3.0/Mac OS: Yes
	MSIE 4.0/Mac OS: Yes
	NN 4.0/Mac OS: Yes
EXAMPLE	{margin-bottom: 0.5in}
TIP	You can use the margin property to set the margin for all four sides at once.

margin-left

PURPOSE	Specifies the width of the box's left margin.
INHERITED	No
VALUES	Specify a length or a percentage of the containing block, or auto.
DEFAULT	0
USED IN	Replaced and block-level elements
SUPPORT	MSIE 3.0/Win95: Yes
	MSIE 4.0/Win95: Yes
	MSIE 5.0/Win98: Yes
	NN 4.0/Win95: Yes
	NN 4.7/Win98: Yes
	MSIE 3.0/Mac OS: Yes
	MSIE 4.0/Mac OS: Yes
	NN 4.0/Mac OS: Yes
EXAMPLE	`{margin-left: 0.5in}`
TIP	You can use the margin property to set the margin for all four sides at once.

margin-right

PURPOSE	Specifies the width of the box's right margin.
INHERITED	No
VALUES	Specify a length or a percentage of the containing block, or auto.
DEFAULT	0
USED IN	Replaced and block-level elements
SUPPORT	MSIE 3.0/Win95: Yes
	MSIE 4.0/Win95: Yes
	MSIE 5.0/Win98: Yes
	NN 4.0/Win95: Yes
	NN 4.7/Win98: Yes
	MSIE 3.0/Mac OS: Yes
	MSIE 4.0/Mac OS: Yes
	NN 4.0/Mac OS: Yes

EXAMPLE	{margin-right: 0.5in}
TIP	You can use the margin property to set the margin for all four sides at once.

margin-top

PURPOSE	Specifies the width of the box's top margin.
INHERITED	No
VALUES	Specify a length or a percentage of the containing block, or auto.
DEFAULT	0
USED IN	Replaced and block-level elements
SUPPORT	MSIE 3.0/Win95: Yes
	MSIE 4.0/Win95: Yes
	MSIE 5.0/Win98: Yes
	NN 4.0/Win95: Yes
	NN 4.7/Win98: Yes
	MSIE 3.0/Mac OS: Yes
	MSIE 4.0/Mac OS: Yes
	NN 4.0/Mac OS: Yes
EXAMPLE	{margin-top: 0.5in}
TIP	You can use the margin property to set the margin for all four sides at once.

max-height

PURPOSE	Specifies the maximum height of an element.
INHERITED	No
VALUES	Specify a length or a percentage of the containing block, or none.
DEFAULT	0
USED IN	Replaced and block-level elements
SUPPORT	MSIE 3.0/Win95: Yes
	MSIE 4.0/Win95: Yes
	MSIE 5.0/Win98: Yes

NN 4.0/Win95: Yes

NN 4.7/Win98: Yes

MSIE 3.0/Mac OS: Yes

MSIE 4.0/Mac OS: Yes

NN 4.0/Mac OS: Yes

EXAMPLE   `{max-height: 50%}`

TIP   You can also set the minimum height of an element
(with min-height).

min-height

PURPOSE   Specifies the minimum height of an element.

INHERITED   No

VALUES   Specify a length or a percentage of the containing block.

DEFAULT   0

USED IN   Replaced and block-level elements

SUPPORT   MSIE 3.0/Win95: Yes

MSIE 4.0/Win95: Yes

MSIE 5.0/Win98: Yes

NN 4.0/Win95: Yes

NN 4.7/Win98: Yes

MSIE 3.0/Mac OS: Yes

MSIE 4.0/Mac OS: Yes

NN 4.0/Mac OS: Yes

EXAMPLE   `{min-height: 50%}`

TIP   You can also set the maximum height of an element
(with max-height).

max-width

PURPOSE   Specifies the maximum width of an element.

INHERITED   No

VALUES   Specify a length or a percentage of the containing block,
or none.

DEFAULT	0
USED IN	Replaced and block-level elements
SUPPORT	MSIE 3.0/Win95: Yes
	MSIE 4.0/Win95: Yes
	MSIE 5.0/Win98: Yes
	NN 4.0/Win95: Yes
	NN 4.7/Win98: Yes
	MSIE 3.0/Mac OS: Yes
	MSIE 4.0/Mac OS: Yes
	NN 4.0/Mac OS: Yes
EXAMPLE	{max-width: 50%}
TIP	You can also set the minimum width of an element (with min-width).

min-width

PURPOSE	Specifies the minimum width of an element.
INHERITED	No
VALUES	Specify a length or a percentage of the containing block.
DEFAULT	0
USED IN	Replaced and block-level elements
SUPPORT	MSIE 3.0/Win95: Yes
	MSIE 4.0/Win95: Yes
	MSIE 5.0/Win98: Yes
	NN 4.0/Win95: Yes
	NN 4.7/Win98: Yes
	MSIE 3.0/Mac OS: Yes
	MSIE 4.0/Mac OS: Yes
	NN 4.0/Mac OS: Yes
EXAMPLE	{min-width: 50%}
TIP	You can also set the maximum width of an element (with max-width).

padding

PURPOSE	Provides a shorthand means of specifying settings for all paddings.
INHERITED	No
VALUES	Specify lengths for the top, right, bottom, and left paddings, in that order. If you specify only one value, it applies to all four sides.
DEFAULT	Not defined
USED IN	Replaced and block-level elements
SUPPORT	MSIE 3.0/Win95: Yes
	MSIE 4.0/Win95: Yes
	MSIE 5.0/Win98: Yes
	NN 4.0/Win95: Yes
	NN 4.7/Win98: Yes
	MSIE 3.0/Mac OS: Yes
	MSIE 4.0/Mac OS: Yes
	NN 4.0/Mac OS: Yes
EXAMPLE	{padding: 0.25in}
TIP	If you specify just one value, it applies to all four paddings.

padding-bottom

PURPOSE	Specifies the width of the box's bottom padding.
INHERITED	No
VALUES	Specify a length or a percentage of the containing block.
DEFAULT	0
USED IN	Replaced and block-level elements
SUPPORT	MSIE 3.0/Win95: Yes
	MSIE 4.0/Win95: Yes
	MSIE 5.0/Win98: Yes
	NN 4.0/Win95: Yes
	NN 4.7/Win98: Yes

MSIE 3.0/Mac OS: Yes

MSIE 4.0/Mac OS: Yes

NN 4.0/Mac OS: Yes

EXAMPLE   `{padding-bottom: 0.5in}`

TIP   You can use the padding property to set the padding for all four sides at once.

padding-left

PURPOSE   Specifies the width of the box's left padding.

INHERITED   No

VALUES   Specify a length or a percentage of the containing block.

DEFAULT   0

USED IN   Replaced and block-level elements

SUPPORT   MSIE 3.0/Win95: Yes

MSIE 4.0/Win95: Yes

MSIE 5.0/Win98: Yes

NN 4.0/Win95: Yes

NN 4.7/Win98: Yes

MSIE 3.0/Mac OS: Yes

MSIE 4.0/Mac OS: Yes

NN 4.0/Mac OS: Yes

EXAMPLE   `{padding-left: 0.5in}`

TIP   You can use the padding property to set the padding for all four sides at once.

padding-right

PURPOSE   Specifies the width of the box's right padding.

INHERITED   No

VALUES   Specify a length or a percentage of the containing block.

DEFAULT   0

USED IN   Replaced and block-level elements

SUPPORT   MSIE 3.0/Win95: Yes

MSIE 4.0/Win95: Yes

MSIE 5.0/Win98: Yes

NN 4.0/Win95: Yes

NN 4.7/Win98: Yes

MSIE 3.0/Mac OS: Yes

MSIE 4.0/Mac OS: Yes

NN 4.0/Mac OS: Yes

EXAMPLE   `{padding-right: 0.5in}`

TIP   You can use the padding property to set the padding for all four sides at once.

padding-top

PURPOSE   Specifies the width of the box's top padding.

INHERITED   No

VALUES   Specify a length or a percentage of the containing block.

DEFAULT   0

USED IN   Replaced and block-level elements

SUPPORT   MSIE 3.0/Win95: Yes

MSIE 4.0/Win95: Yes

MSIE 5.0/Win98: Yes

NN 4.0/Win95: Yes

NN 4.7/Win98: Yes

MSIE 3.0/Mac OS: Yes

MSIE 4.0/Mac OS: Yes

NN 4.0/Mac OS: Yes

EXAMPLE   `{padding-top: 0.5in}`

TIP   You can use the padding property to set the padding for all four sides at once.

width

PURPOSE	Specifies the width of an element.
INHERITED	No
VALUES	Specify a length or a percentage of the containing block, or auto.
DEFAULT	auto
USED IN	Replaced and block-level elements
SUPPORT	MSIE 3.0/Win95: Yes
	MSIE 4.0/Win95: Yes
	MSIE 5.0/Win98: Yes
	NN 4.0/Win95: Yes
	NN 4.7/Win98: Yes
	MSIE 3.0/Mac OS: Yes
	MSIE 4.0/Mac OS: Yes
	NN 4.0/Mac OS: Yes
EXAMPLE	{width: 50%}
TIP	If the width is set to auto, the width is determined by the intrinsic width of the element.

Display Properties

cursor

PURPOSE	Affects the appearance of the mouse pointer as it moves over an object.
INHERITED	Yes
VALUES	auto, crosshair, default, move, pointer, e-resize, ne-resize, nw-resize, n-resize, se-resize, sw-resize, s-resize, w-resize, text, wait, help, url.
DEFAULT	auto
USED IN	All elements
SUPPORT	MSIE 3.0/Win95: No
	MSIE 4.0/Win95: Yes
	MSIE 5.0/Win98: Yes

NN 4.0/Win95: No

NN 4.7/Win98: Yes

MSIE 3.0/Mac OS: No

MSIE 4.0/Mac OS: Yes

NN 4.0/Mac OS: No

EXAMPLE {cursor: crosshair}

TIP This is a cool property because it doesn't require any scripting, but produces dynamic results.

display

PURPOSE Specifies that an object should be hidden in such a way that neither its space nor its content displays.

INHERITED No

VALUES none, block, inline, list-item, marker, run-in,compact, table, inline-table, table-row-group, table-header-group, table-footer-group, table-row, table-column-group

DEFAULT inline

USED IN TABLE, INPUT, TEXTAREA, INPUT type="button", DIV, SPAN, IFRAME, IMG, BODY

SUPPORT MSIE 3.0/Win95: No

MSIE 4.0/Win95: No

MSIE 5.0/Win98: Yes

NN 4.0/Win95: Yes

NN 4.7/Win98: Yes

MSIE 3.0/Mac OS: No

MSIE 4.0/Mac OS: Yes

NN 4.0/Mac OS: No

EXAMPLE {display: none}

TIP To hide an element so that the element's space is still visible, use the visibility property.

visibility

PURPOSE	Specifies that an object should be hidden in such a way that its space is visible even though the content is not.
INHERITED	No
VALUES	inherit (takes on visibility properties of enclosing element), visible, hidden, collapse
DEFAULT	inherit
USED IN	inherit
SUPPORT	MSIE 3.0/Win95: No
	MSIE 4.0/Win95: No
	MSIE 5.0/Win98: Yes
	NN 4.0/Win95: No
	NN 4.7/Win98: Yes
	MSIE 3.0/Mac OS: No
	MSIE 4.0/Mac OS: No
	NN 4.0/Mac OS: No
EXAMPLE	`{visibility: hidden}`
TIP	To hide an element so the element's space is also hidden, use the display property.

Font Properties

font

PURPOSE	Provides a shorthand method for indicating two or more font properties.
INHERITED	Yes
VALUES	List of font properties
DEFAULT	Not defined
USED IN	All elements
SUPPORT	MSIE 3.0/Win95: Yes
	MSIE 4.0/Win95: Yes
	MSIE 5.0/Win98: Yes

NN 4.0/Win95: Yes

NN 4.7/Win98: Yes

MSIE 3.0/Mac OS: Yes

MSIE 4.0/Mac OS: Yes

NN 4.0/Mac OS: Yes

EXAMPLE `{font: 14pt Arial bold}`

TIP If the font name requires two or more words (such as Times Roman), place the name in quotation marks.

font-family

PURPOSE Define font typeface and alternates (in order of preference).

INHERITED Yes

VALUES Font names or font family names, in a comma-separated list (in order of preference). Font family names: serif, sans-serif, cursive, fantasy, monospace.

DEFAULT Determined by browser

USED IN All elements

SUPPORT MSIE 3.0/Win95: Yes

MSIE 4.0/Win95: Yes

MSIE 5.0/Win98: Yes

NN 4.0/Win95: Yes

NN 4.7/Win98: Yes

MSIE 3.0/Mac OS: Yes

MSIE 4.0/Mac OS: Yes

NN 4.0/Mac OS: Yes

EXAMPLE `{font-family: Helvetica, Arial, "sans-serif"}`

TIP If the font name requires two or more words (such as Times Roman), place the name in quotation marks.

font-size

PURPOSE Defines font size.

INHERITED Yes

VALUES	Absolute sizes (xx-small, x-small, small, medium, large, x-large, or xx-large); relative sizes (larger or smaller), font size measurement (in pts, in., cm, px, or em), or percentage in relation to parent element.
DEFAULT	medium
USED IN	All elements
SUPPORT	MSIE 3.0/Win95: Yes
	MSIE 4.0/Win95: Yes
	MSIE 5.0/Win98: Yes
	NN 4.0/Win95: Yes
	NN 4.7/Win98: Yes
	MSIE 3.0/Mac OS: Yes
	MSIE 4.0/Mac OS: Yes
	NN 4.0/Mac OS: Yes
EXAMPLE	{font-size: 14pt}
TIP	Because of inconsistent browser support, avoid using em, ex, or percentage measurements.

font-style

PURPOSE	Defines emphasis options for text.
INHERITED	Yes
VALUES	normal, italic, or oblique.
DEFAULT	normal
USED IN	All elements
SUPPORT	MSIE 3.0/Win95: Yes
	MSIE 4.0/Win95: Yes
	MSIE 5.0/Win98: Yes
	NN 4.0/Win95: Yes
	NN 4.7/Win98: Yes
EXAMPLE	{font-style: italic}
TIP	Oblique is not widely supported.

font-variant

PURPOSE	Enables font variations such as small caps.
INHERITED	Yes
VALUES	normal or small-caps.
DEFAULT	normal
USED IN	All elements
SUPPORT	MSIE 3.0/Win95: No
	MSIE 4.0/Win95: Yes
	MSIE 5.0/Win98: Yes
	NN 4.0/Win95: No
	NN 4.7/Win98: No
	MSIE 3.0/Mac OS: No
	MSIE 4.0/Mac OS: No
	NN 4.0/Mac OS: No
EXAMPLE	`{font-variant: small-caps}`
TIP	This style is not widely supported.

font-weight

PURPOSE	Determines weight (boldness) of font.
INHERITED	Yes
VALUES	normal or bold. You can also specify a numerical weight ranging from 100 (light) to 900 (dark), or relative weights (bolder or lighter).
DEFAULT	normal
USED IN	All elements
SUPPORT	MSIE 3.0/Win95: Yes
	MSIE 4.0/Win95: Yes
	MSIE 5.0/Win98: Yes
	NN 4.0/Win95: Yes
	NN 4.7/Win98: Yes

MSIE 3.0/Mac OS: Yes

MSIE 4.0/Mac OS: Yes

NN 4.0/Mac OS: Yes

EXAMPLE   `{font-weight: bold}`

TIP   Only the normal and bold values are widely supported.

@font-face (CSS Level 2)

PURPOSE   Indicates name and location of a downloadable font.

INHERITED   No

VALUES   Include a font-family descriptor and the URL of the downloadable file, as shown in the following example.

DEFAULT   Determined by browser

USED IN   All elements

SUPPORT   Microsoft Internet Explorer Version 4

EXAMPLE   `@font-face {font-family: Verdana; src: url (http://www.fictitious.org/verdana.eot)}`

TIP   This property is not expected to come into widespread use until Version 5 browsers appear.

Positioning Properties (CSS Level 2)

bottom

PURPOSE   Specifies an offset from the bottom of a positioned element's reference box.

INHERITED   No

VALUES   Specify a length or percentage of the reference box's width.

DEFAULT   0

USED IN   All elements

SUPPORT   MSIE 3.0/Win95: No

            MSIE 4.0/Win95: Yes

            MSIE 5.0/Win98: Yes

            NN 4.0/Win95: No

NN 4.7/Win98: Yes

MSIE 3.0/Mac OS: No

MSIE 4.0/Mac OS: Yes

NN 4.0/Mac OS: No

EXAMPLE   {bottom: 0.5in}

TIP   If you don't specify a height for an absolutely positioned element (using the height property), the width is determined by the top and bottom properties.

clear

PURPOSE   Determines whether an element will allow floating elements on its left side, its right side, or both sides.

INHERITED   No

VALUES   left, right, both, or none.

DEFAULT   none

USED IN   All elements

SUPPORT   MSIE 3.0/Win95: No

MSIE 4.0/Win95: Yes

MSIE 5.0/Win98: Yes

NN 4.0/Win95: No

NN 4.7/Win98: No

MSIE 3.0/Mac OS: No

MSIE 4.0/Mac OS: Yes

NN 4.0/Mac OS: No

EXAMPLE   {clear: left}

TIP   Positioning properties are supported only by Microsoft Internet Explorer Version 4.

float

PURPOSE   Floats an element to the left or right, so text flows around it.

INHERITED   No

VALUES   left, right, or none.

DEFAULT   none

USED IN   All elements

SUPPORT   MSIE 3.0/Win95: No

MSIE 4.0/Win95: Yes

MSIE 5.0/Win98: Yes

NN 4.0/Win95: No

NN 4.7/Win98: No

MSIE 3.0/Mac OS: No

MSIE 4.0/Mac OS: Yes

NN 4.0/Mac OS: No

EXAMPLE   `{float: left}`

TIP   Works inconsistently between Netscape Navigator 4 and Microsoft Internet Explorer 4.

left

PURPOSE   Specifies an offset from the left of a positioned element's reference box.

INHERITED   No

VALUES   Specify a length or percentage of the reference box's width.

DEFAULT   0

USED IN   All elements

SUPPORT   MSIE 3.0/Win95: No

MSIE 4.0/Win95: Yes

MSIE 5.0/Win98: Yes

NN 4.0/Win95: No

NN 4.7/Win98: No

MSIE 3.0/Mac OS: No

MSIE 4.0/Mac OS: Yes

NN 4.0/Mac OS: No

EXAMPLE   `{left: 0.5in}`

TIP   If you don't specify a width for an absolutely positioned element (using the width property), the width is determined by the left and right properties.

position

PURPOSE	Determines whether an element flows with the text (static), occupies a fixed position (absolute), or flows in relation to an absolutely positioned element (relative).
INHERITED	No
VALUES	absolute, relative, fixed, or static.
DEFAULT	static
USED IN	All elements
SUPPORT	MSIE 3.0/Win95: No
	MSIE 4.0/Win95: Yes
	MSIE 5.0/Win98: Yes
	NN 4.0/Win95: No
	NN 4.7/Win98: No
	MSIE 3.0/Mac OS: No
	MSIE 4.0/Mac OS: Yes
	NN 4.0/Mac OS: No
EXAMPLE	`{position: absolute}`
TIP	Positioning properties are supported only by Microsoft Internet Explorer Version 4 and 5.

right

PURPOSE	Specifies an offset from the right of a positioned element's reference box.
INHERITED	No
VALUES	Specify a length or percentage of the reference box's width.
DEFAULT	0
USED IN	All elements
SUPPORT	MSIE 3.0/Win95: No
	MSIE 4.0/Win95: Yes
	MSIE 5.0/Win98: Yes
	NN 4.0/Win95: No
	NN 4.7/Win98: No

MSIE 3.0/Mac OS: No

MSIE 4.0/Mac OS: Yes

NN 4.0/Mac OS: No

EXAMPLE {right: 0.5in}

TIP If you don't specify a width for an absolutely positioned element (using the width property), the width is determined by the left and right properties.

top

PURPOSE Specifies an offset from the top of a positioned element's reference box.

INHERITED No

VALUES Specify a length or percentage of the reference box's width.

DEFAULT 0

USED IN All elements

SUPPORT MSIE 3.0/Win95: No

MSIE 4.0/Win95: Yes

MSIE 5.0/Win98: Yes

NN 4.0/Win95: Yes

NN 4.7/Win98: Yes

MSIE 3.0/Mac OS: No

MSIE 4.0/Mac OS: Yes

NN 4.0/Mac OS: Yes

EXAMPLE {top: 0.5in}

TIP If you don't specify a height for an absolutely positioned element (using the height property), the width is determined by the top and bottom properties.

z-index

PURPOSE Specifies the position of an element in a three-dimensional stack (back to front).

INHERITED No

VALUES auto (stacks elements back to front in the order they appear in the document) or number (overrides default stacking order).

DEFAULT   auto

USED IN   All elements

SUPPORT   MSIE 3.0/Win95: No

                 MSIE 4.0/Win95: Yes

                 MSIE 5.0/Win98: Yes

                 NN 4.0/Win95: No

                 NN 4.7/Win98: No

                 MSIE 3.0/Mac OS: No

                 MSIE 4.0/Mac OS: Yes

                 NN 4.0/Mac OS: No

EXAMPLE   `{z-index: 2}`

TIP   Not supported by Netscape Navigator 4.7.

Printing Properties (CSS Level 2)

page-break-after

PURPOSE   Inserts a page break after the element when the document
                 is printed.

INHERITED   No

VALUES   auto, always, left (insert page breaks until next
                 even-numbered page is reached), right (insert page
                 breaks until next odd-numbered page is reached), avoid.

DEFAULT   auto

USED IN   All elements

SUPPORT   MSIE 3.0/Win95: No

                 MSIE 4.0/Win95: Yes

                 MSIE 5.0/Win98: Yes

                 NN 4.0/Win95: No

                 NN 4.7/Win98: No

                 MSIE 3.0/Mac OS: No

                 MSIE 4.0/Mac OS: Yes

                 NN 4.0/Mac OS: No

EXAMPLE   `{page-break-after: always}`

TIP   You can specify a page break before the element with the page-break-before property.

page-break-before

PURPOSE   Inserts a page break before the element when the document is printed.

INHERITED   No

VALUES   auto, always, left (insert page breaks until next even-numbered page is reached), right (insert page breaks until next odd-numbered page is reached), avoid.

DEFAULT   auto

USED IN   All elements

SUPPORT   MSIE 3.0/Win95: No

MSIE 4.0/Win95: Yes

MSIE 5.0/Win98: Yes

NN 4.0/Win95: No

NN 4.7/Win98: No

MSIE 3.0/Mac OS: No

MSIE 4.0/Mac OS: Yes

NN 4.0/Mac OS: No

EXAMPLE   `{page-break-before: always}`

TIP   You can specify a page break after the element with the page-break-after property.

Text Properties

line-height

PURPOSE   Specifies the height (the distance between the baselines) of each line of text in an element.

INHERITED   Yes

VALUES   Specify a number to multiply the current font height), a length, or a percentage of the current font size, or auto (same as font size).

DEFAULT	auto
USED IN	Replaced and block-level elements
SUPPORT	MSIE 3.0/Win95: Yes
	MSIE 4.0/Win95: Yes
	MSIE 5.0/Win98: Yes
	NN 4.0/Win95: Yes
	NN 4.7/Win98: Yes
	MSIE 3.0/Mac OS: Yes
	MSIE 4.0/Mac OS: Yes
	NN 4.0/Mac OS: Yes
EXAMPLE	`{line-height: 24pt}` or `{line-height: 2}`
TIP	If the height is set to auto, the height is determined by the intrinsic height of the element. If you specify a number, you're specifying the number of times to multiply the current line size set by the height of the font (for a 12pt font, *2* gives you 24pt line heights, or double-line spacing).

letter-spacing

PURPOSE	Adds to the default spacing between characters.
INHERITED	Yes
VALUES	Specify a length, or normal.
DEFAULT	normal
USED IN	Block-level elements
SUPPORT	MSIE 3.0/Win95: No
	MSIE 4.0/Win95: Yes
	MSIE 5.0/Win98: Yes
	NN 4.0/Win95: No
	NN 4.7/Win98: No
	MSIE 3.0/Mac OS: No
	MSIE 4.0/Mac OS: No
	NN 4.0/Mac OS: No
EXAMPLE	`{letter-spacing: 1pt}`
TIP	This property is not well supported.

text-align

PURPOSE	Controls horizontal alignment of text.
INHERITED	Yes
VALUES	left, center, right, or justify.
DEFAULT	0
USED IN	Block-level elements
SUPPORT	MSIE 3.0/Win95: Yes
	MSIE 4.0/Win95: Yes
	MSIE 5.0/Win98: Yes
	NN 4.0/Win95: Yes
	NN 4.7/Win98: Yes
	MSIE 3.0/Mac OS: Yes
	MSIE 4.0/Mac OS: Yes
	NN 4.0/Mac OS: Yes
EXAMPLE	{text-align: 0.5in}
TIP	This property is well supported.

text-decoration

PURPOSE	Adds decorations (such as strikethrough) to text.
INHERITED	No
VALUES	none, underline, overline, line-through, or blink.
DEFAULT	none
USED IN	Block-level elements
SUPPORT	MSIE 3.0/Win95: Yes
	MSIE 4.0/Win95: Yes
	MSIE 5.0/Win98: Yes
	NN 4.0/Win95: Yes
	NN 4.7/Win98: Yes
	MSIE 3.0/Mac OS: Yes
	MSIE 4.0/Mac OS: Yes
	NN 4.0/Mac OS: Yes
EXAMPLE	{text-decoration: underline}
TIP	Only MSIE 4.0/Win95 supports the overline value.

text-indent

PURPOSE	Indents the first line of text.
INHERITED	Yes
VALUES	Any valid length or a percentage of the element's width.
DEFAULT	0
USED IN	Block-level elements
SUPPORT	MSIE 3.0/Win95: Yes
	MSIE 4.0/Win95: Yes
	MSIE 5.0/Win98: Yes
	NN 4.0/Win95: Yes
	NN 4.7/Win98: Yes
	MSIE 3.0/Mac OS: Yes
	MSIE 4.0/Mac OS: Yes
	NN 4.0/Mac OS: Yes
EXAMPLE	`{text-indent: 0.5in}`
TIP	This property is well supported.

text-transform

PURPOSE	Changes case.
INHERITED	Yes
VALUES	capitalize, uppercase, lowercase, none.
DEFAULT	none
USED IN	All elements
SUPPORT	MSIE 3.0/Win95: No
	MSIE 4.0/Win95: Yes
	MSIE 5.0/Win98: Yes
	NN 4.0/Win95: Yes
	NN 4.7/Win98: Yes
	MSIE 3.0/Mac OS: No
	MSIE 4.0/Mac OS: Yes
	NN 4.0/Mac OS: Yes

EXAMPLE   {text-transform: capitalize}

TIP   The capitalize value capitalizes only the first character of each word. Use uppercase to capitalize everything. Because this property is supported inconsistently, you'll be wise to type the characters with the capitalization pattern you prefer.

word-spacing

PURPOSE   Adds to the default spacing between words.

INHERITED Yes

VALUES   Specify a length, or normal.

DEFAULT   normal

USED IN   Block-level elements

SUPPORT   MSIE 3.0/Win95: No

           MSIE 4.0/Win95: Yes

           MSIE 5.0/Win98: Yes

           NN 4.0/Win95: No

           NN 4.7/Win98: No

           MSIE 3.0/Mac OS: No

           MSIE 4.0/Mac OS: No

           NN 4.0/Mac OS: No

EXAMPLE   {word-spacing: 1pt}

TIP   This property is not currently well supported.

white-space (CSS Level 2)

PURPOSE   Controls handling of white space.

INHERITED Yes

VALUES   normal (white space ignored by browser), pre (text spacing retained by browser), nowrap (lines broken only by BR element).

DEFAULT   normal

USED IN   All elements

SUPPORT   MSIE 3.0/Win95: No

           MSIE 4.0/Win95: No

	MSIE 5.0/Win98: No
	NN 4.0/Win95: No
	NN 4.7/Win98: No
	MSIE 3.0/Mac OS: No
	MSIE 4.0/Mac OS: No
	NN 4.0/Mac OS: No
EXAMPLE	{white-space: pre}
TIP	This property is not currently supported.

vertical-align

PURPOSE	Specifies the vertical position of an element relative to the current text baseline.
INHERITED	No
VALUES	baseline, sub (subscript), super (superscript), top (top of the line), text-top (top of the text), middle, bottom, text-bottom. You can also type a length or a percentage of the line height.
DEFAULT	baseline
USED IN	Replaced and block-level elements
SUPPORT	MSIE 3.0/Win95: Yes
	MSIE 4.0/Win95: Yes
	MSIE 5.0/Win98: Yes
	NN 4.0/Win95: Yes
	NN 4.7/Win98: Yes
	MSIE 3.0/Mac OS: Yes
	MSIE 4.0/Mac OS: Yes
	NN 4.0/Mac OS: Yes
EXAMPLE	{vertical-align: 50%}
TIP	This property is most commonly used for superscript and subscript characters in technical documents.

List Properties

These properties affect the appearance of lists in your document.

list-style

PURPOSE	Provides a shorthand method for indicating several list format options.
INHERITED	Yes
VALUES	You can include any of the values from list-style-type, list-style-position, or list-style-image.
DEFAULT	Not defined
USED IN	Elements with the display property set to list-item
SUPPORT	MSIE 3.0/Win95: No
	MSIE 4.0/Win95: Yes
	MSIE 5.0/Win98: Yes
	NN 4.0/Win95: Yes
	NN 4.7/Win98: Yes
	MSIE 3.0/Mac OS: No
	MSIE 4.0/Mac OS: Yes
	NN 4.0/Mac OS: Yes
EXAMPLE	{list-style: upper-roman inside}
TIP	Use the display property to set list elements to the list-item value.

list-style-image

PURPOSE	Specifies a graphic to be used in place of a bullet in an unordered list.
INHERITED	Yes
VALUES	<uri>, none.
DEFAULT	none
USED IN	Elements with the display property set to list-item

SUPPORT	MSIE 3.0/Win95: No
	MSIE 4.0/Win95: Yes
	MSIE 5.0/Win98: Yes
	NN 4.0/Win95: Yes
	NN 4.7/Win98: Yes
	MSIE 3.0/Mac OS: No
	MSIE 4.0/Mac OS: Yes
	NN 4.0/Mac OS: Yes
EXAMPLE	`{list-style-image: url(picture.gif)}`
TIP	Use the display property to set list elements to the list-item value.

list-style-position

PURPOSE	Specifies how the list-item marker (bullet or number) should be positioned relative to the list-item's content.
INHERITED	Yes
VALUES	inside (the marker is placed at the beginning of the element's box) or outside (the marker is placed outside the element's box).
DEFAULT	outside
USED IN	Elements with the display property set to list-item
SUPPORT	MSIE 3.0/Win95: No
	MSIE 4.0/Win95: Yes
	MSIE 5.0/Win98: Yes
	NN 4.0/Win95: Yes
	NN 4.7/Win98: Yes
	MSIE 3.0/Mac OS: No
	MSIE 4.0/Mac OS: Yes
	NN 4.0/Mac OS: Yes
EXAMPLE	`{list-style-position: inside}`
TIP	Use the display property to set list elements to the list-item value.

list-style-type

PURPOSE   Specifies the bullet or number style used in a list.

INHERITED   Yes

VALUES   disc, circle, square, decimal (decimal numbers), lower-roman (lower-case Roman numerals), lower-alpha (lowercase ASCII letters), upper-roman (uppercase Roman numerals), upper-alpha (uppercase ASCII letters), none (no marker).

DEFAULT   disc

USED IN   List elements in which the display property has been set to list-item

SUPPORT   MSIE 3.0/Win95: No

                        MSIE 4.0/Win95: Yes

                        MSIE 5.0/Win98: Yes

                        NN 4.0/Win95: Yes

                        NN 4.7/Win98: Yes

                        MSIE 3.0/Mac OS: No

                        MSIE 4.0/Mac OS: Yes

                        NN 4.0/Mac OS: Yes

EXAMPLE   {list-style-type: disc}

TIP   Use the display property to set list elements to the list-item value.

✦   ✦   ✦

Language Codes Reference

Language Codes are used with the lang and dir attributes. The lang attribute assigns a language to the text in a Web page to be read by the opening browser. The dir attribute assigns a direction, right or left, to the assigned language. For example, Hebrew is not read left to right like English, but right to left.

The Language Codes chart in this Appendix lists the language, the language family, and the name code. The name code is inserted in the <lang=JA> tag for language assignment.

Language Family	Language	Name Code
Amerindian	Aymara	AY
Amerindian	Guarani	GN
Amerindian	Quechua	QU
Asian	Bhutani	DZ
Asian	Bislama	BI [not given]
Asian	Burmese	MY
Asian	Cambodian	KM
Asian	Chinese	ZH
Asian	Japanese	JA
Asian	Korean	KO
Asian	Laotian	LO
Asian	Thai	TH
Asian	Tibetan	BO
Asian	Vietnamese	VI
Baltic	Latvian; Lettish	LV

Continued

Language Family	Language	Name Code
Baltic	Lithuanian	LT
Basque	Basque	EU
Celtic	Breton	BR
Celtic	Irish	GA
Celtic	Gaelic	GD
Celtic	Welsh	CY
Dravidian	Kannada	KN
Dravidian	Malayalam	ML
Dravidian	Tamil	TA
Dravidian	Telugu	TE
Eskimo	Greenlandic	KL
Eskimo	Inupiak	IK
Finno-Ugric	Estonian	ET
Finno-Ugric	Finnish	FI
Finno-Ugric	Hungarian	HU
Germanic	Afrikaans	AF
Germanic	Danish	DA
Germanic	Dutch	NL
Germanic	English	EN
Germanic	Faroese	FO
Germanic	Frisian	FY
Germanic	German	DE
Germanic	Icelandic	IS
Germanic	Norwegian	NO
Germanic	Swedish	SV
Germanic	Yiddish	JI
Hamitic	Afan (Oromo)	OM
Hamitic	Afar	AA
Hamitic	Somali	SO
Ibero-Caucasian	Abkhazian	AB
Ibero-Caucasian	Georgian	KA

Language Family	Language	Name Code
Indian	Assamese	AS
Indian	Bengali; Bangla	BN
Indian	Bihari	BH
Indian	Gujarati	GU
Indian	Hindi	HI
Indian	Kashmiri	KS
Indian	Marathi	MR
Indian	Nepali	NE
Indian	Oriya	OR
Indian	Punjabi	PA
Indian	Sanskrit	SA
Indian	Sindhi	SD
Indian	Singhalese	SI
Indian	Urdu	UR
Indo-European (other)	Albanian	SQ
Indo-European (other)	Armenian	HY
International aux.	Esperanto	EO
International aux.	Interlingua	IA
International aux.	Interlingue	IE
International aux.	Volapük	VO
Iranian	Kurdish	KU
Iranian	Pashto; Pushto	PS
Iranian	Persian (Farsi)	FA
Iranian	Tajik	TG
Latin/Greek	Greek	EL
Latin/Greek	Latin	LA
Negro-African	Hausa	HA
Negro-African	Kinyarwanda	RW
Negro-African	Kurundi	RN

Continued

Language Family	Language	Name Code
Negro-African	Lingala	LN
Negro-African	Sangho	SG
Negro-African	Sesotho	ST
Negro-African	Setswana	TN
Negro-African	Shona	SN
Negro-African	Siswati	SS
Negro-African	Swahili	SW
Negro-African	Tsonga	TS
Negro-African	Twi	TW
Negro-African	Wolof	WO
Negro-African	Xhosa	XH
Negro-African	Yoruba	YO
Negro-African	Zulu	ZU
Oceanic/Indonesian	Fiji	FJ
Oceanic/Indonesian	Indonesian	IN
Oceanic/Indonesian	Javanese	JW
Oceanic/Indonesian	Malagasy	MG
Oceanic/Indonesian	Malay	MS
Oceanic/Indonesian	Maori	MI
Oceanic/Indonesian	Samoan	SM
Oceanic/Indonesian	Sudanese	SU
Oceanic/Indonesian	Tagalog	TL
Oceanic/Indonesian	Tonga	TO
Romance	Catalan	CA
Romance	Corsican	CO
Romance	French	FR
Romance	Galician	GL
Romance	Italian	IT
Romance	Moldavian	MO
Romance	Occitan	OC
Romance	Portuguese	PT

Language Family	Language	Name Code
Romance	Rhaeto-Romance	RM
Romance	Romanian	RO
Romance	Spanish	ES
Semitic	Amharic	AM
Semitic	Arabic	AR
Semitic	Hebrew	IW
Semitic	Maltese	MT
Semitic	Tigrinya	TI
Slavic	Bulgarian	BG
Slavic	Byelorussian	BE
Slavic	Croatian	HR
Slavic	Czech	CS
Slavic	Macedonian	MK
Slavic	Polish	PL
Slavic	Russian	RU
Slavic	Serbian	SR
Slavic	Serbo-Croatian	SH
Slavic	Slovak	SK
Slavic	Slovenian	SL
Slavic	Ukrainian	UK
Turkic/Altaic	Azerbaijani	AZ
Turkic/Altaic	Bashkir	BA
Turkic/Altaic	Kazakh	KK
Turkic/Altaic	Kirghiz	KY
Turkic/Altaic	Tatar	TT
Turkic/Altaic	Turkish	TR
Turkic/Altaic	Turkmen	TK
Turkic/Altaic	Uzbek	UZ

✦　　✦　　✦

Hex Notations Reference

When indicating you would like to assign one of these colors, you must use the Hex notation. The color name provided in the Description column is so you know approximately how the hex code will appear.

Description	Hex Code
Aqua	#00FFFF
Aquamarine	#7FFFD4
Black	#000000
Blue	#0000FF
Blue Violet	#8A2BE2
Brass	#B5A642
Bright Gold	#D9D919
Bronze	#8C7853
Bronze II	#A67D3D
Brown	#A52A2A
Cadet Blue	#5F9EA0
Chocolate	#D2691E
Cool Copper	#D98719
Copper	#B87333
Coral	#FF7F50
Cornflower Blue	#6495ED
Dark Brown	#5C4033
Dark Green	#006400
Dark Green Copper	#4A766E

Continued

Description	Hex Code
Dark Olive Green	#556B2F
Dark Orchid	#9932CD
Dark Purple	#871F78
Dark Slate Blue	#483D8B
Dark Slate Grey	#2F4F4F
Dark Tan	#97694F
Dark Turquoise	#00CED1
Dark Wood	#855E42
Dim Grey	#696969
Dusty Rose	#856363
Faded Brown	#F5CCB0
Feldspar	#D19275
Firebrick	#B22222
Forest Green	#228B22
Fuchsia	#FF00FF
Gold	#FFD700
Goldenrod	#DAA520
Green	#00FF00
Green Copper	#527F76
Green Yellow	#ADFF2F
Grey	#808080
Hunter Green	#215E21
Indian Red	#CD5C5C
Khaki	#F0E68C
Light Blue	#ADD8E6
Light Grey	#D3D3D3
Light Steel Blue	#B0C4DE
Light Wood	#E9C2A6
Lime	#FF0000
Lime Green	#32CD32
Mandaran Orange	#E47833

Description	Hex Code
Maroon	#800000
Medium Aquamarine	#66CDAA
Medium Blue	#0000CD
Medium Forest Green	#6B8E23
Medium Goldenrod	#EAEAAE
Medium Orchid	#BA55D3
Medium Sea Green	#3CB371
Medium Slate Blue	#7B68EE
Medium Spring Green	#00FA9A
Medium Turquoise	#48D1CC
Medium Violet Red	#C71585
Medium Wood	#A68064
Midnight Blue	#191970
Navy Blue	#000080
Neon Blue	#4D4DFF
Neon Pink	#FF6EC7
New Midnight Blue	#00009C
New Tan	#EBC79E
Old Gold	#CFB53B
Orange	#FF7F00
Orange Red	#FF4500
Orchid	#DA70D6
Pale Green	#98FB98
Pink	#FFC0CB
Plum	#DDA0DD
Quartz	#D9D9F3
Red	#008000
Rich Blue	#5959AB
Salmon	#FA8072
Scarlet	#8C1717
Sea Green	#2E8B57

Continued

Description	Hex Code
Semisweet Chocolate	#6B4226
Sienna	#A0522D
Silver	#C0C0C0
Sky Blue	#87CEEB
Slate Blue	#6A5ACD
Spicy Pink	#FF1CAE
Spring Green	#00FF7F
Steel Blue	#4682B4
Summer Sky	#38B0DE
Tan	#D2B48C
Thistle	#D8BFD8
Turquoise	#40E0D0
Very Dark Brown	#5C4033
Very Light Grey	#CDCDCD
Violet	#EE82EE
Violet Red	#CC3299
Wheat	#F5DEB3
White	#FFFFFF
Yellow	#FFFF00
Yellow Green	#9ACD32

✦   ✦   ✦

About the CD-ROM

The CD-ROM in the back of the book contains trial versions of applications, your choice of browsers, and a selection of images and style sheets — all designed to help you get a Web site developed quickly.

Included Software

The CD-ROM that accompanies this book contains demos or trial versions of the following products:

Software Name	Vendor
BBEdit Lite	Bare Bones Software, Inc.
DeBabelizer	Equilibrium
Dreamweaver 3.0	Macromedia, Inc.
Drop Stuff w/ Expander Enhancer	Aladdin Systems
Fireworks 3	Macromedia, Inc.
Flash 4	Macromedia, Inc.
Fusion	NetObjects, Inc.
GIF Movie Gear	Gamani Productions
GraphicConverter 3.2	Lemke Software
HomeSite	Allaire Corporation
HTML Tidy	Dave Raggett
Script Builder	NetObjects, Inc.
Tex-Edit Plus	Trans Tex-Software
TextPad	Helios Software Solutions
WebPosition Gold	FirstPlace Software, Inc.

These products fall into one of three categories of software: Web-development tools, Web-position evaluator, or Web-accessory development tools.

Cross-Reference   Several of the tools listed are the Web-development tools discussed in Chapter 8.

Browsers

Internet Explorer and Netscape Communicator are full-featured Web browsers. They are mentioned throughout this book. While you can download them from their respective Web sites, the file sizes are rather large. Installing from a CD is much faster.

Book files

A PDF version of this book is available on the CD-ROM. In order to open these files, you'll need to install Acrobat Reader, a product by Adobe, which also can be found on the CD.

Finally, there are files discussed in this book. These files are located within folders named by the chapter number in which they are referenced.

✦   ✦   ✦

Index

Continued

Continued

S

IDG Books Worldwide, Inc.
End-User License Agreement

READ THIS. You should carefully read these terms and conditions before opening the software packet(s) included with this book ("Book"). This is a license agreement ("Agreement") between you and IDG Books Worldwide, Inc. ("IDGB"). By opening the accompanying software packet(s), you acknowledge that you have read and accept the following terms and conditions. If you do not agree and do not want to be bound by such terms and conditions, promptly return the Book and the unopened software packet(s) to the place you obtained them for a full refund.

1. **License Grant.** IDGB grants to you (either an individual or entity) a nonexclusive license to use one copy of the enclosed software program(s) (collectively, the "Software") solely for your own personal or business purposes on a single computer (whether a standard computer or a workstation component of a multiuser network). The Software is in use on a computer when it is loaded into temporary memory (RAM) or installed into permanent memory (hard disk, CD-ROM, or other storage device). IDGB reserves all rights not expressly granted herein.

2. **Ownership.** IDGB is the owner of all right, title, and interest, including copyright, in and to the compilation of the Software recorded on the disk(s) or CD-ROM ("Software Media"). Copyright to the individual programs recorded on the Software Media is owned by the author or other authorized copyright owner of each program. Ownership of the Software and all proprietary rights relating thereto remain with IDGB and its licensers.

3. **Restrictions On Use and Transfer.**

    (a) You may only (i) make one copy of the Software for backup or archival purposes, or (ii) transfer the Software to a single hard disk, provided that you keep the original for backup or archival purposes. You may not (i) rent or lease the Software, (ii) copy or reproduce the Software through a LAN or other network system or through any computer subscriber system or bulletin-board system, or (iii) modify, adapt, or create derivative works based on the Software.

    (b) You may not reverse engineer, decompile, or disassemble the Software. You may transfer the Software and user documentation on a permanent basis, provided that the transferee agrees to accept the terms and conditions of this Agreement and you retain no copies. If the Software is an update or has been updated, any transfer must include the most recent update and all prior versions.

4. **Restrictions on Use of Individual Programs.** You must follow the individual requirements and restrictions detailed for each individual program in Appendix H of this Book. These limitations are also contained in the individual

license agreements recorded on the Software Media. These limitations may include a requirement that after using the program for a specified period of time, the user must pay a registration fee or discontinue use. By opening the Software packet(s), you will be agreeing to abide by the licenses and restrictions for these individual programs that are detailed in Appendix H and on the Software Media. None of the material on this Software Media or listed in this Book may ever be redistributed, in original or modified form, for commercial purposes.

5. Limited Warranty.

(a) IDGB warrants that the Software and Software Media are free from defects in materials and workmanship under normal use for a period of sixty (60) days from the date of purchase of this Book. If IDGB receives notification within the warranty period of defects in materials or workmanship, IDGB will replace the defective Software Media.

(b) **IDGB AND THE AUTHORS OF THE BOOK DISCLAIM ALL OTHER WARRANTIES, EXPRESS OR IMPLIED, INCLUDING WITHOUT LIMITATION IMPLIED WARRANTIES OF MERCHANTABILITY AND FITNESS FOR A PARTICULAR PURPOSE, WITH RESPECT TO THE SOFTWARE, THE PROGRAMS, THE SOURCE CODE CONTAINED THEREIN, AND/OR THE TECHNIQUES DESCRIBED IN THIS BOOK. IDGB DOES NOT WARRANT THAT THE FUNCTIONS CONTAINED IN THE SOFTWARE WILL MEET YOUR REQUIREMENTS OR THAT THE OPERATION OF THE SOFTWARE WILL BE ERROR FREE.**

(c) This limited warranty gives you specific legal rights, and you may have other rights that vary from jurisdiction to jurisdiction.

6. Remedies.

(a) IDGB's entire liability and your exclusive remedy for defects in materials and workmanship shall be limited to replacement of the Software Media, which may be returned to IDGB with a copy of your receipt at the following address: Software Media Fulfillment Department, Attn.: *HTML 4 Bible, 2nd Edition*, IDG Books Worldwide, Inc., 10475 Crosspoint Blvd., Indianapolis, IN 46256, or call 1-800-762-2974. Please allow three to four weeks for delivery. This Limited Warranty is void if failure of the Software Media has resulted from accident, abuse, or misapplication. Any replacement Software Media will be warranted for the remainder of the original warranty period or thirty (30) days, whichever is longer.

(b) In no event shall IDGB or the authors be liable for any damages whatsoever (including without limitation damages for loss of business profits, business interruption, loss of business information, or any other pecuniary loss) arising from the use of or inability to use the Book or the Software, even if IDGB has been advised of the possibility of such damages.

(c) Because some jurisdictions do not allow the exclusion or limitation of liability for consequential or incidental damages, the above limitation or exclusion may not apply to you.

7. **U.S. Government Restricted Rights.** Use, duplication, or disclosure of the Software by the U.S. Government is subject to restrictions stated in paragraph (c)(1)(ii) of the Rights in Technical Data and Computer Software clause of DFARS 252.227-7013, and in subparagraphs (a) through (d) of the Commercial Computer — Restricted Rights clause at FAR 52.227-19, and in similar clauses in the NASA FAR supplement, when applicable.

8. **General.** This Agreement constitutes the entire understanding of the parties and revokes and supersedes all prior agreements, oral or written, between them and may not be modified or amended except in a writing signed by both parties hereto that specifically refers to this Agreement. This Agreement shall take precedence over any other documents that may be in conflict herewith. If any one or more provisions contained in this Agreement are held by any court or tribunal to be invalid, illegal, or otherwise unenforceable, each and every other provision shall remain in full force and effect.

Put a serious

dent

in your
workload with
Dreamweaver®
and **Fireworks**®

Introducing Dreamweaver 3 and Fireworks 3

The newest versions of Dreamweaver and Fireworks
work together to give you the power to create
Web sites faster. Design buttons, animations
and page comps in minutes with Fireworks 3.
Mold your graphics and code into completed
Web sites in record time with Dreamweaver 3.
Streamline development with support for the
content creation and Web application software
you use. Together, Dreamweaver and
Fireworks are one awesome team
for rapid Web development.

www.macromedia.com

macromedia®

my2cents.idgbooks.com

Register This Book — And Win!

Visit **http://my2cents.idgbooks.com** to register this book and we'll automatically enter you in our fantastic monthly prize giveaway. It's also your opportunity to give us feedback: let us know what you thought of this book and how you would like to see other topics covered.

Discover IDG Books Online!

The IDG Books Online Web site is your online resource for tackling technology — at home and at the office. Frequently updated, the IDG Books Online Web site features exclusive software, insider information, online books, and live events!

10 Productive & Career-Enhancing Things You Can Do at www.idgbooks.com

- Nab source code for your own programming projects.
- Download software.
- Read Web exclusives: special articles and book excerpts by IDG Books Worldwide authors.
- Take advantage of resources to help you advance your career as a Novell or Microsoft professional.
- Buy IDG Books Worldwide titles or find a convenient bookstore that carries them.
- Register your book and win a prize.
- Chat live online with authors.
- Sign up for regular e-mail updates about our latest books.
- Suggest a book you'd like to read or write.
- Give us your 2¢ about our books and about our Web site.

You say you're not on the Web yet? It's easy to get started with IDG Books' *Discover the Internet*, available at local retailers everywhere.

CD-ROM Installation Instructions

The CD-ROM that accompanies this book contains trial versions of commercial software discussed in the book and two browsers, as well as sample style sheets and sample image files that enable you to complete the exercises in two of the chapters. The CD will work on either a PC or a Mac.

To install any of these programs, place the disc in your CD-ROM drive and run the .exe file. To use the sample style sheets and image files, open the individual chapter folders, Chap3, Chap18, or Chap38 folders and copy these files onto your hard drive.

Web Site Credits